VW Golf & Jetta
Service and Repair Manual

I M Coomber

(1081-320-1Y10)

Models covered

VW Golf & Jetta 'Mk 2' models with petrol engines, including fuel injection, catalytic converter, Formel E, 16-valve and special/limited edition models
1043 cc, 1272 cc, 1595 cc and 1781 cc

Covers mechanical features of Van

Does not cover Convertible, Rallye, Caddy, Diesel engine, four-wheel-drive, 'Mk 1' models or new Golf range introduced in February 1992

© Haynes Publishing 1996

A book in the **Haynes Service and Repair Manual Series**

All rights reserved. No part of this book may be reproduced or transmitted in any form or by any means, electronic or mechanical, including photocopying, recording or by any information storage or retrieval system, without permission in writing from the copyright holder.

ISBN 1 85960 195 2

British Library Cataloguing in Publication Data
A catalogue record for this book is available from the British Library.

ABCDE
FGHIJ
KLMNO
PQRST
3

Printed by **J H Haynes & Co. Ltd, Sparkford, Nr Yeovil, Somerset BA22 7JJ**

Haynes Publishing
Sparkford, Nr Yeovil, Somerset BA22 7JJ, England

Haynes North America, Inc
861 Lawrence Drive, Newbury Park, California 91320, USA

Editions Haynes S.A.
147/149, rue Saint Honoré, 75001 PARIS, France

Contents

LIVING WITH YOUR VOLKSWAGEN
Introduction	Page	0•4
Safety First!	Page	0•5
Dimensions, weights and capacities	Page	0•6

Roadside Repairs
Identifying leaks	Page	0•7
Jacking and towing	Page	0•8
Jump starting	Page	0•9

Routine Maintenance
Routine maintenance *(also see Chapter 13)*	Page	0•10
Tyre checks	Page	0•15
Lubricants and fluids	Page	0•16

Contents

REPAIRS & OVERHAUL

Engine and Associated Systems

Engine *(also see Chapter 12)*	Page	1•1
Cooling system *(also see Chapter 12)*	Page	2•1
Fuel and exhaust systems *(also see Chapter 12)*	Page	3•1
Ignition system *(also see Chapter 12)*	Page	4•1

Transmission

Clutch *(also see Chapter 12)*	Page	5•1
Manual gearbox and automatic transmission *(also see Chapter 12)*	Page	6•1
Driveshafts	Page	7•1

Brakes

Braking system	Page	8•1

Electrical

Electrical system *(also see Chapter 12)*	Page	9•1

Suspension

Suspension and steering *(also see Chapter 12)*	Page	10•1

Body Equipment

Bodywork and fittings *(also see Chapter 12)*	Page	11•1

Additional Information

Supplement: Revisions and information on later models	Page	12•1

Wiring Diagrams

	Page	13•1

REFERENCE

MOT Test Checks

Checks carried out from the driver's seat	Page	REF•1
Checks carried out with the vehicle on the ground	Page	REF•2
Checks carried out with the vehicle raised	Page	REF•3
Checks carried out on your vehicle's exhaust emission system	Page	REF•4
Tools and Working Facilities	Page	REF•5
General Repair Procedures	Page	REF•8
Fault Finding	Page	REF•9
Conversion factors	Page	REF•12
Buying spare parts and vehicle identification numbers	Page	REF•13
Glossary of Technical Terms	Page	REF•14

Index

	Page	REF•19

Introduction

Introduction to the Volkswagen Golf and Jetta

The 'new' Volkswagen Golf and Jetta range of models was introduced in March 1984, a revised body and trim features being the main visual difference to the earlier range of models.

The engine and transmission are mounted transversely at the front, and drive is through the front wheels. Detailed improvements have been made to the mechanics to improve the power output and economy.

As with earlier models the new range is proving popular, giving economy, reliability, comfort and, if previous models can be used as a yardstick, long life.

Acknowledgements

Thanks are due to Champion Spark Plug, who supplied the illustrations showing spark plug conditions. Thanks are also due to Sykes-Pickavant Limited, who provided some of the workshop tools, and all those people at Sparkford who helped in the production of this manual.

VW Golf GL

VW Jetta GLX

We take great pride in the accuracy of information given in this manual, but vehicle manufacturers make alterations and design changes during the production run of a particular vehicle of which they do not inform us. No liability can be accepted by the authors or publishers for loss, damage or injury caused by errors in, or omissions from, the information given.

Safety First! 0•5

Working on your car can be dangerous. This page shows just some of the potential risks and hazards, with the aim of creating a safety-conscious attitude.

General hazards

Scalding
• Don't remove the radiator or expansion tank cap while the engine is hot.
• Engine oil, automatic transmission fluid or power steering fluid may also be dangerously hot if the engine has recently been running.

Burning
• Beware of burns from the exhaust system and from any part of the engine. Brake discs and drums can also be extremely hot immediately after use.

Crushing

• When working under or near a raised vehicle, always supplement the jack with axle stands, or use drive-on ramps. *Never venture under a car which is only supported by a jack.*
• Take care if loosening or tightening high-torque nuts when the vehicle is on stands. Initial loosening and final tightening should be done with the wheels on the ground.

Fire
• Fuel is highly flammable; fuel vapour is explosive.
• Don't let fuel spill onto a hot engine.
• Do not smoke or allow naked lights (including pilot lights) anywhere near a vehicle being worked on. Also beware of creating sparks (electrically or by use of tools).
• Fuel vapour is heavier than air, so don't work on the fuel system with the vehicle over an inspection pit.
• Another cause of fire is an electrical overload or short-circuit. Take care when repairing or modifying the vehicle wiring.
• Keep a fire extinguisher handy, of a type suitable for use on fuel and electrical fires.

Electric shock
• Ignition HT voltage can be dangerous, especially to people with heart problems or a pacemaker. Don't work on or near the ignition system with the engine running or the ignition switched on.

• Mains voltage is also dangerous. Make sure that any mains-operated equipment is correctly earthed. Mains power points should be protected by a residual current device (RCD) circuit breaker.

Fume or gas intoxication
• Exhaust fumes are poisonous; they often contain carbon monoxide, which is rapidly fatal if inhaled. Never run the engine in a confined space such as a garage with the doors shut.
• Fuel vapour is also poisonous, as are the vapours from some cleaning solvents and paint thinners.

Poisonous or irritant substances
• Avoid skin contact with battery acid and with any fuel, fluid or lubricant, especially antifreeze, brake hydraulic fluid and Diesel fuel. Don't syphon them by mouth. If such a substance is swallowed or gets into the eyes, seek medical advice.
• Prolonged contact with used engine oil can cause skin cancer. Wear gloves or use a barrier cream if necessary. Change out of oil-soaked clothes and do not keep oily rags in your pocket.
• Air conditioning refrigerant forms a poisonous gas if exposed to a naked flame (including a cigarette). It can also cause skin burns on contact.

Asbestos
• Asbestos dust can cause cancer if inhaled or swallowed. Asbestos may be found in gaskets and in brake and clutch linings. When dealing with such components it is safest to assume that they contain asbestos.

Special hazards

Hydrofluoric acid
• This extremely corrosive acid is formed when certain types of synthetic rubber, found in some O-rings, oil seals, fuel hoses etc, are exposed to temperatures above 400°C. The rubber changes into a charred or sticky substance containing the acid. *Once formed, the acid remains dangerous for years. If it gets onto the skin, it may be necessary to amputate the limb concerned.*
• When dealing with a vehicle which has suffered a fire, or with components salvaged from such a vehicle, wear protective gloves and discard them after use.

The battery
• Batteries contain sulphuric acid, which attacks clothing, eyes and skin. Take care when topping-up or carrying the battery.
• The hydrogen gas given off by the battery is highly explosive. Never cause a spark or allow a naked light nearby. Be careful when connecting and disconnecting battery chargers or jump leads.

Air bags
• Air bags can cause injury if they go off accidentally. Take care when removing the steering wheel and/or facia. Special storage instructions may apply.

Diesel injection equipment
• Diesel injection pumps supply fuel at very high pressure. Take care when working on the fuel injectors and fuel pipes.

⚠ *Warning: Never expose the hands, face or any other part of the body to injector spray; the fuel can penetrate the skin with potentially fatal results.*

Remember...

DO
• Do use eye protection when using power tools, and when working under the vehicle.
• Do wear gloves or use barrier cream to protect your hands when necessary.
• Do get someone to check periodically that all is well when working alone on the vehicle.
• Do keep loose clothing and long hair well out of the way of moving mechanical parts.
• Do remove rings, wristwatch etc, before working on the vehicle – especially the electrical system.
• Do ensure that any lifting or jacking equipment has a safe working load rating adequate for the job.

DON'T
• Don't attempt to lift a heavy component which may be beyond your capability – get assistance.
• Don't rush to finish a job, or take unverified short cuts.
• Don't use ill-fitting tools which may slip and cause injury.
• Don't leave tools or parts lying around where someone can trip over them. Mop up oil and fuel spills at once.
• Don't allow children or pets to play in or near a vehicle being worked on.

Dimensions, Weights & Capacities

For information applicable to later models, see Supplement at end of manual

Dimensions

Overall length:
- Golf .... 3985 mm (157 in)
- Jetta .... 4315 mm (170 in)

Overall width:
- Golf .... 1665 mm (66 in)
- Jetta .... 1665 mm (66 in)

Overall height:
- Golf .... 1415 mm (56 in)
- Golf GTI .... 1405 mm (55 in)
- Jetta .... 1415 mm (56 in)

Wheelbase:
- All models .... 2475 mm (98 in)

Turning circle:
- All models .... 10.5 m (34.4 ft)

Weights (approximate)

Kerb weight:
- Golf Base model .... 837 kg (1845 lb)
- Golf C and C Formel E:
  - Manual .... 847 kg (1867 lb)
  - Automatic .... 867 kg (1911 lb)
- Golf GL:
  - Manual .... 892 kg (1966 lb)
  - Automatic .... 912 kg (2011 lb)
- Golf GTI .... 1003 kg (2211 lb)
- Jetta C .... 897 kg (1978 lb)
- Jetta CL Formel E .... 897 kg (1978 lb)
- Jetta GL:
  - Manual .... 922 kg (2033 lb)
  - Automatic .... 952 kg (2099 lb)

Trailer load (max) – with brakes:
- 1.05 litre .... 800 kg (1764 lb)
- 1.3 litre .... 1000 kg (2205 lb)
- 1.6 and 1.8 litre .... 1200 kg (2646 lb)

Roof rack load (max):
- All models .... 75 kg (165 lb)

Capacities

Engine oil:
- 1.05 and 1.3 litre:
  - Rocker finger engine:
    - With filter change .... 3.0 litre (5.3 Imp pints)
    - Without filter change .... 2.5 litre (4.4 Imp pints)
  - Hydraulic tappet engine:
    - With filter change .... 3.5 litre (6.2 Imp pints)
    - Without filter change .... 3.0 litre (5.3 Imp pints)
- 1.6 and 1.8 litre:
  - Pre-August 1985:
    - With filter change .... 3.5 litre (6.2 Imp pints)
    - Without filter change .... 3.0 litre (5.3 Imp pints)
  - August 1 985-on:
    - With filter change .... 4.0 litre (7.0 Imp pints)
    - Without filter change .... 3.5 litre (6.2 Imp pints)

Manual gearbox and final drive:
- 4-speed (084 gearbox) .... 2.2 litre (3.9 Imp pints)
- 4-speed (020 gearbox) .... 1.5 litre (2.6 Imp pints)
- 5-speed (085 gearbox) .... 3.1 litre (5.5 Imp pints)
- 5-speed (020 gearbox) .... 2.0 litre (3.5 Imp pints)

Automatic transmission fluid:
- Total from dry .... 6.0 litre (10.6 Imp pints)
- Service (drain and refill) .... 3.0 litre (5.3 Imp pints)
- Final drive capacity .... 0.75 litre (1.3 Imp pints)

Cooling system:
- Total capacity (approx) .... 6.3 litre (11.1 Imp pints)

Fuel tank:
- Total capacity (all models) .... 55 litre (12 gal)

Roadside Repairs 0•7

Puddles on the garage floor or drive, or obvious wetness under the bonnet or underneath the car, suggest a leak that needs investigating. It can sometimes be difficult to decide where the leak is coming from, especially if the engine bay is very dirty already. Leaking oil or fluid can also be blown rearwards by the passage of air under the car, giving a false impression of where the problem lies.

 Warning: Most automotive oils and fluids are poisonous. Wash them off skin, and change out of contaminated clothing, without delay.

Identifying leaks

 HAYNES HiNT *The smell of a fluid leaking from the car may provide a clue to what's leaking. Some fluids are distinctively coloured. It may help to clean the car carefully and to park it over some clean paper overnight as an aid to locating the source of the leak.*
Remember that some leaks may only occur while the engine is running.

Sump oil

Engine oil may leak from the drain plug...

Oil from filter
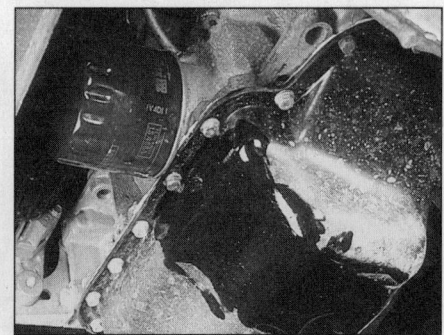
...or from the base of the oil filter.

Gearbox oil

Gearbox oil can leak from the seals at the inboard ends of the driveshafts.

Antifreeze
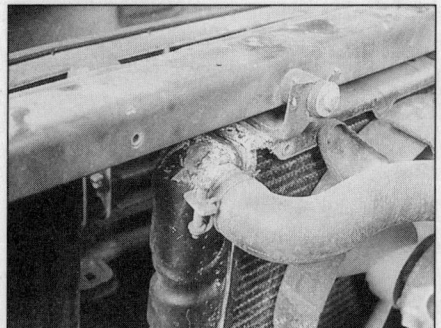
Leaking antifreeze often leaves a crystalline deposit like this.

Brake fluid
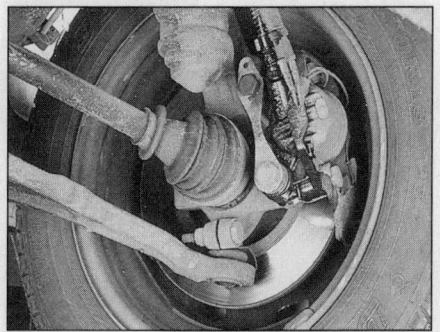
A leak occurring at a wheel is almost certainly brake fluid.

Power steering fluid

Power steering fluid may leak from the pipe connectors on the steering rack.

Roadside Repairs

Jacking and towing

Jacking

The jack supplied in the vehicle tool kit by the manufacturer should only be used for emergency roadside wheel changing unless it is supplemented by safety stands.

The jack supplied is of the half scissors type. Check that the handbrake is fully applied before using the jack, and only jack the vehicle up on firm level ground. If the ground is not firm you will need to position a large flat packing piece under the jack base to provide additional support.

Chock the wheel diagonally opposite the one to be changed. Using the tools provided remove the hub cap where necessary, then loosen the the wheel bolts half a turn. Locate the lifting arm of the jack beneath the reinforced seam of the side sill panel (photo) directly beneath the wedge shaped depression nearest to the wheel to be removed. Turn the jack handle until the base of the jack contacts the ground directly beneath the sill, then continue to turn the handle until the wheel is free of the ground. Unscrew the wheel bolts and remove the wheel. On light alloy wheels prise off the centre trim cap and press it into the spare wheel (photo).

Locate the spare wheel on the hub, then insert and tighten the bolts in diagonal sequence. Lower the jack and fully tighten the bolts. Refit the hub cap where necessary, remove the chock and relocate the tool kit, jack and wheel in the luggage compartment.

When jacking up the car with a pillar or trolley jack, position the jack beneath the reinforced plate behind the front wheel (see illustration) or beneath the reinforced seam at the rear of the side sill panel. Use the same positions when supporting the car with axle stands. *Never jack up the car beneath the suspension or axle components, the sump, or the gearbox.*

Towing

Towing eyes are fitted to the front and rear of the vehicle (photos), the front towing eye being covered by a plastic flap. Compress the flap and pivot it downwards to expose the towing eye. A tow line should not be attached to any other points. It is preferable to use a slightly elastic tow line, to reduce the strain on both vehicles, either by having a tow line manufactured from synthetic fibre, or one which is fitted with an elastic link.

When towing, the following important precautions must be observed:

(a) Turn the ignition key of the vehicle being towed, so that the steering wheel is free (unlocked).
(b) Remember that when the engine is not running the brake servo will not operate, so that additional pressure will be required on the brake pedal after the first few applications.
(c) On vehicles with automatic transmission, ensure that the gear selector lever is at N. Do not tow faster than 30 mph (45 kph), or further than 30 miles (45 km) unless the front wheels are lifted clear of the ground.
(d) On models fitted with power steering, additional force will be required to turn the steering wheel when the engine is not running.

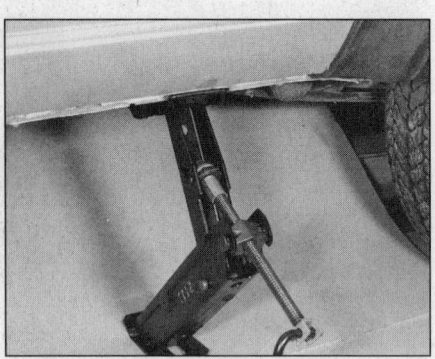
Vehicle jacking position

Removing the wheel centre trim

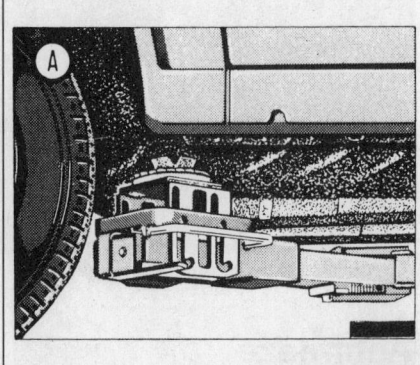

Towing eye – front

Towing eye – rear

Alternative jack location point at front (A) and rear (B)

Roadside Repairs 0•9

Jump starting

Jump starting will get you out of trouble, but you must correct whatever made the battery go flat in the first place. There are three possibilities:

1 The battery has been drained by repeated attempts to start, or by leaving the lights on.

2 The charging system is not working properly (alternator drivebelt slack or broken, alternator wiring fault or alternator itself faulty).

3 The battery itself is at fault (electrolyte low, or battery worn out).

When jump-starting a car using a booster battery, observe the following precautions:

✔ Before connecting the booster battery, make sure that the ignition is switched off.

✔ Ensure that all electrical equipment (lights, heater, wipers, etc) is switched off.

✔ Make sure that the booster battery is the same voltage as the discharged one in the vehicle.

✔ If the battery is being jump-started from the battery in another vehicle, the two vehcles MUST NOT TOUCH each other.

✔ Make sure that the transmission is in neutral (or PARK, in the case of automatic transmission).

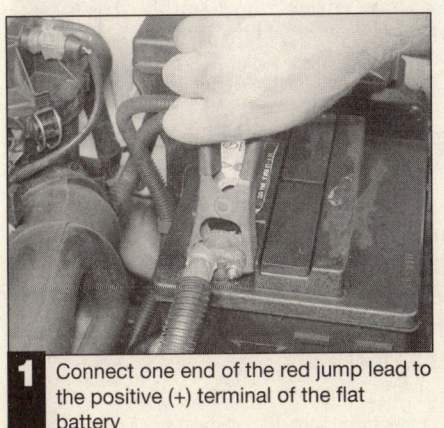

1 Connect one end of the red jump lead to the positive (+) terminal of the flat battery

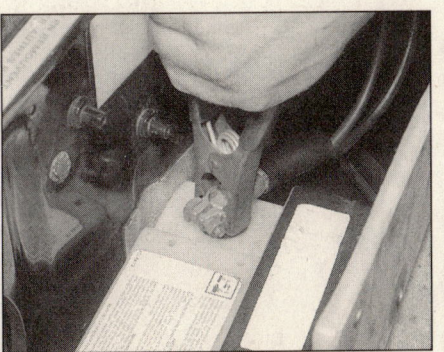

2 Connect the other end of the red lead to the positive (+) terminal of the booster battery.

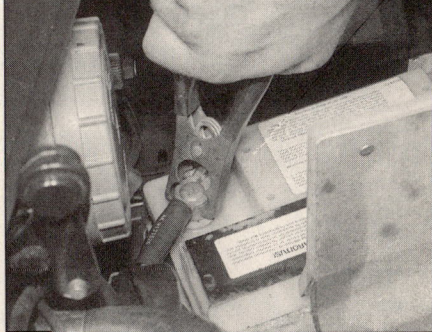

3 Connect one end of the black jump lead to the negative (-) terminal of the booster battery

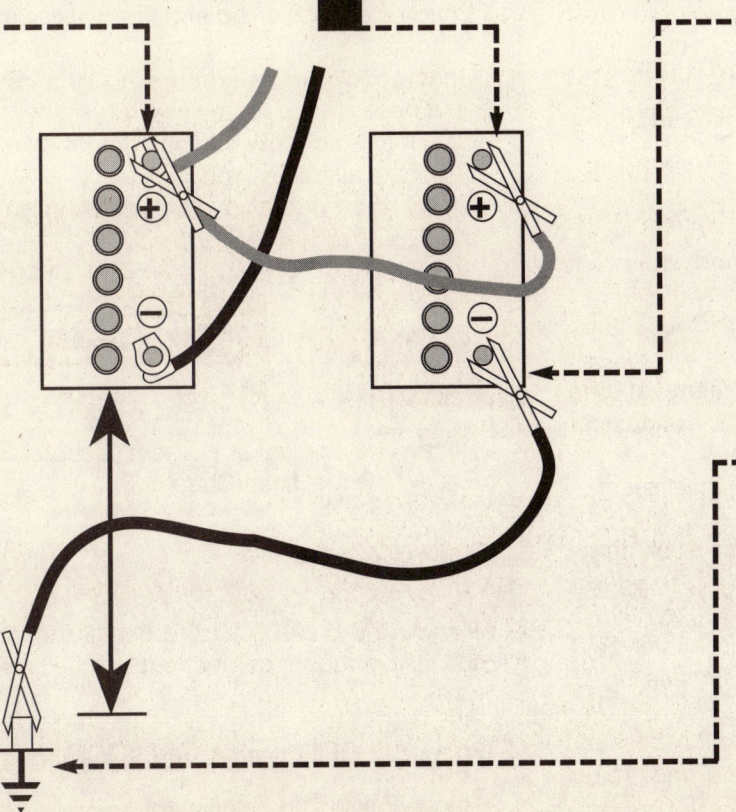

4 Connect the other end of the black jump lead to a bolt or bracket on the engine block, well away from the battery, on the vehicle to be started.

5 Make sure that the jump leads will not come into contact with the fan, drive-belts or other moving parts of the engine.

6 Start the engine using the booster battery, then with the engine running at idle speed, disconnect the jump leads in the reverse order of connection.

Routine Maintenance

For modifications, and information applicable to later models, see Supplement at end of manual

Maintenance is essential for ensuring safety and desirable for the purpose of getting the best in terms of performance and economy from your car. Over the years the need for periodic lubrication has been greatly reduced, if not totally eliminated. This has unfortunately tended to lead some owners to think that because no such action is required, the items either no longer exist, or will last forever. This is certainly not the case; it is essential to carry out regular visual examination as comprehensively as possible in order to spot any possible defects at an early stage, before they develop into major expensive repairs.

Every 250 miles (400 km) or weekly – whichever comes first

- [ ] Check the level of the oil and top up if necessary
- [ ] Check the coolant level and top up if necessary
- [ ] Check the level of electrolyte in the battery and top up if necessary
- [ ] Check the tyre pressures
- [ ] Visually examine the tyres for wear and damage
- [ ] Check that all the lights work
- [ ] Clean the headlamps
- [ ] Check the windscreen/tailgate washer fluid levels and top up if necessary
- [ ] Check the level of fluid in the brake master cylinder reservoir – if topping-up is required, check for leaks

Every 10 000 miles (15 000 km) or 12 months – whichever comes first

- [ ] Check and if necessary adjust the clutch (Chapter 5)
- [ ] Check for oil, fuel and coolant leaks
- [ ] Check antifreeze concentration and adjust if necessary
- [ ] Check valve clearances and adjust if necessary (Chapter 1)
- [ ] Check the condition and adjustment of the alternator, power steering pump and air conditioner compressor drivebelt(s) as applicable
- [ ] Renew the belt(s) or adjust tension, as necessary
- [ ] Renew the spark plugs
- [ ] Renew the contact points and adjust dwell angle (Chapter 4)
- [ ] Adjust ignition timing (Chapter 4)
- [ ] Change engine oil and renew oil filter (Chapter 1)
- [ ] Check exhaust system for leaks and damage
- [ ] Adjust the slow running (Chapter 3)
- [ ] Check the gearbox oil level and top up if necessary
- [ ] Check automatic transmission fluid level and top up if necessary
- [ ] Check the CV joint boots for leaks and damage
- [ ] Check the brake lines, hoses and unions for leaks and damage
- [ ] Check the disc pads and rear brake shoe linings for wear
- [ ] Check the brake fluid level and top up if necessary
- [ ] Check the operation of all electrical components, light bulbs, etc
- [ ] Check the windscreen/rear window washer fluid level and top up if necessary
- [ ] Check the battery electrolyte level and top up with distilled water if necessary
- [ ] Check headlight beam alignment and adjust if necessary
- [ ] Check steering gear bellows for leaks and damage
- [ ] Check steering tie-rod ends for wear and condition of boots
- [ ] Check power-assisted steering fluid level and top up if necessary
- [ ] Check tread depth and condition of tyres
- [ ] Lubricate all hinges and catches
- [ ] Check the underbody for corrosion and damage and reseal as necessary

Every 20 000 miles (30 000 km) or 24 months – whichever comes first

- [ ] Renew the air cleaner element (Chapter 3)
- [ ] Renew the fuel filter (Chapter 3)

Every 2 years

- [ ] Renew the brake fluid and check the condition of the visible rubber components of the brake system

Every 40 000 miles (60 000 km)

- [ ] Renew the timing belt (Chapter 1)

Routine Maintenance 0•11

Engine compartment (1.3 litre) – air cleaner removed

1 Engine oil dipstick
2 Fuel line filter
3 Brake master cylinder reservoir
4 Carburettor
5 Ignition coil
6 Cooling system expansion tank
7 Windscreen/headlight washer reservoir
8 Ignition distributor
9 Battery
10 Cooling fan
11 Engine oil filler cap

0•12 Routine Maintenance

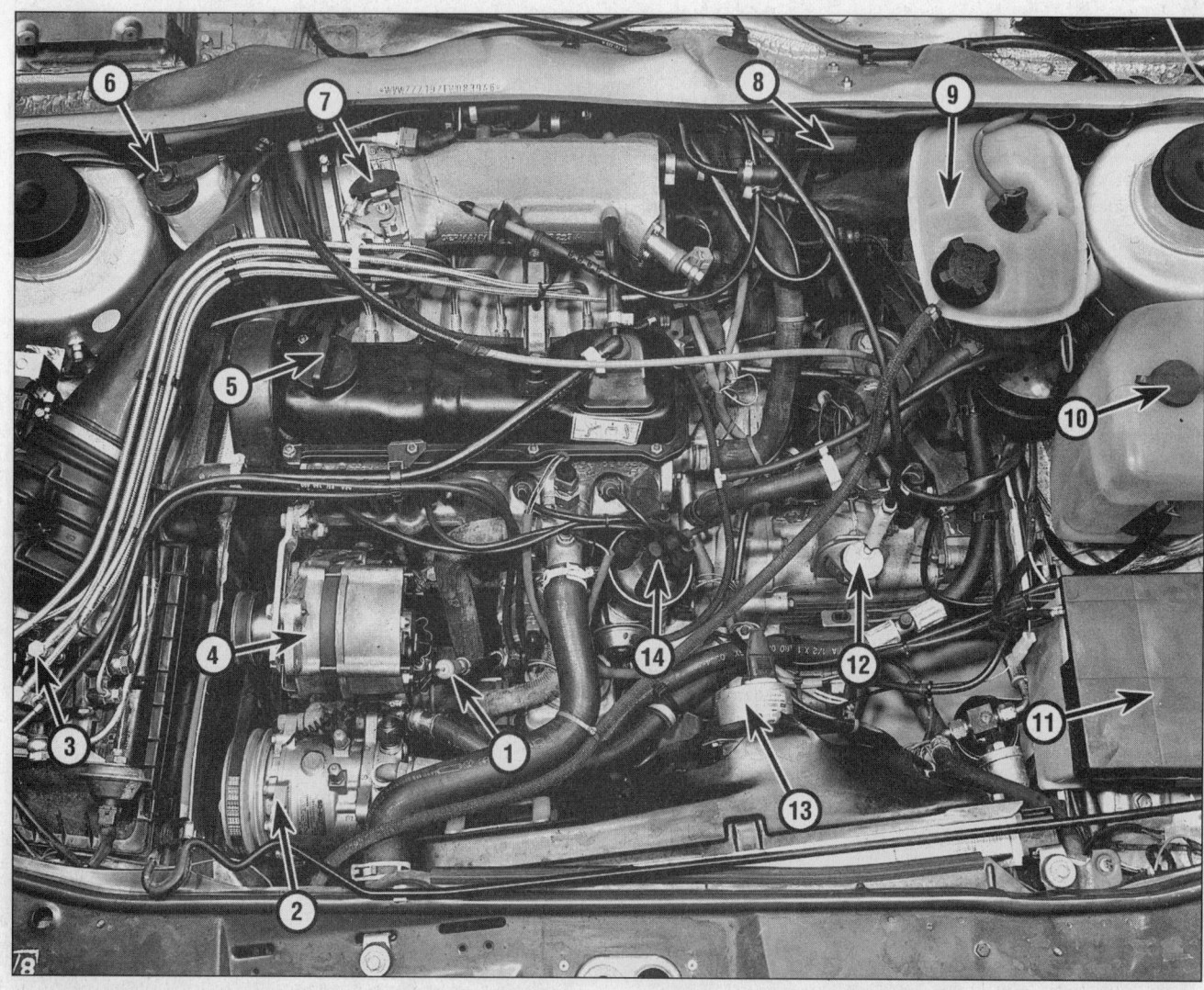

Engine compartment – fuel injection model

1. Engine oil dipstick
2. Compressor (air conditioning)
3. Fuel distributor
4. Alternator
5. Engine oil filler cap
6. Brake master cylinder reservoir
7. Throttle housing
8. Ignition coil
9. Cooling system expansion tank
10. Windscreen/headlamp washer reservoir
11. Battery
12. Clutch cable
13. Cooling fan
14. Ignition distributor

Routine Maintenance 0•13

View from beneath front of 1.3 litre model
1 Alternator
2 Oil filter
3 Driveshaft
4 Front mounting
5 Cooling system bottom hose
6 Gearbox
7 Track control arm
8 Tie-rod
9 Exhaust
10 Engine sump

View from beneath front of fuel injected model
1 Driveshaft
2 Front mounting
3 Starter motor
4 Gearbox
5 Track control arm
6 Tie-rod
7 Anti-roll bar
8 Exhaust system
9 Engine sump

0•14 Routine Maintenance

View from beneath rear of 1.3 litre model
1 Exhaust
2 Fuel tank
3 Rear shock absorber lower mounting
4 Axle beam
5 Handbrake cable (right-hand)
6 Handbrake cable (left-hand)
7 Rear drum brake

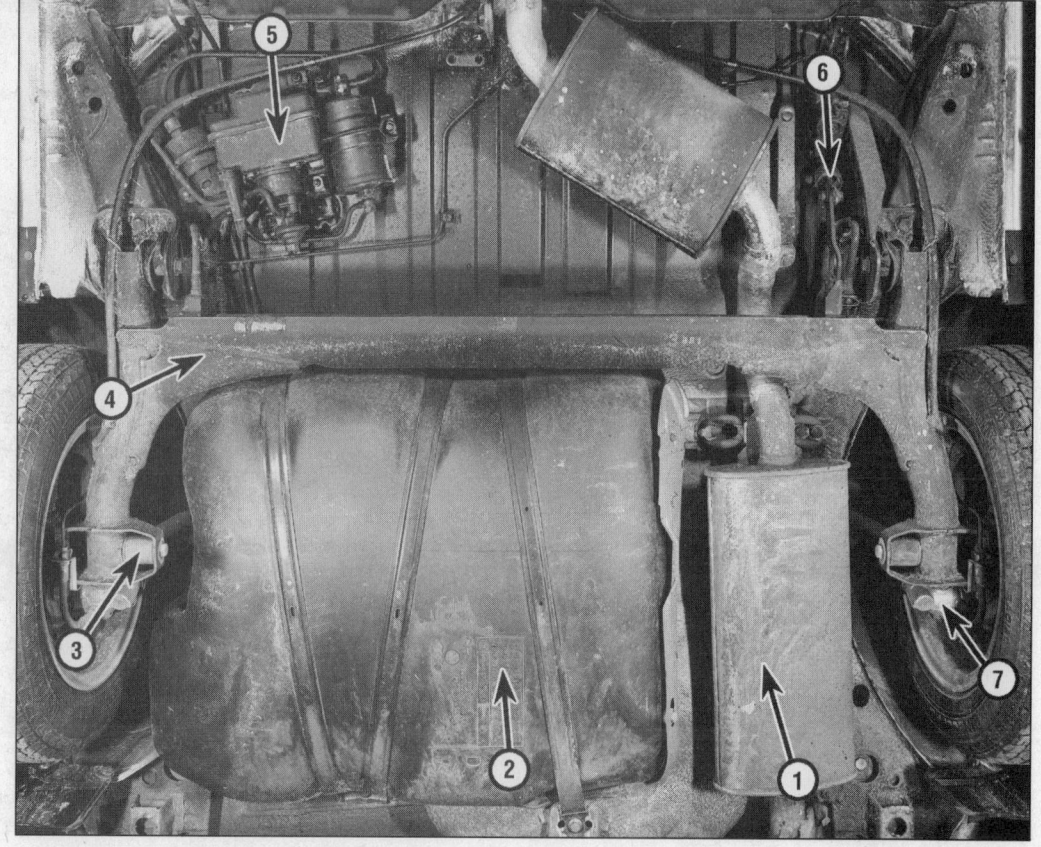

View from beneath rear of fuel injected model
1 Exhaust
2 Fuel tank
3 Rear shock absorber lower mounting
4 Axle beam
5 Fuel pump and associated fittings
6 Brake pressure regulator
7 Rear disc brake

Routine Maintenance 0•15

Tyre conditon and pressure

It is very important that tyres are in good condition, and at the correct pressure - having a tyre failure at any speed is highly dangerous. Tyre wear is influenced by driving style - harsh braking and acceleration, or fast cornering, will all produce more rapid tyre wear. As a general rule, the front tyres wear out faster than the rears. Interchanging the tyres from front to rear ("rotating" the tyres) may result in more even wear. However, if this is completely effective, you may have the expense of replacing all four tyres at once!
Remove any nails or stones embedded in the tread before they penetrate the tyre to cause deflation. If removal of a nail does reveal that the tyre has been punctured, refit the nail so that its point of penetration is marked. Then immediately change the wheel, and have the tyre repaired by a tyre dealer.
Regularly check the tyres for damage in the form of cuts or bulges, especially in the sidewalls. Periodically remove the wheels, and clean any dirt or mud from the inside and outside surfaces. Examine the wheel rims for signs of rusting, corrosion or other damage. Light alloy wheels are easily damaged by "kerbing" whilst parking; steel wheels may also become dented or buckled. A new wheel is very often the only way to overcome severe damage.

New tyres should be balanced when they are fitted, but it may become necessary to re-balance them as they wear, or if the balance weights fitted to the wheel rim should fall off. Unbalanced tyres will wear more quickly, as will the steering and suspension components. Wheel imbalance is normally signified by vibration, particularly at a certain speed (typically around 50 mph). If this vibration is felt only through the steering, then it is likely that just the front wheels need balancing. If, however, the vibration is felt through the whole car, the rear wheels could be out of balance. Wheel balancing should be carried out by a tyre dealer or garage.

1 Tread Depth - visual check
The original tyres have tread wear safety bands (B), which will appear when the tread depth reaches approximately 1.6 mm. The band positions are indicated by a triangular mark on the tyre sidewall (A).

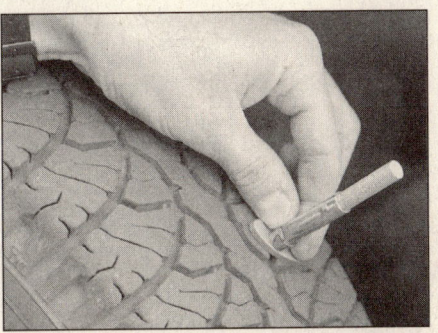

2 Tread Depth - manual check
Alternatively, tread wear can be monitored with a simple, inexpensive device known as a tread depth indicator gauge.

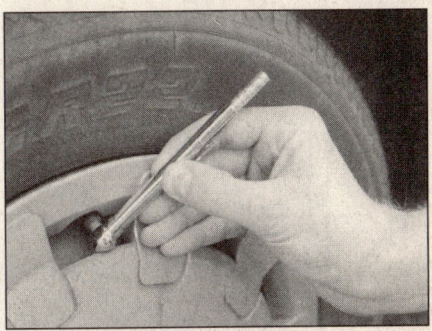

3 Tyre Pressure Check
Check the tyre pressures regularly with the tyres cold. Do not adjust the tyre pressures immediately after the vehicle has been used, or an inaccurate setting will result.

Tyre tread wear patterns

Shoulder Wear

Underinflation (wear on both sides)
Under-inflation will cause overheating of the tyre, because the tyre will flex too much, and the tread will not sit correctly on the road surface. This will cause a loss of grip and excessive wear, not to mention the danger of sudden tyre failure due to heat build-up.
Check and adjust pressures
Incorrect wheel camber (wear on one side)
Repair or renew suspension parts
Hard cornering
Reduce speed!

Centre Wear

Overinflation
Over-inflation will cause rapid wear of the centre part of the tyre tread, coupled with reduced grip, harsher ride, and the danger of shock damage occurring in the tyre casing.
Check and adjust pressures

If you sometimes have to inflate your car's tyres to the higher pressures specified for maximum load or sustained high speed, don't forget to reduce the pressures to normal afterwards.

Uneven Wear

Front tyres may wear unevenly as a result of wheel misalignment. Most tyre dealers and garages can check and adjust the wheel alignment (or "tracking") for a modest charge.
Incorrect camber or castor
Repair or renew suspension parts
Malfunctioning suspension
Repair or renew suspension parts
Unbalanced wheel
Balance tyres
Incorrect toe setting
Adjust front wheel alignment
Note: *The feathered edge of the tread which typifies toe wear is best checked by feel.*

Recommended Lubricants and Fluids

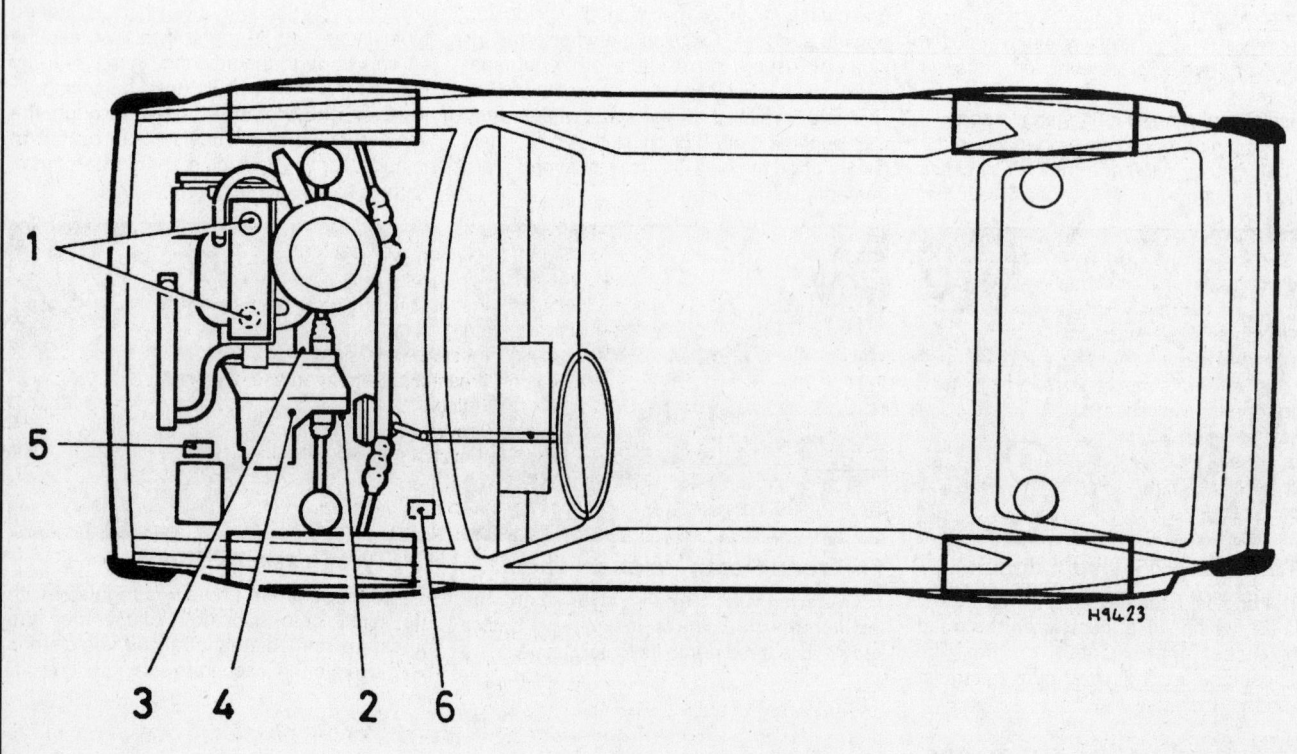

Component or system	Lubricant type/specification
1 Engine	Multigrade engine oil, viscosity SAE 15W/50 or 20W/50
2 Manual gearbox/final drive	Gear oil, viscosity SAE 80
3 Final drive (automatic transmission)	Hypoid gear oil, viscosity SAE 90EP
4 Automatic transmission	Dexron type ATF
5 Power steering To April 1989 April 1989 on	 Dexron type ATF VW oil G 002 000
6 Braking system	Hydraulic fluid to FMVSS 11 6 DOT 4

Chapter 1 Engine

For modifications, and information applicable to later models, see Supplement at end of manual

Contents

Part A: 1.05 and 1.3 litre engine

Camshaft - examination and renovation	29
Camshaft - refitting	37
Camshaft - removal	11
Crankcase ventilation system - description	21
Crankshaft and bearings - examination and renovation	23
Crankshaft and main bearings - refitting	31
Crankshaft and main bearings - removal	19
Crankshaft oil seals - renewal	15
Cylinder block/crankcase - examination and renovation	24
Cylinder head - dismantling, inspection and overhaul	12
Cylinder head - reassembly	36
Cylinder head - refitting	38
Cylinder head - removal	10
Engine - adjustments after major overhaul	43
Engine - refitting	42
Engine - removal	6
Engine ancillary components - removal	9
Engine ancillary components and gearbox - refitting	41
Engine and gearbox - separation	7
Engine dismantling - general	8
Engine reassembly - general	30
Examination and renovation - general	22
Fault finding - engine	See end of Chapter
Flywheel - examination and renovation	27
Flywheel - refitting	35
Flywheel - removal	14
General description	1
Major operation only possible after removal of engine from car	4
Major operations possible with engine in car	3
Method of engine removal	5
Oil filter - renewal	20
Oil pump - examination and renovation	26
Oil pump - refitting	33
Oil pump - removal	17
Pistons and connecting rods - examination and renovation	25
Pistons and connecting rods - refitting	32
Pistons and connecting rods - removal	18
Routine maintenance - engine	2
Sump - refitting	34
Sump - removal	16
Timing belt and sprockets - examination and renovation	28
Timing belt and sprockets - refitting	39
Timing belt and sprockets - removal	13
Valve clearances - checking and adjustment	40

Part B: 1.6 and 1.8 litre engine

Camshaft - removal and refitting	55
Crankcase ventilation system - description	64
Crankshaft and main bearings - examination and renovation	66
Crankshaft and main bearings - refitting	74
Crankshaft and main bearings - removal	60
Crankshaft, camshaft and intermediate shaft oil seals - renewal (engine in car)	63
Cylinder block/crankcase - examination and renovation	67
Cylinder head - dismantling, inspection and overhaul	57
Cylinder head - refitting	78
Cylinder head - removal	56
Engine - adjustments after major overhaul	82
Engine - refitting	81
Engine ancillary components refitting	80
Engine ancillary components - removal	53
Engine and gearbox - separation and reconnection	51
Engine dismantling - general	52
Engine (carburettor) - removal	49
Engine (fuel injection) - removal	50
Engine reassembly - general	73
Examination and renovation - general	65
Fault finding - engine	See end of Chapter
Flywheel/driveplate - examination and renovation	71
General description	44
Intermediate shaft - examination and renovation	70
Intermediate shaft - refitting	75
Intermediate shaft - removal	61
Major operations only possible after removal of engine from car	47
Major operations possible with engine in car	46
Method of engine removal	48
Oil filter - renewal	62
Oil pump - examination and renovation	69
Pistons and connecting rods - examination and renovation	68
Pistons and connecting rods - refitting	76
Pistons and connecting rods - removal	59
Routine maintenance - engine	45
Sump and oil pump - removal and refitting	58
Timing belt and sprockets - examination and renovation	72
Timing belt and sprockets - refitting	79
Timing belt and sprockets - removal	54
Valve clearances - checking and adjustment	77

Degrees of difficulty

| **Easy,** suitable for novice with little experience | **Fairly easy,** suitable for beginner with some experience | **Fairly difficult,** suitable for competent DIY mechanic 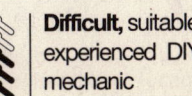 | **Difficult,** suitable for experienced DIY mechanic | **Very difficult,** suitable for expert DIY or professional |

1•2 Engine

Specifications

General
Type	Four-cylinder in-line, water cooled, overhead camshaft
Firing order	1-3-4-2 (No 1 at camshaft sprocket end)

Bore:
- 1043 cc: 75 mm (2.955 in)
- 1272 cc: 75 mm (2.955 in)
- 1595 cc: 81 mm (3.191 in)
- 1781 cc: 81 mm (3.191 in)

Stroke:
- 1043 cc: 59.0 mm (2.325 in)
- 1272 cc: 72.0 mm (2.837 in)
- 1595 cc: 77.4 mm (3.050 in)
- 1781 cc: 86.4 mm (3.404 in)

Compression ratio:
- 1043 cc (engine code GN): 9.5 to 1
- 1272 cc (engine code HK): 9.5 to 1
- 1595 cc (engine code EZ): 9.0 to 1
- 1781 cc (engine code EV Jetronic - fuel injection and GU - carburettor): 10.0 to 1

Compression pressure:

	bar	lbf/in^2
1.05 and 1.3 litre (new)	8 to 10	116 to 145
1.05 to 1.3 litre (minimum)	7	102
1.6 litre (new)	9 to 12	131 to 174
1.6 litre (minimum)	7.5	109
1.8 litre (new)	10 to 13	145 to 189
1.8 litre (minimum)	7.5	109
Maximum permissible difference between any two cylinders	3	44

Crankshaft
- Main journal diameter (standard): 54.0 mm (2.128 in)
- Main journal undersizes: 53.75, 53.50 and 53.25 mm (2.118, 2.108 and 2.098 in)

Crankpin diameter (standard):
- 1.05 and 1.3 litre: 42 mm (1.655 in)
- 1.6 and 1.8 litre: 47.80 mm (1.883 in)

Crankpin journal undersizes:
- 1.05 and 1.3 litre: 41.75, 41.50 and 41.25 mm (1.645, 1.635 and 1.625 in)
- 1.6 and 1.8 litre: 47.55, 47.30 and 47.05 mm (1.873, 1.864 and 1.854 in)

Crankshaft endfloat (maximum):
- 1.05 and 1.3 litre: 0.20 mm (0.0079 in)
- 1.6 and 1.8 litre: 0.25 mm (0.0099 in)

- Crankshaft endfloat (minimum): 0.07 mm (0.0028 in)
- Main bearing running clearance (maximum): 0.17 mm (0.0067 in)

Connecting rods
Big-end running clearance (maximum):
- 1.05 and 1.3 litre: 0.095 mm (0.0037 in)
- 1.6 and 1.8 litre: 0.012 mm (0.0005 in)

Big-end endfloat (maximum):
- 1.05 and 1.3 litre: 0.40 mm (0.0158 in)
- 1.6 and 1.8 litre: 0.37 mm (0.0146 in)

Pistons
- Piston clearance in bore (maximum): 0.07 mm (0.0028 in)
- Piston clearance in bore (minimum): 0.03 mm (0.0012 in)

Piston diameter (standard):
- 1.05 and 1.3 litre: 74.98 mm (2.954 in)
- 1.6 and 1.8 litre: 80.98 mm (3.191 in)

Piston oversize diameters - 1.05 and 1.3 litre
- 1st oversize: 75.23 mm (2.964 in)
- 2nd oversize: 75.48 mm (2.974 in)
- 3rd oversize: 75.98 mm (2.994 in)

Piston oversize diameters - 1.6 and 1.8 litre:
- 1st oversize: 81.23 mm (3.200 in)
- 2nd oversize: 81.48 mm (3.210 in)

Piston wear limit (measured 10 mm from base at right angles to gudgeon pin): 0.04 mm (0.0016 in)

Engine 1•3

Piston rings
Clearance in grooves (maximum) .... 0.15 mm (0.006 in)
End gap - compression rings .... 0.30 to 0.45 mm (0.012 to 0.018 in)
End gap - oil scraper ring .... 0.25 to 0.40 mm (0.010 to 0.016 in)

Gudgeon pin
Fit in piston .... Push fit at 60°C (140°F)

Intermediate shaft (1.6 and 1.8 litre)
Endfloat (maximum) .... 0.25 mm (0.010 in)

Cylinder head
Maximum allowable face distortion .... 0.1 mm (0.004 in)

Camshaft
Run-out at centre bearing:
   1.05 and 1.3 .... 0.02 mm (0.0008 in)
   1.6 and 1.8 .... 0.01 mm (0.0004 in)
Endfloat .... 0.15 mm (0.006 in)

Valves
Seat angle .... 45°

	1.05 and 1.3	1.6 and 1.8
Head diameter:		
Inlet	34.0 mm (1.340 in)	38.0 mm (1.497 in)
Exhaust	28.1 mm (1.107 in)	33.0 mm (1.300 in)
Stem diameter:		
Inlet	7.97 mm (0.314 in)	7.97 mm (0.314 in)
Exhaust	7.95 mm (0.313 in)	7.95 mm (0.313 in)
Overall length (standard):		
Inlet	110.5 mm (4.354 in)	98.70 mm (3.889 in)
Exhaust	110.5 mm (4.354 in)	98.50 mm (3.881 in)

Valve guides
Maximum valve rock (valve stem flush with guide):
   Inlet valve .... 1.0 mm (0.039 in)
   Exhaust valve .... 1.3 mm (0.051 in)

Valve timing (nil valve clearance, at 1 mm valve lift)
1.05 litre:
   Inlet opens .... 9° ATDC
   Inlet closes .... 13° ABDC
   Exhaust opens .... 15° BBDC
   Exhaust closes .... 11° BTDC
1.3 litre:
   Inlet opens .... 3° BTDC
   Inlet closes .... 38° ABDC
   Exhaust opens .... 41° BBDC
   Exhaust closes .... 3° BTDC
1.6 litre:
   Inlet opens .... 5° BTDC
   Inlet closes .... 21° ABDC
   Exhaust opens .... 41° BBDC
   Exhaust closes .... 3° BTDC
1.8 litre (engine code GU):
   Inlet opens .... 1° BTDC
   Inlet closes .... 37° ABDC
   Exhaust opens .... 42° BBDC
   Exhaust closes .... 2° ATDC
1.8 litre (engine code EV):
   Inlet opens .... 2° BTDC
   Inlet closes .... 45° ABDC
   Exhaust opens .... 45° BBDC
   Exhaust closes .... 8° BTDC

1•4 Engine

Valve clearances

	1.05 and 1.3 litre	1.6 and 1.8 litre
Warm:		
Inlet	0.15 to 0.20 mm (0.006 to 0.008 in)	0.20 to 0.30 mm (0.008 to 0.012 in)
Exhaust	0.25 to 0.30 mm (0.010 to 0.012 in)	0.40 to 0.50 m (0.016 to 0.020 in)
Cold:		
Inlet	0.10 to 0.15 mm (0.004 to 0.006 in)	0.15 to 0.25 mm (0.006 to 0.010 in)
Exhaust	0.20 to 0.25 mm (0.008 to 0.010 in)	0.35 to 0.45 mm (0.014 to 0.018 in)

Lubrication

Oil type/specification/filter . . . . Multigrade engine oil, viscosity SAE 15W/50 or 20W/50/Champion C101/C160 (all models)

1.05 and 1.3 litre:
- Oil pump type . . . . Eccentric gear driven by crankshaft
- Oil pressure at 2000 rpm, with oil temperature 80°C/176°F . . . . 2.0 bar (29 lbf/in^2) minimum
- Oil capacity:
  - With filter change . . . . 3.0 litre (5.3 Imp pint)
  - Without filter change . . . . 2.5 litre (4.4 Imp pint)

1.6 and 1.8 litre:
- Oil pump type . . . . Twin gear, driven by intermediate shaft together with distributor
- Oil pressure at 2000 rpm, with oil temperature 80°C/176°F . . . . 2.0 bar (29 lbf/in^2) minimum
- Oil capacity:
  - With filter change . . . . 3.5 litre (6.2 Imp pint)
  - Without filter change . . . . 3.0 litre (5.3 Imp pint)

Torque wrench settings

	Nm	lbf ft
All models (see Figs. 1.1, 1.2 and 12.7)		
Engine mountings (with oiled threads):		
(a) M8 -1.05 and 1.3 litre	25	18
(a) M10 - 1.05 and 1.3 litre	45	33
(a) 1.6 and 1.8 litre	25	18
(b) all models	35	26
(c) all models	45	33
(d) all models	50	37
(e) all models	60	44
(f) all models	70	52
(g) all models	80	59
1.05 and 1.3 litre		
Engine to gearbox	55	41
Exhaust pipe to manifold	25	18
Flywheel bolts	75	55
Clutch bolts	25	18
Sump bolts	20	15
Sump drain plug	30	22
Main bearing cap bolts	65	48
Oil pump bolts	10	7
Connecting rod cap (big-end) nuts (oiled):		
Stage 1	30	22
Stage 2*	Tighten further 1/4 turn (90°)	Tighten further 1/4 turn (90°)
Oil suction pipe to pump	10	7
Oil relief valve plug	25	18
Oil pressure sender switch	25	18
Timing cover	10	7
Valve cover	10	7
Camshaft sprocket bolt	80	59
Crankshaft sprocket/pulley nut	80	59
Coolant pump bolts	10	7
Distributor flange bolts	20	15
Cylinder head bolts (engine cold):		
Stage 1	40	30
Stage 2	60	44
Stage 3	Turn further 1/2 turn (180°)	Turn further 1/2 turn (180°)

Engine 1•5

1.6 and 1.8 litre

Engine to gearbox:		
M10	45	33
M12	75	55
Exhaust manifold nuts	25	18
Exhaust pipe to manifold	10	7
Flywheel/driveplate bolts	20	15
Clutch pressure plate/washer bolts (renew)	100	74
Sump bolts	20	15
Sump drain plug	30	22
Main bearing cap bolts	65	48
Connecting rod big-end cap nuts:		
Stage 1	30	22
Stage 2*	Further tighten 1/4 turn (90°)	Further tighten 1/4 turn (90°)
Oil pump bolts	10	7
Oil pressure switch	25	18
Oil filter flange bolts	25	18
Front seal flange bolts:		
Small	20	15
Large	10	7
Intermediate shaft flange bolts	25	18
Camshaft bearing cap nuts (in sequence)	20	15
Camshaft sprocket bolt	80	59
Valve cover nuts	10	7
Belt tensioner pulley	45	33
Crankshaft sprocket bolt (oiled)	200	148
Intermediate shaft sprocket bolt	80	59
V-belt pulley	20	15
Timing cover	10	7
Rear cover lower bolts	30	22
Rear cover top bolt	10	7
Coolant pump bolts	20	15
Fuel pump bolts	20	15
Distributor clamp bolt	25	18
Cylinder head bolts (engine cold)	As for 1.05 and 1.3 litre engines	

When checking the connecting rod-to-crankshaft journal radial clearance using Plastigage, tighten only to 30Nm (22 lbf ft).

Part A: 1.05 and 1.3 litre engine

1 General description

The engine is of four-cylinder, in-line, overhead camshaft type, mounted transversely at the front of the car. The transmission is attached to the left-hand side of the engine.

The crankshaft is of five bearing type and separate thrust washers are fitted to the central main bearing to control the crankshaft endfloat.

The camshaft is driven by a toothed belt which also drives the water pump - the toothed belt is tensioned by moving the water pump in its eccentric mounting. The valves are operated from the camshaft by rocker fingers which pivot on ball-head studs. The distributor is driven by the camshaft and is located on the left-hand end of the cylinder head.

The oil pump is of the eccentric gear type driven from the end of the crankshaft.

The cylinder head is of crossflow design, with the inlet manifold at the rear and the exhaust manifold at the front.

2 Routine maintenance - engine

The following routine maintenance procedures should be undertaken at the specified intervals given at the start of this manual. The intervals given are those for a vehicle used in normal driving conditions.

2.2 Topping-up engine oil

Where the vehicle is subject to more severe daily use, such as city driving or in a hot dusty climate, then it is advisable to shorten the maintenance intervals accordingly.

Engine oil check

Check the engine oil with the vehicle parked on level ground, the engine switched off and having been stationary for a short period. This will allow oil in the lubrication circuits to return to the sump to provide a true

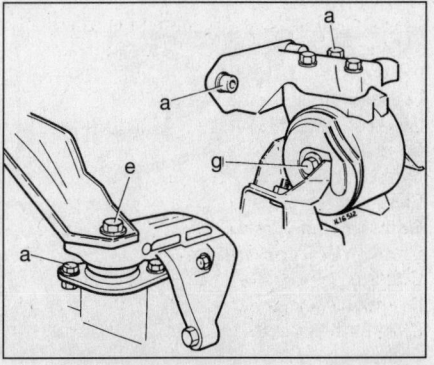

Fig. 1.1 Engine mounting bolts identification - see Specifications for torque settings

1•6 Engine – 1.05 and 1.3 litre

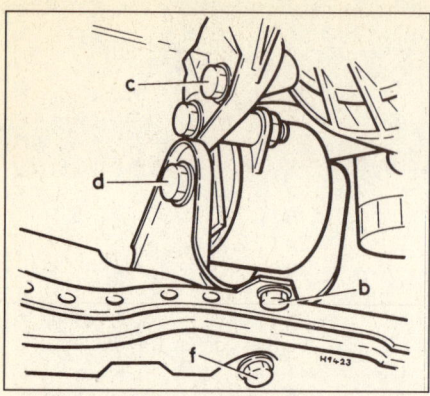

Fig. 1.2 Engine/transmission mounting bolts identification - see Specifications for torque settings

level reading. The dipstick should be withdrawn, wiped clean, fully inserted then withdrawn again to take the oil level reading. The oil level must be kept between the maximum and minimum markings on the dipstick at all times. If the oil level is down to the minimum mark, it will need a litre (1.7 Imp pint) to raise the oil level to the maximum mark. Do not overfill the engine. Top up through the oil filler neck in the cylinder head cover (photo). Check that the cover is firmly refitted and wipe clean any oil spillage. Recheck the oil level on completion.

Engine oil change
With the vehicle standing on level ground, remove the drain plug from the sump and drain the old engine oil into a container of suitable capacity. Draining is best undertaken directly after the vehicle has been used when the engine oil will be hot and will flow more freely. When draining is complete, refit the drain plug (on 1.6 and 1.8 litre models, renew the O-ring) and top up the engine oil to the correct level with the specified grade and quantity of engine oil.

Engine oil filter
The oil filter must be renewed at the specified intervals. The filter is best removed whilst waiting for the engine oil to drain. Renewing the oil filter is described in Section 20 of this Chapter.

Engine general checks
Inspect the engine regularly for any signs of oil, coolant or fuel leaks and if found attend to them without delay.

Valve clearances
The valve clearances must be checked and, if necessary, adjusted at the specified intervals. Refer to Section 40 or 77.

3 Major operation possible with engine in car

The following operations can be carried out without having to remove the engine from the car:
(a) Removal and servicing of the cylinder head, camshaft and timing belt
(b) Removal of the flywheel and crankshaft rear oil seal (after removal of the gearbox)
(c) Removal of the sump
(d) Removal of the piston/connecting rod assemblies (after removal of the cylinder head and sump)
(e) Renewal of the crankshaft front and rear oil seals and the camshaft front oil seal
(f) Renewal of the engine mountings
(g) Removal of the oil pump

4 Major operation only possible after removal of engine from car

The following operation can only be carried out after removal of the engine from the car:
Renewal of crankshaft main bearings

5 Method of engine removal

1 The engine, together with the gearbox, must be lifted from the engine compartment and the engine separated from the gearbox on the bench. Two people will be needed.
2 A hoist, capacity 150 kg (3 cwt), will be needed and the engine must be lifted approximately 1 metre (three feet). If the hoist is not portable, then sufficient room must be left behind the car to push the car back out of the way so that the power unit may be lowered. Blocks will be needed to support the engine after removal.
3 Ideally the car should be over a pit. If this is not possible then the body must be supported on axle stands so that the front wheels may be turned to undo the driveshaft nuts. The left one is accessible from above but the right-hand shaft must be undone from underneath. There are other jobs best done from below. Removal of the shift linkage can only be done from underneath, as can the removal of the exhaust pipe bracket. When all the jobs are done under the car, lower the car back to its wheels.
4 A set of splined keys will be required to remove and refit the socket-head bolts used to secure certain items in the engine, such as the cylinder head bolts (photo).
5 Draining of oil and coolant is best done away from the working area if possible. This saves the mess made by spilled oil in the place where you must work.
6 If an air conditioning system is fitted, observe the cautionary notes in Section 48 of this Chapter.

6 Engine - removal

1 Disconnect the battery negative lead.
2 Remove the bonnet, as described in Chapter 11, and put it in a safe place.
3 Drain the engine coolant and remove the radiator, complete with the cooling fan unit, as described in Chapter 2.
4 Remove the air cleaner unit, as described in Chapter 3.
5 Loosen the clip and disconnect the top hose from the thermostat housing.
6 Place a suitable container beneath the engine then unscrew the sump drain plug and drain the oil (photo). When completed, clean the drain plug and washer and tighten it into the sump.
7 Identify the fuel supply and return hoses

Fig. 1.3 Engine oil level dipstick and markings 1.5 and 1.3 litre (Sec 2)

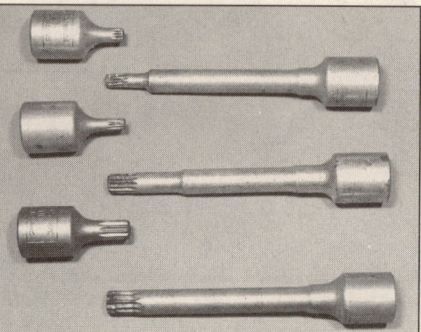

5.4 A splined key set will be required for various overhaul procedures on the car

6.6 Sump drain plug

Engine – 1.05 and 1.3 litre

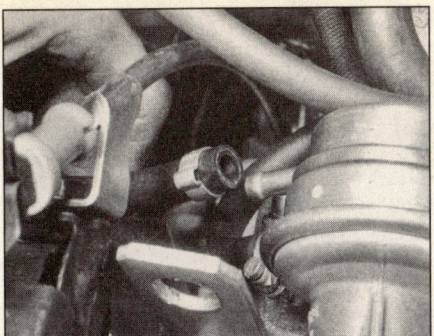
6.7 Detach hoses from fuel pump

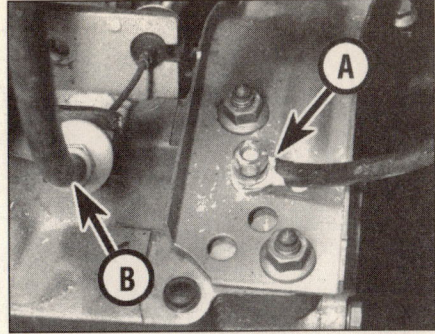
6.14 Earth lead (A) and clutch cable (B)

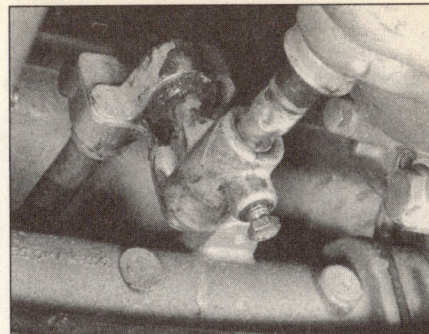
6.18 Shift rod coupling screw

then disconnect them from the fuel pump (photo) and fuel reservoir/carburettor. Plug the hoses to prevent fuel leakage.

8 Loosen the clip and disconnect the bottom hose from the coolant pipe at the rear of the engine.

9 Disconnect the accelerator cable and, where applicable, the choke cable; with reference to Chapter 3.

10 Disconnect the heater hoses from the thermostat housing and rear coolant pipe.

11 Detach the following connections, but identify each lead as it is disconnected to avoid confusion on reassembly:
(a) The oil pressure switches on the rear (carburettor side) of the cylinder head
(b) Inlet manifold preheating element line connector
(c) Thermo-switch leads (coolant hose intermediate piece)
(d) Distributor HT and LT leads
(e) Starter motor
(f) Temperature sender unit (thermostat housing)
(g) Fuel cut-off solenoid valve on carburettor
(h) Earth strap to the gearbox

12 Detach the wiring loom from the location clip on the bottom hose and fold back out of the way.

13 Disconnect and unclip the vacuum hoses from the distributor and inlet manifold as necessary.

14 Disconnect the clutch cable, with reference to Chapter 5 (photo).

15 Disconnect the exhaust downpipe from the exhaust manifold, with reference to Chapter 3.

16 Disconnect the speedometer cable from the gearbox and place it on one side.

17 Apply the handbrake then jack up the front of the car and support it on axle stands.

18 Remove the screw from the shift rod coupling and ease the coupling from the rod (photo). The screw threads are coated with a liquid locking agent, and if difficulty is experienced it may be necessary to heat up the coupling with a blowlamp; *however, take the necessary fire precautions.* Note that once removed this screw should be renewed.

19 Note its orientation then withdraw the shift rod coupling.

20 Unbolt the exhaust steady bracket from the downpipe and clutch housing/starter motor.

21 Detach the reversing light switch lead (photo).

22 Unbolt the driveshafts from the drive flanges, with reference to Chapter 7, and tie them to one side with wire.

23 Attach a suitable hoist to the engine lifting eye brackets (one at each end of the cylinder head on the carburettor side) (photo). Take the weight of the engine and gearbox.

24 Working from above, undo the three engine mounting/bearer retaining bolts (underneath the carburettor) (photo).

25 Undo and remove the gearbox mounting bolt (rear left side of engine compartment).

26 Undo and remove the front engine mounting bolt and then remove the bolts securing the bracket to the engine. Withdraw the mounting (photos).

27 Before lifting out the engine and gearbox

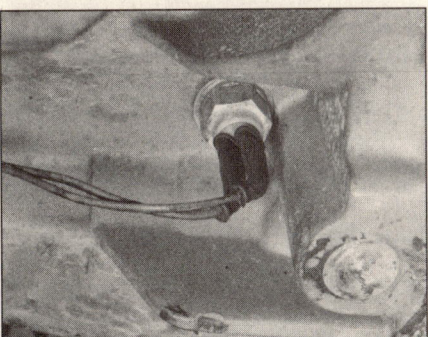
6.21 Reversing light switch

6.23 Engine lifting eye

6.24 Engine mounting/bearer - right-hand

6.26A Undo the front mounting through-bolt

6.26B Unbolt and remove the mounting unit

1•8 Engine – 1.05 and 1.3 litre

6.28 Lifting out the engine and gearbox

7.3 Starter motor and exhaust support bracket

assembly, get an assistant to hold the engine steady and help guide it clear of surrounding components as it is removed.

28 Raise the engine and gearbox assembly from the engine compartment (photo) while turning it as necessary to clear the internally mounted components. Make sure that all wires, cables and hoses have been disconnected.

29 Lower the assembly onto a workbench or large piece of wood placed on the floor.

7 Engine and gearbox - separation

1 The engine must be supported so that the gearbox can be eased away from it. Either support the engine on blocks so that the gearbox overhangs the bench, or do the job while the engine and gearbox are on the hoist.

2 Detach the lead from the alternator then unclip the lead from the locating clips on the sump side walls.

3 Because the rear bearing of the starter armature is in the bellhousing, it is necessary to remove the starter before separating the engine and gearbox. If not already removed, when unbolting the starter motor, also detach the exhaust pipe support bracket (photo).

4 Detach the coolant pipe at its flange on the rear side of the water pump and at the clutch housing.

5 Undo the clutch housing belly plate bolt and withdraw the plate.

6 Undo and remove the remaining engine-to-gearbox securing bolts then pull the gearbox free. **Do not insert wedges, or you will damage the facing;** tap the gearbox gently and wriggle it off the two dowels which locate it. The intermediate plate will remain in position (photos).

7 Reconnection is a reversal of the separating procedure.

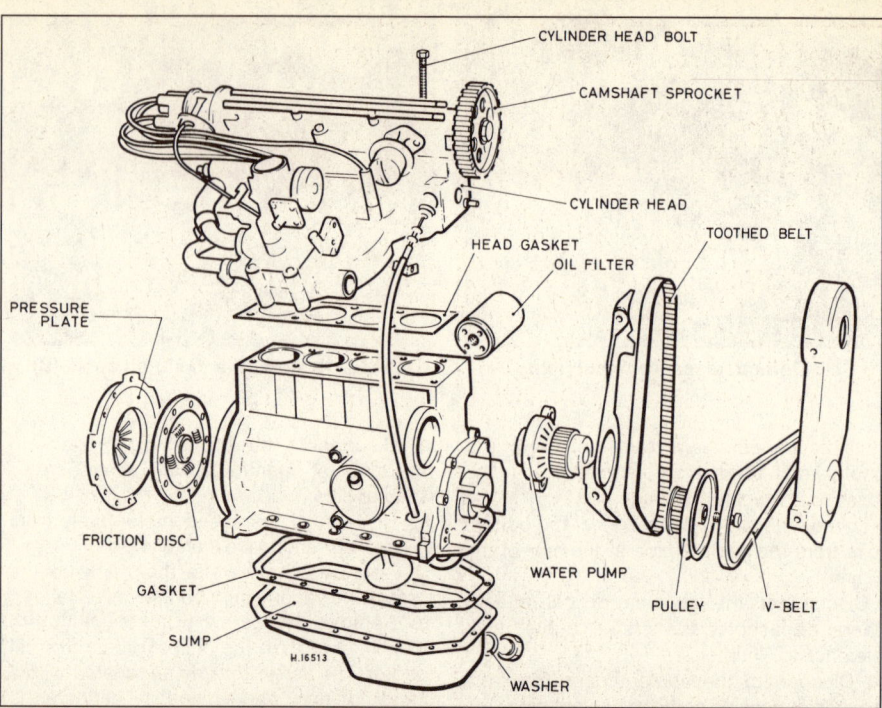

Fig. 1.4 Exploded view of engine main components (Sec 8)

8 Engine dismantling - general

1 If possible, mount the engine on a stand for the dismantling procedure, but failing this, support it in an upright position with blocks of wood.

2 Cleanliness is most important, and if the engine is dirty, it should be cleaned with paraffin while keeping it in an upright position.

3 Avoid working with the engine directly on a concrete floor, as grit presents a real source of trouble.

7.6A Undo the engine/transmission securing bolts...

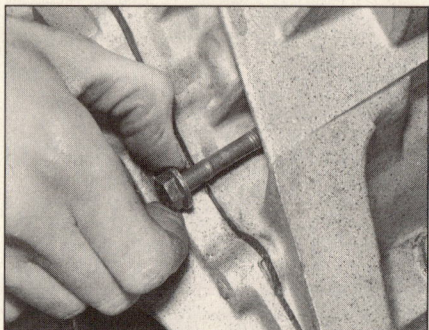

7.6B ...not forgetting the recessed bolt

7.6C ...then separate the engine and transmission

Engine – 1.05 and 1.3 litre 1•9

9.1A Undo the two bolts (arrowed)...

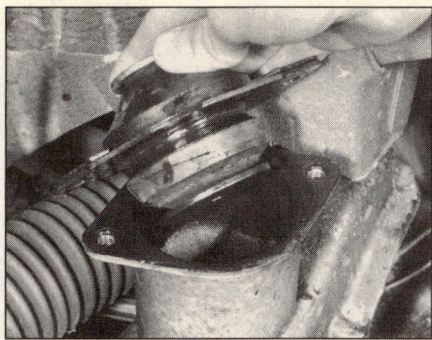
9.1B ...then lift the mounting away

9.1C Right-hand rear mounting viewed from above

9.1D Engine dipstick and tube

9.1E Unscrew the nuts...

9.1F... and remove the engine rear coolant pipe

4 As parts are removed, clean them in a paraffin bath. However, do not immerse parts with internal oilways in paraffin as it is difficult to remove, usually requiring a high pressure hose. Clean oilways with nylon pipe cleaners.

5 It is advisable to have suitable containers to hold small items according to their use, as this will help when reassembling the engine and also prevent possible losses.

6 Always obtain complete sets of gaskets when the engine is being dismantled, but retain the old gaskets with a view to using them as a pattern to make a replacement if a new one is not available.

7 When possible, refit nuts, bolts and washers in their location after being removed, as this helps to protect the threads and will also be helpful when reassembling the engine.

8 Retain unserviceable components in order to compare them with the new parts supplied.

9 Engine ancillary components - removal

With the engine removed from the car and separated from the gearbox, the externally mounted ancillary components should now be removed before dismantling begins. The removal sequence need not necessarily follow the order given:

Alternator and drivebelt (Chapter 9)
Inlet manifold and carburettor (Chapter 3)
Exhaust manifold (Chapter 3)
Distributor (Chapter 4)
Fuel pump (Chapter 3)
Thermostat (Chapter 2)
Clutch (Chapter 5)
Crankcase ventilation hose (Section 21 of this Chapter)
Distributor cap and spark plugs (Chapter 4)
Oil filter (Section 20 of this Chapter)
Engine mountings (photos)
Dipstick (photo)
Oil pressure switches
Water temperature thermo-switch (Chapter 2)
Alternator mounting bracket and engine earth lead
Engine rear coolant pipe (photos)

10 Cylinder head - removal

If the engine is still in the car, first carry out the following operations:
(a) Disconnect the battery negative lead

10.1A Unscrew the nuts and bolts...

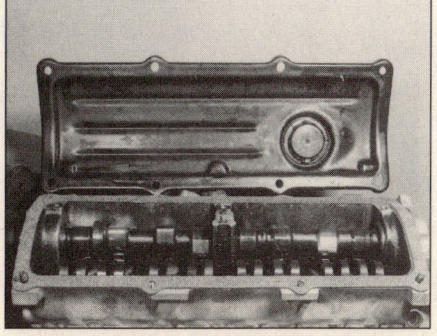
10.1B ...and remove the valve cover...

10.1C ...and gasket

1•10 Engine – 1.05 and 1.3 litre

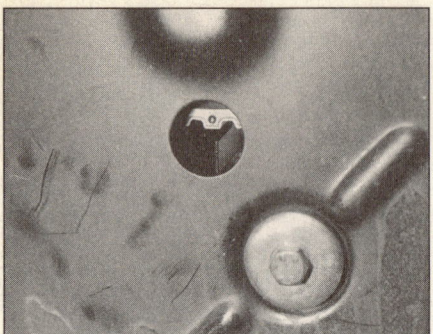

10.2A TDC mark on the camshaft sprocket and pointer

10.2B Crankshaft pulley notch aligned with the TDC pointer

10.3 Removing the timing cover

(b) *Remove the air cleaner and fuel pump (Chapter 3)*
(c) *Drain the cooling system and remove the top hose and thermostat (Chapter 2)*
(d) *Remove the distributor and spark plugs (Chapter 4)*
(e) *Remove the inlet and exhaust manifolds (Chapter 3) although if necessary this can be carried out with the cylinder head on the bench*
(f) *Disconnect the wiring from the coolant temperature sender and oil pressure switch*

1 Unscrew the nuts and bolts from the valve cover and remove the cover together with the gasket and reinforcement strips (photos).
2 Turn the engine until the indentation in the camshaft sprocket appears in the TDC hole in the timing cover, and the notch in the crankshaft pulley is aligned with the TDC pointer on the front of the oil pump (photos). Now turn the crankshaft one quarter of a turn anti-clockwise so that none of the pistons are at TDC.
3 Unbolt and remove the timing cover (photo), noting that the dipstick tube and earth lead are fitted to the upper bolts. On some later 1.3 litre models it is necessary to remove the crankshaft pulley to remove the lower timing belt cover. Pull the dipstick tube from the cylinder block.
4 Using a socket through the hole in the camshaft sprocket, unscrew the timing cover plate upper retaining bolt.

5 Loosen the water pump retaining bolts, then turn the pump body clockwise to release the tension from the timing belt. Remove the timing belt from the camshaft sprocket.
6 Remove the bolts and withdraw the timing cover plate, followed by the water pump if required.
7 Using a splined key, unscrew the cylinder head bolts half a turn at a
time in the reverse order to that shown in Fig. 1.11. Note the location of the engine lifting hooks.
8 Lift the cylinder head from the block (photo). If it is stuck, tap it free with a wooden mallet. **Do not** insert a lever, as damage will occur to the joint faces.
9 Remove the gasket from the cylinder block (photo).

11 Camshaft - removal

If the engine is still in the car, first carry out the following operations:
(a) *Disconnect the battery negative lead*
(b) *Remove the air cleaner and fuel pump (Chapter 3)*
(c) *Remove the distributor and spark plugs (Chapter 4)*

If the cylinder head is still fitted to the engine, first carry out the procedure described in paragraphs 1 to 4 inclusive.

1 Unscrew the nuts and bolts from the valve cover and remove the cover, together with the gasket and reinforcement strips.
2 Turn the engine until the indentation in the camshaft sprocket appears in the TDC hole in the timing cover, and the notch in the crankshaft pulley is aligned with the TDC pointer on the front of the oil pump. Now turn the crankshaft one quarter of a turn anti-clockwise so that none of the pistons are at TDC.
3 Unbolt and remove the timing cover, noting that the dipstick tube and earth lead are fitted to the upper bolts. On some later 1.3 litre models it is necessary to remove the crankshaft pulley to remove the lower timing belt cover.
4 Loosen the water pump retaining bolts, then turn the pump body clockwise to release the tension from the timing belt. Remove the timing belt from the camshaft sprocket.
5 Prise the oil spray tube from the top of the cylinder head (photo).
6 Note how the cam follower clips are fitted then prise them from the ball-studs (photo).
7 Identify each cam follower for location then remove each one by levering with a screwdriver, but make sure that the peak of the relevant cam is pointing away from the follower first by turning the camshaft as necessary (photo).
8 Unscrew the camshaft sprocket bolt and remove the spacer (photo). The sprocket can be held stationary using a metal bar with two

10.8 Removing the cylinder head...

10.9 ...and cylinder head gasket

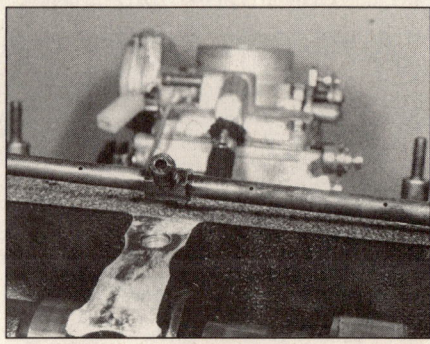

11.5 Removing the oil spray tube

Engine – 1.05 and 1.3 litre 1•11

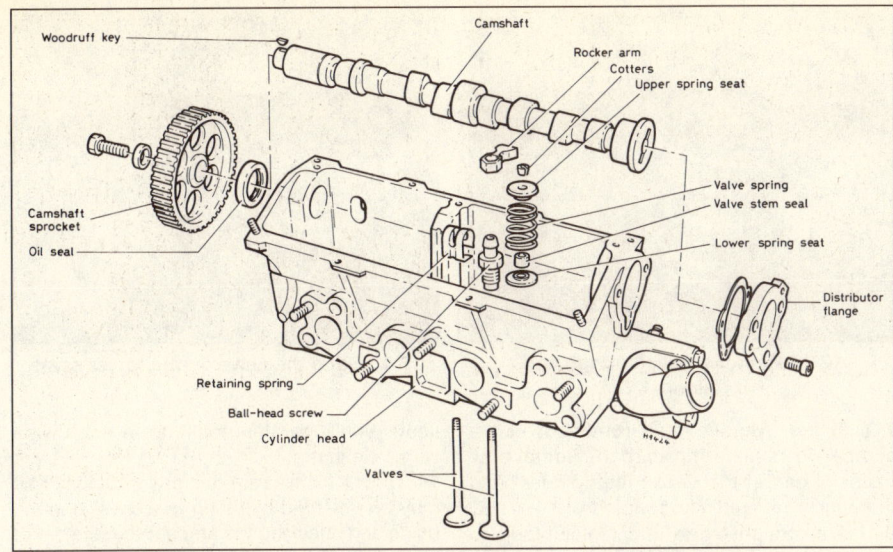

Fig. 1.5 Exploded view of cylinder head components (Sec 11)

11.6 Removing a cam follower clip

11.7 Removing a cam follower

bolts, with one bolt inserted in a hole and the other bolt resting on the outer rim of the sprocket.

9 Tap the sprocket from the camshaft with a wooden mallet and prise out the Woodruff key (photo).

10 Using feeler blades, check the camshaft endfloat by inserting the blade between the end of the camshaft and distributor flanges (photo). If it is more than the amount given in the Specifications the components will have to be checked for wear and renewed as necessary.

11 Using an Allen key, unscrew the bolts and remove the distributor flange (photo). Remove the gasket.

12 Carefully slide the camshaft from the cylinder head, taking care not to damage the three bearing surfaces as the lobes of the cams pass through them (photo).

13 Prise the camshaft oil seal from the cylinder head (photo).

11.8 Unscrew the bolt...

11.9 ...and remove the camshaft sprocket (early type sprocket shown)

11.10 Checking the camshaft endfloat

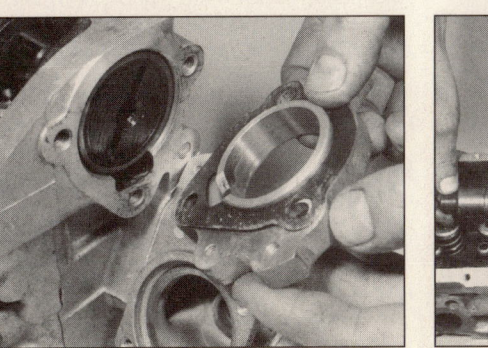

11.11 Removing the distributor flange

11.12 Withdrawing the camshaft

11.13 Removing the camshaft oil seal

12.2A Compressing a valve spring to remove the split collets

12.2B Remove valve springs and retainers...

12.4 ...and the valve spring lower seats

12 Cylinder head - dismantling, inspection and overhaul

1 Remove the cylinder head and camshaft, as described in the previous Sections.
2 Using a valve spring compressor, compress each valve spring in turn until the split collets can be removed. Release the compressor and remove the retainers and springs (photos). If the retainers are difficult to remove do not continue to tighten the compressor, but gently tap the top of the tool with a hammer. Always make sure that the compressor is held firmly over the retainer.
3 Remove each valve from the cylinder head, keeping them identified for location.
4 Prise the valve seals from the valve guides and remove the lower spring seats (photo).
5 Do not remove the cam follower ball-studs unless they are unserviceable, as they are likely to be seized in the head.
6 Decarbonising will normally only be required at comparatively high mileages. However, if performance has deteriorated even though engine adjustments are correct, decarbonising may be required; although this may be attributable to worn pistons and rings.

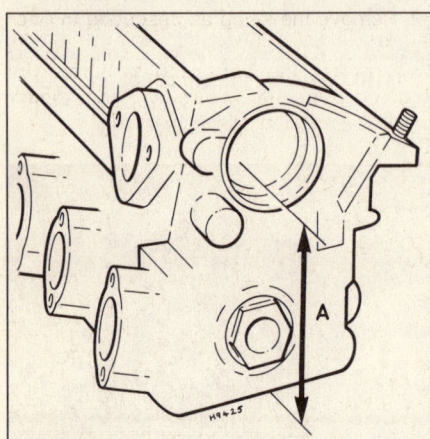

Fig. 1.6 Measure cylinder head depth between the points indicated (Sec 12)

Minimum allowable depth
a = 119.3 mm (4.7 in)

7 With the cylinder head removed, use a scraper to remove the carbon. Remove all traces of gasket then wash the cylinder head thoroughly in paraffin and wipe dry.
8 Use a straight-edge and feeler blade to check that the cylinder head surface is not distorted. If it is, it must be resurfaced by a suitably equipped engineering works. If the cylinder head face is to be resurfaced, this will necessitate the valve seats being re-cut so that they are recessed deeper by an equivalent amount to that machined from the cylinder head. This is necessary to avoid the possibility of the valves coming into contact with the pistons and causing serious damage and is a task to be entrusted to a suitably equipped engine reconditioner.
9 Examine the heads of the valves for pitting and burning, especially the exhaust valve heads. Renew any valve which is badly burnt. Examine the valve seats at the same time. If the pitting is very slight, it can be removed by grinding the valve heads and seats together with coarse, then fine, grinding paste. Note that the exhaust valves should not be re-cut, therefore they should be renewed if the sealing face is excessively grooved as a result of regrinding.
10 Where excessive pitting has occurred, the valve seats must be re-cut or renewed by a suitably equipped engine reconditioner.
11 Valve grinding is carried out as follows. Place the cylinder head upside down on a bench with a block of wood at each end.
12 Smear a trace of coarse carborundum paste on the seat face and press a suction grinding tool onto the valve head. With a semi-rotary action, grind the valve head to its seat, lifting the valve occasionally to redistribute the grinding paste. When a dull matt even surface is produced on both the valve seat and the valve, wipe off the paste and repeat the process with fine carborundum paste as before. A light spring placed under the valve head will greatly ease this operation. When a smooth unbroken ring of light grey matt finish is produced on both the valve and seat, the grinding operation is complete.
13 Scrape away all carbon from the valve head stem, and clean away all traces of grinding compound. Clean the valves and seats with a paraffin-soaked rag, then wipe with a clean rag.
14 Check for wear in the valve guides. This may be detected by fitting a new valve in the guide and checking the amount that the rim of the valve will move sideways, when the top of the valve stem is flush with the top of the valve guide. The rock limit for the inlet valve is 1 mm (0.04 in) and 1.3 mm (0.05 in) for the exhaust valve. This can be measured with feeler gauges if you use a clamp as a datum, but it must be with a new valve. If the rock is at or below this limit with your old valve then this indicates that the existing guide(s) do not need renewal. Check each valve guide in turn, but note that the inlet and exhaust valve stem dimensions differ, so do not get them confused. If the rock exceeds the limit with a new valve this will indicate the need for new valve guides as well. The removal and refitting of new guides is a task which must be entrusted to a suitably equipped engine reconditioner.
15 If possible, compare the length of the valve springs with new ones, and renew them as a set if any are shorter.
16 If the engine is still in the car, clean the piston crowns and cylinder bore upper edges, but make sure that no carbon drops between the pistons and bores. To do this, locate two of the pistons at the top of their bores and seal off the remaining bores with paper and masking tape. Press a little grease between the two pistons and their bores to collect any carbon dust; this can be wiped away when the piston is lowered. To prevent carbon build-up, polish the piston crown with metal polish, but remove all traces of the polish afterwards.

13 Timing belt and sprockets - removal

If the engine is still in the car, first carry out the following operations:
(a) Disconnect the battery negative lead
(b) Remove the air cleaner (Chapter 3)
(c) Remove the alternator drivebelt (Chapter 9)

Engine – 1.05 and 1.3 litre 1•13

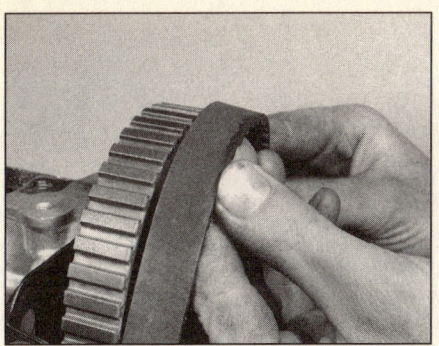

13.3 Releasing the timing belt from the camshaft sprocket

13.6 Crankshaft sprocket bolt and washer removal

14.2 One method of holding the flywheel stationary

1 Turn the engine until the indentation in the camshaft sprocket appears in the TDC hole in the timing cover, and the notch in the crankshaft pulley is aligned with the TDC pointer on the front of the oil pump.
2 Unbolt and remove the timing cover, noting that the dipstick tube and earth lead are fitted to the upper bolts. On some later 1.3 litre models it is necessary to remove the crankshaft pulley to remove the lower timing belt cover (see paragraph 6).
3 Loosen the water pump retaining bolts, then turn the pump body clockwise to release the tension from the timing belt. Remove the timing belt from the camshaft sprocket (photo).
4 Using an Allen key, unbolt the pulley from the crankshaft sprocket, then remove the timing belt.
5 To remove the camshaft sprocket, unscrew the bolt and remove the spacer. Then tap off the sprocket and remove the Woodruff key. Do not turn the camshaft. The sprocket can be held stationary using a metal bar with two bolts, with one bolt inserted through a sprocket hole and the other bolt resting on the outer rim.
6 To remove the crankshaft sprocket, unscrew the bolt and lever the sprocket from the crankshaft (photo). Do not turn the crankshaft otherwise the pistons may touch the valve heads. Hold the crankshaft stationary with a lever inserted in the starter ring gear (remove the starter as applicable). Remove the Woodruff key.

14 Flywheel - removal

1 Remove the clutch, as described in Chapter 5.
2 Hold the flywheel stationary with a lever or angle iron (photo) engaged with the starter ring gear.
3 Unscrew the bolts and lift the flywheel from the crankshaft (photo).
4 Remove the engine plate from the cylinder block (photo).
5 The flywheel bolts must be renewed once they are removed.

15 Crankshaft oil seals - renewal

Front oil seal

1 Remove the crankshaft sprocket with reference to Section 13.
2 If available use VW tool 2085 to remove the oil seal from the oil pump housing. Removal of the seal with the engine and oil pump in position in the car can prove difficult without the special tool. In this instance, an alternative method is to drill two holes, diagonally opposed to each other in the oil seal, insert two self-tapping screws and then pull on the screws using grips to withdraw the seal. If using this method care must be taken not to drill into the housing.
3 If the oil pump is removed from the engine the seal can be prised out and a new seal fitted (photos 33.1A and 33.1B).
4 Clean the recess in the oil pump.
5 Smear a little engine oil on the lip and outer edge of the new oil seal, then fit it with VW tool 10-203 or by tapping it in with a suitable metal tube.
6 Refit the crankshaft sprocket with reference to Section 39.

Rear oil seal

7 Remove the flywheel, as described in Section 14.

Method 1

8 Drill two diagonally opposite holes in the oil seal, insert two self-tapping screws, and pull out the seal with grips.
9 Clean the recess in the housing.
10 Smear a little engine oil on the lip and outer edge of the new oil seal then tap it into the housing using a suitable metal tube.
11 Refit the flywheel, as described in Section 35.

Method 2

12 Remove the sump as described in Section 16.
13 Unscrew the bolts and withdraw the housing from the dowels on the cylinder block. Remove the gasket (photos).

14.3 Removing the flywheel

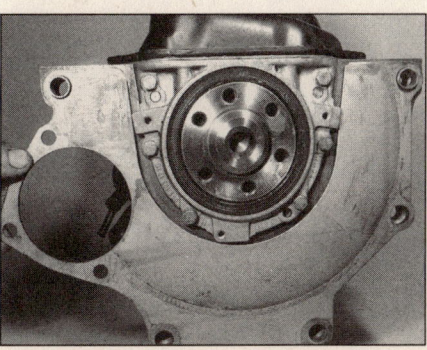

14.4 Removing the engine plate

15.13A Crankshaft rear oil seal and housing

1•14 Engine – 1.05 and 1.3 litre

15.13B Withdraw the crankshaft rear oil seal housing. . .

15.13C . . .and remove the gasket

15.14 Remove the crankshaft rear oil seal from the housing

14 Support the housing and drive out the oil seal (photo).
15 Clean the recess in the housing.
16 Smear a little engine oil on the lip and outer edge of the new oil seal then tap it into the housing using a block of wood (photo).
17 Clean the mating faces then refit the housing, together with a new gasket, and tighten the bolts evenly in diagonal sequence.
18 Refit the sump and flywheel, as described in Sections 34 and 35 respectively.

16 Sump - removal

1 If the engine is still in the car, first carry out the following operations:

(a) Jack up the front of the car and support it on axle stands. Apply the handbrake
(b) Disconnect the right-hand side driveshaft (Chapter 7) and the exhaust system (Chapter 3)
(c) Unclip the alternator wire from the sump (photo)
(d) Drain the engine oil into a suitable container. Clean the drain plug and washer and refit it, tightening it to the specified torque

2 Unscrew the bolts and withdraw the sump from the cylinder block (photo). If it is stuck, lever it away or cut through the gasket with a knife.
3 Scrape the gasket from the sump and cylinder block.

17 Oil pump - removal

1 Remove the timing belt and crankshaft sprocket, as described in Section 13.
2 Remove the sump, as described in Section 16.
3 Unbolt and remove the pick-up tube and strainer from the oil pump and cylinder block. Remove the flange gasket (photos).
4 Unscrew the bolts and withdraw the oil pump from the dowels on the front of the cylinder block. Note that the timing pointed bracket is located on the two upper central bolts, and the timing belt guard on the two left-hand side bolts. Remove the gasket (photos).

15.16 Installing the new crankshaft rear oil seal

16.1 Alternator wire clip on sump

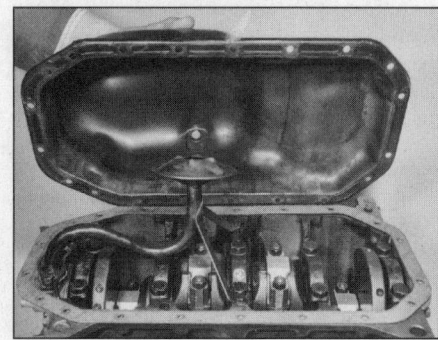
16.2 Removing the sump

17.3A Remove the stay bolts . . .

17 3B . . . flange bolts . . .

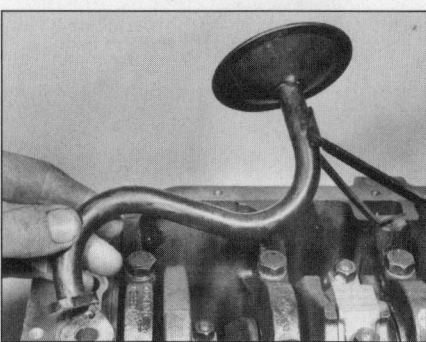
17.3C . . . and remove the oil pump pick-up tube and strainer

Engine – 1.05 and 1.3 litre 1•15

17.4A Removing the oil pump...

17.4B ...and gasket

18.4 Checking the connecting rod endfloat

18 Pistons and connecting rods - removal

1 Remove the cylinder head, as described in Section 10.
2 Remove the sump, as described in Section 16.
3 Unbolt and remove the pick-up tube and strainer from the oil pump and cylinder block. Remove the flange gasket.
4 Using a feeler gauge, check that the connecting rod big-end endfloat on each crankpin is within the limits given in the Specifications (photo). If not, the components must be checked for wear and renewed as necessary.
5 Check the big-end caps and connecting rods for identification marks, and if necessary use a centre punch to mark them for location and position. Note that the cut-outs in the connecting rods and caps face the timing belt end of the engine. The arrows on the piston crown also face the timing belt end of the engine (photo).
6 Turn the crankshaft so that No 1 crankpin is at its lowest point.
7 Unscrew the big-end nuts and tap free the cap, together with its bearing shell (photo).
8 Using the handle of a hammer tap the piston and connecting rod from the bore and withdraw it from the top of the cylinder block (photo).

9 Loosely refit the cap to the connecting rod (photo).
10 Repeat the procedure given in paragraphs 7 to 9 on No 4 piston and connecting rod, then turn the crankshaft through half a turn and repeat the procedure on No 2 and 3 pistons.
11 Note that during reassembly, the connecting rod bolts must be renewed.

19 Crankshaft and main bearings - removal

1 Disconnect the connecting rods from the crankshaft with reference to Section 18.

18, 5 Piston crown showing arrow which points to the timing belt end of the engine

However, it is not essential to remove the pistons or, therefore, to remove the cylinder head.
2 Remove the oil pump, as described in Section 17, and the rear oil seal housing as described in Section 15.
3 Using a feeler gauge check that the crankshaft endfloat is within the limits given in the Specifications (photo). Insert the feeler gauge between the centre crankshaft web and the thrust washers. This will indicate whether new thrust washers are required or not.
4 Check that the main bearing caps are identified for location and position - there should be a cast number in the crankcase ventilation pipe/water coolant pipe side of the

18.7 Withdrawing a big-end cap

18.8 Removing a piston

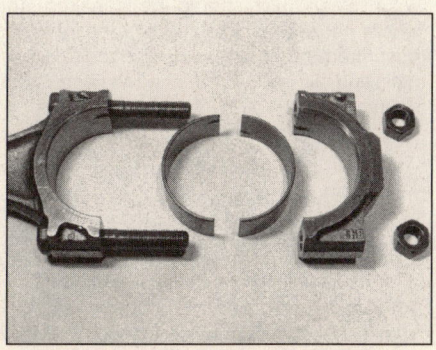
18.9 Big-end bearing components

19.3 Checking the crankshaft endfloat

1•16 Engine – 1.05 and 1.3 litre

19.4 Crankshaft main bearing cap numbering

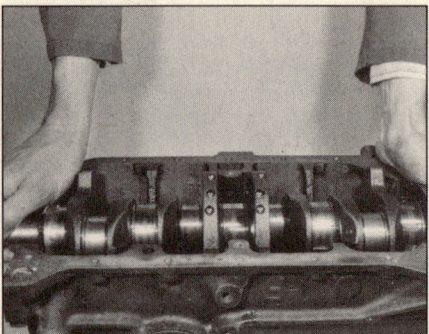

19.6 Removing the crankshaft

caps, numbered from the timing belt end of the engine (photo).
5 Unscrew the bolts and tap the main bearing caps free. Keep the bearing shells and, where fitted, the thrust washers identified for position.
6 Lift the crankshaft from the crankcase and remove the remaining bearing shells and thrust washers, but keep them identified for position (photo).

20 Oil filter - renewal

1 The oil filter is located on the front of the engine beside the alternator (photo).
2 Place a suitable container beneath the filter then, using a suitable tool, unscrew the filter and discard it (photo).

20.1 Oil filter location

20.2 Removing the oil filter using a chain wrench

3 Wipe clean the sealing face on the cylinder block.
4 Smear the sealing rubber on the new filter with engine oil, then fit and tighten the filter by hand only.
5 On completion top up the engine oil level as necessary then wipe clean the filter body. When the engine is restarted, check around the filter joint for any signs of an oil leak.

21 Crankcase ventilation system - description

The crankcase ventilation system is of the positive type and consists of an oil separator on the rear (coolant pipe side) of the cylinder block, connected to the air cleaner by a rubber hose. Vacuum from the air cleaner provides a partial vacuum in the crankcase, and the piston blow-by gases are drawn through the oil separator and into the engine combustion chambers.
Periodically the hose should be examined for security and condition. Cleaning will not normally be necessary except when the engine is well worn.

22 Examination and renovation - general

With the engine completely stripped, clean all the components and examine them for wear. Each part should be checked and where necessary renewed or renovated, as described in the following Sections. Renew main and big-end shell bearings as a matter of course, unless you know that they have had little wear and are in perfect condition

23 Crankshaft and bearings - examination and renovation

1 Examine the bearing surfaces of the crankshaft for scratches or scoring, and using a micrometer, check each journal and crankpin for ovality. Where this is found to be in excess of 0.17 mm (0.0066 in), the crankshaft will have to be reground and undersize bearings fitted.
2 Crankshaft regrinding should be carried out by a suitable engineering works, who will normally supply the matching undersize main and big-end shell bearings.
3 If the crankshaft endfloat is more than the maximum specified amount, new centre main bearing shells with side flanges will have to be fitted to replace the thrust washers. These are usually supplied together with the main and big-end bearings on a reground crankshaft.

24 Cylinder block/crankcase - examination and renovation

1 The cylinder bores must be examined for taper, ovality, scoring and scratches. Start by examining the top of the bores; if these are worn, a slight ridge will be found which marks the top of the piston ring travel. If the wear is excessive, the engine will have had a high oil consumption rate accompanied by blue smoke from the exhaust.
2 If available, use an inside dial gauge to measure the bore diameter just below the ridge and compare it with the diameter at the bottom of the bore, which is not subject to wear. If the difference is more than 0.15 mm (0.006 in) the cylinders will normally require reboring with new oversize pistons fitted.
3 Provided the cylinder bore wear does not exceed 0.20 mm (0.008 in), however, special oil control rings and pistons can be fitted to restore compression and stop the engine burning oil.
4 If new pistons are being fitted to old bores, it is essential to roughen the bore walls slightly with fine glasspaper to enable the new piston rings to bed in properly.
5 Thoroughly examine the crankcase and cylinder block for cracks and damage and use a piece of wire to probe all oilways and waterways to ensure they are unobstructed.
6 Check the core plugs for leaks and security (photo).

24.6 The core plugs in the cylinder block

Engine – 1.05 and 1.3 litre 1•17

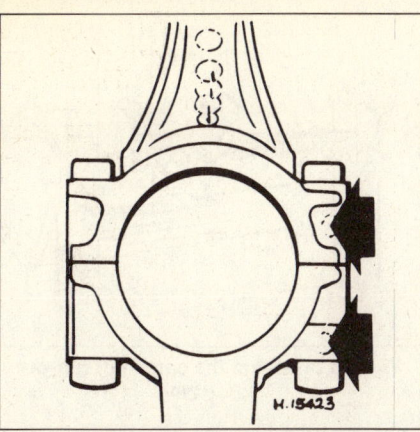

Fig. 1.7 The indentations on the big-end bearings (arrowed) must face the same way as the arrow on the piston crown (Sec 25)

25 Pistons and connecting rods - examination and renovation

1 Examine the pistons for ovality, scoring and scratches. Check the connecting rods for wear and damage.
2 To remove the pistons from the connecting rods, first mark the two components in relation to each other - the indentation on the bearing end of the connecting rod faces the same way as the arrow on the piston crown.
3 Prise out the circlips then dip the piston in hot water (approximately 60°C), press out the gudgeon pin, and separate the piston from the connecting rod.
4 Assemble the pistons in reverse order.
5 If new rings are to be fitted to the original pistons, expand the old rings over the top of the pistons using two or three old feeler blades to prevent the rings dropping into empty grooves.
6 Before fitting the new rings insert each of them into the cylinder bore approximately 15.0 mm (0.6 in) from the bottom and check that the end gaps are as given in the Specifications (photo).
7 When fitting the rings to the pistons make sure that the TOP markings face towards the piston crown, and arrange the end gaps at 120° intervals (photo). Using a feeler gauge check that the clearance of each ring in its groove is within the limits given in Specifications (photo).

25.6 Checking the piston ring gaps

26 Oil pump - examination and renovation

The manufacturer does not supply any clearances for checking the wear of the oil pump gears, so the pump must be assumed to be in good order provided that the oil pressure is as given in the Specifications. This can only be checked with the engine assembled and, as a pressure gauge will not be available to the home mechanic, the work should be entrusted to a VW garage. However, a visual examination of the oil pump can be made if required as follows.

1 Using an Allen key unscrew the relief valve plug and extract the spring and plunger (photos).
2 Using an impact screwdriver, remove the cross-head screws and withdraw the cover from the pump (photos).
3 Remove the rotors, noting that the indentation on the outer rotor faces the cover (photos).
4 Clean the components in paraffin and wipe dry, then examine them for wear and damage. If evident, renew the oil pump complete, but if in good order reassemble the pump in reverse order and tighten the screws and plug.

25.7A Space the ring gaps at 120° intervals

25.7B Checking the piston ring-to-groove wall clearance

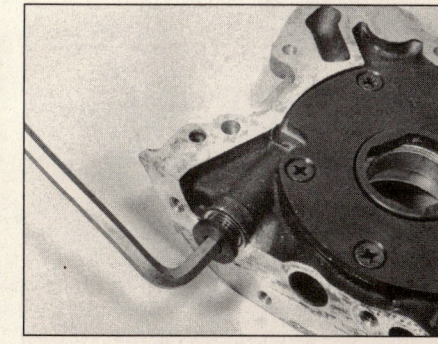

26.1A Unscrew the relief valve plug . . .

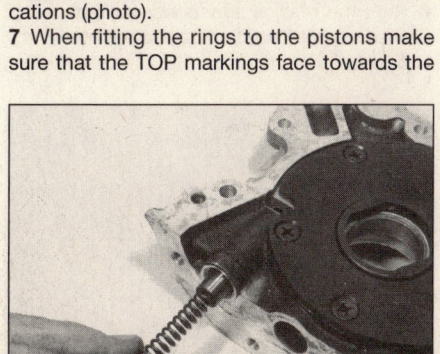

26.1B . . . and remove the spring and plunger

26.2A Use an impact screwdriver to remove the screws . . .

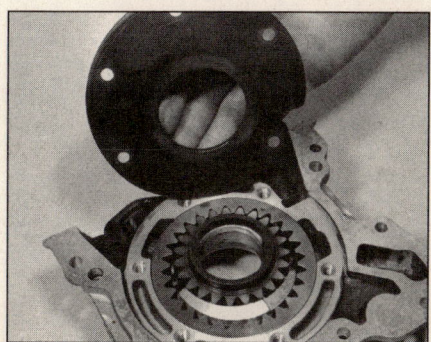

26.2B . . . then remove the oil pump cover. . .

1•18 Engine – 1.05 and 1.3 litre

26.3A ... and rotors

26.3B The outer rotor indentation (arrowed) must face the cover

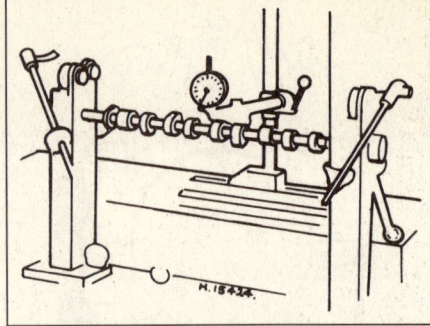

Fig. 1.8 Checking the camshaft run-out (Sec 29)

27 Flywheel - examination and renovation

1 There is not much you can do about the flywheel if it is damaged except renew it.
2 Inspect the starter ring teeth. If these are chipped or worn it is possible to renew the starter ring. This means heating the ring until it may be withdrawn from the flywheel, or alternatively splitting it. A new one must then be shrunk on. If you know how to do this, and you can get a new ring, then the job can be done, but it is beyond the capacity of most owners.
3 Serious scoring on the flywheel clutch facing again requires a new flywheel. **Do not** attempt to clean the scoring off with a scraper or emery.

28 Timing belt and sprockets - examination and renovation

1 The timing belt should be renewed as a matter of course if it has completed more than 20 000 miles (30 000 km) at the time of its removal. Otherwise renew it at 40 000 miles (60 000 km).
2 The camshaft and crankshaft sprockets do not normally require renewal as wear takes place very slowly.

29 Camshaft - examination and renovation

1 Examine the camshaft bearing surfaces, cam lobes, and followers for wear. If excessive renew the shaft and followers.
2 Check the camshaft run-out by turning it between fixed centres with a dial gauge on the centre journal. If the run-out exceeds the amount given in Specifications, renew the shaft.

30 Engine reassembly - general

1 To ensure maximum life with minimum trouble from a rebuilt engine, not only must everything be correctly assembled, but it must also be spotlessly clean. All oilways must be clear, and locking washers and spring washers must be fitted where indicated. Oil all bearings and other working surfaces thoroughly with engine oil during assembly.
2 Before assembly begins, renew any bolts or studs with damaged threads.
3 Gather together a torque wrench, oil can, clean rag, and a set of engine gaskets and oil seals, together with a new oil filter.

31 Crankshaft and main bearings - refitting

1 Clean the backs of the bearing shells and the bearing recesses in the cylinder block and main bearing caps.
2 Press the main bearing shells into the cylinder block and caps and oil them liberally (photo).
3 Where thrust washers are being refitted (instead of a shouldered type number three main bearing shell, a plain shell is used), smear the thrust washers with grease and stick them into position on the side of the centre main bearing and its cap (photo). The washers must be fitted so that their oilways face away from the bearings in the block and cap (photo).
4 Lower the crankshaft into position, then fit the main bearing caps in their previously noted positions (photo). Note that the bearing shell lugs are adjacent to each other.
5 Insert the bolts and tighten them evenly to the specified torque (photo). Check that the crankshaft rotates freely then check that the endfloat is within the limits given in the Specifications by inserting a feeler gauge between the centre crankshaft web and the thrust washers or bearing shoulder, as applicable.
6 Refit the rear oil seal bearing (Section 15) and oil pump (Section 33) and reconnect the connecting rods (Section 32).

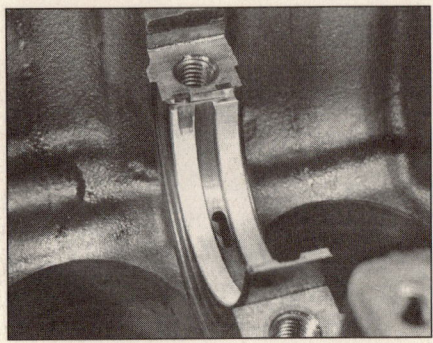

31.2A Fitting the centre main bearing shell

31.2B Oiling the main bearing shells

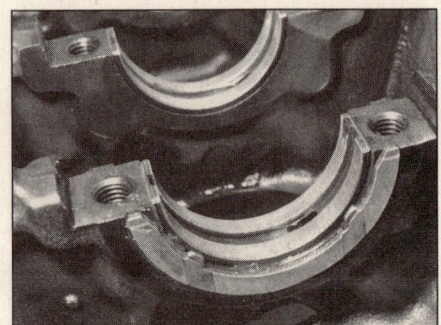

31.3 Thrust washer location on the centre main bearing

Engine – 1.05 and 1.3 litre 1•19

31.4 Fitting the centre main bearing cap

31.5 Tightening the main bearing cap bolts

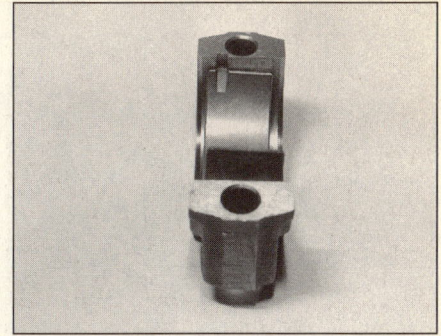
32.3A Fitting a big-end bearing shell

32 Pistons and connecting rods - refitting
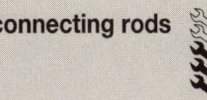

1 As mentioned during removal, the manufacturers recommend that the connecting rod bolts be renewed, so assemble the new bolts to the rods.
2 Clean the backs of the bearing shells and the recesses in the connecting rods and big-end caps.
3 Press the big-end bearing shells into the connecting rods and caps in their correct positions and oil them liberally (photos).
4 Fit a ring compressor to No 1 piston then insert the piston and connecting rod into No 1 cylinder (photo). With No 1 crankpin at its lowest point, drive the piston carefully into the cylinder with the wooden handle of a hammer, and at the same time guide the connecting rod into the crankpin. Make sure that the arrow on the piston crown faces the timing belt end of the engine.
5 Fit the big-end bearing cap in its previously noted position then fit the nuts and tighten them evenly to the specified torque (photo).
6 Check that the crankshaft turns freely and use a feeler gauge to check that the connecting rod endfloat is within the limits given in the Specifications.
7 Repeat the procedure given in paragraphs 3 to 5 for No 4 piston and connecting rod, then turn the crankshaft through half a

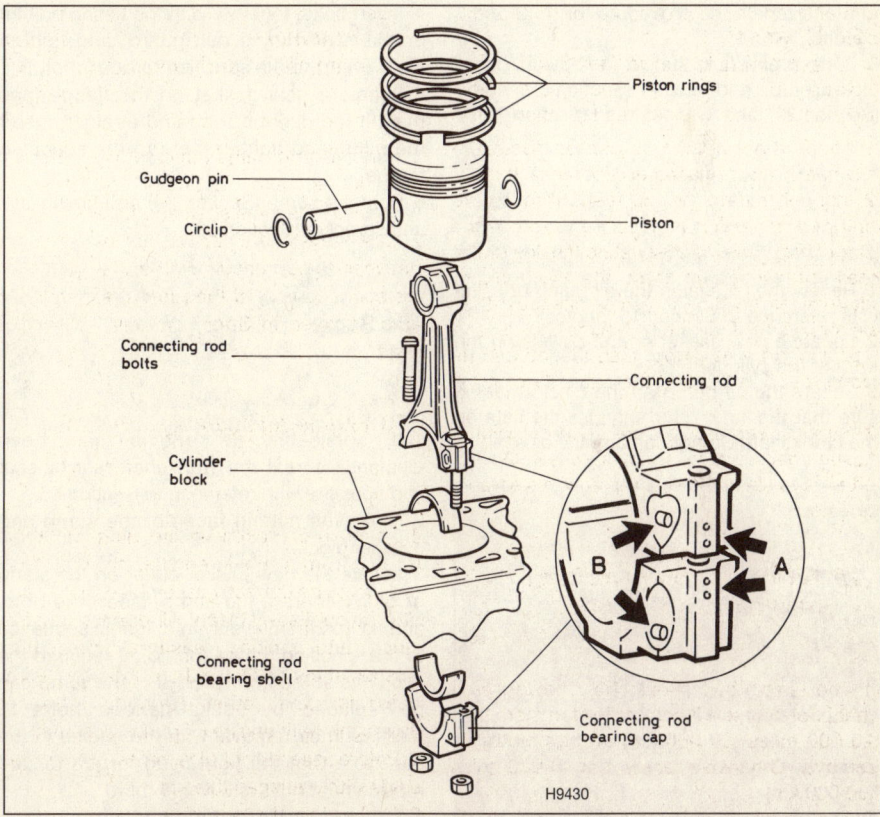
Fig. 1.9 Piston and connecting rod components (Sec 32)
Inset shows cylinder bore number markings (A) and fitting position (B)

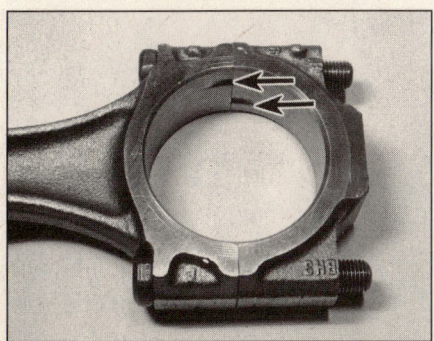
32.3B Correct location of tabs on big-end bearings - arrows

32.4 Using a ring compressor to fit the pistons (No 2 piston shown)

32 5 Tightening the big-end bearing nuts

1•20 Engine – 1.05 and 1.3 litre

33.1A Prising out the oil pump oil seal

33.1B Fitting the new oil seal to the oil pump

33.4 Fitted location of oil pump

turn and repeat the procedure for No 2 and 3 pistons.
8 If the engine is in the car, refit the oil pump pick-up tube and strainer (Section 33), sump (Section 34), and cylinder head (Section 38).

33 Oil pump - refitting

1 Renew the oil seal in the oil pump housing with reference to Section 15 (photos).
2 Locate a new gasket on the dowels on the front of the cylinder block.
3 Locate the oil pump on the block, making sure that the inner rotor engages the flats on the crankshaft. Do not damage the oil seal.

34.3 Fitting the sump gasket

35.3A Apply liquid locking fluid to the flywheel bolts

4 Insert bolts, together with the timing pointer bracket and timing belt guard, and tighten them evenly to the specified torque (photo).
5 Locate a new gasket on the flange face then fit the pick-up tube and strainer, insert the bolts, and tighten them to the specified torque.
6 Refit the sump (Section 34) and timing belt and sprocket (Section 39).

34 Sump - refitting

1 If applicable (ie engine has been dismantled), refit the crankshaft rear oil seal and housing, with reference to Section 15.
2 Clean the mating faces of the sump and cylinder block.
3 Locate the new gasket either on the sump or block, then fit the sump, insert the bolts and tighten them evenly in diagonal sequence to the specified torque (photo). If required the two bolts at the flywheel end of the sump can be replaced by socket-headed bolts to facilitate their removal with the engine in the car. Note that the tightening torque for the replacement bolts is 8 Nm (6 lbf ft).
4 If the engine is in the car refill the engine with oil, fasten the alternator wire to the sump clip, and lower the car to the ground.

35.3B Tightening the flywheel bolts

35 Flywheel - refitting

1 Locate the engine plate on the dowels on the cylinder block.
2 Clean the mating faces of the flywheel and crankshaft, then locate the flywheel in position. Note that the bolt holes only align in one position, as they are offset.
3 Apply liquid locking fluid to the threads of new bolts, then insert them and tighten them in diagonal sequence to the specified torque while holding the flywheel stationary (photos).
4 Refit the clutch, as described in Chapter 5

36 Cylinder head - reassembly

1 Fit the valves in their correct locations in the cylinder head.
2 Working on each valve at a time first locate the valve spring lower seat in position.
3 Before fitting the valve seal, locate the special plastic sleeve provided in the gasket set over the valve stem in order to prevent damage to the seal (photo).
4 Slide the new seal over the valve stem and

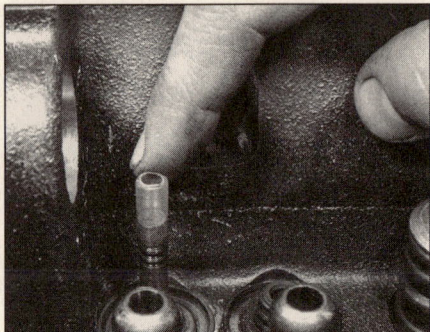
36.3 Locate the plastic sleeve on the valve stem . . .

Engine – 1.05 and 1.3 litre 1•21

36.4 . . . then fit the new oil seal

37.2 Oiling the camshaft bearing surfaces

37.5 Method of tightening the camshaft sprocket bolt

press it firmly onto the guide using a metal tube (photo). Remove the plastic sleeve.
5 Fit the spring and retainer over the valve stem, then compress the spring with the compressor and insert the split collets. Release the compressor and remove it.

HAYNES HiNT *Tap the end of each valve stem with a non-metallic mallet to settle the collets.*

6 Repeat the procedure given in paragraphs 2 to 5 on the remaining valves.
7 Refit the camshaft, as described in Section 37.

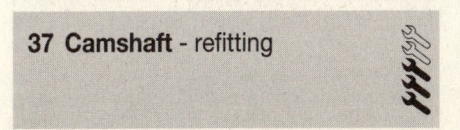

37 Camshaft - refitting

1 Smear a little engine oil on the lip and outer edge of the camshaft oil seal, then drive it squarely into the cylinder head with a block of wood.
2 Oil the camshaft bearing surfaces then slide the camshaft into position, taking care not to damage the oil seal (photo).
3 Fit the distributor flange, together with a new gasket, and tighten the socket-head bolts.
4 Using a feeler gauge, check that the camshaft endfloat is as specified.
5 Fit the Woodruff key then fit the sprocket to the camshaft followed by the spacer and bolt. Tighten the bolt while holding the sprocket stationary with a metal bar and two bolts (photo).
6 Fit the cam followers by turning the camshaft so that the relevant cam lobe peak is pointing away from the valve, then tap the follower between the valve stem and cam, and onto the ball-stud.
7 Slide the cam follower clips into the grooves on the ball studs and locate the upper ends on the cam followers.
8 Adjust the valve clearances, as described in Section 40.
9 Turn the camshaft so that the indentation in the sprocket is pointing downwards and in line with the pointer on the timing cover plate (photo).
10 Turn the crankshaft a quarter of a turn clockwise so that the notch in the crankshaft pulley is aligned with the TDC pointer on the front of the oil pump.
11 Fit the timing belt to the camshaft sprocket and water pump.
12 Using a screwdriver in the water pump, turn the pump anti-clockwise and tension the timing belt until it can just be turned through 90° with the thumb and forefinger midway between the camshaft sprocket and water pump.
13 Tighten the water pump bolts when the belt tension is correct, and check the timing marks are still aligned.
14 Fit the dipstick tube to the cylinder block.
15 Fit the timing cover, insert the bolts with the earth lead and dipstick tube bracket, and tighten the bolts.
16 Press the oil spray tube into the top of the cylinder head.
17 Refit the valve cover with a new gasket, locate the reinforcement strips, and tighten the nuts and bolts.
18 If the engine is in the car reverse the preliminary procedures given in Section 11.

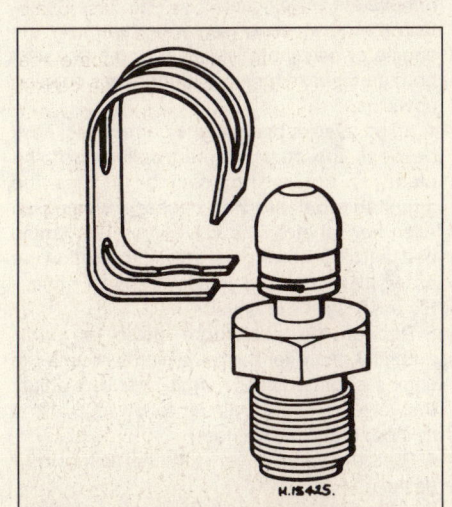

38 Cylinder head - refitting

1 Position Nos 1 and 4 pistons at TDC then turn the crankshaft a quarter of a turn anti-clockwise so that neither of the pistons is at TDC.
2 Make sure that the faces of the cylinder head and block are perfectly clean then locate the new gasket on the block, making sure that all oil and water holes are visible - the gasket part number should be uppermost (photo).
3 Lower the cylinder head onto the gasket,

Fig. 1.10 Cam follower clip and groove in ball-stud (Sec 37)

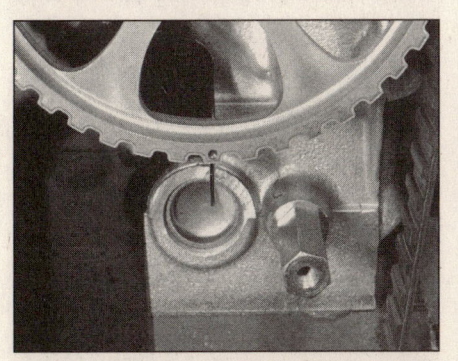

37.9 Camshaft sprocket (later type) with index mark aligned with the timing cover TDC pointer

38.2 Correct fitting of the cylinder head gasket

1•22 Engine – 1.05 and 1.3 litre

38.4 Tightening the cylinder head bolts

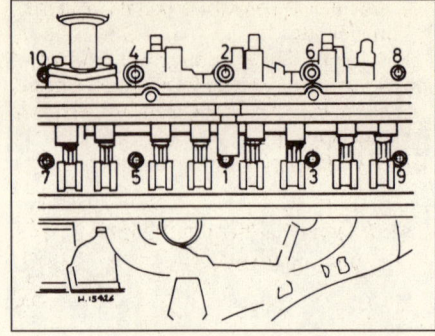

Fig. 1.11 Cylinder head bolt tightening sequence (Sec 38)

38.9 Fitting the crankshaft sprocket and timing belt

then insert the bolts together with the engine lifting hooks.
4 Using a splined key tighten the bolts in the stages given in the Specifications, using the sequence shown in Fig. 1.11 (photo).
5 Refit the water pump, if applicable (Chapter 2).
6 Fit the timing cover plate and insert the water pump bolts loosely.
7 If required, refit the camshaft with reference to Section 37.
8 Refit and tighten the timing cover plate upper retaining bolt.
9 If applicable, refit the crankshaft sprocket and timing belt to the crankshaft as described in Section 39 (photo).
10 Turn the camshaft so that the indentation in the sprocket is aligned with the pointer on the timing cover plate.
11 Turn the crankshaft a quarter of a turn clockwise so that the notch in the crankshaft pulley (temporarily refit if necessary) is aligned with the TDC pointer on the front of the oil pump.
12 Fit the timing belt to the camshaft sprocket and water pump.
13 Using a screwdriver in the water pump, turn the pump anti-clockwise and tension the timing belt until it can just be turned through 90° with the thumb and forefinger midway between the camshaft sprocket and water pump (photo).
14 Tighten the water pump bolts when the tension is correct, and check that the timing marks are still aligned.
15 Fit the dipstick tube to the cylinder block.
16 Fit the timing cover, insert the bolts with the earth lead and dipstick tube bracket, and tighten the bolts.
17 Refit the valve cover with a new gasket, locate the reinforcement strips, and tighten the nuts and bolts.
18 If the engine is in the car reverse the preliminary procedures given in Section 13.

39 Timing belt and sprockets - refitting

1 Fit the Woodruff key in the crankshaft and tap the sprocket into position.
2 Insert the bolt and tighten it to the specified torque while holding the crankshaft stationary with a lever in the starter ring gear.
3 Fit the Woodruff key to the camshaft then fit the sprocket followed by the spacer and bolt. Tighten the bolt while holding the sprocket stationary with a metal bar and two bolts.
4 Locate the timing belt on the crankshaft sprocket then fit the pulley, insert the bolts, and tighten them with an Allen key.
5 Turn the camshaft so that the indentation in the sprocket is aligned with the pointer on the timing cover plate. Check that the notch in the crankshaft pulley is aligned with the TDC pointer on the front of the oil pump
6 Fit the timing belt to the camshaft sprocket and water pump.
7 Using a screwdriver in the water pump, turn the pump anti-clockwise and tension the timing belt until it can just be turned through 90° with the thumb and forefinger midway between the camshaft sprocket and water pump (photo 38.13).
8 Tighten the water pump bolts when the tension is correct, and check that the timing marks are still aligned.
9 Fit the timing cover, insert the bolts with the earth lead and dipstick tube bracket, and tighten the bolts.
10 If the engine is in the car, reverse the preliminary procedures given in Section 13.

40 Valve clearances - checking and adjustment

1 The valve clearances can be checked and adjusted with the cylinder head removed (prior to refitting after overhaul) or in the normal manner such as during a routine service check.
2 Reference to the specifications will show that there are two clearance settings, these being for a cold or warm (coolant temperature above 35°C) engine condition. When the clearances are to be checked with the engine in the vehicle, run the engine up to its normal operating temperature, then switch off and remove the valve cover.
3 With the valve cover removed, turn the engine or camshaft (ie if head removed) until both cam peaks for No 1 cylinder are pointing upwards.
4 Insert a feeler blade of the correct thickness between the cam and cam follower. If the blade is not a firm sliding fit turn the adjustable ball-stud as necessary using an Allen key (photo). The valves from the timing belt end of the engine are in the following order: Inlet - Exhaust - Inlet - Exhaust - Inlet - Exhaust - Inlet - Exhaust.
5 Repeat the procedure given in paragraphs 3 and 4 for the remaining valves. If the engine is rotated in its normal direction, adjust the valves of No 3 cylinder followed by No 4 cylinder and No 2 cylinder.
6 Refit the valve cover, together with a new gasket.
7 If the clearances have been adjusted with the engine cold, recheck the clearances again after 600 miles (900 km) with the engine at its normal operating temperature.

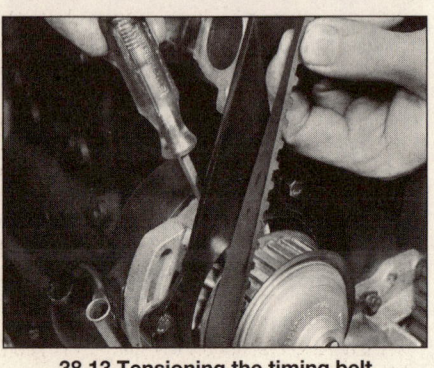

38.13 Tensioning the timing belt

40.4 Adjusting the valve clearances

Engine – 1.05 and 1.3 litre

41 Engine ancillary components and gearbox - refitting

1 Refer to Section 9, and refit the listed ancillary components with reference to the Sections or Chapters as applicable.
2 Refit the gearbox to the engine reversing the procedures described in Section 7.

42 Engine - refitting

Reverse the removal procedure given in Section 6, but note the following additional points:
(a) When lowering the assembly into the engine compartment ensure that the driveshafts are aligned with the flanges
(b) Assemble the engine mountings loosely initially and tighten them only after the assembly is central without straining the mountings
(c) Adjust the clutch, as described in Chapter 5
(d) Adjust the accelerator cable and, where applicable, the choke cable, as described in Chapter 3
(e) Refill the engine with oil and water

43 Engine - adjustments after major overhaul

1 With the engine refitted to the car, make a final check to ensure that everything has been reconnected and that no rags or tools have been left in the engine compartment.
2 If the valve tappets have been renewed, it is essential that no attempt to restart the engine is made for a minimum period of 30 minutes after installation. Failure to observe this precaution may result in engine damage caused by the valves contacting the pistons.
3 If new pistons or crankshaft bearings have been fitted, turn the carburettor engine speed screw in about half a turn to compensate for the initial tightness of the new components.
4 Fully pull out the choke (manual choke models) and start the engine. This may take a little longer than usual as the fuel pump and carburettor float chamber may be empty.
5 As soon as the engine starts, push in the choke to the detent. Check that the oil pressure light goes out.
6 Check the oil filter, fuel hoses and water hoses for leaks.
7 Run the engine to normal operating temperature, then adjust the slow running (idle), as described in Chapter 3.
8 If new pistons or crankshaft bearings have been fitted, the engine must be run-in for the first 500 miles (750 km). Do not operate the engine at full throttle or allow the engine to labour in any gear.
9 Although not strictly essential, it is good practice to change the engine oil and filter after the initial running-in period. This will get rid of the small metallic particles which are produced by new components bedding in to each other.

Part B: 1.6 and 1.8 litre engine

44 General description

The engine is of four-cylinder, in-line, overhead camshaft type, mounted transversely at the front of the car. The gearbox (manual or automatic) is attached to the flywheel/driveplate end of the engine.
The crankshaft is of five main bearing type and the endfloat is controlled by a shouldered centre bearing or by half thrust washers located each side of the centre bearing.
The camshaft is driven by a toothed belt which is tensioned by a tensioner on an eccentric bearing. The valves are operated by bucket type cam followers in direct contact with the camshaft.
An intermediate shaft, which is also driven by the toothed timing belt, drives the distributor and oil pump, and on carburettor engines the fuel pump.
The oil pump is of the twin gear type, driven from the immediate shaft, and it incorporates a pressure relief valve.
The aluminium cylinder head is of conventional design with the inlet and exhaust manifolds mounted on the rear side (as viewed with the engine in the car).

45 Routine maintenance - engine

The procedure is the same as that described for the 1.05 and 1.3 litre variants given in Section 2 of this Chapter.

46 Major operations possible with engine in car

The following operations can be carried out without having to remove the engine from the car:
(a) Removal and servicing of the cylinder head, camshaft, and timing belt
(b) Renewal of the crankshaft rear oil seal (after removal of the gearbox/transmission, driveplate or clutch as applicable)
(c) Removal of the sump and oil pump
(d) Removal of the piston/connecting rod assemblies (after removal of the cylinder head and sump)
(e) Renewal of the crankshaft front oil seal, intermediate shaft front oil seal, and camshaft front oil seal
(f) Renewal of the engine mountings

47 Major operations only possible after removal of engine from car

The following operations can only be carried out after removal of the engine from the car:
(a) Renewal of crankshaft main bearings
(b) Removal and refitting of the crankshaft
(c) Removal and refitting of the intermediate shaft

48 Method of engine removal

1 The engine, together with the gearbox/transmission, must be lifted from the engine compartment, then the engine separated from the gearbox/transmission on the bench. Two people will be needed for some of the time.
2 A hoist, capacity 150 kg (3 cwt) will be needed and the engine must be lifted approximately 1 metre (three feet). If the hoist is not portable and the engine is lifted, then sufficient room must be left behind the car to push the car back out of the way so that the power unit may be lowered. Blocks will be needed to support the engine after removal.
3 Ideally the car should be over a pit. If this is not possible then the body must be supported on axle stands so that the front wheels may be turned to undo the driveshaft nuts. The left one is accessible from above but the right-hand shaft must be undone from underneath. There are other jobs best done from below. Removal of the shift linkage can only be done from underneath, as can the exhaust downpipe-to-manifold detachment.
4 The exhaust downpipe-to-manifold flange connection is secured by special spring clips rather than bolts or studs and nuts. When disconnecting and reconnecting the joint, it will be necessary to use the special VW tool designed for this task, its number being 3049A. Without this tool detachment and certainly reconnection of the joint and clips is virtually impossible, so make arrangements to

1•24 Engine – 1.6 and 1.8 litre

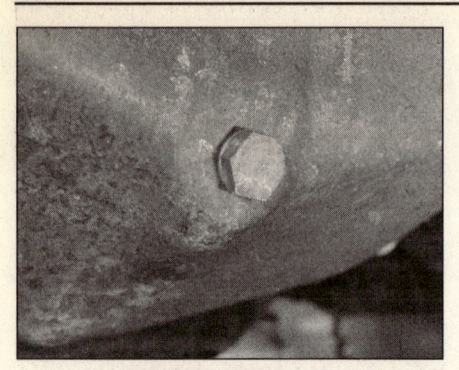

49.4 Sump drain plug

borrow or hire this tool in advance. Refer to Chapter 3 for further details.
5 The only other special tools that will be required will be a set of splined key wrenches which will be needed to remove and refit the socket-head bolts used to secure certain items such as the cylinder head bolts (photo 5.4).
6 Draining of oil and coolant is best done away from the working area if possible. This saves the mess made by spilled oil in the place where you must work.
7 Although not listed as an optional fitting on UK market models, an air conditioning system may have been fitted to some models and, where this is the case, the following special precautions must be taken when handling the refrigerant lines of the system or the system components.
(a) Do not stress or bend the flexible hose lines to a radius of less than 101 mm (4 inches)
(b) The flexible hose lines must be correctly located, must not chafe against adjacent components and must be kept well clear of the exhaust manifold and downpipe.
(c) All metal tubing lines must be kept free of kinks and must be handled with care
(d) Do not disconnect any of the air conditioning supply lines
(e) Do not weld or apply heat in the vicinity of the air conditioning lines or equipment
(f) If any part of the air conditioning system is to be detached and/or removed for any reason it must first be depressurised by

your VW dealer or a competent air conditioning systems engineer The only exception to this rule is the removal refitting and renewal of the compressor drivebelt. This can be achieved in the same manner as that for the alternator drivebelt (refer to Chapter 9)

49 Engine (carburettor) - removal

1 Disconnect the battery negative lead.
2 Remove the bonnet, as described in Chapter 11, and store it in a safe place.
3 Drain the engine coolant, as described in Chapter 2.
4 Position a suitable container beneath the engine then undo the sump drain plug and drain the engine oil (photo). On completion clean the drain plug and refit it. Renew the O-ring.
5 Remove the radiator, together with the cooling fan unit, as described in Chapter 2.
6 On carburettor models remove the air cleaner unit, then disconnect the throttle cable at the carburettor (refer to Chapter 3). Place the cable out of the way.
7 Disconnect the following wiring connections, but identify each lead as it is detached to avoid confusion on reassembly.
(a) Alternator lead
(b) Oil pressure switch lead(s) at cylinder head (photos) and oil filter bracket
(c) Inlet manifold preheater thermo-switch lead
(d) Choke cover thermo-switch lead (where applicable)
(e) Ignition HT and LT leads
(f) Choke cover lead separate connector
(g) Coolant temperature sender unit lead
(h) Earth strap to gearbox (photo) and multi-function switch to gearbox
(i) Starter motor leads
8 Disconnect the fuel supply hose from the fuel pump and the fuel return hose (to the fuel tank). Plug the hoses to prevent fuel leakage.
9 Disconnect the coolant and heater hoses from the engine.
10 On manual transmission models,

disconnect the clutch cable; with reference to Chapter 5.
11 Disconnect the following items from around the carburettor. Identify the connections where necessary to avoid confusion on reassembly:
(a) Thermotime valve
(b) Idle/overrun cut-off valve
(c) Inlet manifold preheater separator connector
(d) Part throttle channel heater separate connector
12 Disconnect the speedometer cable from the transmission.
13 Disconnect and remove the vacuum reservoir.
14 Disconnect the brake vacuum servo hoses and the vacuum hoses from the inlet manifold.
15 Undo and remove the gearbox mounting bolt.
16 Raise and support the vehicle on axle stands, allowing sufficient clearance to work underneath.
17 Disconnect the gearbox linkage, referring to Chapter 6 (manual gearbox).
18 On automatic transmission models select P (Park) then disconnect the throttle and selector cables from the transmission, with reference to Chapter 6.
19 Disconnect the driveshafts from the gearbox/transmission with reference to Chapter 7, and tie them up out of the way.
20 To disconnect the exhaust manifold to downpipe connection VW special tool number 3049A will be required. Although it may be possible to prise the clips free to separate this joint the special tool will definitely be required to refit the springs; see Chapter 3 for further details.
21 The car can now be lowered again; the remaining removal operations being from above.
22 Attach a suitable sling and hoist to the engine and gearbox/transmission unit and take its weight.
23 Disconnect the rear engine bearer by undoing the three bolts (photo 6.24).
24 The engine/gearbox front mounting must now be detached by unscrewing and removing the single through-bolt. It may be

49.7A 0.3 bar oil pressure switch location in rear of cylinder head

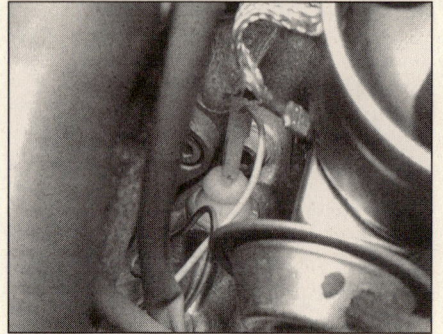

49.7B 1.8 oil pressure switch location in filter mounting

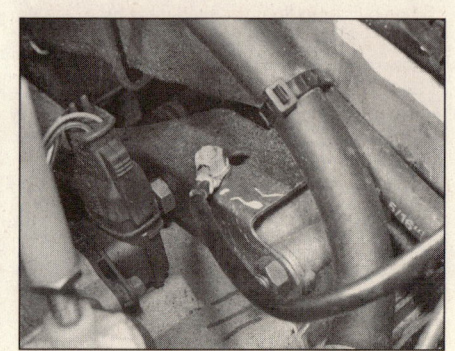

49.7C Earth strap to gearbox

Engine – 1.6 and 1.8 litre 1•25

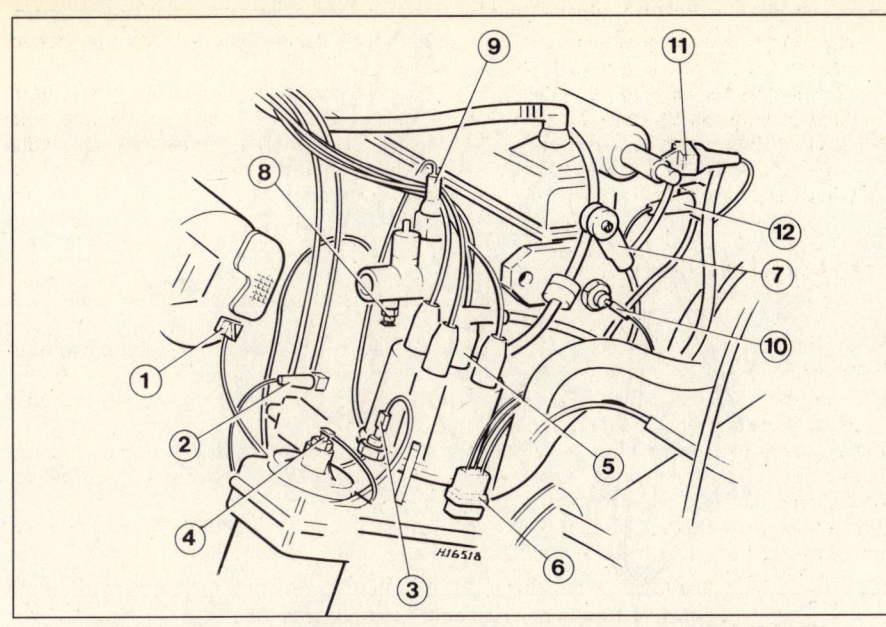

Fig. 1.12 Wiring connections to be detached - fuel injection models (Sec 50)

1 Alternator
2 Warm-up valve
3 1.8 bar oil pressure switch
4 Oil temperature sender
5 Distributor HT cable (terminal 4)
6 Hall sender (distributor)
7 Vacuum switch
8 Coolant temperature sender
9 Thermotime switch
10 0.3 bar oil pressure switch
11 Cold start valve
12 Auxiliary air valve

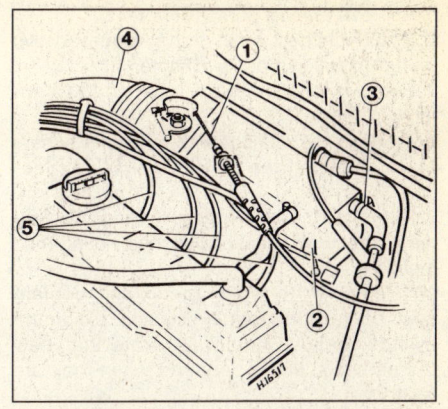

Fig. 1.13 Fuel injection components to be detached (Sec 50)

1 Throttle cable
2 Cold start valve
3 Vacuum hoses
4 Air intake pipe
5 Injectors

necessary to further lift, lower or twist the engine/gearbox unit to allow the through-bolt to be withdrawn (photo 6.26A).

25 The engine/gearbox unit is now ready for lifting out, but first make a final check that all cables, wiring and hoses are clear.

26 Have an assistant at hand to help guide the engine and gearbox unit clear of the surrounding components in the engine compartment as the unit is lifted out. The unit will have to be twisted slightly as it is raised and, once clear of the car, lower it to the ground or to the work area.

50 Engine (fuel injection) - removal

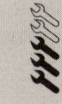

On the fuel injection models, the engine removal procedure closely follows that

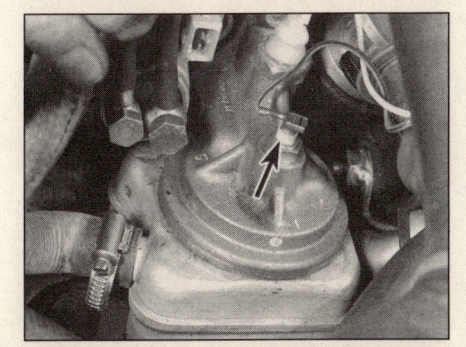

50.11 Oil temperature sender - arrowed (fuel injection models)

described in the previous Section, but disregard those items concerning detachment of the carburettor and associated items. The following fuel injection equipment items will need to be disconnected instead. Refer to Chapter 3 for further details concerning the detachment or removal where necessary of the respective fuel injection items.

1 Disconnect the wires from the warm-up valve (green connector).
2 Disconnect the wiring to the cold start valve (blue connector).
3 Disconnect the wiring to the auxiliary air valve.
4 Disconnect the throttle cable at the fast idle cam and bracket, but do not remove the securing clip.
5 Remove the cold start valve, but leave the fuel lines connected. Place out of the way.
6 Disconnect the air intake pipe at the flexible ducting attached to the throttle housing.
7 Disconnect the vacuum hoses from the inlet manifold and vacuum booster.
8 Leaving the fuel lines connected, undo the retaining bolts and withdraw the warm-up valve from the cylinder block. Position out of the way.
9 Detach the injectors from the cylinder head and plug the holes. Disconnect the injector lines from the locating bracket on the throttle housing and fold them back out of the way.
10 Detach the vacuum hoses to the throttle housing T-piece connector location clip at the bulkhead. Fold the hoses back out of the way.
11 Disconnect the oil temperature switch sender lead (photo).
12 When lifting out the engine and gearbox,

greater care will have to be taken in manoeuvring the combined unit from the engine compartment due to the close proximity of the air inlet manifold to the bulkhead. The unit will need to be pulled forwards first then twisted and lifted.

51 Engine and gearbox - separation and reconnection

The procedure is fully described in Chapter 6, Section 6 (manual gearbox) or Section 10 (automatic transmission). However, it is only necessary to refer to those paragraphs pertinent to the particular method being used. The engine must be supported on blocks, or alternatively the gearbox/transmission can be withdrawn with the engine still on the hoist.

52 Engine dismantling - general

Refer to Section 8 of this Chapter.

53 Engine ancillary components - removal

1 With the engine removed from the car and separated from the transmission, the externally mounted ancillary components can be removed prior to engine dismantling. The removal sequence need not necessarily follow the order given.
2 Remove the alternator and drivebelt (refer to Chapter 9).
3 Unbolt and remove the inlet manifold and carburettor or inlet manifold and throttle housing (fuel injection models). Refer to Chapter 3 as required.
4 Remove the exhaust manifold (Chapter 3).

1•26 Engine – 1.6 and 1.8 litre

5 Remove the fuel pump (Chapter 3).
6 If still attached, remove the warm-up valve on fuel injection models (Chapter 3).
7 Remove the distributor, referring to Chapter 4.
8 Remove the oil filter with oil cooler (where applicable) and the oil filter mounting (Section 62).
9 Remove the oil pressure and coolant temperature and sensor switches, noting their locations.
10 Remove the water pump and coolant hose connectors from the cylinder block and cylinder head (Chapter 2). Note that new O-ring seals will be required when they are refitted.
11 Remove the clutch, as described in Chapter 5, on manual gearbox models, then unbolt the intermediate plate. On automatic transmission models unbolt the driveplate from the crankshaft, noting the location of the spacer and shim(s).

54 Timing belt and sprockets - removal

If the engine is still in the car, first carry out the following operations:
(a) *Disconnect the battery earth lead*
(b) *Remove the alternator drivebelt (Chapter 9)*
(c) *Unbolt and remove the water pump pulley*

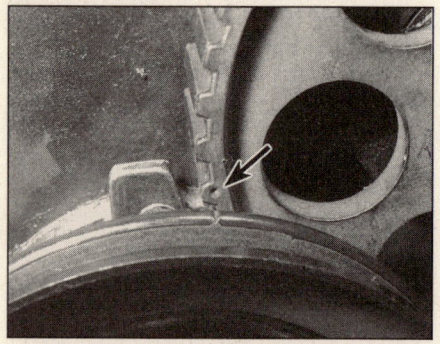

54.5 Intermediate sprocket timing mark (arrowed) aligned with the notch in the crankshaft pulley

54.6 No 1 cylinder cam lobes in valve closed position

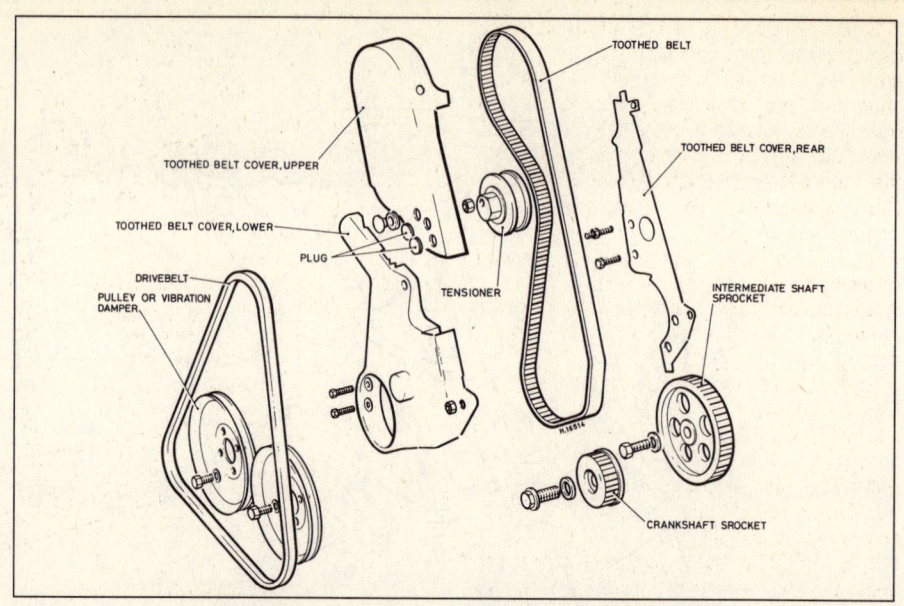

Fig. 1.14 Timing belt and cover components (Sec 54)

1 Depending on type, undo the retaining bolt(s)/nut(s), release the retaining clips and remove the upper timing cover. On some models it will be necessary to remove the bung from the front face of the cover to allow access to the Allen type retaining screw recessed within the cover. On other models, the retaining screw can be seen but its key slot is deeply recessed (access to it being made via the hole in the centre of the screw surround).
2 Unscrew the nuts and bolts from the valve cover and remove the cover, together with the gasket and reinforcement strips. Detach the crankcase emission hose(s) from the rocker cover.
3 Mark the relative positions of the crankshaft pulley and crankshaft sprocket, then undo the four socket-head bolts and withdraw the pulley.
4 Unbolt and withdraw the lower timing cover.

5 The engine must now be set for timing. Temporarily refit the crankshaft pulley. On the intermediate sprocket for the timing belt one tooth has a centre-punch mark. Turn the engine until this mates with a notch on the V-belt pulley bolted to the crankshaft sprocket (photo). To turn the engine over, remove the spark plugs then fit a suitable spanner onto the crankshaft sprocket retaining bolt and turn it in the direction of engine rotation.
6 When these marks match, look at the sprocket on the camshaft. One tooth of this has a centre-punch mark. This should be level with the valve cover flange (Figure 1.15). Having turned the engine until these marks agree now look at the cams for No 1 cylinder, the one nearest the timing belt. They will both be in the 'valve closed' position (photo). Now look through the hole in which the TDC sensor goes where the timing marks show on the periphery of the flywheel and note the reading.

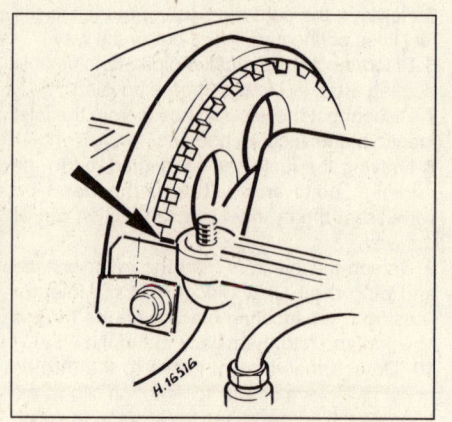

Fig. 1.15 Camshaft sprocket timing mark (arrowed) with No 1 cylinder at TDC on compression (Sec 54)

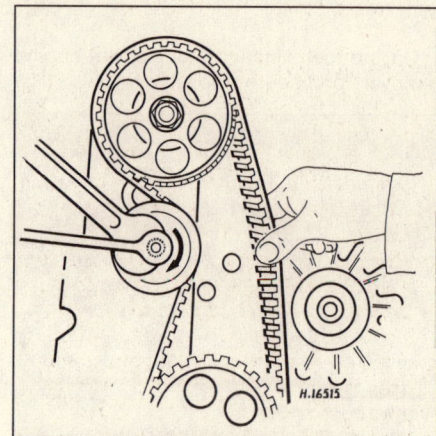

Fig. 1.16 Timing belt tension check method (Secs 54 and 79)

Engine – 1.6 and 1.8 litre 1•27

7 Before removing the timing drivebelt, check its correct tension. If held between the finger and thumb halfway between the intermediate shaft and the camshaft it should be just possible to twist it through 90°. If it is too slack, adjust it by slackening the bolt holding the eccentric cam on the tensioner wheel. If you are satisfied it can be adjusted to the correct tension remove it and examine it for wear. Now is the time to order a new one if necessary.

8 Loosen the tensioner then withdraw the timing belt from the camshaft, intermediate and crankshaft sprockets.

9 Each of the timing belt sprockets is secured by a central bolt and washer. The intermediate, camshaft and crankshaft sprocket (the latter in particular) securing bolts are tightened to a substantial torque and the sprockets will therefore need to be firmly held when undoing the bolts.

10 To remove the camshaft sprocket, unscrew the bolt with the sprocket held stationary by inserting a suitable metal bar through a sprocket hole and resting on the valve cover face of the cylinder head, but take care not to damage the face. Remove the bolt and spacer washer then withdraw the sprocket, tapping it free if necessary. Check the fit of the Woodruff key in the camshaft and if loose in the groove it must be renewed. Lever out the Woodruff key and keep it with the sprocket.

11 To remove the crankshaft sprocket, hold the crankshaft stationary with a lever jammed in the starter ring gear (remove the starter motor as applicable). Do not allow the crankshaft to turn, or the pistons may touch the valve heads. Unscrew the retaining bolt and remove it, together with the spacer washer, then lever the sprocket free from the crankshaft. Check the fit of the Woodruff key (if fitted) in the crankshaft and if loose in its groove it must be renewed. Lever out the Woodruff key and keep it with the crankshaft sprocket.

12 The intermediate shaft sprocket is removed in a similar manner to that for the camshaft sprocket.

55 Camshaft - removal and refitting

To remove the camshaft with the engine in the car, first carry out the following operations:

(a) Remove the timing cover and valve cover, then disconnect the timing belt from the camshaft sprocket, as described in Section 54

(b) If the camshaft oil seal is to be renewed then the camshaft timing sprocket must also be removed

1 Refer to Fig. 1.17 or 1.18. Remove the camshaft bearing caps. These have to go back the same way in the same place. They

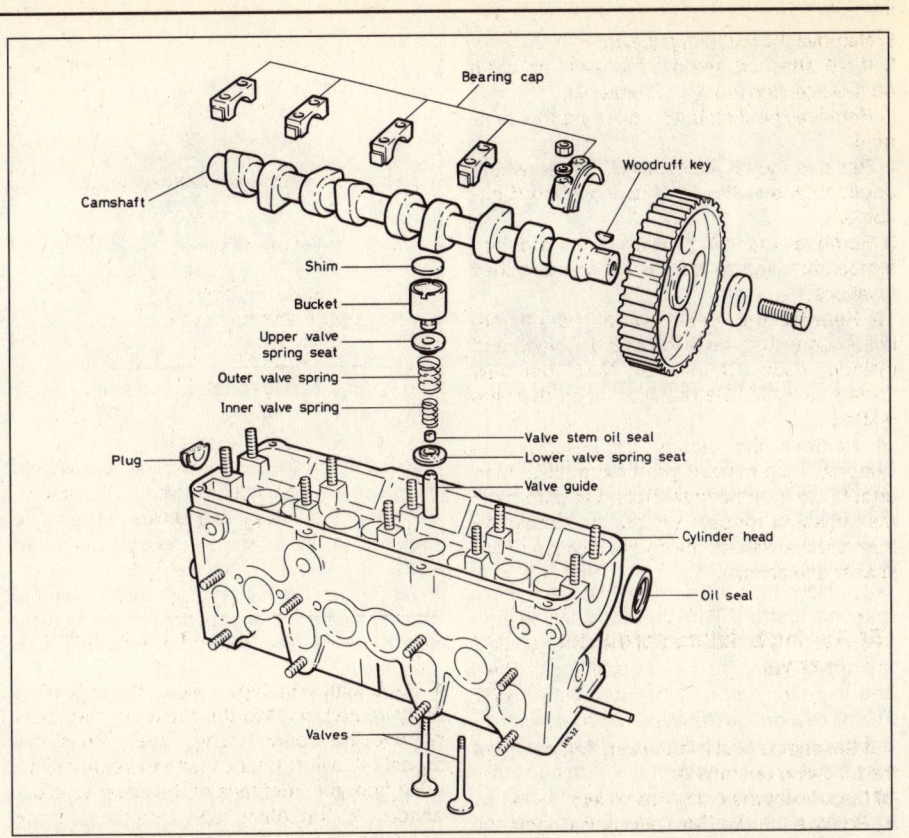

Fig. 1.17 Cylinder head and camshaft components (carburettor engine) (Sec 55)

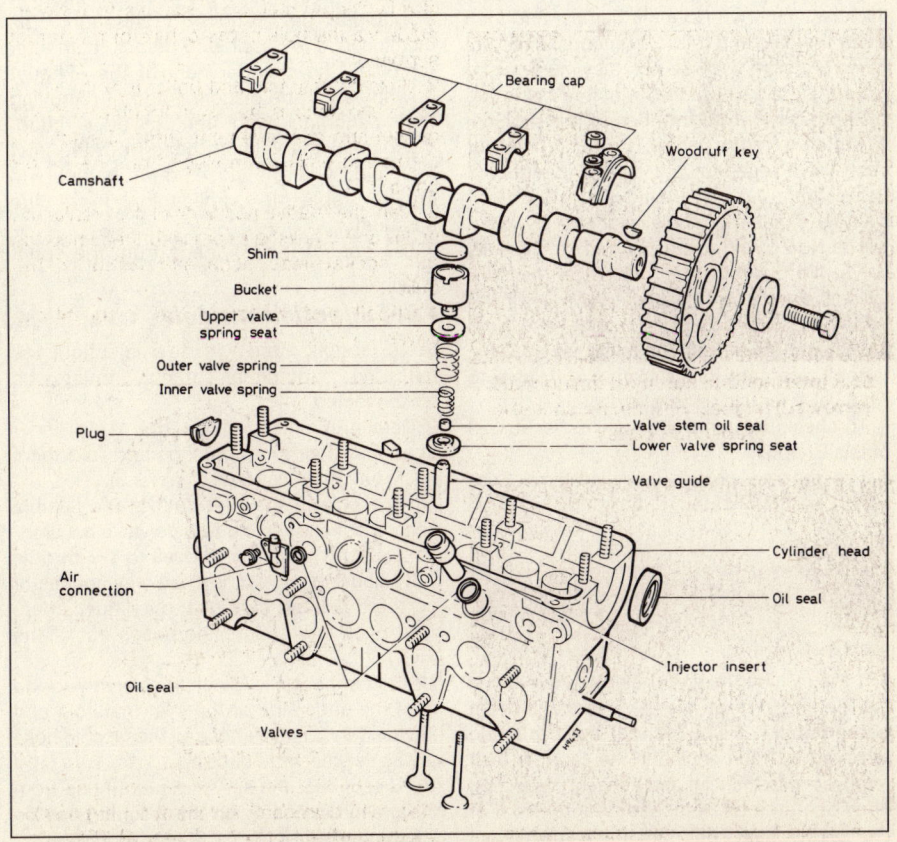

Fig. 1.18 Cylinder head and camshaft components (fuel injection engine) (Sec 55)

1•28 Engine – 1.6 and 1.8 litre

55.1 Removing a camshaft bearing cap

55.3 Tappet bucket and shim

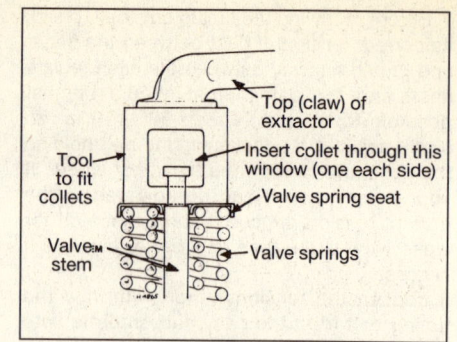

Fig. 1.19 Improvised tool used to remove and refit collets to valve stems (Sec 57)

are numbered (photo), but put a centre-punch on the side nearest the front of the head (where the sprocket was). No 1 is the one with a small oil seal on it.

2 Remove bearing caps 5, 1 and 3 in that order. Now undo the nuts holding 2 and 4 in a diagonal pattern and the camshaft will lift them up as the pressure of the valve springs is exerted. When they are free, lift the caps off and the camshaft may be lifted out as well. The oil seal on the front end will come with it.

3 The tappet buckets are now exposed and may be lifted out (photo). Take each one out in turn, prise the little disc out of the bucket by inserting a small screwdriver either side and lift the disc away. On the reverse the disc is engraved with a size (eg 3.75). This is its thickness number. Note the number and then clean the disc and refit it, number side down. There are eight of these and they must not be mixed. On assembly they must go back into the bore from which they came. This problem exists also for the valves, so a container for each valve assembly and tappet is required. Label them 1 to 8, 1 and 2 will be No 1 cylinder exhaust and inlet respectively. No 3 will be No 2 cylinder exhaust and No 4 its inlet valve. No 5 will be the inlet valve for No 3 cylinder and No 6 its exhaust valve. No 7 will be the inlet valve for No 4 cylinder and No 8 its exhaust valve. Note the thickness of all the tappet clearance discs from No 1 valve to No 8 valve for use on reassembly.

4 To check the camshaft, refer to Section 29 of this Chapter.

5 The refitting procedure is given in Section 57 of this Chapter.

56 Cylinder head - removal

1 If the cylinder head is being removed with the engine out of the car, proceed from paragraph 17. If the cylinder head is being removed with the engine in the car, it is best removed with the inlet and exhaust manifolds. They can then be detached after removal of the cylinder head, but note that a special tool is required to release (and subsequently reconnect) the exhaust downpipe-to-manifold flange retaining clips (refer to Chapter 3, Section 24). A special splined key will also be required to undo/tighten the cylinder head bolts.

2 Disconnect the battery earth lead. Drain the cooling system, then disconnect the cooling and heater hoses from the cylinder head (Chapter 2).

3 Disconnect the thermoswitch and oil pressure lead connections.

4 On carburettor models remove the air cleaner unit (Chapter 3).

5 Disconnect the alternator from the cylinder head attachment brackets and remove the V-belt (Chapter 9).

6 Disconnect/remove the inlet and exhaust manifolds as required although, as mentioned, it is possible to detach them after removing the cylinder head if the exhaust downpipe can be disconnected. If removing the manifolds with the cylinder head, disconnect the vacuum hose from the inlet manifold, and the accelerator cable (and choke cable if applicable) from the carburettor.

7 Disconnect the HT leads from the spark plugs.

Fuel injection models

8 On models fitted with fuel injection, the following additional items must be disconnected.

9 Detach the injector lines from the cylinder head and their location clips and fold them back out of the way (see Chapter 3).

10 Disconnect the inlet duct at the flexible hose connection to the throttle valve housing.

11 Detach the vacuum hoses to the throttle valve housing and at the three-way connector on the bulkhead side of the cylinder head. Fold back and secure the hoses out of the way.

12 Disconnect the auxiliary air valve lead from the underside of the inlet manifold and the auxiliary air valve hose to the flexible hose on the throttle valve housing.

13 Disconnect the servo vacuum hose from the green connector on the flexible hose on the throttle housing.

14 If air conditioning is fitted, detach the hoses from the auxiliary air valve and tube connections.

15 Detach the MFI hose at the servo hose valve connection.

16 Detach the wiring connector from the cold start valve.

All models

17 Remove the timing cover and valve cover, then disconnect the timing belt from the camshaft sprocket, as described in Section 54.

18 Remove the camshaft, as described in Section 55.

19 The next job is to remove the cylinder head bolts. These are recessed in the well of the cylinder head and are socket-head bolts. These must be removed using the correct special splined tool. If an Allen key is used it is likely to strip the socket-head in the bolt and bolt removal will then be virtually impossible without major surgery.

20 The cylinder head bolts must be unscrewed in a progressive manner and in the reverse sequence to that shown in Fig. 1.25.

21 When all ten bolts have been removed, lift the head from the cylinder block. It may need a little tapping to loosen it, but do not try to prise it loose by hammering in wedges. Lift off the gasket and, if the engine is not being dismantled, clean the piston crowns and block face. Note that the cylinder head bolts must not be re-used; a new set will therefore need to be obtained when ordering the cylinder head gasket set.

57 Cylinder head - dismantling, inspection and overhaul

1 Take the cylinder head away from the clean area and, with a wire brush, blunt screwdriver and steel wool, clean off all the carbon from the combustion chambers, valve faces and exhaust ports. When the head is clean and shining, wash your hands and take it back to the work area. Remove the spark plugs for cleaning.

2 The valves are not easy to get out unless a suitable valve spring compressor is available.

Engine – 1.6 and 1.8 litre 1•29

57.3 Valve springs, cap and collets

57.11A Inserting a valve into the cylinder head

57.11B Locate the valve springs and cap

Because the collets and spring caps are set so far down in the head a long claw is necessary on the compressor, and it must be split sufficiently to enable the collets to be removed and inserted. If such a tool is not to hand then find a piece of steel tube about 25 mm (1 in) inside diameter which will fit over the valve stem and press down the spring cover (see Fig. 1.19). The length will depend on the size of the compressor so fit the compressor over the head fully extended, measure the distance between the claw and the valve spring seat and cut the tube to a suitable length.

3 The next step is to cut two windows of suitable size, say 25 mm (1 in) long and 16 mm (0.6 in) wide, in opposite sides of the tube. The tube may then be used with the compressor to extract the collets from each valve stem in turn and the valve, springs, collets and seats may join the tappet in the appropriate receptacle, keeping them strictly together for refitting in the same valve guide from which they were taken (photo).

4 The valve springs must be renewed if they are damaged, distorted or known to have covered a high mileage. If in doubt as to their condition have your VW Dealer check them for compression efficiency using a calibrated valve spring compressor.

5 The valves should be cleaned and checked for signs of wear or burring. Where this has occurred, the inlet valve may be reground on a machine at a dealer, but exhaust valves must not be reground on the machine but ground in by hand. Wear in the valve guides may be detected by fitting a new valve in the guide and checking the amount that the rim of the valve will move sideways, when the top of the valve stem is flush with the top of the valve guide. The valve rock limits are given in the Specifications. New valve guides must be fitted and reamed by your VW dealer.

6 Do not labour away too long grinding in the valves. If the valve seat and valve are not satisfactory after fifteen minutes hard work then you will probably do more harm than good by going on. Make sure both surfaces are clean, smear the grinding paste onto the valve evenly and using a suction type cup work the valve with an oscillating motion lifting the valve away from the seat occasionally to stop ridging. Clean the seat and valve frequently and carry on until there is an even band, grey in colour on both seat and valve then wipe off all the paste.

7 The surface of the head must be checked with a straight-edge and feeler gauge. Place the straight-edge along the centre of the machined face of the head. Make sure there are no ridges at the extreme ends and measure the clearance with feelers between each combustion chamber head. This is the area where the narrowest part of the cylinder head gasket comes and where the gasket is most likely to fail. If the straight-edge is firmly in place and feelers in excess of 0.1 mm (0.004 in) can be put between the head and the straight-edge then the head should be taken to a dealer for servicing or, more probably, a new one.

8 If the cylinder head shows any signs of cracking anywhere have it inspected by your VW dealer to assess its condition for reuse. It may have to be renewed.

9 VW recommend that the valve stem oil seals should always be renewed to prevent possible high oil consumption. Pulling off the old seal is simple with pliers. With a packet of new oil seals is a small plastic sleeve. This is fitted over the valve stem and lubricated, and then the seal should be pushed on over the plastic sleeve until it seats on the guide. This should be done with a special tool (VW 10 204) which fits snugly round the outside of the seal and pushes it on squarely. If the seal is assembled without the plastic sleeve the seal will be damaged and oil consumption will become excessive. If you cannot pull them on properly then ask a dealer to do it for you.

10 Before reassembling the cylinder head, check the condition of the camshaft, as described in Section 29.

11 When all the parts, head, valve, seats, springs, guides, seals and camshaft have been pronounced satisfactory then assembly of the head may commence. Insert the valve in the correct guide (photo), fit the inner seat, valve springs and outer cap (photo), assemble the valve spring compressor and possibly the small tube and compress the valve spring until the collets may be assembled to the valve stem (photo). Assemble the second collet and holding them carefully together in place ease off the compressor until the spring seats the collets home. Remove the compressor, put a rag over the valve stem and tap the stem with a hammer. This is to ensure that the collets are seated correctly. If they are they will not come out. Repeat until all eight valves are in position in the cylinder head.

> **HAYNES HiNT** *If your fingers are too big, put a blob of grease on the collet and pick it up with a small screwdriver, then insert it into the slot on the valve stem.*

12 Refit the tappets in the bores from which they came (photo), then lubricate the camshaft bearing surfaces with oil and fit the camshaft, positioned so that No 1 cylinder cams point upwards.

57.11C ...and valve collets

57.12 Fit the tappet buckets

1•30 Engine – 1.6 and 1.8 litre

57.13 Fit the bearing caps

58.5 Refitting the oil pump

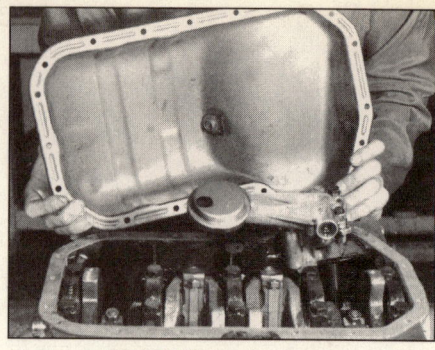

58.6 Refitting the sump

13 Fit a new oil seal at the sprocket end, lubricate the bearings, set the shaft in position, and install bearing caps (photo) Nos 2 and 4, tightening the nuts in a diagonal pattern until the shaft is in place. Now install the other bearing caps, making sure they are the right way round (centre-punch marks towards the drive pulley) and tighten the caps down using a diagonal pattern to the specified torque. Install a new rubber seal at the opposite end to the sprocket.

14 Adjust the valve clearances, with reference to Section 77.

15 To refit the cylinder head, refer to Section 78.

58 Sump and oil pump - removal and refitting

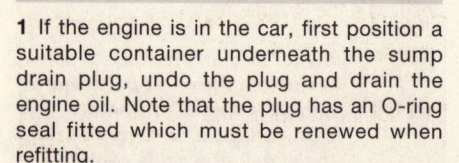

1 If the engine is in the car, first position a suitable container underneath the sump drain plug, undo the plug and drain the engine oil. Note that the plug has an O-ring seal fitted which must be renewed when refitting.

2 Undo the sump retaining bolts and remove the sump from the lower face of the crankcase. Remove the sump gasket. This must also be renewed when refitting the sump.

3 To remove the oil pump, undo the two retaining bolts and lower the pump unit, complete with the oil pick-up pipe and strainer.

4 Dismantling and inspection of the oil pump is dealt with in Section 69.

5 To refit the pump, ensure that the mating faces are clean, locate it into position, fit and tighten the securing bolts to the specified torque (photo).

6 Locate the new sump gasket, but do not apply an adhesive sealant. Refit the sump and tighten the retaining bolts evenly to the specified torque (photo).

7 Refit the oil drain plug fitted with a new O-ring seal and tighten it to the specified torque.

59 Pistons and connecting rods - removal

1 Remove the cylinder head, as described in Section 56.

2 Remove the sump, as described in Section 58.

3 Unscrew the two oil pump unit retaining bolts then lower and remove the pump unit, complete with oil pick-up pipe from the crankcase. Place it on one side for cleaning and inspection.

4 The piston and connecting rod removal procedure now follows that given for the smaller engine variants in Section 18.

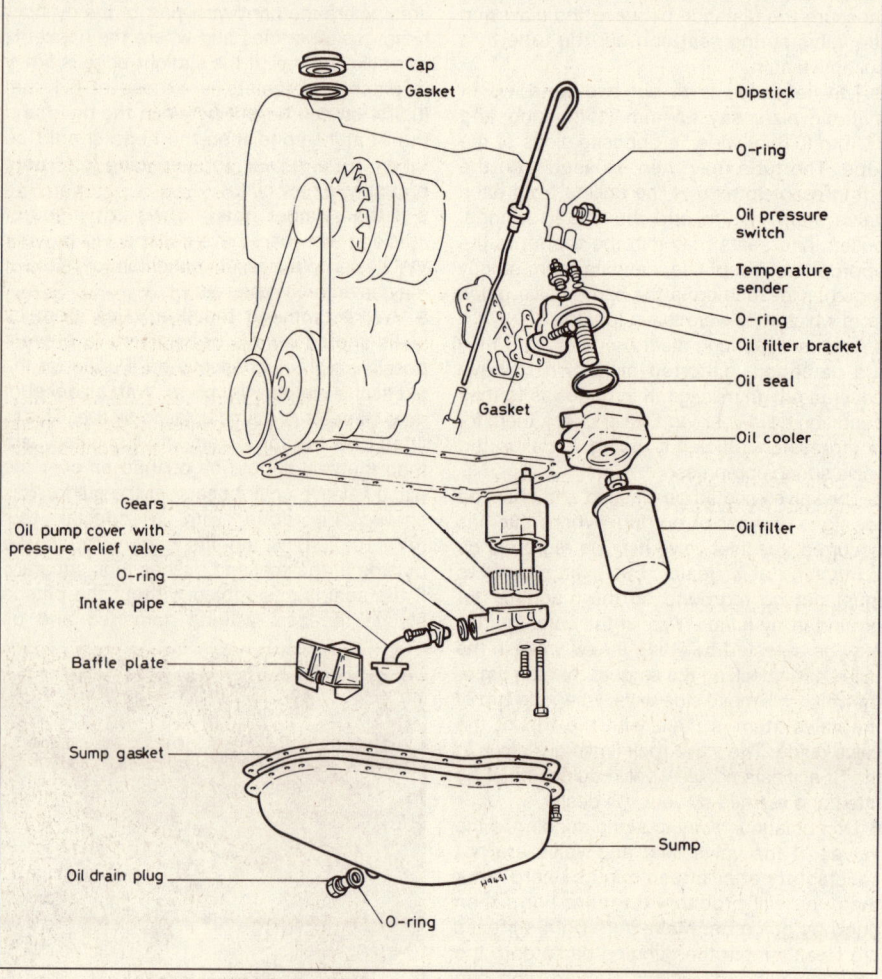

Fig. 1.20 Sump, oil pump and oil filter components (Sec 58)
Fuel injection model shown

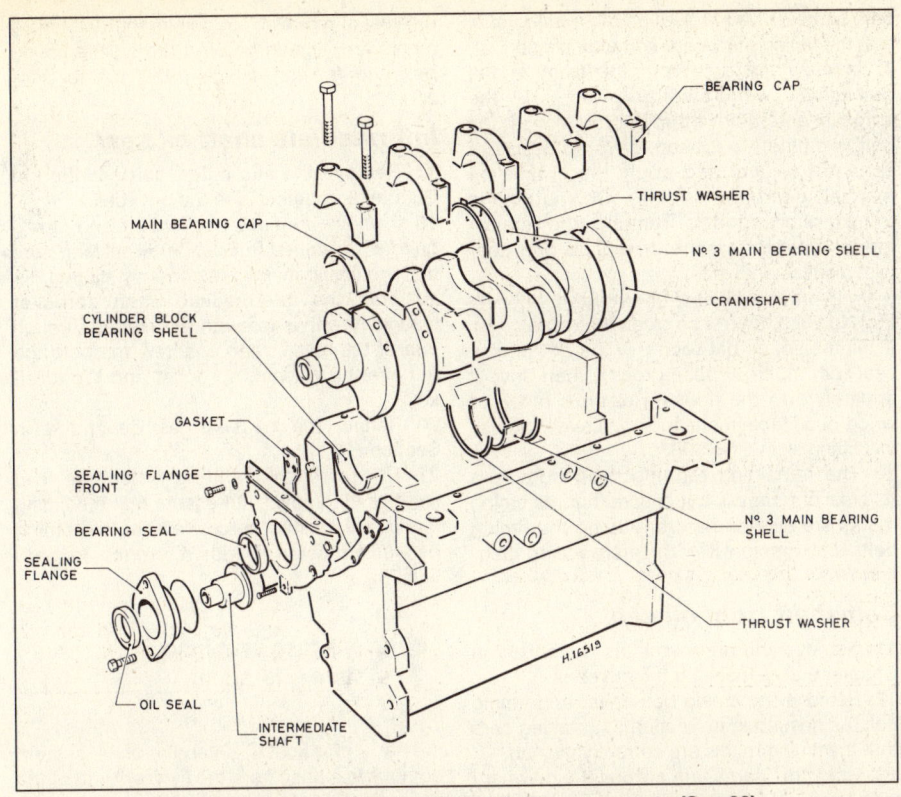

Engine – 1.6 and 1.8 litre 1•31

Fig. 1.21 Crankshaft and cylinder block components (Sec 60)

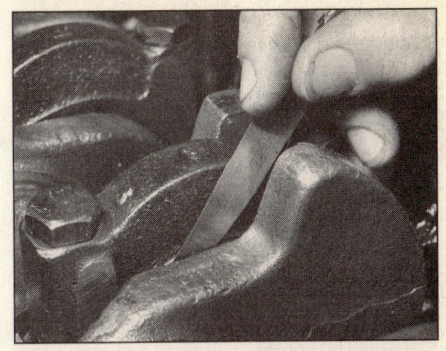

60.3 Checking the crankshaft endfloat at No 3 main bearing

60 Crankshaft and main bearings - removal

1 Disconnect the pistons and connecting rods from the crankshaft, as described in the previous Section. Note that, although the engine has to be removed to remove the crankshaft, the cylinder head, pistons and connecting rods can be left in position.
2 At the flywheel end, undo and remove the six bolts securing the oil seal flange to the crankcase. Withdraw the flange, seal and gasket.
3 Now examine the main bearing caps. It will be seen that the caps are numbered one to five and that the number is on the side of the engine opposite the oil pump position. Identify these numbers. If they are obscured then mark the caps in the same way as the connecting rod caps. Before removing the caps, push the crankshaft to the rear and check the endfloat using a feeler gauge between the thrust washer flanges on No 3 main bearing and the crankshaft web (photo). It must not exceed the specified maximum.
4 Remove the bearing cap retaining bolts, remove the bearing caps and lift out the thrust washers from each side of the centre main bearing.
5 Lift out the crankshaft and then remove the top half bearing shells. If the main bearings are not being renewed make sure the shells are identified so that they go back into the same bearing cap the same way round

61 Intermediate shaft - removal

1 The intermediate shaft can only be withdrawn from the crankcase with the engine removed from the car (Section 49 or 50, as applicable)
2 Remove the timing belt, as described in Section 54.
3 Remove the fuel pump on carburettor models (Chapter 3) and the ignition distributor (Chapter 4).
4 Before removing the intermediate shaft, check that the endfloat does not exceed the maximum allowable amount (see Specifications).
5 Undo the two sealing flange retaining bolts then withdraw the intermediate shaft, complete with sealing flange (photos).
6 Withdraw the sealing flange from the intermediate shaft. The oil seal within the flange and the O-ring must be renewed on reassembly (see Section 70).

62 Oil filter - renewal

1 The oil filter is located on the side of the crankcase beneath the distributor (photo), the filter being a disposable cartridge type which is screwed onto a mounting bracket which is

61.5A Intermediate shaft retaining flange bolts (arrowed)

61.5B Withdrawing the intermediate shaft

62.1 Oil filter location viewed from underneath

1•32 Engine – 1.6 and 1.8 litre

attached to the crankcase. On fuel injection models an oil cooler is fitted between the mounting bracket and the filter cartridge.

2 The filter must be renewed at the specified intervals given in Routine Maintenance at the start of this Manual.

3 Place a suitable container beneath the filter then, using a strap wrench, unscrew the filter and discard it. For better access either jack up the front of the car or position the car on ramps.

4 Wipe clean the sealing faces of the filter and mounting/oil cooler.

5 If the oil cooler is being removed (fuel injection models), drain the cooling system (Chapter 2) and disconnect the coolant hoses from the cooler. The O-ring between the oil cooler and the mounting must be renewed .

6 If the oil filter mounting is to be removed, disconnect the oil pressure switch lead, undo the securing bolts and withdraw the mounting and gasket. The oil pressure switch can be unscrewed from the top face of the mounting if required. Remove and renew the switch O-ring.

7 Refitting is a reversal of the removal procedure. Renew the mounting gasket and O-ring(s) as necessary.

8 Smear the sealing rubber on the new filter with engine oil, then fit and tighten the filter by hand (or as directed on the filter cartridge).

9 Top up the engine oil and coolant (if applicable) levels. Start the engine and check for any signs of oil (or coolant) leaks.

63 Crankshaft, camshaft and intermediate shaft oil seals - renewal (engine in car)

Crankshaft oil seal (flywheel/driveplate end)

1 On manual gearbox models, remove the clutch and pressure plate, as described in Chapter 5. On automatic transmission models, remove the transmission, as described in Chapter 6, then unbolt the driveplate from the crankshaft, noting the location of the spacer and shim(s).

2 On all models, carefully prise out the oil seal with a screwdriver or strong wire and wipe clean the recess.

3 Fill the space between the lips of the new seal with multi-purpose grease, then drive it squarely into the housing using a block of wood or suitable metal tubing If at all possible, use VW fitting sleeve No 2003 to avoid damage to the oil seal lip.

4 Refit the driveplate or clutch using a reversal of the removal procedure, with reference to Chapters 5 and 6 as necessary.

Crankshaft oil seal (timing belt end)

5 Remove the alternator as described in Chapter 9, together with the drivebelt.

6 Remove the timing belt cover and timing belt, as described in Section 54, making sure that the timing marks are correctly aligned.

7 Unscrew the bolt from the front of the crankshaft, withdraw the pulley and the sprocket and remove the Woodruff key. If the belt is difficult to loosen, have an assistant engage top gear and apply the brakes on manual gearbox models. On automatic transmission models remove the starter model and restrain the driveplate ring gear with a suitable lever.

8 Prise out the oil seal or extract it with VW tool No 2085, then wipe clean the recess.

9 Fill the space between the lips of the new seal with multi-purpose grease, then drive it squarely into the housing using a block of wood or suitable metal tubing. If available use VW fitting sleeve No 3083.

10 The remaining refitting procedure is a reversal of removal, but ensure that the timing marks are aligned before refitting the timing belt, and tension it with reference to Section 79.

Camshaft front oil seal

11 Remove the alternator, as described in Chapter 9, together with the drivebelt.

12 Remove the timing belt cover and timing belt, as described in Section 54, making sure that the timing marks are correctly aligned.

13 Hold the camshaft sprocket stationary with a screwdriver inserted through one of the holes, then unscrew the bolt and remove the washer, sprocket and Woodruff key.

14 Prise out the oil seal or alternatively extract it with VW tool No 2085, then wipe clean the recess.

15 Fill the space between the lips of the new seal with multi-purpose grease, then drive it squarely into the cylinder head using a block of wood or suitable metal tubing. If available use VW fitting sleeve No 10-203.

16 The remaining refitting procedure is a

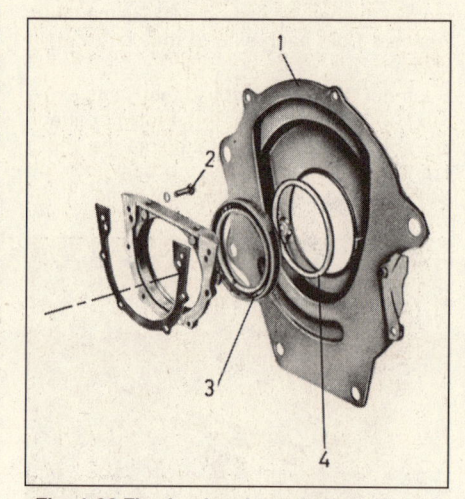

Fig. 1.22 Flywheel end crankshaft oil seal components (Sec 63)

1 Intermediate plate
2 Bolt
3 Oil seal
4 Sealing ring (not fitted to all models)

reversal of removal, but ensure that the timing marks are aligned before refitting the timing belt and tension it with reference to Section 79.

Intermediate shaft oil seal

17 Remove the alternator, as described in Chapter 9, together with the drivebelt.

18 Remove the timing belt cover and timing belt, as described in Section 54 making sure that the timing marks are correctly aligned.

19 Hold the intermediate shaft sprocket stationary with a screwdriver inserted through one of the holes, then unscrew the bolt and remove the washer, sprocket and Woodruff key.

20 Renew the oil seal, as described in Section 70.

21 The remaining refitting procedure is a reversal of removal, but ensure that the timing marks are aligned before refitting the timing belt and tension it with reference to Section 79.

64 Crankcase ventilation system - description

The crankcase ventilation system comprises a hose from the flywheel end of the valve cover to the side of the air cleaner.

On fuel injection models there is a hose to the air inlet manifold and a hose to the air cleaner from a three-way connector on the valve cover.

Periodically the hose(s) should be examined for security and condition. Cleaning will not normally be necessary except when the engine is well worn and sludge has accumulated.

65 Examination and renovation - general

Refer to Section 22 of this Chapter.

Fig. 1.23 VW Tool 2085 for removing crankshaft oil seal (timing belt end) and camshaft oil seal (Sec 63)

Engine – 1.6 and 1.8 litre 1•33

69.2 Examine the face of the oil pump cover for scoring

69.3 Checking the oil pump gear backlash

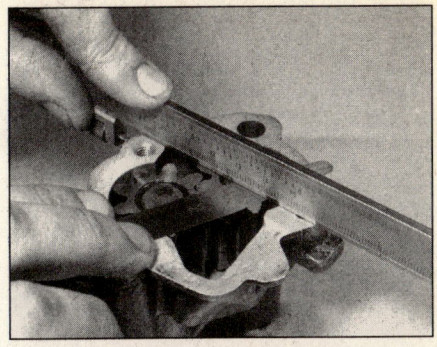

69.4 Checking the oil pump gear endfloat

66 Crankshaft and main bearings - examination and renovation

Refer to Section 23 of this Chapter.

67 Cylinder block/crankcase - examination and renovation

Refer to Section 24 of this Chapter.

68 Pistons and connecting rods - examination and renovation

Refer to Section 25 of this Chapter.

69 Oil pump - examination and renovation

1 With the oil pump on the bench, prise off the cap with a screwdriver and clean the strainer gauze in fuel. Refit the gauze and press on the cap.
2 Remove the two small bolts and take the cover away from the body. Examine the face of the cover (photo). As will be seen in the photograph the gears have marked the cover. If the depth of this marking is significant then the face of the cover must be machined flat again.
3 Remove the gears and wash the body and gears in clean paraffin. Dry them and reassemble the gears, lubricating them with clean engine oil. Measure the backlash between the gears with a feeler gauge (photo). This should be 0.05 to 0.20 mm (0.002 to 0.008 in).
4 Now place a straight-edge over the pump body along the line joining the centre of the two gears and measure with a feeler gauge the axial clearance between the gears and the straight-edge (photo). This must not be more than 0.15 mm (0.006 in).
5 If all is well, check that the shaft is not slack in its bearings, and reassemble the pump for fitting to the engine.
6 If there is any doubt about the pump it is recommended strongly that a replacement be obtained. Once wear starts in a pump it progresses rapidly. In view of the damage that may follow a loss of oil pressure, skimping the oil pump repair is a false economy.

70 Intermediate shaft - examination and renovation

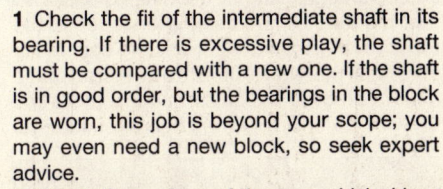

1 Check the fit of the intermediate shaft in its bearing. If there is excessive play, the shaft must be compared with a new one. If the shaft is in good order, but the bearings in the block are worn, this job is beyond your scope; you may even need a new block, so seek expert advice.
2 Check the surface of the cam which drives the fuel pump (where applicable). If serious ridging is present a new shaft is indicated.
3 Check the teeth of the distributor drivegear for scuffing or chipping. Check the condition of the timing belt sprocket.
4 It is unlikely that damage to this shaft has happened, but if it has, seek advice from the VW agent.
5 There is an oil seal in the flange for the intermediate shaft. This may need renewal if there are signs of leakage. To do this remove the timing belt sprocket and withdraw the flange from the shaft. The oil seal may now be prised out and a new one pressed in. Always fit a new O-ring on the flange before assembling it to the cylinder block.

71 Flywheel/driveplate - examination and renovation

1 There is not much you can do about the flywheel if it is damaged.
2 Inspect the starter ring teeth. If these are chipped or worn it is possible to renew the starter ring. This means heating the ring until it may be withdrawn from the flywheel, or alternatively splitting it. A new one must then be shrunk on. If you know how to do this and you can get a new ring then the job can be done but it is beyond the capacity of most owners.
3 Serious scoring on the flywheel clutch facing requires a new flywheel. Do not attempt to clean the scoring off with a scraper or emery. The face must be machined.
4 If it is necessary to fit a new flywheel, the ignition timing mark must be made by the owner. The new flywheel has only the TDC mark as an O on the outer face, therefore punch or scribe the appropriate timing mark for your model (see Chapter 4), to the left of the TDC mark at the appropriate distance (see Fig. 1.24).
5 On automatic transmission models, check the driveplate as described for the flywheel; it will also be necessary to mark a new driveplate for ignition timing.

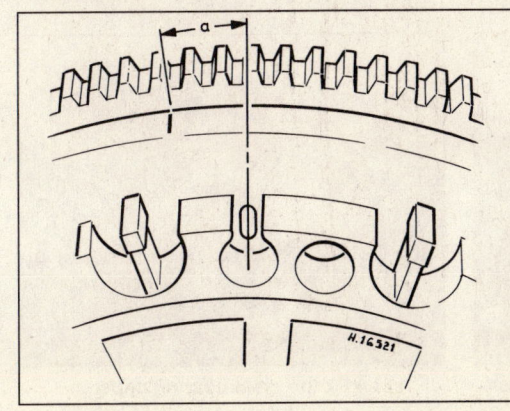

Fig. 1.24 Flywheel/driveplate ignition timing marks (Sec 71)

Engine code EZ (1.6) - flywheel:
  $a = 37.0$ mm (1.46 in) 18° BTDC
Engine code EZ (1.6) - driveplate:
  $a = 42.0$ mm (1.65 in) 18° BTDC
Engine code EV (1.8) - flywheel:
  $a = 12.5$ mm (0.49 in) 6° BTDC
Engine code GU (1.8) - flywheel:
  $a = 37.0$ mm (1.46 in) 18° BTDC
Engine code GU (1.8) - driveplate:
  $a = 42.0$ mm (1.65 in) 18° BTDC

1•34 Engine – 1.6 and 1.8 litre

74.2A Fitting the flanged type centre main bearing into the crankcase

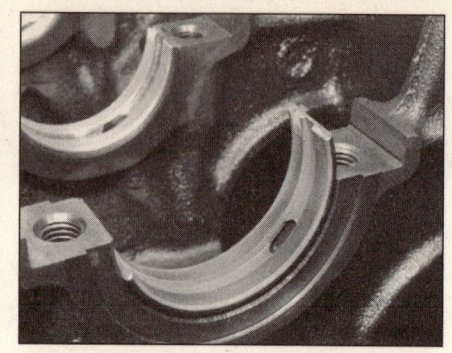

74.2B Fitting the alternative type centre main bearing into the crankcase...

74.2C ...together with its thrust washers

72 Timing belt and sprockets - examination and renovation

Refer to Section 28 of this Chapter. The information given also applies to the intermediate shaft sprocket.

73 Engine reassembly - general

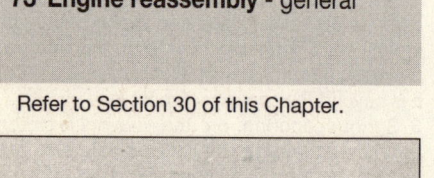

Refer to Section 30 of this Chapter.

74 Crankshaft and main bearings - refitting

1 If a new crankshaft is being fitted to automatic transmission models the needle roller bearing supplied and fitted by the manufacturers will need to be removed from its aperture in the rear end of the crankshaft. It may already have been removed by the supplier, but check anyway.

2 Clean the crankcase recesses and bearing caps thoroughly and fit the bearing shells so that the tang on the bearing engages in the recess in the crankcase or bearing cap. Make sure that the shells fitted to the crankcase have oil grooves and holes, and that these line up with the drillings in the bearing housings. When fitting the bearing shells to the caps, note that bearing numbers 1, 2 and 5 are plain shells whilst bearing number 4 has an oil groove. The bearing shells of the centre bearing (No 3) may either be flanged to act as thrust washers, or may have separate thrust washers. These should be fitted oil groove outwards (photos). Fit the bearing shells so that the ends of the bearing are flush with the joint face (photo).

3 Oil the bearings and journals (photo) then locate the crankshaft in the crankcase.

4 Fit the main bearing caps (with centre main bearing thrust washers if applicable) in their correct positions (photo).

5 Fit the bolts to the bearing caps and tighten the bolts of the centre cap to the specified torque (photo), then check that the crankshaft rotates freely.

74.2D Fitting the flanged type centre main bearing to the cap

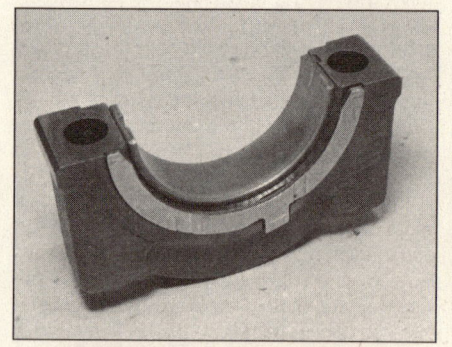

74.2E Fitting the centre bearing and separate thrust washers to the cap

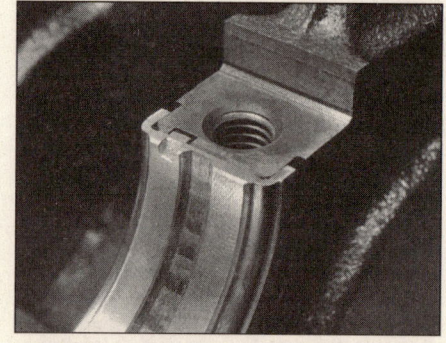

74.2F Ensure that the ends of the bearing are flush with the joint face

74.3 Lubricate the main bearing shells

74.4 Fit the main bearing caps...

74.5 ...and tighten the retaining bolts

Engine – 1.6 and 1.8 litre 1•35

74.8 Crankshaft rear oil seal

HAYNES HiNT *If it is difficult to rotate the crankshaft, check that the bearing shells are seated properly and that the bearing cap is in the correct way round. Rotation will only be difficult if something is incorrect, and the fault must be found. Dirt on the back of a bearing shell is sometimes the cause of a tight main bearing.*

6 Working out from the centre, tighten the remaining bearing caps in turn, checking that the crankshaft rotates freely after each bearing has been tightened.
7 Check that the endfloat of the crankshaft is within specification, by inserting feeler gauges between the crankshaft and the centre bearing thrust face/washer while levering the crankshaft first in one direction and then in the other.
8 Lubricate the rear of the crankshaft and, using a new gasket, install the rear oil seal and flange. Tighten the six bolts.
9 Lubricate the front of the crankshaft and fit the front oil seal and flange with a new gasket. Tighten the bolts to the correct torque.

75 Intermediate shaft - refitting

Lubricate the intermediate shaft, then install it in the block. Fit the O-ring and flange, together with the oil seal, then tighten the bolts. Note that the oil hole must be at the bottom of the flange.

76 Pistons and connecting rods - refitting

1 Proceed as described in Section 32 of this Chapter, paragraphs 2 to 7 inclusive. When refitting the big-end nuts oil the threads.
2 On completion, check the endfloat of each connecting rod in a similar manner to that described for checking the crankshaft enfloat.
3 The oil pump and sump can be refitted, as described in Section 58.

77 Valve clearances - checking and adjustment

1 If a new or reconditioned cylinder head, complete with camshaft, is being fitted, the valve clearances will have been preset.
2 The valve clearances can be checked and if necessary adjusted during a normal routine service check or with the cylinder head removed (prior to refitting after overhaul).
3 Reference to the Specifications will show different clearance requirements for a cold or warm (coolant temperature above 35°C) engine. When the engine is in the vehicle, run it up to its normal operating temperature then switch off and remove the valve cover.
4 Check each valve clearance in turn by rotating the engine so that the valve to be checked has the cam lobe facing upwards. In this position the valve in question is fully closed and a feeler gauge inserted between the heel of the cam lobe and the valve tappet shim within the tappet bucket will give the clearance present. If possible, use a set of metric feeler gauges to avoid the complication of metric/Imperial conversions during subsequent operations. If the engine is fully assembled it will rotate more easily if the plugs are removed, but do not rotate the engine by turning the camshaft sprocket, this will stretch the timing belt. Use the alternator drivebelt (V-belt) or jack up one front wheel and with the engine in gear rotate the roadwheel. Note: *Do not turn the engine with any of the shims removed, otherwise the camshaft may foul the rim at the top of the bucket.*
5 Repeat this measurement for all the valves in turn and then compare the measurements with the Specifications.
6 Make a table of the actual clearances and then calculate the error from those specified. Suppose on No 1 exhaust valve the measured clearance is 0.15 mm. It is 0.3 mm too small so it must be adjusted and a shim 0.3 mm thinner fitted instead of the present one. As the shims are in steps of 0.05 mm variation the required shim can be selected once the size of the shim at present installed is known.

77.4 Checking the valve clearances with a feeler blade

If you have dismantled and reassembled the head then you know the size etched on the back of the shim, but if you do not then the shim must be removed to find out.

TOOL TiP

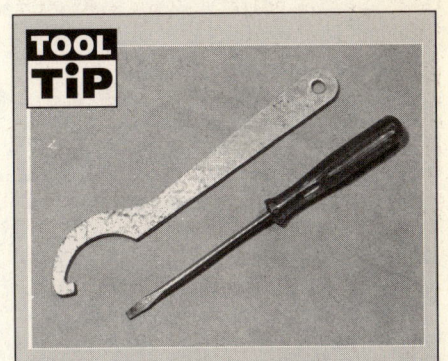

Ideally VW tools 2078 and 10.208 should be used to remove the valve shims, but we managed quite well with these tools: a small electrician's screwdriver and a C-spanner which was just the right size to push the bucket down without pushing the tappet shim (ie pushing the rim down).

With the cam turned to give maximum clearance the tappet is pushed down against the valve springs while the shim is levered out and removed by the VW tool or a screwdriver. Be careful; if the spanner slips when the shim is halfway out, the shim will fly out sharply (photo).
7 Once all the shim sizes are known a table may be constructed and the sizes of the new shims required may be calculated. Going back to the example, if the present shim is marked 3.60 then one marked 3.30 is required. Bucket shims are available in 26 different thicknesses which increase in increments of 0.05 mm from 3.00 mm to 4.25 mm.
8 As it is unlikely that you will have the required shims readily available it will be necessary to wait until they have been obtained before the tappets can be adjusted.
9 When inserting the shims ensure that the face with the thickness etching faces downwards.
10 If adjustment is made when the engine is

77.6 Removing a tappet bucket shim

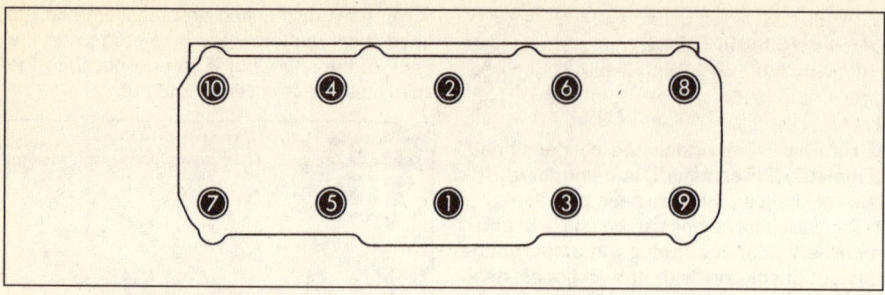

1•36 Engine – 1.6 and 1.8 litre

Fig. 1.25 Cylinder head bolt tightening sequence (Sec 78)

cold then it must be checked again when the engine is hot (coolant above 35°C). If the cylinder head has been overhauled it should be checked again, hot, after 600 miles (900 km). The valve clearances should otherwise normally only need checking at the Routine Maintenance intervals given at the start of this Manual.

11 Once the correct clearances have been achieved, refit the spark plugs and the valve cover (engine in car).

> **HAYNES HiNT** *If you know the sizes of all the valve shims, this information should be kept in a safe place. It will save a lot of time during the next overhaul.*

78 Cylinder head - refitting

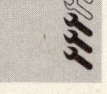

Note: *New cylinder head retaining bolts must be used on refitting*

1 Clean the top face of the block. Make a final inspection of the bores and lubricate them. Turn the crankshaft so that the pistons are in the mid cylinder position.

2 If you look at the edge of the block between No 3 and No 4 cylinders on the side above the distributor, the engine number is stamped on an inclined surface. Using this as a datum, install a new cylinder head gasket so that the word 'OBEN' engraved on the gasket is over this datum point and on the top side of the gasket (photo).

3 Lower the cylinder head into position, locating onto the centring pins where fitted. If the cylinder block does not have centring pins, initially refit new No 8 and No 10 cylinder head bolts. Do not use jointing compound. Check that the gasket is seating correctly and fit the remainder of the new bolts. Now following the sequence in Fig. 1.25 tighten the bolts until the head is firmly held. Using the torque wrench, tighten the bolts in stages to the specified torque following the same sequence (see Specifications).

4 Once the cylinder head has been tightened in stages to the specified torque wrench setting it will not need further tightening.

79 Timing belt and sprockets - refitting

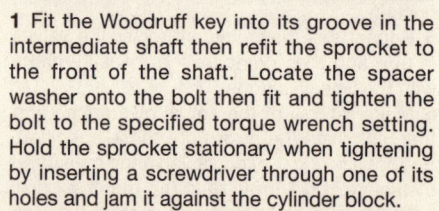

1 Fit the Woodruff key into its groove in the intermediate shaft then refit the sprocket to the front of the shaft. Locate the spacer washer onto the bolt then fit and tighten the bolt to the specified torque wrench setting. Hold the sprocket stationary when tightening by inserting a screwdriver through one of its holes and jam it against the cylinder block.

2 Locate the Woodruff key (if applicable) to the groove at the front of the crankshaft then refit the timing belt sprocket onto the shaft. Lubricate the retaining bolt with oil, locate the spacer washer onto the bolt then fit and tighten it to the specified torque wrench setting. When tightening the bolt, prevent the crankshaft from turning by using the same method as that for its removal.

3 Locate the Woodruff key into its groove on the front of the camshaft then refit the camshaft sprocket. Refit the retaining bolt, together with the spacer washer, and tighten to the specified torque wrench setting. Hold the sprocket stationary when tightening by inserting a screwdriver through one of its holes and jam it against the cylinder block or head.

4 If removed, refit the timing belt rear cover (apply locking compound to the stud thread).

5 Locate the crankshaft pulley onto the sprocket (aligning the marks made previously) using one bolt to secure it temporarily.

6 Turn the camshaft sprocket so that the lobes of No 1 cylinder cams are pointing upwards and the mark on the camshaft sprocket is aligned with the valve cover (Fig. 1.15).

7 Rotate the crankshaft sprocket and the intermediate shaft sprocket until the dot on the intermediate sprocket and the mark on the V-belt pulley coincide. Install the timing belt tensioner loosely and then the timing belt. Making sure the marks are still in place, put a spanner on the adjuster and tighten the belt until it will twist only 90 degrees when held between the finger and thumb halfway between the camshaft and intermediate shaft sprockets. Tighten the eccentric adjuster nut to the specified torque (Fig. 1.16).

8 Unbolt and remove the crankshaft V-belt pulley.

9 Fit the lower timing cover then refit the crankshaft V-belt pulley and tighten its retaining bolts to the specified torque.

10 Locate the new valve cover gasket into position on the cylinder head, the seal to the No 1 camshaft bearing cap and the half round grommet into its location at the rear end of the cylinder head.

11 Fit the valve cover into position, locate the reinforcement strips then refit and tighten the retaining nuts evenly to the specified torque.

12 Refit the upper timing belt cover.

78.2 Cylinder head gasket on the block

78.3A Lowering the cylinder head onto the block

78.3B Tightening the cylinder head bolts

Engine – 1.6 and 1.8 litre 1•37

80 Engine ancillary components - refitting

1 On automatic transmission models, refit the driveplate together with any shims originally located between the crankshaft and the plate. Fit the washer on the transmission side of the driveplate, ensuring that the chamferred side of the washer faces towards the driveplate. Use new bolts and tighten them to the specified torque setting, then using vernier calipers, check the distance between the driveplate and the cylinder block as shown in Fig. 1.26 at three positions. If the clearance is not between 30.5 and 32.1 mm (1.20 and 1.26 in), remove the driveplate, fit shims of suitable thickness between the driveplate and the crankshaft, then refit the driveplate assembly and recheck the clearance. **Note:** *If the engine is a new or reconditioned short block replacement, check that the bore in the rear end does not contain a needle roller bearing. If it does then remove the bearing as this is for manual transmission models only.*

2 On manual gearbox models refit the clutch, as described in Chapter 5, together with the intermediate plate.
3 Refit the inlet and exhaust manifolds, as described in Chapter 3.
4 Refit the water pump and all hoses to the engine, as described in Chapter 2.
5 Refit the alternator and drivebelt as described in Chapter 9.
6 Refit the oil pressure switch to the cylinder head or filter mounting as applicable using a new washer or O-ring seal. Tighten to the specified torque.
7 Fit the oil filter mounting to the cylinder block, together with a new gasket and tighten the bolts. On models fitted with an oil cooler, refit the supply and return hoses to their correct unions.
8 Fit the oil filter, as described in Section 62.
9 Refer to Chapter 4 and refit the distributor.
10 On carburettor models, refit the fuel pump, as described in Chapter 3.
11 On fuel injection models refit the warm-up valve (if the hoses were disconnected).
12 Refit the coolant temperature sender unit and the thermotime switch with new O-ring seals.
13 Refit the spark plugs if not already done and tighten them to the specified torque given in Chapter 4.
14 Refit the gearbox/transmission to the engine with reference to Section 51.

81 Engine - refitting

To refit the engine and gearbox/transmission, reverse the removal procedures given earlier in Section 49 or 50 (as applicable) of this Chapter, but note the following points:
(a) When lowering the assembly into the engine compartment, align the driveshafts with the flanges prior to attaching the respective mountings
(b) Assemble the engine mountings loosely initially and tighten them only after the assembly is central without straining the mountings

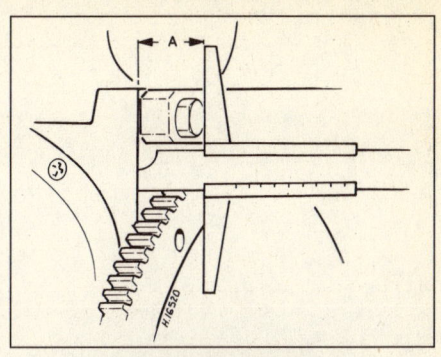

Fig. 1.26 Checking the driveplate-to-cylinder block dimension (A) using vernier calipers (Sec 80)

(c) Adjust the clutch cable (manual transmission) as described in Chapter 5
(d) On models with automatic transmission adjust the throttle and selector cables, as described in Chapter 6
(e) Reconnect and, if necessary, adjust the gear selector linkages on manual transmission models (Chapter 6)
(f) Adjust the throttle cable and, where applicable, the choke cable, with reference to Chapter 3
(g) Refill the cooling system, with reference to Chapter 2
(h) Refill the engine with the correct grade and quantity of oil

82 Engine - adjustments after major overhaul

Refer to Section 43 of this Chapter.

Fault finding - all engines

Engine fails to start
☐ Discharged battery
☐ Loose battery connection
☐ Ignition system fault
☐ Fuel system fault
☐ Low cylinder compressions

Engine idles erratically
☐ Inlet manifold air leak
☐ Leaking cylinder head gasket
☐ Worn camshaft lobes
☐ Faulty fuel pump
☐ Incorrect valve clearances
☐ Mixture adjustment incorrect
☐ Uneven cylinder compressions

Engine stalls
☐ Mixture adjustment incorrect
☐ Inlet manifold air leak
☐ Ignition timing incorrect

Engine misfires
☐ Ignition system fault
☐ Fuel system fault
☐ Burnt valve or valve seating
☐ Leaking cylinder head gasket
☐ Incorrect valve clearances
☐ Uneven cylinder compressions

Excessive oil consumption
☐ Worn pistons and cylinder bores
☐ Valve guides and seals worn
☐ Oil leak (fuel pump vent hole is common)

Engine backfires
☐ Mixture adjustment incorrect
☐ Ignition timing incorrect
☐ Incorrect valve clearances
☐ Exhaust manifold air leak
☐ Sticking or burnt valve

Notes

Chapter 2 Cooling system

For modifications, and information applicable to later models, see Supplement at end of manual

Contents

Antifreeze/corrosion inhibitor mixture - general 6	Radiator - removal, inspection, cleaning and refitting 7
Cooling fan and motor - removal and refitting 8	Routine maintenance - cooling system 2
Cooling fan motor thermo-switch - removal, testing and refitting . . 9	Temperature sender unit/thermo-switch - removal and refitting . . . 14
Cooling system - draining 3	Thermostat (1.05 and 1.3 litre) - removal, testing and refitting 10
Cooling system - filling 5	Thermostat (1.6 and 1.8 litre) - removal, testing and refitting 11
Cooling system - flushing 4	Water pump (1.05 and 1.3 litre) - removal and refitting 12
Fault finding - cooling system . . . . See end of Chapter	Water pump (1.6 and 1.8 litre) - removal and refitting 13
General description 1	

Degrees of difficulty

Easy, suitable for novice with little experience	**Fairly easy,** suitable for beginner with some experience	**Fairly difficult,** suitable for competent DIY mechanic	**Difficult,** suitable for experienced DIY mechanic	**Very difficult,** suitable for expert DIY or professional

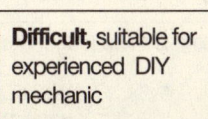

Specifications

General
System type	Pressurised with pump driven by timing or V-belt, front mounted radiator with internal or external expansion tank, electric cooling fan
System capacity (approx)	6.3 litre (11.1 Imp pint)

Radiator/expansion tank cap
Operating pressure	1.2 to 1.5 bar (17.4 to 21.8 lbf/in^2)

Thermostat
	1.05 and 1.3 litre	**1.6 and 1.8 litre**
Opening temperature	92°C (198°F)	85°C (185°F)
Fully open temperature	108°C (226°F)	105°C (221°F)
Minimum stroke	7.0 mm (0.28 in)	7.0 mm (0.28 in)

Cooling fan thermo-switch
Switch-on temperature	93° to 98°C (199° to 208°F)
Switch-off temperature	88° to 93°C (190° to 199°F)

Antifreeze
	Protection down to
Concentration:	
40%	- 25°C (-13°F)
50%	- 35°C (-31°F)
Type/specification	Ethylene glycol, with corrosion inhibitor

Torque wrench settings
	Nm	lbf ft
Temperature sender unit	10	7
Thermo-switch (intake manifold preheater):		
1.6 and 1.8 carburettor models	10	7
1.8 fuel injection models	30	22
Water pump housing (1.6 and 1.8 litre)	20	14
Water pump cover (1.6 and 1.8 litre)	10	7
Water pump pulley bolts (1.6 and 1.8 litre)	20	14
Cooling fan thermo-switch	25	18
Thermostat housing through-bolts (1.05 and 1.3 litre)	20	14
Thermostat housing-to-pipe bolts (1.05 and 1.3 litre)	10	7
Thermostat housing to water pump (1.6 and 1.8 litre)	10	7
Water pump unit (1.05 and 1.3 litre)	10	7

2•2 Cooling system

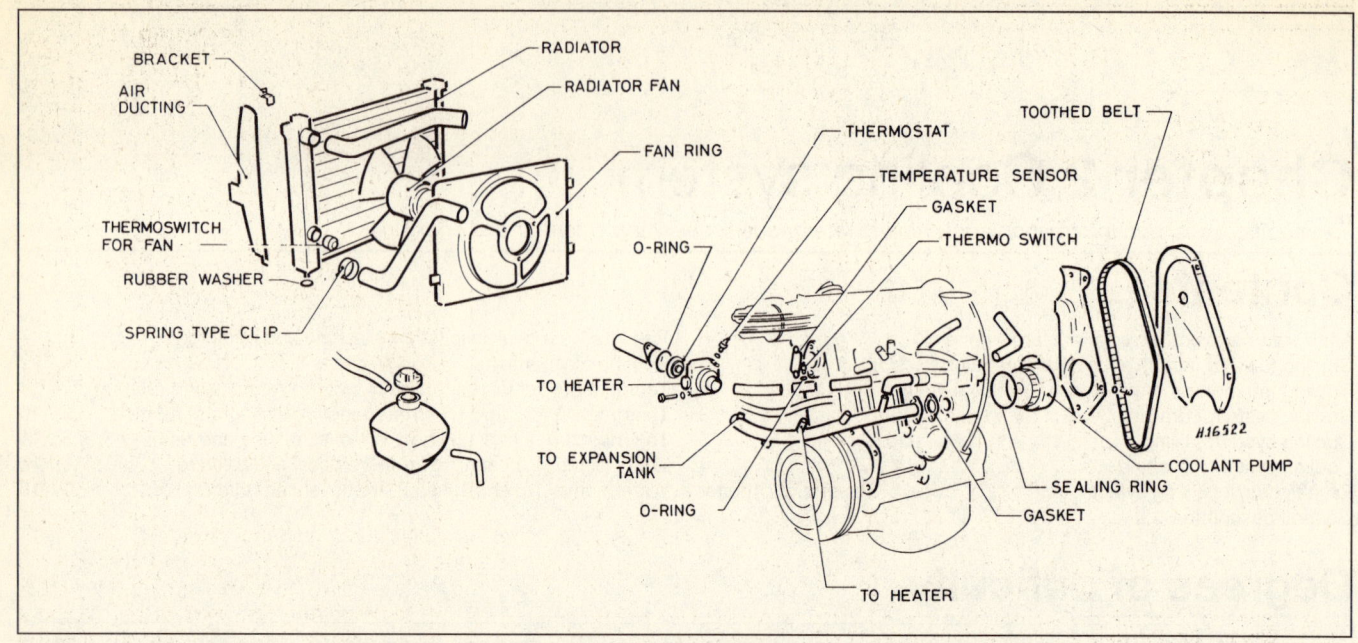

Fig. 2.1 Exploded view of the cooling system – 1.05 and 1.3 litre (Sec 1)

1 General description

The cooling system is of pressurised type and includes a front mounted radiator, water pump, and a thermostatically operated electric cooling fan. Circulation through the radiator is controlled by a thermostat, the location of which differs according to engine. On the 1.05 and 1.3 litre models it is located in a housing on the rear end of the cylinder head (left side of car) below the distributor. On the 1.6 and 1.8 litre models the thermostat is located in the base of the water pump housing which is mounted low down on the front of the engine (timing case end).

The radiator is of aluminium construction and the expansion tank is located separately within the engine compartment.

The fuel injected engine incorporates a water-cooled oil cooler unit which is located between the oil filter and the filter mounting bracket

The system functions as follows. Cold water from the bottom of the radiator circulates through the bottom hose to the water pump, where the pump impeller forces the water around the cylinder block and head passages. After cooling the cylinder bores, combustion surfaces and valve seats, the water reaches the cylinder head outlet and is returned to the water pump via the bypass hoses when the thermostat is closed. A further cylinder head outlet allows water to circulate through the inlet manifold and heater matrix (with heater control on) and it is then returned to the water pump.

When the coolant reaches the predetermined temperature (see Specifications), the thermostat opens and the water then circulates through the top hose to the top of the radiator. As the water circulates down through the radiator, it is cooled by the inrush of air when the car is in forward motion, supplemented by the action of the electric cooling fan when necessary. Having reached the bottom of the radiator, the water is now cooled and the cycle is repeated.

The electric cooling fan is controlled by a thermo-switch located in the left-hand side of the radiator.

2 Routine maintenance - cooling system

1 The cooling system must be regularly checked as part of the vehicle's routine maintenance.
2 A weekly check must be made to ensure that the coolant level is correct in the cooling system expansion tank. When the engine is cold the level of coolant within the expansion tank must be between the MAX and MIN

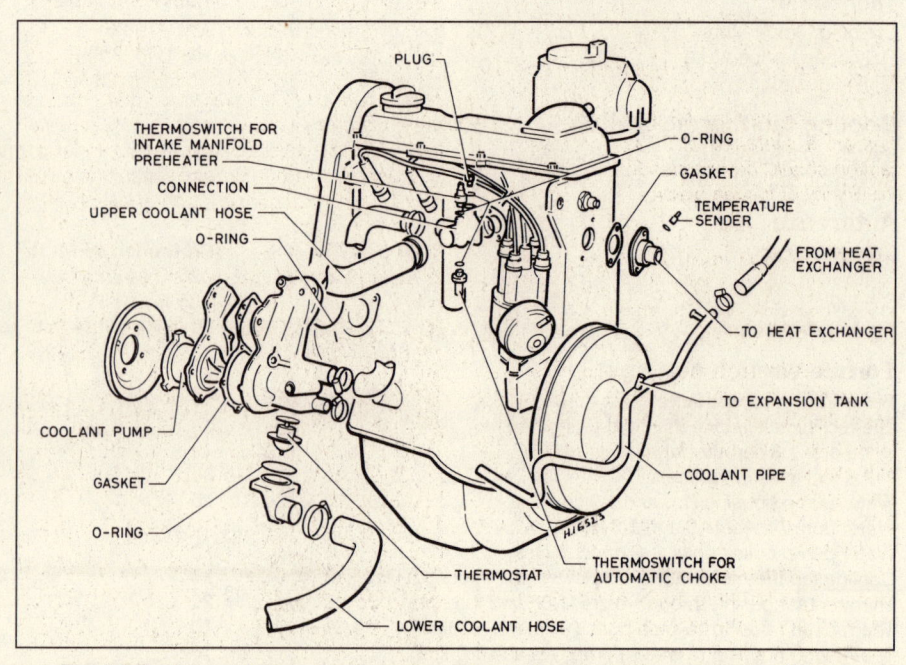

Fig. 2.2 Engine cooling system components – 1.6 and 1.8 litre carburettor (Sec 1)

Cooling system 2•3

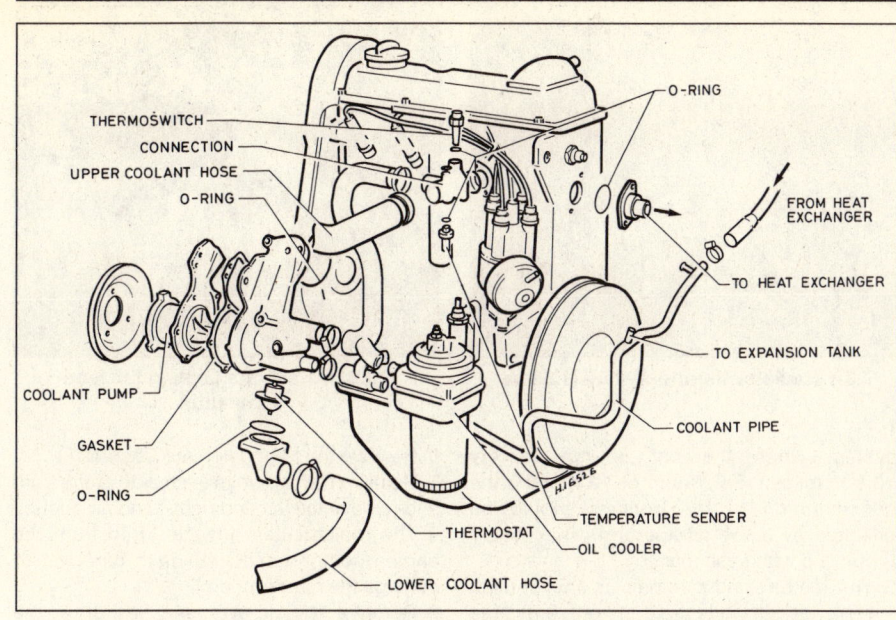

Fig. 2.3 Engine cooling system components – 1.8 litre fuel injection (Sec 1)

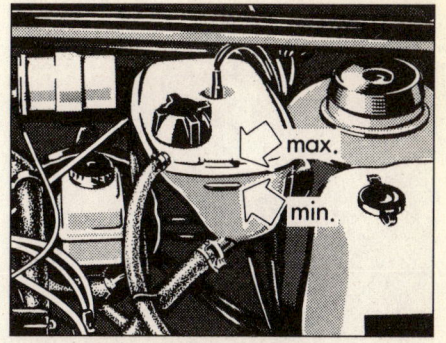

Fig. 2.4 Engine coolant level marks in the expansion tank (Sec 5)

marks. When the coolant level is checked with the engine hot the level of coolant in the expansion tank should be level with, or just above the MAX marking.
3 If a sudden drop in the coolant level should occur, investigate the cause without delay.
4 Periodically check the system hoses and connections for signs of leakage, deterioration and for security.
5 When topping-up the cooling system, use an antifreeze mixture wherever possible to maintain the strength of the antifreeze/corrosion inhibitor within the system (Section 6).
6 Periodically check the wiring connections to the temperature sender units and thermo-switch units are secure. **Note:** the electric cooling fan will operate when the temperature of the coolant in the radiator reaches the predetermined level even if the ignition is switched off. Therefore extreme caution should be exercised when working in the vicinity of the fan blades.

3 Cooling system - draining

1 It is preferable to drain the cooling system when the engine has cooled. If this is not possible, place a cloth over the expansion tank filler cap and turn it *slowly* in an anti-clockwise direction until the pressure starts to escape.
2 When all the pressure has escaped, remove the filler cap.
3 Set the heater controls to maximum heat, then place a suitable container beneath the left-hand side of the radiator.
4 Loosen the clip and ease the bottom hose away from the radiator outlet. Drain the coolant into the container (photos).

4 Cooling system - flushing

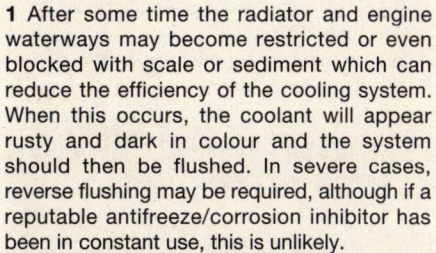

1 After some time the radiator and engine waterways may become restricted or even blocked with scale or sediment which can reduce the efficiency of the cooling system. When this occurs, the coolant will appear rusty and dark in colour and the system should then be flushed. In severe cases, reverse flushing may be required, although if a reputable antifreeze/corrosion inhibitor has been in constant use, this is unlikely.
2 With the coolant drained, disconnect the top hose from the radiator. Insert a garden hose and allow the water to circulate through the radiator until it runs clear from the bottom outlet. If, after a reasonable period the water still does not run clear, the radiator can be flushed with a good proprietary cleaning agent.
3 Disconnect the heater hose from the cylinder head outlet and insert a garden hose in the heater hose. With the heater controls set at maximum heat, allow water to circulate through the heater and out through the bottom hose until it runs clear.
4 In severe cases of contamination the system should be reverse flushed. To do this, remove the radiator, invert it and insert a garden hose in the outlet. Continue flushing until clear water runs from the inlet.
5 The engine should also be reverse flushed. To do this, disconnect the heater hose from the cylinder head outlet and insert a garden hose in the outlet. Continue flushing until clear water runs from the bottom hose.
6 The use of chemical cleaners should only be necessary as a last resort. Regular checking of the antifreeze/corrosion inhibitor concentration at the 10 000 mile (15 000 km) service should prevent the contamination of the system.

5 Cooling system - filling

1 Reconnect all the hoses and check that the heater controls are set to maximum heat.
2 Pour the recommended coolant into the expansion tank until it reaches the maximum mark.
3 Refit and tighten the filler cap then run the engine at a fast idling speed for a few minutes, but keep an eye on the coolant level.
4 Stop the engine and top up the coolant

3.4A Radiator bottom hose connection (1.3 litre)

3.4B Radiator bottom hose connection (1.8 litre)

2•4 Cooling system

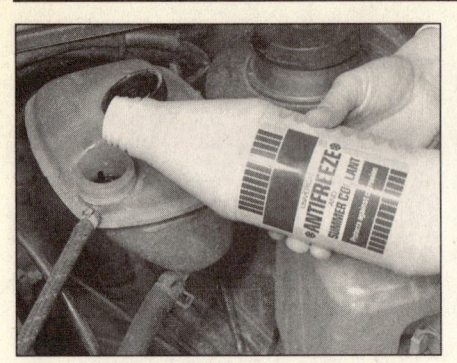

5.4 Topping-up coolant

7.3A Radiator thermo-switch (1.8 litre)

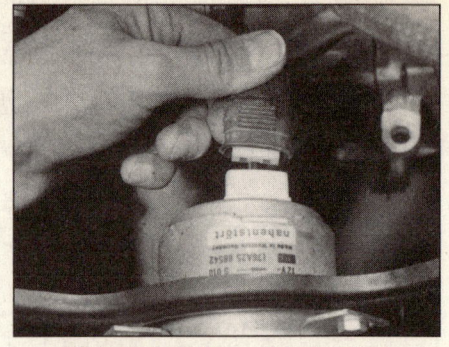

7.3B Detach the cooling fan lead connector

level, as necessary, to the maximum mark (photo). Refit the filler cap.

5 After running the engine up to its normal operating temperature (electric cooling fan cuts into operation), the coolant level should be rechecked. When the engine is warm the level of the coolant in the reservoir should be at (or just above) the MAX level mark. When cool, the coolant level should be between the MIN and MAX level marks.

6 Antifreeze/corrosion inhibitor mixture - general

1 The manufacturers install G10 antifreeze/corrosion inhibitor mixture in the cooling system when the car is new. Every 10 000 miles (15 000 km) or 12 months the concentration of the coolant should be checked by a VW garage and if necessary topped up with fresh mixture.
2 The mixture must remain in the cooling system at all times as it prevents the formation of scale and also provides a higher boiling point than plain water - this maintains the efficiency of the coolant, particularly when the engine is operating at full load.
3 The concentration of the mixture can be calculated according to the lowest ambient temperature likely to be encountered as given in the Specifications. However it should never be less than 40%.
4 Before adding new mixture, check all hose connections for tightness.

7 Radiator - removal, inspection, cleaning and refitting

1 Disconnect the battery negative lead.
2 Drain the cooling system (Section 3).
3 Disconnect the wiring from the thermo-switch and cooling fan motor (photos).
4 Disconnect the top hose and expansion tank hose from the radiator (photo).
5 Undo the two retaining bolts (photo) and remove the insulators and L brackets from the top of the radiator. Note that the longer bracket is the centre one.

6 Remove the front grille (see Chapter 11).
7 Remove the two bolts each side at the front and remove the left and right-hand air ducts.
8 The radiator can now be lifted from the engine compartment, but take care not to damage the matrix (photo).
9 Remove the screws and withdraw the cowling and fan from the radiator.
10 It is not possible to repair this radiator without special equipment, although minor leaks can be cured by using a radiator sealant with the radiator *in situ*.
11 Clean the radiator matrix of flies and small leaves with a soft brush or by hosing, then reverse flush the radiator, as described in Section 4. Renew the hoses and clips if they are damaged or deteriorated.
12 Refitting is a reversal of removal, but if necessary renew the radiator lower mounting rubbers (photo). Fill the cooling system, as described in Section 5.
13 When reconnecting the cooling fan motor wiring, secure the lead to the cowling web (photo).

8 Cooling fan and motor - removal and refitting

1 Disconnect the battery negative lead.
2 Disconnect the wiring from the cooling fan motor and cowling.

7.4 Radiator securing bolt (A), expansion tank hose connection (B) and top hose connection (C)

7.5 Radiator central retaining bolt and bracket

7.8 Lifting out the radiator and cooling fan assembly

7.12 Radiator lower mounting rubber

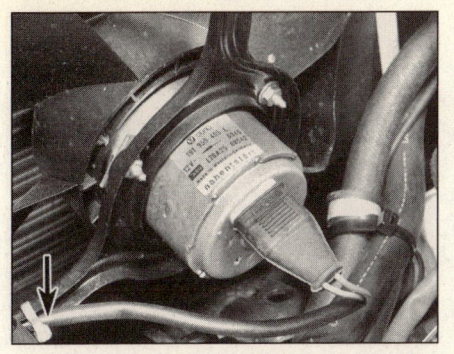

Cooling system 2•5

7.13 Secure the fan lead with a plastic clip (arrowed)

8.4 Cooling fan motor retaining nuts (arrowed)

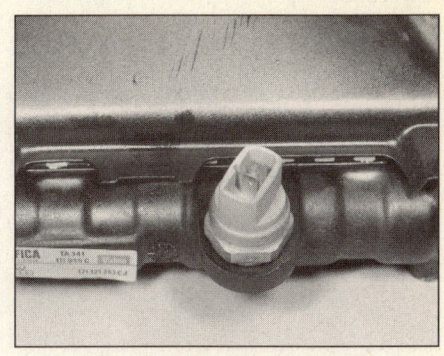

9.3 Cooling fan thermo-switch

3 Remove the bolts and screws and lift the cowling, together with the cooling fan and motor, from the radiator.
4 Remove the nuts and withdraw the cooling fan and motor from the cowling (photo).
5 If necessary the fan can be separated from the motor by prising off the clamp washer. On AEG motors drive out the roll pin, and on Bosch motors remove the shake-proof washer. Assemble the components in reverse order using a new clamp washer.
6 Refitting is a reversal of removal.

9 Cooling fan motor thermo-switch - removal, testing and refitting

1 Disconnect the battery negative lead.
2 Drain the cooling system, as described in Section 3.
3 Unscrew the thermo-switch from the left-hand side of the radiator and remove the sealing ring (photo).
4 To test the thermo-switch, suspend it with a piece of string so that its element is immersed in a container of water. Connect the thermo-switch in series with a 12 volt test lamp and battery. Gradually heat the water and note the temperature with a thermometer. The test lamp should light up at the specified switch-on temperature and go out at the specified switch-off temperature. If not, renew the thermo-switch.

5 Refitting is a reversal of removal, but fit a new sealing ring and tighten the thermo-switch to the specified torque. Fill the cooling system, as described in Section 5.

10 Thermostat (1.05 and 1.3 litre) - removal, testing and refitting

1 The thermostat is located in the outlet housing on the left-hand (rear) end of the cylinder head. To remove it, first drain the cooling system, as described in Section 3.
2 Unscrew the bolts and remove the thermostat cover (photos). Place the cover with top hose still attached to one side.
3 Remove the sealing ring (photo).
4 Extract the thermostat from the outlet housing.
5 To test whether the unit is serviceable, suspend it with a piece of string in a container of water. Gradually heat the water and note the temperature at which the thermostat starts to open. Continue heating the water to the specified fully open temperature then check that the thermostat has opened by at least the minimum amount given in the Specifications. Remove the thermostat from the water and check that it is fully closed when cold.
6 Renew the thermostat if it fails to operate correctly.
7 Clean the thermostat seating and the mating faces of the outlet housing and cover.
8 Refitting is a reversal of removal, but fit a new sealing ring and tighten the cover bolts to the specified torque - the breather hole in the thermostat should face upwards. Fill the cooling system, as described in Section 5.

11 Thermostat (1.6 and 1.8 litre) - removal, testing and refitting

1 The thermostat is located in the bottom of the water pump behind the inlet elbow. To remove it, first drain the cooling system with reference to Section 3.
2 Unbolt the inlet elbow from the water pump and remove the seal and thermostat (photos).

10.2A Unscrew the socket-head bolts . . .

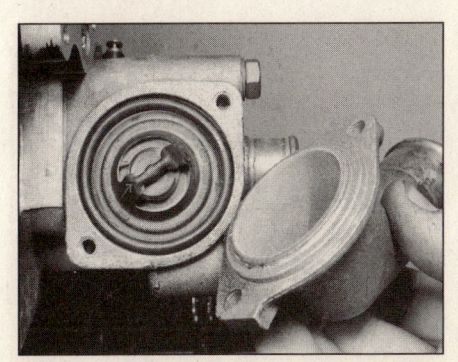

10.2B . . . and remove the thermostat cover

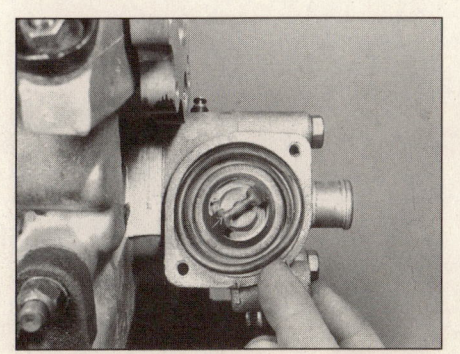

10.3 Removing the thermostat sealing ring

11.2A Thermostat inlet elbow – undo the retaining bolts . . .

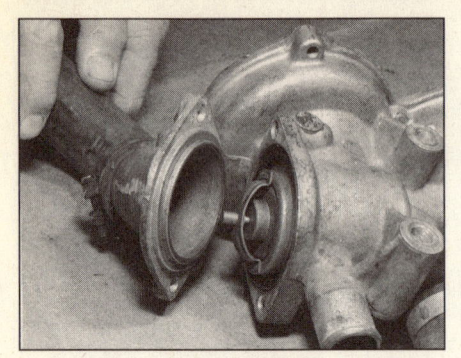

2•6 Cooling system

11.2B ... withdraw the elbow and thermostat ...

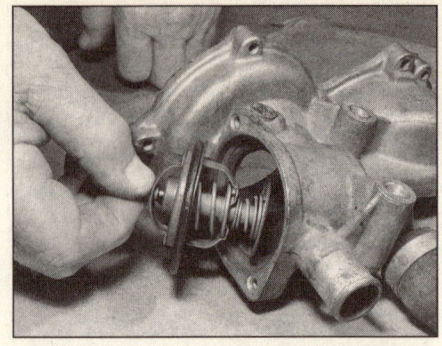

11.2C ... then extract the thermostat and seal

12.5 Disengage the timing belt from the water pump sprocket

3 Clean the water pump and elbow of any scale or corrosion.
4 To test the thermostat proceed as described in paragraphs 5 and 6 in the previous Section.
5 Refitting is a reversal of removal procedure, but always fit a new seal, Fill the cooling system, as described in Section 5.

12 Water pump (1.05 and 1.3 litre) - removal and refitting

1 Drain the cooling system, as described in Section 3.
2 Remove the air cleaner and air ducting, as described in Chapter 3, and disconnect the battery negative lead.
3 Unbolt and remove the timing belt cover. On some later 1.3 litre models it is necessary to remove the crankshaft pulley to remove the lower timing belt cover.
4 Turn the engine with a spanner on the crankshaft pulley until the timing cover plate upper retaining bolt is visible through the camshaft sprocket hole. Unscrew and remove the bolt.
5 Align the timing marks and release the timing belt from the water pump and camshaft sprocket (photo), with reference to Chapter 1.
6 Remove the bolts and withdraw the timing cover plate followed by the water pump (photo). Remove the sealing ring.

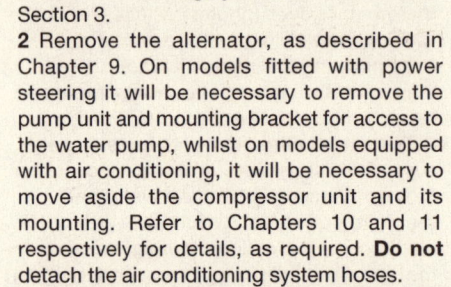

7 It is not possible to repair the water pump, and if faulty it must be renewed. Clean the mating faces of the water pump and cylinder block.
8 Refitting is a reversal of removal, but fit a new sealing ring and refer to Chapter 1 when fitting and tensioning the timing belt. Fill the cooling system, as described in Section 5.

13 Water pump (1.6 and 1.8 litre) - removal and refitting

1 Drain the cooling system, as described in Section 3.
2 Remove the alternator, as described in Chapter 9. On models fitted with power steering it will be necessary to remove the pump unit and mounting bracket for access to the water pump, whilst on models equipped with air conditioning, it will be necessary to move aside the compressor unit and its mounting. Refer to Chapters 10 and 11 respectively for details, as required. **Do not** detach the air conditioning system hoses.
3 Disconnect the three coolant hoses from the pump, then remove the four bolts holding the pump to the cylinder block (photo). The pump will probably be stuck to the block but will come off if tapped gently. Remove the O-ring with the pump.
4 Remove the pulley and then take out the eight bolts which secure the bearing housing

and impeller to the water pump housing. The two halves may now be separated (photo). **Do not** drive a wedge in to break the joint. Clean off the old gasket.
5 Remove the thermostat, with reference to Section 11.
6 The impeller housing and impeller complete with bearings are serviced as one part, so that if the coolant is leaking through the bearing, or the impeller is damaged, the complete assembly must be renewed.
7 Fit a new gasket using jointing compound, then fit the two halves together and tighten the bolts evenly. Fit the thermostat with reference to Section 11. The refitting procedure is a reversal of the removal procedure, but always fit a new O-ring. Fill the cooling system, as described in Section 5, and tension the drivebelt(s), as described in Chapters 9, 10 and 11, as applicable.

14 Temperature sender unit/thermo-switches - removal and refitting

1 It is not necessary to drain the cooling system if some form of plug such as an old sender unit or rubber plug is available. First release any pressure in the system by unscrewing the pressure cap - *if the system is still hot, observe the precaution in Section 3*. With all pressure released, tighten the cap again.

12.6 Withdraw the water pump

13.3 1.6 and 1.8 litre engine water pump location (engine removed from car)

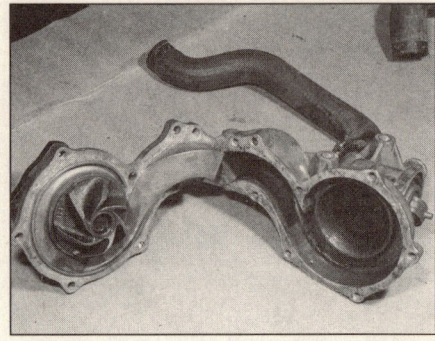

13.4 The two halves of the water pump (1.6 and 1.8 litre)

Cooling system 2•7

14.3 Thermo-switch location (1.05 and 1.3 litre)

14.4 Temperature sensor – arrowed (1.05 and 1.3 litre)

14.8 Temperature sender unit (A) and thermo-switch (B) (1.8 litre fuel injection)

2 The location of the sender unit or thermo-switch is dependent on model but in general they are as follows:

1.05 and 1.3 litre
3 Thermo-switch: Located in the intermediate piece in the hoses between the intake manifold and the thermostat housing (photo).
4 Temperature sensor: Located in the thermostat housing (photo).

1.6 and 1.8 litre carburettor
5 Temperature sender unit: Located in the heat exchanger hose connecting flange on the rear of the cylinder head.
6 Thermo-switch (intake manifold preheater): Located on the top face of the hose connector on the spark plug side of the cylinder head.
7 Thermo-switch (automatic choke): Located in the base of the hose connector on the spark plug side of the cylinder head.

1.8 litre fuel injection
8 Temperature sender unit: Located in the hose connector on the spark plug side of the cylinder head.
9 Thermo-switch: Located on the top face of the hose connector on the spark plug side of the cylinder head.

All models
10 Disconnect the wiring lead from the sender unit/switch concerned.
11 Unscrew and remove the sender unit/switch and plug the aperture.
12 Refitting is the reversal of the removal procedure, but tighten the sender unit/thermo-switch to the specified torque. Check and if necessary top up the cooling system, with reference to Section 5.

Fault finding - cooling system

Overheating
☐ Low coolant level
☐ Faulty pressure cap
☐ Thermostat sticking shut
☐ Open-circuit thermo-switch
☐ Faulty electric cooling fan
☐ Clogged radiator matrix
☐ Retarded ignition timing

Slow warm-up
☐ Thermostat sticking open
☐ Incorrect thermostat

Coolant loss
☐ Damaged or deteriorated hose
☐ Leaking water pump or cylinder head outlet joint
☐ Blown cylinder head gasket
☐ Leaking radiator
☐ Defective core plug
☐ Defective filler cap

Notes

Chapter 3 Fuel and exhaust systems

For modifications, and information applicable to later models, see Supplement at end of manual

Contents

Part A: Carburettor-based fuel system

Accelerator and throttle cables (automatic transmission models) - removal, refitting and adjustment	12
Accelerator cable (manual gearbox models) - removal, refitting and adjustment	11
Accelerator pedal - removal and refitting	13
Air cleaner element - renewal	3
Air cleaner unit - removal and refitting	4
Automatic air cleaner temperature control - checking	5
Carburettor removal and refitting	15
Carburettor (2E2) - dismantling, reassembly and adjustment	20
Carburettor (2E2) - slow running and fast idle speed adjustment	21
Carburettor (2E3) - dismantling, reassembly and adjustment	18
Carburettor (2E3) - slow running and fast idle speed adjustment	19
Carburettor (31 PIC7) - dismantling, reassembly and adjustment	16
Carburettor (31 PIC7) - slow running and fast idle speed adjustment	17
Choke cable (1.05 litre) - removal, refitting and adjustment	14
Exhaust system - checking, removal and refitting	24
Fault finding - fuel system (carburettor models)	See end of Chapter
Fuel filler gravity valve - removal, checking and refitting	10
Fuel gauge sender unit - removal and refitting	9
Fuel pump - testing, removal and refitting	6
Fuel reservoir - removal and refitting	7
Fuel tank - removal and refitting	8
General description	1
Inlet and exhaust manifolds - removal and refitting	23
Inlet manifold preheating - description and testing	22
Routine maintenance - fuel and exhaust system	2

Part B: Fuel injection system

Accelerator cable - removal, refitting and adjustment	32
Air cleaner element - removal, cleaning/renewal and refitting	27
Airflow meter - removal and refitting	40
Airflow sensor plate and control plunger - checking	38
Auxiliary air valve - checking	34
Cold acceleration enrichment system - description and checking	36
Cold start valve and thermotime switch - checking	33
Exhaust manifold - removal and refitting	48
Exhaust system	49
Fault finding - fuel system (fuel injection models)	See end of Chapter
Fuel accumulator - removal and refitting	45
Fuel filter - removal and refitting	44
Fuel injectors - checking	37
Fuel lift pump - checking, removal and refitting	42
Fuel metering distributor - removal and refitting	39
Fuel pump - removal and refitting	43
Fuel tank and associated components - removal and refitting	46
General description	25
Idle mixture - adjustment	31
Idle speed - adjustment	28
Idle speed boost (air conditioned models) - description, checking and idle speed adjustment	30
Increased idling speed valve (air conditioned models) - checking	29
Inlet manifold - removal and refitting	47
Pressure relief valve - removal, servicing and refitting	41
Routine maintenance, adjustments and precautions - fuel injection system	26
Warm-up valve - checking	35

Degrees of difficulty

Easy, suitable for novice with little experience	Fairly easy, suitable for beginner with some experience	Fairly difficult, suitable for competent DIY mechanic	Difficult, suitable for experienced DIY mechanic	Very difficult, suitable for expert DIY or professional

Specifications

General

Air cleaner

Type .. Automatic air temperature control

Air cleaner element

Type ... Renewable paper element
Application:
 1043 cc. Champion WI01
 1272 cc. Champion W102
 1595 cc and 1781 cc. Champion U508
 1781 cc injection (Golf). Champion U506
 1781 cc injection (Jetta). Champion U502

Fuel filter

Application:
 1043 cc, 1272 cc, 1595 cc and 1781 cc Champion L104
 1781 cc injection. Champion L204

Note: *On injection filters new copper washers must be used and these are not supplied with the filter - see Sec 44*

Fuel system
Fuel pump (carburettor engines):
  Type .... Mechanical, diaphragm, operated by plunger from camshaft (1.05 and 1.3 litre) or eccentric on intermediate shaft (1.6 and 1.8 litre)
  Operating pressure at 4000 rpm (return line clamped):
    1.05 and 1.3 litre .... 0.35 to 0.40 bar (5.1 to 5.8 lbf/in^2)
    1.6 and 1.8 litre .... 0.2 to 0.25 bar (2.9 to 3.6 lbf/in^2)
Fuel tank capacity (approx) .... 55 litre (12 gal)
Fuel octane rating (minimum):
  1.05 litre .... 97 RON (4 star)
  1.3 and 1.6 litre .... 91 RON (2 star)
  1.8 litre .... 98 RON (4 star)

Part A: Carburettor system
Carburettor - 1.05 litre
Type	Downdraught with manual or automatic choke
Code	31 PIC-7
Venturi	23
Main jet	X117.5
Air correction jet with emulsion tube	115 Z
Idling fuel jet	45
Idling air jet	135
Auxiliary fuel jet	32.5
Auxiliary air jet	130
Enrichment (primary/secondary)	70/70
Injection capacity (cc/stroke)	0.85 to 1.15
Float needle valve	1.5
Float needle valve washer thickness (mm)	2.0
Fast idle speed (rpm)	2500 to 2700
Choke valve gap (mm)	1.6 to 2.0
Throttle valve gap smooth running detent (mm)	2.2 to 2.8
Idle speed (rpm)	900 to 1000
CO content %	0.5 to 1.5

Carburettor - 1.3 litre
Type	Twin progressive choke downdraught, automatic choke	
Code	2E3	
Jets and settings:	**Stage I**	**Stage II**
Venturi	19	23
Main jet	X95	X110
Air correction jet with emulsion tube	120	130
Idling fuel/air jet	45/130	-
Full throttle enrichment	-	95
Pump injection tube diameter (mm)	0.35	
Choke cover code	276	
Injection capacity (cc/stroke)	0.85 to 1.15	
Locking lever clearance (mm)	0.25 to 0.55	
Full throttle enrichment - height above atomizer (mm)	12	
Choke valve gap (mm)	1.9 to 2.1	
Fast idle speed (rpm)	1900 to 2100	
Idle speed (rpm)	750 to 850	
C0 content %	1.5 to 2.5	

Carburettor - 1.6 litre
Type	Twin progressive choke, downdraught with automatic choke	
Type number	2E2	
Jets and settings:	**Stage I**	**Stage II**
Venturi diameter (mm)	22	26
Main jet	X110	X127
Air correction jet with emulsion tube (mm)	0.75/1.05	1.05
Idle fuel/air jet	42.5	-
Full throttle enrichment	-	0.7
Pump injection tube	0.5	-
Injection capacity (cc/stroke)	0.85 to 1.15	
Choke valve gap (mm) with primary throttle open 45°	6.3 + 0.3	
Fast idle speed (rpm)	2800 to 3200	
Idle speed (rpm)	900 to 1000	
Increased idle speed (rpm):		
Automatic transmission	800	
Air conditioner	900 to 1000	
CO content %	0.5 to 1.5	

Carburettor - 1.8 litre

Type	Twin progressive choke, downdraught with automatic choke	
Type number	2E2	
Jets and settings:	**Stage I**	**Stage II**
Venturi diameter	22	26
Main jet	X105	X120
Air correction jet with emulsion tube (mm)	105	100
Idle fuel/air jet	42.5	-
Full throttle enrichment	-	0.9
Pump injection tube:		
Carburettor part number type 027 129 015	0.35	-
Carburettor part number type 027 129 015 Q	0.5	-
Injection capacity (cc/stroke)	0.95 to 1.25	
Choke valve gap (mm) measured at lower edge:		
Stage 1	2.3 ± 0.15	
Stage 2	4.7 ± 0.15	
Fast idle speed (rpm)	2800 to 3200	
Idle speed (rpm)	900 to 1000	
Increased idle speed (rpm):		
Automatic transmission	800	
Air conditioner	900 to 1000	
CO content %	0.5 to 1.5	

Part B: Fuel injection system

General

Type	K-Jetronic, continuous injection system (CIS)
System pressure	4.7 to 5.4 bar (68 to 78 lbf/in^2)
Idle speed	900 to 1000 rpm
Idle speed - air conditioned models	850 to 1000 rpm
CO content %	0.5 to 1.5

All systems

Torque wrench settings	Nm	lbf ft
1.05 and 1.3 litre		
Carburettor	10	7
Intermediate flange	10	7
Inlet manifold	25	18
Inlet manifold preheater	10	7
Fuel tank strap bolts	25	18
Exhaust manifold	25	18
Exhaust manifold to downpipe	25	18
Exhaust pipe clamp bolts	25	18
1.6 and 1.8 litre (carburettor engines)		
Carburettor	7	5
Fuel pump	20	15
Inlet manifold	25	18
Inlet manifold preheater	10	7
Fuel tank strap bolts	25	18
Exhaust manifold	25	18
Exhaust pipe clip:		
8 mm	25	18
10 mm	40	30
Fuel injection system		
Injector line to injector	25	18
Injector line to fuel metering distributor	10	7
System pressure relief valve	20	15
Cold start valve	10	7
Throttle valve housing to manifold	20	15
Inlet manifold	25	18
Fuel filter clamp	10	7
Union bolt at filter (from fuel accumulator)	25	18
Union nut at accumulator (to filter)	20	15
Union bolt at filter (to metering distributor)	20	15
Fuel pump reservoir mounting	10	7
Fuel pump non-return valve	20	15
Fuel pump damper unit	20	15
Exhaust manifold	25	18
Exhaust heat shield	10	7
Exhaust pipe clamp bolts	40	30

Part A: Carburettor-based fuel system

1 General description

The fuel system consists of a rear-mounted fuel tank, a mechanical diaphragm fuel pump and a downdraught carburettor. The carburettor type is dependent on model; see Specifications.

The fuel pump on 1.05 and 1.3 litre models is operated by means of a plunger activated by the camshaft, whilst on 1.6 and 1.8 litre models the fuel pump is operated direct by an eccentric on the intermediate shaft.

The air cleaner unit contains a renewable paper element and incorporates an automatic temperature control.

A conventional exhaust system is used on all models, being in sections for ease of replacement.

2 Routine maintenance - fuel and exhaust system

1 The following routine maintenance procedures are required for the fuel and exhaust system and must be carried out at the specified intervals given at the start of this Manual. It should be noted that the intervals quoted are those for a vehicle used in normal operating conditions.

> **HAYNES HiNT** *If a vehicle is used in adverse conditions, such as continuous city driving or in a hot dusty climate, then it is advisable to shorten the maintenance intervals accordingly.*

2 **Fuel system, general:** Inspect the fuel system lines, hoses and connections at regular intervals for security and condition. In addition also check the associated vacuum hoses and connections. Occasionally lubricate the accelerator control linkages.

3 **Fuel system adjustments:** Check and if necessary adjust the engine idling speed and, where possible, the exhaust CO content (having first checked ignition timing, as described in Chapter 4).

4 **Air cleaner:** renew air cleaner element, as described in Section 3.

5 **Fuel filter:** The in-line filter should be renewed every 20000 miles (30 000 km). To do this, remove the clips and extract the filter (photo). If necessary renew the crimped type clips with screw type ones. Fit the new filter in a horizontal position with its arrow facing the flow of fuel towards the fuel pump.

6 **Exhaust system:** Inspect the exhaust system for signs of joint leaks, excessive corrosion and general security. Repair if necessary (Section 24).

3 Air cleaner element - renewal

1 A dirty air cleaner element will cause a loss of performance and an increase in fuel consumption. A new element should be fitted at the specified intervals and the element should be cleaned every twelve months or more frequently under dusty conditions.

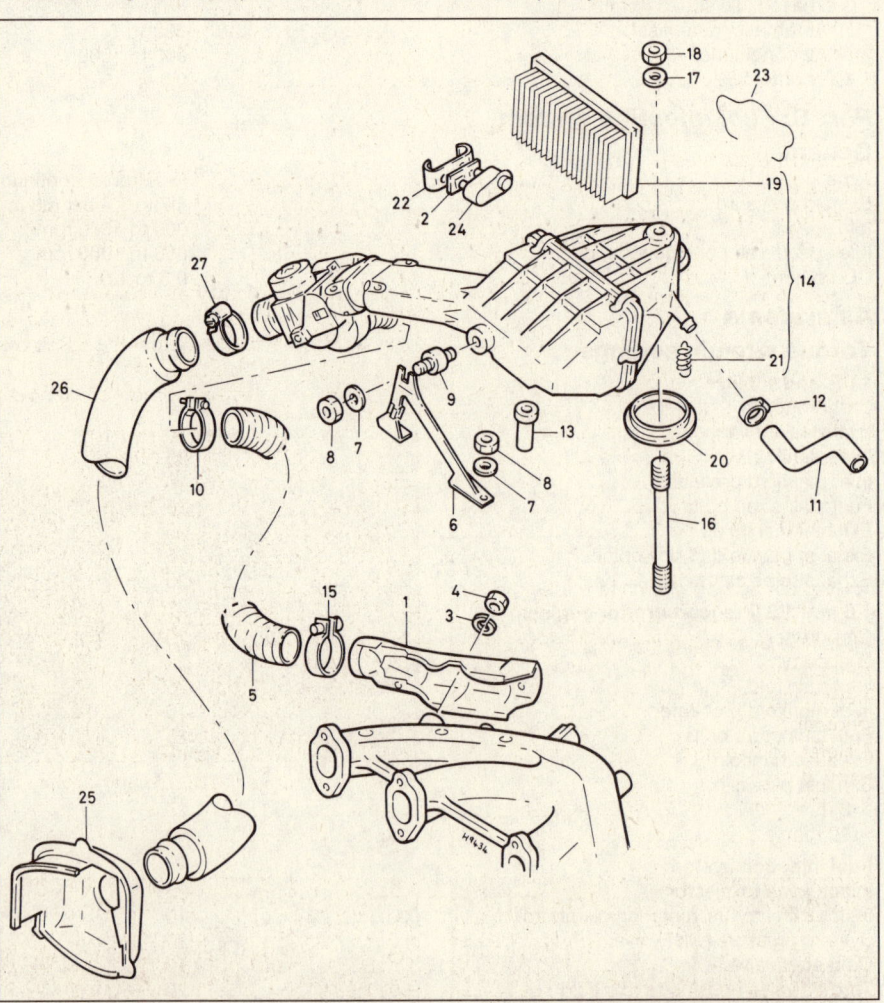

Fig. 3.1 Air cleaner components – 1.6 and 1.8 litre carburettor (Sec 3)

1. Warm air deflector plate
2. Gasket
3. Spring washer
4. Nut
5. Air hose
6. Bracket
7. Washer
8. Nut
9. Bonded rubber mounting
10. Clip
11. Air Hose
12. Clip
13. Spacer tube
14. Air cleaner
15. Clip
16. Stud
17. Washer
18. Self-locking nut
19. Filter element
20. Sealing washer
21. Spring
22. Lockplate
23. Retaining clip
24. Dual thermostat
25. Union
26. Air hose
27. Clip

2.5 Typical fuel system in-line filter

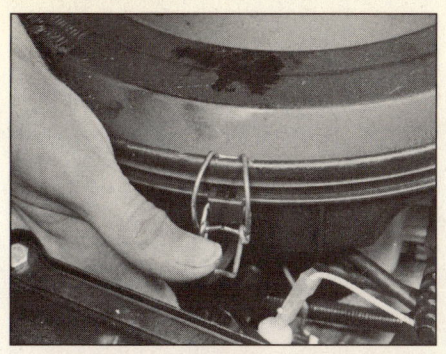

Fuel and exhaust systems – carburettor-based system 3•5

3.2 Removing the air cleaner cover (1.3 litre)

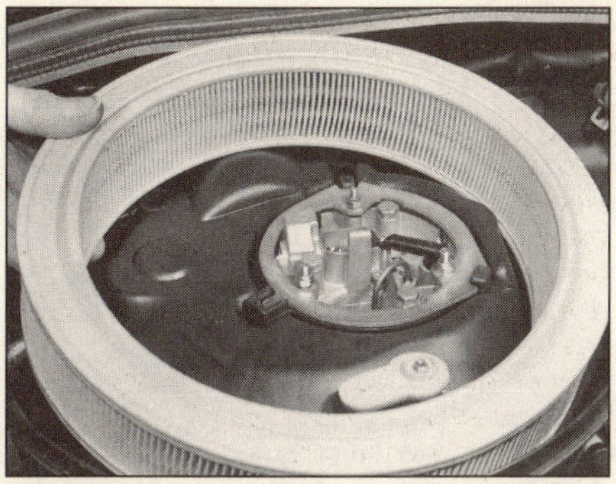

3.3 Removing the air cleaner element (1.3 litre)

3.6A Release the retaining clips . . .

1.05 and 1.3 litre

2 Release the spring clips securing the air cleaner lid and remove the lid (photo).
3 Cover the carburettor entry port to prevent any dirt entering it when the element is lifted out, and remove the element (photo). Wipe the inside of the air cleaner with a moist rag to remove all dust and dirt and then remove the covering from the entry port.
4 If cleaning the element, place well away from the vehicle, then tap the air cleaner element to remove dust and dirt. If necessary use a soft brush to clean the outside or blow air at very low pressure from the inside surface towards the outside.
5 Refit the element, clean the cover and put it in place, then clip the cover down, ensuring that the two arrows are aligned.

1.6 and 1.8 litre

6 To remove the element, unclip and remove the cover and withdraw the element. Note that on some models it is necessary to first loosen the front mounting nut (photos). Clean the interior of the air cleaner with a fuel-moistened cloth, then wipe it dry (photos).
7 Refer to paragraph 4 for cleaning the element.
8 Refit in the reverse order of removal.

4 Air cleaner unit - removal and refitting

1.05 and 1.3 litre

1 Remove the element, as described in Section 3.
2 Unscrew the nut(s) securing the air cleaner body and remove the adaptor or retaining ring (photo).
3 Note the location of all hoses and tubes then disconnect them and withdraw the air cleaner body from the carburettor. Remove the sealing ring (photos).
4 Refit in the reverse order of removal,

3.6B . . . loosen the front mounting nut . . .

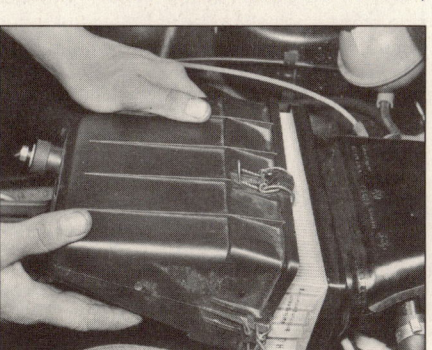

3.6C . . . remove the air cleaner cover . . .

3.6D . . . and withdraw the element (1.6 litre)

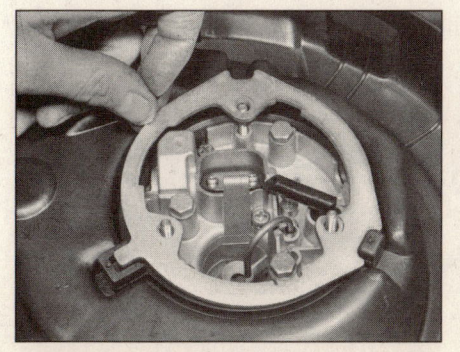

4.2 Remove the air cleaner body retaining ring (1.3 litre)

4.3A Disconnect the temperature sensor hose . . .

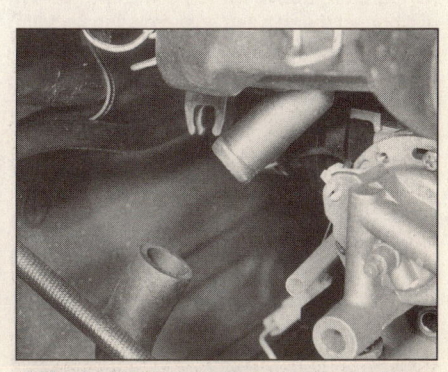

4.3B . . . and the crankcase emission hose (1.3 litre)

3•6 Fuel and exhaust systems – carburettor-based system

5.1 Air cleaner vacuum unit

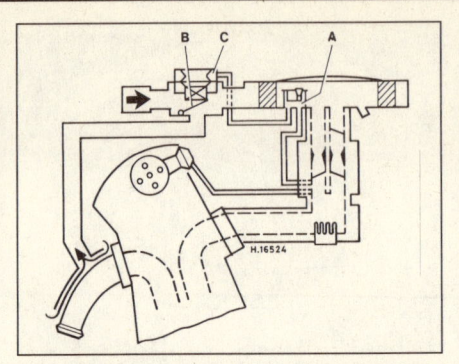

Fig. 3.2 Air cleaner load and temperature control diagram – 1.5 and 1.3 litre (Sec 5)

A Temperature regulator
B Intake pipe with thermostat
C Vacuum unit

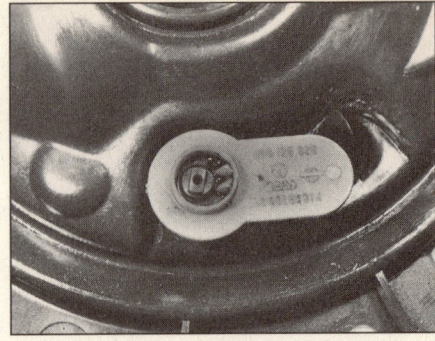

5.5 Upper view of the air temperature sensor (1.3 litre)

ensuring that all hose connections are securely made.

1.6 and 1.8 litre

5 Remove the element, as described in Section 3.
6 Unclip and detach the air hose at the side of the cleaner body.
7 Undo the retaining nut at the top and lift the cleaner unit clear, disconnecting the remaining hoses.
8 Refit in the reverse order of removal. Fit a new sealing washer if the old one has perished or distorted.

5 Automatic air cleaner temperature control - checking

1 Unclip and remove the vacuum unit and intake pipe, but leave the vacuum pipe connected (photo).
2 Suspend a thermometer in the flow of air through the inlet duct then start the engine. Between -20°C (4°F) and 17 to 20°C (63 to 68°F) the control flap in the unit should be a maximum of 2/3rds open to admit hot air from the exhaust manifold. Above 17 to 20° (63 to 68°F) the control flap must close the hot air supply.
3 The control flap movement can be checked by sucking on the vacuum inlet.
4 With the engine running and inlet air temperature above 17 to 20°C (63 to 58°F), disconnect the vacuum hose from the vacuum unit. The control flap should fully open within a maximum of 20 seconds.
5 If the control unit does not operate correctly, renew it, together with the temperature sensor (photo).
6 Refit the vacuum unit and intake pipe.

6 Fuel pump - testing, removal and refitting

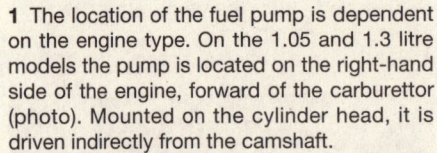

1 The location of the fuel pump is dependent on the engine type. On the 1.05 and 1.3 litre models the pump is located on the right-hand side of the engine, forward of the carburettor (photo). Mounted on the cylinder head, it is driven indirectly from the camshaft.
2 On the 1.6 and 1.8 litre models the fuel pump is located on the side of the cylinder block, next to the oil filter mounting bracket; the pump being driven direct from the intermediate shaft.
3 If the fuel pump is suspected of malfunctioning, disconnect the delivery pipe to the fuel reservoir and connect up a pressure gauge to the delivery pipe/connection from the pump. With the engine running at the specified speed check that the operating pressure of the pump is as given in the Specifications.
4 Alternatively, a less accurate method is to disconnect the supply pipe from the carburettor (air cleaner removed) and also disconnect the LT lead from the coil positive terminal. Spin the engine on the starter while holding a wad of rag near the fuel pipe. Well defined spurts of fuel should be ejected from the pipe if the fuel pump is operating correctly, provided there is fuel in the fuel tank.
5 If the above test indicates that the pump is malfunctioning then it must be renewed, as it is not possible to service or repair it. However, prior to removal of the fuel pump, check the in-line filter for blockage.
6 The in-line filter should either be renewed at the intervals specified in the Routine

6.1 Fuel pump location (1.3 litre)

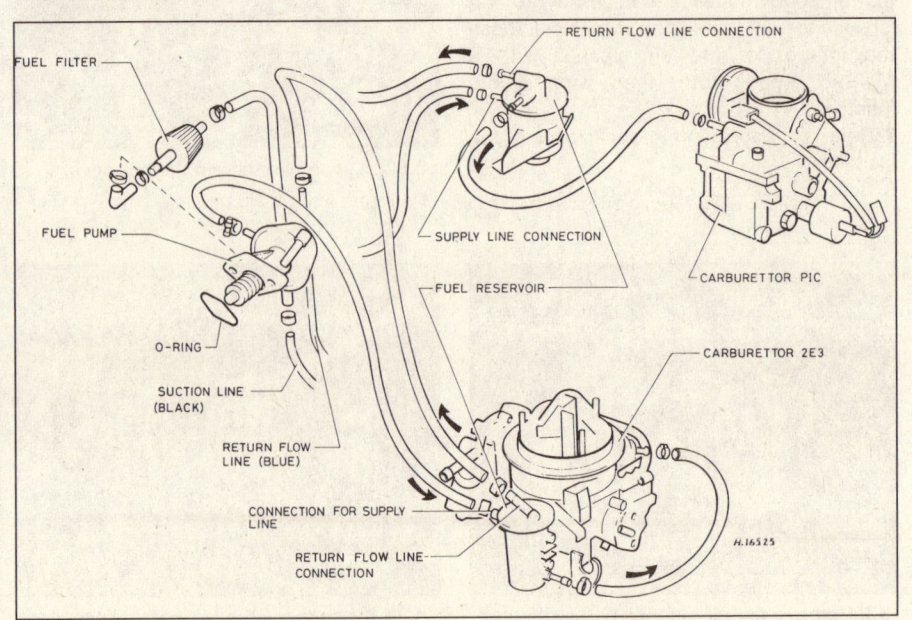

Fig. 3.3 Fuel line attachments – 1.5 and 1.3 litre (Sec 6)

Fuel and exhaust systems – carburettor-based system 3•7

Maintenance Section (Section 2) or if it becomes blocked beforehand.

7 To remove the fuel pump, first identify the hoses for position, then disconnect them from the pump.

8 Using a suitable splined or Allen key, unscrew the pump retaining bolts and withdraw the unit from the cylinder head or cylinder block (as applicable). Remove the sealing ring and, if applicable, note the earth lead location.

9 Clean the mating faces of the pump and cylinder head or cylinder block/seal flange.

10 Refitting is a reversal of the removal procedure. Renew the seal ring and, where crimped type hose clips were used, change them to screw type clips.

11 On completion check all hose connections, with the engine running, and look for any sign of fuel leaks.

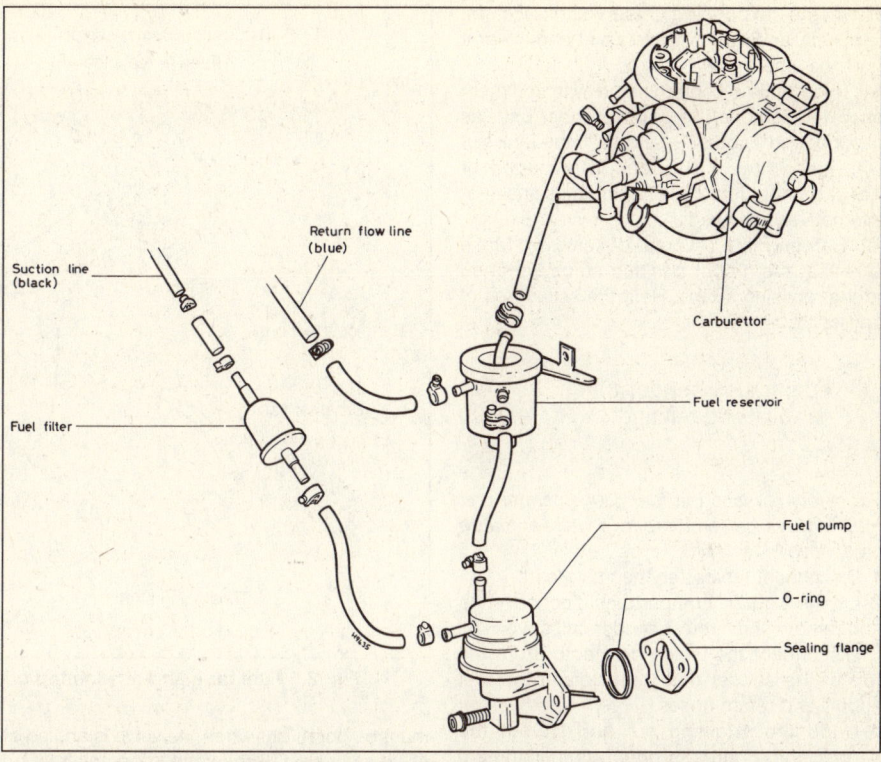

7 Fuel reservoir - removal and refitting

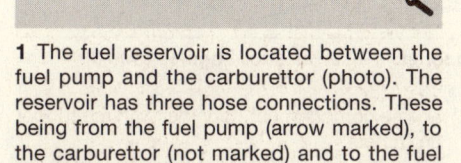

1 The fuel reservoir is located between the fuel pump and the carburettor (photo). The reservoir has three hose connections. These being from the fuel pump (arrow marked), to the carburettor (not marked) and to the fuel return line (marked R).

2 To remove the reservoir, disconnect the three line hoses and plug them to prevent leakage.

Fig. 3.4 Fuel pump and fuel line connections – 1.6 and 1.8 litre carburettors (Sec 6)

3 Remove the support bracket retaining screws and lift away the reservoir. Note the earth lead connection (photo).

4 Refit in the reverse order to removal and then check for any signs of leakage on completion.

8 Fuel tank - removal and refitting

For safety reasons the fuel tank must always be removed in a well ventilated area, never over a pit.

1 Disconnect the battery negative lead.

2 Siphon or pump all the fuel from the fuel tank (there is no drain plug).

3 Lift the floor covering from the luggage compartment then remove the circular sender unit cover.

4 Disconnect the wiring plug from the top of the sender unit, also the fuel feed (to pump) and return (from fuel reservoir) hoses.

5 Jack up the rear of the car and support it on axle stands. Chock the front wheels, remove the right-hand side rear wheel.

6 Disconnect the breather hose from the filler neck (photo).

7 Disconnect the expansion tank-to-filler neck hose and breather pipe.

8 Disconnect the filler neck funnel which is secured by a large C-clip.

9 Support the fuel tank with a trolley jack and length of wood, then unscrew the retaining nuts and bolts, detach the straps (photo) and lower the tank to the ground. On GTI models it will also be necessary to detach the side protector plate.

7.1 Fuel reservoir location (1.3 litre)

7.3 Fuel reservoir retaining screws (arrowed). Note the earth lead connection to the lower screw

8.6 Fuel filler breather valve and hose

8.9 Fuel tank tensioning (retaining) strap-to-floor bolts

3•8 Fuel and exhaust systems – carburettor-based system

10 If the expansion reservoir is to be removed, undo the retaining bolt and lower it from the wheel arch.
11 If the tank is contaminated with sediment or water, remove the gauge sender unit, as described in Section 9, and swill the tank out with clean fuel. If the tank is damaged or leaks, it should be repaired professionally or alternatively renewed.
12 Refitting is a reversal of removal. Make sure that the rubber packing strips are fitted to the retaining straps. Refit the hoses free of any kinks.

9 Fuel gauge sender unit - removal and refitting

For safety reasons the fuel gauge sender unit must always be removed in a well ventilated area, never over a pit.
1 Disconnect the battery negative lead.
2 Lift the luggage compartment floor covering and remove the circular sender unit cover.
3 Disconnect the wiring connector from the top of the sender unit then detach the fuel supply and return hoses.
4 Undo the retaining nut and lift out the sender unit, noting its orientation alignment marking. A suitable wrench may be necessary to loosen the securing nut.
5 Remove and renew the sender unit seal.
6 Refit in the reverse order to removal. Check that the unit is correctly aligned with the markings in register. Renew the crimped supply and return line clips with screw type clips. Check that the wiring connection is secure.

10 Fuel filler gravity valve - removal, checking and refitting

1 The gravity valve is located in the fuel filler neck and is accessible from within the right-hand rear wheel arch.
2 To remove the gravity valve, pull it upwards from the fuel filler neck and unclip it.
3 When the valve is held vertically the valve must be open, but when the valve is angled at 45° it must shut. Renew the valve unit if found to be defective.
4 Refit in the reverse order of removal.

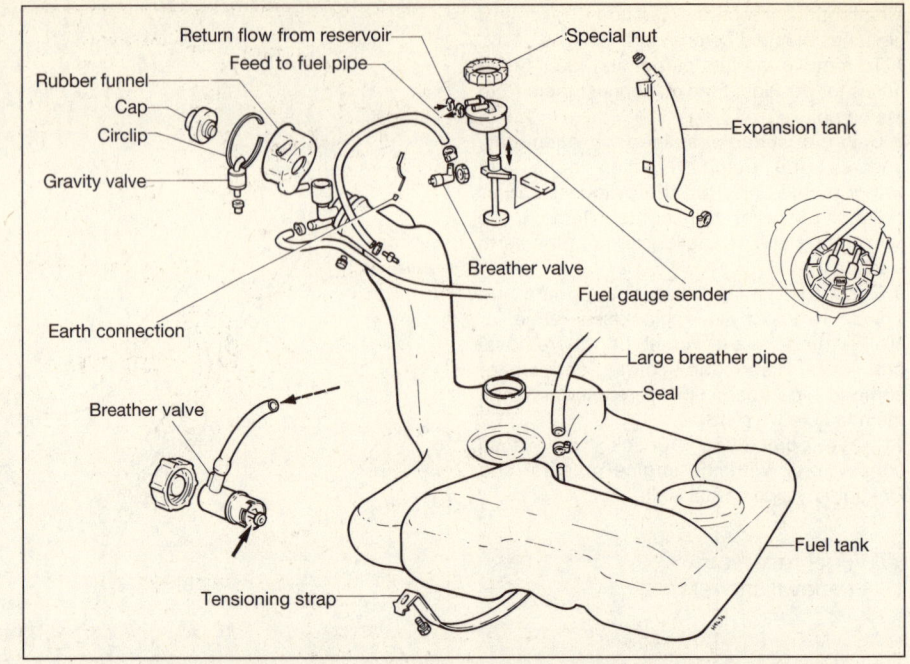

11 Accelerator cable (manual gearbox models) - removal, refitting and adjustment

1 Disconnect the battery earth lead.
2 Remove the air cleaner unit, as described in Section 4.
3 Prise free and release the inner cable securing clip(s) at the carburettor throttle control, noting how the clip(s) are located (photo).
4 Release the cable grommet from the support bracket (photo).
5 Working inside the car, remove the lower facia panel then unclip the inner cable from the accelerator pedal (photo).
6 Withdraw the complete cable into the engine compartment, together with the rubber grommets.
7 Refitting is a reversal of removal, but make sure that it is free of any kinks and correctly aligned. Finally adjust it as follows before refitting the air cleaner.

Adjustment
8 Before adjusting the cable, check that it is correctly aligned over its full length.
9 Have an assistant fully depress the accelerator pedal. Remove the air cleaner.
10 Check that the clearance between the throttle lever at the carburettor and the fully open stop is a maximum of 1.0 mm (0.040 in). Note that the throttle lever must not be hard against the fully open stop (ie there must be a small clearance).
11 There are different cable adjustment arrangements. Where locknuts are provided at the engine end of the outer cable, loosen them, then adjust the cable position and tighten the locknuts. Where a ferrule and

Fig. 3.5 Fuel tank and associated components – carburettor engines (Sec 8)

11.3 Accelerator cable to carburettor throttle control

11.4 Release the cable grommet from the support bracket

11.5 Accelerator cable-to-pedal attachment

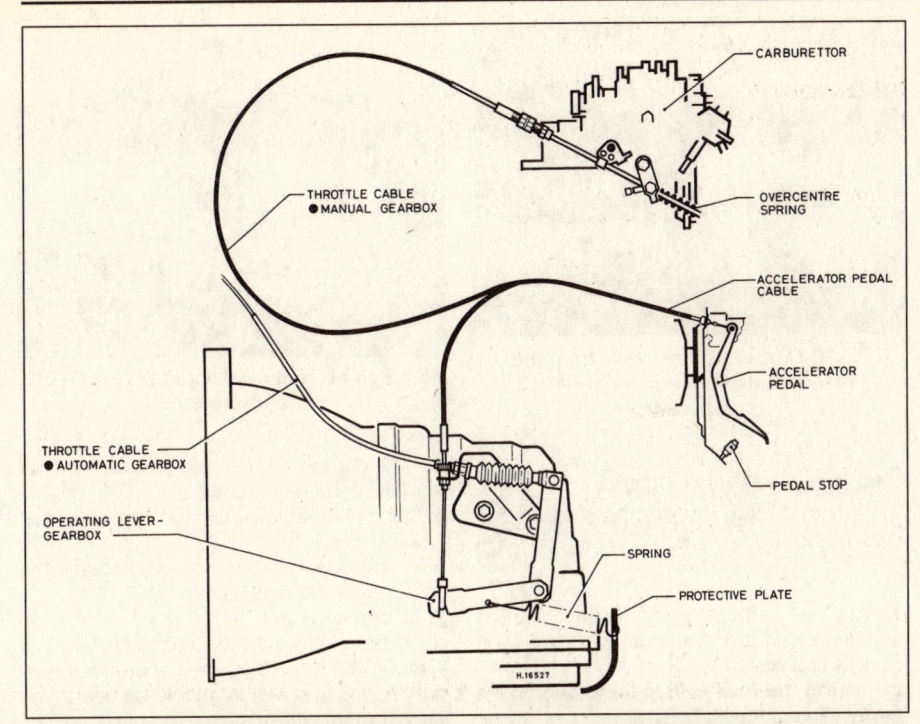

Fuel and exhaust systems – carburettor-based system 3•9

Fig. 3.6 Accelerator/throttle cable connections – manual and automatic gearbox variants with 2E2 carburettor (Sec 12)

circlip are provided, extract the circlip, adjust the cable position then refit the circlip so that it is abutting the ferrule guide. On some models it is necessary to adjust the inner cable by loosening the clamp screw, repositioning the lever while holding the cable taut, then tightening the screw.
12 After adjustment refit the air cleaner.

12 Accelerator and throttle cable (automatic transmission) - removal, refitting and adjustment

1 On automatic transmission models the accelerator pedal activates the accelerator cable which is attached to the operating lever of the gearbox shift control. This simultaneously operates the throttle cable fitted between the shift mechanism and the carburettor.
2 Before removing either cable, select P (Park).
3 To remove the accelerator pedal cable, first loosen the cable adjusting nut, then detach the inner cable from the operating lever clevis and the outer cable from its location bracket. The cable can then be disconnected from the pedal and removed in the same manner as that for manual gearbox models (see previous Section).
4 To remove the throttle cable, loosen the adjuster and locknut at the carburettor support bracket, remove the inner cable retaining clip and then disconnect the cable from the carburettor.
5 At the transmission end, prise free the securing clip and detach the cable from the operating lever and the cable support bracket.
6 Refitting of both cables is a reversal of the removal procedure, but each cable must be adjusted, and this procedure is described in Chapter 6.

13 Accelerator pedal - removal and refitting

1 Remove the lower facia panel.
2 Disconnect the accelerator cable from the pedal
3 Prise out the clip and remove the pivot pin.
4 Remove the accelerator pedal. If necessary press out the pivot pin bushes.
5 Refitting is a reversal of removal, but lubricate the bushes with a little grease. Check the cable adjustment, with reference to Section 12.

14 Choke cable (1.05 litre) - removal, refitting and adjustment

1 Disconnect the battery negative lead
2 Remove the air cleaner, as described in Section 4.
3 Using a screwdriver, loosen the inner and outer cable clamps and disconnect the cable from the carburettor (photo).
4 Working inside the car, remove the lower facia panel.
5 Pull out the clip and remove the choke knob.
6 Unscrew the ring and withdraw the cable from the facia.
7 Disconnect the wiring and withdraw the complete cable from inside the car.
8 Refitting is a reversal of removal, but make sure that the cable is correctly aligned, and that the grommets are firmly fitted in the bulkhead. Finally adjust it as follows before refitting the air cleaner.
9 Locate the outer cable in the clamp so that its end protrudes approximately 12.0 mm (0.47 in). Tighten the clamp with the outer cable in this position.
10 Push the choke knob fully in then pull it out 3.0 mm (0.12 in) - switch on the ignition and check that the warning lamp is not lit.
11 Insert the inner cable into the choke lever clamp and fully open the choke lever by hand. Tighten the inner cable clamp screw in this position.
12 Refit the air cleaner.

15 Carburettor - removal and refitting

1 Disconnect the battery earth lead.
2 Remove the air cleaner unit, as described in Section 4.
3 Disconnect the accelerator cable from the carburettor (Section 11 or 12 as applicable). Disconnect the wiring from the fuel cut-off solenoid, the bypass air cut-off valve, the part throttle channel heater, automatic choke control unit and the earth lead, as applicable.
4 Referring to Chapter 2, drain off half the engine coolant then disconnect the coolant hoses from the automatic choke unit and the expansion element (where applicable).
5 Disconnect the fuel supply and return hoses at the carburettor/fuel reservoir, as necessary, and plug or clamp the hoses to prevent fuel leakage. Note the connections in case of confusion when refitting.
6 Disconnect the vacuum hoses and note their connections.
7 Unscrew the through-bolts or retaining

Fig. 3.7 Choke cable adjustment setting – 1.5 litre (Sec 14)

A Outer cable projection
B Cam and stop
C Choke inner cable connection

3•10 Fuel and exhaust systems – carburettor-based system

15.7A Carburettor securing bolts (arrowed) – 2E3 carburettor

15.7B Carburettor removal from the intermediate flange/manifold – 2E3 carburettor

16.3 Removing the carburettor cover – PIC carburettor

nuts, as applicable, and carefully remove the carburettor from the inlet manifold (photos).
8 To remove the intermediate flange from the manifold, undo the four nuts on the manifold underside and lift the flange clear.
9 Refitting is a reversal of the removal procedure. Ensure that the inlet manifold, intermediate flange and carburettor mating faces are clean, and use new gaskets.
10 On completion, top up the cooling system (Chapter 2), restart the engine and check for fuel and coolant leaks. Adjust the carburettor as necessary.

16 Carburettor (31 PIC7) - dismantling, reassembly and adjustment

1 With the carburettor removed from the engine, clean the external surfaces with paraffin and wipe dry.
2 Remove the screws from the cover, noting the location of the earth lead.
3 Lift off the cover and remove the gasket (photo).
4 Prise out the retainer and remove the float from the carburettor (photos).
5 Clean out the float chamber with clean fuel (photo).
6 If necessary further dismantle the carburettor with reference to Fig. 3.10.
7 To check the bypass air cut-off valve when removed, depress the pin approximately 3 to 4 mm (0.12 to 0.16 in) then energise it with battery voltage. A click should be heard and the pin should move out.
8 To check the cut-off valve for the main jets (where fitted), apply battery voltage. It must

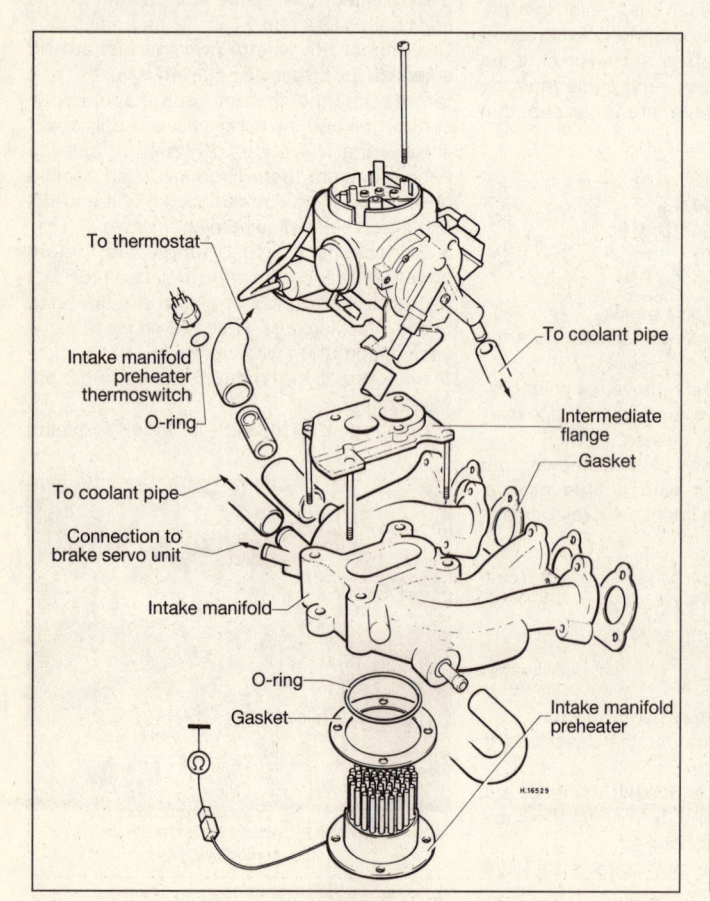

Fig. 3.8 2E3 carburettor, manifold and associated components (Sec 15)

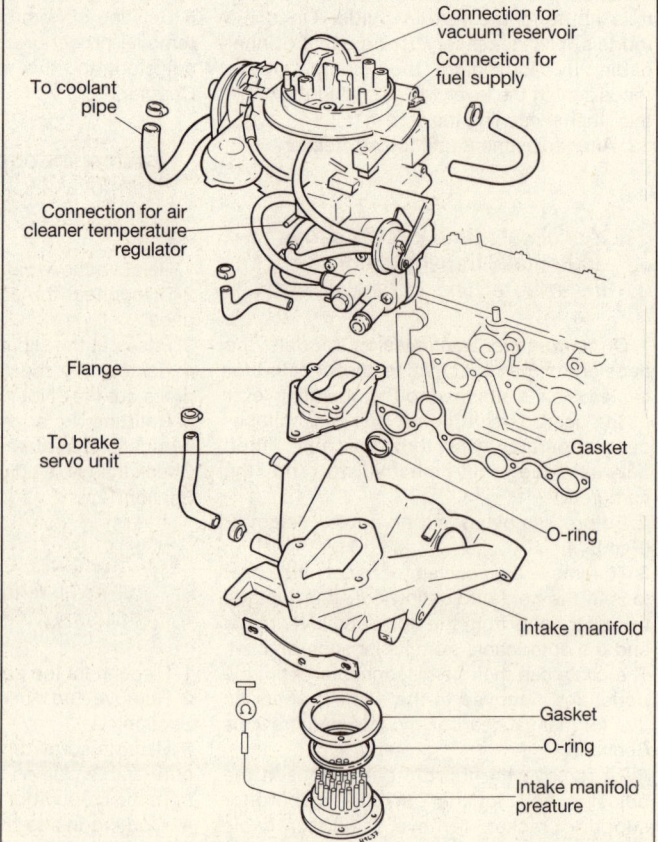

Fig. 3.9 2E2 carburettor, manifold and associated components (Sec 15)

Fuel and exhaust systems – carburettor-based system 3•11

16.4A Prise out the retainer . . .

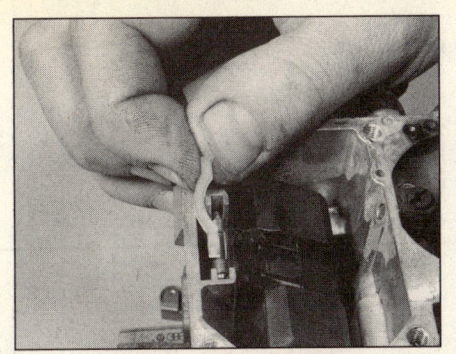

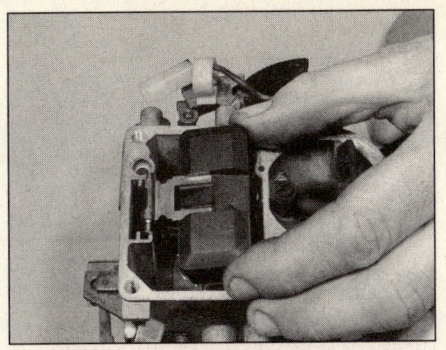

16.4B . . . and remove the float – PIC carburettor

16.5 View of carburettor with cover removed – PIC carburettor

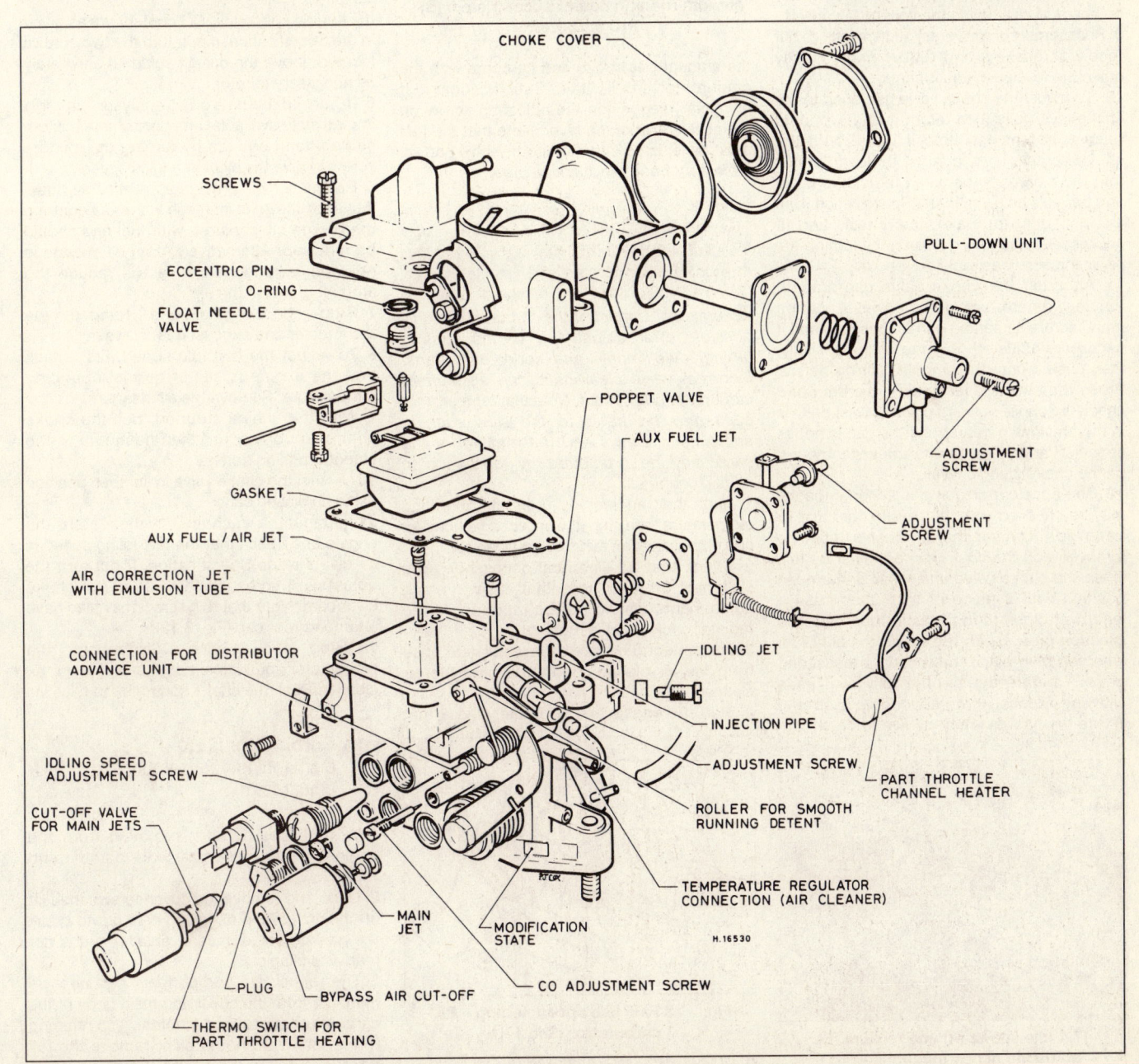

Fig. 3.10 Exploded view of the PIC carburettor (Sec 16)

- CHOKE COVER
- SCREWS
- ECCENTRIC PIN
- O-RING
- FLOAT NEEDLE VALVE
- PULL-DOWN UNIT
- GASKET
- POPPET VALVE
- AUX FUEL JET
- AUX FUEL / AIR JET
- ADJUSTMENT SCREW
- AIR CORRECTION JET WITH EMULSION TUBE
- ADJUSTMENT SCREW
- CONNECTION FOR DISTRIBUTOR ADVANCE UNIT
- IDLING JET
- INJECTION PIPE
- ADJUSTMENT SCREW
- IDLING SPEED ADJUSTMENT SCREW
- PART THROTTLE CHANNEL HEATER
- CUT-OFF VALVE FOR MAIN JETS
- ROLLER FOR SMOOTH RUNNING DETENT
- TEMPERATURE REGULATOR CONNECTION (AIR CLEANER)
- MAIN JET
- MODIFICATION STATE
- PLUG
- BYPASS AIR CUT-OFF
- CO ADJUSTMENT SCREW
- THERMO SWITCH FOR PART THROTTLE HEATING

H.16530

3•12 Fuel and exhaust systems – carburettor-based system

16.10A Checking the choke valve gap with a twist drill – PIC carburettor

16.10B Adjusting screw location for the choke valve gap (A) and choke valve gap smooth running detent eccentric pin (B) – PIC carburettor

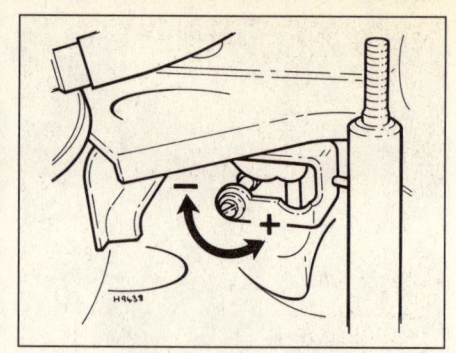

Fig. 3.11 Accelerator pump adjuster screw – PIC carburettor (Sec 16)

be heard to click when the voltage is applied.
9 Reassembly is a reversal of dismantling, but renew all gaskets and rubber rings. Finally make the following adjustments.
10 To adjust the choke valve gap operate the choke lever fully then return it to the smooth running detent and hold it there. With the choke spindle lever against the cam, check that the clearance between the choke valve and barrel is as given in the Specification. Use a twist drill to make the check and if necessary adjust the clearance by turning the adjusting screw as required (photos).
11 Although the choke valve gap smooth running detent position is preset during manufacture its setting can be checked and if necessary adjusted. Pull the choke out fully, then push it onto the smooth running detent. Press the choke lever against the cam and check the choke valve gap with a twist drill, as in the previous paragraph. If the gap is not as specified adjust by turning the eccentric pin on the choke spindle lever.
12 The accelerator pump injection capacity may be checked with the carburettor fitted or removed, however the air cleaner must be removed and the float chamber must be full. Open the choke valve and retain in the open position with a piece of wire, then push a length of close fitting plastic tube over the injection pipe. Operate the throttle until fuel emerges then place the tube in a measuring glass. Operate the throttle fully five times allowing at least three seconds per stroke. Divide the final quantity by five to determine

the amount per stroke and compare with the amount given in the Specifications. If necessary reposition the adjusting screw on the accelerator pump lever. Note that the fuel must be injected into the throttle valve gap - if necessary bend the injection pipe.

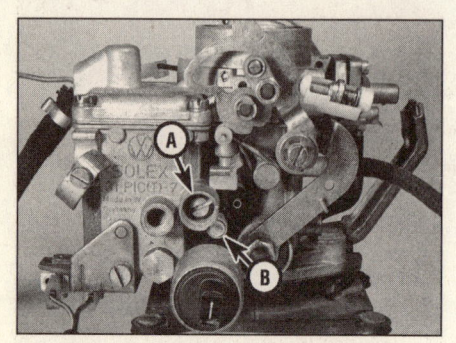

17 Carburettor (31 PIC7) - slow running and fast idle speed adjustments

Accurate adjustment of the carburettor is only possible after adjustment of the ignition timing, dwell angle and spark plug gaps. Incorrect valve clearances can also effect carburettor adjustment. Note that tamperproof caps may be fitted to the slow running adjustment screws and the removal of the caps may be prohibited by legislation in certain countries.

1 Run the engine to normal operating temperature then stop it. Connect a tachometer and, if available, an exhaust gas analyser.
2 Check that all electrical accessories are switched off and note that slow running adjustments should not be made while the radiator cooling fan is running.
3 Disconnect the crankcase ventilation hose from the air cleaner body and plug the air cleaner outlet.
4 Start the engine and let it idle. Check that

17.4 Idle speed (A) and mixture (B) adjusting screw locations – PIC carburettor

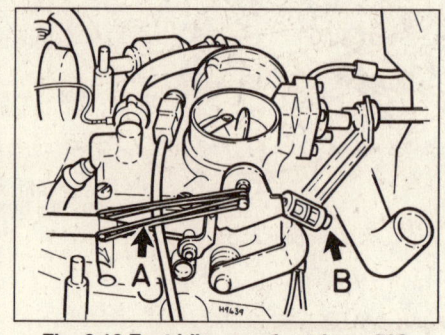

Fig. 3.12 Fast idle speed setting – PIC carburettor (Sec 17)

A Choke valve held open with rubber band
B Adjustment screw

the engine speed and CO content are as given in the Specification. If not, turn the two screws located above the cut-off solenoid alternately as necessary (photo).
5 If an exhaust gas analyser is not immediately available, an approximate mixture setting can be made by turning the mixture screw to give the highest engine speed.
6 Reconnect the crankcase ventilation hose. If this results in an increase in the CO content, the engine oil is diluted with fuel and should be renewed. Alternatively, if an oil change is not due, a long fast drive will reduce the amount of fuel in the oil.
7 Stop the engine and remove the tachometer and exhaust gas analyser.
8 To adjust the fast idle speed, first check that the engine is still at normal operating temperature. Remove the air cleaner.
9 With the engine stopped, pull the choke control knob fully out then push it in to the smooth running detent.
10 Retain the choke valve in its open position using an elastic band.
11 Connect a tachometer then start the engine and check that the fast idling speed is as given in the Specification. If not turn the adjustment screw on the side of the choke lever cam. Note that this screw may also have a tamperproof cap (Fig. 3.12).
12 Stop the engine, disconnect the tachometer and elastic band, and refit the air cleaner. Push the choke control knob fully in.

18 Carburettor (2E3) - dismantling, reassembly and adjustment

1 With the carburettor removed from the engine, clean it externally with paraffin and wipe/blow dry.
2 Undo and remove the cover screws then lift off the cover (photo), taking care not to break the gasket just in case a replacement is not readily available.
3 The respective components can now be removed from the cover and main body of the carburettor as required (photos), also referring to Fig. 3.13. Do not alter or remove the full throttle stop or the Stage II throttle valve adjustment screw settings.

Fuel and exhaust systems – carburettor-based system 3•13

18.2 Top cover securing screws (arrowed) – 2E3 carburettor

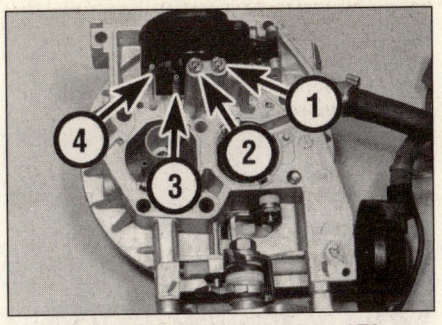

18.3A Underside view of the 2E3 carburettor

1 Stage I main jet   2 Stage II main jet
3 Full throttle enrichment lift pipe
4 Stage II progression lift pipe

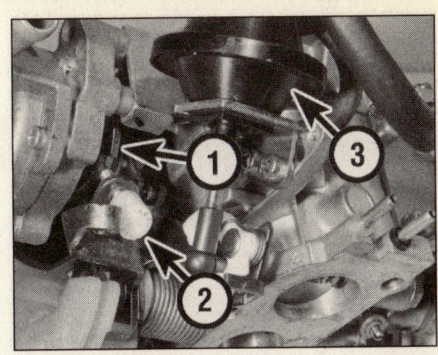

18.3B 2E3 carburettor showing the fast idle cam (1), fast idle adjuster screw (2) and Stage II vacuum unit (3)

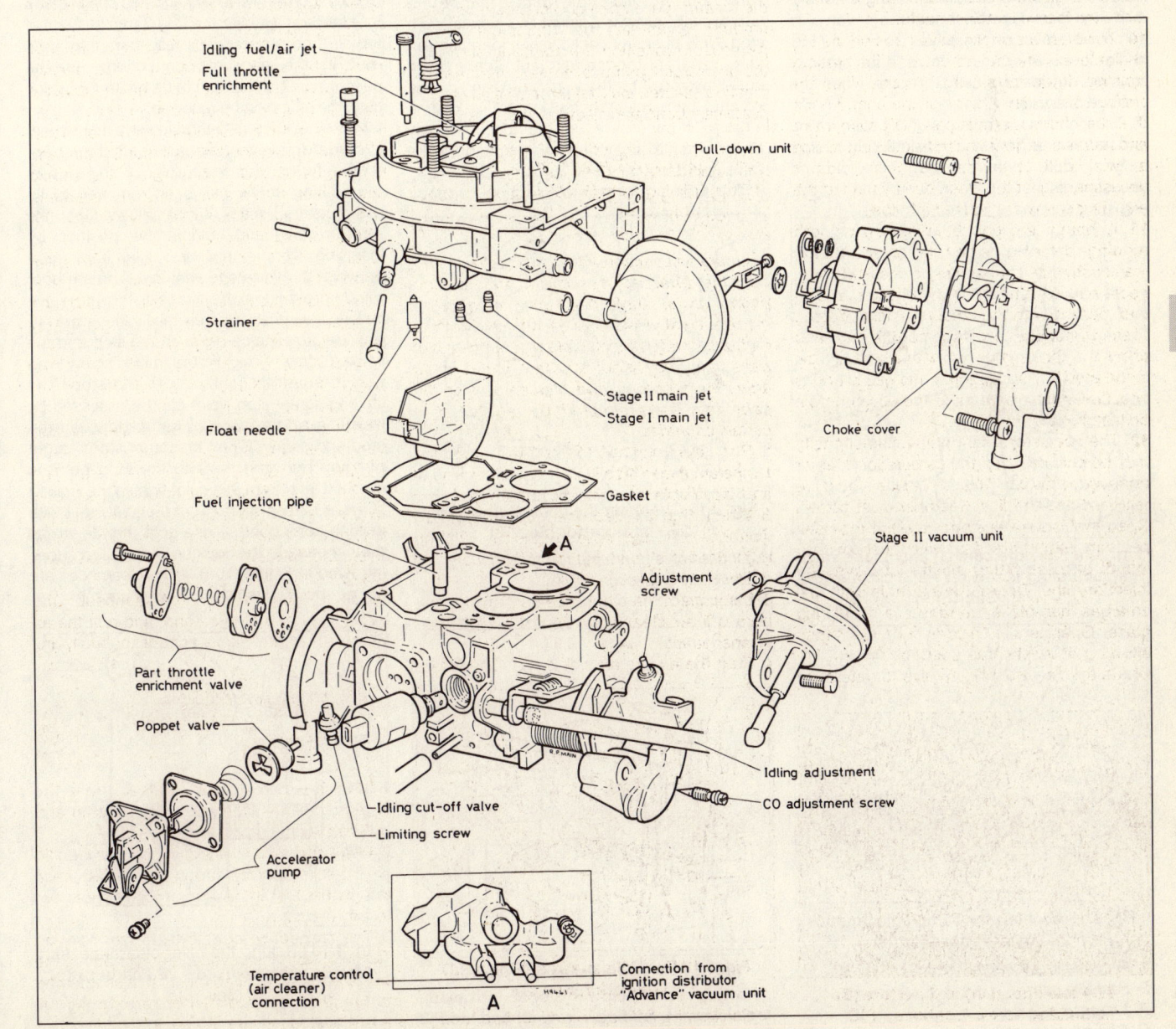

Fig. 3.13 Exploded view of the 2E3 carburettor (Sec 18)

Labels:
- Idling fuel/air jet
- Full throttle enrichment
- Pull-down unit
- Strainer
- Stage II main jet
- Stage I main jet
- Float needle
- Choke cover
- Fuel injection pipe
- Gasket
- Part throttle enrichment valve
- Stage II vacuum unit
- Poppet valve
- Adjustment screw
- Idling cut-off valve
- Idling adjustment
- Limiting screw
- CO adjustment screw
- Accelerator pump
- Temperature control (air cleaner) connection
- Connection from ignition distributor "Advance" vacuum unit

3•14 Fuel and exhaust systems – carburettor-based system

18.9 Acceleration injection pipe must align with recess (arrowed) – 2E3 carburettor

18.10 Choke housing and cover must be correctly aligned – 2E3 carburettor

4 Clean the internal components but do not probe jets and orifices with wire or similar to remove dirt, blow them through using an air line.
5 If the part throttle enrichment valve is removed it must be renewed.
6 To check the cut-off valve, apply battery voltage. It must be heard to click when the voltage is applied.
7 Reassembly is a reversal of the dismantling procedure, but renew all gaskets and rubber rings. Make the following checks and adjustments.
8 To check the choke valve gap the choke cover must be removed. Move the throttle valve and the fast idle cam so that the adjustment screw is against the highest cam stop. Now push the choke valve operating rod fully towards the adjustment screw (and pull-down unit), then check the choke valve-to-barrel clearance using a twist drill as a gauge. If necessary turn the adjuster screw as required to provide the specified choke valve gap (Figs. 3.14 and 3.15).
9 The accelerator pump injection capacity can be checked in the same manner as that described in Section 16, paragraph 12, but allow 1 second per stroke and 3 seconds between strokes (Fig. 3.16).
10 Ensure that the automatic choke cover and the choke housing alignment marks correspond. To check the choke, connect up a test lamp between a battery positive terminal and the choke lead. The test lamp should illuminate, if it doesn't then the choke unit is defective and must be renewed.
11 The choke pulldown unit can be checked whilst it is removed but, as this requires the use of a vacuum pump and gauge, it is a check best entrusted to your VW dealer. The pulldown unit can also be tested when the carburettor is in position in the car. The air cleaner unit must be removed. Run the engine at idle speed then close the choke valve by hand and check that a resistance is felt over the final 3 mm (0.12 in) of travel. If no resistance is felt, there may be a leak in the vacuum connections, or the pulldown unit diaphragm to be broken, in which case the unit must be renewed.
12 The basic Stage II throttle valve adjustment is made during manufacture and should not require further adjustment. If, for any reason, the limiting screw has been removed or its setting altered, readjust it as follows. Open the throttle valve and hold in this position by inserting wooden rod or similar implement between the valve and venturi. Using a rubber band, pretension the Stage II throttle valve locking lever then unscrew the limiting screw to provide a clearance between the stop and the limiting screw. Now turn the limiting screw in so that it is just in contact with the stop. The limiting screw stop point can be assessed by inserting a thin piece of paper between the stop and screw. When the paper starts to get pinched between the two the stop point is reached, and from this point tighten the limiting screw a further quarter turn then secure it with locking compound. Close both throttle valves then measure the locking lever clearances (arrowed in Figure 3.18). If the clearances are not as specified bend them, as necessary.

Fig. 3.14 Fast idle cam (1) and choke valve gap adjusting screw (2) – 2E3 carburettor (Sec 18)

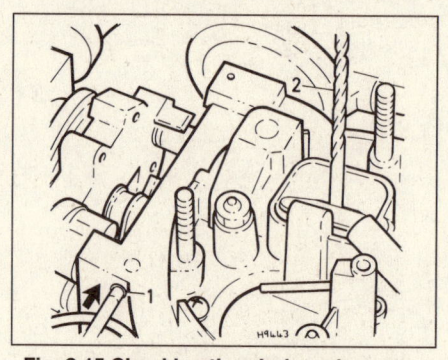

Fig. 3.15 Checking the choke valve gap – 2E3 carburettor (Sec 18)

1 Choke valve operating rod (push in direction of arrow)
2 Twist drill

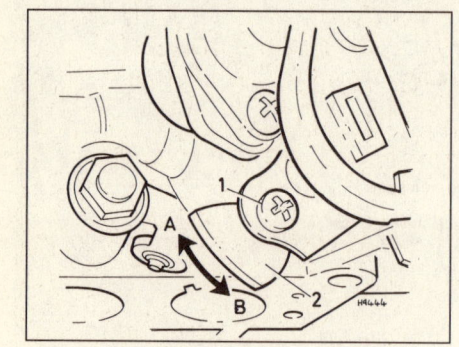

Fig. 3.16 Accelerator pump adjustment – 2E3 carburettor (Sec 18)

1 Fast idle cam clamp screw
2 Fast idle cam
A Increase capacity
B Decrease capacity

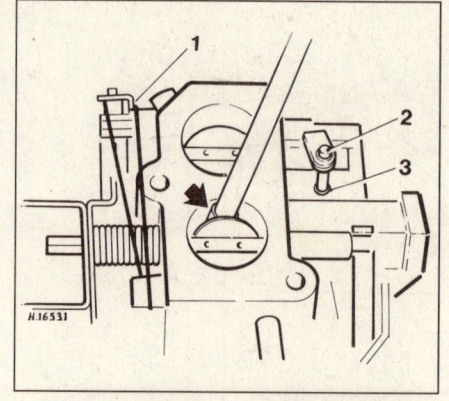

Fig. 3.17 Throttle valve basic setting showing rod to hold valve open (arrowed), lock lever (1), limiting screw (2) and stop (3) – 2E3 carburettor (Sec 18)

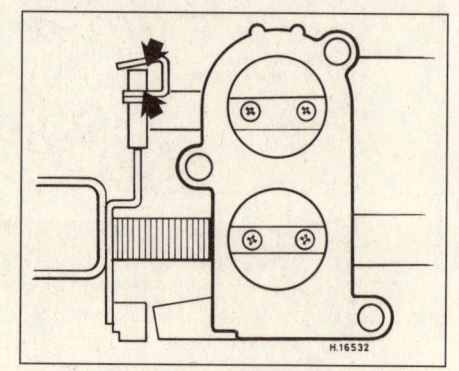

Fig. 3.18 Locking the lever clearance with throttle valves closed – 2E3 carburettor (Sec 18)

Clearance to equal 0.25 to 0.55 mm (each side)

Fuel and exhaust systems – carburettor-based system 3•15

19.1 Idle speed adjustment screw and guide sleeve (A) mixture screw (B) – 2E3 carburettor

Fig. 3.19 Fast idle speed adjustment screw (2) – 2E3 carburettor (Sec 19)

19 Carburettor (2E3) - slow running and fast idle speed adjustment

1 To check and adjust the slow running setting refer to Section 17 and proceed as described in paragraphs 1 to 7 inclusive (photo).
2 To check and adjust the fast idle adjustment, first check that the engine is still at normal operating temperature. The air cleaner must be removed and the other provisional conditions must apply as for the slow running adjustment. Plug the air cleaner temperature control hose.
3 Restart the engine and open the throttle to give an engine speed of 2500 rpm (approximately). Press down the fast idle cam to its stop then move the throttle valve back so that the adjuster screw is on the second highest stop on the fast idle cam. In this position the fast idle speed should be as specified. If the setting is incorrect, turn the adjustment screw in the required direction until it is correct - Fig. 3.19. (Note that the screw may have a tamperproof cap fitted).
4 On completion unplug the temperature control connector and refit the air cleaner.

20 Carburettor (2E2) - dismantling, reassembling and adjustment

1 The dismantling and overhaul procedures for the 2E2 carburettor closely follow those described for the 2E3 carburettor in Section 18. The following checks and adjustments are additional to, or differ from, those given in that Section.
2 **Part throttle channel heater unit:** To check this unit, connect a test lamp between the unit wiring plug and a battery positive terminal. Earth the unit. If the test bulb fails to light the unit is defective and must be renewed. When fitting the unit ensure that it has a good carburettor earth connection.
3 **Choke pull down unit:** This can be checked in the same manner as that for the choke pull down unit on the 2E3 carburettor,

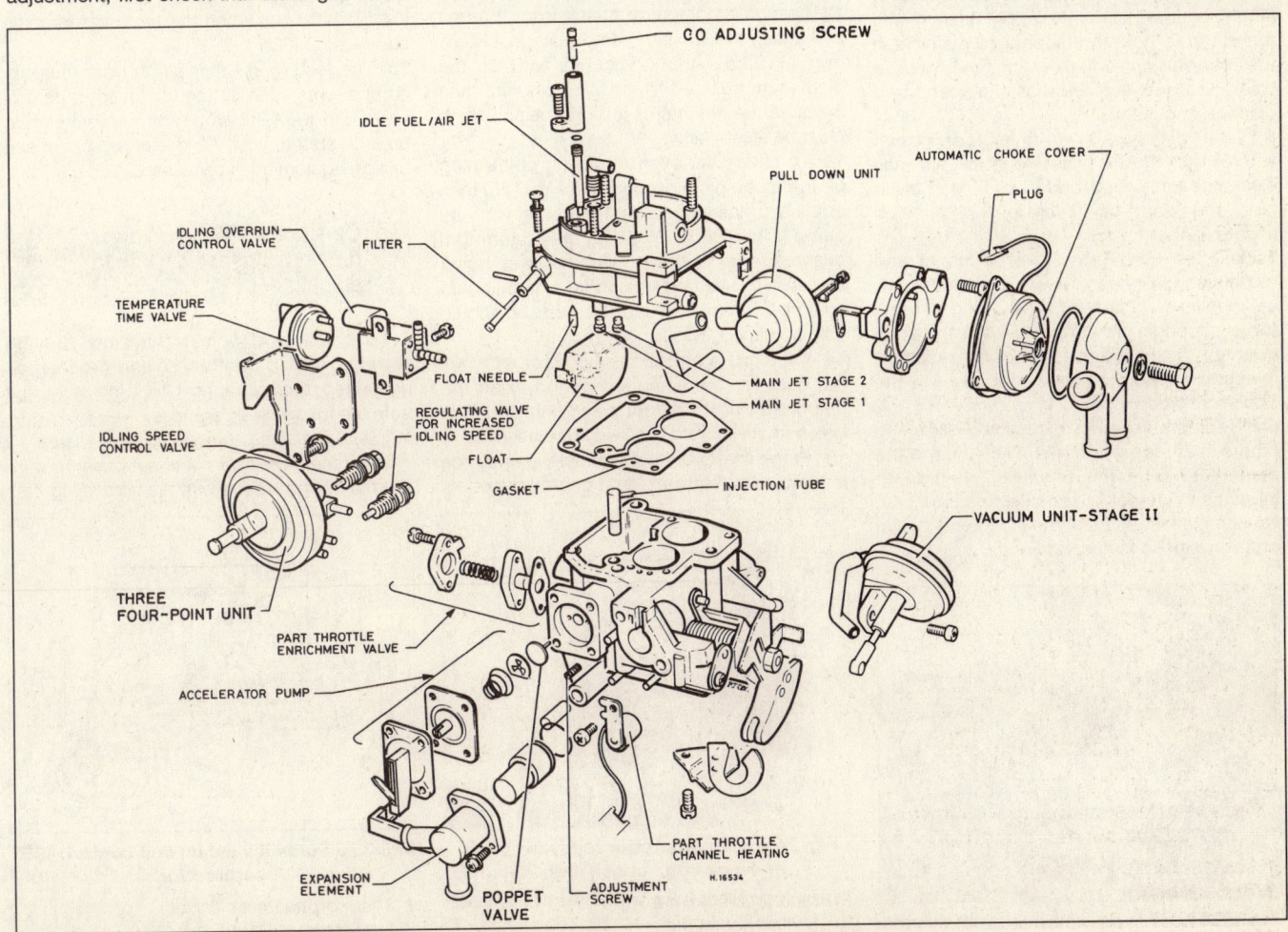

Fig. 3.20 Exploded view of the 2E2 carburettor (Sec 20)

3•16 Fuel and exhaust systems – carburettor-based system

Fig. 3.21 2E2 Carburettor ready for accelerator pump check (Sec 20)

A Vacuum pump connection
B Plug vacuum connection (3-point unit)
C Plug vacuum connection (4-point unit)

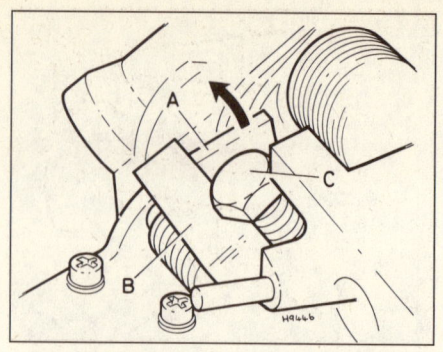

Fig. 3.22 Accelerator pump adjustment check showing warm-up lever (A), lever (B) and bolt (C) – 2E2 carburettor (Sec 20)

Fig. 3.23 Loosen screw (A) and turn cam plate (B) in direction required to adjust accelerator pump injection capacity – 2E2 carburettor (Sec 20)

but note that the resistance felt must be over the final 5 mm (0.20 in) of travel.

4 Accelerator pump (carburettor removed): To make this check, the carburettor must be removed and you will need a vacuum pump and an M8 x 20 mm bolt.

5 Detach the vacuum hoses from the three/four point unit then connect up the vacuum pump to the three/four point unit at A shown in Figure 3.21 and plug connection B (and C on four point unit). Apply vacuum with the pump to hold the diaphragm pushrod in the overrun/cut-off position and give a clearance between the fast idle speed and diaphragm pushrod.

6 Pivot up the warm-up lever to the point where the thottle valve control pin has clearance and insert the M8 x 20 mm bolt to hold the warm-up lever in this position (Figure 3.22).

7 Hold the carburettor over a funnel and measuring glass then slowly open the throttle valve lever fully five times allowing at least three seconds per stroke. Divide the total quantity by five and check the resultant injection capacity against that given in the Specifications.

8 If adjustment is necessary, refer to Figure 3.23, loosen screw A and rotate the cam plate B in the required direction to increase or decrease the injection capacity. On completion retighten the screw and seal in position with locking compound.

9 The accelerator pump injection capacity can also be checked with the carburettor in position in the vehicle, but as specialised equipment is required this is a task best entrusted to your VW dealer.

10 Basic Stage II valve adjustment: Proceed as described in Paragraph 12 of Section 18, and refer to Figs. 3.17 and 3.24.

11 Three/four point unit: To check this unit for satisfactory operation you will need a vacuum pump.

12 Detach the vacuum hoses from the unit and attach the vacuum pump to connection 1 in Fig. 3.25. Apply vacuum to pull the diaphragm pushrod to the idle point and then measure the amount of rod protrusion, which must be as specified.

13 To check the overrun cut-off point, plug off the vacuum connection, 3 in Fig. 3.25, then apply increased vacuum with the vacuum pump. This should cause the diaphragm pushrod to move to the overrun/cut-off point. Measure the rod protrusion (a) which should now be 1.0 mm (0.04 in). The pushrod should hold at this position for one minute.

14 If the rod protrusion is incorrect, or it will not hold for the specified period, then the diaphragm or three/four point unit probably leak and are therefore in need of renewal.

15 Stage II vacuum control unit: This device is fitted to 1.6 litre manual gearbox models

and 1.8 automatic gearbox models from August 1984 on. Its function is to delay the Stage II opening slightly whilst the coolant temperature is below 18°C (64°F). It achieves this by venting the vacuum hose via the thermo-pneumatic valve and the resistor (Fig. 3.26). Check that the straight hose at connection 3 on the thermo-pneumatic valve is not blocked and check the valve itself by blowing through it. It should be open at 18°C (64°F) and close when the temperature rises above 28°C (82°F).

16 The testing of other carburettor ancillary components such as the idle/overrun control valve and the temperature time valve should be entrusted to your VW dealer as specialised testing equipment is necessary.

21 Carburettor (2E2) - slow running and fast idle speed adjustment

1 To check and adjust the slow running setting, refer to Section 17 and proceed as described in paragraphs 1 to 7 inclusive, but note the following differences:
(a) *Before making any adjustments ensure that the three/four point unit pushrod is in the idling position with the cold idling*

Fig. 3.24 Lock lever clearance with throttle valves closed – 2E2 carburettor (Sec 20)

Fig. 3.25 2E2 carburettor ready for the 3- or 4-point unit check (Sec 20)

Pushrod to idle point a = 8.5 mm
1 Vacuum connection
2 and 3 Plug these connections

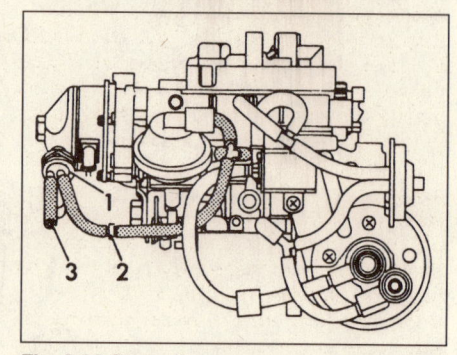

Fig. 3.26 Stage II vacuum unit control – 2E2 carburettor

1 Thermo-pneumatic valve
2 Restrictor
3 Straight connection hose

Fuel and exhaust systems – carburettor-based system 3•17

Fig. 3.27 Three/four point unit with pushrod (A) and cold idling adjusting screw (B) in idling position – 2E2 carburettor (Sec 21)

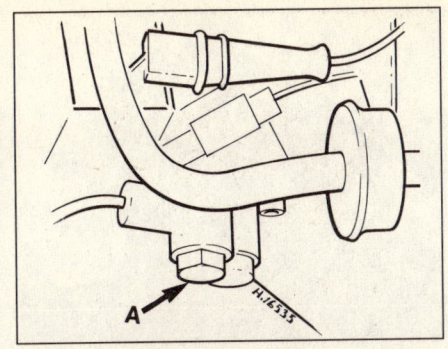

Fig. 3.28 Idling speed control valve (A) – 2E2 carburettor (Sec 21)

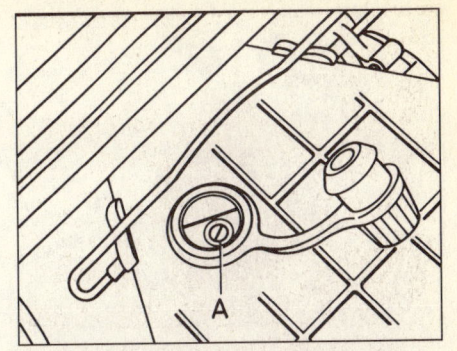

Fig. 3.29 Mixture (CO) adjustment screw (A) – 2E2 carburettor (Sec 21)

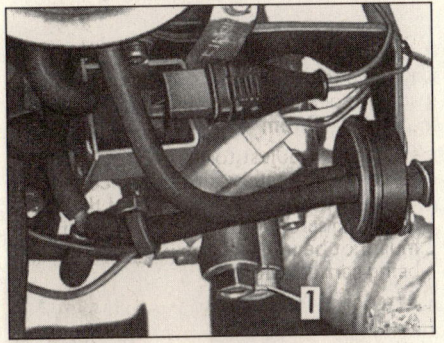

Fig. 3.30 Engine speed regulator valve (1) – 2E2 carburettor (Sec 21)

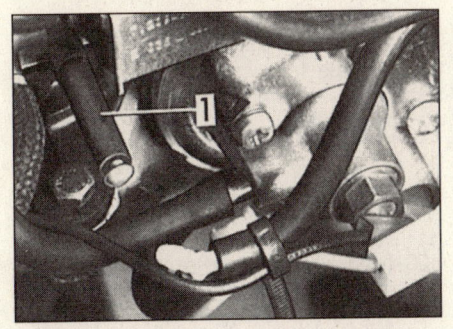

Fig. 3.31 Disconnect and plug vacuum hose (1) to check/adjust fast idle speed adjustment – 2E2 carburettor (Sec 21)

Fig. 3.32 Fast idle adjustment screw (A) – 2E2 carburettor (Sec 21)

adjusting screw touching the pushrod (Fig. 3.27)

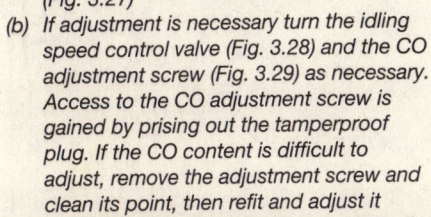

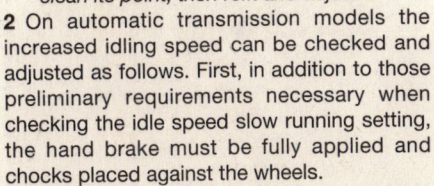

(b) If adjustment is necessary turn the idling speed control valve (Fig. 3.28) and the CO adjustment screw (Fig. 3.29) as necessary. Access to the CO adjustment screw is gained by prising out the tamperproof plug. If the CO content is difficult to adjust, remove the adjustment screw and clean its point, then refit and adjust it

2 On automatic transmission models the increased idling speed can be checked and adjusted as follows. First, in addition to those preliminary requirements necessary when checking the idle speed slow running setting, the hand brake must be fully applied and chocks placed against the wheels.

3 When the engine is started, turn on the fresh air blower (fully), switch on the headlights (high beam) and the heated rear window. Get an assistant to sit in the vehicle and depress the foot brake then select D. Check that the four point unit diaphragm rod is in the increased idling position, the fast idle adjuster screw rests against the diaphragm rod and the engine increased idle speed is not under that specified. Adjust if necessary by altering the regulator valve setting (Figure 3.30).

4 On models fitted with air conditioning the procedure for checking the increased idling speed is similar to that for automatic transmission models except that it is also necessary to switch on the air conditioner and have the control set at maximum cooling at the highest blower speed. The increased idle speed must be as specified and if adjustment is required, alter the regulator valve setting accordingly.

5 With the slow/increased running idle speed adjustment complete the fast idle speed can be checked and, if necessary, adjusted. Check that the engine is still at its normal operating temperature.

6 Detach the Y-piece from the vacuum hose and plug the hose (Fig. 3.31). Connect up a tachometer to the engine. Start and run the engine and check that the fast idle speed is as given in the Specifications, if not turn the adjustment screw on the linkage as necessary. On completion of adjustment apply sealant to the screw threads to lock it in position, unplug and reconnect the Y-piece to the vacuum hose and check that the slow running (idle) speed is as specified.

22 Inlet manifold preheating - description and testing

1 The inlet manifold is preheated by water from the cooling system and by a heater element located in the bottom of the inlet manifold.

2 To check the heater element, the engine should be cold. Disconnect the wire from the element at its inline connector, then attach an ohmmeter between the wire connector from the element and earth - 0.25 to 0.50 ohm should be recorded.

3 To remove the element disconnect the wire, then unscrew the bolts and withdraw the unit. Remove the sealing ring and gasket (photos). When refitting always renew the sealing ring and gasket.

22.3A Unscrew the bolts . . .

22.3B . . . and remove the heater element from the inlet manifold

3•18 Fuel and exhaust systems – carburettor-based system

22.3C Removing the sealing ring from the heater element

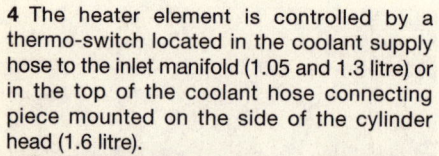

23.5 Inlet manifold support stay (1.3 litre)

23.6 Inlet manifold-to-cylinder head securing nuts and bolts

Note the position of the earth lead spade connector – arrowed (1.3 litre)

4 The heater element is controlled by a thermo-switch located in the coolant supply hose to the inlet manifold (1.05 and 1.3 litre) or in the top of the coolant hose connecting piece mounted on the side of the cylinder head (1.6 litre).

5 Before removing the thermo-switch drain off some engine coolant to reduce spillage when the switch is removed (see Chapter 2).

6 To test the thermo-switch, detach the lead connector. Unscrew and remove the switch from the housing and plug the hole to stop any leakage of coolant.

7 With an ohmmeter connected to the terminals, gradually heat the base of the switch unit in hot water. Below the following temperatures there should be zero resistance (ie internal contacts closed):

1.05 litre 65°C (149°F)
1.3, 1.6 and 1.8 litre 55°C (131°F)

8 Above the following temperatures there should be a maximum resistance (ie internal contacts open).

1.05 litre 75°C (167°F)
1.3, 1.6 an d 1.8 litre 65°C (149°F)

If defective renew the switch.

23 Inlet and exhaust manifolds - removal and refitting

Inlet manifold

1 Remove the carburettor, as described in Section 15.

2 Disconnect the inlet manifold preheater wire at the in-line connector.

3 Drain the cooling system (Chapter 2) and disconnect the coolant hoses from the manifold.

4 Disconnect the manifold vacuum hoses as necessary (Fig. 3.33).

5 Where applicable, disconnect the stay rod between the base of the manifold and the crankcase (photo).

6 Undo the manifold retaining nuts and bolts (photo) noting their respective locations, and carefully withdraw the manifold from the cylinder head.

7 Remove the gasket and clean the mating faces of the manifold and cylinder head.

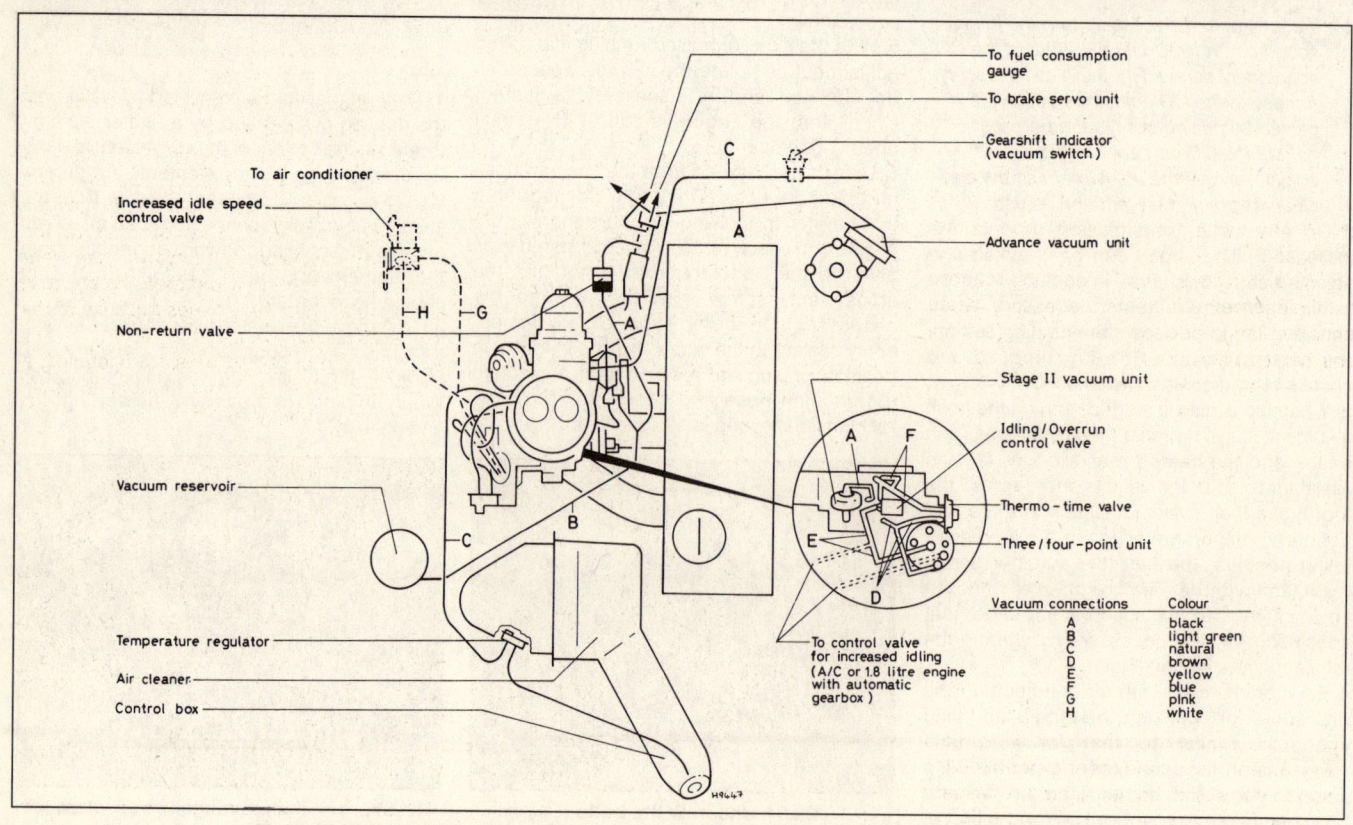

Fig. 3.33 Vacuum hose connections – 1.6 and 1.8 litre with the 2E2 carburettor (Sec 23)

Vacuum connections	Colour
A	black
B	light green
C	natural
D	brown
E	yellow
F	blue
G	pink
H	white

Fuel and exhaust systems – carburettor-based system 3•19

23.10 Warm air deflector plate (1.3 litre)

23.11 Exhaust downpipe-to-manifold flange connection (1.3 litre)

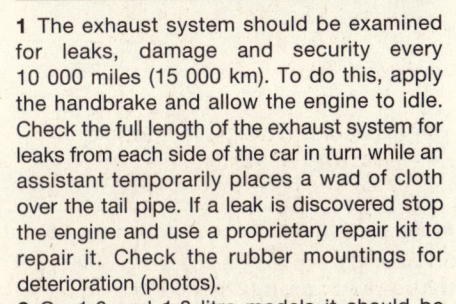

23.13 Exhaust manifold (1.3 litre)

8 Refitting is a reversal of the removal procedure. Use a new manifold gasket and tighten the securing nuts and bolts to the specified torque setting.
9 Refit the carburettor, with reference to Section 15.

Exhaust manifold

10 Undo the retaining nut(s) and withdraw the warm air deflector plate from the exhaust manifold (photo).
11 On 1.05 and 1.3 litre models, unbolt and detach the exhaust downpipe from the manifold joint (photo).
12 On 1.6 and 1.8 litre models, refer to Section 24, paragraph 2.
13 Unscrew and remove the remaining manifold retaining bolts/nuts, then carefully withdraw the manifold from the cylinder head (photo). Remove the gasket.
14 Clean the mating faces of the manifold and cylinder head. Also the exhaust downpipe flange connections.
15 Refit in the reverse order of removal. Use a new gasket and tighten the securing nuts/bolts evenly to the specified torque wrench setting.
16 When reconnecting the downpipe to the manifold, smear a little exhaust jointing paste onto the flange prior to connection. This will ensure a good seal at the joint.

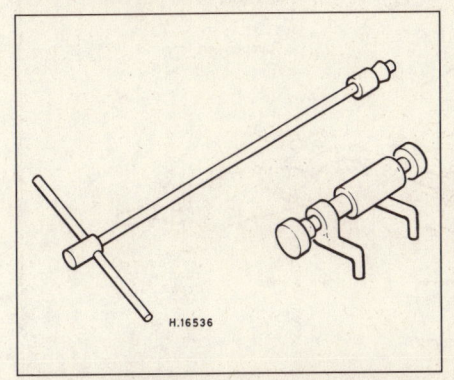

24 Exhaust system - checking, removal and refitting

1 The exhaust system should be examined for leaks, damage and security every 10 000 miles (15 000 km). To do this, apply the handbrake and allow the engine to idle. Check the full length of the exhaust system for leaks from each side of the car in turn while an assistant temporarily places a wad of cloth over the tail pipe. If a leak is discovered stop the engine and use a proprietary repair kit to repair it. Check the rubber mountings for deterioration (photos).
2 On 1.6 and 1.8 litre models it should be noted that if the exhaust system is to be separated at the manifold/downpipe connection, a special VW tool will be necessary to release and subsequently refit the joint retaining clips. Without this tool (VW No 3049A) it is virtually impossible to separate and reassemble the joint without distorting the retaining clips. In view of this, removal and refitting of the system will necessitate detachment of the manifold and front pipe section, or manifold and system complete, and taking the assembly to your VW dealer to separate/reassemble the front joint. If the complete system is in need of replacement it is probably best entrusted to your VW dealer.
3 The exhaust systems are shown in Figs. 3.35 and 3.36.

4 Before doing any dismantling work on the exhaust system, wait until the system has cooled down and then saturate the fixing bolts and joints with a proprietary anti-corrosion fluid.
5 When refitting the system, new nuts and bolts should be used, and it may be found easier to cut through the old bolts with a hacksaw, rather than unscrew them.
6 When removing any part of the exhaust system on 1.05 and 1.3 litre models it is usually easier to undo the manifold-to-front pipe joint and remove the complete system from the car, then separate the various pieces of the system, or cut out the defective part, using a hacksaw.
7 Refit the system a section at a time starting at the front. If the manifold has been removed its gasket must be renewed.
8 Before assembly, smear all joints with a proprietary exhaust sealing compound. This makes it easier to slide the pieces to align them and ensures that the joints will be gas tight. Leave all bolts loose.
9 Run the engine until the exhaust system is at normal temperature and then, with the engine running at idling speed, tighten all the mounting bolts and clips, starting at the manifold and working towards the rear silencer. *Take care to avoid touching any part of the system with bare hands because of the danger of painful burns.*
10 When the bolts and clips are tightened, it is important to ensure that there is no strain on any part of the system

Fig. 3.34 VW special tool number 3049A used to release/fit the exhaust downpipes to manifold clips on the 1.6 and 1.8 litre models (Sec 24)

24.1A Check the exhaust system rubber mountings

24.1B Check the exhaust system joints for leaks and security

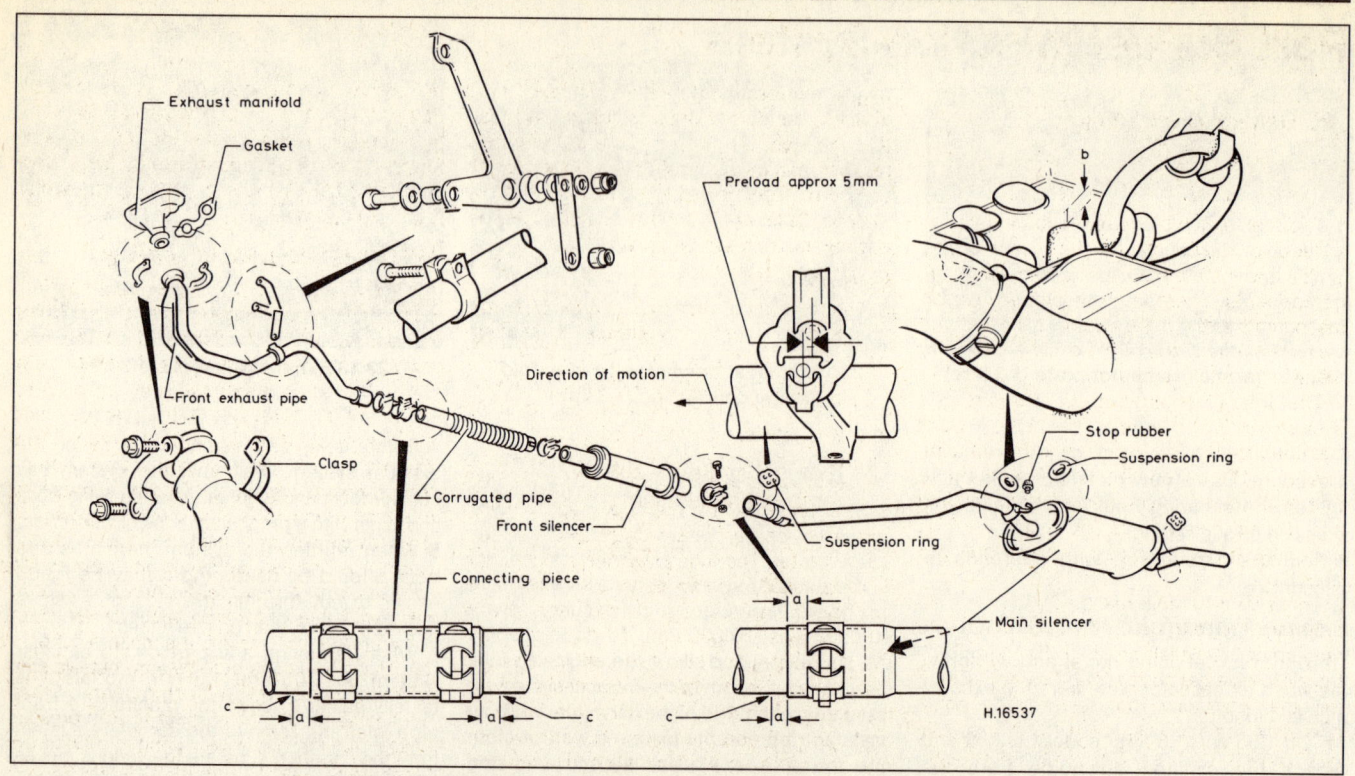

3•20 Fuel and exhaust systems – carburettor-based system

Fig. 3.35 Exhaust system and associated components – 1.5 and 1.3 litre (Sec 24)
Connecting piece and clamp setting dimensions
(a) = 5 mm (0.20 in)   (b) = 12 mm (0.50 in)   (c) Marking (S)

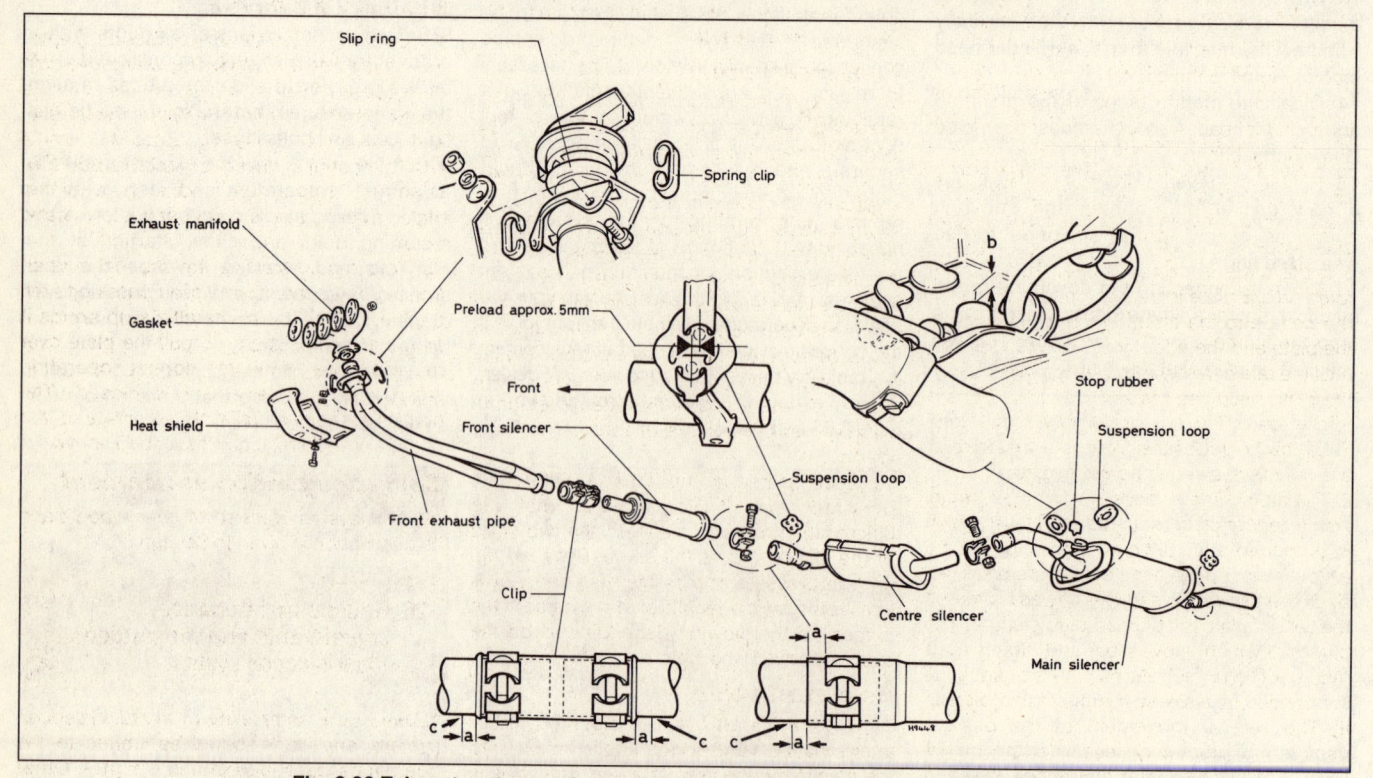

Fig. 3.36 Exhaust system and associated components – 1.6 and 1.8 litre (Sec 24)
Connecting piece and clamp setting dimensions
a = 5 mm (0.20 in)   b = 12 mm (0.50 in)   c Marking (S for manual gearbox or A for automatic transmission)

Part B: Fuel Injection System

25 General description

1 The fuel injection system is known as the K-Jetronic. The principle of the system is very simple and there are no specialised electronic components. There is an electrically driven fuel pump and there are electrical sensors and switches, but these are no different from those in general use on cars.

2 The following paragraphs describe the system and its various elements. Later Sections describe the tests which can be carried out to ascertain whether a particular unit is functioning correctly, but dismantling and repair procedures of units are not generally given because repairs are not possible.

3 The system measures the amount of air entering the engine and determines the amount of fuel which needs to be mixed with the air to give the correct combustion mixture for the particular conditions of engine operation. The fuel is sprayed continuously by an injection nozzle to the inlet port of each cylinder. This fuel and air is drawn into the cylinder when the inlet valves open.

Airflow meter

4 This measures the volume of air entering the engine and relies on the principle that a circular disc, when placed in a funnel through which a current of air is passing, will rise until the weight of the disc is equal to the force on its lower surface which the air creates. If the volume of air is increased, and the plate were to remain in the same place, the rate of flow of air through the gap between the cone and the plate would increase and the force on the plate would increase.

5 If the plate is free to move, then, as the force on the plate increases, the plate rises in the cone and the area between the edge of the plate and the edge of the cone increases, until the rate of air flow and hence the force on the plate becomes the same as it was at the former lower flow rate and smaller cone area. Thus the height of the plate is a measure of the volume of air entering the engine.

6 The airflow meter consists of an air funnel with a sensor plate mounted on a lever which is supported at its fulcrum. The weight of the airflow sensor plate and its lever are balanced by a counterweight and the upward force on the sensor plate is opposed by a plunger. The plunger, which moves up and down as a result of the variations in air flow, is surrounded by a sleeve having vertical slots in it. The vertical movement of the plunger uncovers a greater or lesser length of the slots, which meters the fuel to the injection valves.

7 The sides of the air funnel are not a pure cone because optimum operation of the engine requires a different air/fuel ratio under different conditions such as idling, part load and full load. By making parts of the funnel steeper than the basic shape, a richer mixture can be provided for, at idling and full load. By making the funnel flatter than the basic shape, a leaner mixture can be provided.

Fuel supply

8 The rear-mounted fuel pump operates continuously while the engine is running, excess fuel being returned to the fuel tank. The fuel pump is operated when the ignition switch is in the START position, but once the starter is released a switch, connected to the air plate, prevents the pump from operating unless the engine is running.

9 The fuel line to the fuel supply valve incorporates a filter and also a fuel accumulator. The function of the accumulator is to maintain pressure in the fuel system after the engine has been switched off and so give good hot restarting.

10 Associated with the fuel accumulator is a pressure regulator which is an integral part of the fuel metering device. When the engine is switched off, the pressure regulator lets the pressure to the injection valves fall rapidly to cut off the fuel flow through them and so prevent the engine from 'dieseling' or 'running on'. The valve closes at just below the opening pressure of the injector valves and this pressure is then maintained by the Pressure accumulator.

Fuel distributor

11 The fuel distributor is mounted on the air metering device and is controlled by the vertical movement of the airflow sensor plate. It consists of a spool valve which moves vertically in a sleeve, the sleeve having as many vertical slots around its circumference as there are cylinders on the engine.

12 The spool valve is adjusted to hydraulic pressure on the upper end and this balances the pressure on the air plate which is applied to the bottom of the valve by a plunger. As the spool valve rises and falls, it uncovers a greater or lesser length of metering slot and so controls the volume of fuel fed to each injector.

13 Each metering slot has a differential pressure valve, which ensures that the difference in pressure between the two sides of the slot is always the same. Because the drop in pressure across the metering slot is unaffected by the length of slot exposed, the amount of fuel flowing depends only on the exposed area of the slots.

Cold start valve

14 The cold start valve is mounted in the intake manifold and sprays additional fuel into the manifold during cold starting. The valve is solenoid operated and is controlled by a thermotime switch in the engine cooling system. The thermotime switch is actuated for a period which depends upon coolant temperature, the period decreasing with rise in coolant temperature. If the coolant temperature is high enough for the engine not to need additional fuel for starting, the switch does not operate.

Warm-up regulator (valve)

15 While warming up, the engine needs a richer mixture to compensate for fuel which condenses on the cold walls of the inlet manifold and cylinder walls. It also needs more fuel to compensate for power lost because of increased friction losses and increased oil drag in a cold engine. The mixture is made richer during warming up by the warm-up regulator. This is a pressure regulator which lowers the pressure applied to the control plunger of the fuel regulator during warm-up. This reduced pressure causes the airflow plate to rise higher than it would do otherwise, thus uncovering a greater length of metering slot and making the mixture richer.

16 The valve is operated by a bi-metallic strip which is heated by an electric heater. When the engine is cold the bi-metallic strip presses against the delivery valve spring to reduce the pressure on the diaphragm and enlarge the discharge cross-section. This increase in cross-section results in a lowering of the pressure fed to the control plunger.

Auxiliary air device

17 Compensation for power lost by greater friction is achieved by feeding a larger volume of fuel/air mixture to the engine than is supplied by the normal opening of the throttle. The auxiliary air device bypasses the throttle with a channel having a variable aperture valve in it. The aperture is varied by a pivoted plate controlled by a spring and a bi-metallic strip.

18 During cold starting the channel is open and increases the volume of air passing to the engine, but as the bi-metallic strip bends it allows a control spring to pull the plate over the aperture until at normal operating temperature the aperture is closed. The heating of the bi-metallic strip is similar to that of the warm-up regulator described above.

Cold acceleration enrichment

19 This system is fitted to later models and its description is given in Section 36.

26 Routine maintenance, adjustments and precautions - fuel injection system

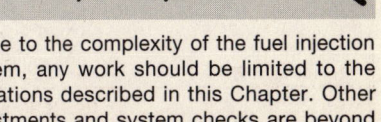

1 Due to the complexity of the fuel injection system, any work should be limited to the operations described in this Chapter. Other adjustments and system checks are beyond the scope of most readers and should be left to your VW dealer.

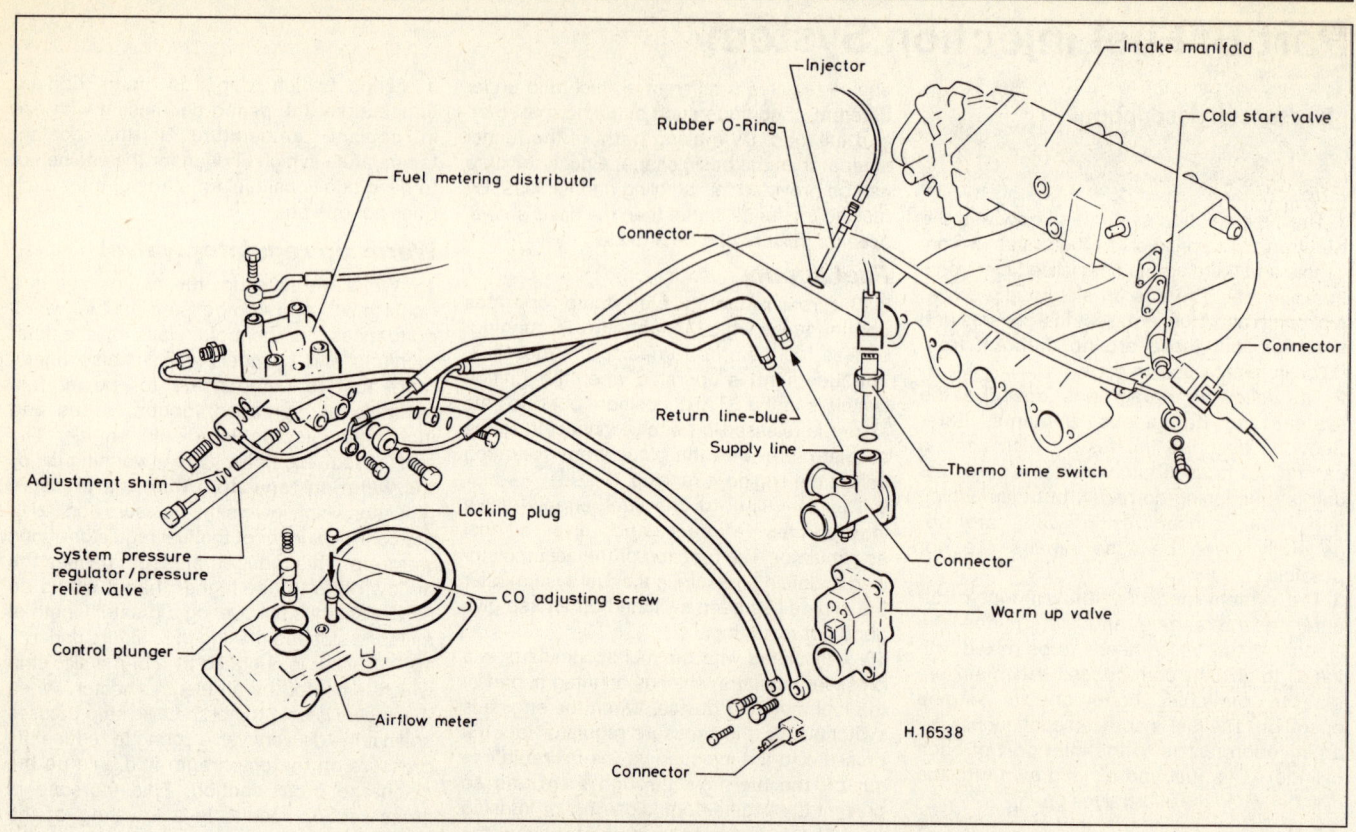

3•22 Fuel and exhaust systems – fuel injection system

Fig. 3.37 Fuel injection system air intake components (Sec 27)

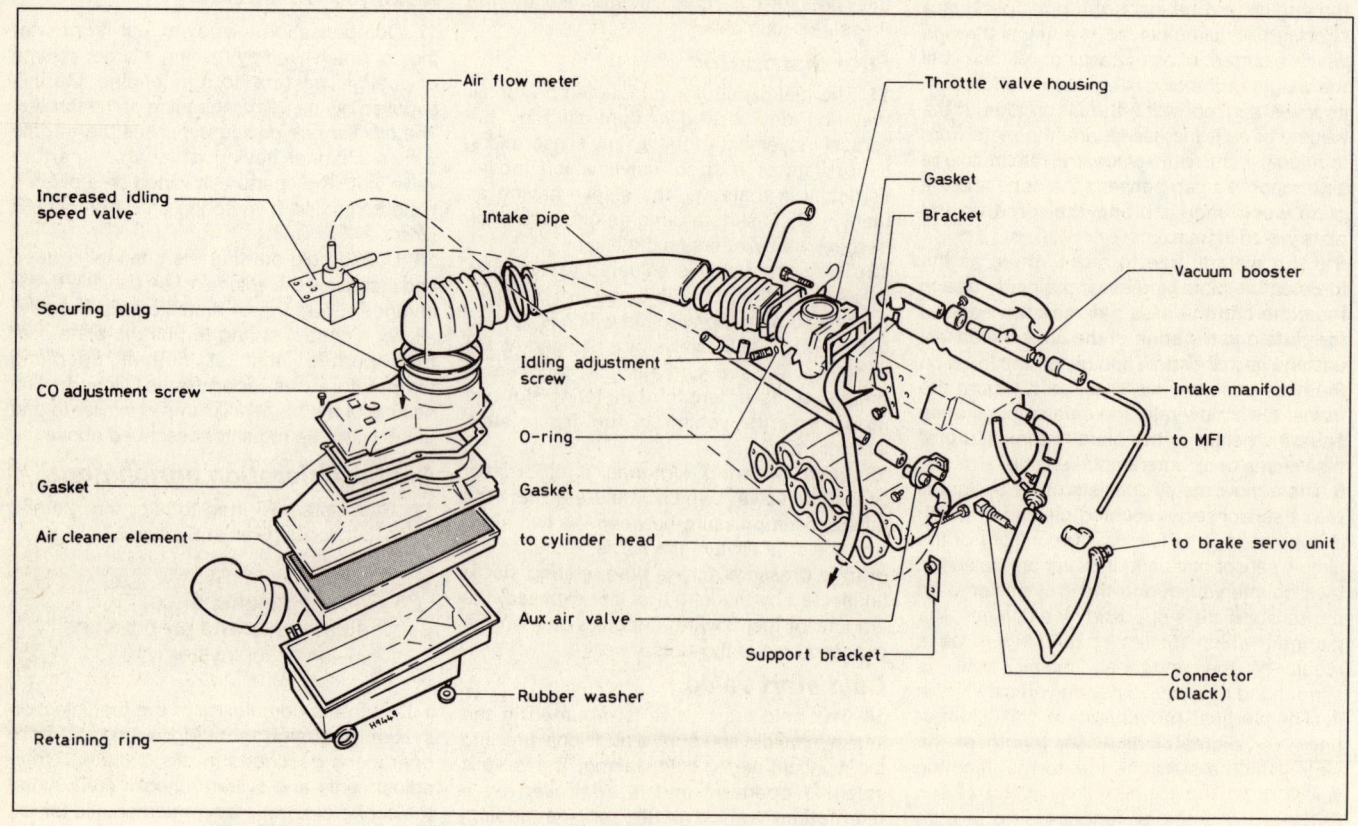

Fig. 3.38 Air cleaner, inlet manifold and associated components – fuel injection system (Sec 27)

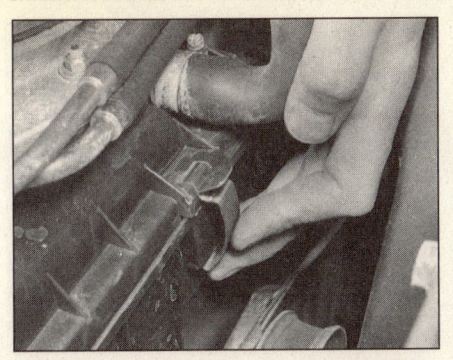

Fuel and exhaust systems – fuel injection system 3•23

27.1 Release the air cleaner retaining clips

27.2 Air cleaner element withdrawal

2 The mixture setting is preset during production of the car and should not normally require adjustment. If new components of the system have been fitted, however, the mixture can be adjusted after reference to Section 31.
3 The only adjustment which may be needed is to vary the engine idle speed by means of the screw mounted in the throttle housing. Use the screw to set the engine speed to that specified when the engine is at the normal operating temperature.
4 Routine servicing of the fuel injection system consists of checking the system components for condition and security, and renewing the air cleaner element at the specified intervals (see Routine Maintenance).
5 Check the system vacuum components for condition and security.
6 In the event of a malfunction in the system, reference should be made to the Fault finding Section at the end of this Chapter, but first make a basic check of the system hoses, connections, fuses and relays for any obvious and immediately visible defects.
7 If any part of the system has to be disconnected or removed for any reason, particular care must be taken to ensure that no dirt is allowed to enter the system.
8 The system is normally pressurised, irrespective of engine temperature, and care must therefore be taken when disconnecting fuel lines; the ignition must be off and the battery disconnected.
9 Before disconnecting any fuel lines, it is advisable to release the pressure in the system by slowly loosening the fuel feed pipe at the warm-up valve and absorb any fuel leakage in a cloth. Remember to retighten the feed pipe connection on completion.

27 Air cleaner element - removal, cleaning/renewal and refitting

1 Release the spring clips securing the air cleaner cover and separate the cover from the airflow meter (photo).
2 Withdraw the element from the housing (photo).
3 If cleaning the element, place well away from the vehicle then tap the air cleaner element to remove dust and dirt. If necessary use a soft brush to clean the outside or blow air at a very low pressure from the inside surface towards the outside.
4 Wipe clean the inside of the cover.
5 Refit the element and secure the cover by pressing the clips.

28 Idle speed - adjustment

1 Run the engine until the oil temperature is at least 80°C (176°F), but do not let the engine coolant temperature rise above normal as the electric radiator fan will run and this should not be operating when checking or adjusting the idle speed.
2 Check the ignition timing and adjust if necessary, as described in Chapter 4.
3 The main headlights should be turned on (except air conditioned models). Disconnect and plug the crankcase breather hose from the valve cover.
4 Where air conditioning is fitted, the system must be switched off during checking and adjustment.
5 If the injector pipes have been disconnected, or possibly renewed, and reconnected just prior to checking and adjustment of the idle speed, run the engine speed up to 3000 rpm a few times and then let it idle for a minimum period of two minutes before checking/adjusting the idle speed.

28.6 Idle speed adjustment screw location in the throttle valve housing (arrowed)

6 If adjustment to the idle speed is necessary, remove the locking cap from the adjustment screw on the throttle assembly and turn the screw to achieve the idle speed given in the Specifications (photo). The adjustments should be made only when the electric radiator fan is stationary.
7 If an exhaust gas analyser is available, check the CO reading and compare it with the specified figure. If necessary adjust the idle mixture as described in Section 31.
8 Air conditioned models will also be fitted with an increased idle speed valve and, in some instances, a second idle speed boost valve as well. To check these, refer to Section 29 or 30 as applicable.

29 Increased idling speed valve (air conditioned models) - checking

1 Start and run the engine at its normal idle speed.
2 With the air conditioner switched off, pinch the hose at the increased idle speed valve (photo). The engine speed should not change.
3 Switch the air conditioning system on and then repeat the test. This time the engine speed should drop. If these tests prove the valve to be faulty it must be renewed.
4 Disconnect the hose, unclip and detach the wiring connector then unbolt and remove the valve from its support bracket.
5 Refit in the reverse order of removal.

30 Idle speed boost (air conditioned models) - checking and adjustment

1 The function of this device is to stabilize the engine speed when it drops below 700 rpm under certain operating conditions. This is achieved by increasing the air supply to the engine which raises the idling speed to approximately 1050 rpm. At this point the air supply valve is cut off and the idle speed then returns to normal. The two valves which control this system are attached to the right-hand front suspension mounting in the engine compartment (Fig. 3.39).

29.2 Increased idling speed valve (air conditioned models)

3•24 Fuel and exhaust systems – fuel injection system

Fig. 3.39 Idle speed boost valve check (Sec 30)

1 Valve No 1   2 Valve No 2   3 Hose

2 Valve number 1 (on the inboard side) increases the engine speed when it drops below 700 rpm, whilst valve number 2 (on the outboard side) increases the idle speed when the air conditioner is switched on.

Valve number 1 - checking and idle speed adjustment

3 Run the engine up to its normal operating temperature, switch off the air conditioner and allow the engine to idle. With the exception of the air conditioner, switch on all electrical consumers (lights, etc), then adjust the idle speed to 700 rpm (see Section 28). When reaching the idle speed, the valve should open and the idle speed increase. Use a pair of pliers and pinch the air hose from the valve and check that the speed drops.
4 Switch off the electrical consumers. Pinch the air hose again and adjust the idle speed to that specified. When the correct idle speed is reached, unclamp the hose. The idle speed should then increase up to about 1050 rpm at which point the valve will close and the speed drop to the specified idle speed setting.

Valve number 2 - checking

5 Run the engine at its normal idle speed with the air conditioner switched off. Pinch the air hose and check that the engine speed remains the same.
6 Now switch the air conditioning on and repeat the test. When the hose is pinched the engine speed should drop.

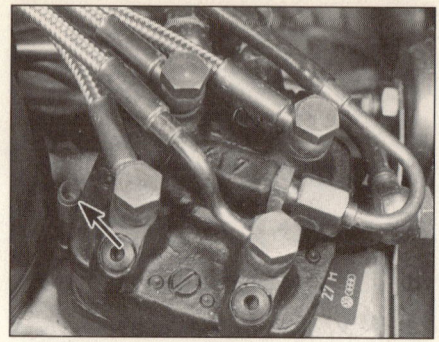

31.2 Idle CO adjustment screw location (arrowed)

7 If the air hose and/or valves number 1 or 2 are disconnected or removed for any reason, it is important when refitting to note that the three-way hose connector large hole must go to valve number 2.

31 Idle mixture - adjustment

Note: accurate idle mixture adjustment can only be made using an exhaust gas analyser

1 The idle CO adjustment screw alters the height of the fuel metering distributor plunger relative to the air control plate of the air flow meter.
2 The screw is accessible by removing the locking plug from between the air duct scoop and the fuel metering distributor on the airflow meter casing (photo).
3 Although a special tool is recommended for this adjustment, it can be made using a long, thin screwdriver.
4 Ensure that the engine is running under the same conditions as those necessary for adjusting the idling speed (see previous Sections, as applicable) and that the idling speed is correct.
5 Connect an exhaust gas analyser to the tailpipe, as directed by the equipment manufacturer, and read the CO level.
6 Turn the adjusting screw clockwise to raise the percentage of CO and anti-clockwise to lower it. It is important that the adjustment is

32.8 Accelerator cable adjuster and support bracket

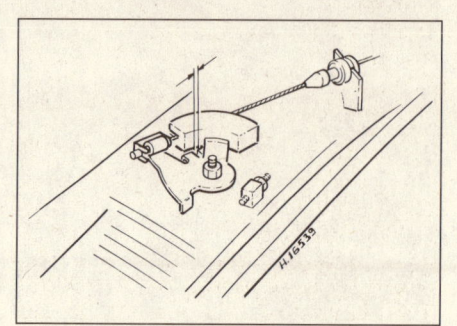

Fig. 3.40 Accelerator cable clearance (1 mm) at full throttle position (Sec 32)

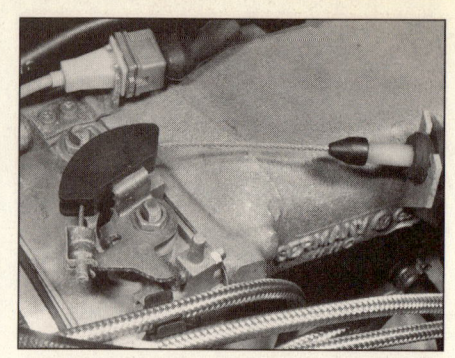

32.2 Accelerator cable connection to the throttle valve

made without pressing down on the adjusting screw, because this will move the airflow sensor plate and affect the adjustment.
7 Remove the tool, accelerate the engine briefly and re-check. If the tool is not removed before the engine is accelerated there is a danger of the tool becoming jammed and getting bent.
8 Recheck that the idle speed is correct and further adjust this if necessary (see previous Sections) to complete.
9 When reconnection of the crankcase ventilation hose results in an increase in the CO content, the engine oil is diluted with fuel and should be renewed. Alternatively, if an oil change is not due, a long fast drive will reduce the amount of fuel in the oil.

32 Accelerator cable - removal, refitting and adjustment

1 Disconnect the battery earth lead.
2 Prise free the inner cable retaining clip from the throttle valve control on the throttle valve housing (photo).
3 Release the inner cable from the control quadrant and the outer cable from the location/adjustment bracket on top of the inlet manifold.
4 Prise free and remove the plastic cover from the top of the bulkhead trough.
5 Working inside the car, remove the lower facia panel on the driver's side.
6 Unclip the inner cable from the accelerator pedal, then withdraw the complete cable into the engine compartment, together with the rubber grommets.
7 Refitting is a reversal of removal, but ensure that the cable run is not kinked and is correctly aligned, then adjust the cable.
8 The accelerator cable is adjusted by getting an assistant to fully depress the accelerator pedal whilst the cable position is set at the throttle valve housing end. When the throttle valve is fully open there should be a 1.0 mm (0.040 in) clearance between the throttle valve lever and the stop (Fig. 3.40). Adjust by altering the cable retainer position at the location/adjustment bracket (photo).

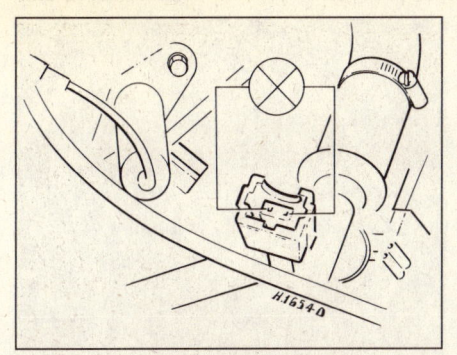

Fuel and exhaust systems – fuel injection system 3•25

Fig. 3.41 Cold start valve check test lamp connections (Sec 33)

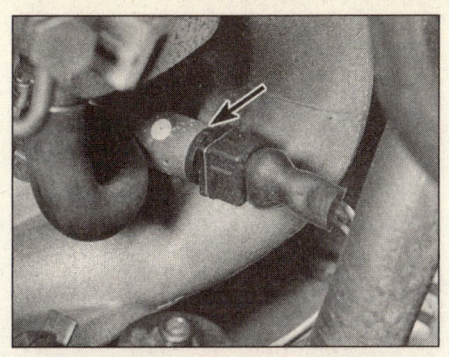

34.2 Auxiliary air valve (arrowed)

33 Cold start valve and thermotime switch - checking

1 The thermotime switch energises the cold start valve for a short time on starting and the time for which the valve is switched on depends upon the engine temperature.
2 This check must only be carried out when the coolant temperature is below 30°C (86°F).
3 Pull the connector off the cold start valve and connect a test lamp across the contacts of the connector (Fig. 3.41).
4 Pull the high tension lead off the centre of the distributor and connect the lead to earth.
5 Pull the connector from the thermotime switch then connect an extension lead from earth to the thermotime switch W terminal (green and white wire). The red and black wire **must not** be earthed.
6 Operate the starter and check that the test lamp lights up. If it doesn't, then there is an open circuit which must be located and repaired.
7 To check the cold start valve, leave the thermotime switch W terminal earthed, remove the cold start valve and re-attach its connector. Take care not to break the gasket when withdrawing the cold start valve from the inlet manifold.
8 With fuel line and electrical connections connected to the valve, hold the valve over a glass jar and operate the starter for 10 seconds. The cold start valve should produce an even cone of spray during the time the thermotime switch is on.
9 Wipe dry the cold start valve nozzle with a clean non-fluffy cloth, then check that the valve does not drip or its body become damp over a period of one minute. If proved defective, renew the valve.
10 To check the thermotime switch, proceed as described in paragraphs 3 to 4 inclusive; the coolant should be at 30°C (86°F). If the switch needs to be cooled down to the temperature specified, remove it and immerse its base in cold water. When cooled, earth the switch to make the test.
11 Operate the starter for 10 seconds. The test lamp should light immediately and stay on for three seconds.
12 Refit the high tension lead onto the distributor, and reconnect the lead to the cold start valve.

34 Auxiliary air valve - checking

1 To carry out this test the engine coolant temperature must be below 30°C (86°F). Detach the distributor HT lead.
2 Detach the auxiliary air valve electrical plug and ensure that the contacts in the plug connector are in good condition (photo).
3 Connect up a voltmeter across the contacts of the plug connectors, start the engine and run at idle speed. The voltage reading must be a minimum of 11.6V. If a voltmeter is not available a test lamp check will suffice to check the voltage supply.
4 With the auxiliary air valve electrical plug still detached, leave the engine running at idle speed and pinch the air intake duct-to-auxiliary valve hose. The engine speed should drop.
5 When the engine is warmed up to its normal operating temperature, reconnect the auxiliary valve plug then pinch the hose again. This time the engine speed should remain unaltered.

35.2 Warm-up valve

35 Warm-up valve - checking

1 Detach the distributor HT lead and earth it.
2 With the engine cold, detach the wiring connector from the warm-up valve (photo).
3 Connect a voltmeter across the terminals of the warm-up valve connector and operate the starter. The voltage across the terminals should be a minimum of 11.5 volts.
4 Switch the ignition off and connect an ohmmeter across the terminals of the warm-up valve (Fig. 3.42). If the meter does not indicate a resistance of about 20 to 26 ohm, the heater coil is defective and a new valve must be fitted.

36 Cold acceleration enrichment system - description and checking

1 When the engine is cold (below 35°C/95°F), acceleration is improved by briefly richening the fuel mixture for a period of approximately 0.4 seconds. This cold acceleration enrichment will only operate if the thermotime switch, the diaphragm pressure switch and the throttle valve switch are shut off.
2 To check the system first check that the cold start valve is operational (Section 32).
3 Detach the wiring connector from the cold start valve and connect up a test lamp to its terminals.
4 Detach the wiring connector from the thermotime switch and connect a length of wire between an earth point and the connector number two terminal W (with the green and white wire). **Do not** earth the G terminal (red and black wire).
5 Run the engine and allow it to idle. The test lamp should not light up, but when the engine

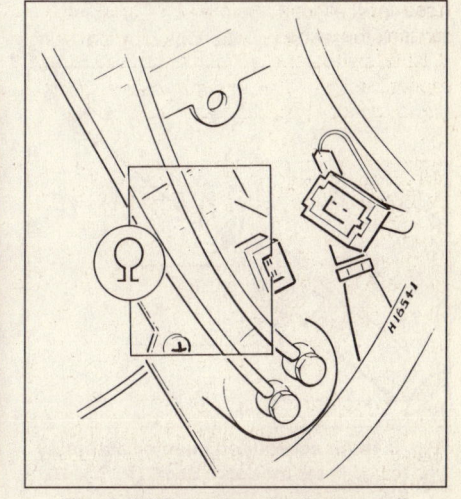

Fig. 3.42 Warm-up valve heater coil resistance test (Sec 35)

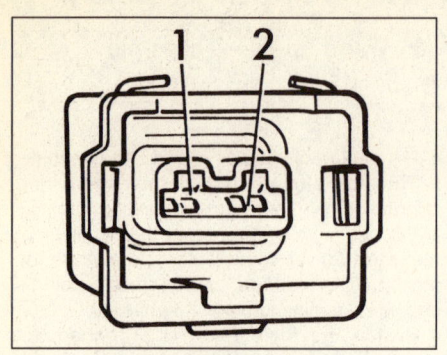

3•26 Fuel and exhaust systems – fuel injection system

Fig. 3.43 Cold acceleration enrichment system check (Sec 36)

Cold start valve connector earth contact (2) (green/white wire to W terminal)
Do not earth contact 1

Fig. 3.44 Diaphragm pressure switch test (Sec 36)

1 Diaphragm pressure switch
2 Vacuum connection for switch (yellow)
3 Vacuum connection for spark control

Fig. 3.45 Throttle valve switch check (Sec 36)

1 Throttle valve switch
a = 0.2 to 0.6 mm (0.08 to 0.24 in)

is quickly accelerated the test lamp should light up briefly (0.4 seconds) (Fig. 3.43).
6 If a fault is evident, check the wiring connections, the throttle valve switch and the diaphragm pressure switch.
7 The diaphragm pressure switch can be checked using an ohmmeter. Detach the wiring connector from the end of the diaphragm pressure switch, then start the engine and allow it to idle. Using the ohmmeter, check the resistance reading between the contacts. An infinity reading should be given.
8 Accelerate the engine briefly and check that the resistance drops briefly and then returns to infinity. (Fig. 3.44).
9 To check the throttle valve switch, detach the switch lead connector and measure the resistance between the switch contacts. An infinity reading should be given.
10 Now slowly open the throttle valve to the point where the switch is heard to operate (it will click at this point). The ohmmeter should give a 0 ohm reading and the clearance between the throttle lever and the idle stop must be between 0.2 to 0.6 mm (0.008 to 0.024 in) see Fig. 3.45.
11 If necessary adjust the switch by loosening the switch (underside of throttle housing) and positioning a feeler gauge blade of 0.4 mm (0.016 in) thickness between the lever and stop. Move the switch towards the lever until the point where the switch is heard to operate, then retighten the switch and check the adjustment.
12 If the throttle valve switch is being removed, prise the connector bracket apart to release the connector.

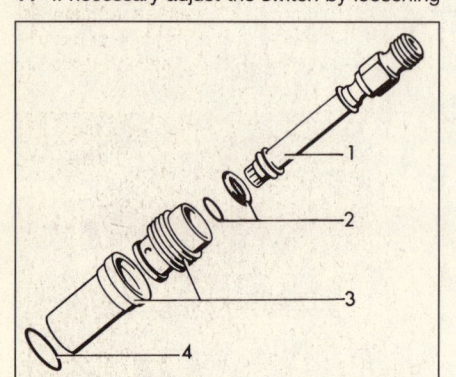

37 Fuel injectors - checking

1 The injector may give trouble for one of four reasons. The spray may be irregular in shape; the nozzle may not close when the engine is shut down, causing flooding when restarting; the nozzle filter may be choked, giving less that the required ration of fuel; or the seal may be damaged, allowing an air leak.
2 To remove an injector for inspection, simply pull it free.
3 Inspect the rubber seal and, if it shows any signs of cracking, distortion or perishing, it must be renewed. If found to be defective check the other injector seals, as they are likely to be in similar condition.
4 To check the performance of an injector, specialised tools are required for an accurate test. However, a basic check can be made as follows.
5 Hold the injector in a suitable measuring glass and plug up the injector location hole. Start the engine and let it idle on three cylinders and look at the shape of the spray. It should be of a symmetrical cone shape. If it is not the injector must be changed because the vibrator pin is damaged or the spring is broken. Shut off the engine and wait for 15 seconds. There must be no leak or dribble from the nozzle. If there is, the injector must be renewed, as dribble will cause flooding and difficult starting.
6 The injector cannot be dismantled for cleaning. If an injector is removed from the line the new one should be fitted and the union tightened to the specified torque.
7 When inserting the injector, lubricate the seal with petrol before fitting.

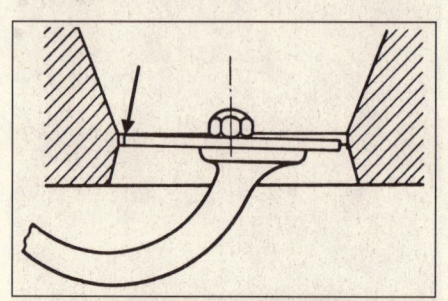

38 Airflow sensor plate and control plunger - checking

1 For the correct mixture to be supplied to the engine it is essential that the sensor plate is central in the venturi and that its height is correct. First run the engine for a period of about one minute.

Fig. 3.46 Air schrouded injector assembly (later models) (Sec 37)

1 Injector   3 Injector insert
2 Rubber rings   4 Washer

Fig. 3.47 Sensor plate position requirement (Sec 38)

Upper edge of plate (arrowed) must be flush with bottom of air cone

38.2 Top view of the airflow sensor plate

Fuel and exhaust systems – fuel injection system 3•27

38.6 Airflow sensor plate adjustment clip (arrowed)

2 Loosen the hose clips at each end of the air scoop and remove the scoop. If the sensor plate appears to be off-centre, loosen its centre screw and carefully run a 0.10 mm (0.004 in) feeler gauge round the edge of the plate to centralise it, then re-tighten the bolt (photo).
3 Raise the airflow sensor plate and then quickly move it to its rest position. No resistance should be felt on the downward movement; if there is resistance, the airflow meter is defective and a new one must be fitted.
4 If the sensor plate can be moved downwards easily, but has a strong resistance to upward movement, the control plunger is sticking. Remove the fuel distributor (Section 39) and clean the control plunger in fuel. If this does not cure the problem, a new fuel distributor must be fitted.
5 Release the pressure on the fuel distributor, as described in Section 39, and then check the rest position of the airflow sensor plate. The upper edge of the plate should be flush with the bottom edge of the air cone. It is permissible for the plate to be lower than the edge by not more than 0.5 mm (0.020 in), but if higher, or lower than the permissible limit, the plate must be adjusted.
6 Adjust the height of the plate by lifting it and bending the wire clips attaching the plate to the balance arm, but take care not to scratch or damage the surface of the air cone (photo).
7 After making the adjustment tighten the warm-up valve union and check the idle speed and CO content.

39 Fuel meter distributor - removal and refitting

1 Disconnect the battery terminals.
2 *Ensure that the vehicle is in a well ventilated space and that there are no naked flames or other possible sources of ignition.*
3 While holding a rag over the joint to prevent fuel from being sprayed out, loosen the control pressure line from the warm-up valve. The control pressure line is the one connected to the large union of the valve.
4 Mark each fuel line, and its port on the fuel distributor. Carefully clean all dirt from around

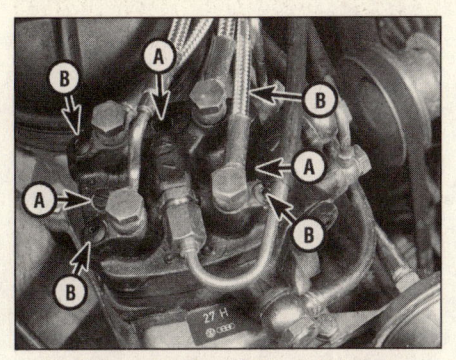

39.6 View showing the fuel distributor retaining screws (A)
Do not remove screws (B)

the fuel unions and distributor ports and then disconnect the fuel lines.
5 Unscrew and remove the connection of the pressure control line to the fuel metering distributor.
6 Remove the locking plug from the CO adjusting screw, then remove the three screws securing the fuel metering distributor (photo).
7 Lift off the fuel metering distributor, taking care that the metering plunger does not fall out. If the plunger does fall out accidentally, clean it in fuel and then re-insert it with its chamfered end downwards.
8 Before refitting the metering distributor, ensure that the plunger moves up and down freely. If the plunger sticks, the distributor must be renewed because the plunger cannot be repaired or replaced separately.
9 Refit the distributor, using a new sealing ring and after tightening the screws, lock them with paint.
10 Refit the fuel lines and the cap of the CO adjusting screw and tighten the union on the warm-up valve.

40 Airflow meter - removal and refitting

1 Remove the fuel lines from the distributor, as described in paragraphs 1 to 5 of the previous Section.

40.3 Airflow meter and fuel distributor unit (inverted)

2 Loosen the clamps at the air cleaner and throttle assembly ends of the air scoop and take off the air scoop.
3 Remove the bolts securing the airflow meter to the air cleaner and lift off the airflow meter and fuel metering distributor (photo).
4 The fuel metering plunger should be prevented from falling out when the fuel metering distributor is removed from the airflow meter (see previous Section).
5 Refitting is the reverse of removing, but it is necessary to use a new gasket between the airflow meter and the air cleaner.

41 Pressure relief valve - removal, servicing and refitting

1 Release the pressure in the fuel system, as described in paragraphs 1 to 3 of Section 39.
2 Unscrew the non-return valve plug and remove the plug and its sealing washer.
3 Take out the O-ring, plunger and O-ring, in that order.
4 When refitting the assembly, use new O-rings and ensure that all
the shims which were removed are refitted. The number of shims fitted determine the system operating pressure. If for any reason the system pressure is suspect, it will be necessary to have a pressure check made by your VW dealer who should have the pressure gauge needed to check the pressure in the system. He will know the amount of shims required to correct the pressure should it be necessary.

42 Fuel lift pump - checking, removal and refitting

1 This is attached to the base of the fuel gauge sender unit fitted to the fuel tank (Fig. 3.49).
2 If this pump is suspected of malfunction, first check that pump wiring does not have an open circuit. Remove the luggage compartment floor covering and the circular cover in

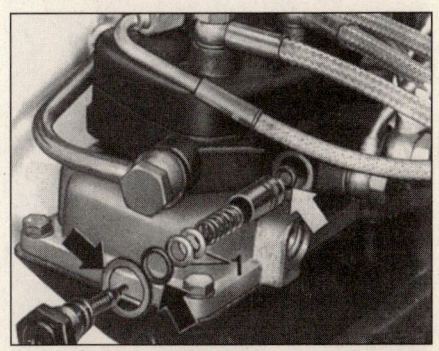

Fig. 3.48 Pressure relief valve components (Sec 41)

1 Shims   Arrows indicate O-rings

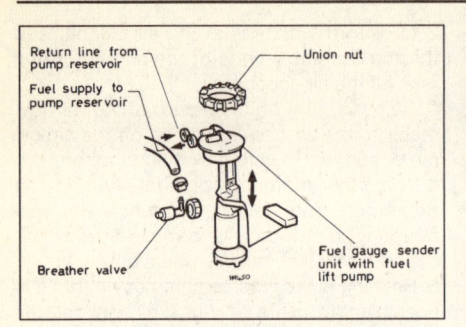

3•28 Fuel and exhaust systems – fuel injection system

Fig. 3.49 Fuel tank sender unit – fuel injection system (Sec 42)

The tank and other associated components are identical to those used for carburettor engines (Fig. 3.5)

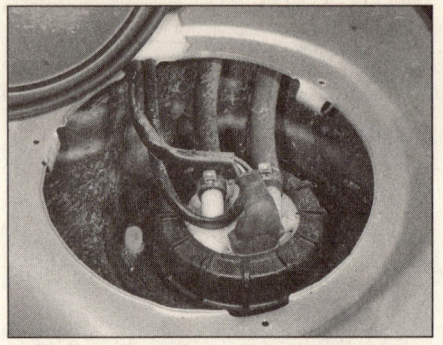

42.2 Fuel tank sender unit and connections

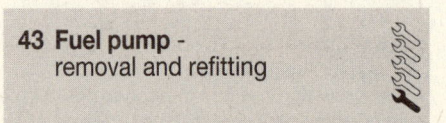

43.1 Fuel pump location and connections viewed from rear

the floor for access to the sender unit and connections. Detach the wiring connector and make a continuity check between the centre wires and the outer (brown) wire of the connector (photo).

3 If the wiring proves correct, then check the pump relay and the pump fuse (number 5). Assuming the fuse to be in order, check the relay by first detaching the Hall sender connector from the distributor (ignition).

4 Remove the fusebox and relay plate cover then pull free the pump relay from position 2.

5 Using a voltmeter, switch on the ignition and check the voltage reading between contact numbers 2 and earth, between contact numbers 2 and 1 and contacts 4 and 1. In each case battery voltage should show. Finally check the voltage between contacts 5 and 1; battery voltage should show.

6 Check that when the central connector wire is earthed briefly, there is a voltage drop. If the voltage does not drop on this test, check the ignition (TCI/H switch) unit. If the voltage does drop, renew the fuel pump relay. If the problem still persists, have the ignition Hall sender unit checked.

7 If after making the above checks and any repairs necessary, the pump still malfunctions remove the sender unit, as described in Section 9 and detach the pump for renewal.

8 Refitting is a reversal of the removal procedure.

43.4 Disconnect the wiring connector from the fuel pump

43 Fuel pump - removal and refitting

1 The fuel pump is located on the underside of the car, forwards of the fuel tank on the right-hand side, the pump being housed in the pump reservoir (photo).

2 Disconnect the battery earth lead.

3 Raise the car at the rear and support it on axle stands.

4 Prise free the retaining clip and detach the pump wiring connector (photo).

5 Unscrew the damper unit from the rear end of the pump and detach the hose union, noting the washer each side of the union.

6 Undo the retaining nuts and washers and remove the adaptor.

7 Undo the three screws securing the pump retaining ring and withdraw the ring, followed by the pump unit.

8 Remove the O-ring and withdraw the strainer.

9 Refitting is a reversal of the removal procedure. Smear the O-ring with petrol when fitting and check that it does not get distorted when fitting.

10 When fitting the pump, position it so that its lug engages with the slot in the retaining ring.

11 If the pump non-return valve was removed from the rear end of the pump, refit it using a new seal washer. Also use a new seal washer each side of the hose union. Tighten the damper unit to the specified torque.

12 On completion check for any signs of leakage of fuel from the connections when the engine is running.

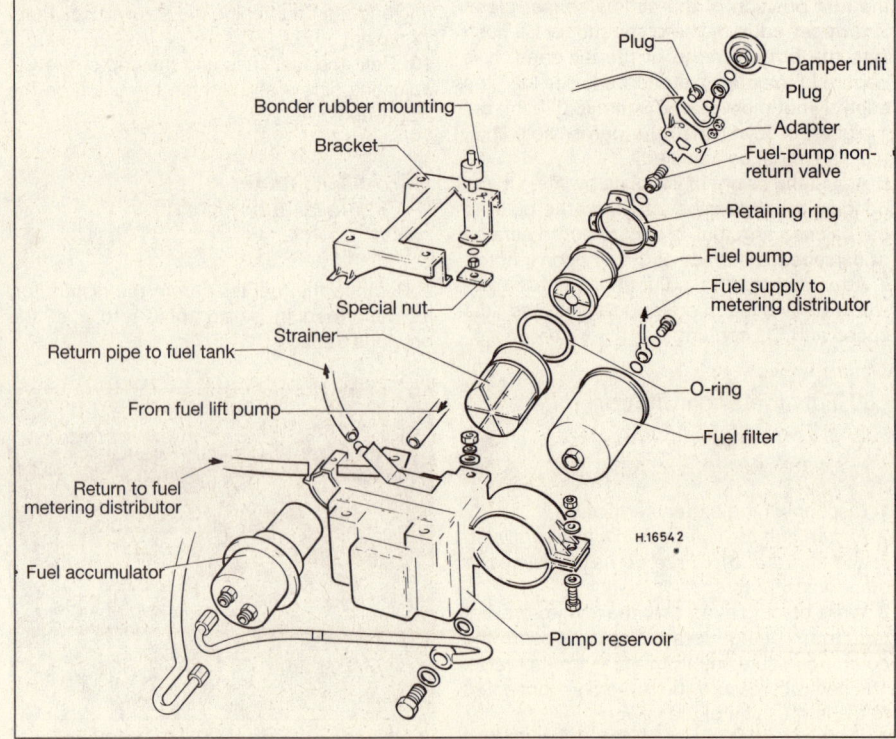

Fig. 3.50 Fuel pump and associated components – fuel injection system (Sec 43)

Fuel and exhaust systems – fuel injection system 3•29

44 Fuel filter – removal and refitting

1 The fuel filter is mounted on the inboard side of the pump reservoir on the underside of the car at the rear just forward of the fuel tank (photo)
2 Disconnect the battery earth lead.
3 Raise the car at the rear and support it on axle stands.
4 At the forward end of the filter, undo the fuel accumulator hose union bolt and detach the union; collecting the washer each side of it.
5 At the rear end of the filter detach the fuel supply hose (to the metering distributor) by undoing the union bolt. Collect the washer each side of the union.
6 Loosen the filter retaining clamp and withdraw the filter.
7 Refitting is a reversal of the removal procedure. Renew the union washers and tighten the union bolts to the specified torque. Check that the arrow on the filter points in the direction of fuel flow.
8 On completion check for any signs of fuel leakage with the engine running.

45 Fuel accumulator – removal and refitting

1 The fuel accumulator is mounted on the outboard side of the fuel pump reservoir on the underside of the car at the rear, just forward of the fuel tank (photo).
2 Disconnect the battery earth lead.
3 Raise the car at the rear and support it on axle stands.
4 Disconnect the fuel pipes from their connections at the front end of the regulator.
5 Undo the clamp bolt and withdraw the accumulator.
6 Refit in the reverse order to removal. Check that the fuel line connections are clean before refitting. Check for fuel leaks on completion with the engine running.

46 Fuel tank and associated components – removal and refitting

1 The fuel tank and associated components can be removed and refitted in the same manner as that described for the carburettor models in Part A of this Chapter.
2 To check the breather valve blow through the hose (dotted arrow in Fig. 3.5) and push the lever in to see if the airflow opens, then shuts off as the lever is released. If defective renew the breather valve.

44.1 Fuel filter unit clamp (A), hose to accumulator (B) and hose to metering valve (C)

47 Inlet manifold – removal and refitting

Access to many of the fastenings and fittings of the manifold, on the bulkhead side in particular, is not good due to the restricted space and close proximity of associated adjacent components, It may therefore be found necessary to at least partially disconnect and remove the engine and gearbox units to gain access to certain items and allow clearance for the removal of the manifold. This being the case, refer to Chapter 1.

1 Disconnect the battery earth lead. Decompress the system as described in Section 39, paragraphs 2 and 3.
2 Disconnect the accelerator cable from the throttle valve and support/adjuster bracket on the manifold (Section 32).
3 Disconnect the wiring connector and the vacuum hose from the auxiliary air valve.
4 Disconnect the wiring and detach the warm-up valve.
5 Undo the hose clips and detach the vacuum hose from the connection on the end of the manifold (left side), and the rear side of the throttle valve housing (photo).
6 Disconnect the vacuum hoses from the front of the throttle housing, noting their connections.
7 Disconnect the injectors and hoses from the cylinder head, release them from the location clips and fold them back out of the way, where they will not get dirty.
8 Unclip and detach the intake ducting from the throttle housing.
9 Remove the bolts and disconnect the support bracket from the accelerator cable support/adjuster bracket and from the cam cover.
10 Disconnect the cam cover-to-inlet manifold breather hose.
11 Undo and remove the inlet manifold retaining bolts then carefully lift the manifold, together with the throttle housing, away from the cylinder head. Disconnect any wiring or hose connections still attached as it is withdrawn.
12 The throttle housing can be unbolted from the manifold and then withdrawn from it.
13 Refitting is a reversal of the removal procedure. Check that the mating faces are clean and use new gaskets. Tighten the securing bolts to the specified torque settings.
14 When reconnecting the accelerator cable, adjust it as described in Section 32.
15 Check that all connections are securely and correctly made before restarting the car.

48 Exhaust manifold – removal and refitting

Before starting to remove the manifold, refer to Section 24, paragraph 2 which concerns details on the special tool required to release and subsequently reconnect the exhaust manifold-to-downpipe securing clips. Unless this tool is available, the manifold is best removed and refitted by your VW dealer.
1 Remove the inlet manifold (Section 47).
2 Removal and refitting of the exhaust manifold is now similar to that described in Section 23 for carburettor variants.

49 Exhaust system

Refer to Section 24.

45.1 Fuel accumulator unit location

47.5 Vacuum hose-to-cylinder connector

Fault finding - fuel system (carburettor models)

Note: *High fuel consumption and poor performance are not necessarily due to carburettor faults. Make sure that the ignition system is properly adjusted, that the brakes are not binding and that the engine is in good mechanical condition before tampering with the carburettor.*

Fuel consumption excessive
- [ ] Air cleaner choked, giving rich mixture
- [ ] Leak from tank, pump or fuel lines
- [ ] Float chamber flooding due to incorrect level or worn needle valve
- [ ] Carburettor incorrectly adjusted
- [ ] Idle speed too high
- [ ] Choke faulty (sticks on)
- [ ] Excessively worn carburettor

Lack of power, stalling or difficult starting
- [ ] Faulty fuel pump
- [ ] Leak on suction side of pump or in fuel line
- [ ] Inlet manifold or carburettor flange gaskets leaking
- [ ] Carburettor incorrectly adjusted
- [ ] Faulty choke

Poor or erratic idling
- [ ] Weak mixture (screw tampered with)
- [ ] Leak in inlet manifold
- [ ] Leak in distributor vacuum pipe
- [ ] Leak in crankcase extractor hose
- [ ] Leak in brake servo hose

Fault finding - fuel system (fuel injection models)

Before assuming that a malfunction is caused by the fuel system, check the items mentioned in the special note at the start of the previous Section.

Engine will not start (cold)
- [ ] Fuel pump faulty
- [ ] Auxiliary air device not opening
- [ ] Start valve not operating
- [ ] Start valve leak
- [ ] Sensor plate rest position incorrect
- [ ] Sensor plate and/or control plunger sticking
- [ ] Vacuum system leak
- [ ] Fuel system leak
- [ ] Thermotime switch remains open

Engine will not start (hot)
- [ ] Faulty fuel pump
- [ ] Warm control pressure low
- [ ] Sensor plate rest position incorrect
- [ ] Sensor plate and/or control plunger sticking
- [ ] Vacuum system leak
- [ ] Fuel system leak
- [ ] Leaky injector valve(s) or low opening pressure
- [ ] Incorrect mixture adjustment

Engine difficult to start (cold)
- [ ] Cold control pressure incorrect
- [ ] Auxiliary air device not opening
- [ ] Faulty start valve
- [ ] Sensor plate rest position faulty
- [ ] Sensor plate and/or control plunger sticking
- [ ] Fuel system leak
- [ ] Thermotime switch not closing

Engine difficult to start (hot)
- [ ] Warm control pressure too high or too low
- [ ] Auxiliary air device faulty
- [ ] Sensor plate/control plunger faulty
- [ ] Fuel or vacuum leak in system
- [ ] Leaky injector valve(s) or low opening pressure
- [ ] Incorrect mixture adjustment

Rough idling (during warm-up period)
- [ ] Incorrect cold control pressure
- [ ] Auxiliary air device not closing (or opening)
- [ ] Start valve leak
- [ ] Fuel or vacuum leak in system
- [ ] Leaky injector valve(s), or low opening pressure

Rough idling (engine warm)
- [ ] Warm control pressure incorrect
- [ ] Auxiliary air device not closing
- [ ] Start valve leaking
- [ ] Sensor plate and/or control plunger sticking
- [ ] Fuel or vacuum leak in system
- [ ] Injector(s) leaking or low opening pressure
- [ ] Incorrect mixture adjustment

Engine backfiring into inlet manifold
- [ ] Warm control pressure high
- [ ] Vacuum system leak

Engine backfiring into exhaust manifold
- [ ] Warm control pressure high
- [ ] Start valve leak
- [ ] Fuel system leak
- [ ] Incorrect mixture adjustment

Engine misfires (on road)
- [ ] Fuel system leak

Engine 'runs on'
- [ ] Sensor plate and or control plunger sticking
- [ ] Injector valve(s) leaking or low opening pressure

Excessive petrol consumption
- [ ] Fuel system leak
- [ ] Mixture adjustment incorrect
- [ ] Low warm control pressure

High CO level at idle
- [ ] Low warm control pressure
- [ ] Mixture adjustment incorrect
- [ ] Fuel system leak
- [ ] Sensor plate and/or control plunger sticking
- [ ] Start valve leak

Low CO level at idle
- [ ] High warm control pressure
- [ ] Mixture adjustment incorrect
- [ ] Start valve leak
- [ ] Vacuum system leak

Idle speed adjustment difficult (too high)
- [ ] Auxiliary air device not closing

Chapter 4 Ignition system

For modifications, and information applicable to later models, see Supplement at end of manual

Contents

Coil - description and testing 13	Fault finding - ignition system . . . . See end of Chapter
Condenser - testing, removal and refitting 5	General discription 1
Contact breaker points - checking and adjustment 3	Ignition timing - checking and adjustment 12
Contact breaker points - renewal 4	Routine maintenance - ignition system 2
Distributor (contact breaker type) - removal, overhaul and refitting 6	Spark plugs and HT leads - general 14
Distributor (transistorized) - dismantling, inspection and	Transistorized ignition Hall sender - testing 9
reassembly 11	Transistorized ignition switch unit - testing 8
Distributor (transistorized) - removal and refitting 10	Transistorized ignition system (TCI-H) - precautions 7

Degrees of difficulty

Easy, suitable for novice with little experience	**Fairly easy,** suitable for beginner with some experience	**Fairly difficult,** suitable for competent DIY mechanic	**Difficult,** suitable for experienced DIY mechanic	**Very difficult,** suitable for expert DIY or professional

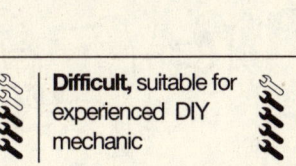

Specifications

General
System type . . . . 12 volt battery and coil, either contact breaker points or transistorized system
Firing order . . . . 1-3-4-2 (No 1 cylinder at crankshaft pulley end)

Coil
	Contact breaker ignition	**Transistorized ignition**
Primary winding resistance	1.7 to 2.1 ohm	0.52 to 0.76 ohm
Secondary winding resistance	7000 to 12 000 ohm	2400 to 3500 ohm

Distributor
Rotor rotation:
  1.05 and 1.3 litre . . . . Anti-clockwise
  1.6 and 1.8 litre . . . . Clockwise
Contact breaker gap (initial setting only) . . . . 0.4 mm (0.016 in)
Dwell angle (1.05, 1.3 and 1.6 litre):
  Setting . . . . 44 to 50° (50 to 56%)
  Wear limit . . . . 42 to 58° (47 to 64%)
Rotor cut-out speed:
  1.05 and 1 3 litre (if applicable) . . . . 6300 to 6700 rpm
  1.6 and 1.8 litre (carburettor engine) . . . . No figures available
  1.8 litre (injection engine) . . . . 6500 to 6900 rpm
Centrifugal advance:
  1.05 litre . . . . Begins at 1100 to 1500 rpm
  1.3 litre . . . . Begins at 1500 to 1900 rpm
  1.6 litre . . . . Begins at 1100 to 1300 rpm
  1.8 litre (carburettor engine) . . . . Begins at 900 to 1100 rpm
  1.8 litre (fuel injection engine) . . . . Begins at 1150 to 1450 rpm

Ignition timing (at idle)
1.05 and 1.3 litre . . . . 4 to 6° BTDC
1.6 and 1.8 litre (carburettor engine) . . . . 17 to 19° BTDC
1.8 litre (fuel injection engine) . . . . 5 to 7° BTDC

Spark plugs
Type:
  1.05 litre . . . . Champion N7YCC or N7YC
  1.3, 1.6, 1.8 litre (to 7/1985) . . . . Champion N7YCC or N7YC
Electrode gap:
  Champion N7YCC and N7BYC . . . . 0.8 mm (0.032 in)
  Champion N7YC . . . . 0.7 mm (0.028 in)

4•2 Ignition system

HT leads

1.05 litre	Champion LS-05 boxed set
1.3, 1.6 and 1.8 litre	Champion LS-07 boxed set

Torque wrench settings

	Nm	lbf ft
Spark plugs	20	15
Distributor clamp bolt:		
1.05 and 1.3 litre	10	7
1.6 and 1.8 litre	25	18

1 General description

The ignition system may be of the conventional contact breaker type or the electronic transistorized type. On 1.05 and 1.3 litre engine variants the distributor is mounted on the left-hand (gearbox) end of the cylinder head and is driven direct from the camshaft. On 1.6 and 1.8 litre engine variants the distributor is mounted at the front (radiator) end of the engine and it is driven by a skew gear in mesh with the intermediate shaft of the engine.

To enable the engine to run correctly, it is necessary for an electrical spark to ignite the fuel/air mixture in the combustion chamber at exactly the right moment in relation to engine speed and load. The ignition system is based on feeding low tension voltage from the battery to the coil, where it is converted to high tension voltage. The high tension voltage is powerful enough to jump the spark plug gap in the cylinders many times a second under high compression, providing that the system is in good condition.

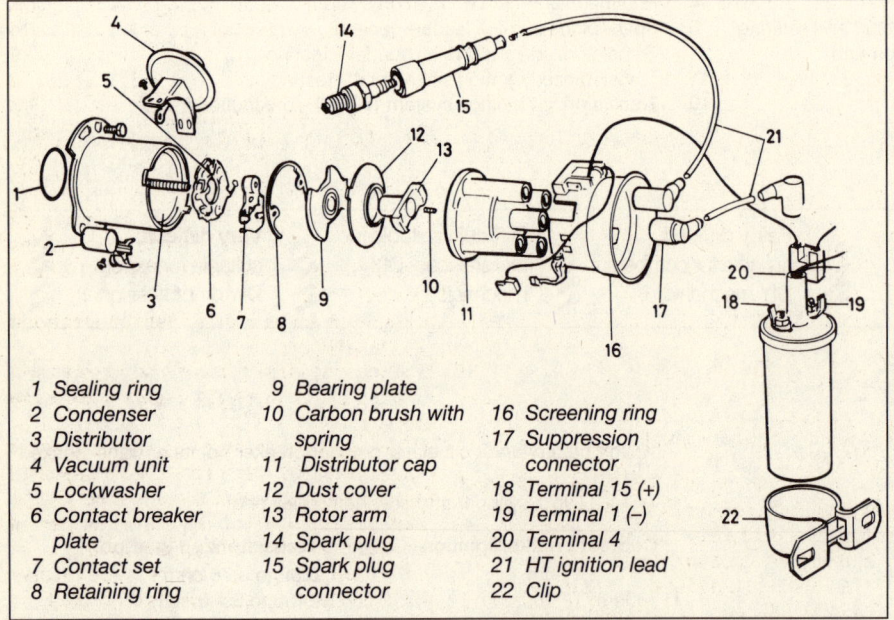

1 Sealing ring
2 Condenser
3 Distributor
4 Vacuum unit
5 Lockwasher
6 Contact breaker plate
7 Contact set
8 Retaining ring
9 Bearing plate
10 Carbon brush with spring
11 Distributor cap
12 Dust cover
13 Rotor arm
14 Spark plug
15 Spark plug connector
16 Screening ring
17 Suppression connector
18 Terminal 15 (+)
19 Terminal 1 (–)
20 Terminal 4
21 HT ignition lead
22 Clip

Fig. 4.1 Contact breaker ignition system with Bosch distributor – 1.05 and 1.3 litre engines (Sec 1)

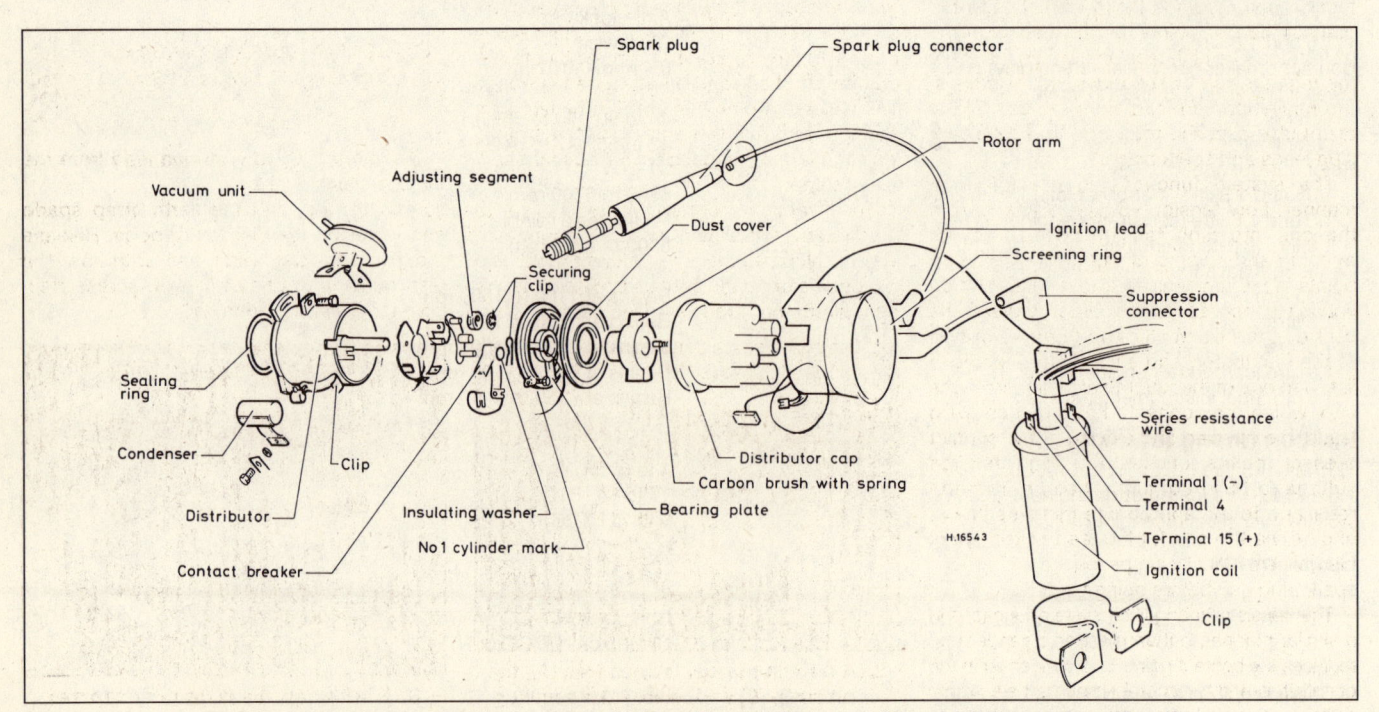

Fig. 4.2 Contact breaker ignition system with Ducellier distributor – 1.05 and 1.3 litre engines (Sec 1)

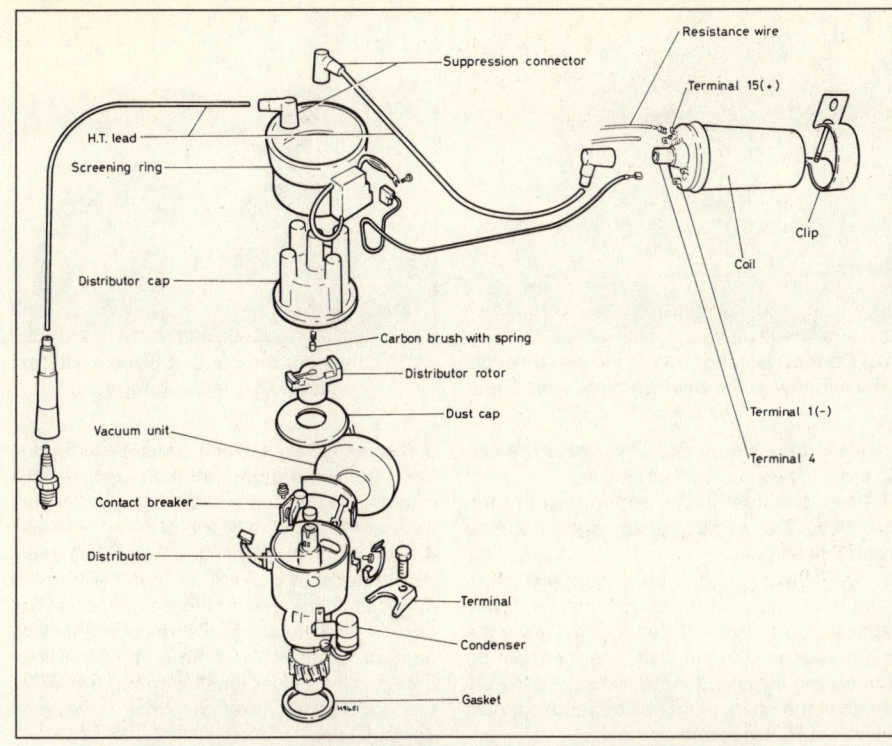

Ignition system 4•3

Fig. 4.3 Contact breaker ignition system – 1.6 litre engine (Sec 1)

With the contact breaker type, the ignition system is divided into two circuits, the low tension circuit and the high tension circuit. The low tension (sometimes known as the primary) circuit consists of the battery, a lead to the ignition switch, a lead from the ignition switch to the low tension or primary coil windings (terminal +) and a lead from the low tension coil windings (coil terminal -) to the contact breaker points and condenser in the distributor. The high tension circuit consists of the high tension or secondary coil windings, the heavy ignition lead from the coil to the distributor cap, the rotor arm and the spark plug leads and spark plugs.

The system functions in the following manner. Low tension voltage is changed in the coil into high tension voltage by the opening and closing of the contact breaker points in the low tension circuit. High tension voltage is then fed via the carbon brush in the centre of the distributor cap to the rotor arm of the distributor, and each time it comes in line with one of the four metal segments in the cap, which are connected to the spark plug leads, the opening and closing of the contact breaker points causes the high tension voltage to build up, jump the gap from the rotor arm to the appropriate metal segment, and so via the spark plug lead to the spark plug, where it finally jumps the spark plug gap before going to earth.

The transistorized ignition system functions in a similar manner, but an electronic sender unit replaces the contact points and condenser in the distributor, and a remotely-mounted electronic switch unit controls the coil primary circuit.

The ignition timing is advanced and retarded automatically, to ensure that the spark occurs at just the right instant for the particular load at the prevailing engine speed.

The ignition advance is controlled both mechanically and by a vacuum-operated system. The mechanical governor mechanism comprises two weights, which move out from the distributor shaft as the engine speed rises due to centrifugal force. As they move outwards they rotate the cam relative to the distributor shaft, and so advance the spark. The weights are held in position by two light springs, and it is the tension of the springs which is largely responsible for correct spark advancement.

The vacuum control consists of a diaphragm, one side of which is connected via a small bore pipe to the inlet manifold, and the other side to the contact breaker plate, or baseplate on transistorized distributors.

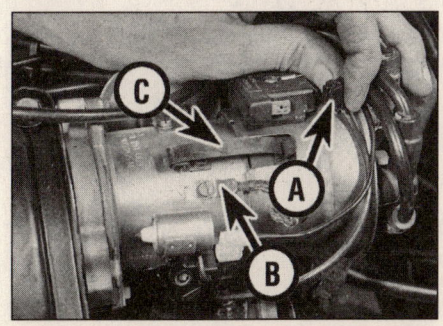

3.1A Detach the low tension lead (A), the earth strap (B) and release the securing clips (C)

3.1B Withdraw the distributor cap and screen ring

Depression in the inlet manifold, which varies with engine speed and throttle opening, causes the diaphragm to move, so moving the contact breaker plate or baseplate, and advancing or retarding the spark. A fine degree of control is achieved by a spring in the vacuum assembly.

The contact breaker ignition system incorporates a ballast resistor or resistive wire in the low tension circuit, which is in circuit all the time that the engine is running. When the starter is operated, the resistance is bypassed to provide increased voltage at the spark plugs for easier starting.

2 Routine maintenance - ignition system

The following routine maintenance procedures must be carried out at the specified intervals given at the start of this manual.

1 Renew the spark plug. Set the electrode gap before fitting.
2 Clean and inspect the ignition system HT and LT lead connections. Renew if defective in any way.
3 Clean and inspect the contact breaker points midway between their specified renewal intervals. Check the adjustment of the contact breaker points and adjust if necessary, as described in Section 3.
4 Remove and renew the contact breaker points at the specified intervals (Section 4).
5 Check and, if necessary, adjust the ignition timing, as described in Section 12.

3 Contact breaker points - checking and adjustment

1 Disconnect the low tension lead from the terminal block on the
screening ring, and the earth strap spade connector on the distributor body. Release the two retaining clips and withdraw the distributor cap, complete with screen ring, from the distributor (photos).

4•4 Ignition system

3.2 Remove the rotor arm

3.3 Contact breaker points viewed through the window in the bearing plate – arrowed (Ducellier)

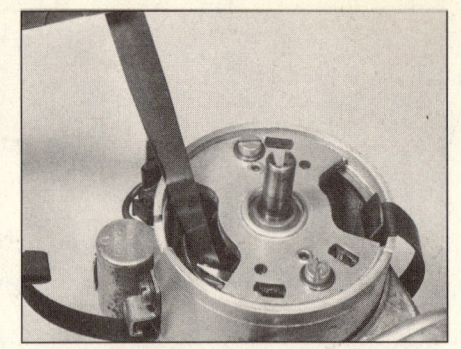

3.5A Checking the contact breaker points gap with a feeler gauge

2 Pull off the rotor arm and remove the dust cover (photo).

3 Using a screwdriver, prise open the points and check the condition of the faces (photo). If they are pitted and discoloured, remove them, as described in Section 4, and dress them using emery tape or a grindstone making sure that the surfaces are flat and parallel with each other. If the points are worn excessively, renew them. If the points are in good condition check their adjustment as follows.

Adjustment

4 Turn the engine with a spanner on the crankshaft pulley bolt until the moving contact point is fully open with the contact heel on the peak of one of the cam lobes.

5 Using a feeler blade, check that the gap between the two points is as given in the Specifications (photo). If not, loosen the fixed contact screw and reposition the fixed contact until the feeler blade is a firm sliding fit between the two points. In order to make a fine adjustment slightly loosen the screw then position the screwdriver in the fixed contact notch and the two pips on the contact plate. With the gap adjusted tighten the screw (photos)

6 Using a dwell meter, check that the dwell angle of the contact points is as given in the Specifications while spinning the engine on the starter. If not, readjust the points gap as necessary - reduce the gap in order to increase the dwell angle, or increase the gap in order to reduce the dwell angle.

7 Clean the dust cover and rotor arm then refit them. Do not remove any metal from the rotor arm segment.

8 Wipe clean the distributor cap and make sure that the carbon brush moves freely against the tension of the spring. Clean the metal segments in the distributor cap, but do not scrape away any metal, otherwise the HT spark at the spark plugs will be reduced. Also clean the HT leads and coil tower.

9 Refit the distributor cap and interference screen.

10 Start the engine and check that the dwell angle is as given in the Specifications both at idling and higher engine speeds. A decrease in dwell angle at high engine speeds indicates a weak spring on the moving contact points.

11 After making an adjustment to the contact points the ignition timing should be checked and adjusted as described in Section 12.

4 Contact breaker points - renewal

1 Proceed as described in paragraphs 1 and 2 in the previous Section.

2 Remove the screws and withdraw the bearing plate - 1.05 and 1.3 litre variants only (photo).

3 Disconnect the moving contact low tension lead from the terminal then remove the retaining screw and withdraw the contact breaker set from the distributor.

4 Wipe clean the contact breaker plate in the distributor and make sure that the contact surfaces of the new contact breaker set are clean. Lubricate the arm surface and moving contact pivot with a little multi-purpose grease. Use only a small amount, otherwise the contact points may become contaminated.

5 Fit the contact set on the baseplate and refit the retaining screw. Connect the low tension lead to the terminal.

6 Refit the bearing plate and tighten the screws (where applicable).

7 Adjust the contact breaker points as described in Section 3, paragraphs 4 to 11 inclusive.

5 Condenser - testing, removal and refitting

1 The condenser is fitted in parallel with the contact points and its purpose is to reduce arcing between the points and also to accelerate the collapse of the coil low tension magnetic field. A faulty condenser can cause the complete failure of the ignition system, as

3.5B Adjusting the contact breaker points gap

3.5C Showing the two pips and notch for inserting a screwdriver when adjusting the contact breaker points gap

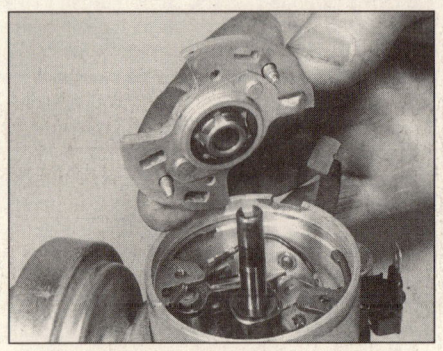

4.2 Removing the bearing plate (1.05 and 1.3 litre)

Ignition system 4•5

5.5 Condenser location

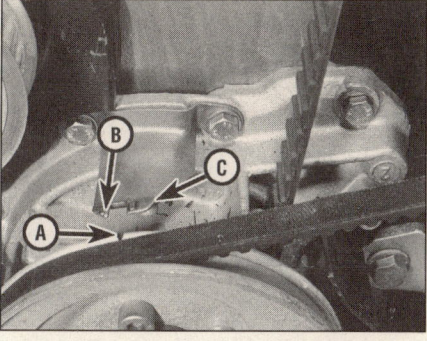

6.4 Crankshaft pulley mark (A), timing mark (B) and TDC mark (C) on the 1.3 litre engine (timing cover removed)

6.5 Removing the distributor (1.05 and 1.3 litre)

the points will be prevented from interrupting the low tension circuit.

2 To test the condenser, remove the distributor cap, rotor arm and dust cover and rotate the engine until the contact points are closed. Switch on the ignition and separate the points - if this is accompanied by a *strong* blue flash the condenser is faulty (a *weak* white spark is normal).

3 A further test can be made for short circuiting by removing the condenser and connecting a test lamp and leads to the supply lead and body (ie connecting the condenser in series with a 12 volt supply). If the test lamp lights, the condenser is faulty.

4 If the correct operation of the condenser is in doubt, substitute a new unit and check whether the fault persists.

5 To remove the condenser, unscrew the condenser retaining screw and disconnect the low tension supply lead (at the coil on some models) (photo).

6 Withdraw the condenser far enough to disconnect the moving contact supply lead then withdraw the condenser. If the moving contact supply lead has insufficient length it will be necessary to remove the distributor cap, rotor arm, dust cover and bearing plate (if applicable) first.

7 Refitting is a reversal of removal.

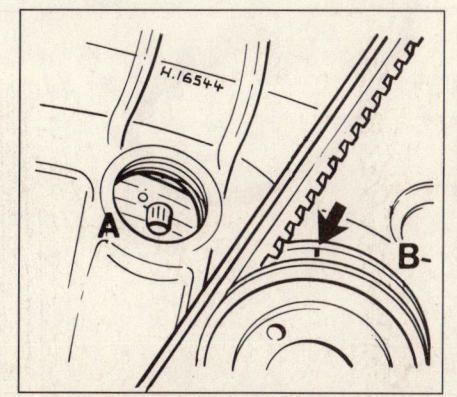

6 Distributor (contact breaker type) - removal, overhaul and refitting

1 Disconnect the battery earth lead, then remove the distributor cap and screening ring (Section 3, paragraph 1).

2 Disconnect the vacuum hose.

1.05 and 1.3 litre engine

3 The distributor driveshaft is located in the end of the camshaft by an offset centre key and therefore the procedures described in paragraphs 4 and 5 are only necessary for checking purposes, such as when fitting a new distributor.

4 Turn the engine with a spanner on the crankshaft pulley bolt until the rotor arm points to the No 1 spark plug lead position. On some models a TDC groove is provided on the distributor body rim and the rotor arm must align with this. The mark on the crankshaft pulley should be aligned with the TDC pointer with No 1 piston (timing belt end) at TDC compression (photo).

5 Mark the distributor flange and cylinder head in relation to each other, then unscrew the bolts and withdraw the distributor (photo).

1.6 and 1.8 litre engine

6 Unscrew and remove the TDC sensor or blanking plug from the top of the gearbox (or automatic transmission) then turn the engine over so that TDC O mark on the flywheel or driveplate is visible and aligned with the timing pointer. The crankshaft pulley timing notch should be aligned with the TDC arrow mark on the timing case (Fig. 4.4). The rotor arm should be pointing to the timing mark on the top rim of the distributor body (Fig. 4.5).

7 Mark the distributor body in line with the tip of the rotor arm, and also mark the distributor body and cylinder block in relation to each other, then unscrew the clamp bolt and withdraw the clamp, followed by the distributor from the cylinder block. Note by how much the rotor turns clockwise. Remove the distributor body sealing washer (fit a new one on refitting).

All models

8 The dismantling and overhaul of the distributor is similar on all models. The accompanying photos illustrate the distributor fitted to the 1.05 and 1.3 litre engine types.

9 Remove the contact breaker points (see Section 4).

10 On the Bosch distributor, mark the position of the guide pin then remove the bearing plate retaining ring (photos).

11 Before removing the vacuum unit on the Ducellier distributor, mark the adjustment segment position so that it can be correctly repositioned when reassembling.

12 Extract the circlip securing the vacuum unit arm to the contact breaker plate.

Fig. 4.4 TDC timing marks on the 1.6 and 1.8 litre engines (Secs 6 and 10)

A Flywheel/driveplate   B Crankshaft pulley

Fig. 4.5 Rotor arm aligned with TDC mark on the distributor body – 1.6 and 1.8 litre engines (Secs 6 and 12)

6.10A Correct fitted position of the bearing plate retaining ring (Bosch)

4•6 Ignition system

6.10B Removing the bearing plate retaining ring

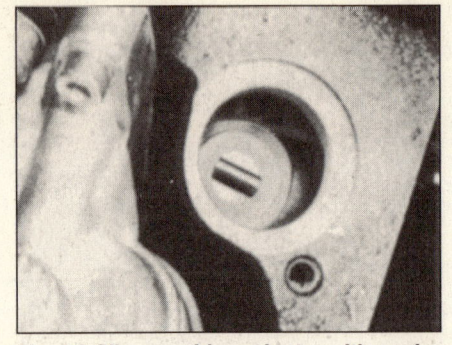

Fig. 4.6 Oil pump drive spigot position prior to refitting the distributor – 1.6 and 1.8 litre engines (Secs 6 and 12)

13 Remove the retaining screws, then unhook the arm and withdraw the vacuum unit. Note that the screws may also secure a suppression choke unit to the distributor body.
14 Remove the side screws, noting the location of the earth lead terminal, then remove the contact breaker plate by turning it anti-clockwise to align the lugs with the cut-outs (if applicable).
15 Wipe clean all the electrical components. Clean the distributor body assembly with paraffin then wipe dry.
16 Check all components for wear and damage referring to Sections 3 and 5 for the contact breaker points, distributor cap, rotor and condenser.
17 Reassembly is a reversal of the dismantling procedure.
18 Realign the vacuum unit adjuster segment with the mark made when removing it (Ducellier).
19 On the Bosch distributor, locate the retaining ring guide pin as previously marked.
20 Lubricate the centrifugal mechanism and the contact breaker plate with a little multi-purpose grease Adjust the contact breaker points, as described in Section 3.
21 To refit the 1.05 and 1.3 litre distributor reverse the removal procedure and align the timing marks made during removal before tightening the clamp bolts.
22 To refit the distributor on the 1.6 litre engine, first check that the oil pump drive spigot is correctly positioned with the spigot parallel to the crankshaft. This is visible through the distributor aperture (Fig. 4.6).

Check that the TDC O mark is still aligned. Set the rotor arm to the position noted in paragraph 7, align the distributor body and cylinder block marks and insert the distributor. As the gears mesh, the rotor will turn anti-clockwise and point to the previously made mark. Refit the clamp and tighten the bolt. Reconnect the vacuum hose, and low tension lead or multi-plug (as applicable). Refit the TDC sensor or blanking plug.
23 Refit the distributor cap, then reconnect the battery negative terminal.
24 Check and if necessary adjust the ignition timing, as described in Section 12.

7 Transistorized ignition system (TIC-H) - precautions

1 On models equipped with transistorised ignition, certain precautions must be observed in order to prevent damage to the semi-conductor components and in order to prevent personal injury.
2 Before disconnecting wires from the system make sure that the ignition is switched off.
3 When turning the engine at starter speed without starting, the HT lead must be pulled from the centre of the distributor cap and kept earthed to a suitable part of the engine or bodywork.
4 Disconnect the battery leads before

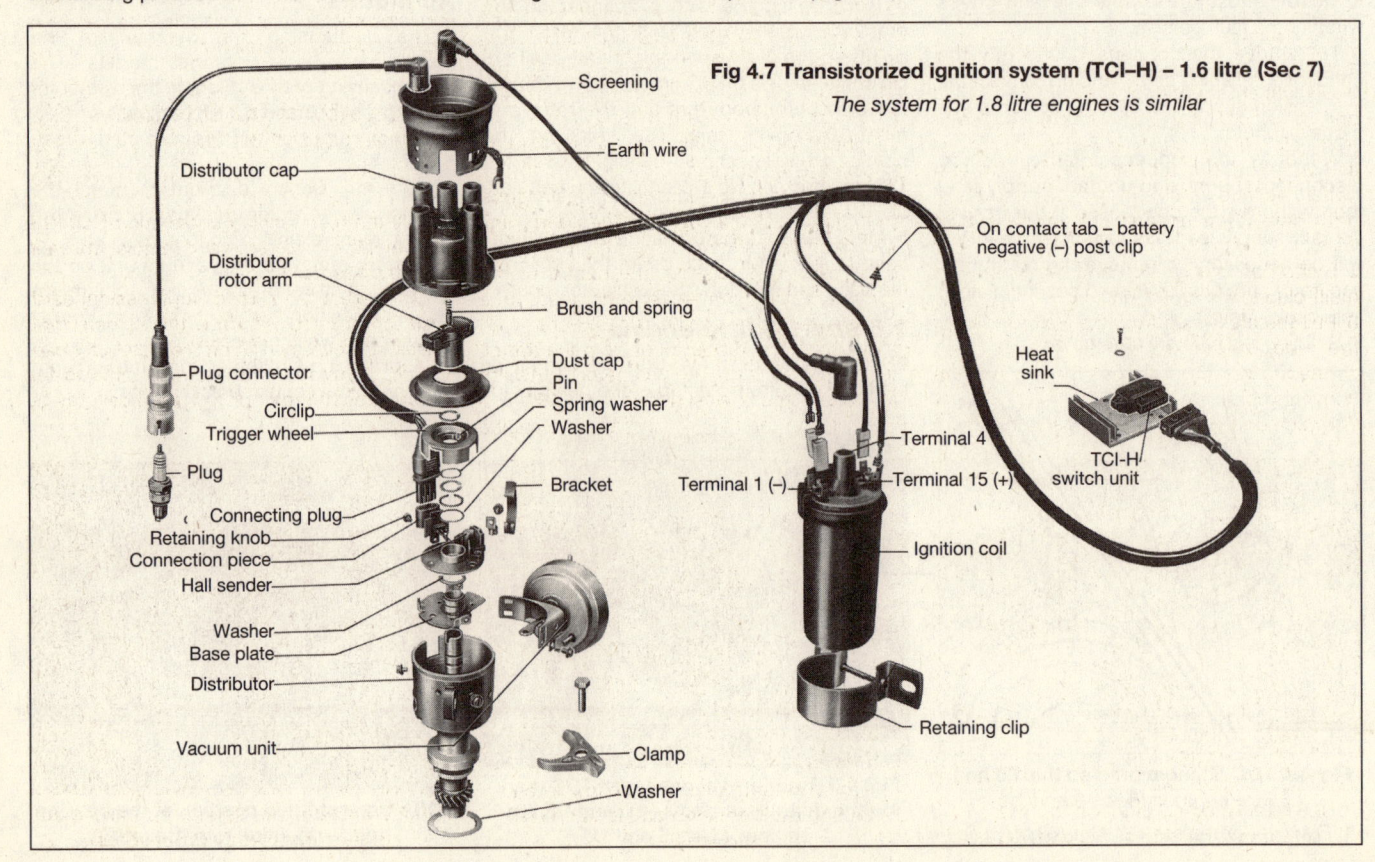

Fig 4.7 Transistorized ignition system (TCI–H) – 1.6 litre (Sec 7)
The system for 1.8 litre engines is similar

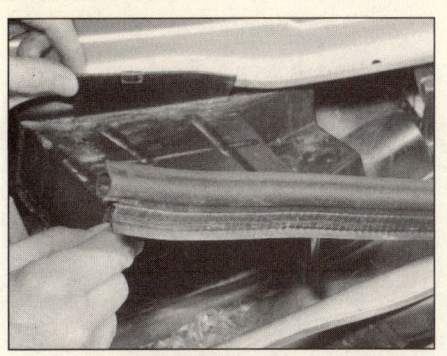

Ignition system 4•7

8.2A Carefully prise free the plastic cover . . .

8.2B . . . for access to the transistorized ignition switch

Fig. 4.8 Voltmeter connection when testing the transistorized ignition switch unit (Sec 8)

carrying out electric welding on any part of the car.
5 If the system develops a fault and it is necessary to tow the car with the ignition key switched on, the wiring must be disconnected from the TCI-H switch unit.
6 Do not under any circumstances connect a condenser to the coil terminals.
7 Take care to avoid receiving electric shocks from the HT system.

8 Transistorized ignition switch unit - testing

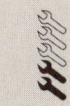

1 When making this test the coil must be in good condition (Section 13).
2 Remove the plastic cover on the right-hand side of the plenum chamber for access to the switch unit (photos).
3 Disconnect the multi-plug from the switch unit and connect a voltmeter between terminals 4 and 2, as shown in Fig. 4.8.
4 Switch on the ignition and check that battery voltage, or slightly less, is available. If not, there is an open-circuit in the supply wires.
5 Switch off the ignition and reconnect the multi-plug to the switch unit.
6 Pull the multi-plug from the Hall sender on the side of the distributor (photo), then connect a voltmeter across the low tension terminals on the coil (Fig. 4.9).
7 Switch on the ignition and check that there is initially 2 volts, dropping to zero after 1 to 2 seconds. If this is not the case, renew the switch unit and coil.
8 Using a length of wire, earth the centre terminal of the distributor multi-plug briefly; the voltage should rise to at least 2 volts. If not, there is an open-circuit or the switch unit is faulty.
9 Switch off the ignition and connect the voltmeter across the outer terminals of the distributor multi-plug.
10 Switch on the ignition and check that 5 volts is registered on the voltmeter.
11 If a fault still exists, renew the switch unit.
12 Switch off the ignition, remove the voltmeter, and reconnect the distributor multi-plug.

9 Transistorised ignition Hall sender - testing

1 Check that the ignition system wiring and plugs are fitted correctly.
2 The coil must be known to be in good condition (Section 13), also the TCI-H unit (see previous Section).
3 Pull the HT lead from the centre of the distributor cap, and earth the lead to a suitable part of the engine or bodywork.
4 Pull back the rubber boot from the switch unit and connect a voltmeter between terminals 6 and 3, as shown in Fig. 4.10.
5 Switch on the ignition and turn the engine by hand in its normal direction of rotation. The voltage should alternate from between 0 and a minimum of 2 volts. If not, the Hall sender is faulty and must be renewed.

Fig. 4.9 Voltmeter connection to the coil when testing the transistorized ignition switch unit and coil (Sec 8)

10 Distributor (transistorized) - removal and refitting

1 Pull the high tension connection from the centre of the ignition coil and remove the caps from the spark plugs.
2 Disconnect the screen (suppression) earth lead (photo) and withdraw the screen, then release the clips and lift off the distributor cap. Do not allow the cap retaining clips to fall inwards, as the rotor or trigger wheel may be damaged.

8.6 Multi-plug connection to the Hall sender on the side of the distributor

Fig. 4.10 Voltmeter connection when testing the transistorized ignition Hall sender (Sec 9)

10.2 Transistorized distributor earth lead connection to body (from screen)

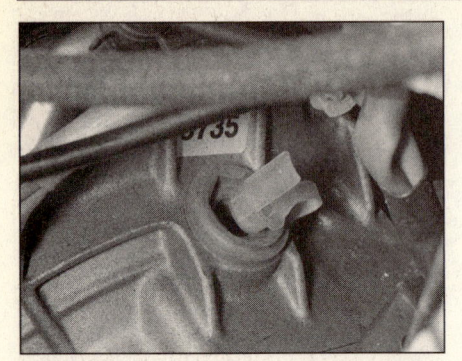

4•8 Ignition system

10.4 TDC blanking plug – manual gearbox

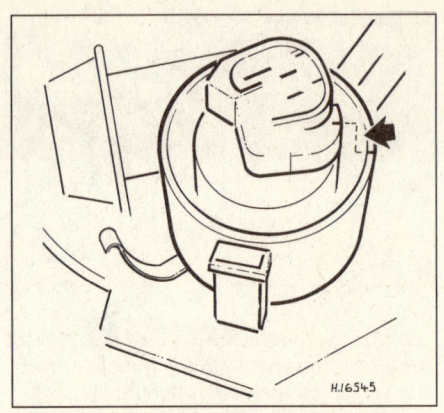

Fig. 4.11 Rotor arm position when at TDC – transistorized ignition – 1.8 litre engine (Sec 10)

10.6A Transistorized distributor removal (1.8 litre)

3 Disconnect the control unit lead multi-plug by releasing the wire retaining clip.
4 Unscrew and remove the TDC sensor or blanking plug from the top of the gearbox or automatic transmission (photo) then turn the engine over until the TDC O mark is aligned with the timing pointer (see Fig. 4.4). If not already marked, scribe an alignment mark on the distributor body in line with the tip of the rotor arm. Also mark the distributor body and cylinder block in relation to each other.
5 Pull the vacuum pipe(s) from the vacuum control unit, marking the position of the pipes if there is more than one.
6 Remove the bolt and washer from the distributor clamp plate and remove the clamp plate. Withdraw the distributor and remove the gasket (this must be renewed) (photos).
7 Refitting is a reversal of the removal procedure. When the distributor is in position, check that the rotor arm points to the No 1 cylinder mark before tightening the clamp plate bolt.
8 On completion check and if necessary adjust the ignition timing, as described in Section 12.

11 Distributor (transistorized) - dismantling, inspection and reassembly

Note: *Before commencing work, check that spare parts are available for this distributor. Specify whether the parts required will be for the 1.6 or 1.8 litre engine distributor.*

1 Wipe clean the exterior of the distributor.
2 Pull the rotor arm from the driveshaft then lift off the dust cover. Do not allow the cap retaining clips to touch the rotor during subsequent operations (photos).
3 Prise out the locking ring and withdraw the rotor up the shaft. Collect the locating pin (photos).
4 Undo the retaining screws securing the vacuum unit. Remove the vacuum unit, disengaging its operating arm (photo).
5 Remove the locking ring and collect the washers from the shaft.
6 Undo the cap clip and baseplate retaining screws from the body and lift out the Hall sender unit and the baseplate (photo).
7 Clean all the components and examine them for wear and damage.
8 Inspect the inside of the distributor cap for

10.6B The gasket must be removed

11.2A Pull free the rotor . . .

11.2B . . . and lift off the dust cap

11.3A Remove the locking ring and rotor

11.3B . . . and the locating pin from the shaft groove (arrowed)

11.4 Vacuum unit removal

Ignition system 4•9

signs of burning, or tracking. Make sure that the small carbon brush in the centre of the distributor cap is in good condition and can move up and down freely under the influence of its spring.

9 Check that the rotor arm is not damaged. Use an ohmmeter to measure the resistance between the brass contact in the centre of the rotor arm and the brass contact at the edge of the arm. The measured value of resistance should be between 600 and 1400 ohm.

10 Suck on the pipe connection to the vacuum diaphragm and check that the operating rod of the diaphragm unit moves. Retain the diaphragm under vacuum to check that the diaphragm is not perforated.

11 Reassemble the distributor in reverse order of dismantling, but smear a little grease on the bearing surface of the baseplate and the Hall sender bearing surfaces.

12 Before fitting the rotor (trigger wheel) back over the shaft, locate the small engagement pin in the groove in the shaft. Smear the pin with grease to retain it in position. Align the indent in the rotor inner bore with the groove in the shaft and slide it down into position over the pin (photo).

13 On completion, rotate the distributor shaft by hand to ensure that it moves freely. If it doesn't then the rotor is possibly distorted and will need renewal.

12 Ignition timing - checking and adjustment

Note: *Accurate ignition timing is only possible using a stroboscopic timing light, although on some models a DC sender unit is located on the top of the gearbox casing and may be used with a special VW tester to give an instant read-out. However, this tester will not normally be available to the home mechanic. For initial setting-up purposes of the conventional ignition system, the test bulb method can be used, but this must always be followed by the stroboscopic timing light method.*

Test bulb method (conventional ignition system only)

1 Remove the No 1 spark plug (crankshaft pulley end) and place the thumb over the aperture.

2 Turn the engine in the normal running direction (clockwise viewed from the crankshaft pulley end) until pressure is felt in No 1 cylinder, indicating that the piston is commencing its compression stroke. Use a spanner on the crankshaft pulley bolt, or engage top gear and pull the car forwards.

3 Continue turning the engine until the line on the crankshaft pulley is aligned with the pointer on the timing cover. If there are no marks on the timing cover, unscrew and remove the DC sensor or blanking plug from the top of the gearbox or automatic

11.6 Hall sender unit, retaining ring and washers

transmission and align the timing mark (see Specifications) with the timing pointer. Refer to photo 6.4 or Figs. 4.4 and 4.5, as applicable.

4 Remove the distributor cap and check that the rotor arm is pointing toward the No 1 HT lead location in the cap.

5 Connect a 12 volt test bulb between the coil LT negative terminal and a suitable earthing point on the engine.

6 Loosen the distributor clamp retaining bolt.

7 Switch on the ignition. If the bulb is already lit, turn the distributor body slightly clockwise until the bulb goes out.

8 Turn the distributor body anti-clockwise until the bulb just lights up, indicating that the points have just opened. Tighten the clamp retaining bolt.

9 Switch off the ignition and remove the test bulb.

10 Refit the distributor cap and No 1 spark plug and HT lead. Once the engine has been started, check the timing stroboscopically, as follows, and adjust as necessary.

Stroboscopic timing light method

11 Run the engine until its normal operating temperature is reached.

12 On 1.05, 1.3 and 1.8 fuel injection engines disconnect and plug the distributor vacuum hose.

13 If there are no timing marks on the timing cover and crankshaft pulley, unscrew and

11.12 Align the rotor indent with the groove in the shaft when refitting

remove the TDC sensor or blanking plug from the top of the gearbox or automatic transmission.

14 Connect the timing light to the engine in accordance with the manufacturer's instructions.

15 Connect a tachometer to the engine in accordance with the manufacturer's instructions.

16 Start the engine and run it at idling speed.

17 Point the timing light at the timing mark and pointer; they should appear to be stationary and aligned. If adjustment is necessary (ie the marks are not aligned), loosen the clamp retaining bolt and turn the distributor body to correct the ignition timing.

18 Gradually increase the engine speed while still pointing the timing light at the timing marks. The mark on the flywheel (or driveplate) or pulley should appear to move opposite to the direction of rotation, proving that the centrifugal weights are operating correctly. If not, the centrifugal mechanism is faulty and the distributor should be renewed.

19 Accurate checking of the vacuum advance (and retard where fitted) requires the use of a vacuum pump and gauge. However, providing that the diaphragm unit is serviceable, the vacuum hose(s) firmly fitted, and the internal mechanism not seized, the system should work correctly.

20 Switch off the engine, remove the timing light and tachometer, and refit the vacuum hose (where applicable).

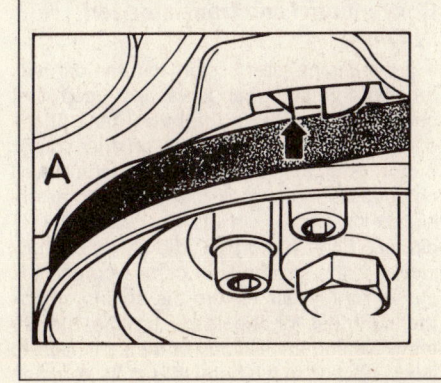

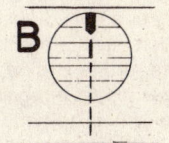

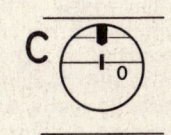

A 1.05 and 1.3 litre
B 1.6 and 1.8 litre (carburettor models)
C 1.8 litre (fuel injection models)

Fig. 4.12 Ignition timing marks (Sec 12)

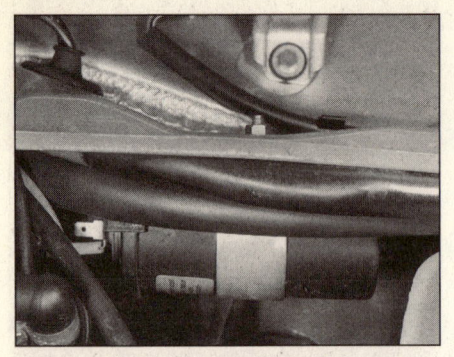

4•10 Ignition system

13.1 Ignition coil location

13 Coil - description and testing

1 The coil is located on the bulkhead under the plenum chamber (photo). It should be periodically wiped clean to prevent high tension voltage loss through possible arcing.
2 To ensure the correct HT polarity at the spark plugs, the coil LT leads must always be connected correctly. The ignition lead from the fusebox must be connected to the positive (+) terminal 15, and the distributor lead (usually green) must be connected to the negative (-) terminal 1. Incorrect connections can cause bad starting, misfiring, and short spark plug life.
3 Complete testing of the coil requires special equipment. However, if an ohmmeter is available, the primary and secondary winding resistances can be checked and compared with those given in the Specifications. During testing the LT and HT wires must be disconnected from the coil. To test the primary winding, connect the ohmmeter between the two LT terminals. To test the secondary winding, connect the ohmmeter between the negative (-) terminal 1 and the HT terminal.

14 Spark plugs and HT leads - general

1 The correct functioning of the spark plugs is vital for the correct running and efficiency of the engine. It is essential that the plugs fitted are appropriate for the engine, and the suitable type is specified at the beginning of this chapter. If this type is used and the engine is in good condition, the spark plugs should not need attention between scheduled replacement intervals. Spark plug cleaning is rarely necessary and should not be attempted unless specialised equipment is available as damage can easily be caused to the firing ends.
2 The condition of the spark plugs will also tell much about the overall condition of the engine.
3 If the insulator nose of the spark plug is clean and white, with no deposits, this is indicative of a weak mixture, or too hot a plug. (A hot plug transfers heat away from the electrode slowly - a cold plug transfers it away quickly.)
4 If the tip and insulator nose are covered with hard black-looking deposits, then this is indicative that the mixture is too rich. Should the plug be black and oily, then it is likely that the engine is fairly worn, as well as the mixture being too rich.
5 If the insulator nose is covered with light tan to greyish brown deposits, then the mixture is correct and it is likely that the engine is in good condition.
6 The spark plug gap is of considerable importance, as, if it is too large or too small, the size of the spark and its efficiency will be seriously impaired. The spark plug gap should be set to the figure given in the Specifications at the beginning of this Chapter.
7 To set it, measure the gap with a feeler gauge, and then bend open, or close, the outer plug electrode until the correct gap is achieved. The centre electrode should never be bent as this may crack the insulation and cause plug failure, if nothing worse.
8 Always tighten the spark plugs to the specified torque.
9 Periodically the spark plug leads should be wiped clean and checked for security.

HAYNES HINT

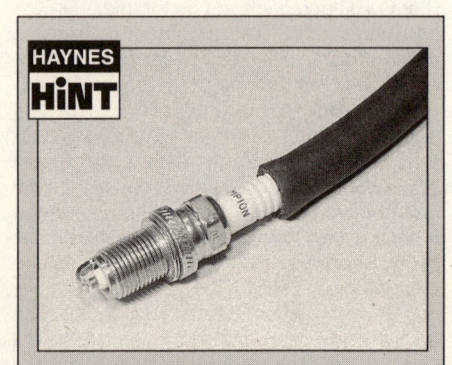

It is very often difficult to insert spark plugs into their holes without cross-threading them. To avoid this possibility, fit a short length of 5/16 inch internal diameter rubber hose over the end of the spark plug. The flexible hose acts as a universal joint to help align the plug with the plug hole. Should the plug begin to cross-thread, the hose will slip on the spark plug, preventing thread damage to the cylinder head.

Fault finding - ignition system

By far the majority of breakdown and running troubles are caused by faults in the ignition system either in the low tension or high tension circuit. There are two main symptoms indicating ignition fault. Either the engine will not start or fire, or the engine is difficult to start and misfires. If it is a regular misfire, i.e. the engine is only running on two or three cylinders, the fault is almost sure to be in the secondary, or high tension circuit. If the misfiring is intermittent, the fault could be in either the high or low tension circuits. If the car stops suddenly or will not start at all it is likely that the fault is in the low tension circuit. Loss of power and overheating, apart from faulty carburation settings, are normally due to faults in the distributor or incorrect ignition timing.

Engine fails to start

Conventional and transistorized systems

1 If the engine fails to start and the car was running normally when it was last used, first check there is fuel in the petrol tank. If the engine turns over normally on the starter motor and the battery is evidently well charged, then the fault may be in either the high or low tension circuits. First check the HT circuit. If the battery is known to be fully charged, the ignition light comes on and the starter motor fails to turn the engine, check the tightness of the leads on the battery terminals and the security of the earth lead to its connection to the body. It is quite common for the leads to have worked loose, even if they look and feel secure. If one of the battery terminal posts gets very hot when trying to work the starter motor, this is a sure indication of a faulty connection to that terminal.
2 One of the most common reasons for bad starting is wet or damp spark plug leads and distributor. If the engine fails to start due to either damp HT leads or distributor cap, a moisture dispersant can be very effective to prevent the problem recurring.
3 If the engine on models fitted with conventional ignition still fails to start, check that current is reaching the plugs by disconnecting each plug lead in turn at the spark plug end. Hold the end of the cable with an insulated tool about 5 mm (0.2 in) away from the cylinder block, then spin the engine on the starter motor.

Ignition system 4•11

4 On engines with transistorized ignition remove each plug in turn and earth it to a suitable part of the engine with the HT cable connected. Spin the engine on the starter motor.

5 Sparking at the cables or plugs should be fairly strong, with a regular blue spark. If necessary remove the plugs for cleaning and regapping. The engine should now start.

Conventional system only

6 If there is no spark at the plug leads, take off the HT lead from the centre of the distributor cap and hold it to the block as before. Spin the engine on the starter once more. A rapid succession of blue sparks between the end of the lead and the block indicates that the coil is in order and that the distributor cap is cracked, the rotor arm faulty or the carbon brush in the top of the distributor cap is not making good contact with the rotor arm.

7 If there are no sparks from the end of the lead from the coil, check the connections at the coil end of the lead. If this is in order start checking the low tension circuit. Commence by cleaning and gapping the points (Section 3).

8 Use a 12 volt voltmeter, or a 12 volt bulb and two lengths of wire. With the ignition switch on and the points open, test between the low tension wire to the coil (it is marked -) and earth. No reading indicates a break in the supply from the ignition switch. Check the connections at the switch to see if any are loose. Refit them, and the engine should run. A reading shows a faulty coil or condenser or broken lead between the coil and the distributor.

9 Remove the condenser from the distributor body, but leave the wiring connected. With the points open, test between the moving point and earth. If there now is a reading then the fault is in the condenser. Fit a new one and the fault is cleared.

10 With no reading from the moving point to earth, take a reading between earth and the negative (-) terminal of the coil. A reading here indicates a broken wire which must be renewed between the coil and distributor. No reading confirms that the coil has failed and must be renewed. For these tests it is sufficient to separate the contact breaker points with a piece of paper.

11 If the engine starts when the starter motor is operated, but stops as soon as the ignition key is returned to the normal running position the ballast resistor may have an open-circuit. Connect a temporary lead between the coil positive (+) terminal and the battery positive (+) terminal. If the engine now runs correctly, renew the resistor. Note that the ballast resistor or resistive wire must not be permanently bypassed otherwise the coil will overheat and be damaged.

Engine misfires
Conventional system only

12 If the engine misfires regularly, run it at a fast idling speed. Pull off each of the plug caps in turn and listen to the note of the engine. Hold the plug cap in a dry cloth or with a rubber glove as additional protection against a shock from the HT supply.

13 No difference in engine running will be noticed when the lead from the defective circuit is removed. Removing the lead from one of the good cylinders will accentuate the misfire.

14 Remove the plug lead from the end of the defective plug and hold it about 5 mm (0.2 in) away from the block. Restart the engine. If the sparking is fairly strong and regular, the fault must lie in the spark plug.

Conventional and transistorized systems

15 The plug may be loose, the insulation may be cracked, or the points may have burnt away, giving too wide a gap for the spark to jump. Worse still, one of the points may have broken off. Either renew the plug, or clean it, reset the gap and then test it.

16 Check the HT lead from the distributor to the plug. If the insulation is cracked or perished, renew the lead. Check the connections at the distributor cap.

17 Examine the distributor cap carefully for tracking. This can be recognised by a very thin black line running between two or more electrodes, or between an electrode and some other part of the distributor. These lines are paths which now conduct electricity across the cap, thus letting it run to earth. The only answer in this case is a new distributor cap.

18 Apart from the ignition timing being incorrect, other causes of misfiring have already been dealt with under the paragraphs dealing with the failure of the engine to start. To recap, these are that:
(a) The coil may be faulty giving an intermittent misfire
(b) There may be a damaged wire or loose connection in the low tension circuit
(c) The condenser may be short-circuiting (where applicable)
(d) There may be a mechanical fault in the distributor (broken driving spindle or contact breaker spring where applicable).

19 If the ignition timing is too far retarded it should be noted that the engine will tend to overheat, and there will be a quite noticeable drop in power. If the engine is overheating and the power is down, and the ignition timing is correct, then the carburettor should be checked as it is likely that this is where the fault lies.

Notes

Chapter 5 Clutch

For modifications, and information applicable to later models, see Supplement at end of manual

Contents

Clutch - adjustment	2	Clutch pedal - removal and refitting	4
Clutch (020 gearbox) - inspection	9	Clutch release mechanism (020 gearbox) - removal and refitting	10
Clutch (020 gearbox) - removal and refitting	8	Clutch release mechanism (084 gearbox) - removal, checking and refitting	7
Clutch (084 gearbox) - inspection	6		
Clutch (084 gearbox) - removal and refitting	5	Fault finding - clutch	See end of Chapter
Clutch cable - renewal	3	General description	1

Degrees of difficulty

Easy, suitable for novice with little experience	**Fairly easy,** suitable for beginner with some experience	**Fairly difficult,** suitable for competent DIY mechanic	**Difficult,** suitable for experienced DIY mechanic	**Very difficult,** suitable for expert DIY or professional

Specifications

General

Type	Single dry plate, diaphragm spring pressure plate, cable operation. Automatic adjustment on 1.8 litre models
Free play at clutch pedal	15 to 20 mm (0.6 to 0.8 in)

Clutch friction disc diameter:
084 gearbox	180 mm (7.09 in)
020 4-speed gearbox	190 mm (7.49 in)
020 5-speed gearbox (4+E)	200 mm (7.88 in)
020 5-speed gearbox (Sports)	210 mm (8.27 in)

Clutch components

Maximum inward taper:
084 gearbox	0.3 mm (0.012 in)
020, 4 and 5-speed gearbox	0 2 mm (0.008 in)

Maximum run-out allowance - measured 2.5 mm (0.099 in) from outer edge:
084 gearbox	0.4 mm (0.016 in)
020, 4 and 5-speed gearbox	0.3 mm (0.012 in)

Diaphragm spring finger scoring depth (maximum):
084 gearbox	0.3 mm (0.012 in)

Torque wrench settings

	Nm	lbf ft
084 gearbox		
Pressure plate	25	18
Flywheel	75	55
Guide sleeve	15	11
020, 4 and 5-speed gearbox		
Flywheel	20	15
Pressure plate:		
Bolt without shoulder	75	55
Bolt with shoulder	100	74

5•2 Clutch

1 General description

The type of clutch fitted depends upon the gearbox; two distinct types of clutch type being used.

Clutch unit - 084 gearbox

With the gearbox, the clutch is of single dry plate type with a diaphragm spring pressure plate, and actuation is by cable. The pressure plate assembly is bolted to the flywheel and transmits drive to the friction disc which is splined to the gearbox input shaft. Friction linings are riveted to each side of the disc and radial damper springs are incorporated in the hub in order to cushion rotational shocks.

When the clutch pedal is depressed, the cable pulls the arm on the release shaft, and the release bearing is pushed along the guide sleeve against the diaphragm spring fingers. Further movement causes the diaphragm spring to withdraw the pressure plate from the friction disc which also moves along the splined input shaft away from the flywheel. Drive then ceases to be transmitted to the gearbox.

When the clutch pedal is released, the diaphragm spring forces the pressure plate back into contact with the friction disc which then moves along the input shaft into engagement with the flywheel. Drive is then transmitted directly through the clutch to the gearbox.

Wear of the friction disc linings causes the pressure plate to move closer to the flywheel and the cable free play to decrease. Cable adjustment must therefore be carried out as described in Section 2.

Clutch unit - 020, 4 and 5-speed gearbox

Unlike the more conventional clutch used on models with the 084 gearbox, on the 020 gearbox the clutch pressure plate is bolted to the crankshaft flange and the flywheel, which is dish shaped, is bolted to the pressure plate with the friction disc being held between them. This is in effect the reverse of the more conventional arrangement where the flywheel is bolted to the crankshaft flange and the clutch pressure plate bolted to the flywheel.

The release mechanism consists of a metal disc, called the release plate, which is clamped in the centre of the pressure plate by a retaining ring. In the centre of the release plate is a boss into which the clutch pushrod is fitted. The pushrod passes through the centre of the gearbox input shaft and is actuated by a release bearing located in the gearbox end housing. A single finger lever presses on this bearing when the shaft to which it is spliced is turned by operation of the clutch pushrod, which in turn pushes the centre of the release plate inwards towards the crankshaft. The outer edge of the release plate presses on the pressure plate fingers forcing them back towards the engine and removing the pressure plate friction face from the friction disc, thus disconnecting the drive. When the clutch pedal is released the pressure plate reasserts itself, clamping the friction disc firmly against the flywheel and restoring the drive.

As the friction linings on the disc wear, the pressure plate will gradually move closer to the flywheel and the cable free play will decrease. Periodic adjustment must therefore be carried out as described in Section 2.

2 Clutch - adjustment

1 On some 1.6 and 1.8 litre models the clutch is automatically adjusted by means of a segment and pawl at the pedal end of the clutch cable. The only adjustment necessary with this type is when the cable has been disconnected for any reason or renewed; adjustment being made by depressing the clutch pedal several times once it is reconnected.
2 On all other models the clutch adjustment is made manually.
3 The clutch cable adjustment must be checked at the specified intervals given in Routine Maintenance at the front of this Manual. To do this, check the free play at the clutch pedal by measuring the distance it has to be moved in order to take up the slack in the cable. If the distance is not as given in the Specifications adjust the cable as follows.

084 gearbox

4 Locate the release arm on the gearbox clutch housing then turn the adjusting nut and half-round seating until the adjustment is correct (photo). Depress the arm if necessary to enable the nut to be turned
more easily, and if the nut is tight on its thread, hold the inner cable with a spanner.
5 Make sure that the adjusting nut is correctly seated in the release arm before finally checking the adjustment.

020 gearbox (manual adjustment)

6 Loosen the outer cable lockout at the gearbox bracket, then turn the serrated disc while holding the outer cable stationary until the pedal free play is correct (photo).
7 Fully depress the pedal several times and recheck the adjustment, then tighten the locknut. Lubricate the exposed part of the inner cable with a little multi-purpose grease.

3 Clutch cable - renewal

1 Loosen the cable at the gearbox end, then disconnect the inner and outer cable from the release lever and support bracket (photo).
2 On models with an automatic adjustment clutch cable, pivot the segment forwards and retain it with the pawl, then disengage the cable from it. Withdraw the cable. On models with a manually adjusted clutch cable, unhook the inner cable from the clutch pedal, then withdraw the cable.
3 If necessary, prise the guide sleeve from the rubber washer on the gearbox bracket, then remove the washer.
4 Check that the cable locating grommet and washer are secure in the bulkhead.
5 Fit the new cable using a reversal of the removal procedure. Check that the sealing ring is correctly located on the bulkhead end

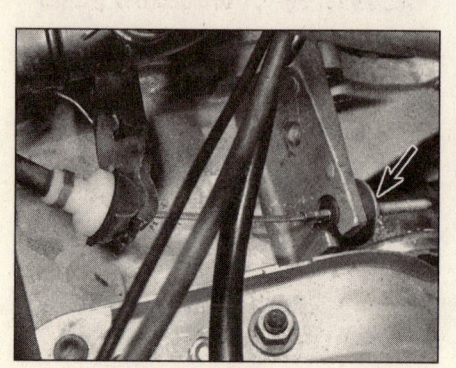

2.4 Clutch cable and release arm adjustment nut – arrowed (084 gearbox)

2.6 Clutch cable adjuster (020 gearbox)

3.1 Inner cable to release lever viewed from underneath (020 gearbox)

Clutch 5•3

of the outer cable, and lightly lubricate the exposed parts of the inner cable with multi-purpose grease. Make sure that the inner sealing lip of the rubber washer on the gearbox bracket is parallel to the end cap, otherwise the gearbox breather may become blocked with foreign matter. Finally adjust the cable, as described in Section 2, or, on models with an automatic adjustment cable, simply depress the clutch pedal several times.

4 Clutch pedal - removal and refitting

1 Detach the clutch cable from the release arm on the gearbox clutch housing and then from the clutch pedal, as described in the previous Section.
2 On models with a manually adjusted clutch, prise free the clip from the end of the pedal shaft then carefully slide the pedal free from the shaft.
3 On models fitted with an automatic cable adjuster mechanism, you will need to disconnect the steering column and move it to the left to allow pedal removal (refer to Chapter 10). When the steering column is moved to the left, you will then need to tension the over-centre spring and hold it under tension during its removal. A suitable spring retainer will therefore be required; if possible use VW special tool 3113.
4 With the over-centre spring held under tension, remove the clip, the over-centre spring and retainer. Now remove the circlip securing the pedal unit and withdraw the pedal, together with the segment and pawl.
5 Examine the shaft and pedal bush for wear and renew them if necessary. The bush is an interference fit in the pedal and can be removed or installed using a soft metal drift - make sure that the ends of the bush are flush with the ends of the pedal tube.
6 If dismantling the segment and panel on the automatic adjuster clutch type, note the orientation of the segment and pawl spring prior to dismantling. Check the pawl bush for excessive wear and renew any parts as necessary.
7 Refitting is a reversal of the removal procedure on both pedal types. Lubricate the pivot shaft with a little multi-purpose grease, also the pawl bush (automatic adjuster).
8 On manual cable adjuster models, recheck and adjust the cable, as described in Section 2. On models fitted with an automatic adjuster depress the pedal a few times to take up the adjustment.

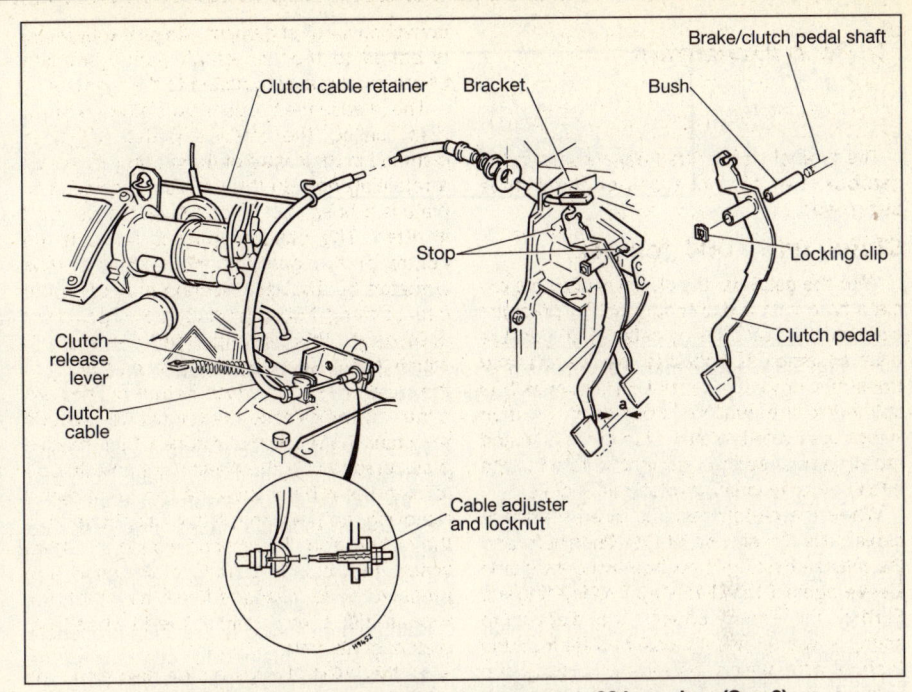

Fig. 5.1 Clutch pedal and cable components – 084 gearbox (Sec 3)

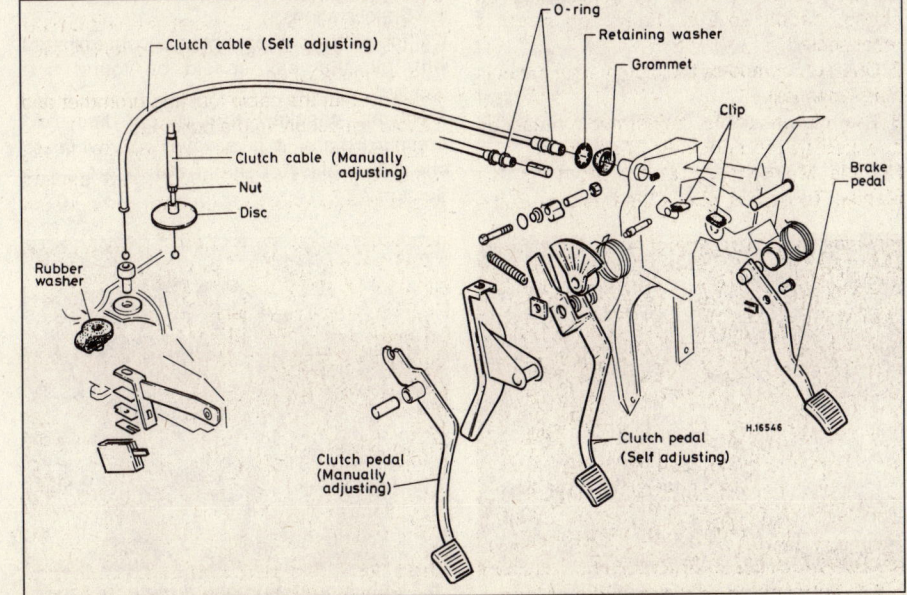

Fig. 5.2 Clutch pedal and cable components – 020 gearbox (Sec 3)

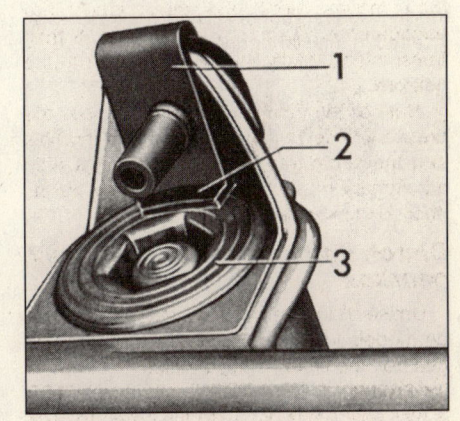

Fig. 5.3 Clutch cable guide rubber washer (1), sealing lip (2), and selector shaft end cap (3) – 020 gearbox (Sec 3)

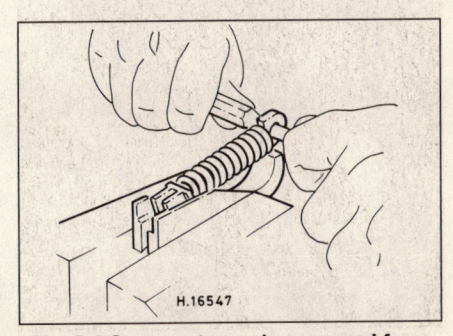

Fig. 5.4 Over-centre spring removal from retainer using VW tool 3113 (Sec 4)

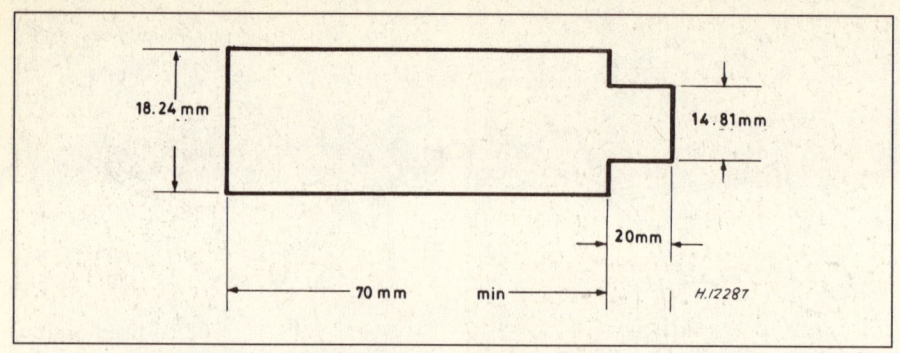

5•4 Clutch

Fig. 5.5 Wooden mandrel dimensions for centralising the clutch friction disc – 084 gearbox (Sec 5)

5 Clutch (084 gearbox) - removal and refitting

1 Remove the gearbox, as described in Chapter 6.
2 Mark the pressure plate cover and flywheel in relation to each other.
3 Using an Allen key, unscrew the bolts securing the pressure plate cover to the flywheel in diagonal sequence one turn at a time (photo). If the key handle is pressed towards the centre of the flywheel it should be possible to loosen the bolts while holding the cover stationary by hand. If necessary hold the flywheel stationary using a screwdriver inserted in the starter ring gear teeth.
4 Withdraw the pressure plate assembly and the friction disc from the flywheel. Note that the friction disc hub extension containing the cushion springs faces the pressure plate.
5 Check the clutch components, as described in Section 6.
6 Before commencing the refitting procedure a tool must be obtained for centralising the friction disc, otherwise difficulty will be experienced when refitting the gearbox. Unlike the normal arrangement, the gearbox input shaft does not enter a bush or bearing in the rear of the crankshaft. If, however, the friction disc is not centralised the gearbox dowels will not be aligned correctly. If a centralising tool is not available a wooden mandrel may be made to the dimensions shown in Fig. 5.5.
7 Clean the friction faces of the flywheel and pressure plate, then fit the centralising tool to the crankshaft and locate the friction disc on it with the hub extension outwards (photo).
8 Fit the pressure plate assembly to the flywheel (in its original position if not renewed), then insert the bolts and tighten them evenly in diagonal sequence to the specified torque (photos).
9 Check the release bearing, as described in Section 7, before refitting the gearbox, as described in Chapter 6.

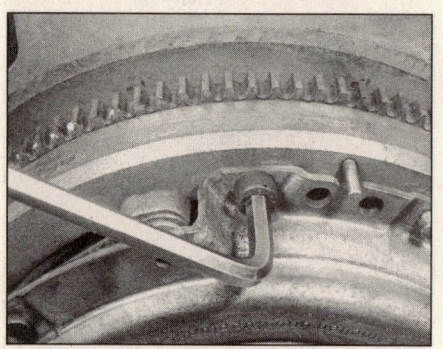

6 Clutch (084 gearbox) - inspection

1 Examine the surfaces of the pressure plate and flywheel for signs of scoring. Light scoring is normal, but if excessive the pressure plate must be renewed and the flywheel either machined or renewed.
2 Check the pressure plate diaphragm spring fingers for wear caused by the release bearing. If the scoring exceeds the maximum depth given in the Specifications, renew the assembly.
3 Using a straight-edge and feeler blade, check that the inward taper of the pressure plate does not exceed the maximum amount given in the Specifications (photo). Also check for loose riveted joints and for any cracks in the pressure plate components.
4 Check the friction disc linings for wear, and renew the disc if the linings are worn to within 1.0 mm (0.04 in) of the rivets.
5 Check that the friction disc damper springs and all rivets are secure, and that the linings are not contaminated with oil. Temporarily fit the disc to the gearbox input shaft and check that the run-out does not exceed that given in the Specifications.
6 If the clutch components are contaminated with oil, the leak should be found and rectified.
7 Having checked the clutch disc and pressure plate, it is always worthwhile to check the release bearing with reference to Section 7.

5.3 Removing the pressure plate bolts (084 gearbox)

5.7 The friction disc and centralising tool (084 gearbox)

5.8A Fitting the pressure plate assembly (084 gearbox)

5.8B Clutch unit reassembled (084 gearbox)

6.3 Checking the pressure plate for taper

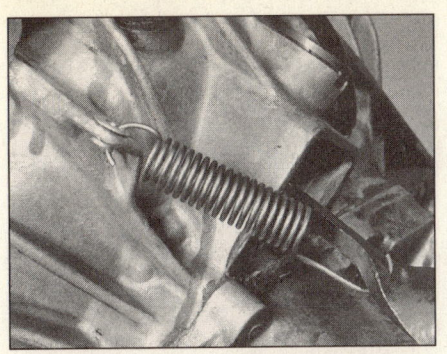

Clutch 5•5

7.1 Clutch release arm return spring (084 gearbox)

7.2A The release bearing fitted to the arm (084 gearbox)

7.2B Release bearing and retaining clips (084 gearbox)

7 Clutch release mechanism (084 gearbox) - removal, checking and refitting

1 With the gearbox removed, unhook the return spring from the release arm (photo).
2 Turn the release arm to move the release bearing up the guide sleeve, then disengage the two spring clips from the release fork and withdraw the bearing (photos).
3 Note how the springs and clips are fitted then prise the clips from the release bearing.
4 Spin the bearing by hand and check it for roughness, then attempt to move the outer race laterally against the inner race. If any excessive roughness or wear is evident, renew the bearing. Do not wash the bearing in solvent if it is to be re-used.
5 Using a spliced key, unbolt and remove the guide sleeve from the clutch housing (photos).
6 Using a narrow drift, drive the release shaft outer bush from the clutch housing. Alternatively prise out the bush.
7 Pull the release shaft from the inner bearing then withdraw the shaft and arm from the housing (photo).
8 Check the bushes and bearing surfaces of the shaft for wear and also check the guide sleeve for scoring. The inner bush may be removed using a soft metal drift and the new bush driven in until flush.
9 Refitting is a reversal of removal, but lubricate all bearing surfaces with a little high melting-point grease. Make sure that the release shaft outer bush is correctly sealed with the tab located in the cut-out in the clutch housing (photo).

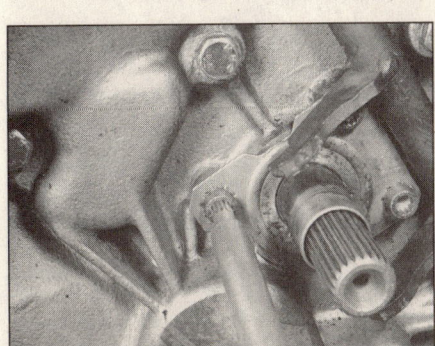

7.5A Unscrew the splined-head bolts (084 gearbox)

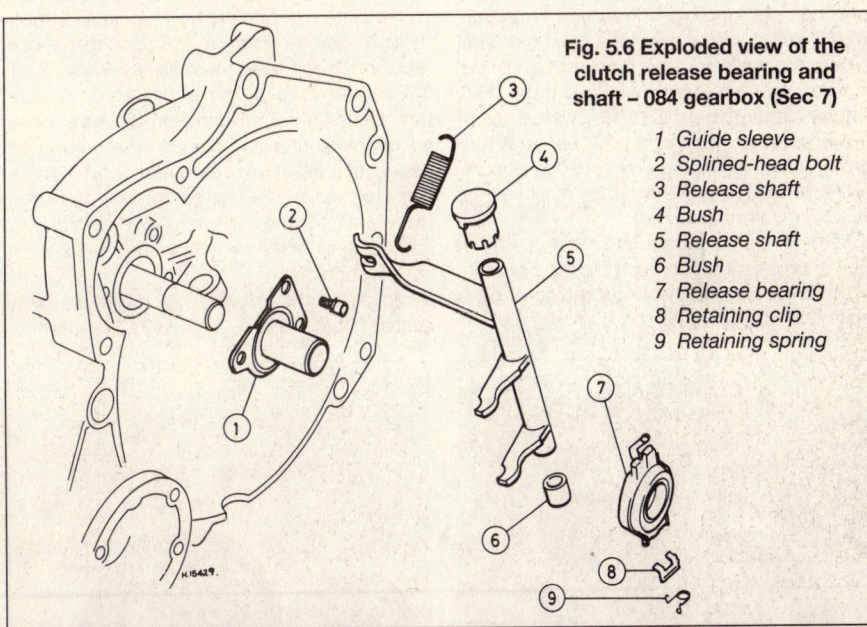

Fig. 5.6 Exploded view of the clutch release bearing and shaft – 084 gearbox (Sec 7)

1 Guide sleeve
2 Splined-head bolt
3 Release shaft
4 Bush
5 Release shaft
6 Bush
7 Release bearing
8 Retaining clip
9 Retaining spring

7.5B Withdraw the guide sleeve (084 gearbox)

7.7 Removing the release shaft (084 gearbox)

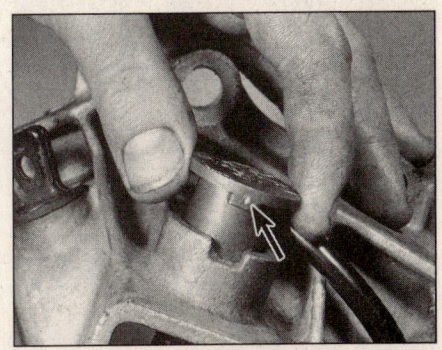

7.9 The location tab on the release shaft outer bush (084 gearbox)

5•6 Clutch

8.2 Flywheel expanding peg for centring the pressure plate (020 gearbox)

8.4A Removing the clutch release plate (020 gearbox)

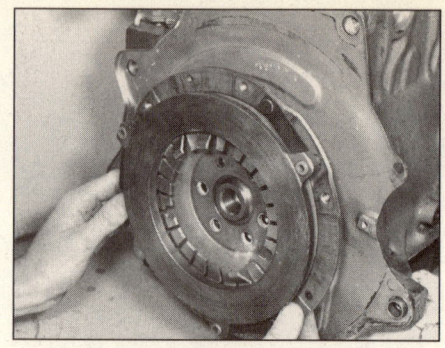

8.4B Removing the clutch pressure plate (020 gearbox)

8 Clutch (020 gearbox) - removal and refitting

1 Remove the gearbox, as described in Chapter 6.
2 Clamp the flywheel to prevent it turning, then undo the flywheel-to-pressure plate bolts in a progressive and diagonal sequence, releasing each one half a turn at a time until they are all slack and then take them out. The flywheel and the friction disc may now be removed, but note which way round the disc is fitted and also mark the flywheel and pressure plate in relation to each other, although centring pins are provided to ensure that the TDC mark on the flywheel is positioned correctly (photo).
3 Examine the pressure plate surface. If it is clean and free from scoring there is no reason to remove it unless the friction disc shows signs of oil contamination.
4 If the plate surface is defective then it must be removed. Note exactly where the ends of the retaining ring are located (the ring must be refitted this way later), and prise the ring out with a screwdriver. The release plate may now be removed (photo). The pressure plate is held to the crankshaft flange by six bolts fitted using a thread locking compound. These will be difficult to remove as they were tightened to a high torque before the locking fluid set, so the plate must be held with a clamp similar to that shown in Fig. 5.8 (photo). Once removed, these bolts must be renewed.
5 Refitting is a reversal of removal. Use thread locking compound on the **new** bolts securing the pressure plate to the crankshaft flange (if they were removed), and tighten them to the specified torque (photo). Note that the bolt torque wrench setting differs according to bolt type, which may or may not have a shoulder.
6 Make sure that the retaining ring is correctly seated (Figs. 5.9 and 5.10). Take care that no oil or grease is allowed to get onto the pressure plate or friction surfaces. Where a new pressure plate is being fitted, wipe the protective coating from the friction surfaces.
7 Lubricate the splines of the friction disc hub with a Moly paste or spray lubricant, but do not get any lubricant onto the linings.
8 When refitting the friction disc, make sure the greater projecting boss which incorporates the cushion springs is furthest from the engine, then fit the flywheel over the pressure plate. Fit the securing bolts and tighten them finger tight only.
9 The next operation is to centre the friction disc. If this is not done accurately the gearbox mainshaft will not be able to locate in the

Fig. 5.8 Special VW tool for holding the pressure plate stationary while unscrewing or tightening the retaining bolts – 020 gearbox (Sec 8)

Fig. 5.7 Exploded view of the clutch components – 020 gearbox (Sec)

1 Pressure plate assembly
2 Packing plate
3 Bolt
4 Release plate (200 and 210 mm diameter clutch)
5 Release plate (190 mm diameter clutch)
6 Retaining ring (200 and 210 mm diameter clutch)
7 Retaining ring (190 mm diameter clutch)
8 Friction disc
9 Pushrod
10 Bolt

8.5 Tightening the clutch pressure plate retaining bolts (020 gearbox)

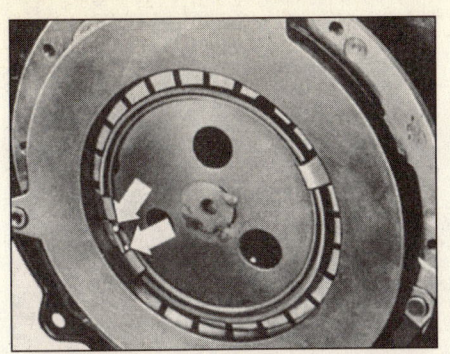

Fig. 5.9 Correct location of release plate retaining ring ends (arrowed) on the 190 mm clutch – 020 gearbox (Sec 8)

Fig. 5.10 Correct location of the release plate retaining ring ends (arrowed) on the 200 and 210 mm diameter clutch – 020 gearbox (Sec 8)

Fig. 5.11 Using VW tool 547 to centre the clutch friction disc – 020 gearbox (Sec 8)

splines of the clutch disc hub, and it will be impossible to fit the gearbox. The best centralising tool is VW 547 which fits in the flywheel and has a spigot which fits exactly in the centre of the clutch disc hub (Fig. 5.11). If you cannot borrow or hire tool VW 547 then we suggest you make up a tool as shown in Fig. 5.12. Alternatively centre the disc using vernier calipers (photo). Once the friction disc is centred correctly, tighten the securing bolts in a diagonal sequence to the specified torque and check the centralisation again.

10 When refitting the transmission, put a smear of lithium based grease on the end of the clutch pushrod at the release plate end.

9 Clutch (020 gearbox) - inspection

1 The most probable part of the clutch to require attention is the friction disc. Normal wear will eventually reduce its thickness. The lining must stand proud of the rivets by not less than 0.6 mm (0.025 in). At this measurement the lining is at the end of its life and a new friction disc is needed.

2 The friction disc should be checked for run-out if possible. Mount the disc between the centres of a lathe and measure the run-out at the specified dimension from the outer edge, then compare the result with the Specifications. However, this requires a dial gauge and a mandrel. If the clutch has not shown signs of dragging then this test may be passed over, but if it has we suggest that expert help be sought to test the run-out.

3 Examine the pressure plate. There are three important things to check. Put a straight-edge across the friction surface and measure any bow or taper with feeler gauges (see photo 6.3).

4 The rivets which hold the spring fingers in position must be tight. If any of them are loose the pressure plate must be scrapped. Finally, the condition of the friction surface. Ridges or scoring indicate undue wear and unless they can be removed by light application of emery paper it would be better to renew the plate.

5 The flywheel friction surface must be similarly checked.

6 So far the inspection has been for normal wear. Two other types of damage may be encountered. The first is overheating due to clutch slip. In extreme cases the pressure plate and flywheel may have radial cracks. Such faults mean that they require renewal. The second problem is contamination by oil or grease. This will cause clutch slip; but probably without the cracks. There will be shiny black patches on the friction disc which will have a glazed surface. There is no cure for this, a new friction disc is required. In addition it is imperative that the source of contamination be located and rectified. It will be either the crankshaft oil seal or the gearbox input shaft oil seal (or both!). Examine them and renew them as necessary.

7 Whilst the gearbox is removed, it is as well to check the release bearing for satisfactory condition - see Section 10.

10 Clutch release mechanism (020 gearbox) - removal and refitting

1 The clutch release mechanism is located in the gearbox end housing and is accessible after the removal of the end cover or plate (as applicable).

2 On 4-speed gearbox models, unbolt the end cover from the gearbox and remove the gasket (photo).

3 On 5-speed gearbox models, first support the engine/gearbox unit with a trolley jack, then disconnect the engine/gearbox front mounting and the gearbox rear mounting (see Chapter 1). Lower the jack a few inches to gain access to the end plate in the gearbox housing cover. Using a sharp instrument, pierce the endplate and lever it out from the gearbox. A new plate must be obtained (Fig. 5.13).

4 On both 4 and 5-speed gearboxes the release lever is located on the shaft by two circlips. Extract the circlips (photo).

5 With the clutch cable disconnected (see

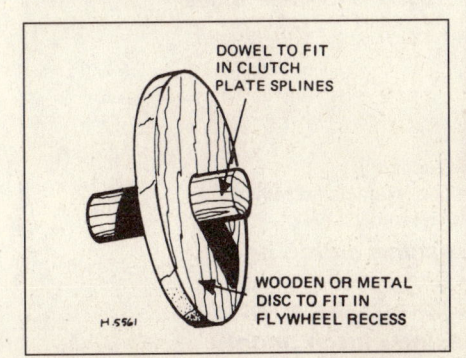

Fig. 5.12 Home-made tool for centralising the clutch friction disc – 020 gearbox (Sec 8)

8.9 Using vernier calipers to check the friction disc centralisation

10.2 Removing the gearbox end cover (020 4-speed gearbox)

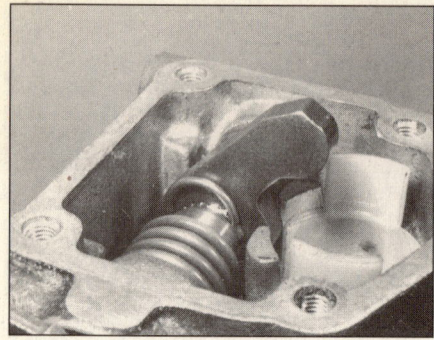

5•8 Clutch

10.4 Extracting the clutch release lever location circlips (020 4-speed gearbox)

10.5 Withdrawing the clutch release arm and shaft (020 4-speed gearbox)

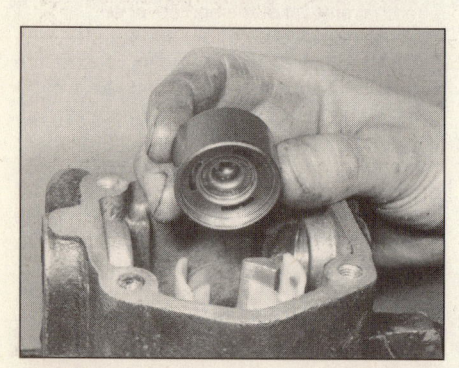

10.6 Removing the clutch release bearing (020 4-speed gearbox)

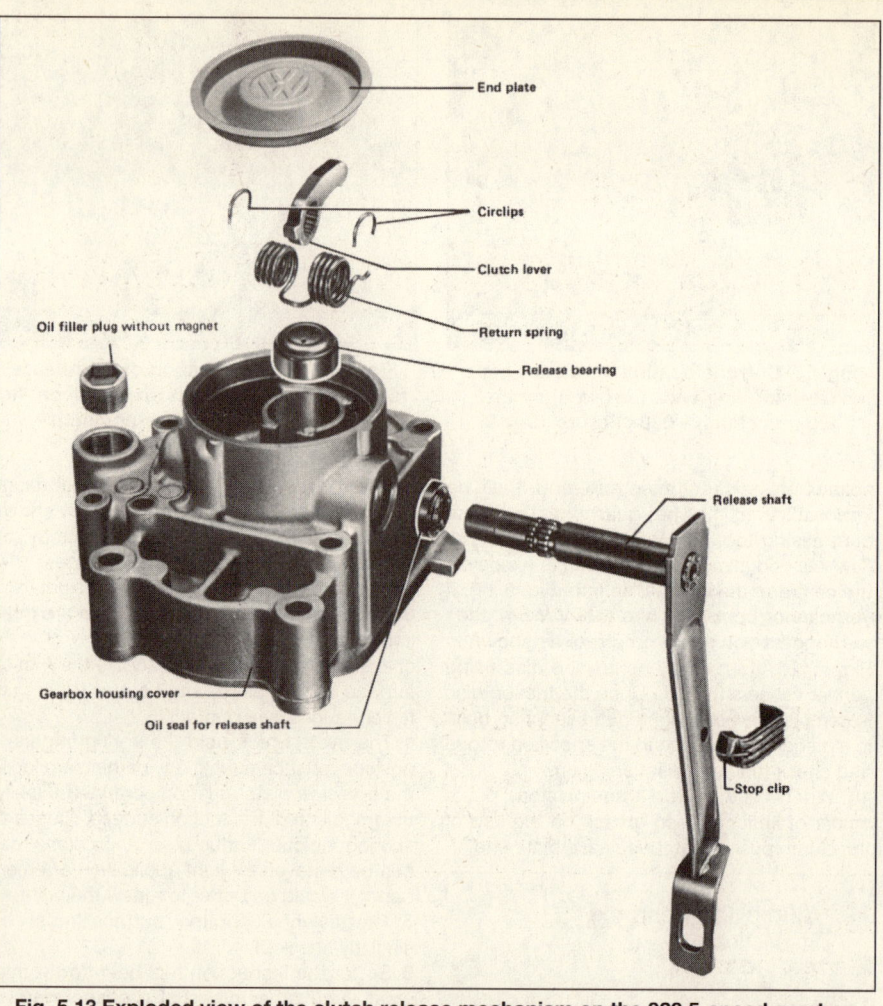

Fig. 5.13 Exploded view of the clutch release mechanism on the 020 5-speed gearbox (Sec 10)

Section 3) withdraw the release arm and shaft from the gearbox and remove the lever and spring (photo).

6 Remove the release bearing (photo) and, on 4-speed models only, extract the guide sleeve. Removal of the pushrod on the 4-speed gearbox is not possible unless the unit is lowered.

7 Rotate the release bearing and check it for wear and roughness; renew it if necessary. Check the shaft oil seal for wear or deterioration, and if necessary prise it out and drive in a new seal squarely using a suitable length of metal tubing. Fill the space between the seal lips with multi-purpose grease.

8 Refitting is a reversal of removal. Note that the release lever and shaft have a master spline, and when fitting the return spring ensure that the bent ends bear against the casing with the centre part hooked over the release lever. Always fit a new gasket to the end cover on 4-speed models, and use a suitable length of metal tubing to drive the new endplate into the housing on 5-speed models.

Fault finding - clutch

Judder when taking up drive
☐ Loose engine/gearbox mountings
☐ Friction linings worn or contaminated with oil
☐ Worn splines on gearbox input shaft or friction disc

Clutch fails to disengage
☐ Incorrect cable adjustment
☐ Friction disc sticking on input shaft splines (may be due to rust if car off road for long period)
☐ Faulty pressure plate assembly

Clutch slips
☐ Incorrect cable adjustment
☐ Friction linings worn or contaminated with oil
☐ Faulty pressure plate assembly

Noise when depressing clutch pedal
☐ Worn release bearing
☐ Worn splines on gearbox input shaft or friction disc

Noise when releasing clutch pedal
☐ Distorted friction disc
☐ Broken or weak friction disc cushion springs

Chapter 6
Manual gearbox and automatic transmission

For modifications, and information applicable to later models, see Supplement at end of manual

Contents

Automatic transmission - general description	8
Automatic transmission - removal and refitting	10
Automatic transmission - stall test	11
Automatic transmission - selector cable - removal, refitting and adjustment	12
Automatic transmission throttle and accelerator pedal cables (2E2 carburettor) - adjustment	13
Fault finding - manual gearbox and automatic transmission	See end of Chapter
Gearshift mechanism (020 gearbox, 4 and 5-speed) - removal, refitting and adjustment	7
Gearshift mechanism (084 gearbox) - removal, refitting and adjustment	5
Manual gearbox - general description	1
Manual gearbox - overhaul (general)	3
Manual gearbox (020, 4 and 5-speed) - removal and refitting	6
Manual gearbox (084) - removal and refitting	4
Routine maintenance - automatic transmission	9
Routine maintenance - manual gearbox	2

Degrees of difficulty

Easy, suitable for novice with little experience | **Fairly easy,** suitable for beginner with some experience | **Fairly difficult,** suitable for competent DIY mechanic | **Difficult,** suitable for experienced DIY mechanic | **Very difficult,** suitable for expert DIY or professional

Specifications

Manual gearbox
Type .... Four or five-speed (all synchromesh) and reverse. Drive to the front wheels by double CV jointed driveshafts

Gearbox identification codes
Four-speed (1.05 litre)	084 (6F)
Four-speed (1.3 litre)	084 (4F or 5F)
Four-speed (1.6 litre)	020 (4R)
Five-speed (1.6 litre)	020 (4T or 9A)
Five-speed (1.8 litre)	020 (9A)

Lubrication
Oil capacity:
- 084 gearbox .... 2.2 litre (3.9 Imp pint)
- 020 gearbox (four-speed) .... 1.5 litre (2.6 Imp pint)
- 020 gearbox (five-speed) .... 2.0 litre (3.5 Imp pint)

Lubricant type .... Gear oil, viscosity SAE 80

Ratios (:1)

	084 (All)	020 (4R)	020 (4T)	020 (9A)
1st	3.45	3.45	3.45	3.45
2nd	1.95	1.94	1.94	2.11
3rd	1.25	128	1.28	1.44
4th	0.89	0.90	0.90	1.12
5th	-	-	0.74	0.89
Reverse	3.38	3.16	3.16	3.16
Final drive	3.88 (4F)	3.66	3.66	3.66
	4.06 (5F)			
	4.57 (6F)			
Overall ratio in top gear	3.47 (4F)	3.33	2.73	3.27
	3.64 (5F)			
	3.82 (6F)			

Wear limits

084 gearbox:
Synchro ring gap clearance . . . . 0.5 mm (0.0197 in)
Input and output shaft maximum endfloat . . . . 0.5 mm (0.0197 in)

020, 4 and 5-speed gearbox:
Synchro-ring gap clearance . . . . 0.5 mm (0.0196 in)
3rd gear axial play circlips available: **Thickness**
   Brown . . . . 2.5 mm (0.099 in)
   Black . . . . 2.6 mm (0.102 in)
   Bright . . . . 2.7 mm (0.106 in)
   Copper . . . . 2.8 mm (0.110 in)
   Brass . . . . 2.9 mm (0.114 in)
   Blue . . . . 3.0 mm (0.118 in)

Automatic transmission

Type
Type . . . . 3-speed epicyclic geartrain type, incorporating multi-plate clutches and brake, and one brake band. Drive from engine transmission by torque converter

Identification
Gearbox code number 010
Gearbox code letters:
   1.6 litre . . . . TKA
   1.8 litre . . . . TJA
Torque converter code letter:
   1.6 litre . . . . M
   1.8 litre . . . . K

Ratios (:1)
1st 2.71
2nd 1.50
3rd 1.00
Reverse 2.43
Final drive:
   1.6 litre 3.41
   1.8 litre 3.12

Lubrication
Lubricant type:
   Gearbox . . . . Dexron type ATF
   Final drive . . . . Hypold gear oil viscosity SAE 90EP
Capacity:
   Total (from dry) . . . . 6.0 litre (10.6 Imp pint)
   Service (drain and refill) . . . . 3.0 litre (5.3 Imp pint)
   Final drive oil capacity . . . . 0.75 litre (1.3 Imp pint)

All transmissions

Torque wrench settings

	Nm	lbf ft
084 gearbox		
Clutch guide sleeve to gearbox	15	11
Gear lever stop plate nuts	10	7
Shift rod mounting coupling screw (new)	20	15
Shift rod clip nut	20	15
Gearshift housing bolts	15	11
Gearbox to engine:		
M12	75	55
M10	45	33
Driveshaft to gearbox	45	33
Bracket to engine	45	33
Gearbox mountings	60	44
Drive flange bolt	25	18
Clutch housing-to-gearbox bolts	25	18
Gearbox housing cover bolts	25	18
Relay lever bolt	35	26
Oil filler plug	25	18
Oil drain plug	25	18
Selector finger (to inner shift lever)	25	18

Manual gearbox and automatic transmission 6•3

Torque wrench settings (continued)

	Nm	lbf ft
020 four-speed gearbox		
Gearbox to engine (M12)	75	55
Starter motor to gearbox/engine	60	44
Driveshafts to flange	45	33
Left console to gearbox	35	26
Left console to subframe	60	44
Rear right console to engine	25	18
Gearbox to clutch housing	25	18
Peg bolt for selector shaft	20	15
Reverse shaft set screw:		
Hex head type	20	15
Torx head type	30	22
Selector shaft end cap	50	37
Output shaft bearing plate bolts	40	30
Input shaft bearing clamp screw nut	15	11
020 five-speed gearbox		
Gear lever retaining plate nuts	10	7
Selector shaft lever nut	15	11
Gearbox housing cover bolts	25	18
Gearbox-to-clutch housing bolts	25	18
Selector shaft end cap	50	37
Reverse shaft securing bolt	20	15
Selector shaft securing bolt	20	15
First gear synchronizer screw	150	111
Bearing plate bolts	40	30
Oil filler plug	25	18
Automatic transmission		
Selector lever cable clamp nut	8	6
Driveshaft to flange	45	33
Converter to driveplate	35	26
Gearbox to engine	75	55
Left-hand gearbox mounting to gearbox	60	44
Left-hand gearbox mounting to console	35	26
Console (rear right) to engine	25	18
Oil pan bolts	20	15
Oil strainer (filter) cover bolts	3	2

1 Manual gearbox - general description

The manual gearbox is VW type 084 or 020, according to model. It incorporates four or five forward speeds and one reverse speed, with synchromesh engagement on all forward gears. The clutch withdrawal mechanism comprises a release arm and lever located at the outer end of the gearbox and a pushrod located in the input shaft.

Gearshift is by means of a floor-mounted lever connected by a remote control housing and shift rod to the gearbox selector shaft and relay lever.

The differential (final drive) unit is integral with the main gearbox and is located between the main casing and the bearing housing.

Drain and filler/level plugs are screwed into the main gearbox casing.

2 Routine maintenance - manual gearbox

The manual gearbox requires the minimum amount of maintenance, only the following checks need be made at the specified intervals given at the front of this manual (see Routine Maintenance).

1 Check gearbox for signs of oil leaks: If possible run the vehicle over an inspection pit or raise and support it on axle stands to make this (and the following) check. Inspect the gearbox casing for any signs of serious oil leaks. Oil leakage from the transmission will necessitate further investigation and, if serious, must be remedied without delay. A very minor leak may be permissible providing regular checks are made to ensure that the leak does not get any worse and to ensure that the gearbox oil level is maintained. Do not confuse gearbox oil leaks with engine oil leaks which may have sprayed onto the gearbox casing.

2 Check the gearbox oil level. The vehicle must be parked level for this check. Remove the oil level/filler plug from the gearbox (photo and Fig. 6.1) and check that the oil level is up to the base of the filler orifice. If not, top up with the specified grade of oil and refit the plug.

2.2 Using a key to remove the gearbox filler plug (020 5-speed gearbox)

Fig. 6.1 Gearbox filler plug location (arrowed) – 084 gearbox (Sec 2)

6•4 Manual gearbox and automatic transmission

3 Although not specified as being necessary during normal service procedures, the transmission oil can be drained and renewed. Drain the oil into a suitable container by undoing the drain plug in the lower part of the differential housing. Refit the plug and refill with the specified type and quantity of oil.

3 Manual gearbox - overhaul (general)

Overhauling a manual transmission unit is a difficult and involved job for the DIY home mechanic. In addition to dismantling and reassembling many small parts, clearances must be precisely measured and, if necessary, changed by selecting shims and spacers. Internal transmission components are also often difficult to obtain, and in many instances, are extremely expensive. Because of this, if the transmission develops a fault or becomes noisy, the best course of action is to have the unit overhauled by a specialist repairer, or to obtain an exchange reconditioned unit.

Nevertheless, it is not impossible for the more experienced mechanic to overhaul the transmission, provided the special tools are available, and that the job is done in a deliberate step-by-step manner so that nothing is overlooked.

The tools necessary for an overhaul may include internal and external circlip pliers, bearing pullers, a slide hammer, a set of pin punches, a dial test indicator, and possibly a hydraulic press. In addition, a large, sturdy workbench and a vice will be required.

During dismantling of the transmission, make careful notes of how each component is fitted, to make reassembly easier and accurate.

Before dismantling the transmission, it will help if you have some idea which area is malfunctioning. Certain problems can be closely related to specific areas in the gearbox, which can make component examination and replacement easier.

4 Manual gearbox (084) - removal and refitting

The following paragraphs describe how to remove the gearbox leaving the engine in situ. However, if work is necessary on the engine as well, the engine and gearbox can be removed as one unit then separated on the bench, as described in Chapter 1.

1 The gearbox is removed downwards, so the vehicle must be raised from the ground sufficiently to withdraw the box from underneath. The ideal is to work over a pit, but axle stands or similar support under the body can be arranged. However, note that you must be able to turn the wheels to disconnect the driveshafts. Do not raise it too much or you will be unable to get at the box through the opening in the engine compartment. About 600 mm (24 in) clearance is required.

2 Since the engine will be left unsupported at the rear it is necessary to make provision to take the weight of it. If you have a block and tackle or a garage crane this will be simple, but if not it is possible to make a simple support similar to that used in the VW agency. Fig. 6.2 shows a simple beam which is supported on either side of the vehicle in the channels which house the bonnet sides on the top of the wings. Alternatively the engine can be supported from underneath with blocks placed under the sump, but this method means that the car cannot be moved while the transmission is out of the car.

3 Remove the bonnet, as described in Chapter 11, and place it safely out of the way.

4 Having supported the engine, disconnect the battery negative lead.

5 For the purposes of this Section the front is the engine end of the gearbox, left and right are as if you are standing at the side of the car behind the gearbox looking towards the engine.

6 Remove the left gearbox mounting complete and take it away. Unscrew the drain plug from the differential housing, drain the oil into a suitable container, then refit the plug (photo).

7 Disconnect the clutch cable from the gearbox, with reference to Chapter 5.

8 Disconnect the earth strap at the gearbox support.

9 Unbolt and remove the starter motor, with reference to Chapter 9.

10 Disconnect the reversing light lead from the gearbox (photo).

11 Disconnect the speedometer drive cable from the gearbox by undoing the collar.

12 Unscrew and remove the upper engine-to-gearbox securing bolts.

13 Disconnect the inner ends of the drive shafts from the gearbox flanges, with reference to Chapter 7 and tie them out of the way.

14 Unbolt and remove the cover plate from the clutch housing (photo).

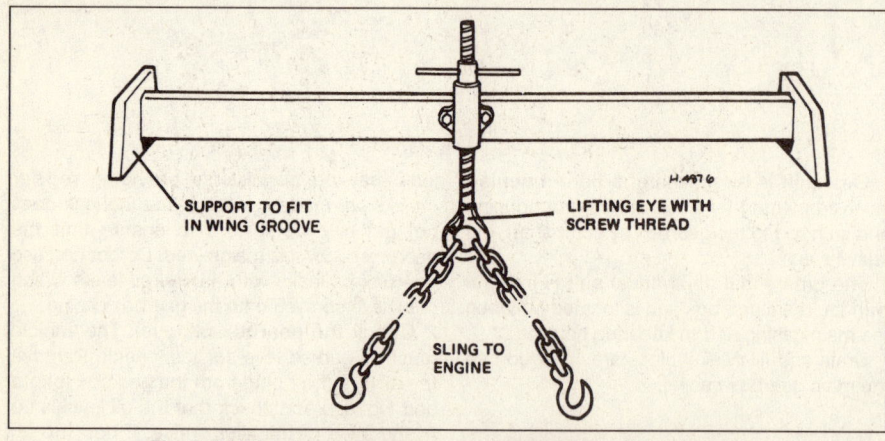

Fig. 6.2 Lifting bar arrangement to support the engine (Sec 4)

4.6 Gearbox drain plug (084 gearbox)

4.10 Disconnecting the reversing light switch wiring (084 gearbox)

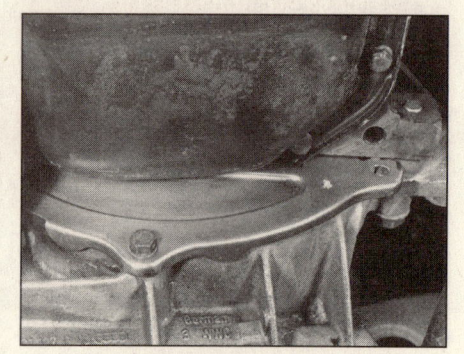

4.14 Clutch housing cover plate (084 gearbox)

Manual gearbox and automatic transmission 6•5

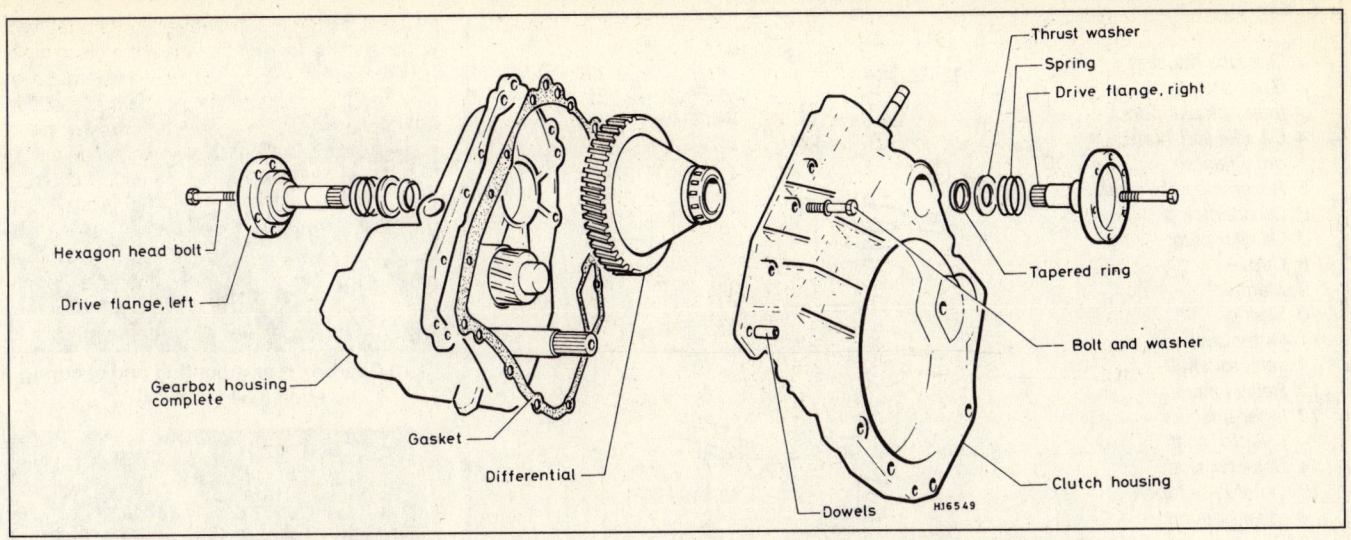

Fig. 6.3 Gearbox, clutch housing and associated components – 084 gearbox (Sec 4)

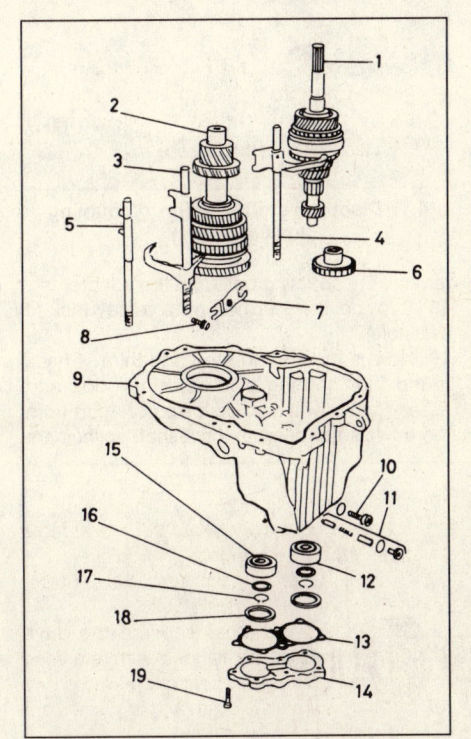

Fig. 6.4 Input and output shafts and selector rod locations in the gearbox housing – 084 gearbox (Sec 4)

1 Input shaft
2 Output shaft
3 Selector rod and fork, 1st and 2nd gears
4 Selector rod and fork, 3rd and 4th gears
5 Selector rod, reverse gear
6 Reverse gear
7 Relay lever
8 Pin for relay lever
9 Gearbox housing
10 Bolt – relay lever
11 Gear detent
12 Input shaft bearing
13 Gasket
14 Bearing cover
15 Output shaft bearing
16 Small shim
17 Circlip
18 Large shim
19 Hexagon bolt

Fig. 6.5 Exploded view of the clutch housing – 084 gearbox (Sec 4)

1 Needle bearing
2 Switch
3 Extension pin
4 Clutch housing
5 Breather connection
6 Plug
7 Breather pipe
8 Input shaft pinion
9 Starter bush
10 Input shaft seal
11 Guide sleeve
12 Release bearing
13 Driveshaft oil seal
14 Seal
15 Bush
16 Inner shift lever
17 Outer race taper roller bearing
18 Selector finger
19 Needle bearing
20 Seal sleeve

6•6 Manual gearbox and automatic transmission

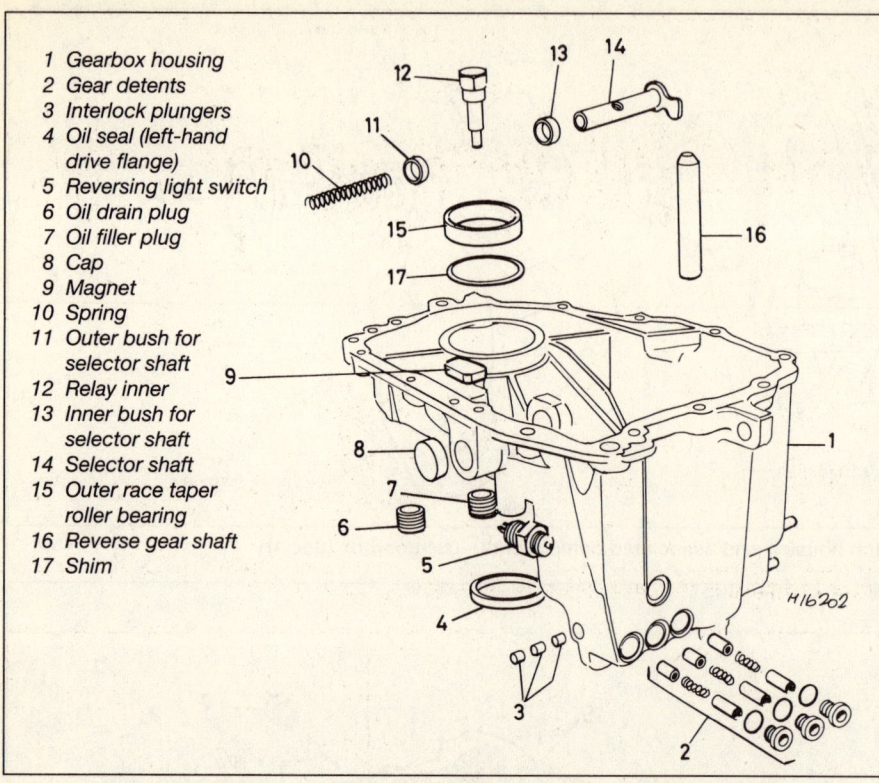

Fig. 6.6 Exploded view of the gearbox housing – 084 gearbox (Sec 4)

1 Gearbox housing
2 Gear detents
3 Interlock plungers
4 Oil seal (left-hand drive flange)
5 Reversing light switch
6 Oil drain plug
7 Oil filler plug
8 Cap
9 Magnet
10 Spring
11 Outer bush for selector shaft
12 Relay inner
13 Inner bush for selector shaft
14 Selector shaft
15 Outer race taper roller bearing
16 Reverse gear shaft
17 Shim

4.16 Gearbox rear mounting and securing bolt (084 gearbox)

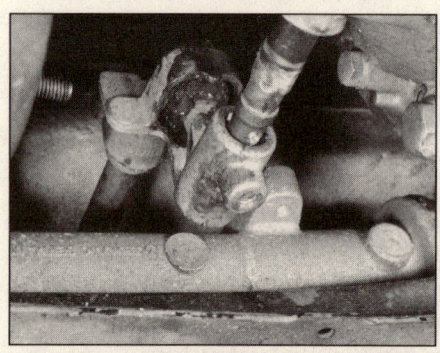

4.17 Disconnect the shaft rod coupling (084 gearbox)

15 Unscrew and remove the remaining engine-to-gearbox bolts, noting the location of the rear mounting bracket.
16 Unscrew the rear mounting nut and remove the bracket, or leave the mounting on the bracket and remove the mounting bolts (photo).
17 Remove the screw from the shaft rod coupling and ease the coupling from the rod (photo). The screw threads are coated with a liquid locking agent and, if difficulty is experienced, it may be necessary to heat up the coupling with a blowlamp; *however, take the necessary fire precautions*. If required, remove the coupling ball from the adaptor.
18 Support the gearbox on a trolley jack (if available).
19 Now is the time to stop and think. Check round that nothing else holds the box and assess just how it is to be lowered. Apart from the dowels the gearbox driveshaft splines are

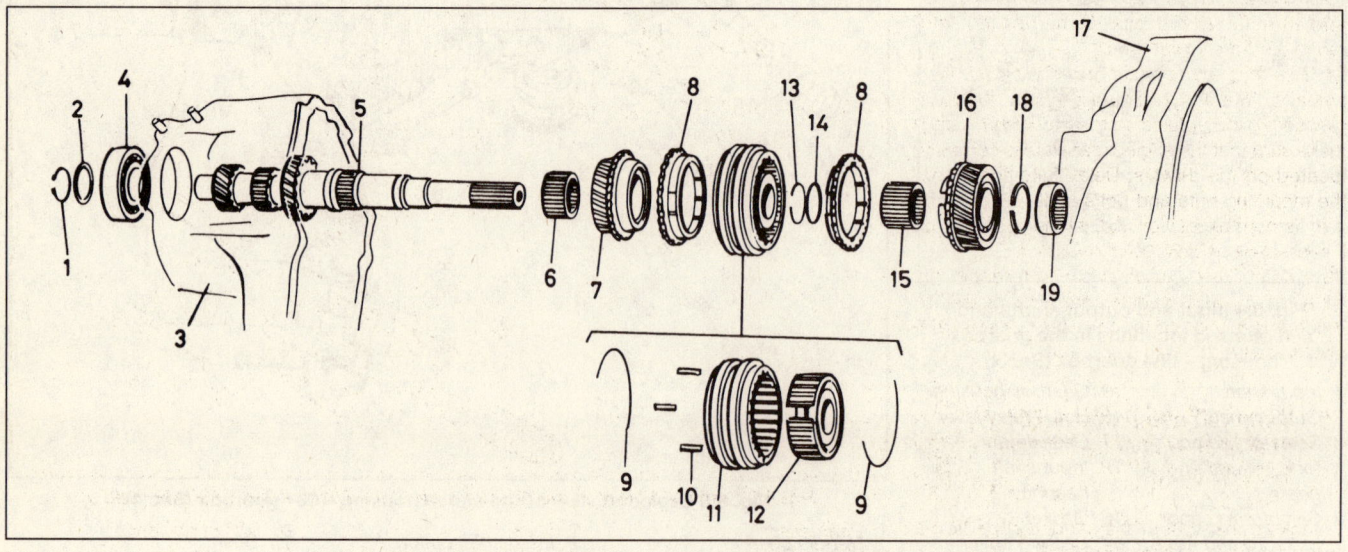

Fig. 6.7 Exploded view of the input shaft assembly – 084 gearbox (Sec 4)

1 Circlip
2 Shim
3 Gearbox housing
4 Grooved ball-bearing
5 Input shaft
6 Needle bearing for 3rd gear
7 3rd speed gear
8 Synchro-rings for 3rd and 4th gears
9 Spring
10 Key
11 Sleeve
12 Synchro-hub
13 Circlip
14 Thrust washer
15 Needle bearing for 4th gear
16 4th gear
17 Clutch housing
18 Circlip
19 Needle bearing

Manual gearbox and automatic transmission 6•7

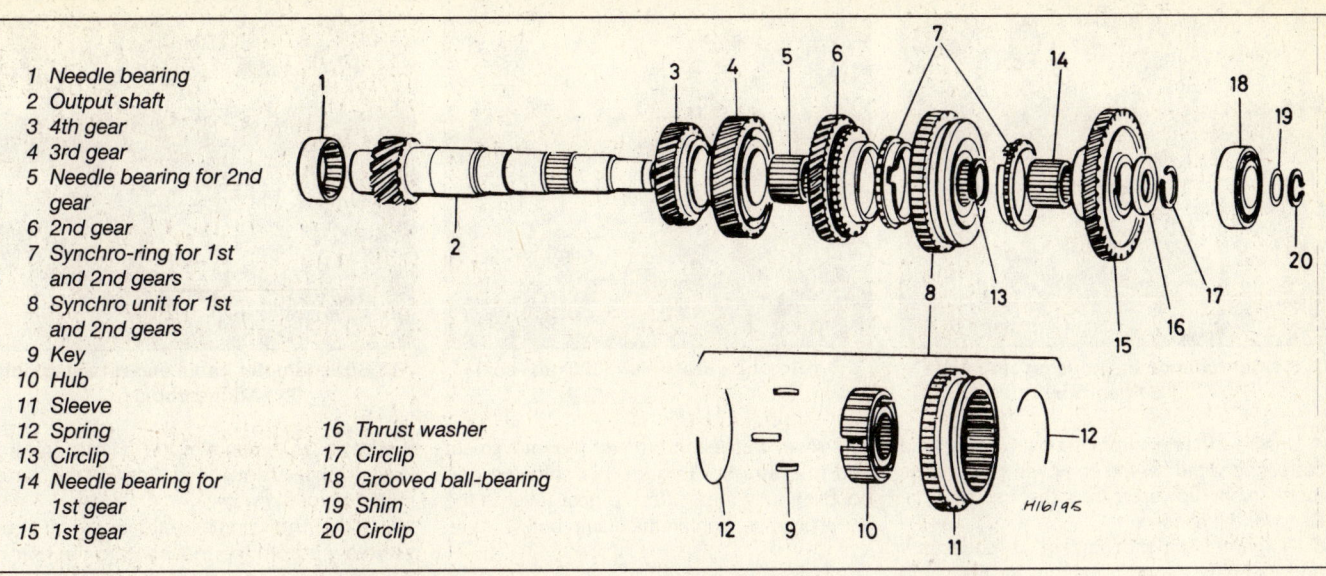

Fig. 6.8 Exploded view of the output shaft assembly – 084 gearbox (Sec 4)

1 Needle bearing
2 Output shaft
3 4th gear
4 3rd gear
5 Needle bearing for 2nd gear
6 2nd gear
7 Synchro-ring for 1st and 2nd gears
8 Synchro unit for 1st and 2nd gears
9 Key
10 Hub
11 Sleeve
12 Spring
13 Circlip
14 Needle bearing for 1st gear
15 1st gear
16 Thrust washer
17 Circlip
18 Grooved ball-bearing
19 Shim
20 Circlip

engaged in the friction disc of the clutch and the box must be pulled back to withdraw the shaft from the boss of the disc. This must be done carefully or there will be damage to the friction disc. In fact, if the box is not kept level the shaft will jam in the splines.

20 **Do not** try to separate the box from the engine by driving a wedge between the flanges, this will damage the castings. This box can be pulled backwards easily enough if it is kept level. The dowels are a tight fit and when they come out of the dowel holes the weight of the box will be felt suddenly. **Do not** let the box drop at all or you will damage the gear driveshaft splines, but move it away from the engine until you can see the shaft clear and then lower the box to the ground and remove it from under the car.

21 Refitting is a reversal of removal, but first smear a little molybdenum disulphide based grease on the splines of the input shaft, and make sure that the engine rear plate is correctly located on the dowels. Delay fully tightening the mounting nuts and bolts until the gearbox is in its normal position. Adjust the gearchange if necessary, as described in Section 5.

22 Adjust the clutch with reference to Chapter 5, and check that the gearshift mechanism operates correctly. Refill the gearbox with oil.

5 Gearshift mechanism (084 gearbox) - removal, refitting and adjustment

1 Jack up the front of the car and support on axle stands. Apply the handbrake.
2 With neutral selected, mark the shift rod and coupling in relation to each other, then unscrew the coupling clamp and pull out the shift rod.
3 Working inside the car, unscrew the gear knob and remove the gaiter.

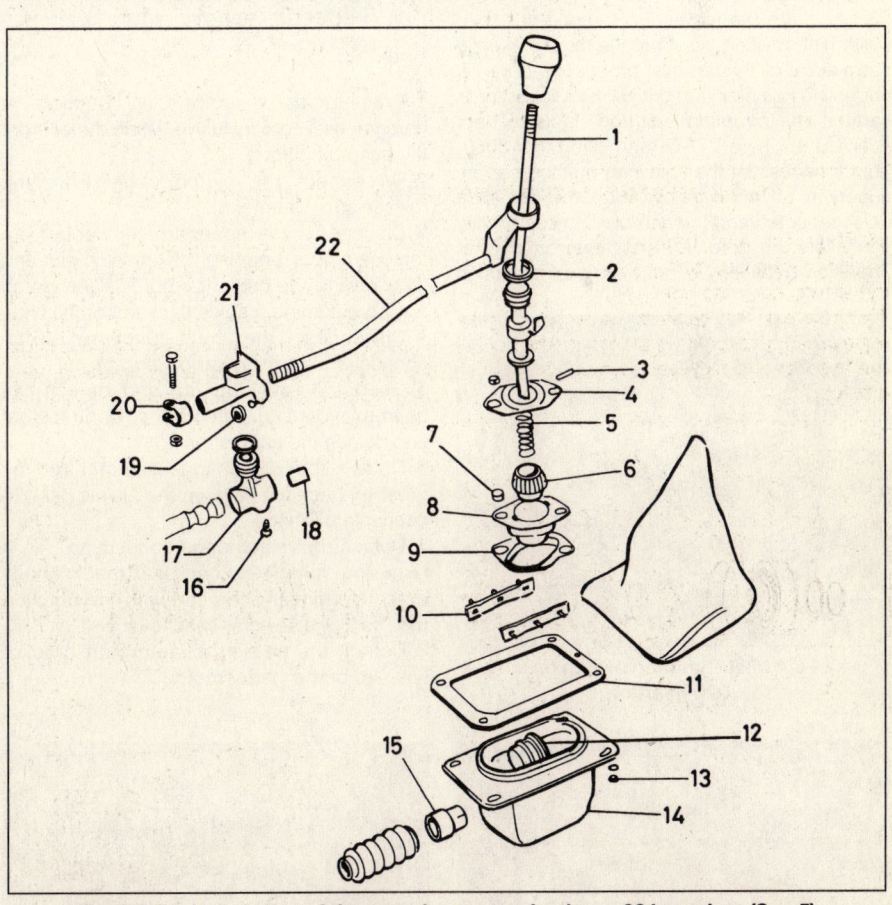

Fig. 6.9 Exploded view of the gearchange mechanism – 084 gearbox (Sec 5)

1 Gear lever
2 Plastic ring
3 Pin
4 Stop plate
5 Spring
6 Ball
7 Spacer
8 Ballhousing
9 Seal
10 Stop
11 Seal
12 Bearing race
13 Self-locking nut
14 Housing
15 Bush
16 Mounting screw
17 Coupling
18 Bush
19 Foam plastic washer
20 Clip
21 Shift finger
22 Shift rod

6•8 Manual gearbox and automatic transmission

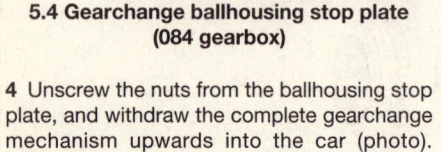

5.4 Gearchange ballhousing stop plate (084 gearbox)

6.1 Gearbox drain plug (020 gearbox)

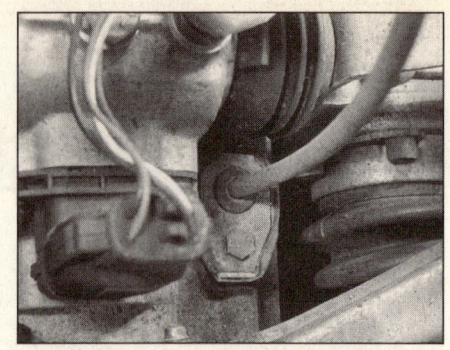

6.3 Speedometer cable and retaining bolt (020 gearbox)

4 Unscrew the nuts from the ballhousing stop plate, and withdraw the complete gearchange mechanism upwards into the car (photo). Recover the spacers.
5 Dismantle the mechanism as necessary and examine the components for wear and damage. Renew as necessary.
6 Lubricate the joints and bearing surfaces with high melting-point grease then refit using a reversal of the removal procedure. If a new coupling has been fitted it will be necessary to adjust the coupling position - this is best carried out by a VW garage using tool 3069, but if necessary the following method can be used in an emergency. With the coupling disconnected and the gearbox in neutral have an assistant hold the gear lever in neutral position between 3rd and 4th gear positions (ie halfway between front and rear movement and to the right). Engage the shift rod and coupling fully and, with the gear lever in the same position, tighten the clamp bolt.

6 Manual gearbox (020, 4 and 5-speed) - removal and refitting

1 Proceed as described in Section 4, paragraphs 1 to 5 inclusive. Drain the oil from the gearbox (photo).
2 Disconnect the clutch cable from the release arm (Chapter 5).
3 Disconnect the speedometer cable from the gearbox by undoing the retaining bolt and withdrawing the cable (photo). Tie the clutch and speedometer cables back out of the way.
4 Disconnect the multi-function switch connector from the gearbox (photo).
5 Undo the retaining nut and detach the gearbox mounting support arm. Undo the nut and detach the earth strap.
6 Detach the gearchange selector rod by pressing back the clips on the plastic balljoint connectors (photo).
7 Detach the gearchange connecting link. If removing completely note that the link ends differ in angle and the end with the notched mark is at the selector shaft lever end.
8 Detach the heater hose support bracket (inboard of the starter motor).
9 Unbolt and remove the starter motor, leaving the leads attached. Position the starter motor out of the way.
10 Undo the single retaining bolt and withdraw it from the mounting to the rear of the left-hand driveshaft (right rear of gearbox looking from left side of car).
11 Unbolt and remove the engine/gearbox mounting on the left-hand side (front of car) - photo.
12 Unscrew and remove the engine-to-gearbox attachment bolts at the top.
13 Working underneath the vehicle, detach the right and left-hand driveshafts at their driveshaft flanges. Tie up the driveshafts to support them. Refer to Chapter 7 for further details.
14 Detach and remove the wheel arch cover on the left-hand side.
15 Unbolt and remove the clutch housing cover plate bolts (photo).
16 Unscrew and remove the lower engine-to-gearbox attachment bolt (under the right-hand drive flange) and the cover plate bolts.
17 Disconnect the exhaust downpipe from the manifold flange (see Chapter 3).
18 Unbolt and detach, but do not remove, the engine mounting unit (between the engine and the bulkhead) - photo. This will allow the engine to be pivoted to allow gearbox removal.
19 Lower the engine and gearbox a little and

6.4 Multi-function switch on 020 gearbox

6.6 Gearchange connecting rod links and plastic balljoint (020 gearbox)

6.11 Front engine/gearbox mounting viewed from underneath (1.8 litre)

6.15 Clutch housing cover plate (020 gearbox)

Manual gearbox and automatic transmission 6•9

6.18 Right-hand rear engine mounting viewed from underneath (1.8 litre gearbox)

Fig. 6.10 Remove cover plate from the driveshaft flange (arrowed) – 020 gearbox (Sec 6)

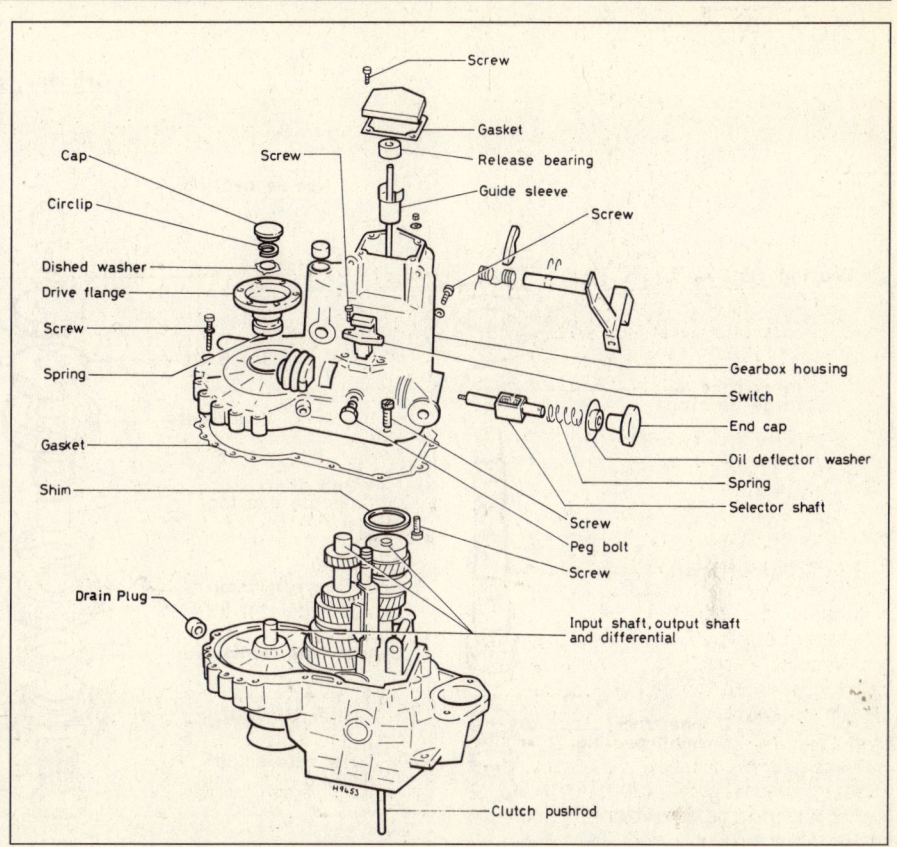

Fig. 6.11 Exploded view of the 020 4-speed gearbox (Sec 6)

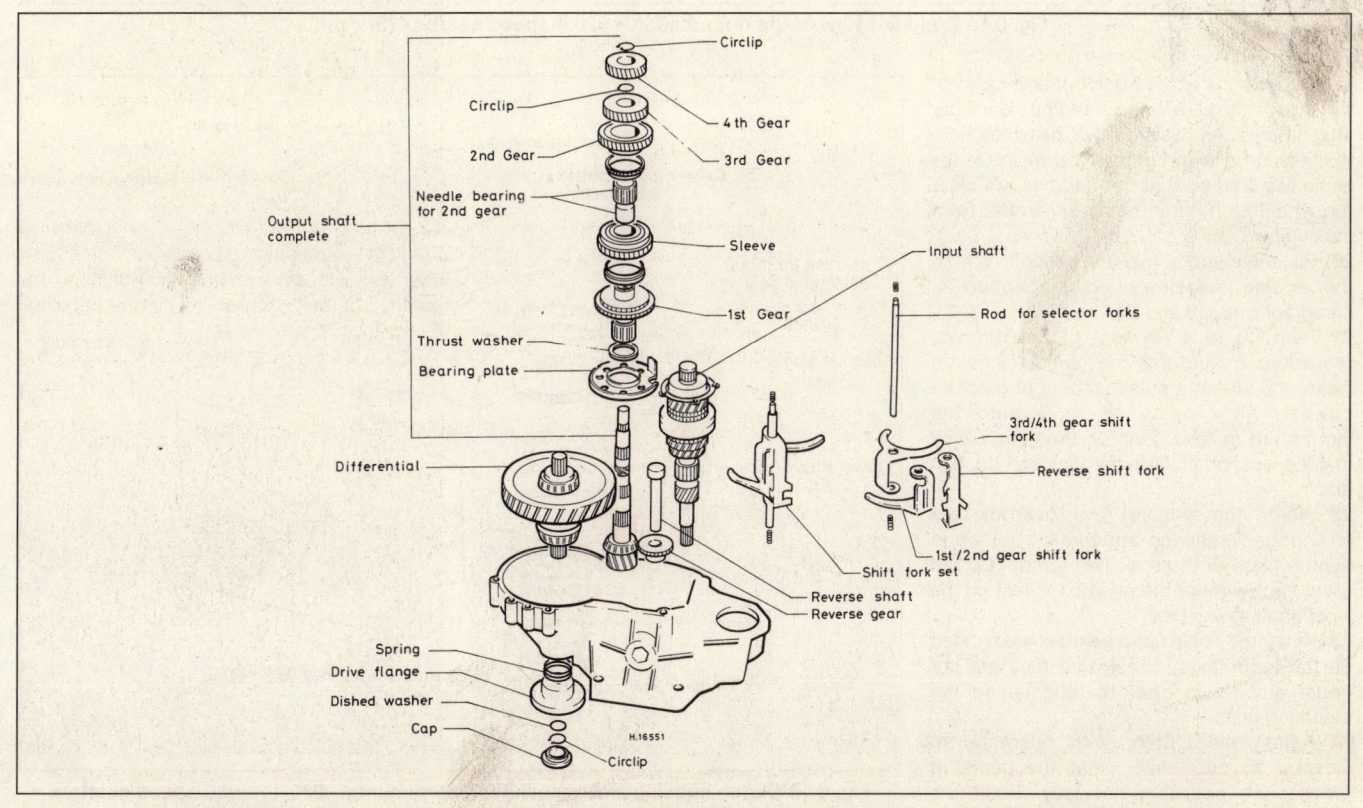

Fig. 6.12 Exploded view of the gear assemblies and clutch housing components – 020 4-speed gearbox (Sec 6)

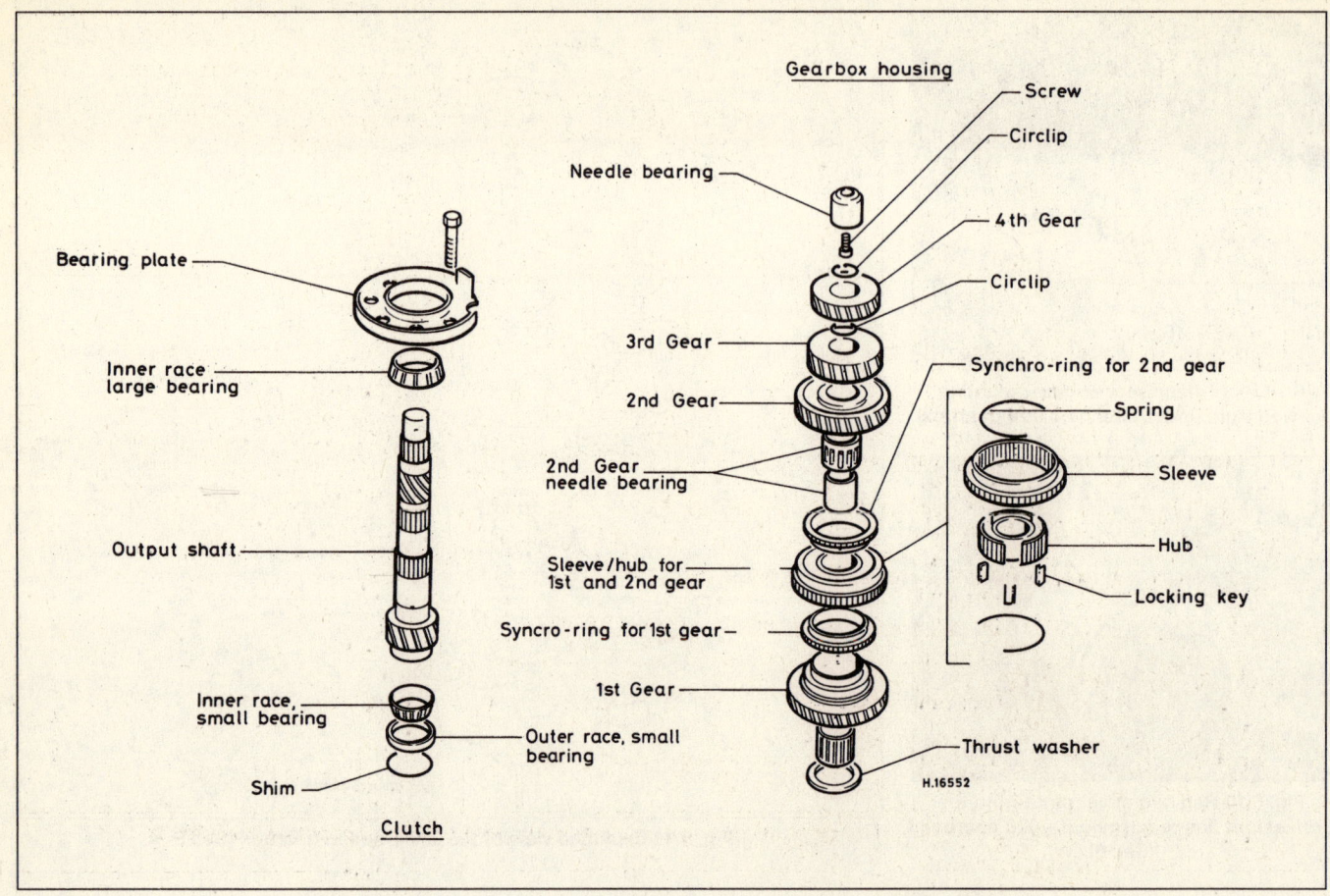

6•10 Manual gearbox and automatic transmission

Fig. 6.13 Exploded view of the output shaft – 020 4-speed gearbox (Sec 6)

pull the gearbox to the front, but take care not to strain any of the engine ancillary attachments. An assistant will be useful here to check on this and to hold the engine at the angle required so that the gearbox will clear the wheel arch when being separated from the engine.

20 Pull the gearbox free and separate it from the engine, as described in Section 4, paragraphs 18, 19 and 20.

21 Refitting is a reversal of the removal procedure. Ensure that the joint surfaces are clean and smear a small amount of graphite powder, Moly paste or spray onto the input shaft splines. Line up the gearbox so that the input shaft will enter the clutch friction disc.

22 When the engine and gearbox are re-engaged, refit the attachment bolts and tighten them to the specified torque. Do not allow the weight of the gearbox to rest on the input shaft at any time.

23 When the engine and gearbox are located on the mountings, check that they are not under any strain prior to retightening the mounting bolts.

24 Adjust the clutch, with reference to Chapter 5, and check that the gearshift mechanism operates correctly. Refill the gearbox with oil.

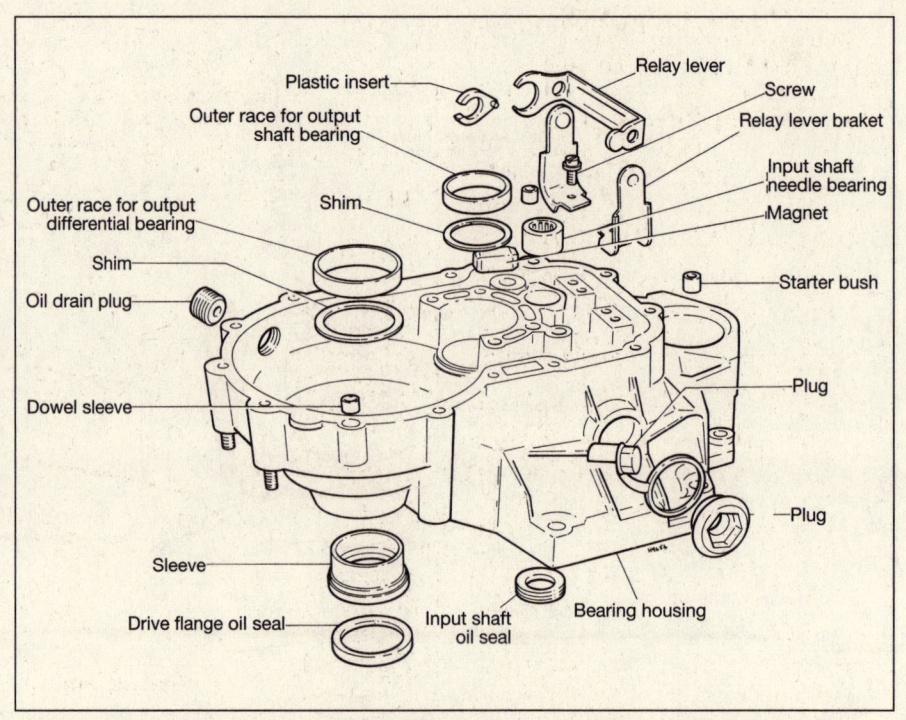

Fig. 6.14 Clutch housing and associated components – 020 4- and 5-speed gearbox (Sec 6)

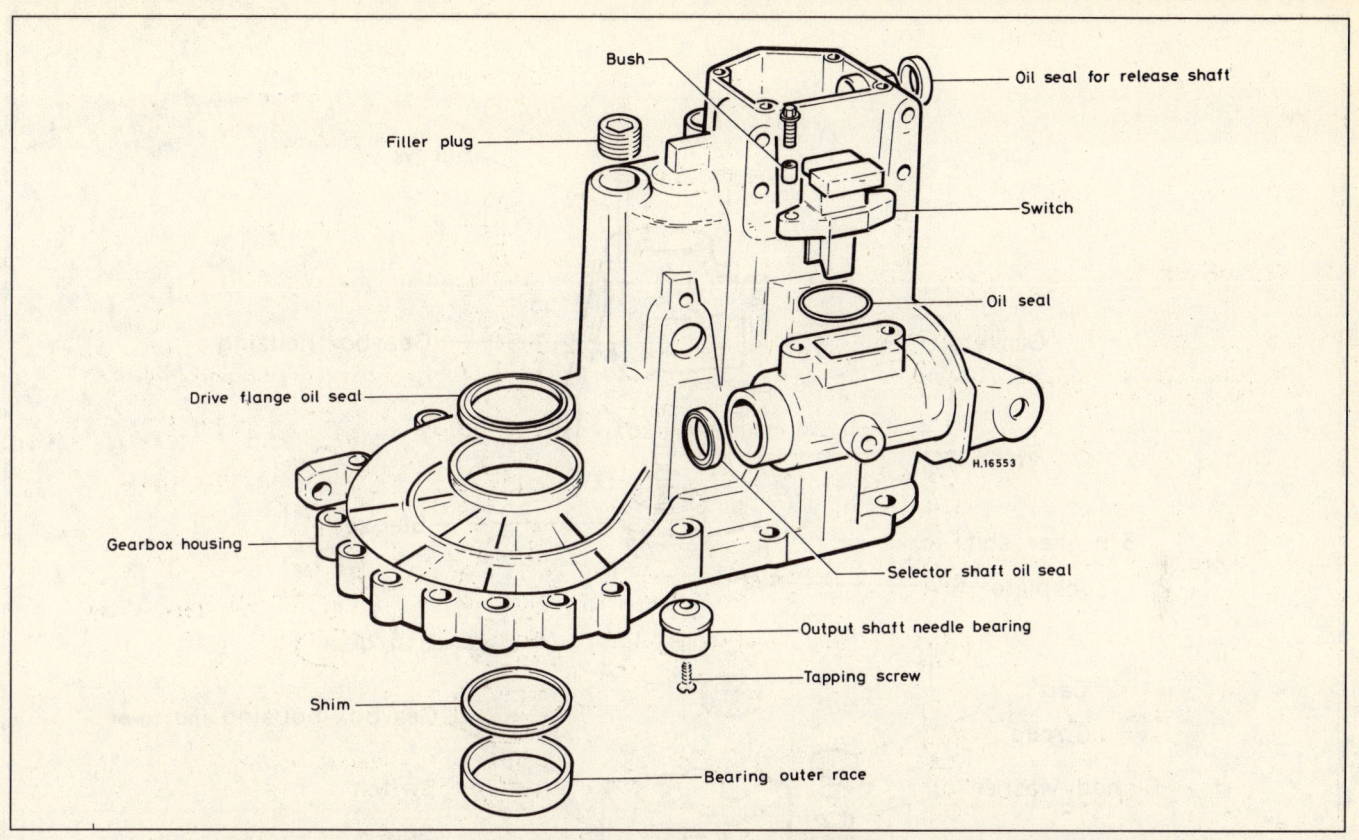

Manual gearbox and automatic transmission 6•11

Fig. 6.15 Gearbox housing (gear carrier housing) and associated components – 020 4-speed gearbox (Sec 6)

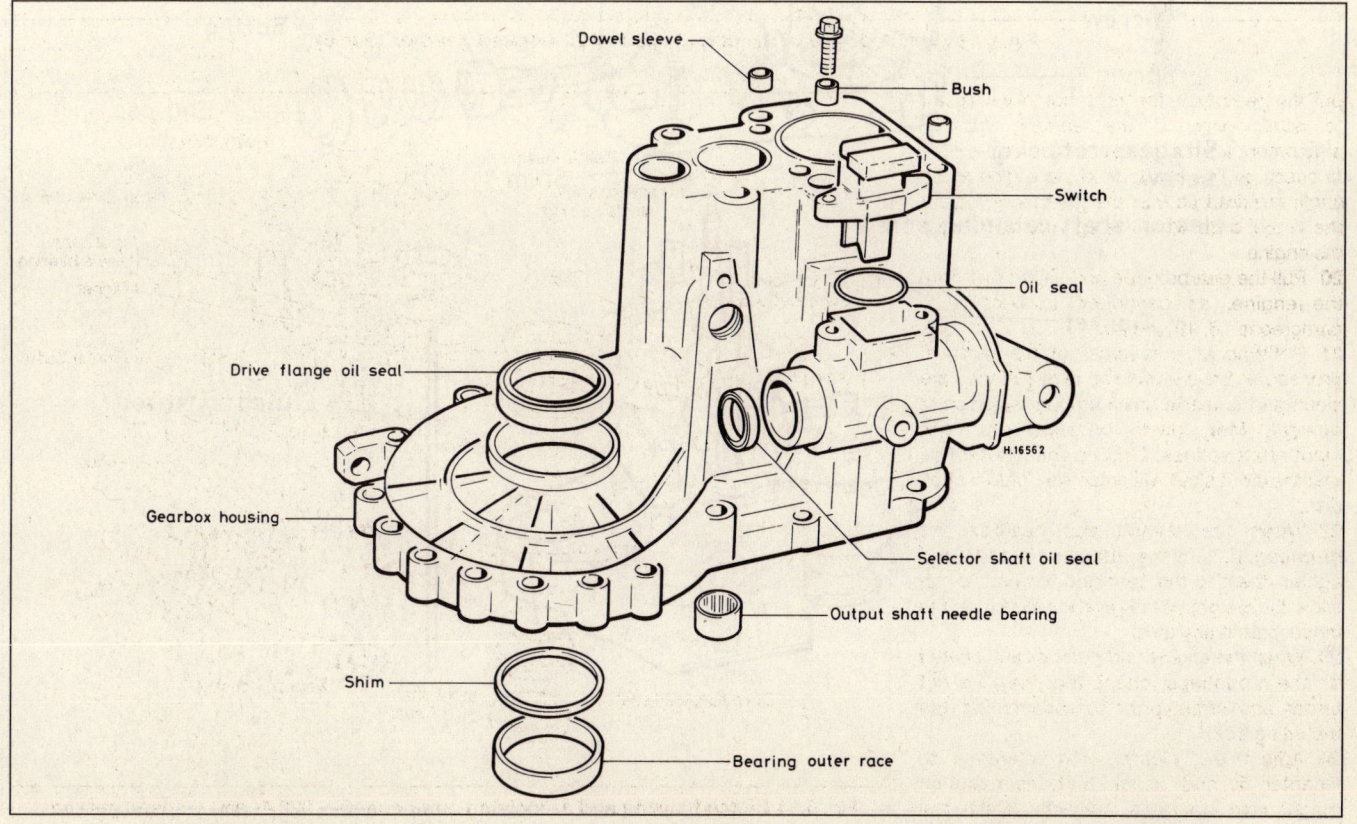

Fig. 6.16 Gearbox housing (gear carrier housing) and associated components – 020 5-speed gearbox (Sec 6)

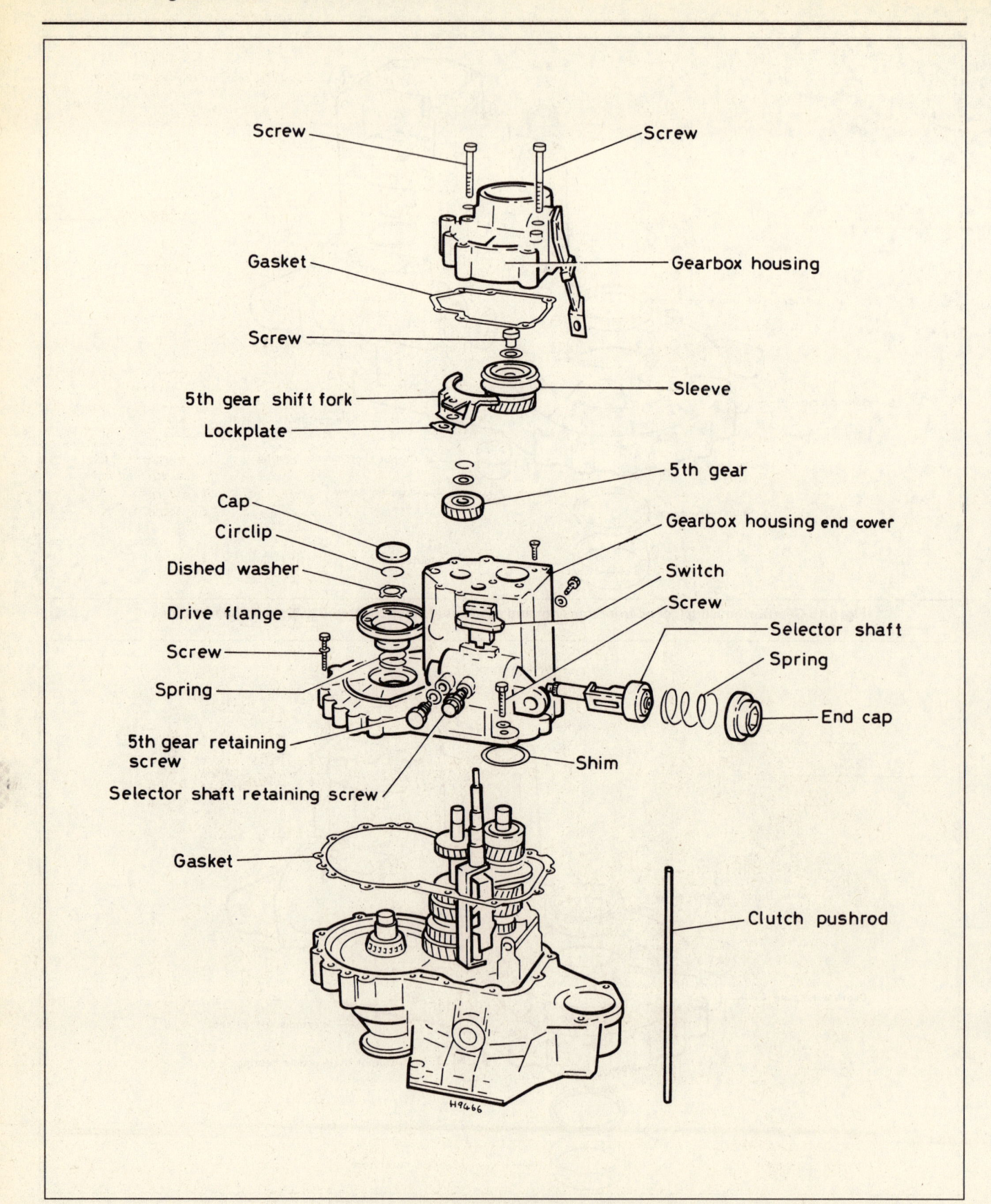

6•12 Manual gearbox and automatic transmission

Fig. 6.17 Exploded view of the 020 5-speed gearbox (Sec 6)

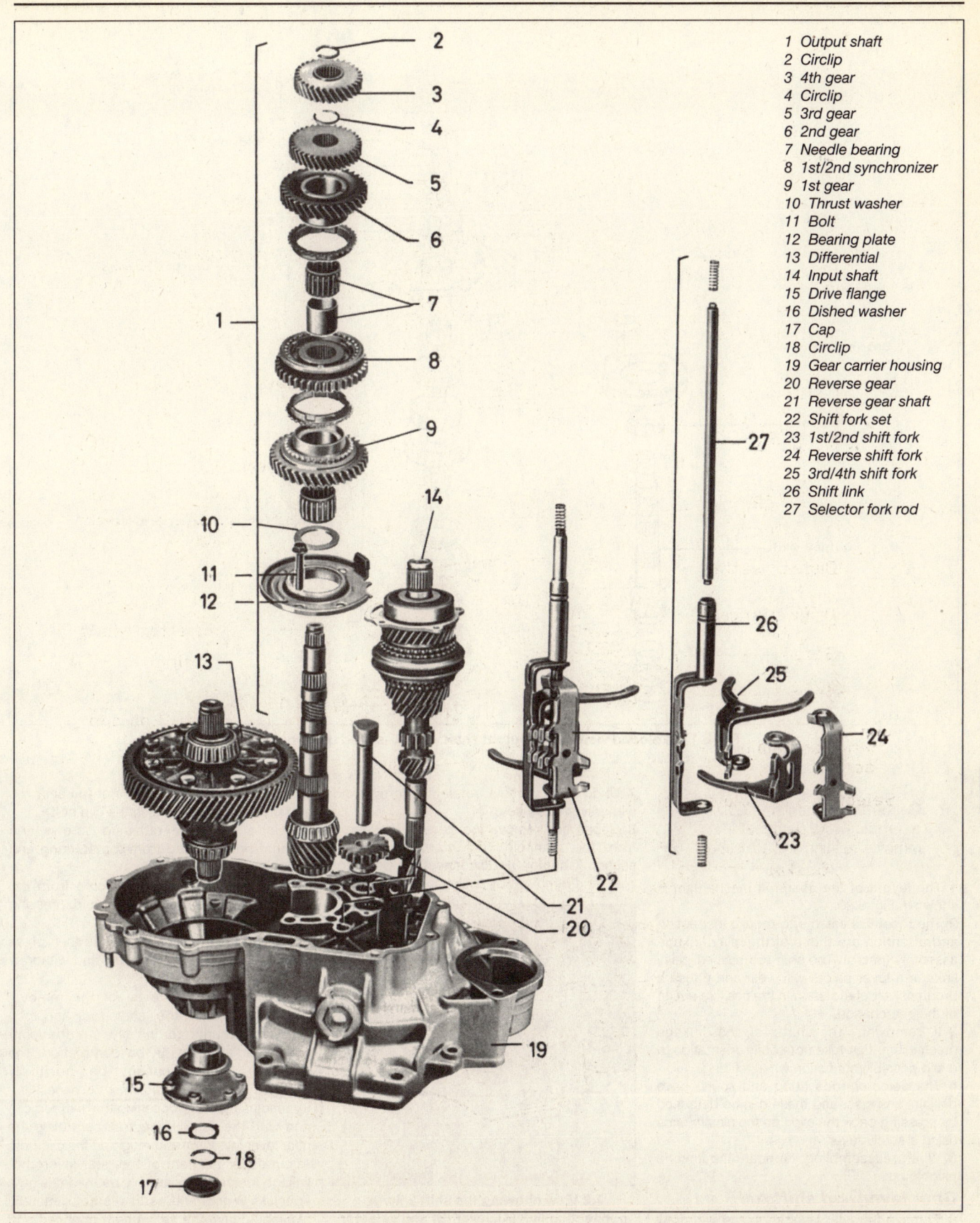

Manual gearbox and automatic transmission 6•13

1 Output shaft
2 Circlip
3 4th gear
4 Circlip
5 3rd gear
6 2nd gear
7 Needle bearing
8 1st/2nd synchronizer
9 1st gear
10 Thrust washer
11 Bolt
12 Bearing plate
13 Differential
14 Input shaft
15 Drive flange
16 Dished washer
17 Cap
18 Circlip
19 Gear carrier housing
20 Reverse gear
21 Reverse gear shaft
22 Shift fork set
23 1st/2nd shift fork
24 Reverse shift fork
25 3rd/4th shift fork
26 Shift link
27 Selector fork rod

Fig. 6.18 Exploded view of the gear carrier (clutch) housing and associated components – 020 5-speed gearbox (Sec 6)

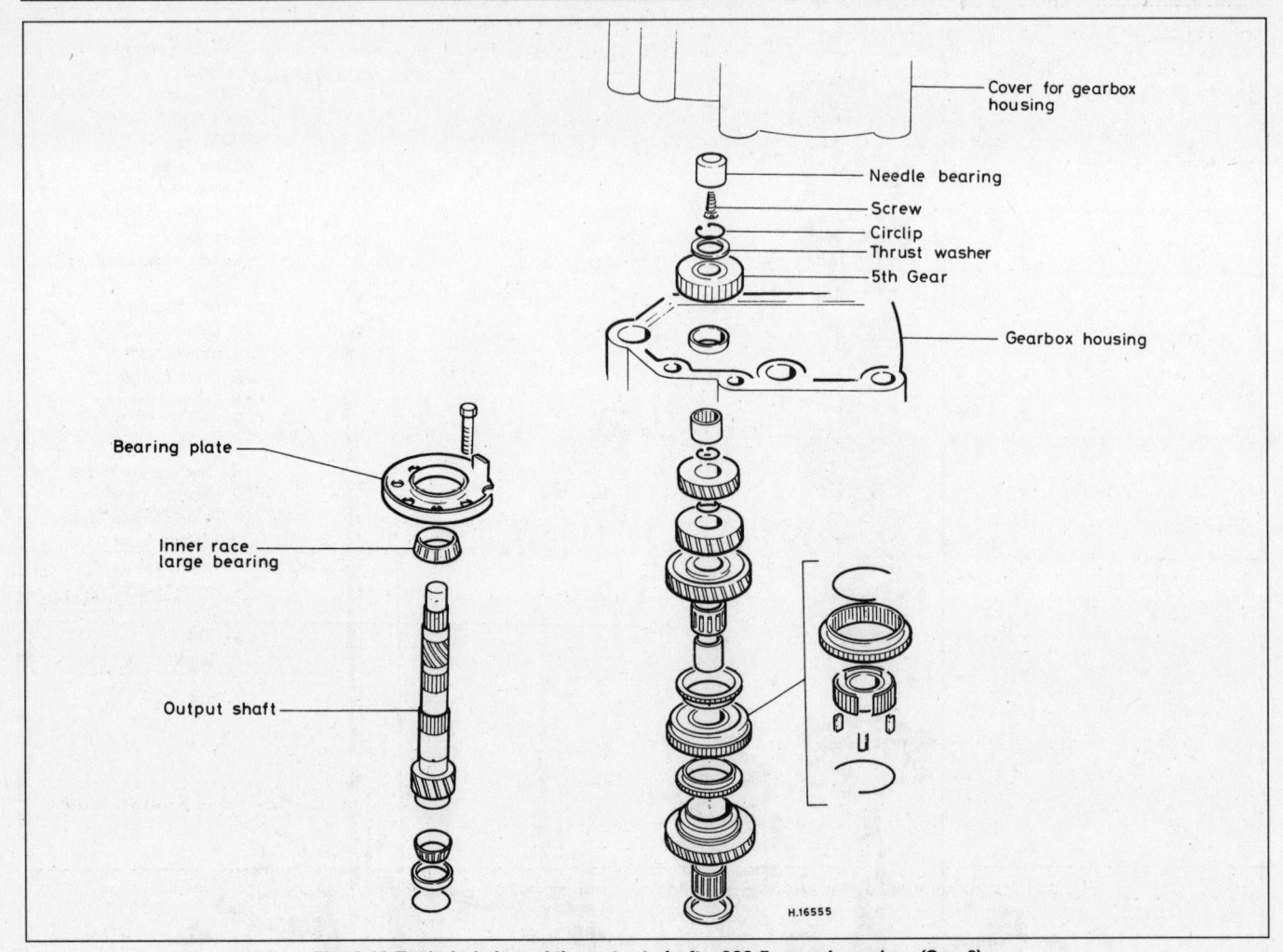

Fig. 6.19 Exploded view of the output shaft – 020 5-speed gearbox (Sec 6)

7 Gearshift mechanism (020 gearbox, 4 and 5-speed) - removal, refitting and adjustment

1 The layout of the gearshift mechanism is shown in Fig. 6.20.
2 The most likely items to require inspection and attention are those of the relay linkage assembly (photo). The shift rod bushes, relay links and lever pivots will wear and cause a progressive deterioration in the positive action of the gearchange.
3 If removing any parts of the linkage mechanism, first take note of its orientation to avoid possible confusion when refitting.
4 The selector rods (long and short) have balljoint linkages, and these can be detached by pressing back the clips on the plastic ends using a screwdriver.
5 When reassembling, lubricate the linkage pivot joints.

Gear lever and shift rod

6 Remove the gear lever knob and withdraw the rubber boot.
7 Undo the console retaining screw and withdraw the console.
8 Unbolt and remove the exhaust downpipe from the manifold and intermediate pipe section (Chapter 3). Disconnect the deflector plate and remove it by pulling it forwards.

7.2 View showing the shift linkage connecting link (A), lever (B) and selector rod (C)

9 Mark the relative positions of the shift rod and front clips, then loosen the clip bolt.
10 Undo the three retaining screws and detach the mounting from the steering and remove from the shift rod.
11 Disconnect the lever housing from the body, pull the housing forwards and, pressing it downwards, remove it.
12 Disconnect the retaining plate then press out the shift rod bush (inwards) and withdraw the rod from the housing.
13 Refitting is a reversal of the removal procedure. Align the shift rod and clip alignment marks to initially set the shift linkage adjustment. If, on completion, the respective gears cannot be positively engaged and further adjustment is necessary, try readjustment by loosening the shift rod clip and with the gears in neutral, centralise the gear lever in neutral and retighten the clip bolt. Accurate adjustment of the gear lever/shift linkage mechanism can only be made using a special VW tool and as this is not generally available, have the adjustment checked and set by your VW dealer.

Manual gearbox and automatic transmission 6•15

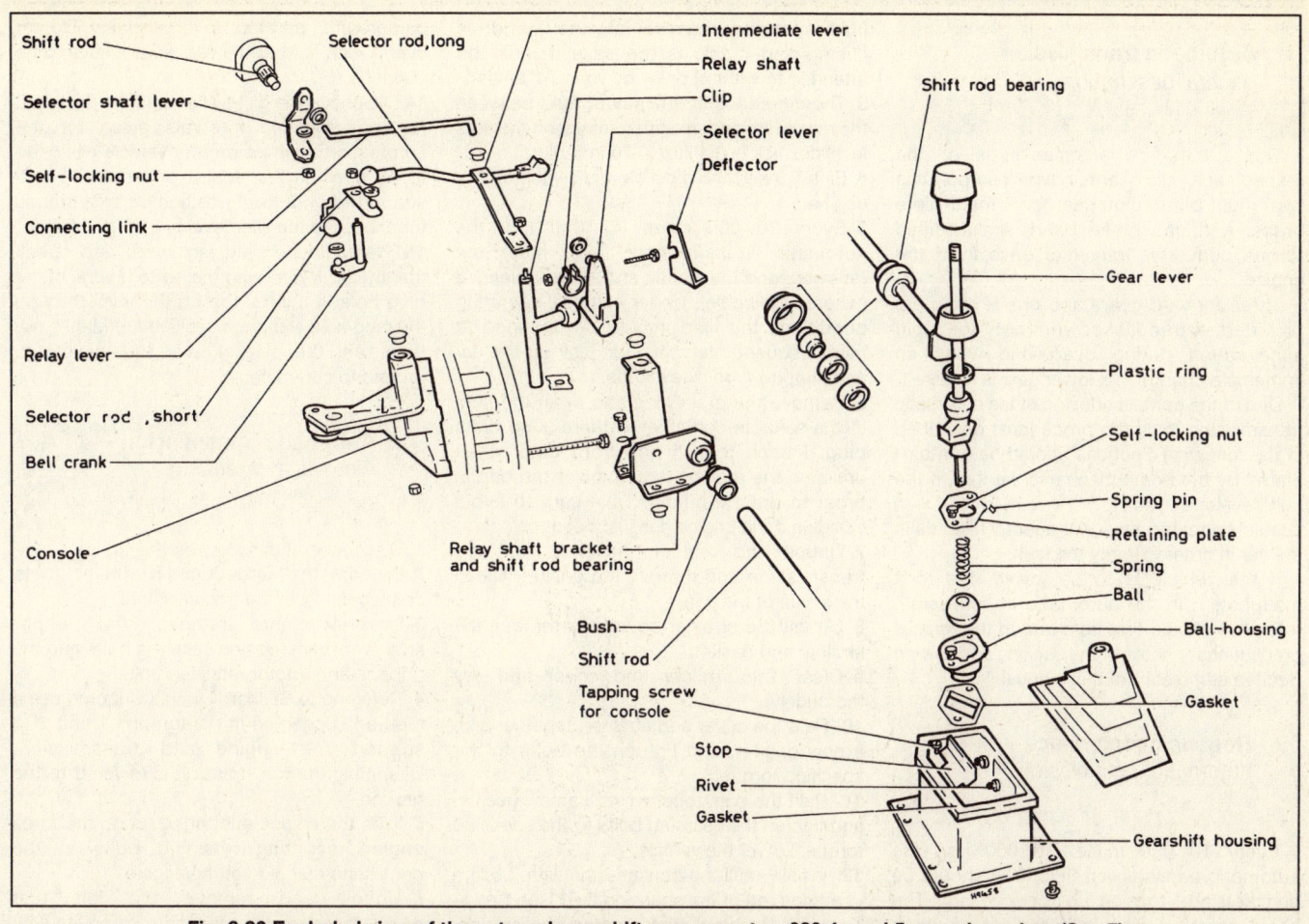

Fig. 6.20 Exploded view of the external gearshift components – 020 4- and 5-speed gearbox (Sec 7)

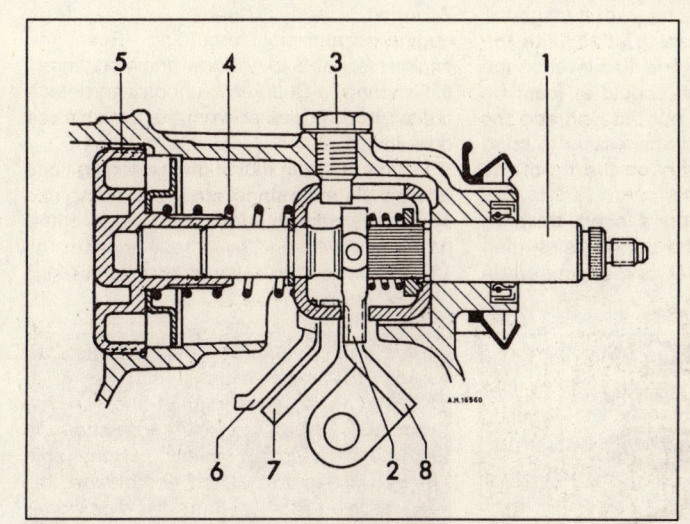

Fig. 6.21 Sectional view of gearshift internal linkage – 020 4-speed gearbox (Sec 7)

1 Selector shaft
2 Shift finger
3 Peg bolt
4 Spring
5 End cap
6 Reverse gear shift fork
7 1st/2nd gear shift fork
8 3rd/4th gear shift fork

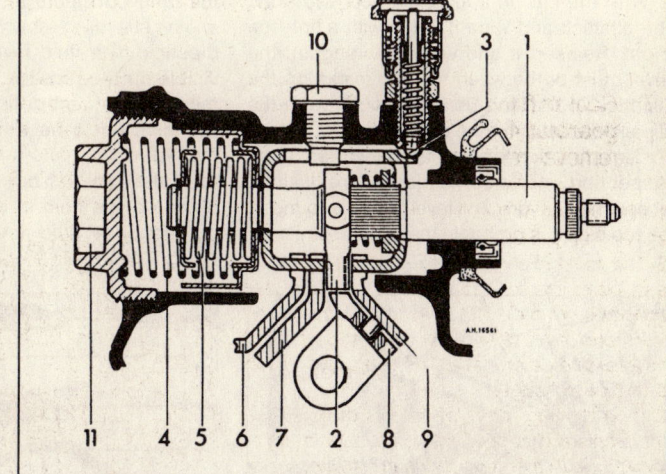

Fig. 6.22 Sectional view of the gearshift internal linkage – 020 5-speed gearbox (Sec 7)

1 Selector shaft
2 Shift finger
3 5th gear
4 Spring (large)
5 Spring (small)
6 Reverse gear shift fork
7 1st/2nd gear shift fork
8 3rd/4th gear shift fork
9 5th gear shift link
10 Peg bolt
11 End cap

6•16 Manual gearbox and automatic transmission

8 Automatic transmission - general description

The automatic transmission is of the 3-speed epicyclic geartrain type incorporating two multi-plate clutches, one multi-plate brake, and one brake band. A fluid-filled torque converter transmits drive from the engine.

Three forward gears and one reverse are provided, with a kickdown facility for rapid acceleration during overtaking when an immediate change to a lower gear is required.

Due to the complex design of the automatic transmission, only the procedures described in the following Sections should be contemplated by the home mechanic. Further, if the unit develops a fault it should be tested by a VW agent while still in the car in order to verify the fault.

If the vehicle is to be towed due to a malfunction in the automatic transmission, reference should first be made to the special precautionary notes in the *Jacking and towing* Section at the start of this manual.

9 Routine maintenance - automatic transmission

1 Every 10 000 miles (15 000 km) the automatic transmission fluid level should be checked and topped up if necessary. The check must be made with the engine warm and idling, with the selector lever in position N (neutral) and the handbrake firmly applied.
2 With the car on a level surface, withdraw the dipstick and wipe it clean with a lint-free cloth. Reinsert it and withdraw it again; the level must be between the two marks on the dipstick. If not, top up the level through the dipstick tube using the specified fluid. Check for leaks if much topping-up is required. If, on inspection, no external leaks are visible, check the final drive oil level. If this is found to be too high it is probable that the transmission fluid is leaking internally into the final drive casing and if this is the case it must be attended to without delay by your VW dealer.
3 The difference in quantity of fluid between the maximum and minimum marks on the fluid level dipstick is 0.4 litre (0.70 Imp pint).
4 Finally insert the dipstick and switch off the engine.
5 Every 30 000 miles (45 000 km) the automatic transmission fluid must be renewed, and the oil pan and strainer cleaned (where applicable). Under extreme operating conditions the fluid should be changed at more frequent intervals. First jack up the car and support it on axle stands.
6 Remove the drain plug and drain the fluid into a suitable container. If there is no drain plug, loosen the oil pan front bolts, then unscrew the rear bolts and lower the pan in order to drain the fluid. Take care to avoid scalding if the engine has just been run.
7 Unbolt and remove the pan from the transmission and remove the gasket. Clean the inside of the pan.
8 Unbolt the strainer cover and remove the strainer and gasket.
9 Clean the strainer and cover and dry thoroughly.
10 Refit the cover and strainer, together with a new gasket, and tighten the bolts to the specified torque.
11 Refit the pan, together with a new gasket, and tighten the securing bolts to the specified torque. Lower the vehicle.
12 Initially refill the transmission with 2.5 litre (4.4 Imp pint) of transmission fluid (see Specifications for type), then restart the engine. Check that the handbrake is still fully applied then move the gear selector lever through the full range of gears finishing at N. With the engine still idling, check the fluid level on the dipstick. The fluid level should at least be visible on the dipstick, but if it isn't add the minimum amount of fluid necessary to bring the level up to be visible on the tip of the dipstick.
13 Take the vehicle on a short drive to warm-up the fluid in the transmission then recheck the fluid level, as described in paragraph 2, and top up if necessary. Do not overfill with fluid or the excess will have to be drained off.
14 To check the oil level in the final drive unit (at the specified intervals given for the automatic transmission) the vehicle will need to be over an inspection pit or raised and supported on a level position on axle stands for access to the filler/level plug (Fig. 6.25).
15 Remove the plug (arrowed) and check that the oil is level with the bottom edge of the plug hole. If it isn't, top up the level through the plug hole with the specified lubricant type, then refit the plug. Lower the vehicle to ground to complete.

10 Automatic transmission - removal and refitting

1 Disconnect the battery earth lead.
2 Detach the speedometer drive cable connection from the transmission.
3 Unscrew and remove the upper engine-to-transmission securing bolts and the upper starter motor retaining bolt.
4 Referring to Section 4 in this Chapter, use a method suggested in paragraphs 1 and 2 to support the engine and transmission. Ultimately the transmission is lowered to the ground.
5 With the engine supported, undo the three engine mounting retaining bolts at the right-hand rear side of the engine.
6 Unbolt and remove the left rear engine/transmission mounting, complete with support.
7 Unbolt and remove the front engine/transmission mounting. Push the engine rearwards to withdraw the mounting.
8 Referring to Chapter 7, unbolt and detach the left-hand driveshaft from the transmission drive flange.
9 Undo the starter motor lower retaining bolts and withdraw the starter motor.
10 Unbolt and withdraw the engine sump protector plate.
11 Check that the selector lever is in the P

Fig. 6.23 Automatic transmission fluid level dipstick – remove in direction of arrow (Sec 9)

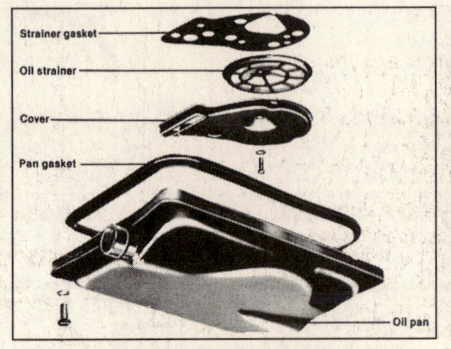

Fig. 6.24 Automatic transmission oil pan and strainer (Sec 9)

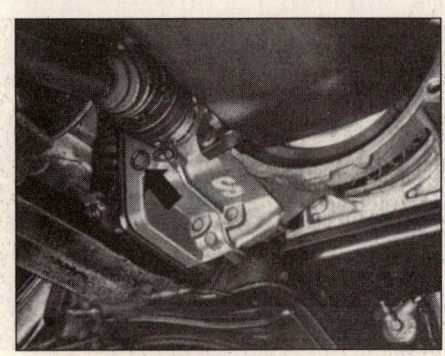

Fig. 6.25 Final drive oil lever/filler plug location (arrowed) – automatic transmission (Sec 9)

Manual gearbox and automatic transmission 6•17

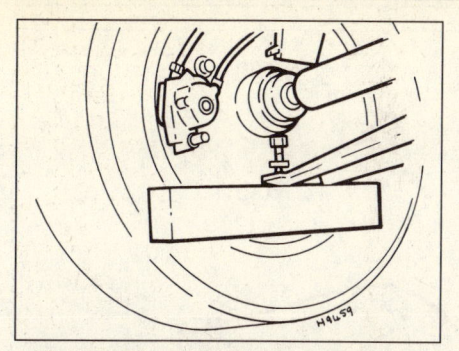

Fig. 6.26 Disconnect and support lower balljoint/track control arm with block of wood (Sec 10)

position then detach the drive range selector cable (see Section 12).
12 Detach the cables support bracket from the transmission.
13 Disconnect the throttle and accelerator pedal cables, but do not alter their settings.
14 Working through the hole left by the starter, locate and undo the three bolts holding the torque converter to the driveplate. These can be seen also in the gap when the bottom cover plate is removed.
15 Unbolt and detach the right-hand driveshaft (Chapter 7).
16 Detach the lower balljoint from the track control arm (wishbone) then support it at the outboard end (Fig. 6.26). Take care not to damage the driveshaft gaiter.
17 Now push the engine and transmission unit to the right as far as the stop then lift and tie up the left-hand driveshaft out of the way.

18 Locate a trolley jack under the transmission for support.
19 Undo and remove the remaining engine-to-transmission bolts at the bottom then check that all other transmission attachments are disconnected.
20 The transmission may now be removed. Lift a little and push the driveshaft up and out of the way. Pull the transmission off the dowels and lower it gently, at the same time supporting the torque converter, which will fall out if not held in place in the transmission. There are two shafts and two sets of splines; be careful not to bend either of them or you will have a leaking torque converter.
21 The transmission is too heavy for one person to lift so a sling and tackle must be used to support and lower the transmission if a suitable trolley jack is not available.
22 When the transmission is separated from the engine, it can be lowered and manoeuvred from beneath the vehicle.
23 Position a suitable support plate across the torque converter housing to retain the torque converter in position whilst the transmission is removed.
24 Refitting is the reversal of removal. Ensure that the torque converter remains fully engaged when attaching the engine and transmission.
25 Semi-tighten the respective mountings as they are attached then, when fully located, remove the engine/transmission supports and fully tighten the mounting bolts to the specified torque wrench settings.
26 If a new transmission unit has been fitted it will be necessary to readjust the throttle cable (Section 13).
27 Check the selector cable adjustment, as described in Section 12.
28 Refill the transmission with the correct quantity of fluid and recheck the fluid level, as described in Section 9.
29 Remove the final drive filler/level plug and check that the oil level is to the bottom of the hole. If necessary top up the level with the specified oil, then refit the plug.

11 Automatic transmission - stall test

1 The stall test is used to check the performance of the torque converter and the results can also indicate certain faults in the automatic transmission.
2 Connect a tachometer to the engine, then run the engine until warm.
3 Finally apply the handbrake and footbrake, and select position D.
4 Fully depress the accelerator pedal and record the engine speed, then release the pedal. **Do not** depress the pedal for any period longer than five seconds otherwise the torque converter will overheat. After a period of twenty seconds repeat the test. According to gearbox type the stall speeds should be as follows:

TJA   2390 to 2640 rpm
TKA   2340 to 2590 rpm

Note: Deduct 125 rpm per 1000 m (3200 feet) altitude.

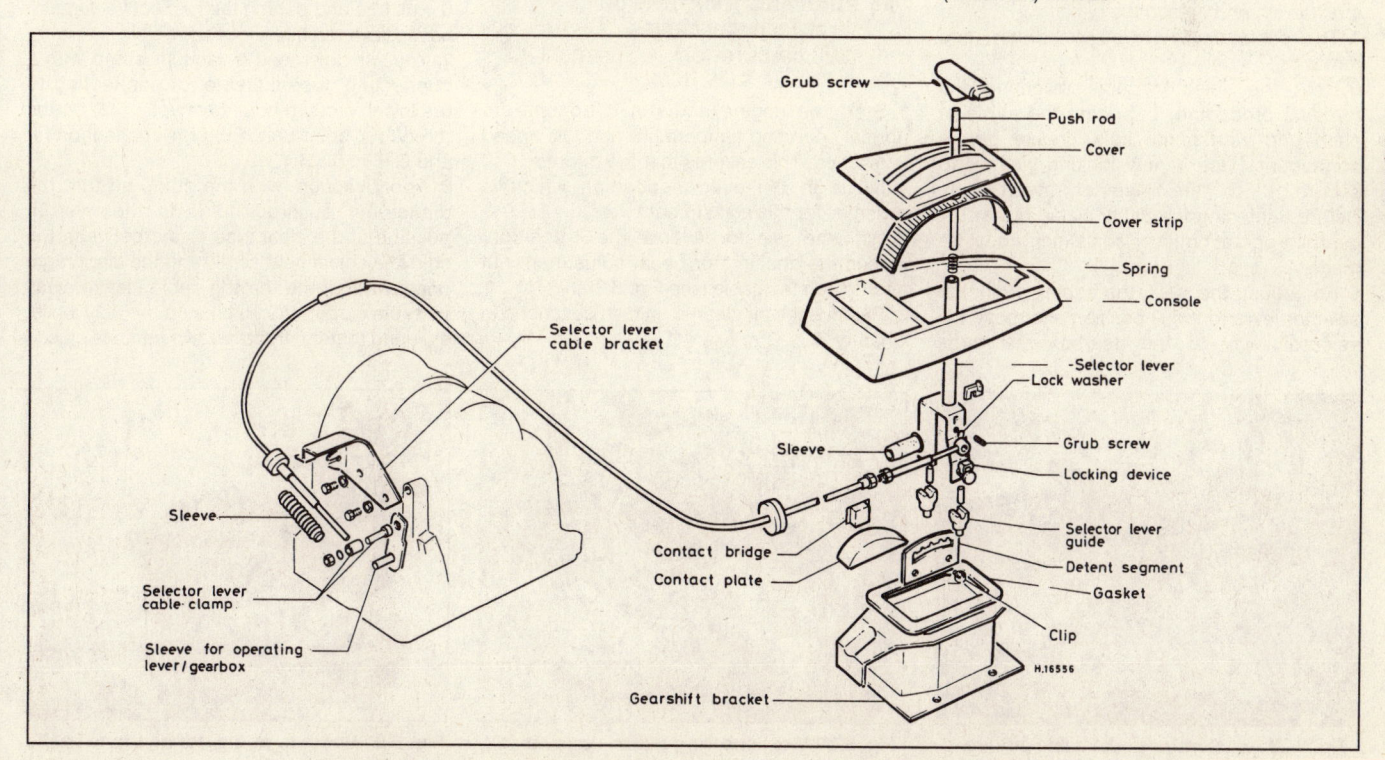

Fig. 6.27 Automatic transmission selector cable and shift mechanism (Sec 12)

6•18 Manual gearbox and automatic transmission

5 If the stall speed is higher than the speed given above then the forward clutch or 1st gear one-way clutch may be slipping. Repeat the test in position 1; if the stall speed is now correct the 1st gear one-way clutch is faulty, but if the speed is still too high, the forward clutch is faulty.
6 A stall speed up to 200 rpm below the specified amount indicates poor engine performance, and the engine should therefore be tuned up as necessary.
7 If the stall speed is more than 200 rpm below the specified amount, the torque converter stator one-way clutch is faulty and the torque converter should be renewed, but first ensure that the engine is tuned correctly and, if adjustments are necessary, recheck the stall speed.
8 Switch off the engine and disconnect the tachometer.

12 Automatic transmission selector cable - removal, refitting and adjustment

1 At the transmission end of the cable, undo the cable clamp nut and detach the cable from the selector lever cable bracket.
2 Working inside the car, remove the retaining screws securing the selector lever cover to the console, lift the cover up the lever and turn it to one side.
3 Prise free the retaining clip (locking washer) securing the selector cable to the shift mechanism and detach the cable.
4 The cable can now be withdrawn and removed.
5 Refit the selector cable reversing the removal procedure. Lubricate the cable at each end with some light grease before connecting. Use a new locking washer to secure it to the selector mechanism. Before tightening the cable clamp nut at the gearbox operating lever adjustment must be made.
6 To adjust the selector cable, push the selector lever to the P position and move the selector lever at the gearbox rearwards against the stop to the corresponding P position. Check that the cable is not kinked or bent at any point through its run then tighten the clamp nut.

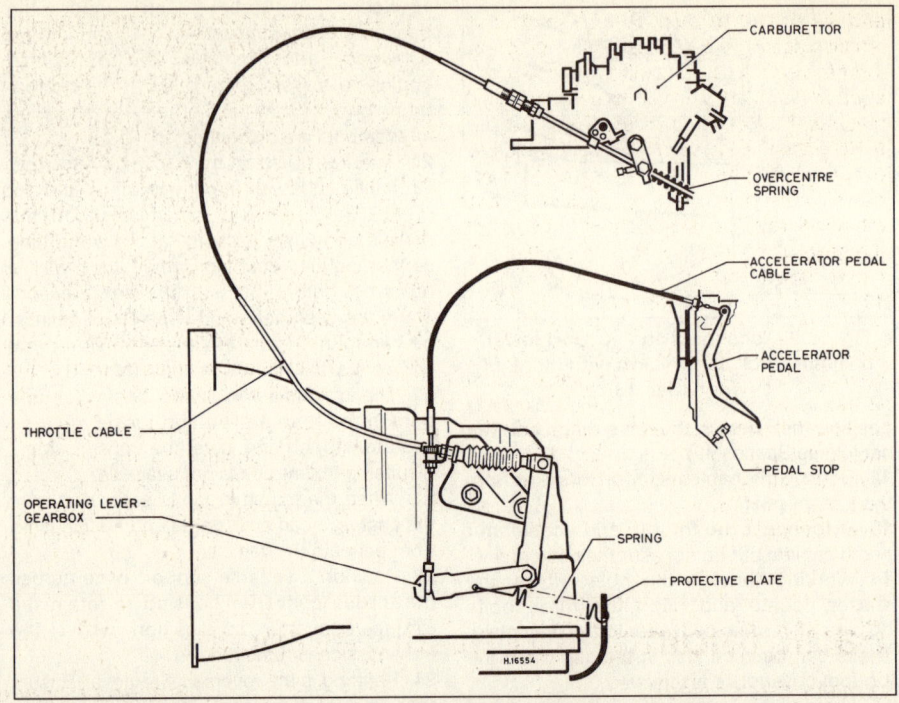

Fig. 6.28 Automatic transmission throttle and accelerator pedal cables (Sec 13)

13 Automatic transmission throttle pedal cables (2E2 carburettor) - adjustment

1 Start the engine and run it up until its normal operating temperature and idle speed is reached. This ensures that the throttle valve is in the overrun position which is essential for this adjustment.
2 With the selector lever at the P position, loosen the accelerator pedal adjustment nut and detach the cable (see Fig. 6.29).
3 Remove the air cleaner unit, as described in Chapter 3.
4 Loosen the throttle cable nut at the support bracket at the carburettor.
5 Referring to Fig. 6.30 rotate the warm-up lever A so that the throttle control pin is not touching it, then retain the lever in this position by moving lever C with a screwdriver.
6 Pull free and detach the respective vacuum hoses from the three/four point unit.
7 You will now need a vacuum pump with a connecting hose suitable for connecting to the lower vacuum hose connection (E) on the three/four point unit. Plug off connections F and G (Fig. 6.31).
8 Apply vacuum with the pump so that the diaphragm pushrod holds in the overrun position and a clearance exists between the cold idle adjustment screw and the diaphragm pushrod. Pull the throttle cable sleeve away from the carburettor to take up the play whilst ensuring that the throttle valve remains closed

Fig. 6.29 Accelerator pedal cable adjusting nut and operating lever connection (arrowed) – automatic transmission (Sec 13)

Fig. 6.30 View showing warm-up lever (A), throttle valve control pin (B), lever (C) and screwdriver location (D) (Sec 13)

Fig. 6.31 Vacuum pump connections to the three/four-point vacuum unit (Sec 13)

and the operating lever at the transmission remains against the overrun stop. Tighten the throttle cable adjuster so that it contacts the support bracket and is stress-free, then retighten the locknut to secure (Fig. 6.32).
9 Reconnect the accelerator pedal cable then get an assistant to press the accelerator pedal down to the kickdown stop position. Rotate the accelerator pedal adjustment nut so that the gearbox operating lever is in contact with the kickdown stop, then tighten the locknut.
10 To check the adjustment is correctly made, the throttle must be in the overrun position and the gearbox operating lever must be in contact with the overrun stop. Get an assistant to depress the accelerator pedal until the full throttle pressure point is reached (not kickdown), then check that the throttle lever is resting against the full throttle stop and that the over-centre spring is not compressed.

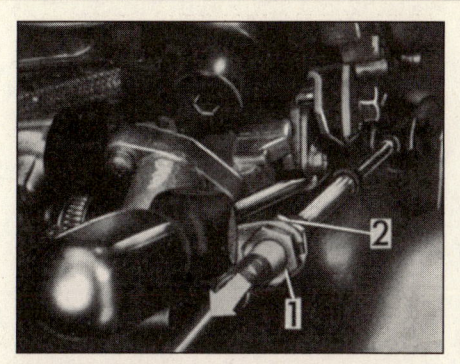

Fig. 6.32 Throttle cable adjuster nut (1) and locknut (2) (Sec 13)

11 Next depress the accelerator pedal past the full throttle position to the kickdown position and then check that the gearbox operating lever rests against the kickdown stop, and the over-centre spring is

Fig. 6.33 Throttle cable over-centre spring compression point (a) (Sec 13)

compressed approximately 8 mm (0.3 in) (Fig. 6.33).
12 On completion refit the air cleaner to the carburettor, with reference to Chapter 3.

Fault finding - manual gearbox

Jumps out of gear
☐ Worn synchro-hubs or baulk rings
☐ Worn selector shaft detent plunger or spring
☐ Worn selector forks

Difficulty in engaging gears
☐ Clutch fault
☐ Gearshift mechanism out of adjustment
☐ Worn synchro-hubs or baulk rings

Gearbox noisy in neutral
☐ Mainshaft (input shaft) bearings worn

Gearbox noisy only when moving (in all gears)
☐ Pinion shaft (output shaft) bearings worn
☐ Differential bearings worn

Gearbox noisy in only one gear
☐ Worn, damaged, or chipped gearteeth

Ineffective synchromesh
☐ Worn baulk rings or synchro-hubs

Fault finding - automatic transmission

Shift speeds too high or too low
☐ Throttle and pedal cables out of adjustment

Loss of drive
☐ Fluid level too low
☐ Driveplate-to-torque converter bolts fallen out
☐ Internal fault

Erratic drive
☐ Fluid level too low
☐ Dirty oil pan filter

Gear selection jerky
☐ Fluid level too low
☐ Idle speed too high

Poor acceleration
☐ Faulty torque converter
☐ Throttle and pedal cables out of adjustment
☐ Brakes sticking on

6•20 Manual gearbox and automatic transmission

Notes

Chapter 7 Driveshafts

Contents

Drive flange oil seals - renewal 4
Driveshaft - dismantling and reassembly 3
Driveshaft - removal and refitting 2
Fault finding - driveshafts .... See end of Chapter
General description 1

Degrees of difficulty

| Easy, suitable for novice with little experience | Fairly easy, suitable for beginner with some experience | Fairly difficult, suitable for competent DIY mechanic | Difficult, suitable for experienced DIY mechanic | Very difficult, suitable for expert DIY or professional |

Specifications

Type .... Solid (left) and tubular (right) driveshafts with constant velocity (CV) joints at each end. Vibration damper fitted to right-hand driveshaft on 55 and 66 kW engine models

Length   **Left-hand**   **Right-hand**
084 gearbox .... 465 mm (18.32 in)   677.2 mm (26.68 in)
020 gearbox:
  Not GTI models .... 443 mm (17.45 in)   677.2 mm (26.68 in)
  GTI models .... 447 mm (17.61 in)   681.2 mm (26.84 in)
010 gearbox (automatic) .... 443 mm (17.45 in)   677.2 mm (26.68 in)

Torque wrench settings   **Nm**   **lbf ft**
Driveshaft to flange 45   33
Driveshaft/hub nut 265   195
Drive flange retaining bolt (1.05 and 1.3 litre) ... 25   18

1 General description

Drive from the differential unit to the roadwheels is provided by two driveshafts. Each driveshaft has a constant velocity (CV) joint at each end, the inner end being flanged and secured to the final drive flange by bolts and the outer end being splined to the hub.

The left-hand driveshaft is of solid construction and is shorter than the tubular right-hand driveshaft.

The driveshaft joints are sealed and require no maintenance apart from checking the rubber boots at the specified routine maintenance intervals for any sign of leakage or damage, in which case they must be renewed (photo).

If the joints are suspected of excessive wear, noticeable when changing from acceleration to overrun and vice versa, the shafts should be removed and the joints dismantled to inspect for wear or damage, and overhauled or renewed as necessary.

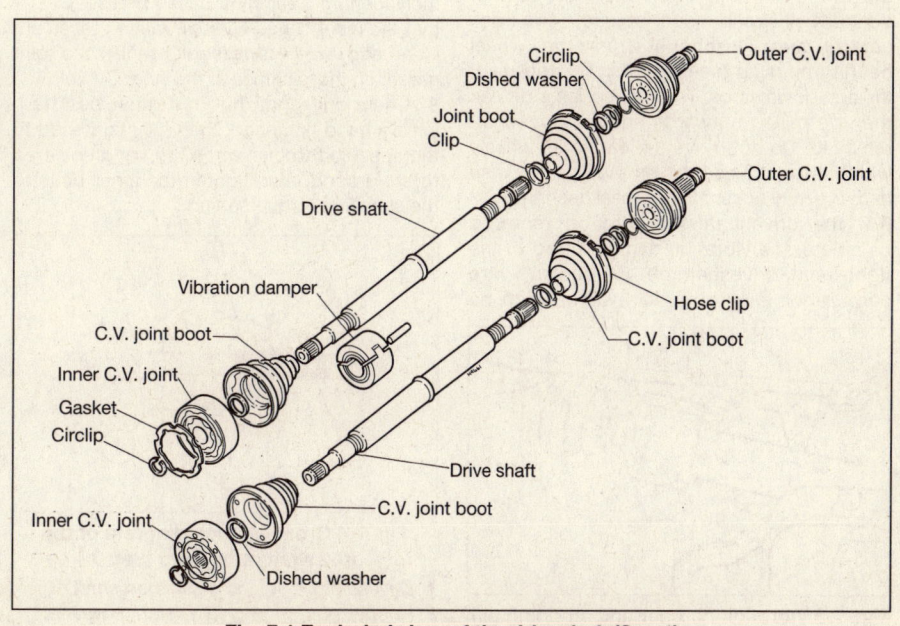

Fig. 7.1 Exploded view of the driveshaft (Sec 1)

Upper GTI models   Lower Other models

7•2 Driveshafts

1.3 Check the condition of the driveshaft rubber boots

2.4A Driveshaft-to-final drive flange socket-head bolts

2.4B Removal of the socket-head bolts and spacer plates

2 Driveshaft - removal and refitting

1 The driveshafts are secured to the drive flanges at the gearbox end by socket-head bolts, the removal of which will require the use of a special splined key. Whilst an Allen key may suffice, it is also likely to strip the socket in the bolts.
2 Remove the wheel trim from the relevant wheel. With the handbrake applied, loosen the driveshaft nut. The nut is tightened to a high torque and a socket extension may be required.
3 Jack up the front of the car and support it on axle stands. Remove the roadwheel.
4 Using a splined tool, remove the socket-head bolts holding the inner CV joint to the final drive flange. Be careful to use a proper key for if the socket head is damaged the result will be time consuming to say the least. These bolts are quite tight (photos).
5 Once all the bolts are removed the CV joint may be pulled away from the final drive and the shaft removed from the hub joint. If difficulty is experienced, separate the track control arm (wishbone) from the wheel bearing housing (see Chapter 11) and pivot the arm downwards. The suspension strut can then be pulled outwards and the driveshaft removed. Do not move the car on its wheels with either driveshaft removed, otherwise damage may occur to the wheel bearings.
6 If the driveshaft(s) are to be renewed complete, the vibration damper fitted to the right-hand driveshaft on 1.6 and 1.8 litre carburettor engine models will have to be transferred to the new shaft. To remove the damper, use a pin punch and drive out one of the retaining spring pins. The damper can then be pivoted open and removed from the driveshaft. Note the position of the damper unit on the shaft as it must be refitted in the same position.
7 Before fitting the vibration damper, check that the adhesive tape on its inner diameter is still sticky. Renew the tape if necessary. It is also advisable to renew the spring pin when refitting the damper. When the damper is in position check it for security.
8 Refitting of the driveshaft is a reversal of the removal procedure. The hub and driveshaft splines must be clean and lubricated with a little molybdenum disulphide based grease. Check that the inner flange/CV joint mating faces are clean and, where applicable, renew the joint gasket on the joint face of the inner CV unit.
9 A new driveshaft/hub nut must be fitted, initially hand tightened, then fully tightened to the specified torque when the car is lowered to the ground. Also tighten the inner bolts to the specified torque setting.

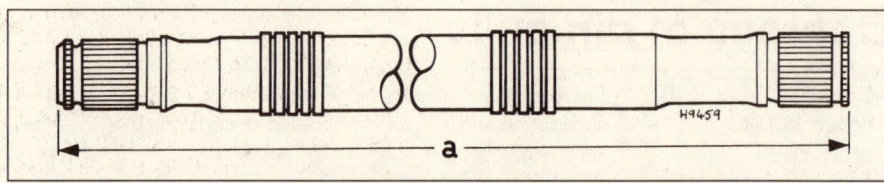

Fig. 7.2 Measure new driveshaft between points indicated (a) to ensure correct length for your model (Sec 2)

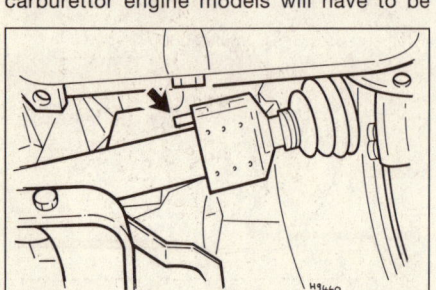

Fig. 7.3 Vibration damper and retaining pin (arrowed) – 1.6 and 1.8 litre carburettor models (Sec 2)

3 Driveshaft - dismantling and reassembly

1 Having removed the shaft from the car it may be dismantled for the individual parts to be checked for wear.
2 The rubber boots, clips and thrust washers may be renewed if necessary but the CV joints may only be renewed as complete assemblies. It is not possible to fit new hubs, outer cases, ball cages or balls separately for they are mated to a tolerance on manufacture. A replacement CV joint assembly kit will include the rubber boot and a tube of special grease, but you will need to specify which car model you have as the CV joints differ.

Outer joint

3 Loosen the rubber boot clips and release the large diameter end of the boot from the joint.
4 Using a soft-faced mallet, drive the outer joint from the driveshaft.
5 Extract the circlip from the driveshaft and remove the spacer (if fitted) and dished

Fig. 7.4 Cross-section diagram of the driveshaft outer joint (Sec 3)

1 Driveshaft
2 Rubber boot
3 Worm drive clip
4 Bearing race
5 Splined shaft
6 Distance washer
7 Dished washer

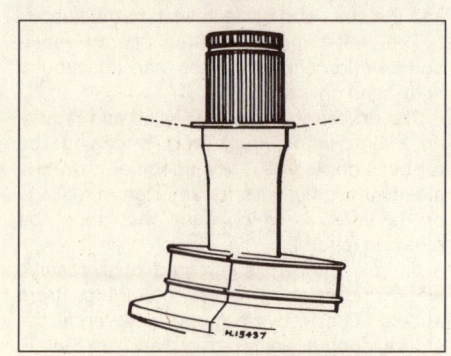

Fig. 7.5 Correct fitment of the dished washer (Sec 3)

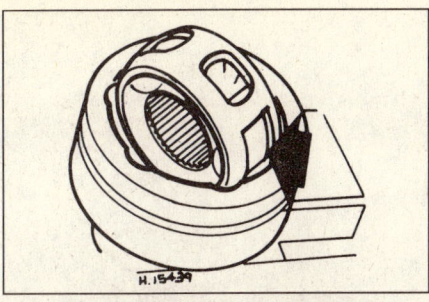

Fig. 7.6 Removing the cage and hub from the outer joint housing (Sec 3)
Arrow shows rectangular aperture

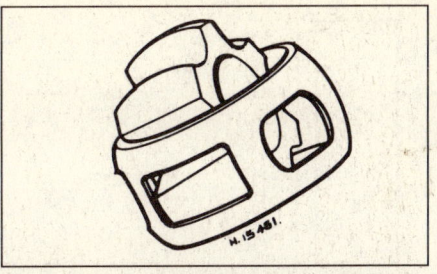

Fig. 7.7 Removing the outer joint hub from the cage (Sec 3)

3.21 Driveshaft inner joint retaining clip (arrowed) – 1.3 litre

washer; noting that the concave side faces the outboard end of the driveshaft.
6 Slide the rubber boot and clips from the driveshaft.
7 Mark the hub in relation to the cage and joint housing.
8 Swivel the hub and cage until the rectangular apertures are aligned with the housing then withdraw the cage and hub.
9 Turn the cage until the rectangular apertures are aligned with the housing then withdraw the cage and hub.
10 Turn the hub and insert one of the segments into one of the rectangular apertures, then swivel the hub from the cage.
11 Note that the joint components including the balls form a matched set and must only be fitted to the correct side.
12 Clean the components in paraffin and examine them for wear and damage. Excessive wear will have been evident when driving the car, especially when changing from acceleration to overrun. Renew the components as necessary.
13 Commence reassembly by inserting half the amount of special grease (ie 45g) into the joint housing.
14 Fit the hub to the cage by inserting one of the segments into the rectangular aperture.
15 With the rectangular apertures aligned with the housing, fit the hub and cage to the housing in its original position.
16 Swivel the hub and cage and insert the balls from alternate sides.
17 Fit the rubber boot and clips on the driveshaft.
18 Fit the dished washer and spacer (if applicable) to the driveshaft and insert the circlip in the groove.
19 Locate the outer joint on the driveshaft and, using a soft-faced mallet, drive it fully into position until the circlip is engaged.
20 Insert the remaining grease in the joint then locate the boot and tighten the clips. On models fitted with the 90 mm (3.55 in) diameter CV joint, ventilate the joint briefly prior to tightening the small hose clip, to balance the pressure in the joint.

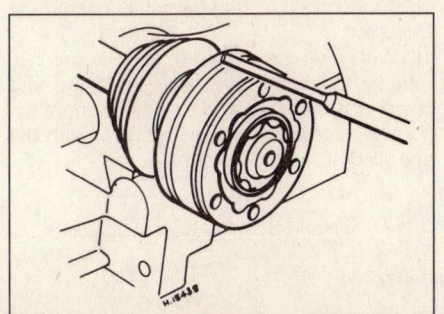

Inner joint - models except GTI

21 Extract the retaining clip (photo).
22 Where applicable, use a small drift to drive the plastic cap from the joint housing.
23 Mark the exact location of the rubber boot end face relative to the driveshaft. A length of insulation tape or quick-drying paint applied to the shaft will suffice. This will show the exact location for the rubber boot on the shaft when refitting (particularly important on the GTI model).
24 Loosen the clip and slide the rubber boot away from the joint.
25 Support the joint over the jaws of a vice and, using a soft metal drift, drive out the driveshaft.
26 Remove the dished washer from the driveshaft, noting that the concave side faces the end of the driveshaft.
27 Slide the rubber boot and clip from the driveshaft.
28 Mark the hub in relation to the cage and joint housing.
29 Turn the hub and cage 90° to the housing and press out the hub and cage.
30 Extract the balls then turn the hub so that one of the track grooves is located on the rim of the cage, and withdraw the hub.
31 Note that the joint components including the balls form a matched set and must only be fitted in the correct side.
32 Clean the components in paraffin and examine them for wear and damage. Excessive wear will have been evident when driving the car, especially when changing from acceleration to overrun. Renew the components as necessary.
33 Commence reassembly by fitting the hub to the cage.
34 Insert the balls into position using the special grease to hold them in place.
35 Press the hub and cage into the housing, making sure that the wide track spacing on the housing will be adjacent to the narrow spacing on the hub (see Fig. 7.10) when fully assembled. Note also that the chamfer on the hub splines must face the large diameter side of the housing.
36 Swivel the cage ahead of the hub so that the balls enter their respective tracks then align the hub and cage with the housing.
37 Check that the hub can be moved freely through its operating arc.
38 Fit the rubber boot and clip to the driveshaft followed by the dished washer.
39 Mount the driveshaft in a vice then drive the joint onto the driveshaft using a suitable metal tube on the hub.
40 Fit the retaining circlip in its groove.
41 Insert the remaining grease in the joint then tap the plastic cap into position (where applicable).
42 Reposition the driveshaft boot, ensuring

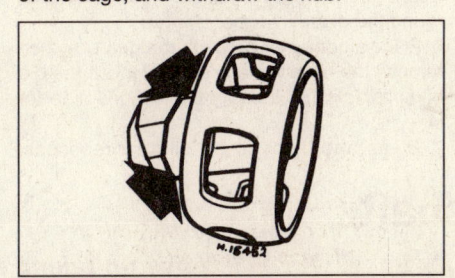

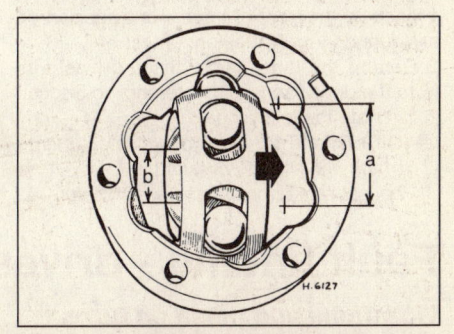

Fig. 7.8 Removing the plastic cap from the inner joint housing (Sec 3)

Fig. 7.9 Removing the inner joint hub from the cage (Sec 3)
Align the grooves – arrowed

Fig. 7.10 Assembly of the inner joint cage and hub to the housing (Sec 3)
a must be aligned with b

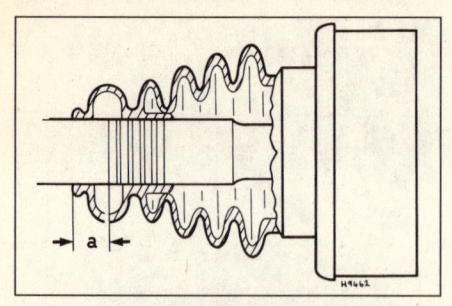

7•4 Driveshafts

Fig. 7.11 Inner CV joint boot installation position – GTI models (Sec 3)

a = 17 mm (0.669 in) on left-hand shaft

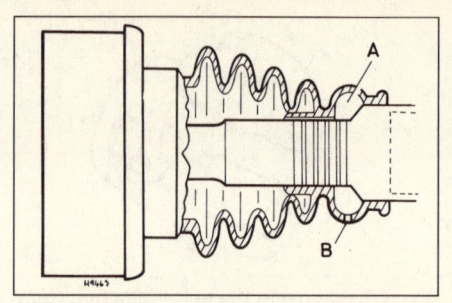

Fig. 7.12 Inner CV joint boot installation position on the right-hand driveshaft – GTI models (Sec 3)

A Ventilation chamber   B Ventilation hole

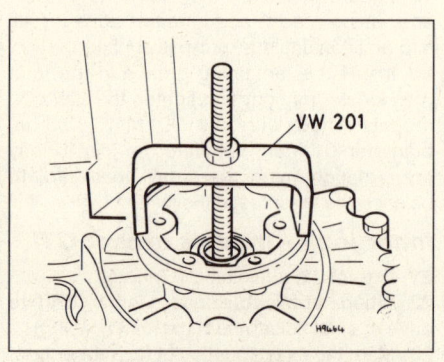

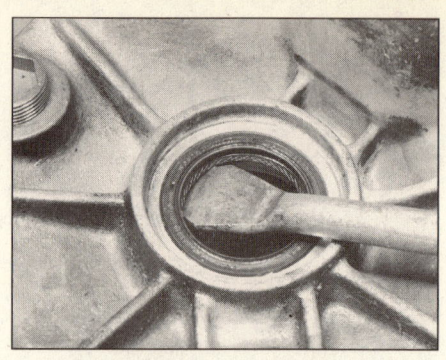

4.6 Prising out the drive flange oil seal from the gearbox housing

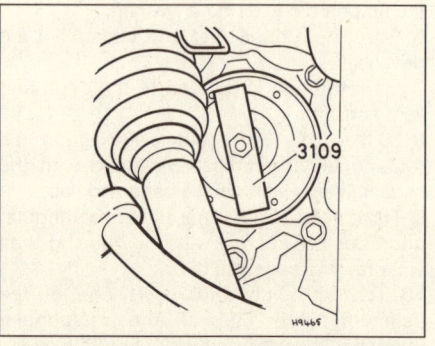

Fig. 7.13 Drive flange removal using VW tool (Sec 4)

Gearbox 020

Fig. 7.14 Drive flange refitting using VW tool (Sec 4)

Gearbox 020

Fig. 7.15 Drive flange refitting using VW tool (Sec 4)

Automatic transmission

that when fitted it is not twisted or distorted abnormally and that the outer end aligns with the mark made during removal.

Inner joint - GTI

43 Proceed as described for other models, but note that a gasket is located on the drive flange end face of the inner joint. This gasket must be renewed. Wipe dry the mating face on the joint, peel the protective foil from the gasket and carefully locate it onto the inner face of the joint.

44 When refitting the driveshaft boot its fitting position is critical and is shown in Figs. 7.11 and 7.12.

4 Drive flange oil seals - renewal

1 Jack up the front of the car and support on axle stands. Apply the handbrake.
2 Detach the inner ends of the driveshafts from the drive flange with reference to Section 2, but note the following:
(a) On 1.05 and 1.3 litre models detachment of the right-hand driveshaft will necessitate unbolting the anti-roll bar from its body mounting and disconnecting the track control arm from the suspension strut on that side (see Chapter 11 for details). Pivot the track control arm downwards.
(b) On automatic transmission models, detachment of the left-hand driveshaft will necessitate disconnecting the track control arm from the suspension strut on that side (see Chapter 11 for details). Pivot the track control arm downwards.
3 With the driveshaft disconnected from the drive flange tie it up out of the way.
4 On 1.05 and 1.3 litre models, unscrew the bolt from the centre of the drive flange using a bar and two temporarily inserted bolts to hold the flange stationary.
5 On other models, prise off the cap (where fitted) and extract the circlip and dished washer from the drive flange. Note which way round the dished washer is fitted.
6 Place a container beneath the gearbox then remove the drive flanges and lever out the old oil seals (photo). Identify the flanges side for side.
7 Clean and inspect the oil seal recesses.

Where applicable, renew the sleeve in the recess if it is damaged.

8 Fill the space between the lips of the new seal with multi-purpose grease, then drive it fully into the housing using a suitable length of metal tube.
9 Refit the drive flange, taking care not to damage the oil seal lips. If available use VW special tool to fit the flange.
10 With the drive flange in position, refit and tighten the securing bolt to the specified torque wrench setting (1.05 and 1.3 litre) or locate the dished washer (ensuring correct orientation noted when removing) and the circlip on other models.
11 Refit the cap (where applicable) and the driveshaft with reference to Section 2. Reconnect the track control arm to the suspension strut and the anti-roll bar to the body mounting, where applicable, referring to Chapter 11.
12 With the car lowered to the ground, remove the final drive filler/level plug and check that the oil level is to the bottom of the hole. If necessary top up the level with the specified oil, then refit the plug.

Fault finding - driveshafts

Vibrations and noise on turns
☐ Worn driveshaft joints

Noise on taking up drive
☐ Worn driveshaft joints
☐ Worn drive flange and/or driveshaft splines
☐ Loose driveshaft bolts or nut

Chapter 8 Braking system

Contents

Brake drum - examination and renovation 11
Brake pressure regulator - general 13
Fault finding - braking system . . . . See end of Chapter
Footbrake pedal - removal and refitting 18
Front brake disc - examination, removal and refitting 5
Front brake disc caliper - removal, overhaul and refitting 4
Front brake disc pads - inspection and renewal 3
General description 1
Handbrake cables - removal, refitting and adjustment 17
Handbrake lever - removal and refitting 16
Hydraulic pipes and hoses - inspection and renewal 14
Hydraulic system - bleeding 15
Master cylinder - removal and refitting 12
Rear brake disc and hub bearings - examination, removal
  and refitting 8
Rear brake disc caliper - removal, overhaul and refitting 7
Rear brake disc pads - inspection and renewal 6
Rear drum brake shoes - inspection and renewal 9
Rear wheel cylinder - removal, overhaul and refitting 10
Routine maintenance - braking system 2
Vacuum servo unit - description and testing 19
Vacuum servo unit - removal and refitting 20

Degrees of difficulty

Easy, suitable for novice with little experience	Fairly easy, suitable for beginner with some experience	Fairly difficult, suitable for competent DIY mechanic	Difficult, suitable for experienced DIY mechanic	Very difficult, suitable for expert DIY or professional

Specifications

General
System type . . . . Hydraulic, dual circuit, split diagonally, pressure regulator on some models. Cable-operated handbrake on rear wheels. Disc front brakes on all models, drum or disc rear brake according to model
Master cylinder diameter . . . . 20.65 mm (0.814 in)
Brake wheel cylinder diameter . . . . 14.29 mm (0.563 in)
Brake servo unit diameter:
  Manual transmission . . . . 178 mm (7.0 in)
  Automatic transmission . . . . 228 mm (9.0 in)
Brake fluid type . . . . Hydraulic fluid to FMVSS 116 DOT 4

Front brakes
Disc thickness (new):
  1.05 and 1.3 litre . . . . 10 mm (0.394 in)
  1.6 and 1.8 litre . . . . 12 mm (0.473 in)
  1.8 litre with ventilated discs . . . . 20 mm (0.790 in)
Disc thickness (minimum):
  1.05 and 1.3 litre . . . . 8 mm (0.315 in)
  1.6 and 1.8 litre . . . . 10 mm (0.394 in)
  1.8 litre with ventilated discs . . . . 18 mm (0.709 in)
Disc pad thickness - new (excluding backplate):
  1.05 and 1.3 litre . . . . 12 mm (0.473 in)
  1.6 and 1.8 litre . . . . 14 mm (0.552 in)
  1.8 litre with ventilated discs . . . . 10 mm (0.394 in)
Disc pad thickness - minimum (including backplate):
  All models . . . . 7 mm (0.276 in)

Rear brakes - disc
Disc thickness (new) . . . . 10.0 mm (0.394 in)
Disc thickness (minimum) . . . . 8.0 mm (0.315 in)
Maximum disc run-out . . . . 0.06 mm (0.002 in)
Disc pad thickness - new (including backplate) . . . . 12.0 mm (0.473 in)
Disc pad thickness - minimum (including backplate) . . . . 7.0 mm (0.28 in)

8•2 Braking system

Rear brakes - drum
Drum internal diameter (new) .... 180.0 mm (7.092 in)
Drum internal diameter (maximum) .... 181.0 mm (7.131 in)
Maximum drum run-out:
   Radial (at friction surface) .... 0.05 mm (0.002 in)
   Lateral (wheel contact surface) .... 0.2 mm (0.008 in)
Lining thickness:
   Minimum (including shoe) .... 5.00 mm (0.20 in)
   Minimum (excluding shoe) .... 2.5 mm (0.10 in)

Torque wrench settings

	Nm	lbf ft
Caliper upper securing bolt	25	19
Caliper lower securing bolt	25	19
Master cylinder securing nuts	20	15
Servo unit securing nuts	20	15
Splash guard to strut	10	7
Backplate to rear axle	60	44
Rear disc brake guide pin (self-locking)	35	26
Rear disc brake carrier bolts	65	48
Rear disc brake cover plate-to-axle bolts	60	44
Roadwheel bolt	110	81

1 General description

The braking system is of hydraulic, dual circuit type with discs at the front and drum or disc brakes (according to model) at the rear. The hydraulic circuit is split diagonally so that with the failure of one circuit, one front and one rear brake remain operative. A load-sensitive pressure regulator is incorporated in the rear hydraulic circuits on some models to prevent the rear wheels locking in advance of the front wheels during heavy application of the brakes. The regulator proportions the hydraulic pressure between the front and rear brakes according to the load being carried.

The handbrake operates on the rear wheels only and the lever incorporates a switch which illuminates a warning light on the instrument panel when the handbrake is applied. The same warning light is wired into the low hydraulic fluid switch circuit.

2 Routine maintenance - braking system

1 The brake fluid level should be checked every week - the reservoir is translucent and the fluid level should be between the MIN and MAX marks. If necessary, top up with the specified brake fluid (photo). However, additional fluid will only be necessary if the hydraulic system is leaking, therefore the source of the leak must first be traced and rectified. Note that the level will drop slightly as the front disc pads wear, but in this case it is not necessary to top up the level.
2 Every 10 000 miles (15 000 km) or 12 months, if this occurs sooner, the hydraulic pipes and unions should be checked for chafing, leakage, cracks and corrosion. At the same time check the operation of the brake pressure regulator and check the disc pads and rear brake linings for wear. Also check the servo vacuum hose for condition and security.
3 Check the brake warning device for correct operation by switching the ignition on and releasing the handbrake. Now press the contact on the reservoir filler cap down and get an assistant to check that the handbrake and dual circuit warning lamp light up (photo).
4 Renew the brake fluid every 2 years.

3 Front brake disc pads - inspection and renewal

1 The disc pad lining wear can be checked by viewing through a hole in the wheel rim and by using a mirror on the inside of the wheel (photo). The use of a torch may also be necessary. If the thickness of any disc pad is less than the minimum amount given in the Specifications, renew the front pads as a set. Where the thickness is more than the minimum amount, due consideration must be given to whether there is sufficient lining left until the next service: 1 mm (0.04 in) of lining will last for approximately 6000 miles (10 000 km).

2.1 Topping-up brake fluid

2.3 Press contact (arrowed) to check the brake warning device

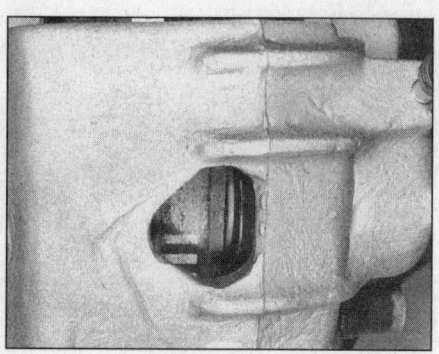

3.1 Front brake pad inspection aperture in caliper

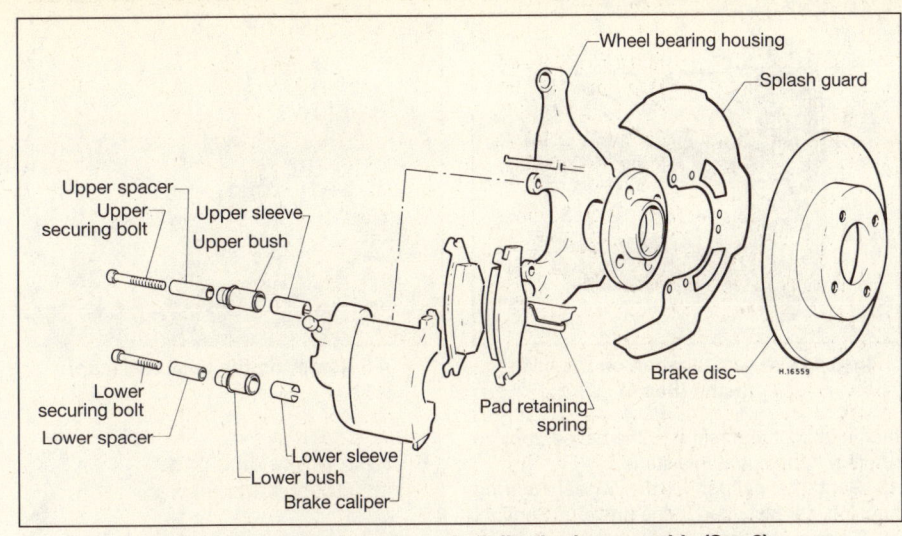

Braking system 8•3

Fig. 8.1 Exploded view of a typical disc brake assembly (Sec 3)

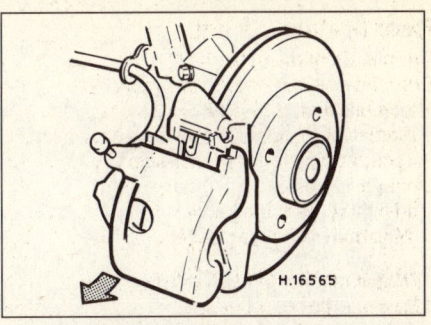

Fig. 8.2 Caliper removal – pivot outwards from the bottom (Sec 3)

2 To remove the disc pads, first jack up the front of the car and support it on axle stands. Apply the handbrake and remove both front wheels.
3 Use an Allen key and unscrew the upper and lower caliper securing bolts (photo). Withdraw the caliper and tie it up out of the way. Do not allow the weight of the caliper to stretch or distort the brake hose (photo).
4 Withdraw each pad by sliding it sideways from the wheel bearing housing, noting that the pads differ, the pad with the larger friction area being fitted to the outside.
5 The retaining spring can be detached from the wheel bearing housing, but note its orientation (photo). Replace the spring when renewing the pads.
6 Brush the dust and dirt from the caliper, piston, disc and pads, *but do not inhale it as it is injurious to health.* Scrape any scale or rust from the disc and pad backing plates.
7 If the pads are to be renewed, they must be replaced as a set on both sides at the front. If the original pads are to be re-used they must be refitted to their original positions each side.
8 Using a piece of wood, push the piston back into the caliper, but while doing this check the level of the fluid in the reservoir and if necessary draw off some with a pipette or release some from the caliper bleed screw. Tighten the screw immediately afterwards.
9 Relocate the retaining spring (photo).
10 Refit the inner pad (smaller friction area), followed by the outer pad. Locate the pad backing plate notches as shown (photo).
11 Refit the brake caliper, locating it at the top end first. Pivot the bottom end into position, align the upper and lower retaining bolt holes, then insert the bolts. Take care not to press the caliper in more than is necessary when fitting the bolts or the retainer springs may be distorted which, in turn, will give noisy braking. Tighten the bolts to the specified torque.
12 On completion, the brake pedal should be depressed firmly several times with the car stationary so that the brake pads take up their normal running positions. Also check the brake hydraulic fluid level in the master cylinder reservoir and top up if necessary.

4 Front brake disc caliper - removal, overhaul and refitting

1 Unbolt and remove the caliper from the wheel bearing housing, as described in the previous Section.
2 If available fit a hose clamp to the caliper flexible brake hose. Alternatively remove the

3.3A Caliper securing bolt removal

3.3B Removing the caliper

3.5 Removing the retaining spring

3.9 Pad retaining spring is located as shown

3.10 Refitting the front brake disc pads

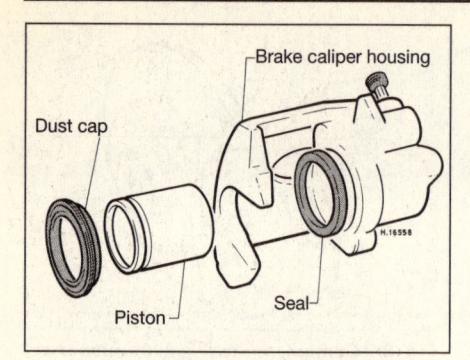

8•4 Braking system

Fig. 8.3 Front disc brake caliper components (Sec 4)

Fig. 8.4 Dust seal location on the caliper piston (Sec 4)

4.5 Removing the dust seal (cap)

fluid reservoir filler cap and tighten it down onto a piece of polythene sheet in order to reduce the loss of hydraulic fluid.
3 Loosen and detach the brake hose union at the caliper; allow for a certain amount of fluid spillage, and plug the hose union to prevent the ingress of dirt.
4 Clean the external surfaces of the caliper with paraffin and wipe dry; plug the fluid inlet during this operation.
5 Prise free and remove the dust seal from the piston (photo).
6 Using air pressure from a foot pump in the fluid inlet blow the piston from the cylinder, but take care not to drop the piston. Prise the sealing ring from the cylinder bore. Take care not to scratch the cylinder bore.
7 Clean the components with methylated spirit and allow to dry. Inspect the surfaces of the piston, cylinder and frames for wear, damage and corrosion. If evident renew the caliper, but if the components are in good condition obtain a repair kit of seals.
8 Dip the new sealing ring in brake fluid and locate it in the cylinder bore groove using the fingers only to manipulate it.
9 Manipulate the new dust cap into position on the piston, the inner seal lip engaging in the piston groove. Use a suitable screwdriver to ease it into position, but take care not to damage the seal or scratch the piston.
10 Smear the piston with brake fluid and press it into position in the caliper bore.
11 Check that the brake hose union is clean, then unplug it and refit it to the caliper, but do not fully tighten it at this stage.
12 Refit the caliper to the wheel bearing housing, as described in the previous Section.
13 Tighten the brake hose union so that the hose is not twisted or in a position where it will chafe against surrounding components.
14 Remove the hose clamp or polythene sheet from the reservoir. Top up the brake fluid reservoir and bleed the brakes, described in Section 15.

5 Front brake disc - examination, removal and refitting

1 Remove the disc pads and caliper, as described in Section 3 leaving the brake hose attached to the caliper. Support the caliper to prevent straining the hose.
2 Rotate the disc and examine it for deep scoring or grooving.
3 Using a micrometer, check that the disc thickness is not less than the minimum amount given in the Specifications.
4 Remove the cross-head screw and withdraw the brake disc from the hub (photo).
5 If necessary the splash guard can be removed from the wheel bearing housing by unscrewing the three bolts.
6 Refitting is a reversal of removal, but make sure that the mating faces of the disc and hub are clean. Refer to Section 3 when refitting the disc pads and caliper.

6 Rear brake disc pads - inspection and renewal

1 To check the rear brake disc pads for wear, refer to Section 3, paragraph 1.
2 To remove the disc pads, chock the front wheels, jack up the rear of the car and support it on axle stands. Remove both rear wheels.
3 Release the handbrake then detach the handbrake cable from the caliper (photo).
4 If the brake hydraulic hose connects to the underside of the caliper, undo the caliper upper retaining bolt (photo). If the hydraulic hose connects to the top of the caliper, undo both caliper retaining bolts. Note that these self-locking bolts must be renewed on reassembly.
5 If the upper retaining bolt was removed, pivot the caliper downwards. If both bolts were removed, carefully lift off and support the caliper.
6 Before removing each brake pad, if they are to be re-used, mark them for identification to ensure that they are refitted to their original location, their positions must not be changed.
7 Brush the dust and dirt from the caliper, piston, disc and pads, *but do not inhale it as it is injurious to health.* Scrape any scale or rust from the disc and pad backing plates.
8 Move the piston back into the caliper by turning it clockwise using either an Allen key

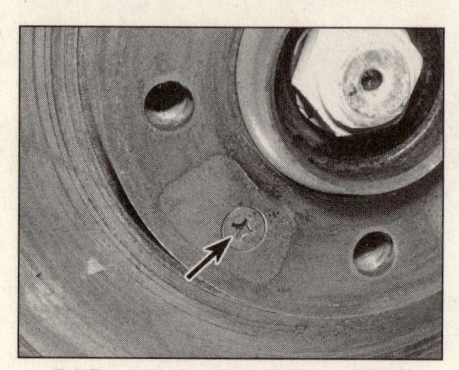

5.4 Front brake disc retaining screw (arrowed)

6.3 Release the handbrake cable (arrowed) from the caliper

6.4 Rear caliper bolt removal – prevent the guide pin from turning with open-ended spanner

Braking system 8•5

6.5 Rear brake caliper removal

6.6 Removing the rear disc brake pads

6.8A Retracting the caliper piston using an Allen key

or a pair of angled circlip pliers according to caliper type (photos). As the piston moves back into the caliper, check the fluid level in the master cylinder and if necessary draw some off with a pipette or release some from the caliper bleed screw. Tighten the screw immediately afterwards.

9 Locate the respective brake pads into position (photo).

10 Before refitting the caliper the piston position must be set to provide a 1.0 mm (0.04 in) clearance between the outer brake pad and the caliper. Check the adjustment by temporarily refitting the caliper and retaining bolts (use the old ones) and check the clearance with a feeler gauge as shown in Fig 8.6. If adjustment is necessary, remove the caliper and rotate the piston clockwise or anti-clockwise until the correct clearance is achieved.

11 Refit the caliper and insert the new self-locking bolts when the adjustment is correct. Tighten the bolts to the specified torque setting.

12 If new brake pads and/or discs have been fitted it is necessary to carry out a basic rear wheel brake adjustment before reconnecting the handbrake cable. To do this apply a medium pressure to the brake pedal and depress it a total of 40 times (car stationary).

13 Reconnect the handbrake cable to the caliper.

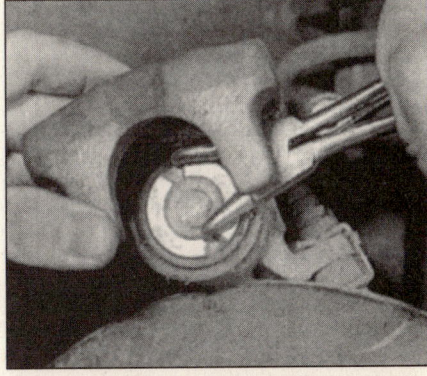

14 On completion check the handbrake adjustment, as described in Section 17

6.8B Retracting the caliper piston using a pair of angled circlip pliers

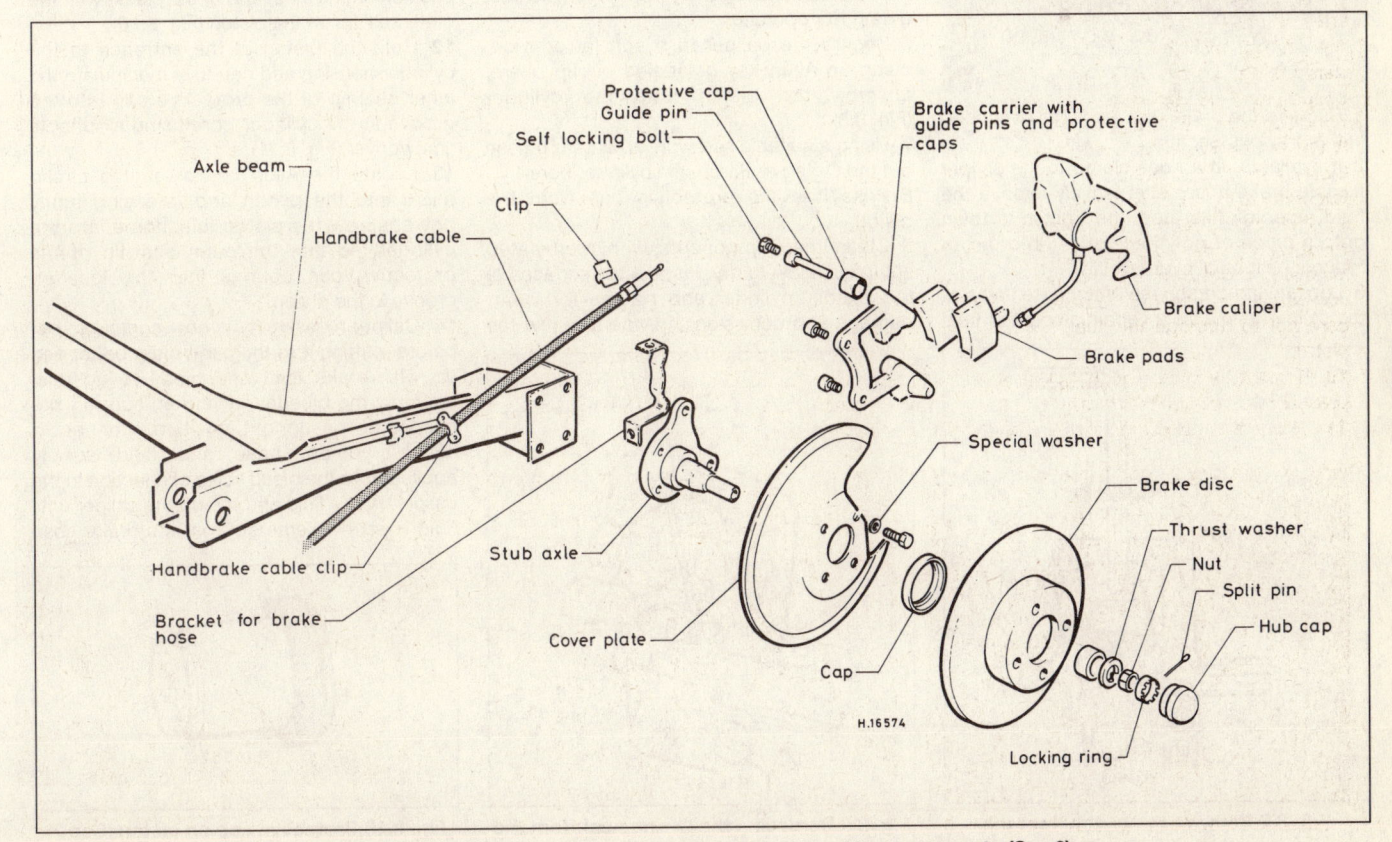

Fig. 8.5 Exploded view of the rear disc brake assembly components (Sec 6)

8

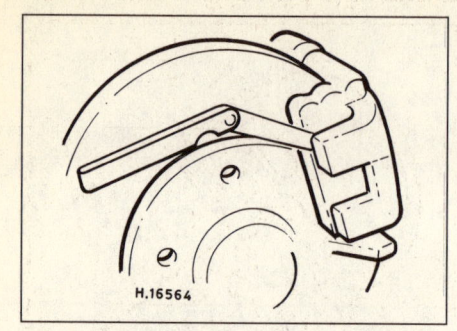

8•6 Braking system

Fig. 8.6 Checking the outer brake pad-to-caliper clearance (Sec 6)

7.4 Rear brake caliper removal

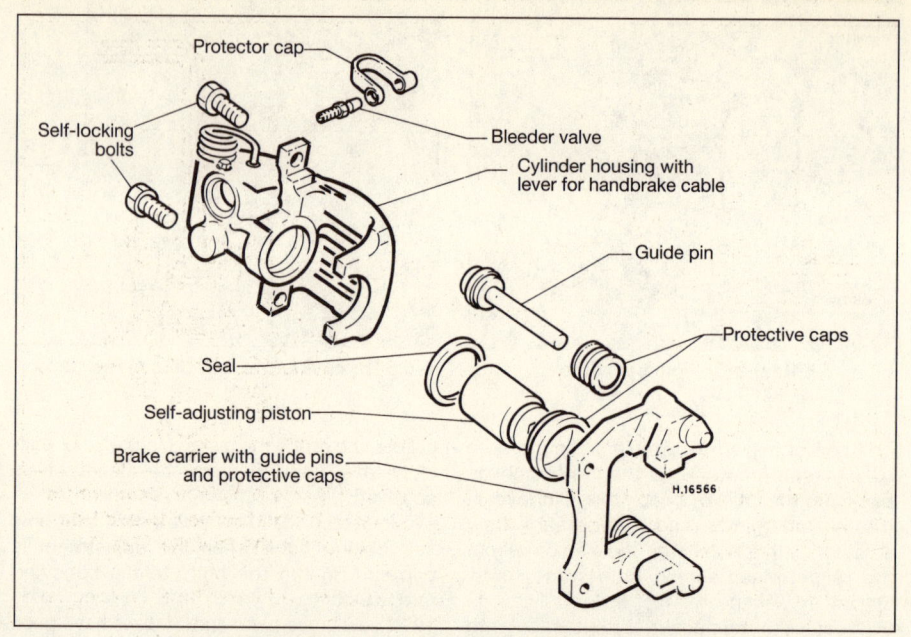

Fig. 8.7 Exploded view of the rear disc brake caliper (Sec 7)

- Protector cap
- Self-locking bolts
- Bleeder valve
- Cylinder housing with lever for handbrake cable
- Guide pin
- Protective caps
- Seal
- Self-adjusting piston
- Brake carrier with guide pins and protective caps

7 Rear brake disc caliper - removal, overhaul and refitting

1 Remove the brake disc pads, as described in the previous Section.
2 If available, fit a hose clamp to the caliper flexible brake hose. Alternatively remove the fluid reservoir filler cap and tighten it down onto a piece of polythene sheet in order to reduce the loss of hydraulic fluid.
3 Loosen and detach the brake hose union at the caliper. Allow for a certain amount of fluid spillage and plug the hose union to prevent the ingress of dirt.
4 Unscrew and remove the lower caliper retaining bolt (where applicable) and remove the caliper (photo). This self-locking bolt must be removed.
5 Clean the external surfaces of the caliper with paraffin and wipe dry - plug the fluid inlet during this operation.
6 Secure the caliper in a soft-jawed vice, using an Allen key or angled circlip pliers, unscrew the piston from the cylinder (Fig. 8.8).
7 Using a suitable screwdriver, carefully ease out the O-ring seal from the cylinder bore.
8 Prise free the protective cap from the piston.
9 Clean the components with methylated spirit and allow to dry. Inspect the surfaces of the piston, cylinder and frames for wear, damage and corrosion. If evident renew the caliper, but if the components are in good condition obtain a repair kit of seals.
10 Dip the new sealing ring in brake fluid and locate it in the cylinder bore groove using the fingers only to manipulate it.
11 Smear the piston with brake fluid then manipulate the new protective cap into position on the inner end of the piston with the outer seal lip on the piston (Fig. 8.10).
12 Hold the piston at the entrance to the cylinder housing and carefully manipulate the inner seal lip of the protective cap into the groove in the cylinder bore using a suitable screwdriver (Fig. 8.11).
13 Locate the Allen key or angled circlip pliers into the piston and, pressing firmly down, screw the piston fully home into the cylinder, so that the outer seal lip of the protective cap springs into the location groove in the piston.
14 Caliper reassembly is now complete, but before refitting it to the car it must be topped up with brake fluid and bled. To do this, unscrew the bleeder valve then support the caliper in the upright position. Connect a suitable union, hose and fluid supply applicator to the bleed valve connection in the caliper. Apply fluid and top up the caliper until fluid is seen to emerge from the brake hose

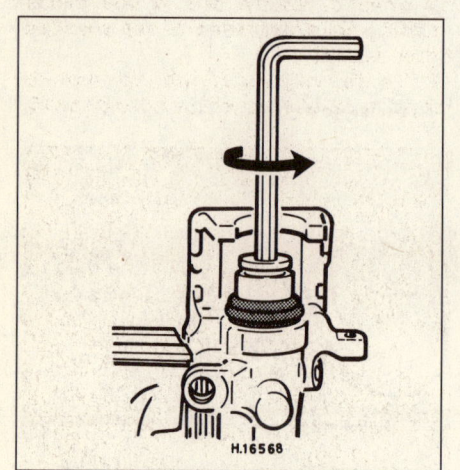

Fig. 8.8 Remove the piston from the cylinder (Sec 7)

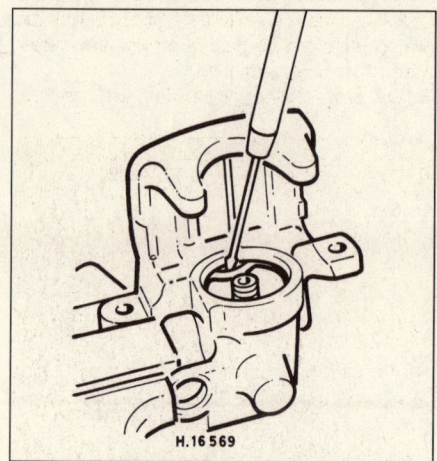

Fig. 8.9 Removing the O-ring seal from the cylinder (Sec 7)

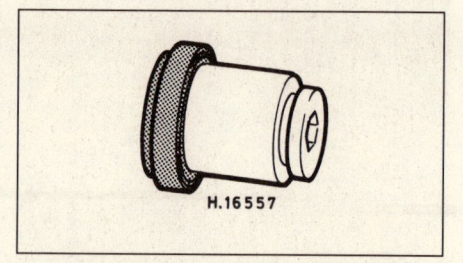

Fig. 8.10 Protective cap on piston (Sec 7)

Braking system 8•7

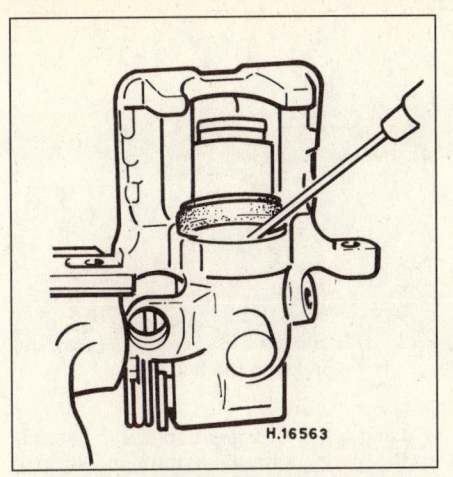

Fig. 8.11 Manipulating the inner seal lip of the protective cap into the cylinder bore groove (Sec 7)

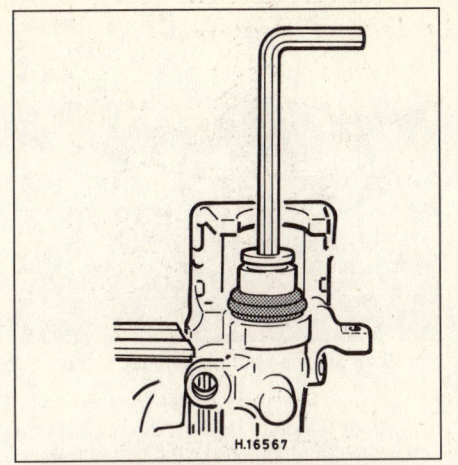

Fig. 8.12 Screw the piston downwards through the protective cap and into position in the cylinder (Sec 7)

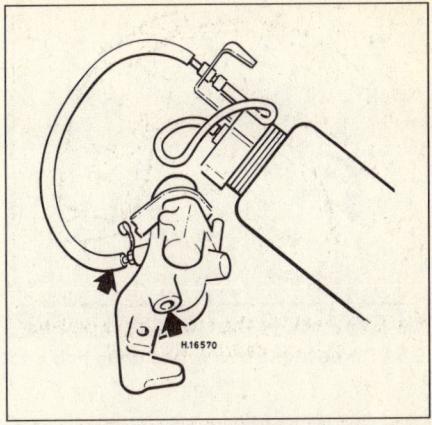

Fig. 8.13 Bleed the rear brake caliper unit prior to refitting (Sec 7)
Arrows indicate brake bleed valve and brake hose connection point

connection without air bubbles. Tighten the bleed valve and plug the brake hose connection aperture.
15 The caliper can now be refitted to the car, as described in Section 6, paragraph 8 to 14 inclusive.

8 Rear brake disc and hub bearings - examination, removal and refitting

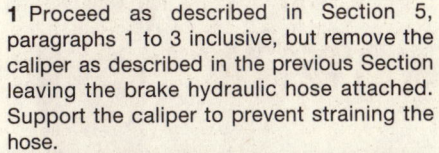

1 Proceed as described in Section 5, paragraphs 1 to 3 inclusive, but remove the caliper as described in the previous Section leaving the brake hydraulic hose attached. Support the caliper to prevent straining the hose.
2 Using a dial gauge or metal block and feeler gauges, check that the disc run-out measured on the friction surface does not exceed the maximum amount given in the Specifications.
3 Unbolt and remove the rear brake carrier. Use a screwdriver and prise free the hub cap (photo).
4 Straighten and extract the split pin, then withdraw the locking ring (photo).
5 Undo the hub nut and then withdraw the thrust washer and outer taper bearing race (photo).
6 Withdraw the disc from the stub axle.
7 The inner bearing can now be removed from the disc by levering free the cap then prising out the oil seal. The bearing can then be extracted.
8 The bearing outer races can be removed from the disc, by drifting them out using a soft drift whilst supporting the disc.
9 If required the brake cover plate can be unbolted, together with the stub axle, from the axle beam. Note that the retaining bolts have high tension spring washers fitted.
10 Unless a disc is being renewed after a fairly low mileage due to damage or other defect, both rear brake discs must be renewed at the same time (rather than one).
11 Commence reassembly by refitting the stub axle and splash guard. Tighten the securing bolts to the specified torque setting.
12 Check that the bearing recesses in the disc are clean, then support the disc and drive the new bearing outer races into position using a suitable tube drift. Ensure that they are fully home. If re-using the old bearings be sure to keep the original bearings and races together when assembling.
13 Lubricate the inner bearing with grease and locate it onto its outer race. The oil seal can now be driven into position. Lubricate its seal lip when fitted. Drive the dust cap into position using a suitable tube drift.
14 Lubricate the stub axle with grease then refit the rear brake disc over it, taking care not to damage the inner oil seal lips.
15 Lubricate the outer taper roller bearing with grease and then locate it onto the stub axle against its bearing outer race.
16 Refit the thrust washer, engaging the inner lug with the groove in the stub axle, then hand tighten the securing nut to the point where the thrust washer can just be moved with a screwdriver and finger pressure but **without** levering it. Check that the disc rotates freely without binding or excessive endfloat, then locate the locking ring over the nut and insert a new split pin to secure.
17 Half fill the hub cap with bearing grease and tap it carefully into position.
18 Before refitting the brake carrier, check that the protective caps and guide pins are not damaged. If they are then the carrier must be renewed. Locate and fit the carrier retaining bolts, tightening to the specified torque setting.
19 The disc caliper and pads can now be refitted, as described in Section 7, paragraph 15.

8.3 Prise free the hub cap (rear disc brake)

8.4 Remove the split pin and lock ring

8.5 Remove the outer washer and bearing

8•8 Braking system

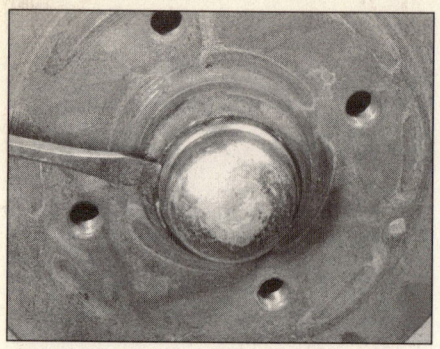

9.4A Remove the rear brake drum hub cap and ...

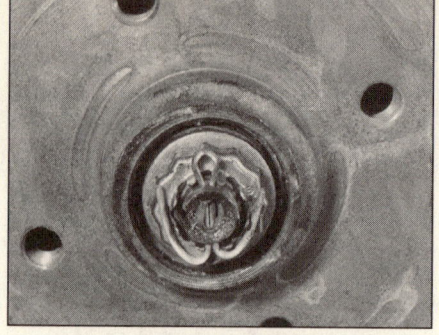

9.4B ... the split pin and lock ring

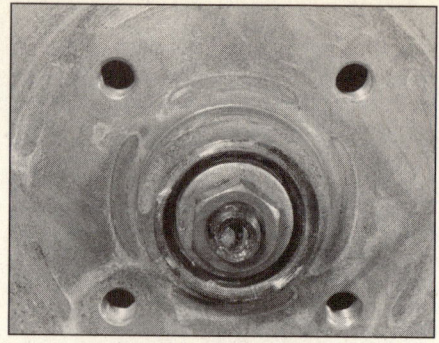

9.5A Undo the hub nut ...

9 Rear drum brake shoes - inspection and renewal

1 Jack up the rear of the car and support it on axle stands. Chock the front wheels.
2 Working beneath the car remove the rubber plugs from the front of the backplates and check that the linings are not worn below the minimum thickness given in the Specifications. If necessary use a torch. Refit the plugs.
3 To remove the rear brake shoes first remove the wheels.
4 Prise off the hub cap then extract the split pin and remove the locking ring (photos).
5 Unscrew the hub nut and remove the thrust washer and outer wheel bearing (photos).
6 Check that the handbrake is fully released, then withdraw the brake drum. If difficulty is experienced, the brake shoes must be backed away from the drum first. To do this, insert a screwdriver through one of the bolt holes and push the automatic adjuster wedge upwards against the spring tension. This will release the shoes from the drum.
7 Brush the dust from the brake drum, brake shoes and backplate, *but do not inhale it as it is injurious to health.* Scrape any scale or rust from the drum. Note that the rear brake shoes should be renewed as a set of four.
8 Using a pair of pliers depress the steady spring cups, turn them through 90° and remove the cups, springs and pins (photo).
9 Note the location of the return springs and strut on the brake shoes, then lever the shoes from the bottom anchor. Unhook and remove the lower return spring (photo).
10 Disengage the handbrake cable from the lever on the trailing brake shoe (photo).
11 Release the brake shoes from the wheel

9.5B ... remove the thrust washer ...

9.5C ... and outer bearing

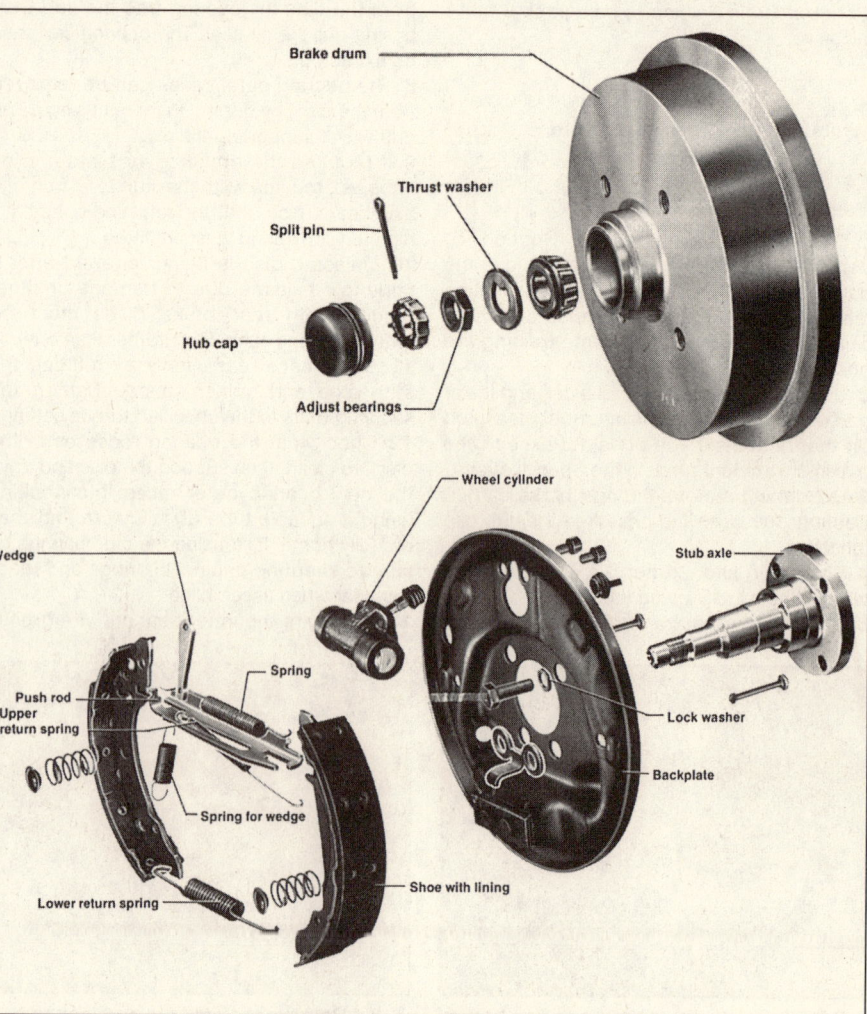

Fig. 8.14 Rear drum brake assembly components (Sec 9)

9.8 Brake shoe steady spring and cup (arrowed)

9.9 Lower return spring fixing points to the brake shoes

9.10 Handbrake cable attachment point to trailing brake shoe (arrowed)

cylinder, unhook the wedge spring and upper return spring and withdraw the shoes (photo).
12 Grip the strut in a vice and release the shoe, then remove the wedge and spring. The backplate and stub axle may be removed, if necessary, by unscrewing the four bolts after removing the wheel cylinder (Section 10). Note the location of the handbrake cable bracket. If the wheel cylinder is being left in position, retain the pistons with an elastic band. Check that there are no signs of fluid leakage and, if necessary, repair or renew the wheel cylinder, as described in Section 10.
13 Fit the new brake shoes using a reversal of the removal procedure, but note that the lug on the wedge faces the backplate.
14 Check the brake drum for wear and damage, as described in Section 11.
15 Before refitting the brake drum, smear the lips of the oil seal with a little grease.
16 Refit the drum onto the stub axle, taking care not to damage the oil seal, then lubricate the outer taper roller bearing and fit it onto the stub axle.
17 Fit the thrust washer and hub nut, and tighten the nut hand tight.
18 Refit the wheel.
19 With the hub cap, split pin, and locking ring removed, tighten the hub nut firmly while turning the wheel in order to settle the bearings.
20 Back off the nut then tighten it until it is just possible to move the thrust washer laterally with a screwdriver under finger

pressure. Do not twist the screwdriver or lever it.
21 Fit the locking ring, together with a new split pin, then tap the hub cap into the drum with a mallet.
22 Check that the brake drum rotates freely then refit the roadwheel(s) and lower the car to the ground. Finally, fully depress the brake pedal several times in order to set the shoes in their correct position.

10 Rear wheel cylinder - removal, overhaul and refitting

1 Remove the rear brake shoes, as described in Section 9.
2 If available, fit a hose clamp to the flexible brake hose. Alternatively remove the fluid reservoir filler cap and tighten it down onto a piece of polythene sheet in order to reduce the loss of hydraulic fluid.
3 Unscrew the hydraulic pipe union from the rear of the cylinder, and plug the end of the pipe.
4 Remove the two screws and withdraw the wheel cylinder from the backplate.
5 Prise off the dust caps then remove the pistons, keeping them identified for location. If necessary, use air pressure from a foot pump in the fluid inlet.

9.11 View showing wheel cylinder, upper return spring and pushrod assembly

6 Remove the internal spring and, if necessary, unscrew the bleed valve.
7 Clean all the components in methylated spirit and allow to dry. Examine the surfaces of the piston and cylinder bore for wear, scoring and corrosion. If evident, renew the complete wheel cylinder. If the components are in good condition, discard the seals and obtain a repair kit.
8 Dip the inner seals in clean brake fluid and fit them to the grooves on the pistons using the fingers only to manipulate them. Make sure that the larger diameter ends face the inner ends of the pistons.
9 Smear brake fluid on the pistons then insert the spring and press the pistons into the cylinder, taking care not to damage the seal lips.
10 Locate the dust caps on the pistons and in the grooves on the outside of the cylinder.
11 Insert and tighten the bleed valve.
12 Clean the mating faces then fit the wheel cylinder to the backplate and tighten the screws.
13 Refit the hydraulic pipe and tighten the union. Remove the hose clamp or polythene sheet.
14 Refit the rear brake shoes, as described in Section 9.
15 Top up the brake fluid reservoir and bleed the valves, as described in Section 15.

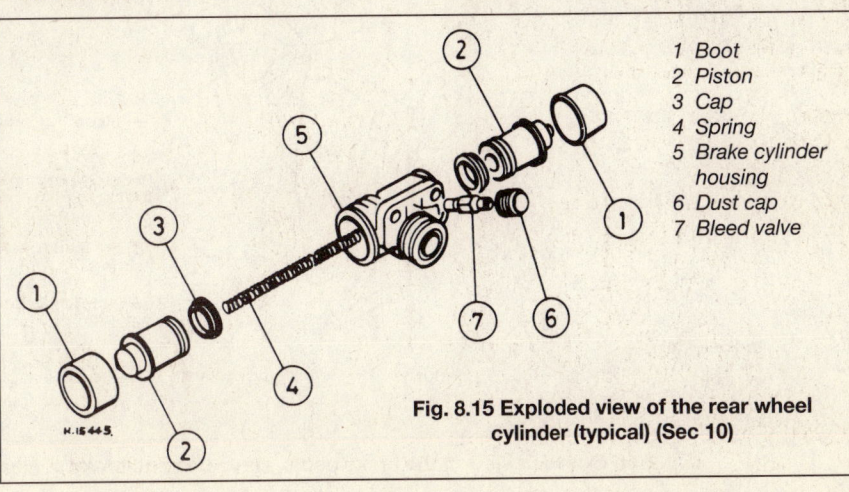

1 Boot
2 Piston
3 Cap
4 Spring
5 Brake cylinder housing
6 Dust cap
7 Bleed valve

Fig. 8.15 Exploded view of the rear wheel cylinder (typical) (Sec 10)

8•10 Braking system

11.3 Prising out the brake drum oil seal

12.6 Master cylinder and brake line connections

11 Brake drum - examination and renovation

1 Whenever the brake drums are removed, they should be checked for wear and damage. Light scoring of the friction surface is normal, but if excessive the drums must either be renewed as a pair or reground provided that the maximum internal diameter given in the Specifications is not exceeded.

2 After a high mileage the drums may become warped and oval. The run-out can be checked with a dial gauge and, if in excess of the maximum amounts given in the Specifications, the drums should be renewed as a pair.
3 The inner oil seal should be checked for condition and if necessary removed and renewed. Prise out the old seal using a screwdriver (photo). Drive the new seal into position so that it is flush with the boss face.

12 Master cylinder - removal and refitting

1 Disconnect the battery negative lead.
2 Disconnect the wiring from the fluid level switches on the master cylinder and fluid reservoir filler cap.
3 On carburettor models, remove the air cleaner, as described in Chapter 3.
4 On fuel injection models detach the injection hoses from the retaining clips on the intake ducting, then unclip and detach the intake duct between the fuel distributor unit and the throttle housing.

5 Place a suitable container beneath the master cylinder and place some cloth on the surrounding body to protect it from any spilled brake fluid.
6 Unscrew the unions and disconnect the hydraulic fluid pipes from the master cylinder (photo).
7 Unscrew the mounting nuts and withdraw the master cylinder from the servo unit. Remove the spacer and seal where applicable.
8 Remove the master cylinder from the

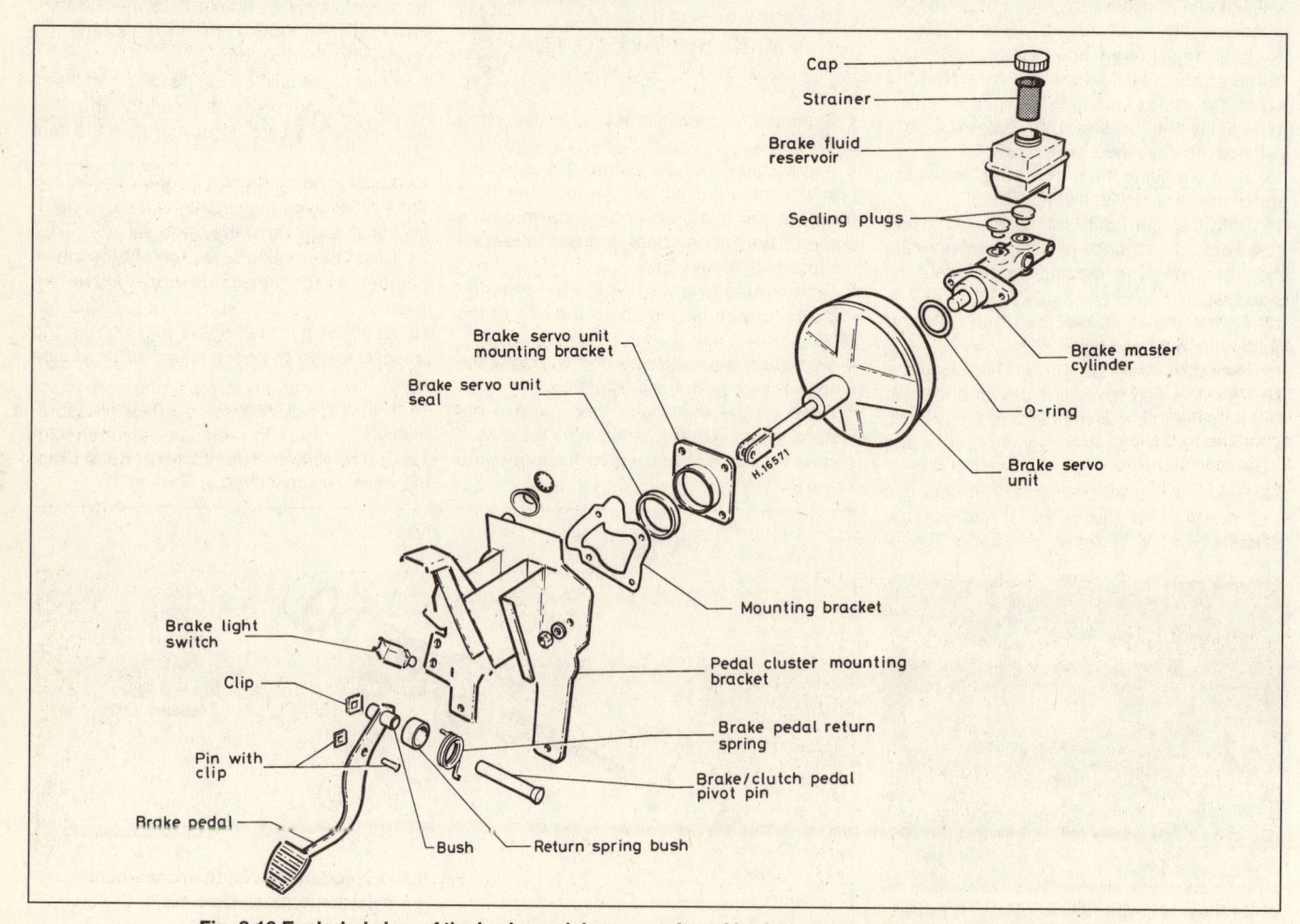

Fig. 8.16 Exploded view of the brake pedal, servo unit and brake master cylinder assembly (Sec 12)

Braking system 8•11

13.2 Brake pressure regulator unit (fitted to some models)

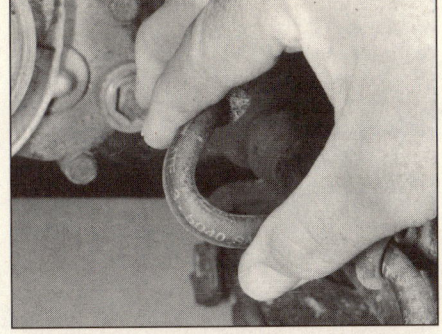

14.1A Bend flexible brake hose to check for signs of cracks

14.1B Flexible hose retaining clip (to front strut)

engine compartment, taking care not to spill any hydraulic fluid on the body paintwork.
9 Clean the exterior of the master cylinder with paraffin and wipe dry.
10 If the master cylinder is defective it cannot be overhauled and must be renewed as a unit. This being the case, remove the reservoir by pulling it free from the rubber grommets, then prise free the grommets from the cylinder.
11 Commence reassembly by smearing the rubber grommets in brake fluid and press them into the cylinder, then press the reservoir into the grommets.
12 Refitting the master cylinder is otherwise a reversal of the removal procedure, but fit a new mounting seal between the cylinder and servo unit. On completion, bleed the brake hydraulic system, as described in Section 15.

13 Brake pressure regulator - general

1 A brake pressure regulator is fitted in the rear brake circuit of some models and its purpose is to prevent the rear wheels locking in advance of the front wheels during heavy application of the brakes. The regulator is also load sensitive in order to vary the pressure according to the load being carried.
2 The regulator is located on the under-body, in front of the left-hand rear wheel (photo).
3 Checking of the regulator is best left to a VW garage, as special pressure gauges and spring tensioning tools are required. Adjustment is made by varying the spring tension, but this must be carried out by the garage.
4 Removal and refitting are straightforward but, after fitting, bleed the hydraulic system, as described in Section 15, and have the regulator adjusted by a garage.
5 When bleeding the hydraulic system of cars fitted with a pressure regulator, the lever of the regulator should be pressed toward the rear axle.

14 Hydraulic pipes and hoses - inspection and renewal

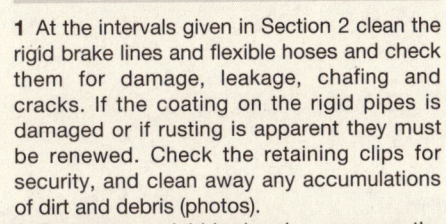

1 At the intervals given in Section 2 clean the rigid brake lines and flexible hoses and check them for damage, leakage, chafing and cracks. If the coating on the rigid pipes is damaged or if rusting is apparent they must be renewed. Check the retaining clips for security, and clean away any accumulations of dirt and debris (photos).
2 To remove a rigid brake pipe, unscrew the union nuts at each end and where necessary remove the line from the clips. Refitting is a reversal of removal.
3 To remove a flexible brake hose, unscrew the union nut securing the rigid brake pipe to the end of the flexible hose and remove the spring clip and hose end fitting from the bracket (photo). Unscrew the remaining end from the component or rigid pipe according to position. Refitting is a reversal of removal.
4 Bleed the complete hydraulic system, as described in Section 15, after fitting a rigid brake pipe or flexible brake hose.

15 Hydraulic system - bleeding

1 This is not a routine operation, but will be required after any component in the system has been removed and refitted or any part of the hydraulic system has been 'broken'. When an operation has only affected one circuit of the hydraulic system, then bleeding will normally only be required to that circuit (front and rear diagonally opposite).

> **HAYNES HiNT** *Take great care not to spill brake fluid onto the paintwork as it will act as a paint stripper. If any is spilled, wash it off at once with cold water.*

2 If the master cylinder or the pressure regulating valve have been disconnected and reconnected, then the complete system must be bled. Note that where a brake pressure regulator is fitted, the regulator lever should be pressed toward the rear axle during the bleeding of the rear brakes.
3 One of three methods can be used to bleed the system.

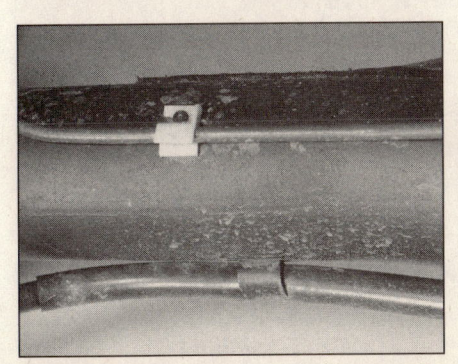

14.1C Rigid pipe retaining clip (to rear axle beam)

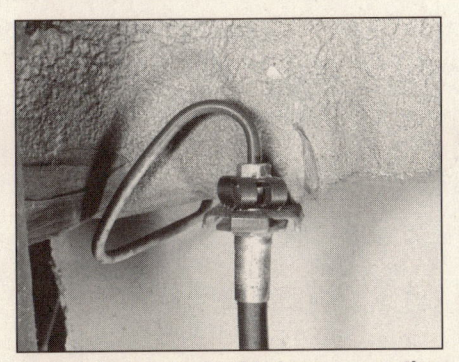

14.3 Rigid pipe-to-flexible hose connection

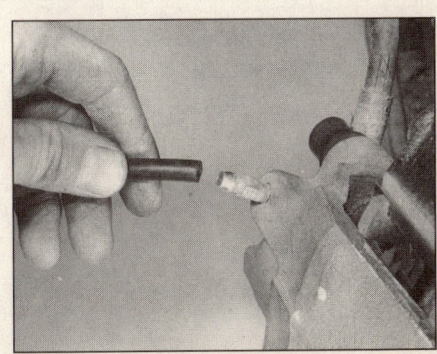

15.5 Connect the bleed tube to the bleed valve

8•12 Braking system

Bleeding - two-man method

4 Gather together a clean jar and a length of rubber or plastic bleed tubing which will fit the bleed valve tightly. The help of an assistant will be required.
5 Clean around the bleed valve on the rear brake and attach the bleed tube to the valve (photo)
6 Check that the master cylinder reservoir is topped up and then destroy the vacuum in the brake servo (where fitted) by giving several applications of the brake foot pedal.
7 Immerse the open end of the bleed tube in the jar, which should contain 50 to 76 mm (2 to 3 in) of hydraulic fluid. The jar should be positioned about 300 mm (12.0 in) above the bleed valve to prevent any possibility of air entering the system down the threads of the bleed valve when it is slackened.
8 Open the bleed valve half a turn and have your assistant depress the brake pedal slowly to the floor and then quickly remove his foot to allow the pedal to return unimpeded. Tighten the bleed valve at the end of each downstroke to prevent expelled air and fluid being drawn back into the system.
9 Observe the submerged end of the tube in the jar. When air bubbles cease to appear, fully tighten the bleed valve when the pedal is being held down by your assistant.
10 Top up the fluid reservoir. It must be kept topped up throughout the bleeding operations. If the connecting holes in the master cylinder are exposed at any time due to low fluid level, then air will be drawn into the system and work will have to start all over again.
11 Repeat the operation on the diagonally opposite front brake. If the whole system is being bled, follow the sequence given below.
12 On completion, remove the bleed tube. Discard the fluid which has been bled from the system unless it is required for bleed jar purposes, **never** use it for filling the system.

Bleeding - with one-way valve

13 There are a number of one-man brake bleeding kits currently available from motor accessory shops. It is recommended that one of these kits should be used whenever possible as they greatly simplify the bleeding operation and also reduce risk of expelled air or fluid being drawn back into the system.
14 Connect the outlet tube of the bleeder device to the bleed valve and then open the valve half a turn. Depress the brake pedal to the floor and slowly release it. The one-way valve in the device will prevent expelled air from returning to the system at the completion of each stroke. Repeat this operation until clean hydraulic fluid, free from air bubbles, can be seen coming through the tube. Tighten the bleed screw and remove the tube.
15 Repeat the procedure on the remaining bleed nipples in the order described in paragraph 11. Remember to keep the master cylinder reservoir full.

Bleeding - with pressure bleeding kits

16 These are available from motor accessory shops and are usually operated by air pressure from the spare tyre.
17 By connecting a pressurised container to the master cylinder fluid reservoir, bleeding is then carried out by simply opening each bleed valve in turn and allowing the fluid to run out, rather like turning on a tap, until no air bubbles are visible in the fluid being expelled.
18 Using this system, the large reserve of fluid provides a safeguard against air being drawn into the master cylinder during the bleeding operations.
19 This method is particularly effective when bleeding 'difficult' systems or when bleeding the entire system at routine fluid renewal.

All methods

20 If the entire system is being bled the procedures described above should now be repeated at each wheel. The correct sequence is as follows.
   Right-hand rear wheel
   Left-hand rear wheel
   Right-hand front wheel
   Left-hand front wheel

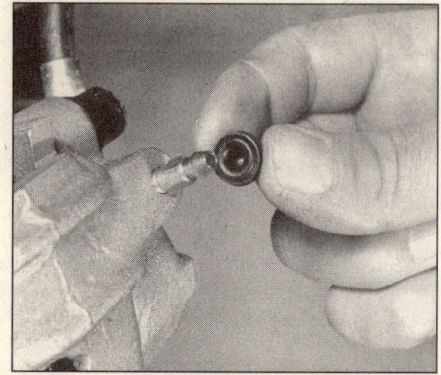

15.23 Fit the protector caps on completion

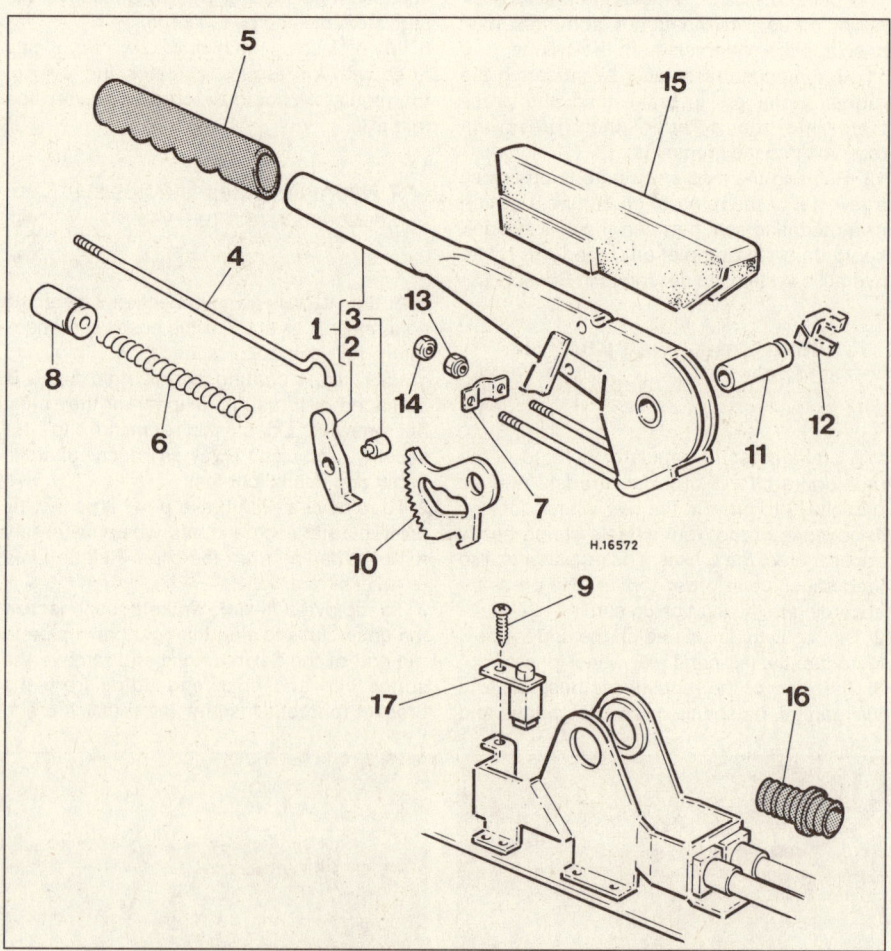

Fig. 8.17 Exploded view of the handbrake assembly (Sec 16)

1 Handbrake lever	7 Compensator lever	13 Adjusting nut
2 Pawl	8 Press stud	14 Locknut
3 Pin	9 Screw	15 Cover boot
4 Rod	10 Ratchet	16 Grommet
5 Handle	11 Pin	17 Switch
6 Pressure spring	12 Clamp	

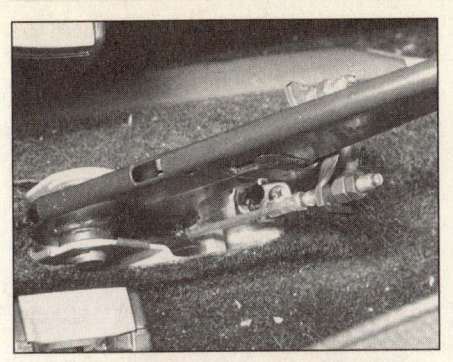

16.2 Handbrake lever and cables with adjuster and locknuts

The handbrake lever ON switch retaining screw is just visible underneath the lever

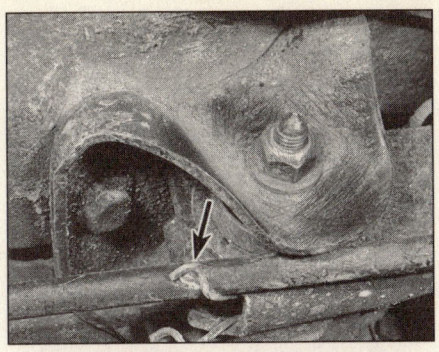

17.6 Handbrake cable retaining clip (arrowed) at rear axle beam pivot

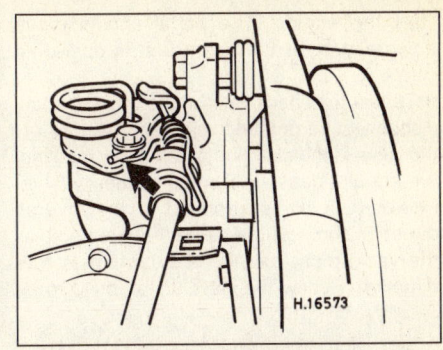

Fig. 8.18 Handbrake adjustment on rear disc brakes – lever on caliper (arrowed) should be just clear of stop (Sec 17)

Do not forget to recheck the fluid level in the master cylinder at regular intervals and top up as necessary.

21 When completed, recheck the fluid level in the master cylinder, top up if necessary and refit the cap. Check the 'feel' of the brake pedal which should be firm and free from any 'sponginess' which would indicate air still present in the system.

22 Discard any expelled hydraulic fluid as it is likely to be contaminated with moisture, air and dirt which makes it unsuitable for further use.

23 On completion refit the rubber protector caps over each bleed valve (photo).

16 Handbrake lever - removal and refitting

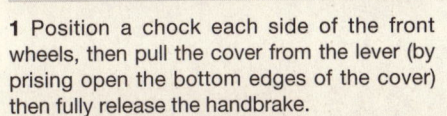

1 Position a chock each side of the front wheels, then pull the cover from the lever (by prising open the bottom edges of the cover) then fully release the handbrake.

2 Undo each cable locknut and adjuster nut and disconnect the cables from the compensating lever (photo).

3 Prise free the lever retaining clamp on the right-hand side, then withdraw the pivot pin and remove the lever.

4 If required remove the screw from the lever switch, disconnect the wiring, and remove the switch.

5 Refitting is a reversal of removal. Lubricate the pivot pin and, on completion, adjust the handbrake cables, as described in Section 17.

17 Handbrake cables - removal, refitting and adjustment

1 Chock the front wheels, then jack up the rear of the car and support it on axle stands. Release the handbrake.

2 Remove the cover from the handbrake lever then undo the locknut and adjuster nut from the cable concerned.

3 Remove the rear roadwheel(s).

4 On drum brake models, remove the brake drum and disconnect the cable from the shoe operating lever, as described in Section 9. Detach the cable from the backplate.

5 On models fitted with disc brakes at the rear, disengage the cable from the caliper lever, then prise free the outer cable retaining clip from the caliper. Note how the clip is located.

6 Release the cable from its retaining clips and then carefully withdraw it from under the car (photo).

7 Refitting is a reversal of removal, but adjust the cable as follows before lowering the car.

Cable adjustment - drum brakes

8 With the handbrake lever fully released, depress the footbrake applying firm pressure, once only. Now pull the handbrake up onto its second notch position.

9 Tighten the adjuster nut on the cable concerned so that the rear roadwheel is just felt to bind when rotated. Fully release the handbrake lever, then check that the roadwheel spins freely without binding. Tighten the locknut against the adjuster nut, then apply the handbrake and check that the wheel is locked. Repeat the procedure with the other cable.

Cable adjustment - disc brakes

10 Before checking and adjusting the handbrake cables, first check the outer brake pad to caliper clearance, as described in Section 6.

11 Fully release the handbrake lever then tighten the cable adjuster nut to the point where the caliper lever just separates from its stop (Fig. 8.18). An assistant is useful here to ensure that, as the nut is tightened, the lever-to-stop clearance does not exceed 1 mm (0.04 in). Tighten the locknut then fully release the handbrake and check that the roadwheel rotates freely then apply the handbrake and check that the roadwheel is locked.

12 Repeat the procedure on the other side.

18 Footbrake pedal - removal and refitting

1 The brake and clutch pedals share a common bracket assembly and pivot shaft.

2 Remove the clutch pedal, as described in Chapter 5.

3 Extract the clip and withdraw the clevis pin securing the servo pushrod.

4 Extract the clip from the pivot shaft, unhook the return spring, withdraw the pivot shaft and remove the pedal.

5 Check the pedal bushes for wear. If necessary drive them out from each side and press in new bushes using a soft-jawed vice.

6 Refitting is a reversal of removal, but lubricate the pivot shaft with a little multi-purpose grease.

19 Vacuum servo unit - description and testing

1 The vacuum servo unit is located between the brake pedal and the master cylinder and provides assistance to the driver when the brake pedal is depressed. The unit operates by vacuum from the inlet manifold.

2 The unit basically consists of a diaphragm and non-return valve. With the brake pedal released, vacuum is channelled to both sides of the diaphragm, but when the pedal is depressed, one side is opened to the atmosphere. The resultant unequal pressures are harnessed to assist in depressing the master cylinder pistons.

3 Normally, the vacuum servo unit is very reliable, but if the unit becomes faulty, it should be renewed. In the event of a failure, the hydraulic system is in no way affected, except that higher pedal pressures will be necessary.

4 To test the vacuum servo unit depress the brake pedal several times with the engine switched off to dissipate the vacuum. Apply moderate pressure to the brake pedal then

start the engine. The pedal should move down slightly if the servo unit is operating correctly.

5 To test the check valve in the vacuum hose, disconnect it from the hose then blow through the valve in the direction of the arrow marking. Air should pass through the check valve. However, if air is supplied in the reverse direction through the valve it should not, as the valve must be closed to airflow in that direction. Renew the valve unit if found to be defective.

20 Vacuum servo unit - removal and refitting

1 Remove the brake master cylinder as described in Section 12.
2 Pull the vacuum hose free from the servo unit connector and, where applicable, the non-return valve.
3 Working inside the vehicle, detach the lower trim panel on the driver's side.
4 Disconnect the pushrod clevis from the brake pedal by releasing the clip and withdrawing the clevis pin.
5 Unscrew the mounting nuts and withdraw the servo unit from the bulkhead into the engine compartment.
6 Refitting is a reversal of removal. Lubricate the clevis pin with a little molybdenum disulphide based grease. The mounting nuts are self-locking and should always be renewed.

Fault finding - braking system

Excessive pedal travel
☐ Brake fluid leak
☐ Air in hydraulic system
☐ Worn rear brake shoes

Brake judder
☐ Worn drums and/or discs
☐ Loose suspension anchor point
☐ Loose rear brake backplate

Brake pedal feels spongy
☐ Air in hydraulic system
☐ Faulty master cylinder seals

Uneven braking and pulling to one side
☐ Contaminated linings
☐ Seized wheel cylinder or caliper
☐ Incorrect and unequal tyre pressures
☐ Loose suspension anchor point
☐ Different lining material at each wheel

Excessive effort to stop car
☐ Seized wheel cylinders or calipers
☐ Incorrect lining material
☐ Contaminated linings
☐ New linings not yet bedded-in
☐ Excessively worn linings

Chapter 9 Electrical system

For modification, and information applicable to later models, see Supplement at end of manual

Contents

Alternator - maintenance and special precautions	7
Alternator - removal and refitting	10
Alternator - testing	9
Alternator (Bosch) - overhaul	11
Alternator drivebelt - adjustment	8
Alternator (Motorola) - overhaul	12
Automatic stop-start system - general	16
Battery - charging	6
Battery - electrolyte replenishment	5
Battery - maintenance	4
Battery - removal and refitting	3
Cigarette lighter - removal and refining	25
Combination switches - removal and refitting	21
Courtesy and luggage compartment light switches - removal and refitting	24
Direction indicators and hazard flasher system - general	19
Electrically-operated door mirror motor - removal and refitting	35
Electrical system - maintenance	2
Facia switches - removal and refitting	22
Facia trim panel - removal and refitting	29
Fault finding - electrical system	See end of Chapter
Foglight (front) bulb and unit - removal and refitting	33
Fuses and relays - general	18
Gearchange and consumption gauge - general	17
General description	1
Headlamp bulbs and headlamps - removal and refining	30
Headlamp range control - removal and refitting	32
Headlamps - adjustment	31
Horn - removal and refitting	42
Ignition switch/steering column lock - removal and refitting	20
Instrument panel - dismantling, testing and reassembly	28
Instrument panel cluster - removal and refitting	27
Lamp bulbs - renewal	34
Loudspeakers - removal and refitting	44
Radio/cassette player - removal and refining	43
Rear window wiper motor - removal and refitting	39
Speedometer cable - removal and refitting	26
Starter motor - overhaul	15
Starter motor - removal and refitting	14
Starter motor - testing in the car	13
Warning lamp cluster - removal and refitting	23
Windscreen, headlamp and rear window washer system - general	41
Windscreen wiper linkage - removal and refitting	40
Windscreen wiper motor - removal and refitting	38
Wiper arms - removal and refitting	37
Wiper blades - renewal	36
Wiring diagrams	See end of Manual

Degrees of difficulty

Easy, suitable for novice with little experience	Fairly easy, suitable for beginner with some experience	Fairly difficult, suitable for competent DIY mechanic	Difficult, suitable for experienced DIY mechanic	Very difficult, suitable for expert DIY or professional

Specifications

System type . . . . 12 volt, negative earth

Battery . . . . 36 amp hour or 45 amp hour
Minimum voltage (under load) . . . . 9.6 volts at 110 amps

Alternator
Type . . . . Bosch or Motorola
Maximum output (amps) . . . . 55, 65 or 90
Minimum allowable brush length . . . . 5 mm (0.2 in)

Rotor winding resistance (ohms): **Bosch**   **Motorola**
  55 amp . . . . 2.9 to 3.2   3.1 to 3.3
  65 amp . . . . 2.8 to 3.1   3.9 to 4.1
  90 amp . . . . 3.0 to 4.0   -

9•2 Electrical system

Starter motor
Type.	Pre-engaged
Model:	VW part/type number
1.05 and 1.3 litre	036 911 023 G
1.3 litre	036 911 023 H
1.6 litre:	
Manual gearbox	055 911 023 G
Automatic transmission	055 911 023 A
1.8 litre	027 911 023

Fuses

Fuse number	Component	Rating (amps)
1	Radiator fan	30
2	Brake light	10
3	Cigarette lighter, radio, clock, interior light, central locking, boot light (Jetta)	15
4	Emergency light system	15
5	Fuel pump	15
6	Foglights (main current)	15
7	Tail and sidelights, left	10
8	Tail and sidelights, right	10
9	High beam right, high beam warning lamp	10
10	High beam, left	10
11	Windscreen wipers and washer, headlight washer	15
12	Rear wiper and washer, seat heater control, electric mirror control	15
13	Rear window heating, mirror heating	15
14	Blower, glovebox light	20
15	Reversing lights, shift pattern illumination (automatic gearbox)	10
16	Horn	15
17	Carburettor	10
18	Horn (dual tone), coolant level warning lamp	15
19	Turn signals, stop-start system, brake warning lamp	10
20	Number plate light, foglights (switch current)	10
21	Low beam, left, headlight range control, left	10
22	Low beam right, headlight range control, right	10

Additional fuses (In separate holders above the fusebox)	**Rating (amps)**
Rear foglight	10
Electric windows	30
Air conditioner	30

Relays
See wiring diagrams at end of Manual

Bulbs
	Wattage
Headlamps (halogen)	60/55
Sidelight	4
Tail light	5
Stop-light	21
Direction indicators	21
Foglight (rear)	21
Reversing light	21
Instrument light	1.2

Wiper blades
Champion X-4503

Torque wrench settings
	Nm	lbf ft
Starter motor:		
1.05 and 1.3 litre	20	15
1.6 and 1.8 litre (manual gearbox)	60	44
1.6 litre (automatic transmission)	20	15
Alternator:		
Pulley nut	40	30
Mounting (to engine) bolts	45	33
Mounting/alternator pivot bolt	45	33
Adjuster strap bolts	25	18

Electrical system 9•3

1 General description

The electrical system is of 12 volt negative earth type. The battery is charged by a belt-driven alternator which incorporates a voltage regulator. The starter motor is of pre-engaged type incorporating a solenoid which moves the drive pinion into engagement with the flywheel/driveplate ring gear before the motor is energised.

Although repair procedures are given in this Chapter, it may well be more economical to renew worn components as complete units.

2 Electrical system - maintenance

The following routine maintenance procedures should be undertaken at the specified intervals given at the start of this manual.
1 **Battery:** Refer to Section 4 in this Chapter.
2 **Alternator:** Refer to Section 7 in this Chapter.
3 **Alternator drivebelt:** Check condition and adjustment of the drivebelt, as described in Section 8 of this Chapter.
4 **Vehicle lighting:** Periodically check that all of the front and rear lights are functioning correctly. The headlights and (where applicable) the foglights should be checked for alignment, as described in Section 31. Renew any defective bulbs.
5 **Windscreen/rear window wipers:** Check their operation (having wet the glass first) and also the condition of the wiper blade rubbers. Renew if necessary. At the same time, check that the windscreen, rear window and headlamp washers (as applicable) operate in a satisfactory manner. Check and, when necessary, top up the fluid reservoirs.
6 **Wiring:** Periodically check the wiring and connections for condition and security.

3 Battery - removal and refitting

1 The battery is located in the engine compartment on the left-hand side.
2 Loosen the battery terminal clamp nuts and disconnect the negative lead followed by the positive lead (photo).
3 Unscrew the bolt and remove the battery retaining clamp (photo).
4 Lift the battery from its platform; taking care not to spill any electrolyte on the bodywork.
5 Refitting is a reversal of removal, but make sure that the leads are fitted to their correct terminals, and do not overtighten the lead clamp nuts or the battery retaining clamp bolt. Finally smear a little petroleum jelly on the terminals and clamps.

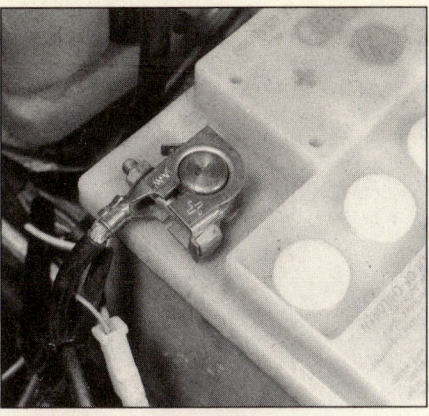

3.2 Battery positive terminal and lead connection

3.3 Battery retaining clamp and bolt

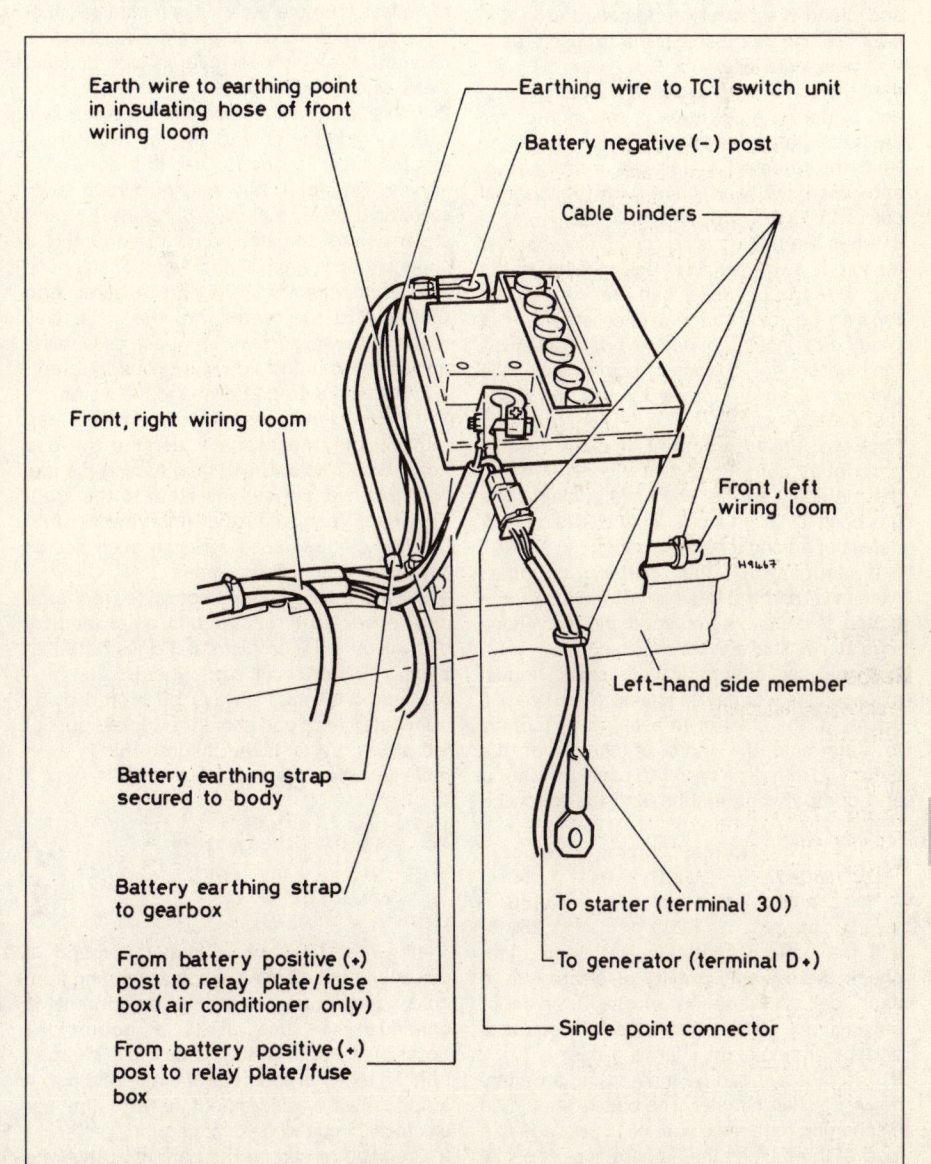

Fig. 9.1 Battery and lead connection (Sec 3)

- Earth wire to earthing point in insulating hose of front wiring loom
- Earthing wire to TCI switch unit
- Battery negative (-) post
- Cable binders
- Front, right wiring loom
- Front, left wiring loom
- Left-hand side member
- Battery earthing strap secured to body
- Battery earthing strap to gearbox
- To starter (terminal 30)
- To generator (terminal D+)
- From battery positive (+) post to relay plate/fuse box (air conditioner only)
- Single point connector
- From battery positive (+) post to relay plate/fuse box

4 Battery - maintenance

1 Where a conventional battery is fitted, the electrolyte level of each cell should be checked every month and, if necessary, topped up with distilled or de-ionized water until the separators are just covered. On some batteries the case is translucent and incorporates minimum and maximum level marks. The check should be made more often if the car is operated in high ambient temperature conditions.
2 Where a low maintenance battery is fitted, it is not necessary to check the electrolyte level.
3 Every 10 000 miles (15 000 km) or 12 months, whichever occurs first, disconnect and clean the battery terminals and leads. After refitting them, smear the exposed metal with petroleum jelly.
4 At the same time, inspect the battery clamp and platform for corrosion. If evident, remove the battery and clean the deposits away, then treat the affected metal with a proprietary anti-rust liquid and paint with the original colour.
5 When the battery is removed, for whatever reason, it is worthwhile checking it for cracks and leakage. Cracks can be caused by topping-up the cells with distilled water in winter *after* instead of *before* a run. This gives the water no chance to mix with the electrolyte, so the former freezes and splits the battery case. If the battery case is fractured, it may be possible to repair it with a proprietary compound, but this depends on the material used for the case. If electrolyte has been lost from a cell, refer to Section 5 for details of adding a fresh solution.
6 If topping-up the battery becomes excessive and the case is not fractured, the battery is being over-charged and the voltage regulator will have to be checked.
7 If the car covers a very small annual mileage, it is worthwhile checking the specific gravity of the electrolyte every three months to determine the state of charge of the battery. Use a hydrometer to make the check, and compare the results with the following table.

	Normal climates	Tropics
Discharged	1.120	1.080
Half charged	1.200	1.160
Fully charged	1.280	1.230

8 If the battery condition is suspect, first check the specific gravity of electrolyte in each cell. A variation of 0.040 or more between any cells indicates loss of electrolyte or deterioration of the internal plates.
9 A further test can be made using a battery heavy discharge meter. The battery should be discharged for a maximum of 15 seconds at a load of three times the ampere-hour capacity (at the 20 hour discharge rate). Alternatively connect a voltmeter across the battery terminals and spin the engine on the starter with the ignition disconnected (see Chapter 4), and the headlamps, heated rear window and heater blower switched on. If the voltmeter reading remains above 9.6 volts, the battery condition is satisfactory. If the voltmeter reading drops below 9.6 volts, and the battery has already been charged as described in Section 6, it is faulty and should be renewed.

5 Battery - electrolyte replenishment

Note: *This Section is not applicable to maintenance-free batteries.*

1 If the battery has been fully charged, but one cell has a specific gravity of 0.025 or more less than the others it is most likely that electrolyte has been lost from the cell at some time and the acid over-diluted with distilled water when topping-up.
2 In this case, remove some of the electrolyte with a hydrometer and top up with fresh electrolyte. It is best to get this done at a service station, for making your own electrolyte is messy, dangerous, and expensive for the small amount you need. If you must do it yourself add 1 part of sulphuric acid (concentrated) to 2.5 part of water. **Add the acid to the water,** not the other way round or the mixture will spit back as water is added to acid and you will be badly burnt. Add the acid a drop at a time to the water.
3 If topping-up is needed, the battery cap removal may necessitate piercing the cap notch with a screwdriver then turning the cap (with screwdriver still inserted) to the stop. The caps can then be unscrewed. Add distilled or de-ionized water to each cell as necessary then refit the caps.
4 Having added fresh electrolyte, recharge and recheck the readings. In all probability this will cure the problem. If it does not, then there is a short-circuit somewhere.
5 Electrolyte must always be stored away from other fluids and should be locked up, not left about. If you have children this is even more important.

6 Battery - charging

1 In winter time when heavy demand is placed upon the battery, such as starting from cold, and much electrical equipment is continually in use, it is a good idea occasionally to have the battery fully charged from an external source at the rate of 3.5 to 4 amps. Always disconnect it from the car electrical circuit when charging.
2 Continue to charge the battery at this rate until no further rise in specific gravity is noted over a four hour period.
3 Alternatively, a trickle charger, charging at

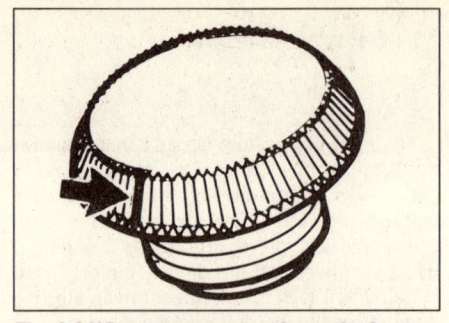

Fig. 9.2 Where necessary, pierce the battery cap notch (arrowed) with a screwdriver when removing the caps (Sec 5)

the rate of 1.5 amps, can be safely used overnight. Disconnect the battery from the car electrical circuit before charging or you will damage the alternator.
4 Specially rapid 'boost' charges which are claimed to restore the power of the battery in 1 to 2 hours can cause damage to the battery plates through overheating. Maintenance-free batteries should not be rapid charged.
5 While charging the battery note that the temperature of the electrolyte should never exceed 37.8°C (100°F).
6 Make sure that your charging set and battery are set to the same voltage.
7 'Maintenance-free' batteries must **only** be trickle charged and may require twice the charging period of a normal battery.

7 Alternator - maintenance and special precautions

1 Periodically wipe away any dirt which has accumulated on the outside of the unit, and also check that the plug is pushed firmly on the terminals. At the same time check the tension of the drivebelt and adjust it if necessary as described in Section 8.
2 Take extreme care when making electrical circuit connections on the car, otherwise damage may occur to the alternator or other electrical components employing semiconductors. Always make sure that the battery leads are connected to the correct terminals. Before using electric arc welding equipment to repair any part of the car, disconnect the battery leads and alternator multi-plug. Disconnect the battery leads before using a mains charger. Never run the alternator with the multi-plug or a battery lead disconnected.

8 Alternator drivebelt - adjustment

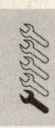

1 The alternator drivebelt should be adjusted at the specified Routine Maintenance intervals. To check its tension, depress the belt firmly with a finger or thumb midway between the alternator and crankshaft pulleys

Electrical system 9•5

8.1 Checking the alternator drivebelt tension

8.2A Alternator adjustment link – 1.8 litre

8.2B Alternator adjustment link – 1.3 litre

(photo). The belt should deflect approximately 5 mm (0.2 in). If a new drivebelt has been fitted the initial adjustment should give a deflection of 2 mm (0.08 in) then, after a suitable running in period of about 500 miles (750 km), the belt adjustment should be rechecked and, if necessary, adjusted to deflect 5 mm (0.2 in).
2 If adjustment is necessary, loosen the nut on the adjusting link (photos) and pivot bolt, then lever the alternator away from the cylinder block until the belt is tensioned correctly, using a lever at the pulley end of the alternator.
3 Tighten the nut and bolt after adjusting the drivebelt.

9 Alternator - testing

Accurate testing of the alternator is only possible using specialised instruments and is therefore best left to a qualified electrician. If, however, the alternator is faulty the home mechanic should dismantle it, with reference to Section 11 or 12, and check the condition of the brushes, soldered joints, etc. If the fault cannot be found, refit the alternator and have it checked professionally.

10 Alternator - removal and refitting

1 Disconnect the battery negative lead.
2 Release the clip and pull the multi-plug from the rear of the alternator (photo).
3 Loosen the pivot and adjustment bolts (photo) then push the alternator in towards the engine and slip the drivebelt from the alternator.
4 Remove the adjustment link nut and washer.
5 Support the alternator then remove the pivot bolt and withdraw the unit from the engine.
6 Refitting is a reversal of removal but, before fully tightening the pivot and adjustment bolts, tension the drivebelt, as described in Section 8.

11 Alternator (Bosch) - overhaul

1 Wipe clean the exterior surfaces of the alternator.
2 Remove the two screws and withdraw the voltage regulator and brush assembly from the rear of the alternator (photos).
3 Mark the end housings and stator in relation to each other, then unscrew the through-bolts and tap the drive end housing from the stator and end housing.
4 Grip the pulley in a soft-jawed vice and unscrew the nut. Tap the rotor shaft through the pulley and remove the spacers and fan; noting the direction or rotation arrow on the front of the fan.
5 Using a three-arm puller, press the rotor shaft out of the drive end housing. Note that the arms of the pulley must be located on the bearing retainer otherwise damage may occur to the retainer screws.
6 Remove the screws and the retainer and use a soft metal drift to drive out the bearing.
7 Using a puller, remove the bearing from the end of the rotor shaft.
8 If necessary the stator and diode plate can

10.2 Rear view of Bosch alternator showing lead multi-plug and retaining clip (arrowed)

10.3 Alternator pivot bolt and bracket – 1.3 litre

11.2A Voltage regulator location (arrowed) – Bosch

11.2B Removing the voltage regulator and brush assembly – Bosch

9•6 Electrical system

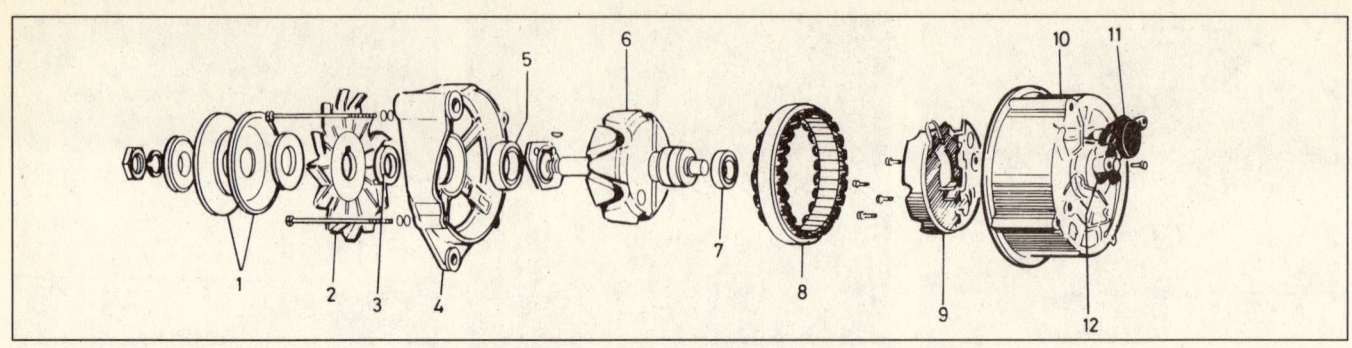

Fig. 9.3 Exploded view of the Bosch alternator (Sec 11)

1 Belt pulley	3 Spacer	5 Bearing	7 Bearing	9 Diode plate	11 Regulator
2 Fan	4 Drive housing	6 Rotor	8 Stator	10 Housing	12 Regulator brushes

be removed from the end housing after removing the retaining screws.

9 Clean all the components in paraffin or petrol and wipe them dry.

10 Check that the length of the carbon brushes is not less than the minimum amount given in the Specifications (photo). If necessary unsolder the leads and remove the old brushes then clean the housing, insert the new brushes, and solder the new leads into position.

11 The rotor bearings should be renewed as a matter of course.

12 To check the stator, first identify the wire positions then unsolder them using long-nosed pliers to dissipate heat from the diode plate. Check the windings for short circuits by connecting an ohmmeter between each of the four wires (ie between wires 1 and 2, wires 1 and 3, wires 1 and 4, then wires 2 and 3, wires 2 and 4 and wires 3 and 4). In each case a 0 ohm reading must be given. Check the windings for insulation by connecting a 12 volt test lamp and leads between each of the wires and the stator ring. If the lamp illuminates, the windings are faulty.

13 Check the rotor windings for continuity by connecting an ohmmeter to the two slip rings. A reading of 2.9 to 3.2 ohms should be obtained for the 55 amp alternator or 2.8 to 3.1 ohms for the 65 amp alternator. Check the windings for insulation by connecting a 12 volt test lamp and leads between each of the slip rings and the winding core. If the lamp illuminates, the windings are faulty.

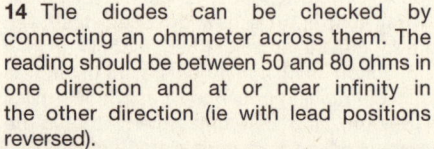

14 The diodes can be checked by connecting an ohmmeter across them. The reading should be between 50 and 80 ohms in one direction and at or near infinity in the other direction (ie with lead positions reversed).

15 Clean the slip rings with fine glass paper and wipe clean with a fuel-moistened cloth.

16 Reassemble the alternator using a reversal of the dismantling procedure. When fitting the bearing to the rotor shaft, drive it on with a metal tube located on the inner race. If the diode plate has been renewed, a suppression condenser should (if not already) be fitted to the rear of the alternator as shown in Fig. 9.4 - check this with your dealer.

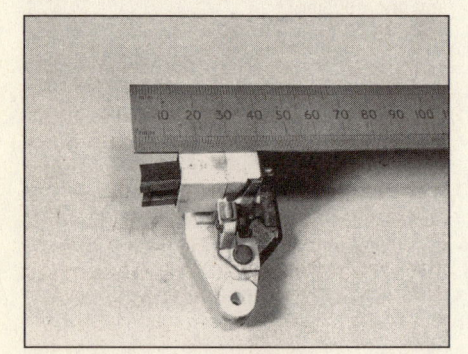

11.10 Checking the length of the alternator brushes

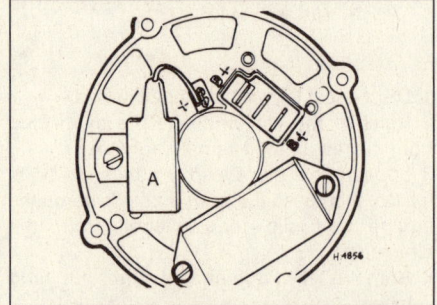

Fig. 9.4 Location of the suppression condenser (A) on the rear of the Bosch alternator (Sec 11)

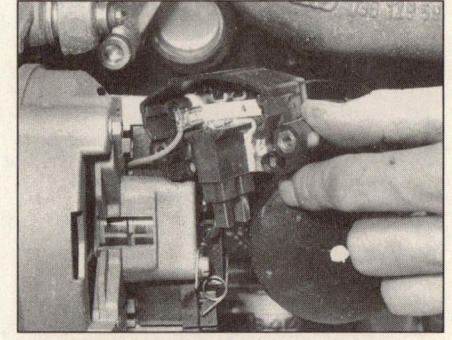

12.1 Voltage regulator/brush unit removal from the Motorola alternator

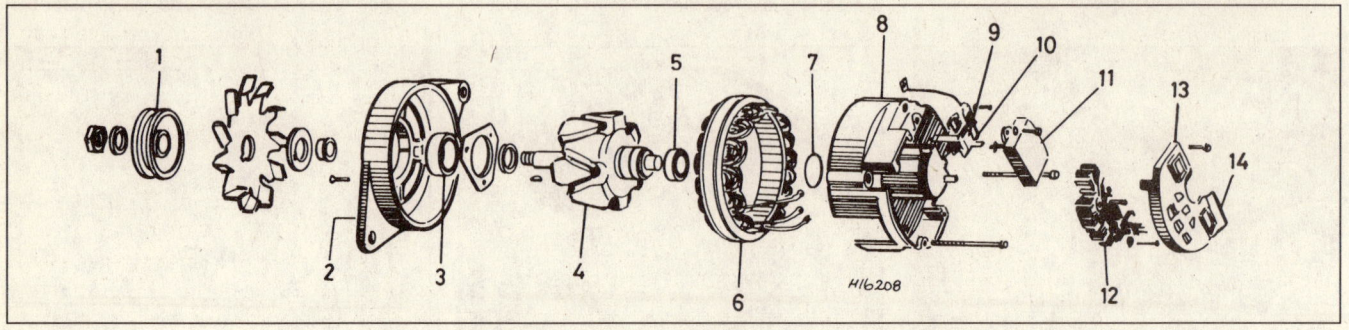

Fig. 9.5 Exploded view of the Motorola alternator (Sec 12)

1 Belt pulley	4 Rotor	6 Stator	9 Brush holder	11 Regulator	13 Cover
2 Drive-end housing	5 Bearing (slip ring end)	7 O-ring	10 D + connecting plate	12 Diode plate	14 Wire clip
3 Bearing (drive end)		8 Housing			

Electrical system 9•7

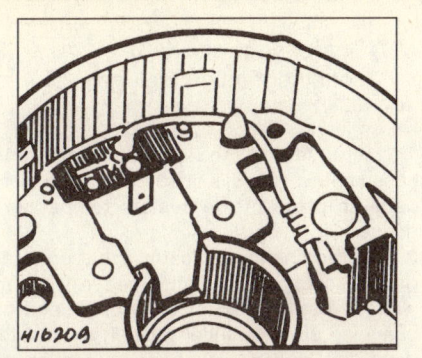

Fig. 9.6 The correct routing of the D + wire on the Motorola alternator (Sec 12)

14.4 Wiring connections to the starter motor solenoid – 1.3 litre

12 Alternator (Motorola) - overhaul

1 The procedure is similar to that described in Section 11, and the exploded diagram of this alternator is shown in Fig. 9.5. Identify the regulator wires for position before disconnecting them (photo).
2 The stator windings are checked in the same manner as that described for the Bosch alternator, but a 0 ohm reading should be given between each of the three leads (not four).
3 When checking the rotor windings for continuity, the 55 amp alternator should give a reading of 3.1 to 3.3 ohms and the 65 amp alternator a reading of 3.9 to 4.1 ohms.
4 On the 65 amp version the DT wire must be routed as shown in Fig. 9.6.

13 Starter motor - testing in the car

1 If the starter motor fails to operate, first check the condition of the battery by switching on the headlamps. If they glow brightly, then gradually dim after a few seconds, the battery is in an uncharged condition.
2 If the battery is in good condition, check the wiring connections on the starter for security and also check the earth wire between the gearbox and body.
3 If the starter still fails to turn, use a voltmeter or 12 volt test lamp and leads to check that current is reaching the main terminal (terminal 30) on the starter solenoid.
4 With the ignition switched on and the ignition key in the start position, check that current is reaching the remaining terminals on the solenoid. Also check that an audible click is heard as the solenoid operates indicating that the internal contacts are closed and that current is available at the field windings terminal.
5 Failure to obtain current at terminal 50 indicates a faulty ignition switch.
6 If current at the correct voltage is available at the starter motor, yet it does not operate, the unit is faulty and should be removed for further investigation.

14 Starter motor - removal and refitting

1 Disconnect the earth lead from the battery.
2 Jack up the front of the car and support it on axle stands. Apply the handbrake.
3 Where a heat deflector plate is fitted, undo the retaining nuts and remove the plate.
4 Identify the wiring for position then disconnect it from the solenoid (photo).
5 Where applicable, unbolt and detach the support bracket.
6 Undo the retaining bolts and withdraw the starter motor. On 1.6 and 1.8 litre models, move the steering fully to the right and if necessary detach the right-hand driveshaft at the gearbox drive flange to allow room for removal.
7 Refitting is a reversal of removal, but tighten the bolts to the specified torque. Where a support bracket is fitted, do not fully tighten the nuts and bolts until the bracket is correctly located and free of any tension.

15 Starter motor - overhaul

1 Wipe clean the exterior surfaces of the starter motor.
2 Unscrew the terminal nut and disconnect the field windings lead from the solenoid.
3 Unscrew the bolts and withdraw the solenoid from the housing, then unhook the solenoid core from the operating lever.
4 Remove the screws and lift off the end cap, then prise out the circlip and remove the shims.
5 Unscrew the through-bolts and remove the end cover.
6 Lift the springs and remove the carbon brushes from the brush holder, then withdraw the holder.
7 Remove the field coil housing from the end housing.
8 Using a metal tube drive the stop ring towards the pinion, then remove the circlip and stop ring.
9 Slide the armature from the pinion, and withdraw the pinion.
10 Prise the rubber pad from the end housing.
11 Unscrew and remove the pivot bolt and withdraw the operating lever.
12 Clean all the components in paraffin and wipe dry. Check the pinion teeth for wear and pitting and check that the one-way clutch only allows the pinion to turn in one direction. Clean the commutator with a fuel-moistened cloth and, if necessary, use fine glass paper to remove any carbon deposits. If the commutator is worn excessively it cannot be machined and renewal is necessary.
13 Check the brushes for excessive wear

1 Pinion
2 Mounting bracket
3 Operating lever
4 Solenoid
5 Armature
6 Housing with windings
7 Carbon brushes
8 Brush plate
9 Brush
10 Spacers
11 Through-bolt

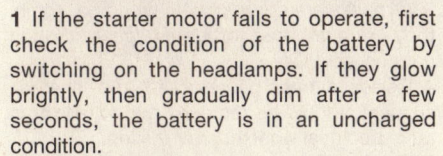

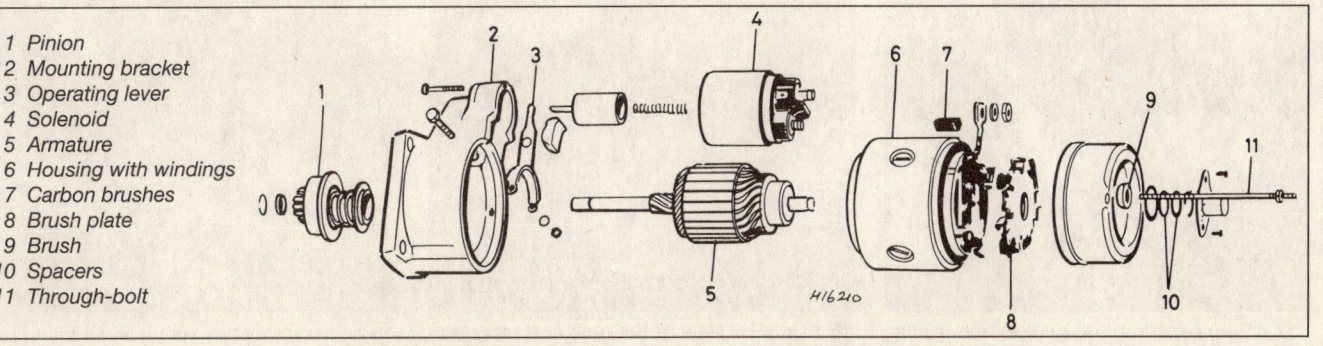

Fig. 9.7 Exploded view of the starter motor (typical) (Sec 15)

9•8 Electrical system

and if in doubt renew them. To do this, crush the old brushes with a pair of pliers and clean the leads. Insert the leads into the new brushes and splay out the ends. Solder the wires in position but grip the wire next to the brush with long-nosed pliers in order to prevent the solder penetrating the flexible section of the wire. File off any surplus solder.

14 Check the bush in the end cover and if necessary drive it out with a soft metal drift. Soak the end cover in hot oil for five minutes before driving the new bush into it.

15 Assemble the starter motor in reversal of the dismantling procedure but note that the unit must be sealed with suitable sealant on the surfaces shown in Fig. 9.8. Lubricate the pinion drive with a little molybdenum disulphide grease. Make sure that the stop ring is fitted from the inside of the circlip with the annular groove facing outwards,

and also make sure that the stop ring turns freely on the shaft. Lubricate the solenoid and operating lever with a little molybdenum disulphide grease. When fitting the brush holder, the springs may be held in a raised position by using two lengths of bent wire.

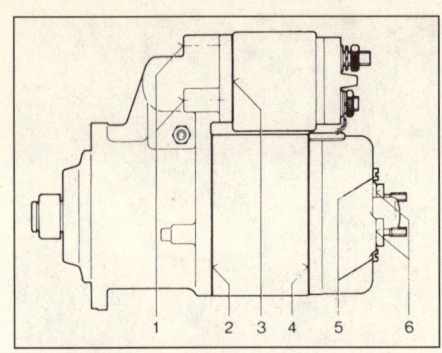

16 Automatic stop-start system - general

This system is fitted as optional equipment to some models and is a fuel economy device. Activated by a control switch, the system automatically switches off the engine when the vehicle is stationary during traffic delays.

The system is switched on and off by means of a switch on the dash insert between the instrument panel and the heater/fresh air control panel. A warning light in the switch advises when the system is switched on.

The system should only be used when the vehicle has reached its normal operating temperature. When activated, the system will automatically stop the engine when the vehicle speed drops below 3.1 mph (5 kph) and has run at its normal idle speed for a period of at least 2 seconds. In addition the vehicle must previously have been driven at a speed in excess of 3.1 mph (5 kph). When the

Fig. 9.8 Surface to be sealed when reassembling the starter motor (Sec 15)

1 Solenoid securing screws
2 Starter/mounting surface
3 Solenoid joint
4 Starter/end cap joint
5 Through-bolts
6 Shaft cover joint and screws

engine is stopped by the system, the rear window heater will automatically cut out.

When traffic conditions permit, the engine can be restarted by depressing the clutch pedal and moving the gear lever fully to the left in neutral. Once the engine has restarted, the gear engagement can be made in the normal manner. If for any reason the engine stalls or stops after restarting, the restart procedure should be repeated, but the gear lever must be moved back into neutral within 6 seconds.

The following safety precautions should be noted when using the system, these being:

(a) Do not use the system when the engine temperature is below 55°C (131°F) or when the ambient temperature is very low as the engine will take longer to warm up
(b) Do not allow the vehicle to roll when the engine is switched off, check that the handbrake is fully applied
(c) During extended delays switch the engine off in the normal manner with the ignition key, as electrical accessories will otherwise be left on and the battery run down
(d) If leaving the vehicle for any length of time, switch off the system and always take the ignition key with you

17 Gearchange and consumption gauge - general

1 When fitted, the gearchange and consumption gauge is fitted in the instrument panel in place of the coolant temperature gauge.
2 The gearchange indicator lights up in all gears except top gear when better economy without loss of power can be obtained by changing up to a higher gear. The indicator does not operate during acceleration or deceleration, or on carburettor engines when the engine is cold.
3 The gearchange indicator light goes out when a higher gear is engaged.
4 On automatic transmission models the gearchange indicator is non-operational since all forward gears are automatically changed in accordance with engine speed/output and vehicle speed.
5 The fuel consumption indicator operates only in top gear (D in automatic transmission models), and indicates the actual fuel consumption in mpg.
6 The gearchange and consumption gauge is operated by a switch
on the gearbox and a sender in the vacuum line to the distributor (photo).

18 Fuses and relays - general

1 The fuses and relays are located under the facia panel on the right-hand side (photo).
2 The fuses are numbered consecutively for identification. Always renew a fuse with one of identical rating and never renew it more than once without finding out the source of the trouble (usually a short circuit).
3 All relays are of the plug-in type and, again, they are numbered for identification, though not consecutively.
4 Relays cannot be repaired and, if at all suspect, should be removed and taken to an auto-electrical workshop for testing.
5 The fuse/relay unit holder complete can be

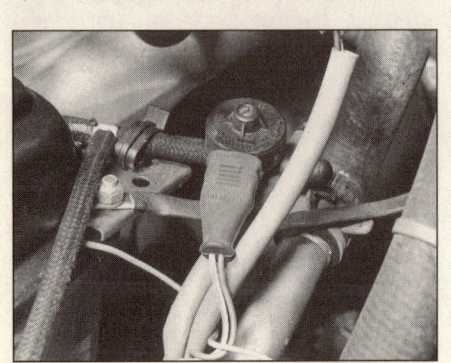

17.6 Fuel consumption gauge sender unit

18.1 General view of the fuse and relay box unit

18.5 Fuse/relay box removal, showing rear connections

Electrical system 9•9

18.6 Typical relay installation in the engine compartment

21.4 Combination switch retaining screws (arrowed)

21.5 Combination switch multi-plug connections

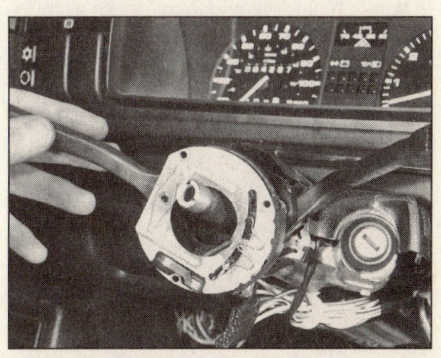

removed by twisting the securing knob on the lower right-hand side and removing the knob. Twist the slotted retainer on the left-hand side and withdraw the fuse/relay box. The various connectors on the rear face of the unit are then accessible for detachment as required (photo).

6 In addition to those fuses and relays located at the main fuse/relay unit, some models will have in-line fuses and relays fitted to some circuits, these being shown in the wiring diagrams and photo 18.6.

19 Direction indicators and hazard flasher system - general

1 The direction indicators are controlled by the left-hand column switch.
2 A switch on the facia board operates all four flashers simultaneously, and although the direction indicators will not work when the ignition is switched off, the emergency switch overrides this and the flasher signals continue to operate.
3 All the circuits are routed through the relay on the console and its fuse.
4 If the indicators do not function correctly, a series of tests may be done to find which part of the circuit is at fault.
5 The most common fault is in the flasher lamps, defective bulbs, and dirty or corroded contacts or mountings. Check these first, then test the emergency switch. Remove it from the circuit and check its operation. If the switch is in good order, refit it and again turn on the emergency lights. If nothing happens then the relay is not functioning properly and it should be renewed. If the lights function on emergency but not on operation of the column switch then the wiring and column switch are suspect (see Section 21).

20 Ignition switch/steering column lock - removal and refitting

The procedure is described in Chapter 10 for the removal and refitting of the steering lock.

21 Combination switches - removal and refitting

1 Remove the steering wheel, as described in Chapter 10.
2 Disconnect the battery negative lead.
3 Remove the screws and withdraw the steering column lower shroud.
4 Remove the three screws securing the combination switch (photo).
5 Disconnect the multi-plugs (photo).
6 Rotate the indicator switch clockwise and withdraw it, noting location of the plastic retaining arms (photo).

21.6 Removing the indicator switch ...

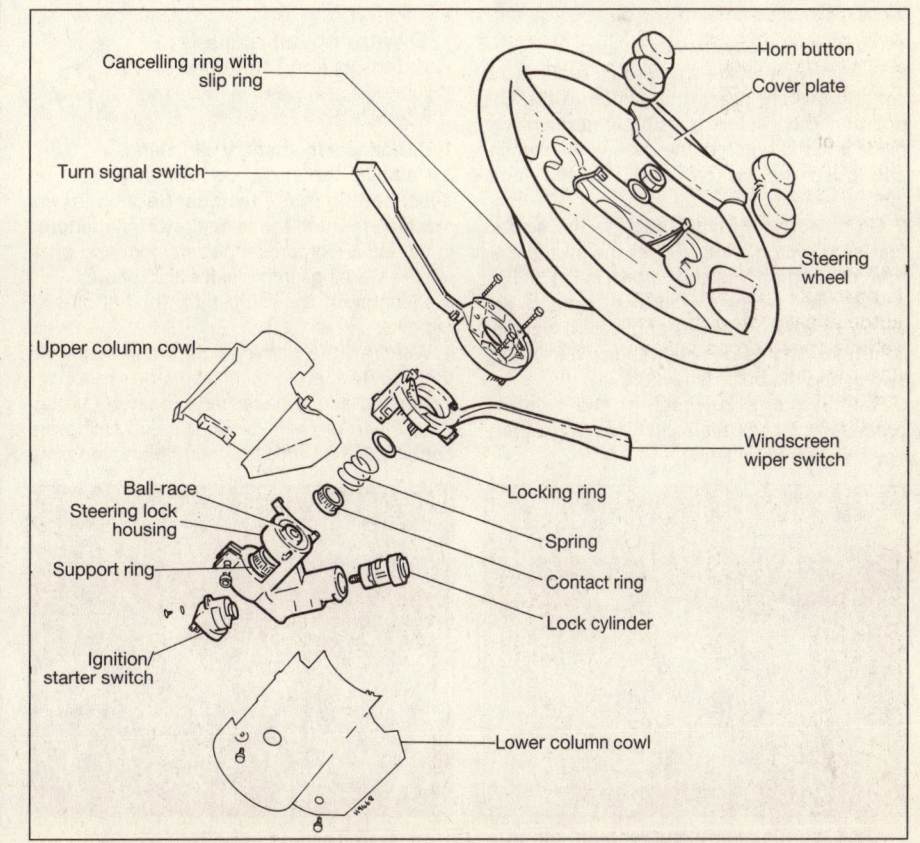

Fig. 9.9 Steering column combination switches and associated components (Sec 21)

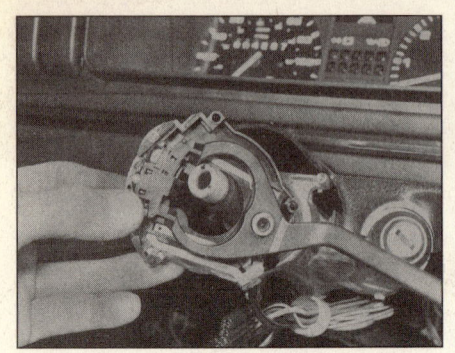

9•10 Electrical system

21.7A . . . and wiper control switch

21.7B Additional under dash wiring connection and insulator – GTI

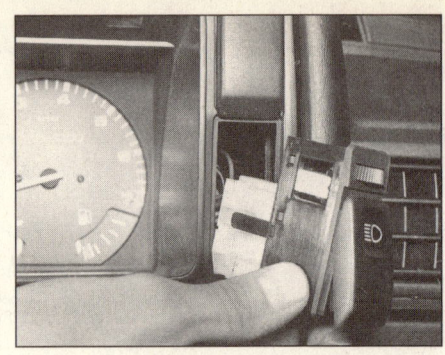

22.2 Facia switch removal

7 Withdraw the wiper control switch from the column. Full removal of the switch of GTI models will necessitate detaching the additional wire from its connector under the dash panel (photo).
8 Refitting is a reversal of the removal procedure. Check that the indicator switch is centralised before fitting the steering wheel otherwise the cancelling cams could be damaged.
9 Refit the steering wheel, with reference to Chapter 10.
10 On completion check the operation of the switches.

22 Facia switches - removal and refitting

1 Disconnect the battery earth lead.
2 To remove a rocker type switch such as the lighting switch, press the switch to the ON position then insert a suitable screwdriver blade into the notch at the base of the switch, and prise the switch free from the facia (photo).
3 On other switch types such as the heated rear seat switch, simply lever the switch free from the bottom edge, as shown in Fig. 9.10.
4 With the switch withdrawn, detach the wiring connector. Where applicable, warning light bulb holders can be withdrawn from the switch and the bulb removed.
5 Refitting is a reversal of the removal procedure. Check the switch for satisfactory operation on completion.

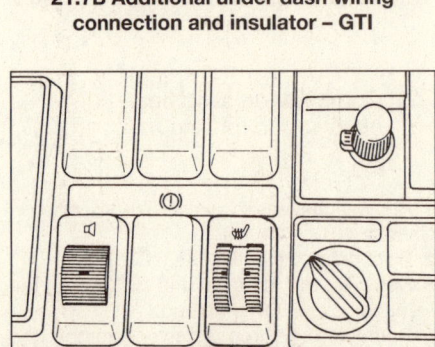

Fig. 9.10 Prise free the switch from the bottom edge (Sec 22)

23 Warning lamp cluster - removal and refitting

1 Disconnect the battery earth lead.
2 Remove the facia control switches, as described in the previous Section, then, reaching through the vacant switch apertures in the facia, compress the retainers and push out the warning lamp cluster unit (photo).
3 Disconnect the multi-plug for full cluster removal.
4 Withdraw the warning light bulbholder from the cluster and pull free the bulb for inspection and, if necessary, renewal (photo). Where two or more warning lamp bulbs are contained in a single mounting plate, the plate unit complete must be renewed as it is not possible to renew a single bulb in this instance.
5 Refit in the reverse order of removal and, on completion, check the operation of the switches and warning light bulb(s).

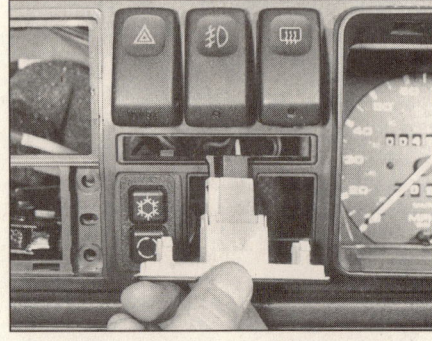

23.2 Warning lamp cluster removal

24 Courtesy and luggage compartment light switches - removal and refitting

1 Disconnect the battery negative lead.
2 Open the door, boot lid or tailgate (as applicable) and unscrew the cross-head screw from the switch (photo).
3 Withdraw the switch and disconnect the wiring. Tie a loose knot in the wire to prevent it from dropping into the door pillar (photo).

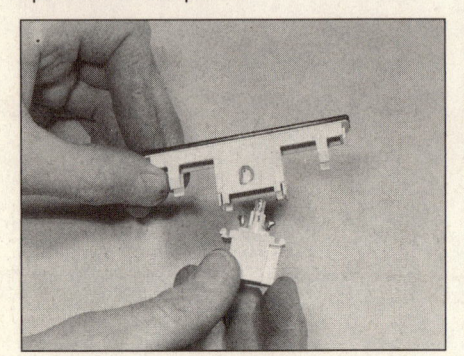

23.4 Warning lamp cluster bulbholder removal

24.2 Tailgate actuated luggage compartment light switch

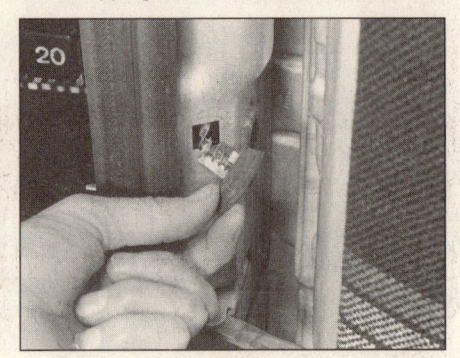

24.3 Door courtesy light switch removal

Electrical system 9•11

27.3 Instrument panel screws removal

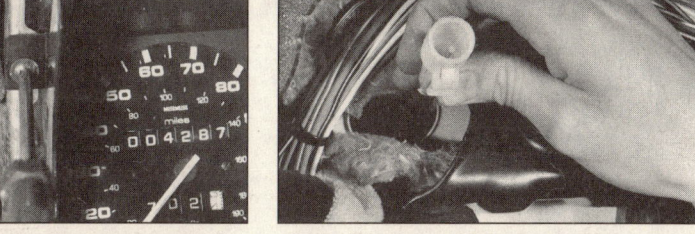

27.4A Disconnect the speedometer cable

27.4B Rear view of the instrument panel cluster

4 Check the switch seal for condition and renew it, if necessary.
5 Refitting is a reversal of removal.

25 Cigarette lighter - removal and refitting

1 Disconnect the battery negative lead.
2 Remove the lower facia panel then reach up and disconnect the wiring from the cigarette lighter.
3 Remove the retaining ring and withdraw the cigarette lighter from the facia.
4 Refitting is a reversal of removal.

26 Speedometer cable - removal and refitting

1 Open the bonnet and then reach down and unscrew the speedometer cable nut from the transmission.
2 Withdraw the instrument panel far enough to disconnect the cable; with reference to Section 27.
3 Remove the air cleaner, as described in Chapter 3.
4 Carefully unclip and detach the plastic cover from the top edge of the bulkhead. Pull the speedometer cable through the bulkhead and withdraw it from the engine compartment side.
5 Refitting is a reversal of removal. Make sure that the grommet is correctly fitted in the bulkhead and that there are no sharp bends in the cable. **Do not** grease the cable ends.

27 Instrument panel cluster - removal and refitting

1 Disconnect the battery earth lead.
2 Remove the facia panel, as described in Section 29.
3 Remove the instrument panel retaining screws - one each side at the top (photo).
4 Prise the panel away, tilting from the top edge. Reach behind the panel and disconnect the speedometer cable (photo) and, where applicable, the vacuum hose from the vacuum sender. Detach the wiring multi-connectors from the rear lower edge then lift the instrument panel out; taking care not to damage the printed circuit on its rear face (photo).
5 The individual circuits of the printed circuit foil can be checked for continuity using an ohmmeter. For circuit identification refer to the wiring diagram.
6 Refitting is a reversal of the removal sequence, but make sure that all connections are securely made. Check instruments for satisfactory operation on completion.

28 Instrument panel - dismantling, testing and reassembly

1 Remove the instrument panel cluster, as described in Section 27
2 Remove the relevant instrument, with reference to Figs. 9.11 or 9.12, but take particular care not to damage the printed circuit foil.
3 To test the voltage stabilizer, connect a voltmeter between the terminals shown in Fig. 9.13 with a 12 volt supply to the remaining terminal. A constant voltage of 10 volts must be registered. If the voltage is above 10.5 volts or below 9.5 volts renew the voltage stabilizer.
4 The accuracy of the fuel gauge can be checked by draining the fuel tank and then adding exactly 5 litres of fuel. After leaving the ignition switched on for at least two minutes the fuel gauge needle should be level with the upper edge of the red reserve zone. If not, either the fuel gauge or tank unit is faulty.
5 If renewing the gearchange/consumption indicator avoid touching the back of the gauge. Removal necessitates detaching the printed circuit and the vacuum sender unit then undoing the three securing screws (Fig. 9.14). Renew the diode (LED) or consumption indicator unit, as necessary.
6 When renewing the normal type clock (which incorporates the fuel gauge) it is important to ensure the correct printed circuit connections when refitting. The connections are shown in Fig. 9.15.
7 The digital type clock is secured by two retaining screws. When removing the clock take care not to allow the adjuster pins for the hours and minutes to fall out.
8 The warning lamp LED indicators in the lamp housing are positioned as shown in Fig. 9.16. When renewing the LEDs, each diode can be pulled free from the retainer plate, but note that one of the connector prongs is wider. This is the negative connection and it is important that it is correctly refitted. If necessary the diode holder unit can be removed by carefully levering it free from the warning lamp housing.
9 The individual circuits of the printed circuit foil can be checked for continuity using an ohmmeter and referring to the appropriate wiring diagram.
10 If renewing the printed circuit foil it should be noted that a common type may be supplied for all models. If fitting a new printed circuit foil to the dash insert on models with a normal type clock it may be necessary to cut off the connector pins used for the digital clock and vice versa for models with the digital clock. Check this with your supplier.
11 To remove the plug housing from the instrument panel insert, press the plastic rib on the housing (using a screwdriver) over the engagement lugs and pull the housing with printed circuit in the direction of the arrow (Fig. 9.17). The plug housing can be removed from the printed circuit by pressing free the engagement lugs and pulling the housing away from the printed circuit in the direction of the arrow shown in Fig. 9.18.
12 If removing the tachometer, first remove the gearshift and fuel consumption indicator (paragraph 5) then undo the two retaining screws and remove the tachometer, together with the multi-function indicator (printed circuit). The VDO type multi-function indicator can then be removed by undoing the retaining screws, pressing the retaining lugs from the

9•12 Electrical system

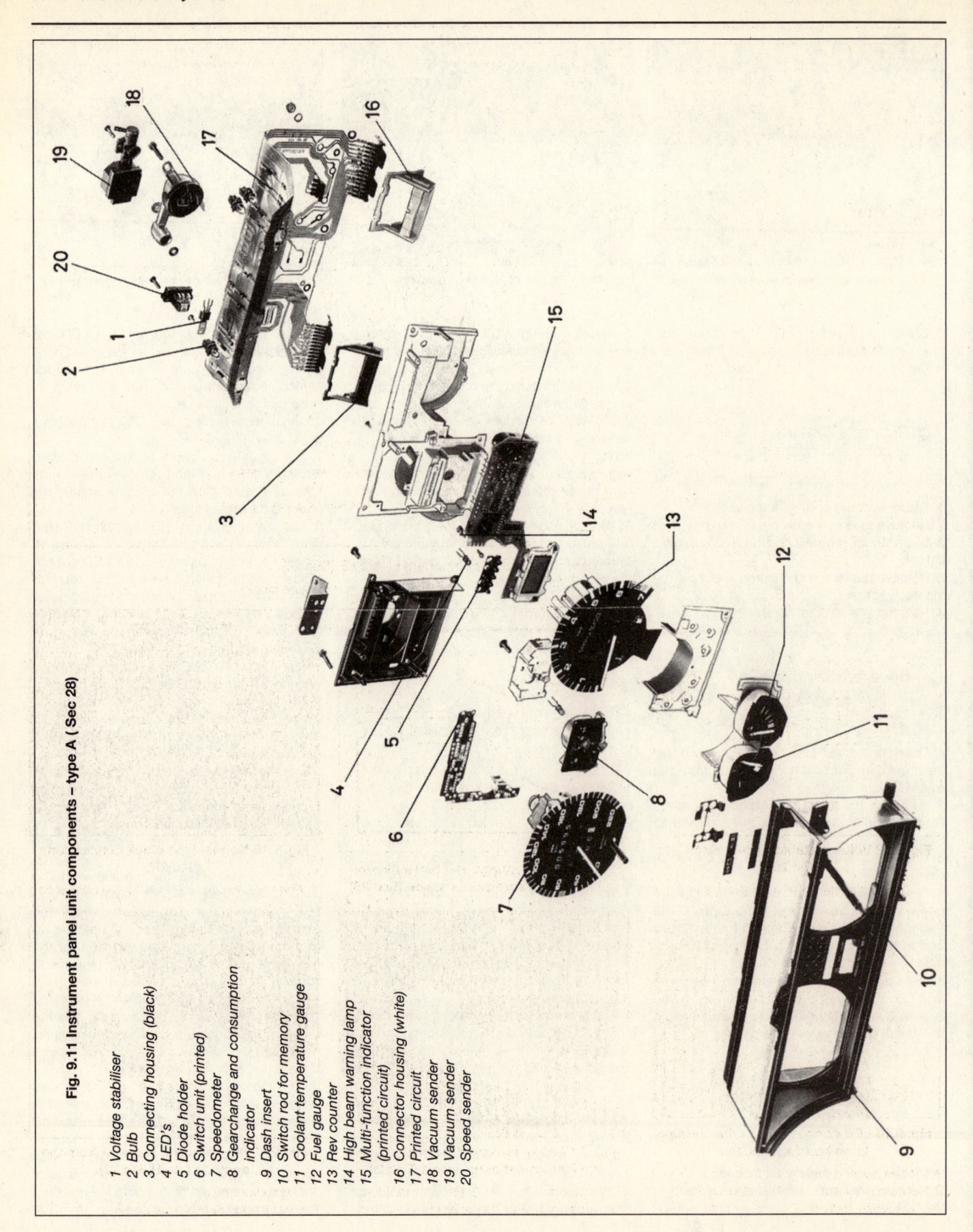

Fig. 9.11 Instrument panel unit components – type A (Sec 28)

1 Voltage stabiliser
2 Bulb
3 Connecting housing (black)
4 LED's
5 Switch unit (printed)
6 Speedometer
7 Gearchange and consumption indicator
8 Dash insert
9 Switch rod for memory
10 Coolant temperature gauge
11 Fuel gauge
12 Rev counter
13 High beam warning lamp
14 Multi-function indicator (printed circuit)
15 Connector housing (white)
16 Printed circuit
17 Vacuum sender
18 Vacuum sender
19 Vacuum sender
20 Speed sender

Electrical system 9•13

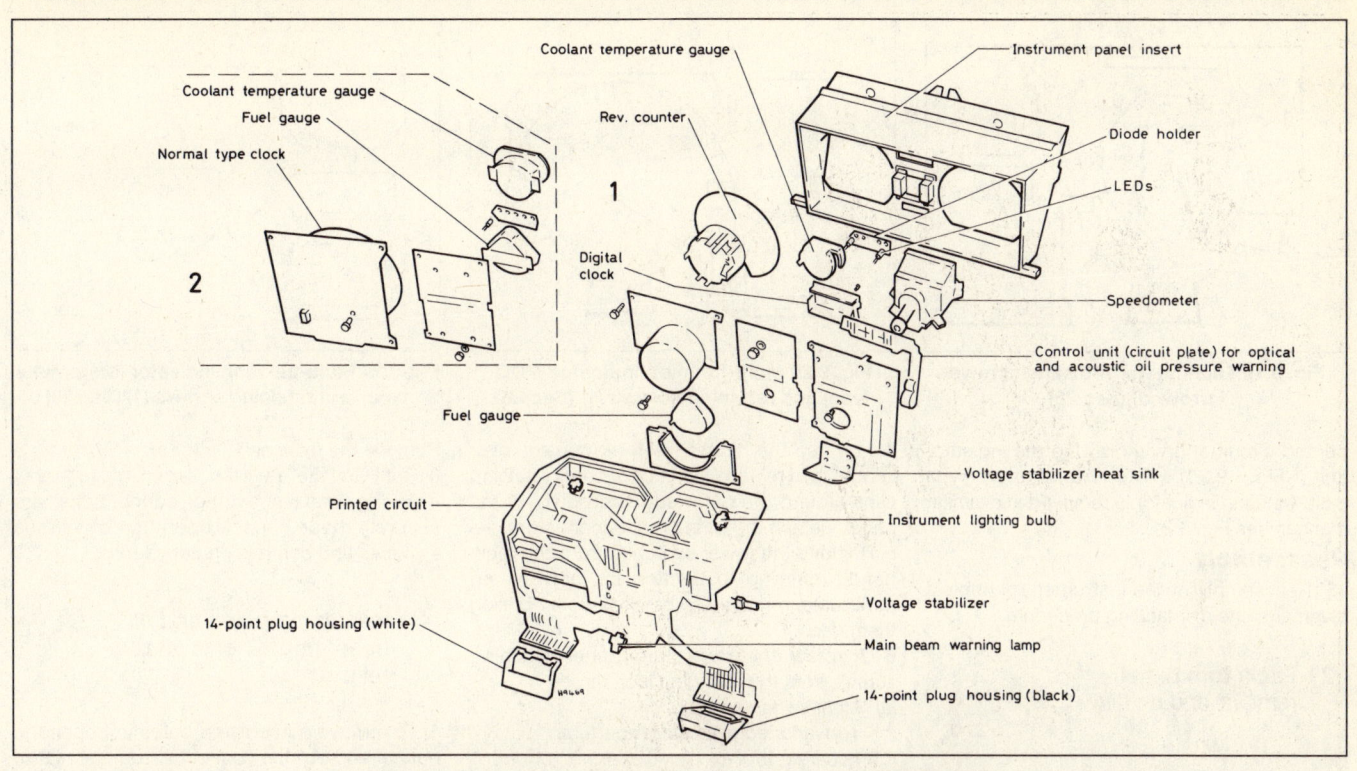

Fig. 9.12 Instrument panel unit components – type B (Sec 28)

1 With rev counter and digital clock 2 With normal type clock

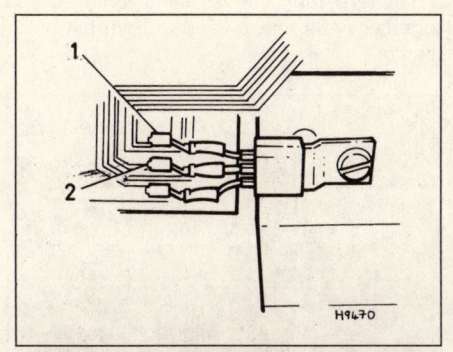

Fig. 9.13 Voltage stabilizer test terminals (Sec 28)

Connect a voltmeter between 1 and 2

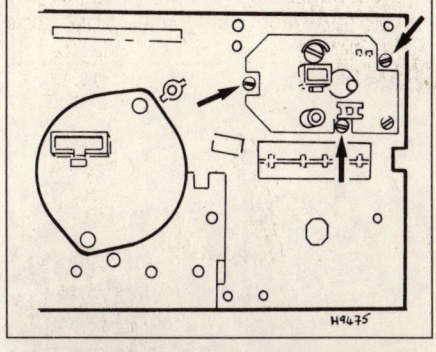

Fig. 9.14 Gearchange and fuel indicator unit retaining screws – arrowed (Sec 28)

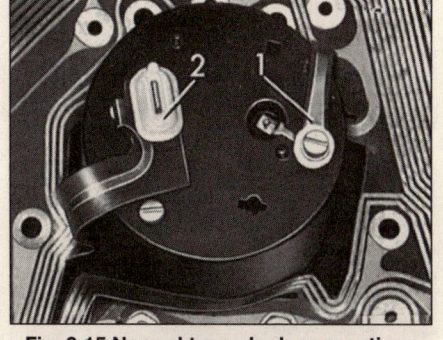

Fig. 9.15 Normal type clock connections (Sec 28)

1 Earth connection 2 Plus (+) live connection

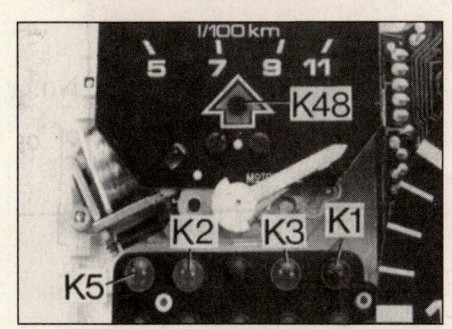

Fig. 9.16 LED connections in the warning lamp housing (Sec 28)

K1 Main beam (blue) K5 Indicators (green)
K2 Alternator (red) K48 Gearchange
K3 Oil pressure (red) indicator (yellow)

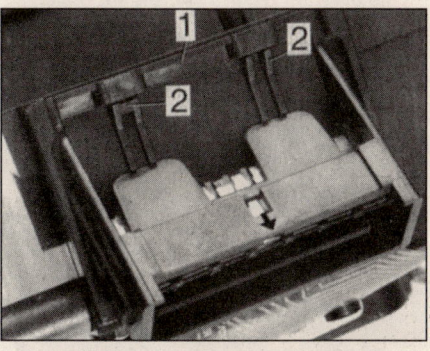

Fig. 9.17 Plug housing detachment from the instrument panel insert (Sec 28)

1 Plastic rib 2 Engagement lugs
Pull housing in direction of arrow

Fig. 9.18 Plug housing removal from the printed circuit (Sec 28)

1 Engagement lugs
Pull housing in direction of arrow

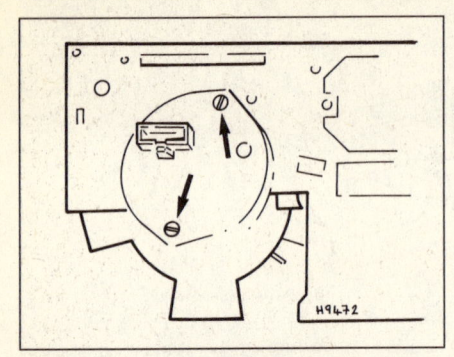

9•14 Electrical system

Fig. 9.19 Tachometer retaining screws (arrowed) (Sec 28)

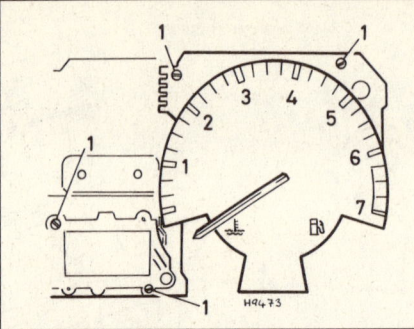

Fig. 9.20 Multi-function indicator (VDO type) and retaining screws (1) (Sec 28)

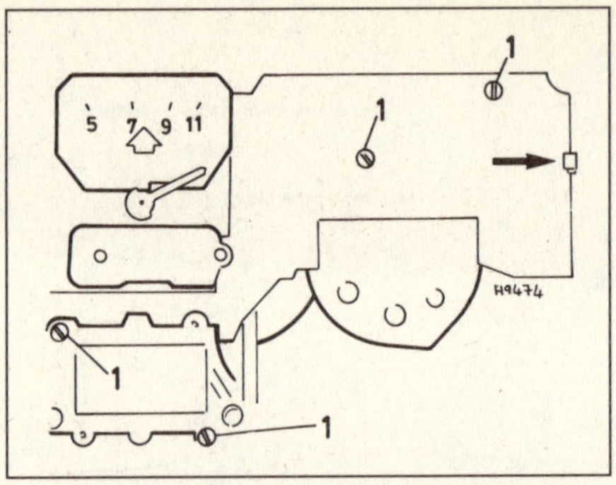

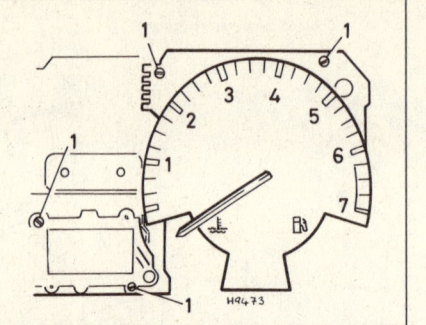

Fig. 9.21 Multi-function indicator (Motometer type) and retaining screws (1) (Sec 28)

printed circuit and withdrawing the indicator unit (Fig. 9.20). The Motometer type multi-function indicator is removed in a similar manner (see Fig. 9.21).

Reassembly
13 Reassembly of the instrument panel is a reversal of the dismantling procedure.

29 Facia trim panel - removal and refitting

1 Disconnect the battery earth lead.
2 To improve accessibility, remove the steering wheel, as described in Chapter 10.
3 Remove the radio, referring to Section 43 for details.
4 Pull free the heater/fresh air control lever knobs, then release the control panel retaining clips around the outer edge and pull out the panel. Detach the wiring multi-connectors.
5 Remove the lower switches from the facia panel, referring to Section 22, and, where applicable, remove the blank pads by prising them free.
6 Unscrew the facia trim panel retaining screws from the following locations:
   (a) Light switch aperture
   (b) Top inner edge of radio aperture
   (c) Fader control (or blank) aperture (photo)
   (d) Heater control panel aperture
   (e) Top of the instrument panel (photo)
   (f) Top left side of panel
7 Partially withdraw the panel and detach any remaining switch lead multi-connectors.

Remove the facia panel (photo).
8 Refit in the reverse order of removal, ensuring that all wiring connections are securely made. Check operation of various switches and controls on completion.

30 Headlamp bulbs and headlamps - removal and refitting

1 To remove a headlamp bulb, first open the bonnet and pull the connector from the rear of the headlamp (photos).
2 Prise off the rubber cap.
3 Squeeze the bulb retaining spring clips together and release the clip from the bulb (photo).

29.6A Facia trim panel retaining screw through fader control aperture

29.6B Remove the instrument panel retaining screws at the top

29.7 Facia trim panel removal

30.1A Rear view of headlight (round type) showing wiring connectors

30.1B Detaching the headlamp bulb connector

30.3 Squeeze the bulb retaining clips free . . .

Electrical system 9•15

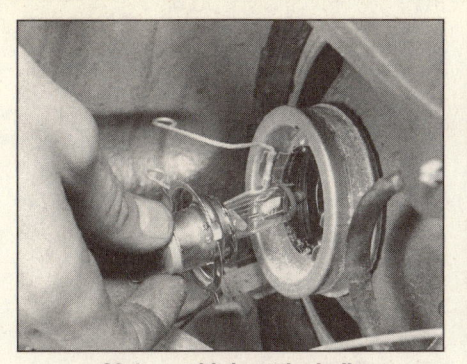

30.4 . . . withdraw the bulb

30.6 Front view of the round type headlamp unit

31.5 Headlamp alignment adjuster screw locations (arrowed)

4 Withdraw the bulb, but do not touch its glass with your fingers if it is to be re-used (photo).
5 To remove the headlamp unit, first remove the radiator grille, as described in Chapter 11.
6 With the headlamp bulb removed, unscrew the screws securing the carrier plate to the front panel, and withdraw the unit (photo).
7 Refitting is a reversal of removal, but check and, if necessary, adjust the beam alignment, as described in Section 31.

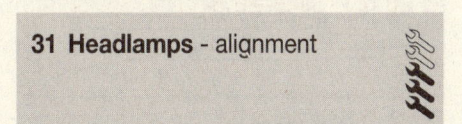

31 Headlamps - alignment

1 The headlamp beam alignment should be checked and if necessary adjusted every 10 000 miles (15 000 km).
2 It is recommended that the alignment is carried out by a VW garage using modern beam setting equipment. However, in an emergency, the following procedure will provide an acceptable light pattern.
3 Position the car on a level surface with tyres

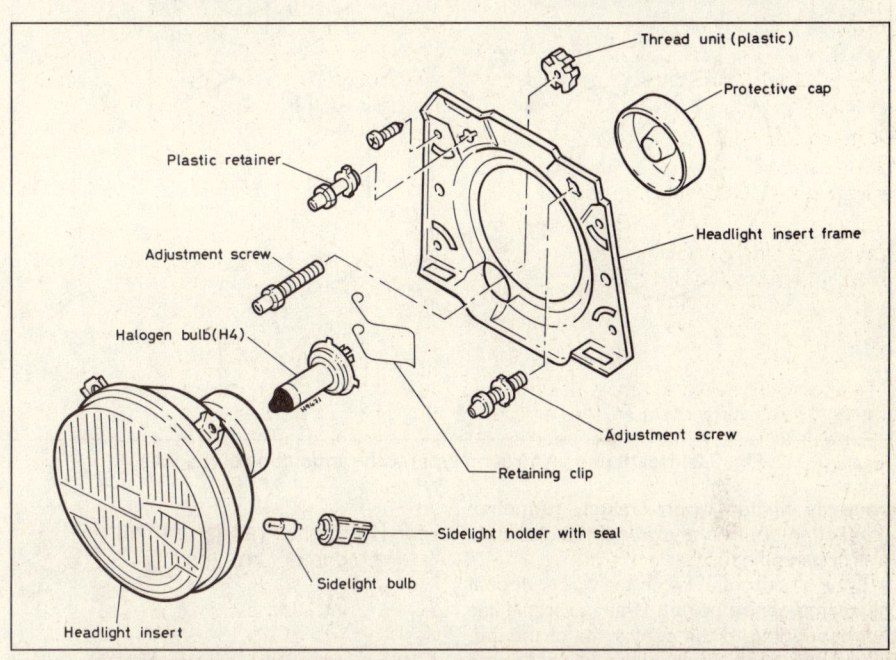

Fig. 9.22 Headlamp unit (round type) and associated components (Sec 30)

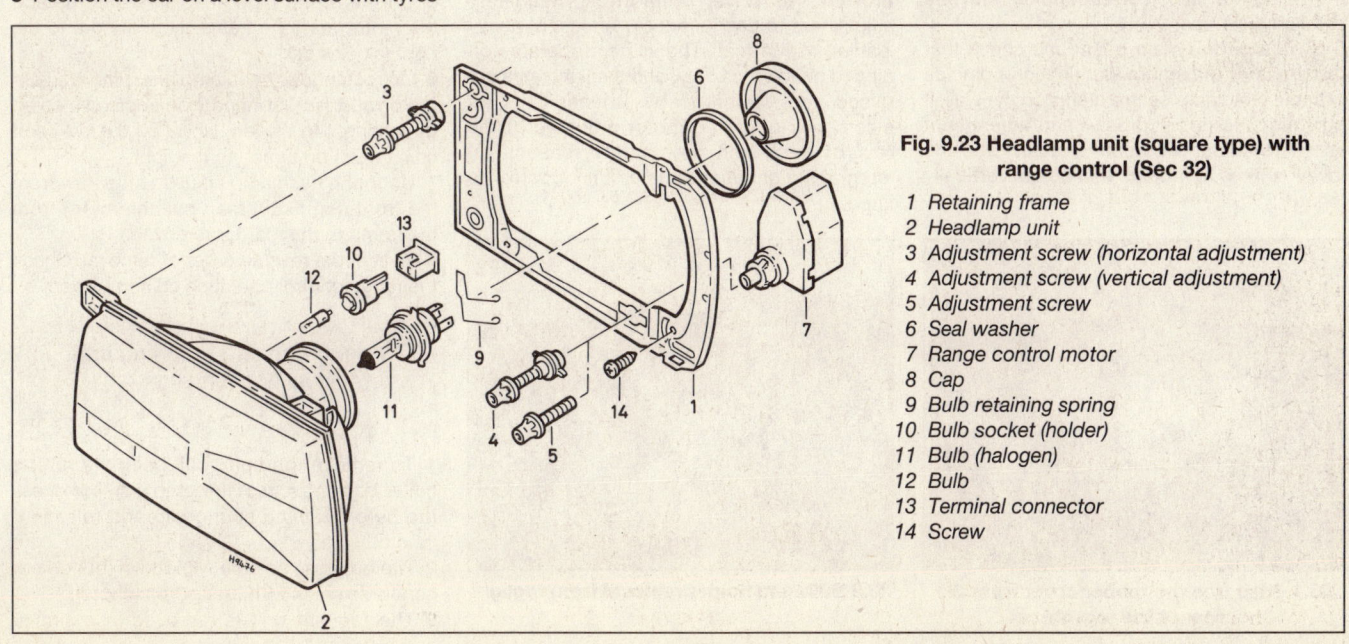

Fig. 9.23 Headlamp unit (square type) with range control (Sec 32)

1 Retaining frame
2 Headlamp unit
3 Adjustment screw (horizontal adjustment)
4 Adjustment screw (vertical adjustment)
5 Adjustment screw
6 Seal washer
7 Range control motor
8 Cap
9 Bulb retaining spring
10 Bulb socket (holder)
11 Bulb (halogen)
12 Bulb
13 Terminal connector
14 Screw

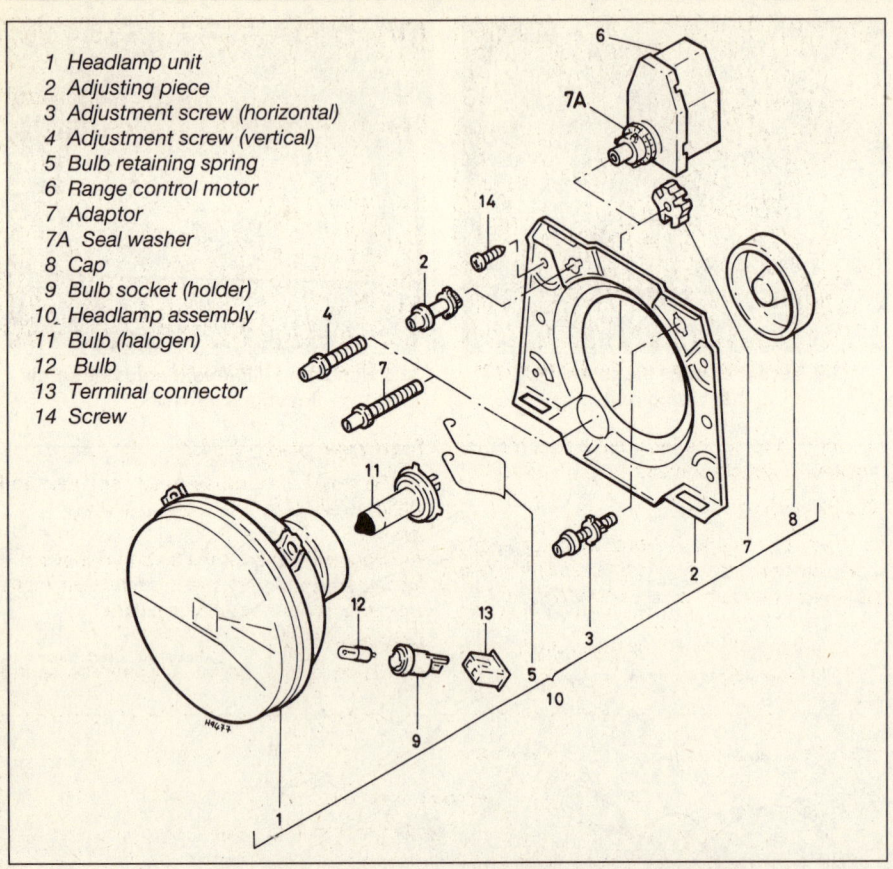

9•16 Electrical system

Fig. 9.24 Headlamp unit (round type) with range control (Sec 32)

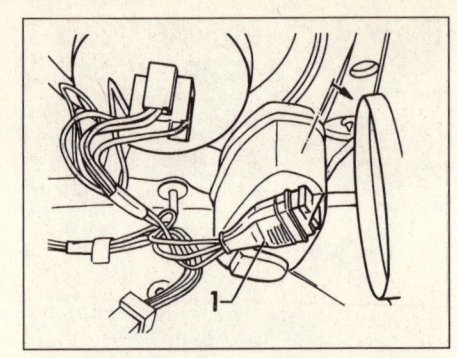

1 Headlamp unit
2 Adjusting piece
3 Adjustment screw (horizontal)
4 Adjustment screw (vertical)
5 Bulb retaining spring
6 Range control motor
7 Adaptor
7A Seal washer
8 Cap
9 Bulb socket (holder)
10 Headlamp assembly
11 Bulb (halogen)
12 Bulb
13 Terminal connector
14 Screw

Fig. 9.25 Range control motor and terminal multi-connector (1) – round unit type (Sec 32)

Detach motor by rotating clockwise – arrowed

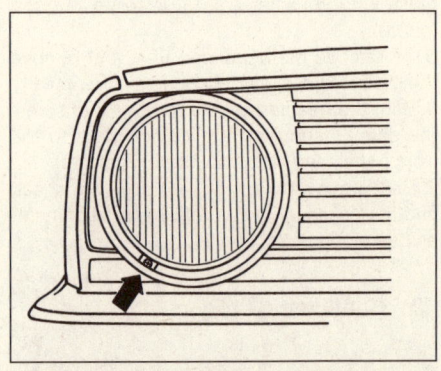

Fig. 9.26 Remove headlamp adjuster screw (arrowed) (Sec 32)

correctly inflated, approximately 10 metres (33 feet) in front of, and at right-angles to, a wall or garage door.
4 Draw a horizontal line on the wall or door at headlamp centre height. Draw a vertical line corresponding to the centre line of the car, then measure off a point either side of this, on the horizontal line, corresponding with the headlamp centres.
5 Switch on the main beam and check that the areas of maximum illumination coincide with the headlamp centre marks on the wall. If not, turn the upper cross-head adjustment screw to adjust the beam laterally, and the lower screw to adjust the beam vertically (photo).

32 Headlamp range control - removal and refitting

1 Where fitted, the system is designed to provide the driver with in-car headlamp adjustment to counteract the effects of heavy loading at the rear. The system operates on dipped headlamps only, and the light units are raised or lowered by means of an electrically-operated motor mounted at the rear of each unit. For safety reasons an integral height adjustment limit control is fitted.

2 The range control switch can be removed in the manner described in Section 22.
3 To remove a range control motor from the rear of a headlamp unit first disconnect the battery earth lead.
4 Pull free the plug connector from the rear of the motor unit.
5 On the round type headlamp unit, detach the motor from the frame by twisting it to the right (clockwise).
6 On rectangular headlamp units, the adjuster motor on the right-hand side is disconnected by turning it to the left, whilst on the left-hand unit it must be turned to the right.
7 Undo the headlamp adjustment screw from the front (Fig. 9.26) then pull the motor from the frame to the rear for removal.
8 Refit in the reverse order of removal. Check the range control operation on completion.

33 Foglight (front) bulb and unit - removal and refitting

1 To remove the bulb, pull back the rubber cover from the rear of the lamp unit, compress the bulb retaining spring clip and release it (photo).
2 The bulb can now be withdrawn, but do not handle its glass with the fingers (photo).
3 The foglight unit is removed in a similar

33.1 Prise free the rubber cover from the rear of the foglight

33.2 Bulb and holder removal from foglight

Electrical system 9•17

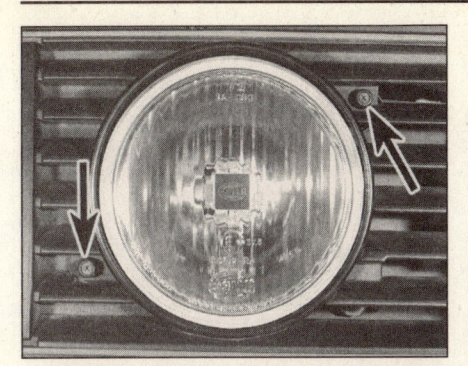

33.4 Foglight beam alignment adjuster screws (arrowed)

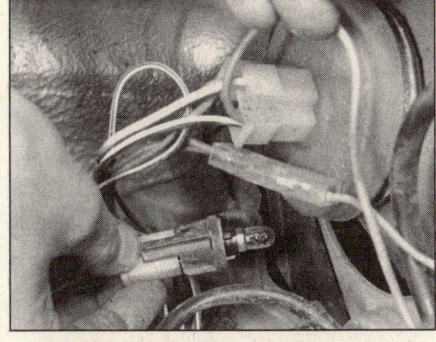

34.2 Sidelight bulb and holder removal

34.4 Front indicator lens removal

manner to that described for the headlamps (Section 30).
4 Refit in the reverse order of removal and check operation of lamp on completion. If necessary adjust the lamp beam alignment by means of the adjustment screws (photo).
5 Foglight alignment should be carried out by a VW dealer with the proper beam setting equipment. In an emergency follow the procedure for headlamps given in Section 31.

34 Lamp bulbs - renewal

Note: Lamp bulbs should always be renewed with ones of similar type and rating, as listed in the Specifications.

Sidelights
1 Open the bonnet and pull the connector from the sidelight bulbholder located beneath the headlamp bulb.
2 Turn the bulbholder anti-clockwise and remove it from the reflector (photo).
3 Depress and twist the bulb to remove it.

Front indicator lights
4 Remove the cross-head screws and withdraw the lens (photo).
5 Depress and twist the bulb to remove it (photo).
6 If necessary the lamp unit can be withdrawn from the bumper and the wiring disconnected (photo).

7 When refitting the lens make sure that the gasket is correctly located.

Rear lights
8 Open the tailgate or bootlid, as applicable, and compress the bulb carrier securing tabs to release the bulb carrier, and withdraw it for bulb inspection/renewal.
9 Depress and twist the relevant bulb to remove it (photo).

Number plate light
10 Remove the cross-head screws and withdraw the lens and cover (photo).
11 Depress and twist the bulb to remove it.
12 When refitting the lens and cover make sure that the lug is correctly located.

Interior light
13 Using a screwdriver, depress the spring

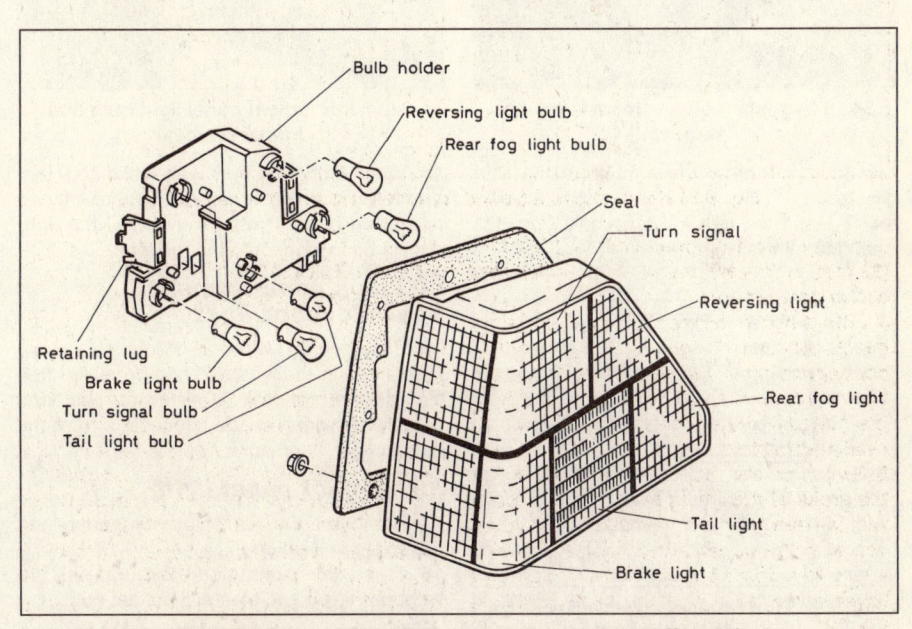

Fig. 9.27 Rear combination light unit components (Sec 34)

Bulb holder — Reversing light bulb — Rear fog light bulb — Seal — Turn signal — Reversing light — Rear fog light — Tail light — Brake light — Retaining lug — Brake light bulb — Turn signal bulb — Tail light bulb

34.5 Front indicator lamp bulb

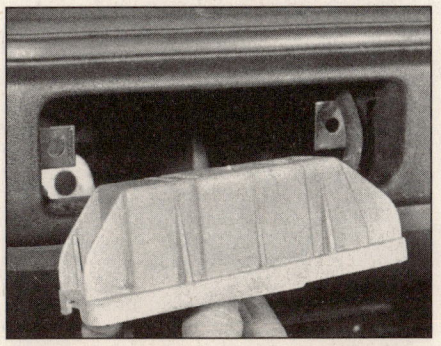

34.6 Front indicator lamp unit removal

34.9 Rear combination light unit and bulbs

9•18 Electrical system

34.10 Number plate lens removal

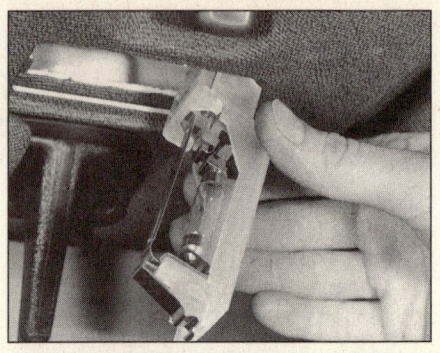

34.13A Interior light removal – 1.8 litre

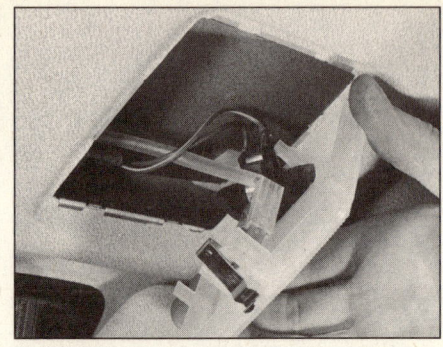

34.13B Interior light removal – 1.3 litre

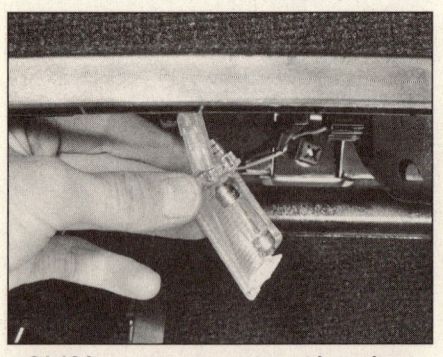

34.16 Luggage compartment lamp lens removal

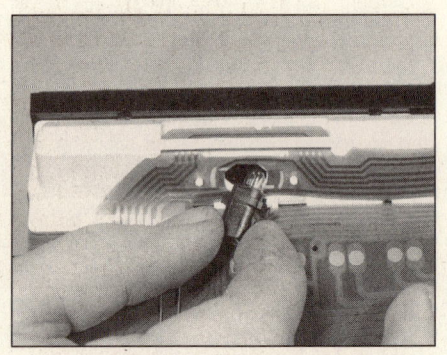

34.18 Instrument panel light bulb and holder removal

clip then withdraw the light from the roof (photos).
14 Release the festoon type bulb from the spring terminals.

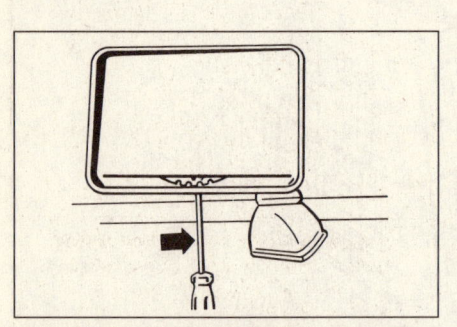

15 When fitting the new bulb make sure that the terminals are tensioned sufficiently to retain the bulb. The switch end of the light should be inserted into the roof first.

Luggage compartment light/glovebox light

16 Prise free and withdraw the lens. The bulb is retained in the lens and can be pulled free for renewal (photo). If renewing the lens detach the wiring spade connectors from the lens.

Instrument panel light

17 Remove the instrument panel, as described in Section 27.
18 Twist the bulbholder through 90° to withdraw it (photo), then pull out the bulb.

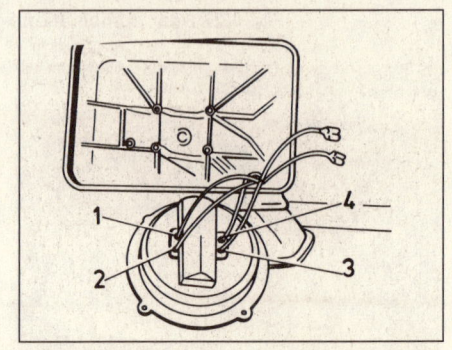

Facia switch lights

19 Remove the relevant facia switch, as described in Section 22.
20 Remove the bulb from the switch or connector as applicable.

35 Electrically-operated door mirror motor - removal and refitting

1 Disconnect the battery earth lead.
2 Release the mirror glass by rotating the retainer anti-clockwise as shown in Fig. 9.28, using a suitable screwdriver.
3 Remove the mirror and disconnect the wiring.
4 Undo the four retaining screws and withdraw the mirror motor. Detach the wiring from the motor.
5 Carefully lever free the door mirror adjuster switch from the trim panel and withdraw it so that the multi-connector plug can be detached.
6 Further removal of the wiring will necessitate door trim removal; see Chapter 11
7 Refitting is a reversal of the removal procedure. Note that the mirror motor wires are colour-coded for correct reconnection (Fig. 9.30).
8 When refitting the mirror glass, rotate the retainer in a clockwise direction to its full extent, then carefully insert the glass into its housing.

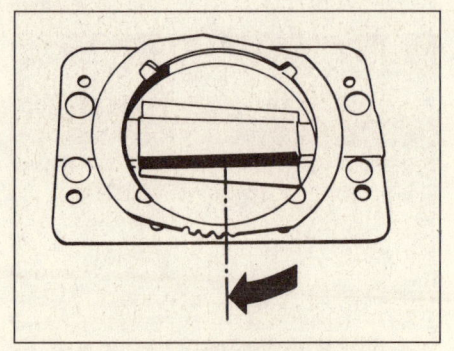

Fig. 9.28 Turn retainer anti-clockwise for electrically-operated door mirror removal (Sec 35)

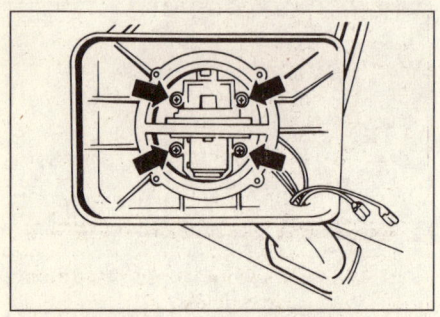

Fig. 9.29 Mirror motor retaining screws (arrowed) (Sec 35)

Fig. 9.30 Door mirror wiring identification (Sec 35)

1 Blue 2 Brown 3 White 4 Black

Fig. 9.31 Rotate retainer clockwise before fitting the glass (Sec 35)

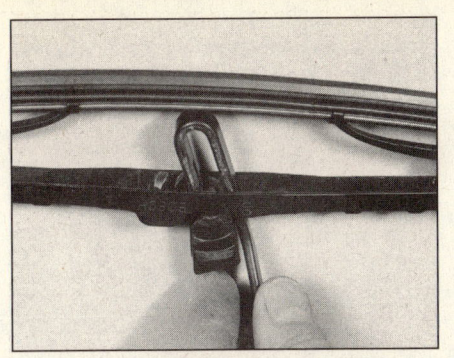

Electrical system 9•19

36.1 Wiper blade removal from arm

36 Wiper blades - renewal

1 To remove a wiper blade pull the arm from the windscreen/rear window as far as possible, then depress the plastic clip and slide the blade from the arm (photo).
2 If necessary the wiper rubber may be renewed separately. To do this use pliers to compress the rubber so that it can be removed from the blade.
3 Refitting is a reversal of removal.

37 Wiper arms - removal and refitting

1 Make sure that the wiper arms are in their parked position then remove the wiper blade, as described in Section 36.
2 Lift the hinged cover and unscrew the nut (photo).
3 Ease the wiper arm from the spindle, taking care not to damage the paintwork (photo).
4 Refitting is a reversal of removal. In the parked position, the end of the wiper arm (ie middle of the blade), should be as shown in Fig. 9.33. On the rear window the dimension should be measured at the points shown in Fig. 9.35.

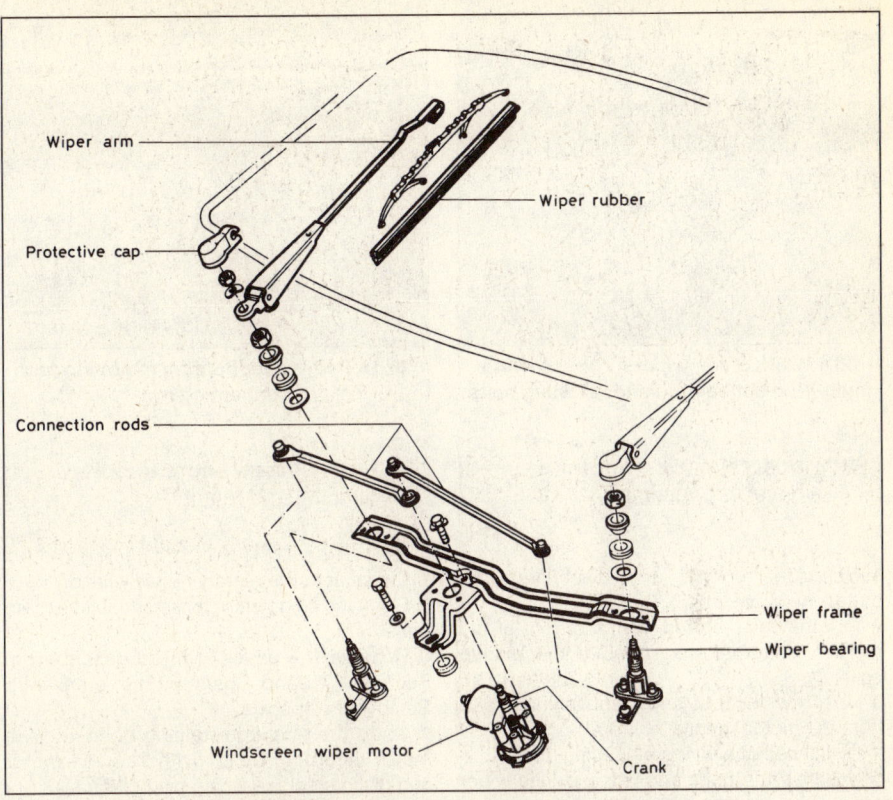

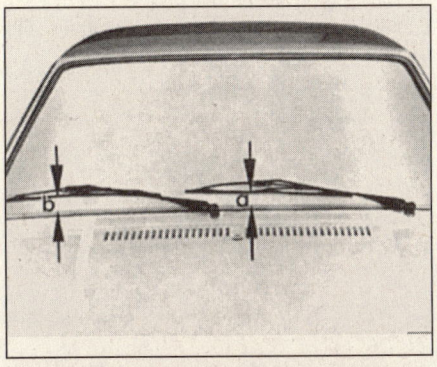

Fig. 9.32 Windscreen wiper components (Sec 37)

Wiper arm — Wiper rubber — Protective cap — Connection rods — Wiper frame — Wiper bearing — Windscreen wiper motor — Crank

Fig. 9.33 Windscreen wiper blade setting positions (Sec 37)

a = 55 mm (2.16 in)   b = 59 mm (2.32 in)

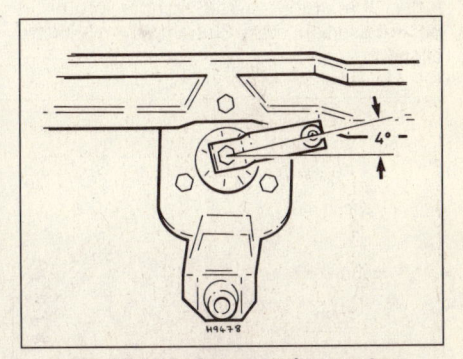

Fig. 9.34 Windscreen wiper motor bellcrank angle (with motor at rest) (Sec 37)

37.2 Undo the wiper arm nut . . .

37.3 . . . and withdraw the arm from the spindle

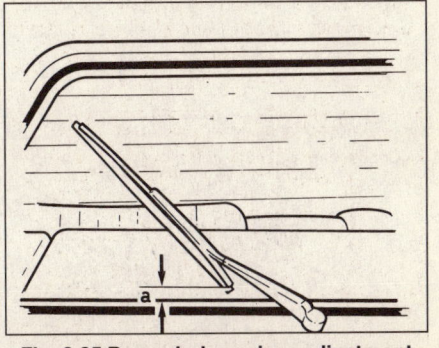

Fig. 9.35 Rear window wiper adjustment position (Sec 37)

a = 15 mm (0.60 in)

9•20 Electrical system

38.4 Windscreen wiper motor showing multi-plug connection and retaining bolts

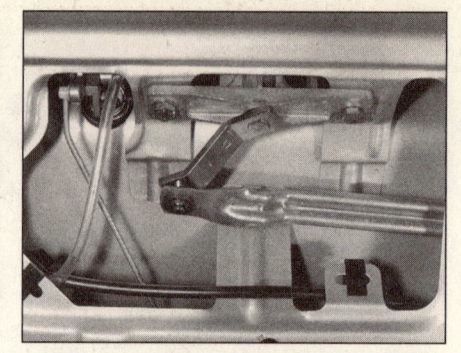

39.4A Rear wiper bearing mounting and connecting rod

39.4B Rear wiper motor mounting in tailgate

38 Windscreen wiper motor - removal and refitting

1 Open the bonnet and disconnect the battery negative lead.
2 Pull the weatherstrip from the front of the plenum chamber and remove the plastic cover.
3 Unscrew the nut and remove the crank from the motor spindle.
4 Disconnect the wiring multi-plug (photo).
5 Unscrew the bolts and withdraw the wiper motor from the frame.
6 Refitting is a reversal of removal, but when fitting the crank to the spindle (motor in parked position) make sure that the marks are aligned.

39 Rear window wiper motor - removal and refitting

1 Disconnect the battery negative lead.
2 Open the tailgate and prise off the inner trim panel.
3 Remove the wiper arm, as described in Section 37, and unscrew the outer nut. Remove the spacers.
4 Undo the bearing retaining bolts and the motor mounting bolts. Withdraw the motor and disconnect the wiring plug (photos).
5 If detaching the crank and connecting rod from the wiper motor pivot, mark a corresponding alignment position across the crank arm and pivot end face. Undo the nut to detach the crank arm.
6 The wiper motor is secured to the mounting by three bolts.
7 Refitting is a reversal of the removal procedure. Correctly align the crank arm when refitting so that the wiper arm will park correctly (Fig. 9.37).

40 Windscreen wiper linkage - removal and refitting

1 Disconnect the battery negative lead.
2 Remove the wiper arms, as described in Section 37, then unscrew the bearing nuts and remove the spacers.
3 Pull the weatherstrips from the front of the plenum chamber and remove the plastic cover.
4 Disconnect the wiring multi-plug.
5 Unscrew the frame mounting bolt, then withdraw the assembly from the bulkhead.
6 Prise the pullrods from the motor crank and bearing levers.
7 Unbolt the wiper motor from the frame.
8 Refitting is a reversal of removal, but lubricate the bearing units and pullrod joints with molybdenum disulphide grease.

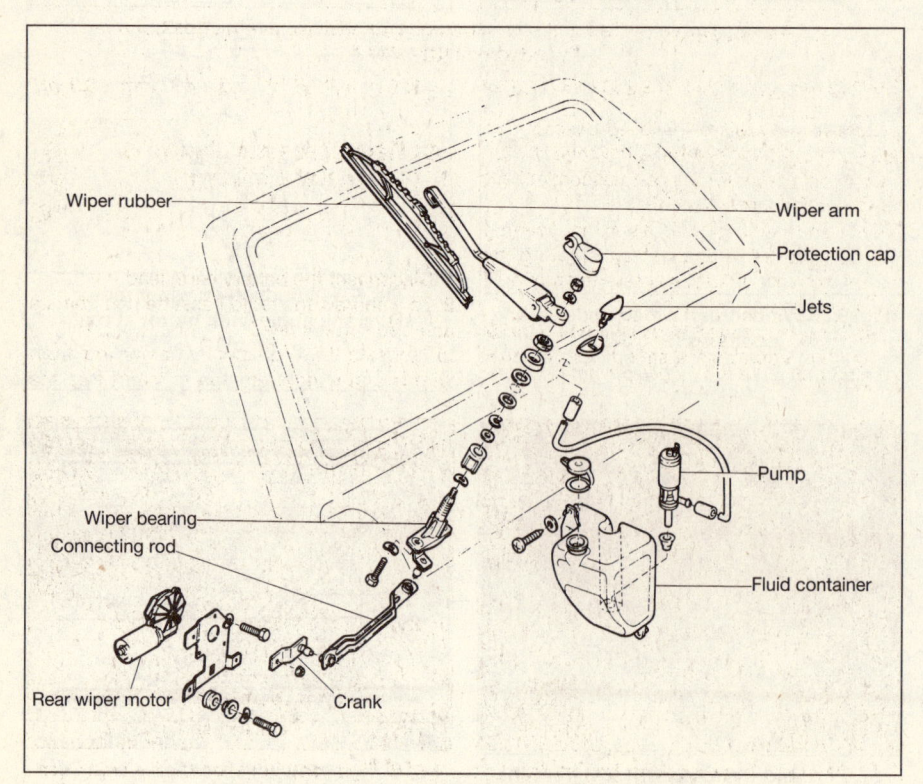

Fig. 9.36 Rear window wiper components (Sec 39)

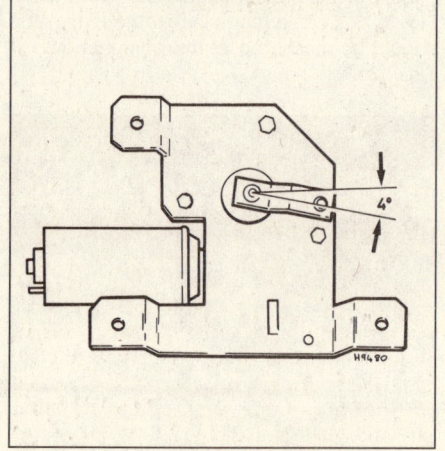

Fig. 9.37 Rear wiper motor bellcrank angle (Sec 39)

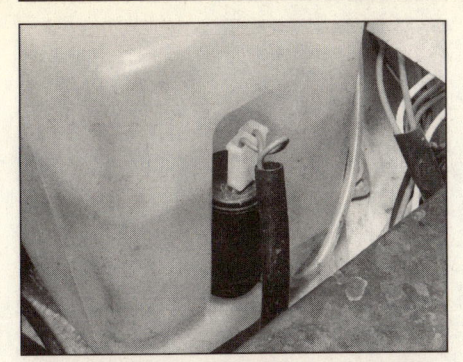

Electrical system 9•21

41.1 Windscreen washer pump and wire connector

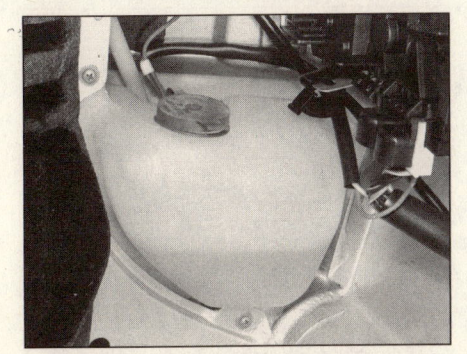

41.2 Rear window washer reservoir unit location

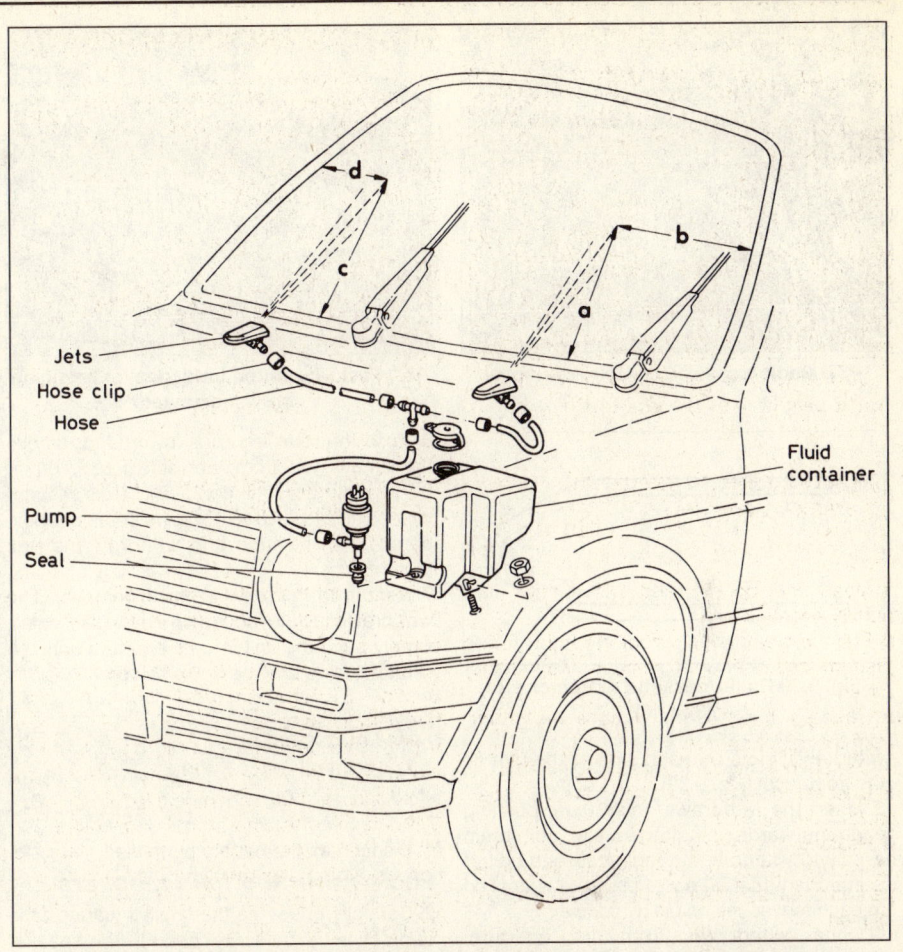

41 Windscreen, headlamp and rear window washer system - general

1 The windscreen washer fluid reservoir is located on the left-hand side of the engine compartment, and the pump and motor are fitted to the side of the reservoir (photo).
2 The rear window washer reservoir is located on the right-hand side rear corner of the luggage compartment, the pump and motor being attached to the side of the reservoir (photo).
3 The reservoir should be regularly topped up with a suitable washer fluid.
4 To adjust the jets, use a needle to direct the spray into the centre of the wiped area (Fig. 9.38). A special tool (VW tool 301 9A) is necessary to direct the headlight washer spray to the centre of the headlights although a needle may be used as an alternative.

42 Horn - removal and refitting

1 If a single horn is fitted it will be located behind the radiator grille. On models with two horns the additional high tone horn is located under the forward section of the front left-hand wheel arch (photos).
2 To remove the horn, first disconnect the battery negative lead.

Fig. 9.38 Windscreen washer system components with jet aiming positions on windscreen (Sec 41)

a = 345 mm (13.5 in)   b = 300 mm (11.8 in)   c = 320 mm (12.5 in)   d = 420 mm (16.5 in)

3 Remove the radiator grille, as described in Chapter 11 (for access to the low tone horn).
4 Unscrew the mounting bolt, disconnect the wires, and withdraw the horn.
5 If the horn emits an unsatisfactory sound it may be possible to adjust it by removing the sealant from the adjusting screw and turning it one way or the other.
6 Refitting is a reversal of removal. Check that horn(s) operate in a satisfactory manner on completion.

43 Radio/cassette player - removal and refitting

1 Disconnect the battery earth lead.
2 To withdraw the radio/cassette unit from its aperture you will need to fabricate the U-shaped extractor tool from wire rod of suitable gauge to insert into the

42.1A Single horn location behind front grille

42.1B High tone horn location – twin horn installation

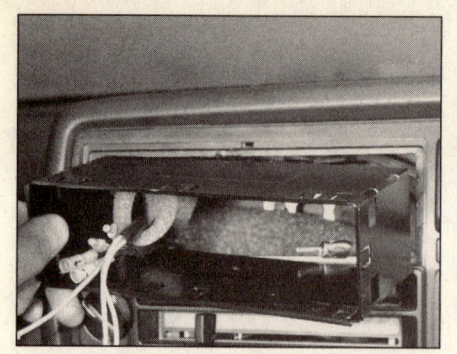

9•22 Electrical system

43.6 Radio/cassette container removal

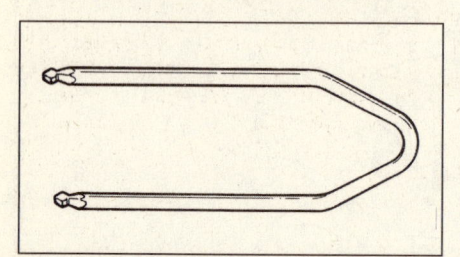

44.3 Facia-mounted loudspeaker retaining screws (arrowed)

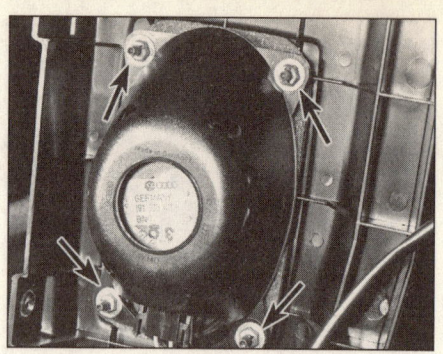

44.5 Luggage compartment loudspeaker retaining nuts (arrowed)

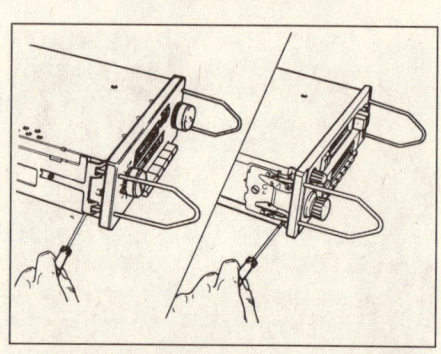

Fig. 9.39 Radio/cassette extractor tool (Sec 43)

withdrawal slots on each side of the unit (in the front face) (Fig. 9.39).
3 Insert the withdrawal tools then, pushing each outwards simultaneously, pull them evenly to withdraw the radio/cassette unit. It is important that an equal pressure is applied to each tool as the unit is withdrawn.
4 Once withdrawn from its aperture, disconnect the aerial cable, the power lead, the aerial feed, the speaker plugs, the earth lead and the light and memory feed (where applicable).

5 Push the retaining clips inwards to remove the removal tool from each side (Fig. 9.40).
6 The radio/cassette container box is secured by locking tabs. To remove the container box, bend back the tabs and withdraw the box (photo).
7 Refit in the reverse order of removal. The withdrawal tools do not have to be used, simply push the unit into its aperture until the securing clips engage in their slots.

44 Loudspeaker - removal and refitting

1 Disconnect the battery earth lead.

Facia-mounted loudspeakers

2 Carefully prise free the small square plastic cap covering the screw head in the speaker grille then undo and remove the screw Lift the speaker grille clear.
3 Undo the two screws securing the speaker unit and lift the speaker out far enough to

Fig. 9.40 Releasing the extractor tool (Sec 43)

enable the leads to be disconnected (photo).
4 Refit in the reverse order of removal.

Luggage compartment loudspeakers

5 Undo the retaining nuts from underneath, withdraw the loudspeaker unit and detach the wiring connector (photo).
6 Refit in reverse order of removal.

Fault finding - electrical system

Starter fails to turn engine
☐ Battery discharged or defective
☐ Battery terminal and/or earth leads loose
☐ Starter motor connections loose
☐ Starter solenoid faulty
☐ Starter brushes worn or sticking
☐ Starter commutator dirty or worn
☐ Starter field coils earthed

Starter turns engine very slowly
☐ Battery discharged
☐ Starter motor connections loose
☐ Starter brushes worn or sticking

Starter noisy
☐ Pinion or flywheel ring gear badly worn
☐ Mounting bolts loose

Ignition lights stays on
☐ Alternator faulty
☐ Alternator drivebelt faulty

Ignition lights fails to come on
☐ Warning bulb blown
☐ Alternator faulty

Battery will not hold charge
☐ Battery defective
☐ Electrolyte level too low
☐ Battery terminal leads loose
☐ Alternator drivebelt slipping
☐ Alternator or regulator faulty
☐ Short circuit in wiring

Fuel and temperature readings increase with engine speed
☐ Voltage stabiliser faulty

Lights inoperative
☐ Fuse blown
☐ Bulb blown
☐ Switch faulty
☐ Connections or wiring faulty

Failure of component motor
☐ Commutator dirty or burnt
☐ Armature faulty
☐ Brushes sticking or worn
☐ Armature bearings seized
☐ Fuse blown

Failure of individual component
☐ Wiring loose or broken
☐ Fuse blown
☐ Switch faulty
☐ Component faulty

Chapter 10 Suspension and steering

For modifications, and information applicable to later models, see Supplement at end of manual

Contents

Fault finding - suspension and steering . . . . See end of Chapter	Steering column - removal, overhaul and refitting 13
Front anti-roll bar - removal and refitting 5	Steering gear bellows - renewal 15
Front suspension strut - removal and refitting 3	Steering gear (manual) - adjustment 18
Front suspension strut and coil spring - separation and assembly. . 4	Steering gear (power-assisted) - adjustment 19
Front wheel bearing - removal and refitting 7	Steering gear unit - removal and refitting 20
Front wheel bearing housing - removal and refitting 6	Steering lock - removal and refitting 14
General description 1	Steering wheel - removal and refitting 12
Maintenance - suspension and steering 2	Tie-rods and balljoints (manual steering) - removal and refitting . . . 16
Power steering fluid - level check, draining and refilling 21	Tie-rods and balljoints (power steering) - removal and refitting 17
Power steering pump - removal, refitting and adjustment 22	Track control arm (wishbone) - removal and refitting 8
Rear axle beam - removal and refitting 10	Wheel alignment - checking and adjustment 23
Rear suspension strut and coil spring - removal and refitting 9	Rear wheel hub bearings - removal and refitting 11
Roadwheels and tyres - general 24	

Degrees of difficulty

Easy, suitable for novice with little experience	**Fairly easy,** suitable for beginner with some experience	**Fairly difficult,** suitable for competent DIY mechanic	**Difficult,** suitable for experienced DIY mechanic	**Very difficult,** suitable for expert DIY or professional

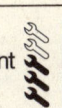

Specifications

Front suspension

Type . . . . Independent with spring struts, lower track control arms (wishbones), anti-roll bar on some models. Telescopic shock absorbers incorporated in struts

Rear suspension

Type . . . . Semi-independent incorporating torsion axle beam, trailing arms and spring struts/shock absorbers. Anti-roll bar on some models

Steering

Type . . . . Rack and pinion with safety column. Power steering optional on Golf GL models
Turning circle (approx) . . . . 10.5 m (34.4 ft)
Steering roll radius . . . . Negative 8.2 mm (0.323 in)
Steering wheel turns lock to lock:
  Standard 3.83
  Power-assisted 3.17
Steering ratio:
  Standard 20.8
  Power-assisted 17.5
Power-assisted steering fluid type . . . . Dexron type ATF

Front wheel alignment

Total toe . . . . 0° ± 10'
Camber (in straight-ahead position):
  All models except Golf GTI and Jetta GT . . . . - 30' ± 20'
  Golf GTI and Jetta GT . . . . - 35' ± 20'
  Golf/Jetta 16V . . . . - 40' ± 20
Maximum difference side-to-side . . . . 30'
Castor (not adjustable):
  All models except Golf GTI and Jetta GT . . . . 1°30' ± 30'
  Golf GTI and Jetta GT . . . . 1°35' ± 30'
Maximum difference - side to side . . . . 1°

Note: *The camber and castor settings may differ on some variants - check with your VW dealer*

Rear wheel alignment (not adjustable)
Total toe . . . . 25' ± 15'
Maximum deviation in adjustment . . . . 25'
Camber . . . . -1° 40' ± 20'
Maximum difference - side-to-side . . . . 30'

Wheels
Golf base, C, CL and C Formel E . . . . 5J x 13
Golf GL . . . . 5½J x 13
Golf GTI . . . . 5½ or 6J x 14
Jetta . . . . 5½J x 13 or 6J x 14

Tyres
Type . . . . Radial ply
Size:
  Golf base, C, GL and C Formel E . . . . 155 SR 13
  Golf GL . . . . 175/70 SR 13
  Golf GTI . . . . 185/60 HR 14
  Jetta . . . . 175/70 SR 13
  Golf/Jetta GTI 16V . . . . 185/60 VR 14
Tyre pressures - bar (lbf/in^2): **Front** **Rear**
  Golf and Jetta:
    1.05 and 1.3 litre:
      Half load 1.8 (26)   1.8 (26)
      Full load 1.8 (26)   2.4 (35)
    All other models:
      Half load 2.0 (29)   1.8 (26)
      Full load 2.0 (29)   2.4 (35)
  Temporary spare wheel (space saver) 4.2 (61)
  Normal spare wheel 2.4 (35)

Torque wrench settings | Nm | lbf ft
Front suspension
Strut to body 60   44
Strut to wheel bearing housing:
  19 mm nut 80   59
  18 mm nut 95   70
Lower track control arm:
  Pivot bolt to subframe 130   96
  Lower balljoint bolts 35   26
Track control arm/subframe bolts 130   96
Subframe rear mounting strut to body 80   59
Shock absorber slotted nut 40   30
Anti-roll bar eye bolt nut 25   18
Hub nut 265   195

Rear suspension
Mounting bracket shouldered bolt 85   63
Shock absorber lower mounting nut 70   52
Stub axle 60   44
Axle beam/mounting bracket pivot bolt nut 60   44
Brake pressure regulator spring bracket 35   26
Shock absorber top cover nut 15   11
Shock absorber spacer retaining nut 15   11

Steering
Steering wheel 40   30
Column tube mounting bracket 20   15
Tie-rod inner 35   26
Tie-rod balljoint 35   26
Tie-rod balljoint locknut 50   37
Rack mounting clip 30   22
Steering column joint 30   22
Power steering pressure and return hose unions 20   15
Power steering pump and swivel bracket bolts 20   15
Power steering pump tensioner/bracket 20   15
Power steering pump pulley 20   15
Power steering tie-rod to rack 70   52
Roadwheels 110   81

Suspension and steering 10•3

1 General description

The front suspension is of independent type, incorporating coil struts and lower wishbones. The struts are fitted with telescopic shock absorbers and both front suspension units are mounted on a subframe. An anti-roll bar is fitted to the track control arm (wishbone) on some models.

The rear suspension consists of a transverse torsion axle with trailing arms rubber-bushed to the body. The axle is attached to the lower ends of the shock absorbers, which act as struts, since they incorporate mountings for the coil springs (Figure 10.2).

The steering is of rack and pinion type mounted on the front subframe. The tie-rods are attached to a single coupling which is itself bolted to the steering rack. Power assistance is fitted to some models.

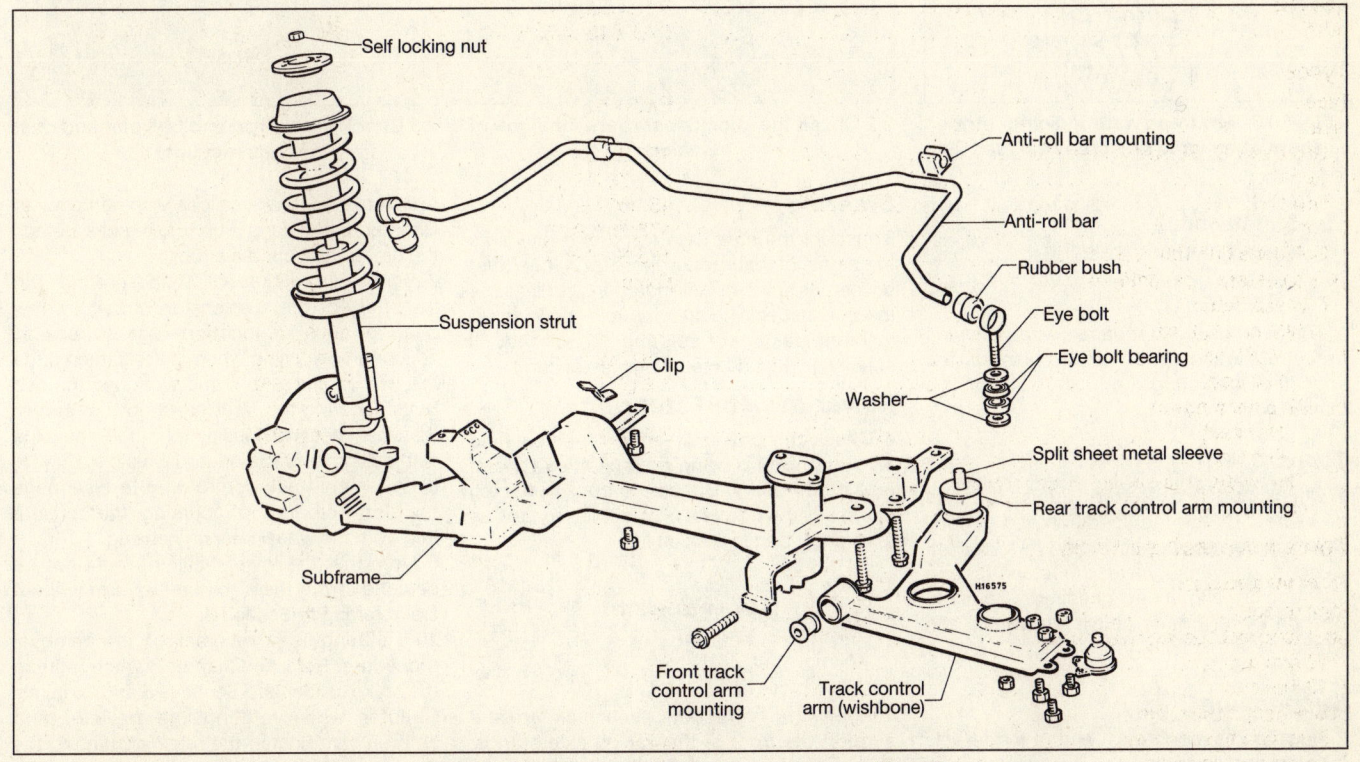

Fig. 10.1 Front suspension main components (Sec 1)

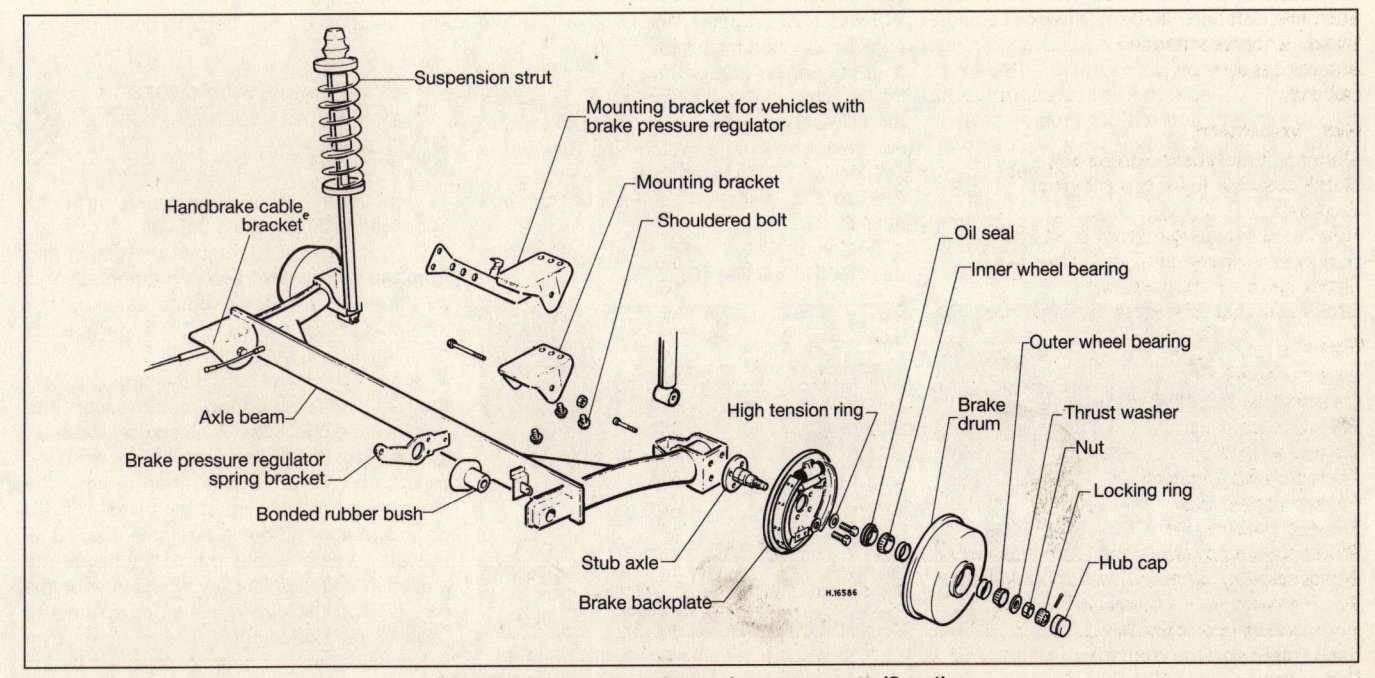

Fig. 10.2 Rear suspension main components (Sec 1)

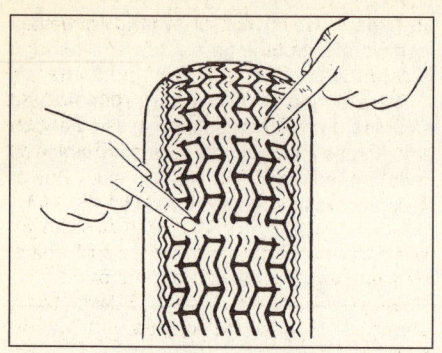

10•4 Suspension and steering

Fig. 10.3 Tyre tread wear indicator strips show when tyres need renewal (Sec 2)

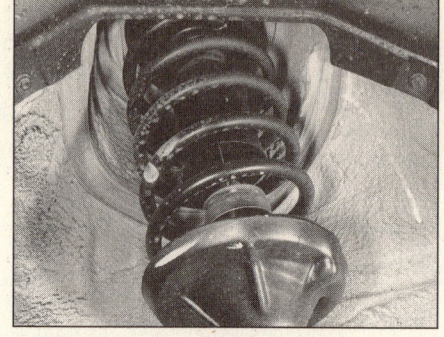

2.2 Check the shock absorbers for signs of leaking

2.3 Check the tie-rod end balljoint and dust caps regularly

2 Maintenance - suspension and steering

The following routine maintenance procedures should be undertaken at the specified intervals given at the start of this manual.

Tyres

1 Check and if necessary adjust the tyre pressures. Check the condition and general wear characteristics of the tyres and, if wearing unevenly, have the steering and suspension alignment checked. Refer to Section 24 for further details on wheels and tyres.

Suspension

2 Raise and support each end of the vehicle in turn and inspect the suspension and steering components for signs of excessive wear or damage. Inspect the suspension balljoints for wear and the dust covers for any signs of splits or deterioration. Renew if necessary. Check the track control arm (wishbone) and anti-roll bar mounting/pivot bushes for signs of excessive wear and/or deterioration and again renew if necessary. Check the shock absorbers for signs of leakage and the suspension to subframe and body mountings for signs of corrosion (photo).

Steering

3 Inspect the steering tie-rod end balljoints for signs of excessive wear and the dust covers for splits or deterioration and leakage (photo). Inspect the steering gear bellows for signs of leakage or splitting. Check that all steering joints and mountings are secure.

Power-assisted steering

4 Check the power steering reservoir fluid level and top up using the specified type of fluid if necessary. Check the power steering pump drivebelt. Adjust or, if necessary, renew it, as described in Section 22.

3 Front suspension strut - removal and refitting

1 Apply the handbrake then jack up and support the front of the car on axle stands. Remove the roadwheel on the side concerned.
2 Position a jack under the outer end of the track control arm for support.
3 In the engine compartment, prise the cap from the top of the strut (photo) and unscrew the self-locking nut whilst holding the piston rod stationary with an Allen key. Renew the self-locking nut once removed.
4 Undo and remove the anti-roll bar eye bolt nut (see Section 5).
5 Detach the steering tie-rod balljoint, as described in Section 16.
6 Remove the brake caliper, with reference to Chapter 8, and hang it up to one side. Detach the brake line from the strut.
7 Scribe an alignment mark around the periphery of the suspension strut-to-wheel bearing housing location lugs to ensure accurate positioning when refitting, then undo the two retaining nuts and withdraw the two bolts securing the strut at its bottom end to the wheel bearing housing (photo). Renew the self-locking nuts and special washers.
8 Lower the track control arm to disengage the strut from its top mounting, then prise it free from the wheel bearing housing.
9 Note that the lower balljoint must not be detached from the track control arm without first referring to Section 8.
10 Refitting is a reversal of the removal procedure. Refer to Chapter 8 when refitting the brake caliper and Sections 5 and 16 in this Chapter when refitting the balljoint and anti-roll bar. Tighten the retaining nuts to the specified torque. Use only new self-locking nuts with special washers to secure the strut-to-wheel bearing housing bolts.

4 Front suspension strut and coil spring - separation and assembly

1 Remove the front suspension strut, as described in the previous Section.
2 Do not attempt to remove the coil spring from the strut unless a spring compressor is available. If a suitable compressor is not available, take the strut to a garage for dismantling and assembly.
3 Support the lower end of the strut in a vice, then fit the coil spring compressor into position and check that it is securely located.
4 Compress the spring until the upper spring retainer is free of tension, then remove the slotted nut from the top of the piston rod. To do this, a special tool is available (Fig. 10.5). However, it is possible to hold the piston rod stationary with an Allen key, or spanner on the flats (as applicable) and use a peg spanner to unscrew the slotted nut.
5 Remove the strut bearing, followed by the spring retainer.

3.3 Removing the front suspension strut top cap

3.7 Strut-to-front wheel bearing housing retaining nuts/bolts

Suspension and steering 10•5

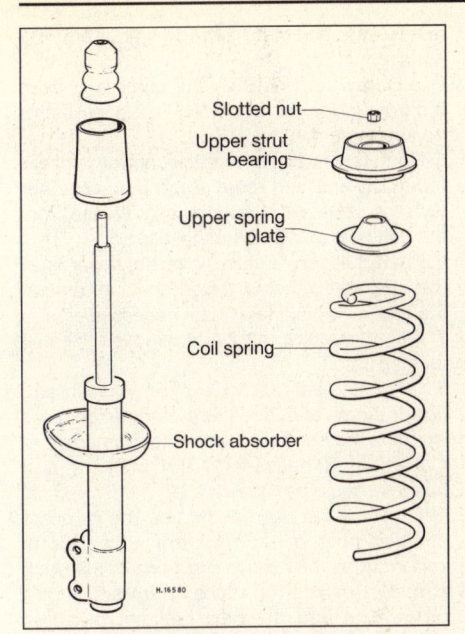

Fig. 10.4 Front suspension strut and coil spring components (Sec 4)

- Slotted nut
- Upper strut bearing
- Upper spring plate
- Coil spring
- Shock absorber

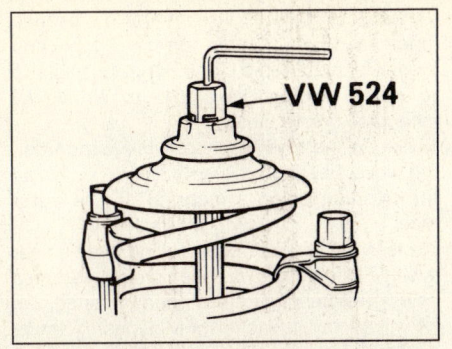

Fig. 10.5 Using the special tool to unscrew the slotted nut from the front suspension. A peg spanner and Allen key or suitable spanner will suffice if necessary – see text (Sec 4)

6 Lift the coil spring from the strut with the compressor still in position. Mark the top of the spring for reference.
7 Withdraw the bump stop components from the piston rod, noting their order of removal.
8 Move the shock absorber piston rod up and down through its complete stroke and check that the resistance is even and smooth. If there are any signs or seizing or lack of resistance, or if fluid has been leaking excessively, the shock absorber/strut unit should be renewed.
9 The coil springs are normally colour-coded and if the springs are to be renewed (it is advisable to renew the spring each side at the same time), be sure to get the correct replacement type with the identical colour code.
10 Reassembly is a reversal of removal. Tighten the slotted nut to the specified torque before releasing the spring compressor.

5 Front anti-roll bar - removal and refitting

1 Apply the handbrake then jack up the front of the car and support it on axle stands.
2 Undo and remove the anti-roll bar eye bolt nuts from the underside of the track control arm each side (photo).
3 Position a jack under the subframe and raise to support it.
4 Undo the subframe-to-body strut retaining bolt at the rear end, loosen the front bolt and swing the strut round to allow the anti-roll bar and bush clearance for removal. Repeat on the other side.
5 Lift the anti-roll bar eye bolts and disengage them from the anti-roll bar (photo). Note the location and orientation of the eye bolt bushes and washers. Remove the anti-roll bar.
6 Renew the anti-roll bar if it is damaged or distorted. Renew the bushes if they are perished or worn.
7 Refitting is a reversal of the removal procedure. Check that the eye bolt bushes are fitted with their conical face towards the washers, the cover faces of which must face away from the bush mountings.
8 Do not fully tighten the retaining nuts and bolts until the vehicle is free standing and has been bounced a few times to settle the mountings.

6 Front wheel bearing housing - removal and refitting

1 Refer to Chapter 7, Section 2 and proceed as described in paragraphs 1 to 5 inclusive to remove the driveshaft on the side concerned.
2 Refer to Section 16 in this Chapter and disconnect the tie-rod balljoint from the wheel bearing housing.
3 Refer to Chapter 8, Section 4 and remove the brake caliper. Leave the brake hydraulic line connected to the caliper and hang up the caliper to support it. Disconnect the hydraulic line location bracket from the strut.

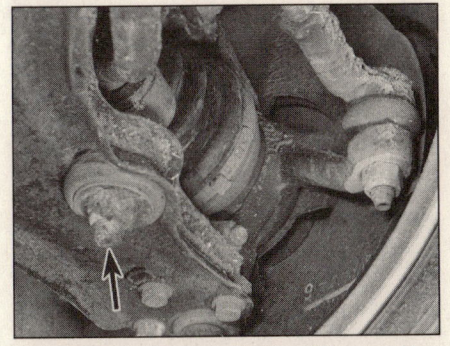

5.2 Anti-roll bar eye bolt nut (arrowed)

5.5 Anti-roll bar location in eye bolt

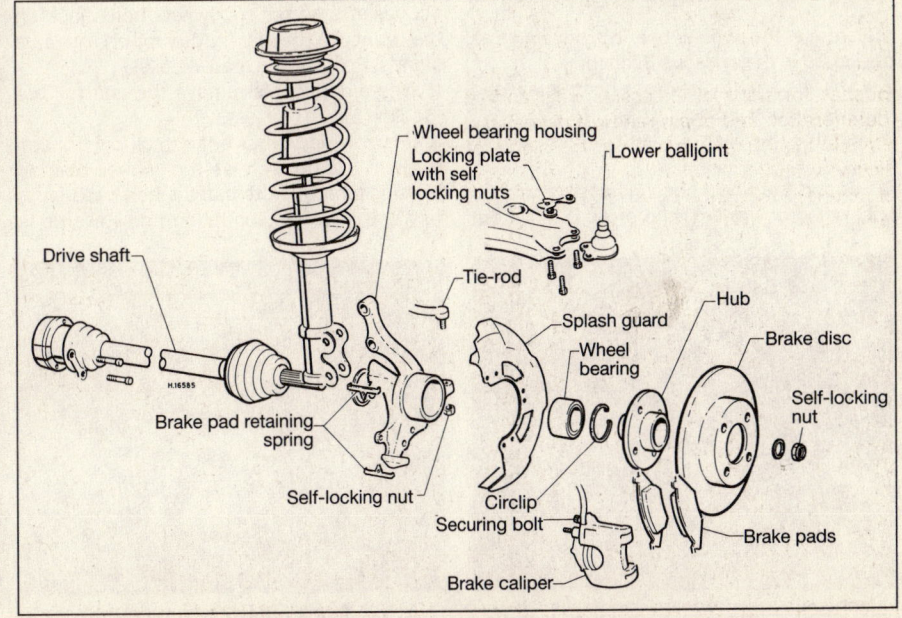

Fig. 10.6 Exploded view of the wheel bearing housing and associated components (Sec 6)

- Drive shaft
- Wheel bearing housing
- Locking plate with self locking nuts
- Lower balljoint
- Tie-rod
- Splash guard
- Hub
- Wheel bearing
- Brake disc
- Brake pad retaining spring
- Self-locking nut
- Circlip
- Securing bolt
- Brake caliper
- Brake pads
- Self-locking nut

10•6 Suspension and steering

4 Undo the retaining screw and remove the brake disc.
5 Scribe an alignment mark around the periphery of the suspension strut-to-wheel bearing housing location lugs, to ensure accurate positioning when refitting.
6 Undo the two suspension arm-to-wheel bearing retaining bolt nuts and remove them, together with their special washers. These nuts must be renewed when refitting. Withdraw the bolts and separate the wheel bearing housing from the suspension strut.
7 If the wheel bearing housing is to be renewed, remove the wheel bearing, as described in Section 7, then fit the bearing and hub to the new housing, with reference to the same Section.
8 Refitting is a reversal of the removal procedure. Renew all self-locking nuts.
9 When refitting the suspension strut to the wheel bearing housing, check that they are correctly positioned according to the alignment scribe marks made during dismantling before tightening the securing bolts and nuts to the specified torque setting.
10 Refit the driveshaft, as described in Section 2 of Chapter 7.
11 Reconnect the tie-rod balljoint and the anti-roll bar (where applicable) to the track control arm with reference to Sections 5 and 8 respectively.
12 Refit the brake disc and caliper, with reference to the appropriate Sections in Chapter 8.
13 On completion, lower the car to the ground and tighten the hub nut to the specified torque wrench setting.

7 Front wheel bearing - removal and refitting

1 Remove the wheel bearing housing, as described in the previous Section.
2 If still fitted, undo the cross-head screw and remove the brake disc.
3 Remove the screws and withdraw the splash guard.
4 Support the wheel bearing housing with the hub facing downward, and press or drive out the hub, using a suitable mandrel. The bearing inner race will remain on the hub, and therefore, once removed, it is not possible to re-use the bearing. Use a puller to remove the inner race from the hub.
5 Extract the circlips, then, while supporting the wheel bearing housing, press or drive out the bearing, using a mandrel on the outer race.
6 Clean the recess in the housing, then smear it with a little general purpose grease. Where a new wheel bearing kit has been obtained, the kit will contain a sachet of Molypaste. Smear some Molypaste onto the bearing seat (not the bearing).
7 Fit the outer circlip, then support the wheel bearing housing and press or drive in the new bearing, using a metal tube *on the outer race only*.
8 Fit the inner circlip, making sure that it is correctly seated.
9 Position the hub with its bearing shoulder facing upward, then press or drive on the bearing and housing, using a metal tube *on the inner race only*.
10 Refit the splash guard and brake disc, then refit the wheel bearing housing, as described in the previous Section.
11 On completion, lower the car to the ground and tighten the hub nut to the specified torque setting. If the bearings have been renewed, it is advisable to raise the car at the front again after the hub nut has been tightened and check that the front roadwheel and hub can be spun freely without excessive binding or lateral play.

8 Track control arm (wishbone) - removal, overhaul and refitting

1 Loosen the front roadwheel bolts, jack up the front of the car and support on axle stands. Remove the roadwheel(s).
2 Where applicable remove the anti-roll bar (Section 5).
3 Unscrew and remove the track control arm balljoint clamp bolt at the wheel bearing housing (photo). Note that the bolt head faces forwards. Tap the control arm downwards to release the balljoint from the wheel bearing housing.
4 Unscrew and remove the pivot bolt from the front inboard end of the track control arm (to subframe) (photo).
5 Undo and remove the track control arm rear mounting bolt and remove the bolt, together with the strut. Withdraw the split sleeve from the bolt hole using suitable pliers.
6 Pivot the track control arm downwards at the front and withdraw it from the subframe at the rear mounting, levering if necessary.
7 With the track control arm removed, clean it for inspection.
8 Check the balljoint for excessive wear, and check the pivot bushes for deterioration. Also examine the track control arm for damage and distortion. If necessary, the balljoint and bushes should be renewed.
9 To renew the balljoint, first outline its exact position on the track control arm. This is important as the relative positions of the track control arm and the balljoint are set during production and the new balljoint must be accurately positioned when fitting it. Unscrew the nuts and remove the balljoint and clamp plate. Fit the new balljoint in the exact outline, and tighten the nuts. If fitting a new track control arm, locate the balljoint centrally in the elongated hole.
10 To renew the front pivot bush, use a long bolt, together with a metal tube and washers, to pull the bush from the track control arm. Fit the new bush using the same method but, to ease insertion, dip the bush into soapy water first.
11 The rear mounting bonded rubber bush can be removed by prising free but, failing this, you will need to carefully cut through its rubber and steel sections to split and release it by driving it out. The latter course of action should only be necessary if it is badly corroded into position.
12 Press or drive the new mounting bush into position from the top end of the control arm but ensure that it is positioned correctly, as shown in Fig. 10.7.

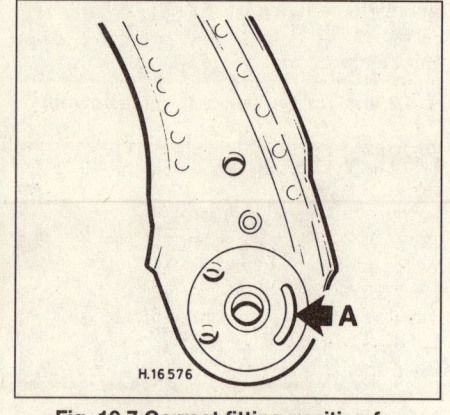

Fig. 10.7 Correct fitting position for mounting bush in the control arm (Sec 8)

Opening A to be located on inboard side of vehicle

8.3 Track control arm balljoint and clamp bolt

8.4 Track control arm pivot bolt

Suspension and steering 10•7

9.4 Removing the rear suspension strut top cap

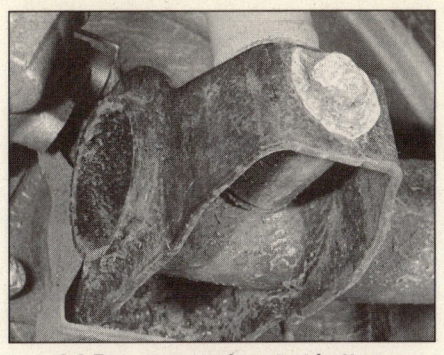

9.6 Rear suspension strut bottom mounting

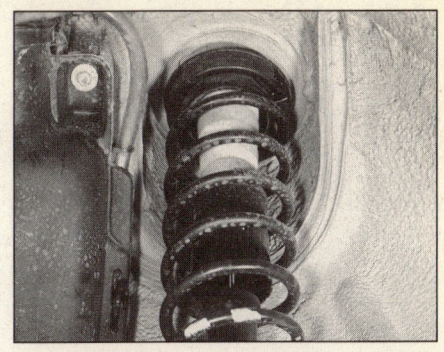

9.7 Remove the rear suspension strut and coil spring downwards

13 Refitting the track control arm is a reverse of removal, but delay tightening the pivot bolts until the weight of the car is on the suspension. Refer to Section 5 when refitting the anti-roll bar. Have the front wheel camber angle checked and, if necessary, adjusted by a VW dealer.

9 Rear suspension strut and coil spring - removal and refitting

1 Detach the trim panel from the top of the rear suspension strut within the luggage compartment.
2 Chock the front roadwheels and then jack up the rear of the car and support on axle stands. Remove the roadwheel(s) at the rear for improved access.
3 Support the weight of the trailing arm with a trolley jack.
4 Remove the cap from the top of the strut (photo), then unscrew the upper securing nut from the top of the strut, if necessary holding the rod stationary with a spanner.
5 Withdraw the dished washer then undo the second retaining nut and withdraw the thrust washer and upper bearing ring.
6 At the bottom end of the strut, engage a spanner on the self-locking nut retaining the mounting bolt; access being through the trailing arm tube (photo). Undo the bolt and withdraw it.
7 Lower the trailing arm as far as possible and withdraw the strut assembly (photo).
8 To remove the coil spring from the strut, undo the retaining nut then withdraw the spacer sleeve, lower bearing ring, upper spring seat and packing. Note how the packing is fitted for correct direction on reassembly.
9 Withdraw the coil spring, rubber stop and ring with protective tube, bottom cap, packing piece and lower spring seat.
10 If the shock absorber is faulty it will normally make a knocking noise as the car is driven over rough surfaces. However, with the unit removed, uneven resistance tight spots will be evident as the central rod is operated. Check the condition of the buffers, bump stop and associated components and renew them as necessary.
11 Coil springs should only be renewed as a pair at the rear and it is important to fit the correct replacements. The springs are colour-coded for identification.
12 Refitting is a reversal of removal, but make sure that the coil spring is correctly located in the seats. Delay tightening the lower mounting bolt until the full weight of the car is on the roadwheels.
13 If new coil springs have been fitted it is advisable to have a rear wheel alignment check made by your VW dealer after an initial distance of 1000 miles (1500 km) has been covered and the springs have settled.

10 Rear axle beam - removal and refitting

Note: *If the axle beam is suspected of being distorted it should be checked in position by a VW garage using an optical alignment instrument.*

1 Remove the rear stub axles, as described in Section 11.
2 Support the weight of the trailing arms with axle stands then disconnect the struts/shock absorbers by removing the lower mounting bolts.

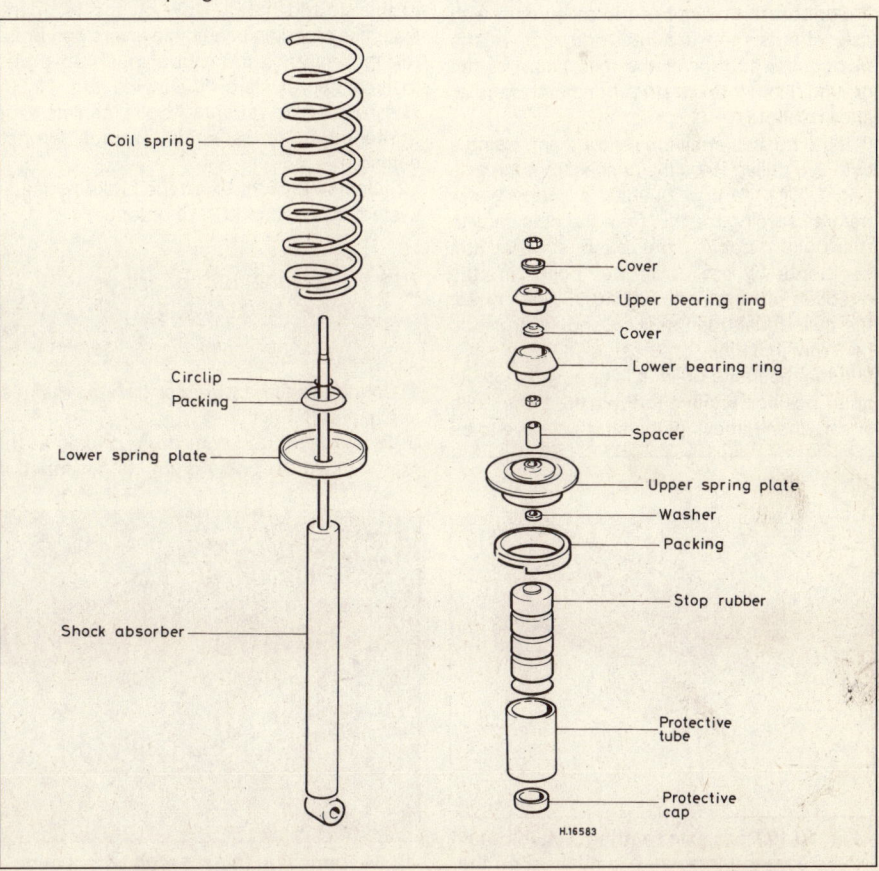

Fig. 10.8 Rear suspension strut and coil spring components (Sec 9)

10•8 Suspension and steering

10.3 Brake pressure regulator unit showing spring bracket

10.7 Axle beam pivot bolt heads to be as shown

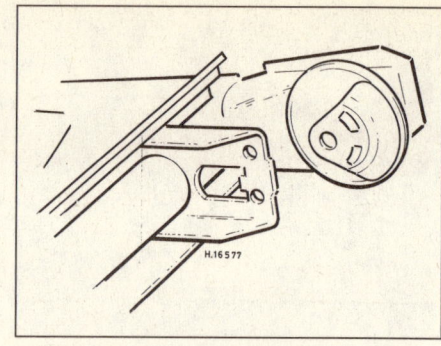

Fig. 10.9 Rear axle bonded rubber bush orientation – protruding segments to face forwards (Sec 10)

3 On models fitted with a brake pressure regulator unit, unbolt the spring bracket from the axle beam (photo).
4 Disconnect the handbrake cables from the axle beam and from the left-hand side and underbody bracket with reference to Chapter 8.
5 Remove the brake fluid reservoir filler cap and tighten it down onto a piece of polythene sheet in order to reduce the loss of hydraulic fluid.
6 Lower the axle beam and disconnect the brake hydraulic hoses with reference to Chapter 8. Plug the hoses to prevent the ingress of dirt.
7 Support the weight of the axle beam with axle stands then unscrew and remove the pivot bolts and lower the axle beam to the ground. Note that the pivot bolt heads face as shown (photo).
8 If the bushes are worn renew them. Using a two-arm puller, force the bushes from the axle beam. Dip the new bushes in soapy water before pressing them in from the outside with the puller. Locate the bush so that the segments which protrude point in the direction of travel, see Fig. 10.9. When fitted, the cylindrical bush section should protrude by 8 mm (0.31 in).
9 If the mounting bracket is removed, note its fitted position relative to the axle. If the bolts shear when removing, the stud will have to be accurately drilled out and the resultant hole tapped for a 12 mm x 1.5 thread. Be careful to drill in the centre of the broken stud since misalignment of the hole will in turn mean misalignment of the axle. Unless you have experience in this type of work it is best entrusted to a trained mechanic.
10 When the mounting bracket is refitted its inclination angle to the axle beam should be 12° ± 2°.
11 Refitting is a reversal of removal, but note the following. When the axle is fitted into position with the mountings under tension, locate the securing bolts then align the right side mounting so that the bolts are centralised in the slotted holes. Now on the left-hand side, use a couple of suitable levers and press the mounting to the rubber bush so that a minimal gap exists on the inside (Fig. 10.10). The respective retaining bolts can now be tightened to the specified torque wrench setting.
12 On completion, bleed the brake hydraulic system, as described in Chapter 8.

11 Rear wheel hub bearings - removal and refitting

1 On models fitted with rear disc brakes refer to Chapter 8, Section 8.
2 On models fitted with drum brakes at the rear, remove the brake drum, as described in Section 9 of Chapter 8. The bearings and oil seal can be removed in the same manner as that given for the corresponding components in the rear brake disc in Section 8 of Chapter 8.
3 Refit the brake disc or drum, as applicable, and adjust the bearing as described in the appropriate Section (8 or 9) in Chapter 8.

12 Steering wheel - removal and refitting

1 Disconnect the battery earth lead.
2 Set the front roadwheels in the straight-ahead position.
3 Prise free the cover from the centre of the steering wheel. Where the cover is the horn push button, note the location of the wires and disconnect them from the terminals on the cover (photos).
4 Mark the steering wheel and inner column in relation to each other, then unscrew the nut and withdraw the steering wheel (photo). Remove the washer.
5 Refitting is a reversal of removal, but make sure that the turn signal lever is in its neutral position, otherwise damage may occur in the cancelling arm. The cancelling ring tongue points to the left. Tighten the retaining nut to the specified torque.
6 On completion reconnect the battery and check that the horn and column switches operate satisfactorily.

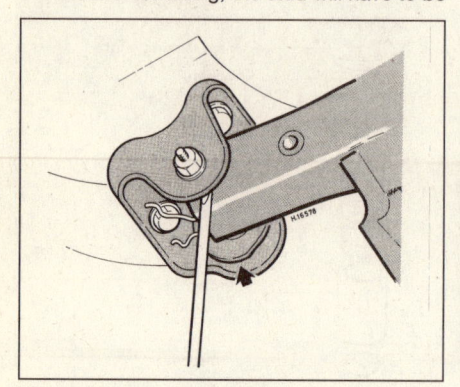

Fig. 10.10 Rear axle refitting – check that the clearance (arrowed) is minimal on the left-hand mounting inner side (Sec 10)

12.3A Removing the steering wheel centre cover – GTI

12.3B Removing the steering wheel centre cover – 1.3 litre

Suspension and steering 10•9

12.4 Undoing the steering wheel retaining nut

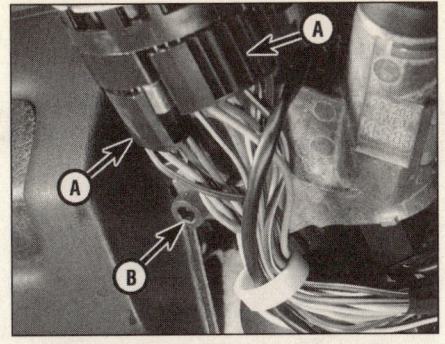

13.4 Detach the multi-function switch wiring connectors (A)
Steering column mounting bolt is also shown (B)

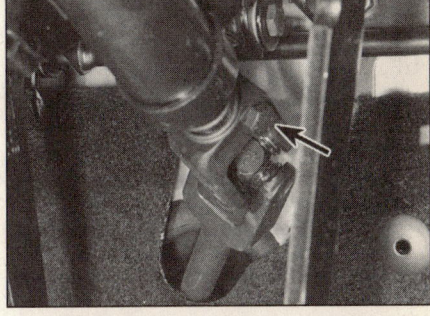

13.7 Steering column universal joint (upper). Clamp bolt is arrowed

13 Steering column - removal, overhaul and refitting

1 Disconnect the battery negative lead.
2 Remove the steering wheel, as described in Section 12.
3 Remove the screws and withdraw the steering column lower shroud.
4 Remove the three screws and withdraw the combination switch. Disconnect the wiring multi-connectors (photo).
5 Remove the screws and withdraw the lower facia trim panel.
6 Remove the column mounting bolts. Where shear-head bolts have been fitted, it will be necessary to drill off the heads and unscrew the threaded portions, or use a centre punch to unscrew them. On some models one of the mounting bolts may be a socket-head type, in which case use an Allen key to unscrew it.
7 Undo and withdraw the universal joint-to-column clamp bolt (photo). Undo the lower mounting-to-column transverse bolt then withdraw the column from the universal joint, and collect the coil spring.
8 On early (pre-July 1984) models, a two section column is fitted. With this type push the two sections together to disengage the rectangular engagement pins within the housing, collect the rubber insulation caps and withdraw the lower section upwards through the housing tube.
9 Check the various components for excessive wear. If the column has been damaged in any way it must be renewed as a unit. If renewing the earlier type column as a unit the later telescopic type column unit may be fitted, in which case a new lower mounting must also be fitted as the earlier type is not compatible with the later type.
10 To dismantle the top housing (both types), prise free the lockwasher from the inner column and withdraw the spring and contact ring. (Renew the lockwasher.)
11 Check the condition of the flange tube bushes and if necessary renew them. Lever the old bushes out with a screwdriver then press in the new bushes after dipping them in soapy water. Unscrew the old shear bolt(s) and obtain new bolts.
12 Using an Allen key, unscrew the clamp bolt securing the steering lock and withdraw the lock. Note that the ignition key must be inserted and the lock released.
13 Withdraw the inner column from the outer columns and remove the support ring.
14 Clean the components and examine them for wear. Renew them as necessary.
15 Reassembly is a reversal of dismantling, but lubricate bearing surfaces with multi-purpose grease and renew the inner column lockwasher.
16 On later models with the telescopic single section column reassembly differs. Secure the lower end of the column in a vice (with soft jaws) so that the upper section rests on the jaws and the two halves of the column cannot be slid together. The small lug in the lower part must be visible through the hole in the upper part (arrowed in Fig. 10.12). Assemble the support ring with the column switch and lock housing, the contact ring, spring and locking washer.
17 On both steering column types the locking washer is fitted by driving it down the shaft until it is completely pressed on. On the earlier two section type column, compress the two columns together using a suitable pair of pliers as the washer is driven into position.
18 Check that the column alignment is correct when connecting it to the universal joint. Tighten the retaining nuts and bolts to the specified torque setting. Tighten the shear bolt(s) until their head(s) break off.

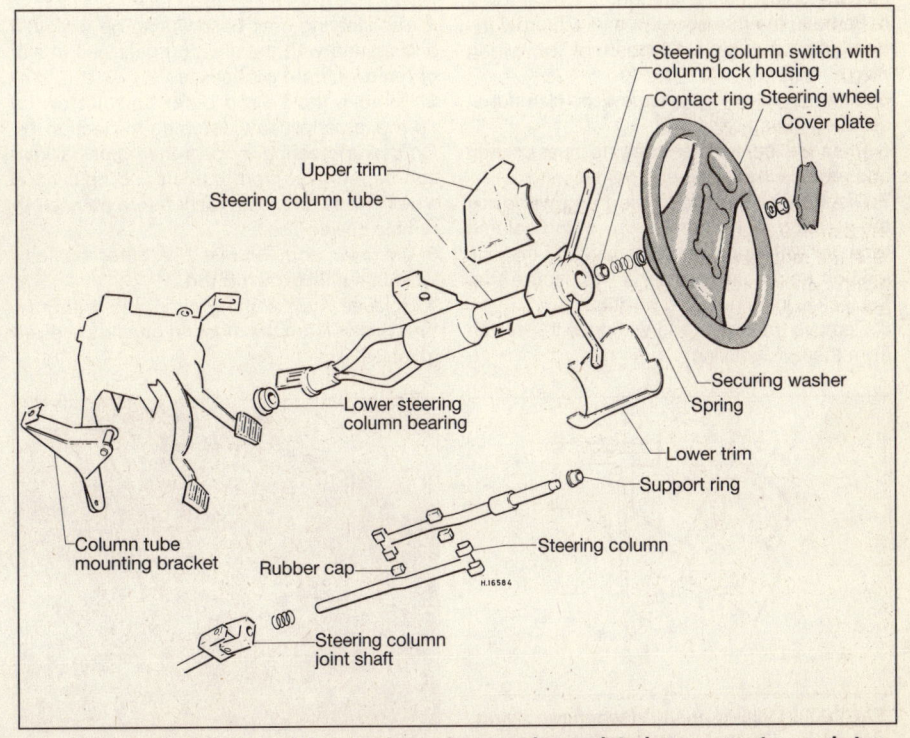

Fig. 10.11 Exploded view of the steering column and associated components – early two section type column (Sec 13)

10•10 Suspension and steering

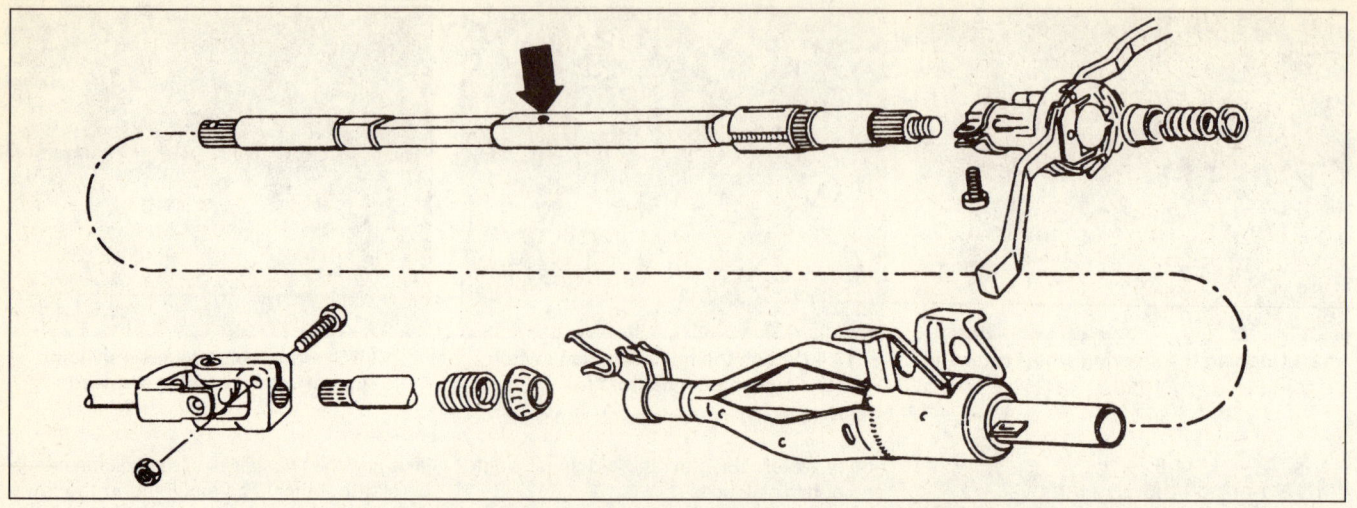

Fig. 10.12 Exploded view of the later steering column type (Sec 13)
Reassembly alignment hole arrowed

19 On completion check that the operation of the steering and various steering column switches and the horn are satisfactory.

14 Steering lock - removal and refitting

1 Disconnect the battery negative lead.
2 Remove the steering wheel, as described in Section 12.
3 Remove the screws and withdraw the steering column lower shroud.
4 Remove the three screws and withdraw the combination switch. Disconnect the wiring plug.
5 Using an Allen key, unscrew the clamp bolt securing the steering lock.
6 Prise the lockwasher from the inner column and remove the spring and contact ring.
7 Disconnect the wiring plug and withdraw the steering lock from the top of the column together with the upper shroud. Note that the ignition key must be inserted to ensure that the lock is in its released position.
8 Remove the screw and withdraw the switch from the lock housing.

9 To remove the lock cylinder, drill a 3.0 mm (0.118 in) diameter hole in the location shown in Fig. 10.13, depress the spring pin, and extract the cylinder.
10 Refitting is a reversal of removal, but renew the inner column lockwasher and press it fully onto the stop while supporting the lower end of the column.

15 Steering gear bellows - renewal

1 The steering gear bellows can be removed and refitted with the steering gear unit *in situ* or removed from the vehicle.
2 Remove the tie-rod outer balljoint or the tie-rod, as applicable, referring to Section 16. On power steering models the outer balljoint can be removed from the left and right-hand side tie-rods and there is therefore no need to remove the tie-rod.
3 Unscrew and remove the outer balljoint locknut nut from the tie-rod.
4 Release the retaining clips and withdraw the bellows from the steering gear and tie-rod (photo).

5 Refit in the reverse order of removal. Smear the inner bore of the bellows with lubricant prior to fitting to ease its assembly. Renew the balljoint locknuts.
6 On completion check the front wheel alignment, as described in Section 23.

16 Tie-rods and balljoints (manual steering) - removal and refitting

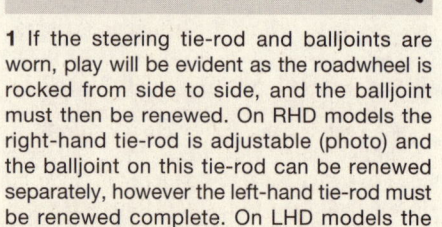

1 If the steering tie-rod and balljoints are worn, play will be evident as the roadwheel is rocked from side to side, and the balljoint must then be renewed. On RHD models the right-hand tie-rod is adjustable (photo) and the balljoint on this tie-rod can be renewed separately, however the left-hand tie-rod must be renewed complete. On LHD models the tie-rods are vice versa.
2 Jack up the front of the car and support on axle stands. Apply the handbrake and remove the front wheel(s).
3 If removing the tie-rod end balljoint, measure the distance of the exposed thread inboard of the locknut. Make a note of the distance then loosen the locknut.

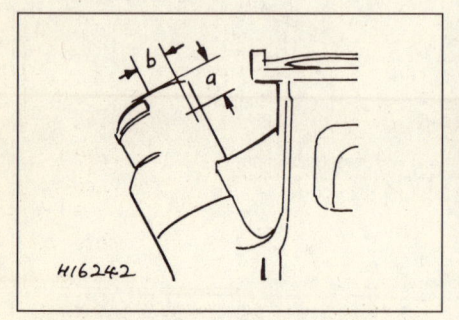

Fig. 10.13 Drilling position when removing steering lock cylinder (Sec 14)
a = 12 mm (0.473 in)   b = 10 mm (0.394 in)

15.4 Steering tie-rod bellows and retaining clip

16.1 Right-hand balljoint (adjustable)

Suspension and steering 10•11

16.4 Balljoint separator tool in position on left-hand balljoint (not adjustable)

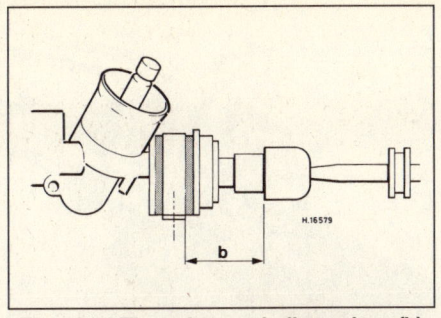

Fig. 10.14 Tie-rod-to-rack dimensions (b) to be as follows (Sec 16)

All models: b = 70.5 mm (2.78 in)

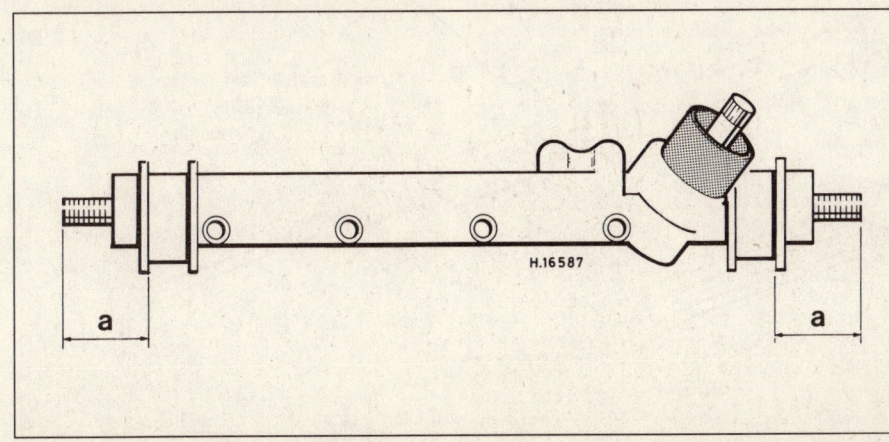

4 Unscrew the balljoint nut on the side concerned then use a balljoint nut separator tool to release the joint from the wheel bearing housing (photo). With the tie-rod outer joint separated from the wheel bearing housing, the outer balljoint can be unscrewed from the tie-rod (where applicable).

5 To remove the tie-rod, release the retaining clips from the steering gear bellows then slide the bellows outwards along the tie-rod to expose the inner balljoint.

6 Loosen the inner joint locknut then unscrew the tie-rod from the steering rack. The steering gear bellows can then be withdrawn from the inboard end of the tie-rod. Renew the bellows if they are damaged or perished.

7 Refitting is a reversal of the removal procedure, but note the following special points.

8 Clean the old locking fluid from the steering rack, and from the old tie-rod if it is being refitted. Smear both threads with a locking solution prior to assembly.

9 Lubricate the inner bore of the gaiter ends before sliding it onto the tie-rod.

10 When reconnecting the tie-rod to the rack, screw it in to give the specified dimension 'b' as shown in Fig. 10.14. Where both tie-rods (left and right) are being refitted to the rack, centralise the rack so that dimension 'a' shown in Fig. 10.15 is equal on each side.

11 Centralise the steering, then set the length of the left-hand tie-rod at a distance 'a' shown in Fig. 10.16, measured between the centre of the outer balljoint and the steering gear stop face on the inboard end of the driveshaft, When the distance is correct, tighten the locknut against the tie-rod end to set it at the specified 'fixed' length, Set the right-hand tie-rod to the original length measured on dismantling, This will provide an approximate initial setting only, On completion, it will be necessary to check the toe-in setting as described in Section 23. If further minor adjustment is required, adjust the right-hand tie-rod to provide the specified front wheel toe-in alignment, Any subsequent adjustments to the track setting must only be made by altering the length of the right-hand tie-rod,

12 Alternatively, screw on the balljoint to give the exposed thread dimension noted during removal, then tighten the locknut. Check that the steering gear-to-inner balljoint distance is as previously specified then lock the inner locknut. Refit the steering gear bellows and ensure that they are not distorted.

13 Reconnect the outer balljoints to the wheel bearing housing and tighten the locknuts to the specified torque wrench settings. Always fit new locknuts if refitting the old balljoints/tie-rod.

14 On completion check the front wheel alignment, as described in Section 23.

17 Tie-rods and balljoints (power steering) - removal and refitting

1 Remove the steering gear unit, together with the tie-rods from the car. This is necessary to avoid damaging the rack and pinion. Refer to Section 20 for removal details.

2 With the steering gear removed, clean it externally, then release the clips and slide the bellows outwards along the tie-rods away from the inner joints.

3 Support the steering gear in a soft jaw vice with the steering rack in the jaws. Do not clamp the rack into a vice not fitted with protective jaws.

4 Each tie-rod and the outer balljoint can be removed in a similar manner to that described for the manual steering gear unit type (see previous Section).

5 Refit the steering tie-rods to the rack, as described in the previous Section, and adjust the fitted lengths as given. Tighten the tie-rods to the specified torque when the settings are correct.

6 Refit the steering gear and tie-rods, as described in Section 20.

7 On completion check the front wheel alignment, as described in Section 23.

18 Steering gear (manual) - adjustment

1 If there is any undue slackness in the steering gear, resulting in noise or rattles, the steering gear should be adjusted as follows, with reference to the photo.

2 Raise and support the car at the front end on axle stands.

3 With the wheels in the straight-ahead position, tighten the self-locking adjustment screw by 20° (approximately).

4 Lower the vehicle to the ground then road test the car. If the steering fails to self-centre after cornering, loosen the adjustment screw a fraction at a time until it does.

5 If, when the correct self-centring point is reached, there is still excessive wear in the

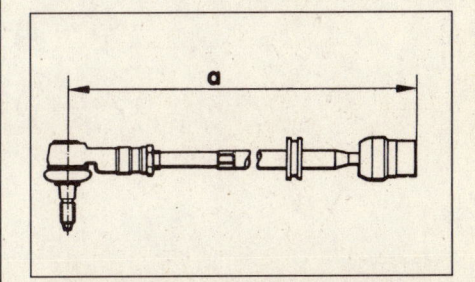

Fig. 10.15 Steering rack is centralised when dimension (a) is equal on each side (Sec 16)

Fig. 10.16 Check that the fixed length of the left-hand driveshaft is as specified between the points indicated (Sec 16)

Distance 'a' must be 410 mm (16.1 in)

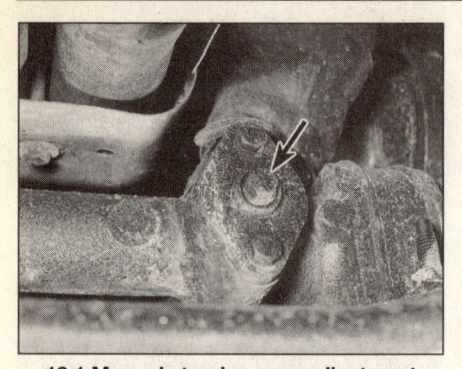

10•12 Suspension and steering

18.1 Manual steering gear adjustment screw (arrowed)

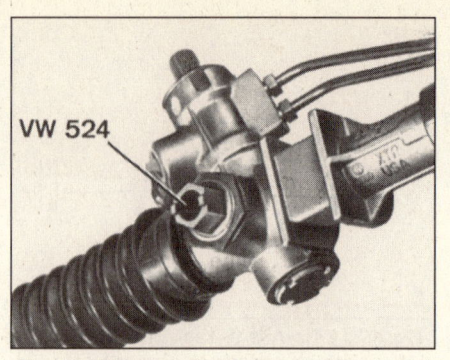

Fig. 10.17 Power steering gear adjustment – use VW special tool if available (Sec 19)

20.6 Steering gear pinion-to-lower column joint

steering, retighten the adjuster nut a fraction to take up the play.

6 If the adjustment procedures listed above do not provide satisfactory steering adjustment it is probable that the steering gear is worn beyond an acceptable level and it must be removed and overhauled.

19 Steering gear (power-assisted) - adjustment

1 Remove the steering gear unit, as described in Section 20.
2 Loosen the adjuster screw locknut then turn the adjustment screw in to the point where the rack can just be moved by hand without binding or sticking (see Fig. 10.17). Retighten the locknut.
3 Refit the steering gear to the car.

20 Steering gear unit - removal and refitting

1 Apply the handbrake, jack up the front of the car, and support it on axle stands. Remove the roadwheels.
2 Disconnect the inner ends of the tie-rods described in Section 16.
3 On power steering models, detach the fluid suction hose at the pump unit end by loosening the hose clip, withdrawing the hose from the pump and draining the fluid into a suitable container.
4 Disconnect the steering tie-rod outer balljoints, with reference to Section 16.
5 Where applicable, disconnect the gearshift securing bracket from the steering gear.
6 Undo and remove the steering gear pinion-to-lower column joint clamp bolt (photo). Prise free the joint shaft bellows and pull the bellows up the shaft for access to the clamp bolt.
7 Undo and remove the steering gear unit retaining clamp nuts and withdraw the clamps. Note that the retaining bolts remain in the subframe. If necessary the bolts can be removed by driving them out downwards using a soft metal drift.
8 On power steering models, disconnect the pressure and return flow fluid hoses at the union connections to the steering gear unit.
9 To enable the steering unit to be withdrawn it may be necessary to detach and withdraw the steering column a sufficient amount to enable the pinion shaft to disengage from the lower column joint; in which case refer to Section 13. Before disengaging the pinion from the lower column joint it is advisable to

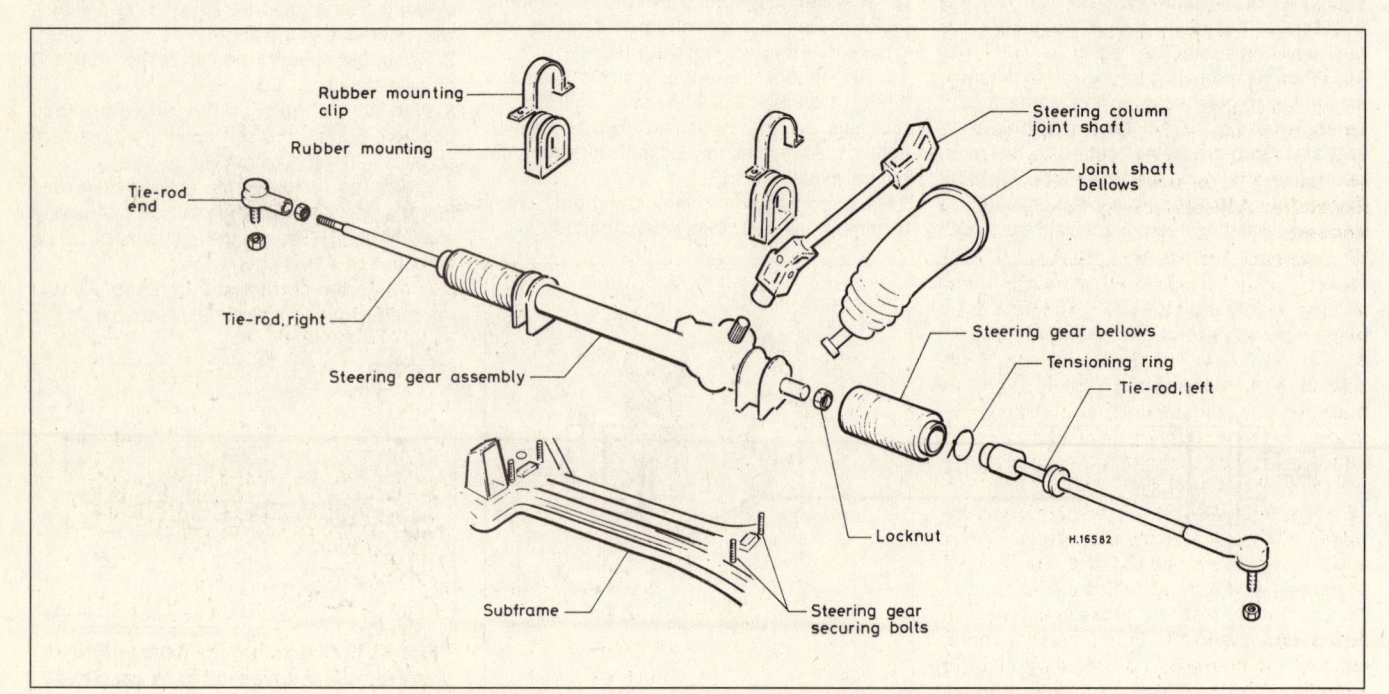

Fig. 10.18 Exploded view of the manual steering gear (Sec 20)

Suspension and steering 10•13

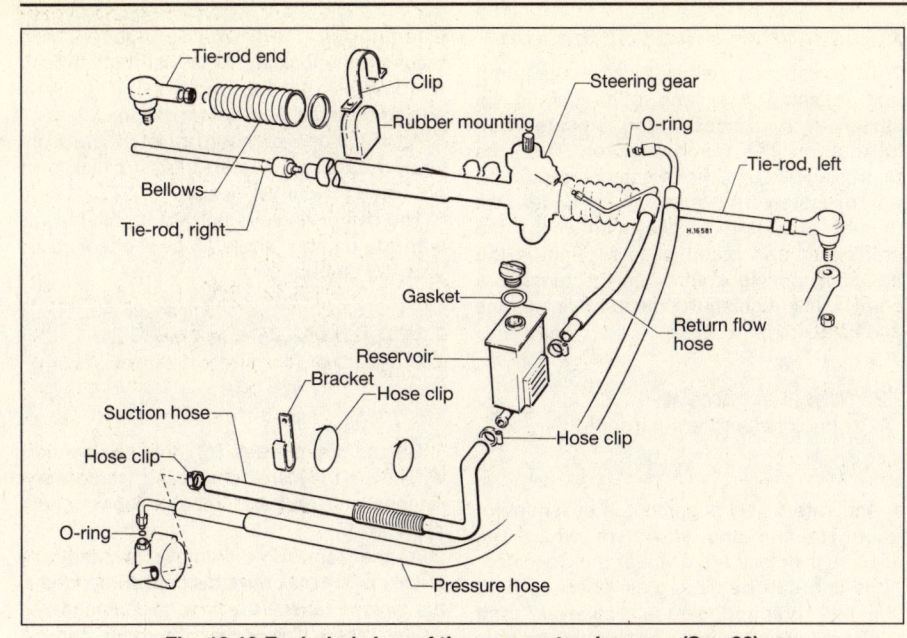

Fig. 10.19 Exploded view of the power steering gear (Sec 20)

Fig. 10.20 Fluid level marks on the power steering fluid reservoir (Sec 21)

make an index mark between the two to ensure correct alignment when refitting.

10 On power steering models support the weight of the engine and gearbox units using a hoist (see Chapter 1) then unscrew and remove the left-hand subframe bolt. Loosen but do not remove the right-hand subframe retaining bolt.

11 On manual steering models withdraw the steering gear unit through the aperture in the left-hand side wheel arch.

12 On power steering models remove the steering gear unit from the left side, guiding it past the partially lowered subframe. Plug the power steering fluid hoses whilst the steering gear is removed to prevent the ingress of dirt.

13 Remove the tie-rods from the steering gear, described in Section 16.

14 Refitting is a reversal of the removal procedure. All self-locking nuts must be renewed.

15 Lubricate the steering gear rack with steering gear grease before refitting the tie-rods. Adjust the tie-rods when fitting them to the rack, as described in Section 16.

16 Establish that the pinion shaft-to-lower column alignment is correctly made to ensure that the correct steering centralisation is made. If a new steering gear unit is being fitted, centralise the rack and the steering column before assembly.

17 Delay tightening all nuts and bolts until the weight of the car is on the suspension. Check and, if necessary, adjust the front wheel alignment, as described in Section 23.

18 On power steering models unplug the hoses and reservoir cap ventilation hole, connect the hoses taking care not to let dirt enter the system. Top up the system fluid, as described in Section 21, and check for any signs of leakage on completion.

21 Power steering fluid - level checks, draining and refitting

1 The power steering fluid level is checked with the roadwheel in the straight-ahead position and the engine running. Check that the fluid level in the reservoir is between the MAX and MIN marks. If necessary, top up the level using only the specified fluid through the reservoir filler neck.

2 If the system is in need of constant topping-up, check for signs of leakage at the pump, reservoir and steering gear unit hose unions and make repairs as necessary.

3 To drain the fluid from the system, detach the fluid suction hose at the pump unit and drain the fluid into a container for disposal. When draining, turn the steering wheel from lock to lock to expel as much fluid as possible.

4 After draining off the fluid, reconnect the suction hose to the pump unit then fill the reservoir to the top with new fluid. Restart the engine and switch off as soon as it fires, repeating the starting and stopping sequence several times; this will cause fluid to be drawn into the system quickly.

5 Watch the level of fluid and keep adding fluid so that the reservoir is never sucked dry. When the fluid ceases to drop as a result of the start/stop sequence, start the engine and allow it to run at idling speed.

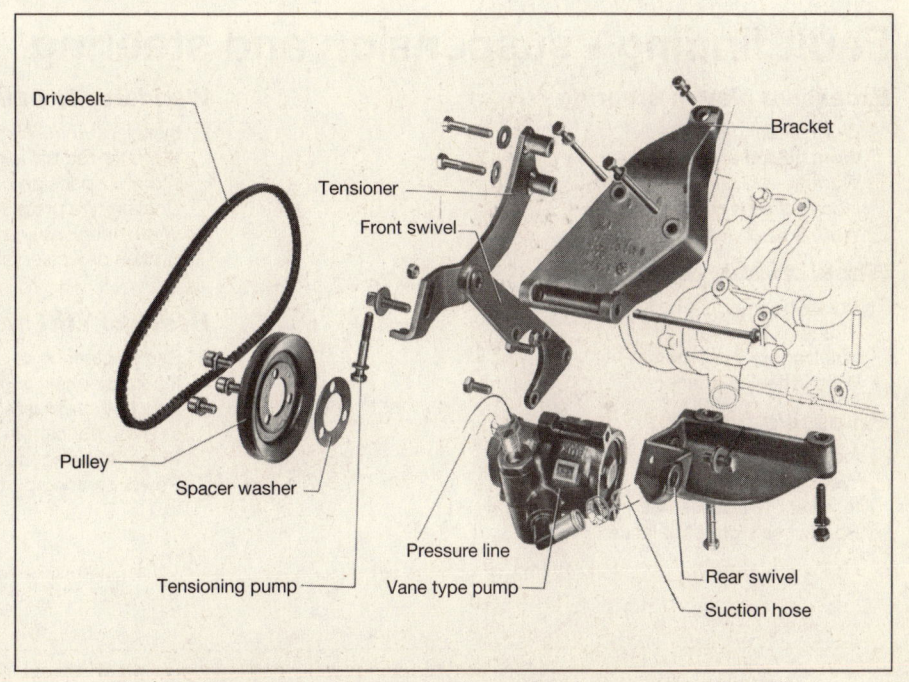

Fig. 10.21 Power steering pump and associated components (Sec 22)

10•14 Suspension and steering

6 Turn the steering from lock to lock several times, being careful not to leave the wheels on full lock because this will cause the pressure in the system to build up.
7 Watch the level of the fluid in the reservoir and add fluid if necessary to keep the level at the MAX mark.
8 When the level stops falling and no more air bubbles appear in the reservoir, switch the engine off and fit the reservoir cap. The level of fluid will rise slightly when the engine is switched off.

22 Power steering pump - removal, refitting and adjustment

1 If the power steering is suspected of malfunction have the supply and system pressure checked by your VW dealer. The pump unit cannot be overhauled or repaired and if defective it must be renewed as a unit.
2 To remove the pump unit, first drain the system fluid, as described in the previous Section.
3 Disconnect the pressure hose from the pump unit.
4 Loosen the pump unit retaining bolts and pivot the pump so that the drivebelt can be disconnected from the pulley.
5 Support the pump, withdraw the retaining bolts and withdraw the pump unit.
6 Refitting is a reversal of removal, but tension the drivebelt as described in paragraph 7 and top up with new fluid and bleed the system as described in the previous Section.

Adjusting the drivebelt tension

7 To adjust the drivebelt tension, the pump unit retaining nuts and bolts should be loosened. Also loosen the adjuster bolt locknut on the pump bracket. Turn the tensioning bolt until the belt can be depressed approximately 10.0 mm (0.4 in) under firm thumb pressure midway between the crankshaft and pump pulleys. Tighten the adjusting bolt locknut when the tension is correct. Also tighten the pump retaining nuts and bolts.

23 Wheel alignment - checking and adjustment

1 Accurate wheel alignment is essential for good steering and slow tyre wear. The alignment details are given in the Specifications and can be accurately checked by a suitably equipped garage. However, front wheel alignment gauges can be obtained from most motor accessory stores, and the method of using one is as follows.
2 Check that the car is only loaded to kerbside weight, with a full fuel tank and the tyres correctly inflated.
3 Position the car on level ground, with the wheels straight-ahead, then roll the car backwards 4 m (12 ft) and forwards again.
4 Using a wheel alignment gauge in accordance with the manufacturer's instructions, check that the front wheel toe dimension is as given in the Specifications. If adjustment is necessary, loosen the balljoint-to-tie-rod locknut on the right-hand side and turn the tie-rod as required, then retighten the locknut. Note that the left-hand tie-rod is set at a specified length (Fig. 10.16) and its setting should not be changed.
5 Although the camber angle of the front wheels can be adjusted this is a task best entrusted to your VW dealer.
6 The castor angle is not adjustable but, as with the camber angle, is best checked by your VW dealer.

24 Roadwheels and tyres - general

1 Clean the insides of the roadwheels whenever they are removed. If necessary, remove any rust and repaint them, where applicable.
2 At the same time, remove any flints or stones which may have become embedded in the tyres. Examine the tyres for damage and splits. Where the depth of tread is almost down to the legal minimum, renew them.
3 The wheels should be rebalanced half way through the life of the tyres to compensate for loss of rubber.
4 Check and adjust the tyre pressures regularly, and make sure that the dust caps are correctly fitted. Do not forget to check the spare tyre.
5 If interchanging steel or alloy roadwheels from other models in the range, it may be necessary to change the retaining bolts. Check with your VW dealer.
6 The use of a temporary (space saver) spare wheel may contravene the law.

Fault finding - suspension and steering

Excessive play in steering
☐ Worn steering gear
☐ Worn tie-rod end balljoints
☐ Worn tie-rod bushes
☐ Incorrect rack adjustment
☐ Worn suspension balljoints

Wheel wobble and vibration
☐ Roadwheels out of balance
☐ Roadwheel damaged
☐ Weak shock absorbers
☐ Worn wheel bearings

Excessive tyre wear
☐ Incorrect wheel alignment
☐ Weak shock absorbers
☐ Incorrect tyre pressures
☐ Roadwheels out of balance

Wanders, or pulls to one side
☐ Incorrect wheel alignment
☐ Worn tie-rod balljoints
☐ Worn suspension balljoints
☐ Uneven tyre pressures
☐ Weak shock absorbers
☐ Broken or weak coil spring

Heavy or stiff steering
☐ Seized steering or suspension balljoint
☐ Incorrect wheel alignment
☐ Low tyre pressures
☐ Leak of lubricant in steering gear
☐ Power steering faulty (where applicable)
☐ Power steering pump drivebelt broken (where applicable)

Chapter 11 Bodywork and fittings

For modifications, and information applicable to later models, see Supplement at end of manual

Contents

Air conditioning system - general	40
Body protective and decorative trim fittings - removal and refitting	30
Bonnet - removal, refitting and adjustment	8
Bonnet lock and release cable - removal and refitting	9
Boot lid - removal, refitting and adjustment	14
Boot lid lock and lock cylinder - removal and refitting	15
Bumpers - removal and refitting	25
Bumper trim covering - removal and renewal	26
Centre console - removal and refitting	32
Door - removal and refitting	19
Door handle (exterior) - removal and refitting	18
Door handle (interior) - removal and refitting	17
Door lock - removal and refitting	21
Door rattles - tracing and rectification	7
Door striker - adjustment	20
Door trim panel - removal and refitting	16
Drivebelt - air conditioning system	41
Exterior mirrors - removal and refitting	27
Facia panel - removal and refitting	33
Front seats - removal and refitting	34
Front wheel housing liner - removal and refitting	28
Front wing - removal and refitting	29
General description	1
Heater and fresh air blower unit - removal and refitting	38
Heater controls - removal and refitting	37
Heat exchanger/fresh air box - removal and refitting	39
Instrument panel - removal and refitting	33
Maintenance - bodywork and underframe	2
Maintenance - hinges and locks	6
Maintenance - upholstery and carpets	3
Major body damage - repair	5
Minor body damage - repair	4
Radiator grille - removal and refitting	10
Rear seat - removal and refitting	35
Seat belts- maintenance	36
Sunroof - removal, refitting and adjustment	31
Tailgate - removal and refitting	12
Tailgate lock, grip and lock cylinder - removal, refitting and adjustment	13
Tailgate support strut - removal and refitting	11
Window regulator (electric) - removal and refitting	23
Window regulator (manual) - removal and refitting	22
Windows - removal and refitting	24

Degrees of difficulty

Easy, suitable for novice with little experience	Fairly easy, suitable for beginner with some experience	Fairly difficult, suitable for competent DIY mechanic	Difficult, suitable for experienced DIY mechanic	Very difficult, suitable for expert DIY or professional

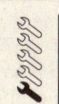

Specifications

Torque wrench settings

	Nm	lbf ft
Front bumper bracket bolts	82	61
Rear bumper bracket bolts	70	52
Tailgate spider nut	6	4
Front seat cap nut	1.5	1.1
Seat belt anchor bolts	40	30

1 General description

The body is of all-steel unit construction with impact-absorbing front and rear crumple zones which take the brunt of any accident, leaving the passenger compartment with minimum distortion. The front crumple zones take the form of two corrugated box sections in the scuttle and firewall.

The Golf is available in two or four-door hatchback versions, and all models have a large tailgate which is propped open with a steel rod or a gas-filled telescopic strut.

The Jetta is only available as a four-door 'notchback' incorporating a conventional boot and lid.

On all models the front wings are bolted to the body and can easily be renewed in the event of damage.

2 Maintenance - bodywork and underframe

The general condition of a vehicle's bodywork is the one thing that significantly affects its value. Maintenance is easy, but needs to be regular. Neglect, particularly after minor damage, can lead quickly to further deterioration and costly repair bills. It is important also to keep watch on those parts of the vehicle not immediately visible, for instance the underside, inside all the wheel arches, and the lower part of the engine compartment.

The basic maintenance routine for the bodywork is washing - preferably with a lot of water, from a hose. This will remove all the loose solids which may have stuck to the vehicle. It is important to flush these off in such a way as to prevent grit from scratching the finish. The wheel arches and underframe need washing in the same way, to remove any accumulated mud, which will retain moisture and tend to encourage rust. Paradoxically enough, the best time to clean the underframe and wheel arches is in wet weather, when the

11•2 Bodywork and fittings

mud is thoroughly wet and soft. In very wet weather, the underframe is usually cleaned of large accumulations automatically, and this is a good time for inspection.

Periodically, except on vehicles with a wax-based underbody protective coating, it is a good idea to have the whole of the underframe of the vehicle steam-cleaned, engine compartment included, so that a thorough inspection can be carried out to see what minor repairs and renovations are necessary. Steam-cleaning is available at many garages, and is necessary for the removal of the accumulation of oily grime, which sometimes is allowed to become thick in certain areas. If steam-cleaning facilities are not available, there are some excellent grease solvents available which can be brush-applied; the dirt can then be simply hosed off. Note that these methods should not be used on vehicles with wax-based underbody protective coating, or the coating will be removed. Such vehicles should be inspected annually, preferably just prior to Winter, when the underbody should be washed down, and any damage to the wax coating repaired. Ideally, a completely fresh coat should be applied. It would also be worth considering the use of such wax-based protection for injection into door panels, sills, box sections, etc, as an additional safeguard against rust damage, where such protection is not provided by the vehicle manufacturer.

After washing paintwork, wipe off with a chamois leather to give an unspotted clear finish. A coat of clear protective wax polish will give added protection against chemical pollutants in the air. If the paintwork sheen has dulled or oxidised, use a cleaner/polisher combination to restore the brilliance of the shine. This requires a little effort, but such dulling is usually caused because regular washing has been neglected. Care needs to be taken with metallic paintwork, as special non-abrasive cleaner/polisher is required to avoid damage to the finish. Always check that the door and ventilator opening drain holes and pipes are completely clear, so that water can be drained out. Brightwork should be treated in the same way as paintwork. Windscreens and windows can be kept clear of the smeary film which often appears, by the use of proprietary glass cleaner. Never use any form of wax or other body or chromium polish on glass.

3 Maintenance - upholstery and carpets

Mats and carpets should be brushed or vacuum-cleaned regularly, to keep them free of grit. If they are badly stained, remove them from the vehicle for scrubbing or sponging, and make quite sure they are dry before refitting. Seats and interior trim panels can be kept clean by wiping with a damp cloth. If they do become stained (which can be more apparent on light-coloured upholstery), use a little liquid detergent and a soft nail brush to scour the grime out of the grain of the material. Do not forget to keep the headlining clean in the same way as the upholstery. When using liquid cleaners inside the vehicle, do not over-wet the surfaces being cleaned. Excessive damp could get into the seams and padded interior, causing stains, offensive odours or even rot.

> **HAYNES HiNT** *If the inside of the vehicle gets wet accidentally, it is worthwhile taking some trouble to dry it out properly, particularly where carpets are involved. Do not leave oil or electric heaters inside the vehicle for this purpose.*

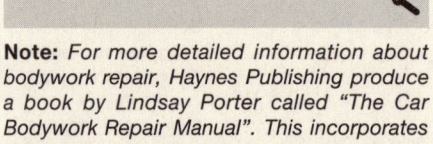

4 Minor body damage - repair

Note: *For more detailed information about bodywork repair, Haynes Publishing produce a book by Lindsay Porter called "The Car Bodywork Repair Manual". This incorporates information on such aspects as rust treatment, painting and glass-fibre repairs, as well as details on more ambitious repairs involving welding and panel beating.*

Repairs of minor scratches in bodywork

If the scratch is very superficial, and does not penetrate to the metal of the bodywork, repair is very simple. Lightly rub the area of the scratch with a paintwork renovator, or a very fine cutting paste, to remove loose paint from the scratch, and to clear the surrounding bodywork of wax polish. Rinse the area with clean water.

Apply touch-up paint to the scratch using a fine paint brush; continue to apply fine layers of paint until the surface of the paint in the scratch is level with the surrounding paintwork. Allow the new paint at least two weeks to harden, then blend it into the surrounding paintwork by rubbing the scratch area with a paintwork renovator or a very fine cutting paste. Finally, apply wax polish.

Where the scratch has penetrated right through to the metal of the bodywork, causing the metal to rust, a different repair technique is required. Remove any loose rust from the bottom of the scratch with a penknife, then apply rust-inhibiting paint to prevent the formation of rust in the future. Using a rubber or nylon applicator, fill the scratch with bodystopper paste. If required, this paste can be mixed with cellulose thinners to provide a very thin paste which is ideal for filling narrow scratches. Before the stopper-paste in the scratch hardens, wrap a piece of smooth cotton rag around the top of a finger. Dip the finger in cellulose thinners, and quickly sweep it across the surface of the stopper-paste in the scratch; this will ensure that the surface of the stopper-paste is slightly hollowed. The scratch can now be painted over as described earlier in this Section.

Repairs of dents in bodywork

When deep denting of the vehicle's bodywork has taken place, the first task is to pull the dent out, until the affected bodywork almost attains its original shape. There is little point in trying to restore the original shape completely, as the metal in the damaged area will have stretched on impact, and cannot be reshaped fully to its original contour. It is better to bring the level of the dent up to a point which is about 3 mm below the level of the surrounding bodywork. In cases where the dent is very shallow anyway, it is not worth trying to pull it out at all. If the underside of the dent is accessible, it can be hammered out gently from behind, using a mallet with a wooden or plastic head. Whilst doing this, hold a suitable block of wood firmly against the outside of the panel, to absorb the impact from the hammer blows and thus prevent a large area of the bodywork from being "belled-out".

Should the dent be in a section of the bodywork which has a double skin, or some other factor making it inaccessible from behind, a different technique is called for. Drill several small holes through the metal inside the area - particularly in the deeper section. Then screw long self-tapping screws into the holes, just sufficiently for them to gain a good purchase in the metal. Now the dent can be pulled out by pulling on the protruding heads of the screws with a pair of pliers.

The next stage of the repair is the removal of the paint from the damaged area, and from an inch or so of the surrounding "sound" bodywork. This is accomplished most easily by using a wire brush or abrasive pad on a power drill, although it can be done just as effectively by hand, using sheets of abrasive paper. To complete the preparation for filling, score the surface of the bare metal with a screwdriver or the tang of a file, or alternatively, drill small holes in the affected area. This will provide a really good "key" for the filler paste.

To complete the repair, see the Section on filling and respraying.

Repairs of rust holes or gashes in bodywork

Remove all paint from the affected area, and from an inch or so of the surrounding "sound" bodywork, using an abrasive pad or a wire brush on a power drill. If these are not available, a few sheets of abrasive paper will do the job most effectively. With the paint removed, you will be able to judge the severity of the corrosion, and therefore decide whether to renew the whole panel (if this is possible) or to repair the affected area. New body panels are not as expensive as most people think, and it is often quicker and more satisfactory to fit a new panel than to attempt to repair large areas of corrosion.

Remove all fittings from the affected area, except those which will act as a guide to the original shape of the damaged bodywork (eg headlight shells etc). Then, using tin snips or a hacksaw blade, remove all loose metal and any other metal badly affected by corrosion. Hammer the edges of the hole inwards, in order to create a slight depression for the filler paste.

Wire-brush the affected area to remove the powdery rust from the surface of the remaining metal. Paint the affected area with rust-inhibiting paint, if the back of the rusted area is accessible, treat this also.

Before filling can take place, it will be necessary to block the hole in some way. This can be achieved by the use of aluminium or plastic mesh, or aluminium tape.

Aluminium or plastic mesh, or glass-fibre matting, is probably the best material to use for a large hole. Cut a piece to the approximate size and shape of the hole to be filled, then position it in the hole so that its edges are below the level of the surrounding bodywork. It can be retained in position by several blobs of filler paste around its periphery.

Aluminium tape should be used for small or very narrow holes. Pull a piece off the roll, trim it to the approximate size and shape required, then pull off the backing paper (if used) and stick the tape over the hole; it can be overlapped if the thickness of one piece is insufficient. Burnish down the edges of the tape with the handle of a screwdriver or similar, to ensure that the tape is securely attached to the metal underneath.

Bodywork repairs - filling and respraying

Before using this Section, see the Sections on dent, deep scratch, rust holes and gash repairs.

Many types of bodyfiller are available, but generally speaking, those proprietary kits which contain a tin of filler paste and a tube of resin hardener are best for this type of repair. A wide, flexible plastic or nylon applicator will be found invaluable for imparting a smooth and well-contoured finish to the surface of the filler.

Mix up a little filler on a clean piece of card or board - measure the hardener carefully (follow the maker's instructions on the pack), otherwise the filler will set too rapidly or too slowly. Using the applicator, apply the filler paste to the prepared area; draw the applicator across the surface of the filler to achieve the correct contour and to level the surface. As soon as a contour that approximates to the correct one is achieved, stop working the paste - if you carry on too long, the paste will become sticky and begin to "pick-up" on the applicator. Continue to add thin layers of filler paste at 20-minute intervals, until the level of the filler is just proud of the surrounding bodywork.

Once the filler has hardened, the excess can be removed using a metal plane or file. From then on, progressively-finer grades of abrasive paper should be used, starting with a 40-grade production paper, and finishing with a 400-grade wet-and-dry paper. Always wrap the abrasive paper around a flat rubber, cork, or wooden block - otherwise the surface of the filler will not be completely flat. During the smoothing of the filler surface, the wet-and-dry paper should be periodically rinsed in water. This will ensure that a very smooth finish is imparted to the filler at the final stage.

At this stage, the "dent" should be surrounded by a ring of bare metal, which in turn should be encircled by the finely "feathered" edge of the good paintwork. Rinse the repair area with clean water, until all of the dust produced by the rubbing-down operation has gone.

Spray the whole area with a light coat of primer - this will show up any imperfections in the surface of the filler. Repair these imperfections with fresh filler paste or bodystopper, and once more smooth the surface with abrasive paper. Repeat this spray-and-repair procedure until you are satisfied that the surface of the filler, and the feathered edge of the paintwork, are perfect. Clean the repair area with clean water, and allow to dry fully.

> **HAYNES HINT** *If bodystopper is used, it can be mixed with cellulose thinners to form a really thin paste which is ideal for filling small holes.*

The repair area is now ready for final spraying. Paint spraying must be carried out in a warm, dry, windless and dust-free atmosphere. This condition can be created artificially if you have access to a large indoor working area, but if you are forced to work in the open, you will have to pick your day very carefully. If you are working indoors, dousing the floor in the work area with water will help to settle the dust which would otherwise be in the atmosphere. If the repair area is confined to one body panel, mask off the surrounding panels; this will help to minimise the effects of a slight mis-match in paint colours. Bodywork fittings (eg chrome strips, door handles etc) will also need to be masked off. Use genuine masking tape, and several thicknesses of newspaper, for the masking operations.

Before commencing to spray, agitate the aerosol can thoroughly, then spray a test area (an old tin, or similar) until the technique is mastered. Cover the repair area with a thick coat of primer; the thickness should be built up using several thin layers of paint, rather than one thick one. Using 400-grade wet-and-dry paper, rub down the surface of the primer until it is really smooth. While doing this, the work area should be thoroughly doused with water, and the wet-and-dry paper periodically rinsed in water. Allow to dry before spraying on more paint.

Spray on the top coat, again building up the thickness by using several thin layers of paint. Start spraying at one edge of the repair area, and then, using a side-to-side motion, work until the whole repair area and about 2 inches of the surrounding original paintwork is covered. Remove all masking material 10 to 15 minutes after spraying on the final coat of paint.

Allow the new paint at least two weeks to harden, then, using a paintwork renovator, or a very fine cutting paste, blend the edges of the paint into the existing paintwork. Finally, apply wax polish.

Plastic components

With the use of more and more plastic body components by the vehicle manufacturers (eg bumpers, spoilers, and in some cases major body panels), rectification of more serious damage to such items has become a matter of either entrusting repair work to a specialist in this field, or renewing complete components. Repair of such damage by the DIY owner is not really feasible, owing to the cost of the equipment and materials required for effecting such repairs. The basic technique involves making a groove along the line of the crack in the plastic, using a rotary burr in a power drill. The damaged part is then welded back together, using a hot-air gun to heat up and fuse a plastic filler rod into the groove. Any excess plastic is then removed, and the area rubbed down to a smooth finish. It is important that a filler rod of the correct plastic is used, as body components can be made of a variety of different types (eg polycarbonate, ABS, polypropylene).

Damage of a less serious nature (abrasions, minor cracks etc) can be repaired by the DIY owner using a two-part epoxy filler repair material. Once mixed in equal proportions, this is used in similar fashion to the bodywork filler used on metal panels. The filler is usually cured in twenty to thirty minutes, ready for sanding and painting.

If the owner is renewing a complete component himself, or if he has repaired it with epoxy filler, he will be left with the problem of finding a suitable paint for finishing which is compatible with the type of plastic used. At one time, the use of a universal paint was not possible, owing to the complex range of plastics encountered in body component applications. Standard paints, generally speaking, will not bond to plastic or rubber satisfactorily. However, it is now possible to obtain a plastic body parts finishing kit which consists of a pre-primer treatment, a primer and coloured top coat. Full instructions are normally supplied with a kit, but basically, the method of use is to first

11•4 Bodywork and fittings

8.2 Bonnet hinge

8.3 Disconnecting the windscreen washer tubes from the bonnet

8.5 Bonnet rubber buffer

apply the pre-primer to the component concerned, and allow it to dry for up to 30 minutes. Then the primer is applied, and left to dry for about an hour before finally applying the special-coloured top coat. The result is a correctly-coloured component, where the paint will flex with the plastic or rubber, a property that standard paint does not normally possess.

5 Major body damage - repair

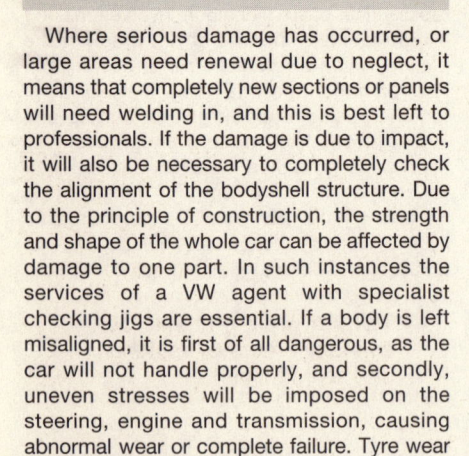

Where serious damage has occurred, or large areas need renewal due to neglect, it means that completely new sections or panels will need welding in, and this is best left to professionals. If the damage is due to impact, it will also be necessary to completely check the alignment of the bodyshell structure. Due to the principle of construction, the strength and shape of the whole car can be affected by damage to one part. In such instances the services of a VW agent with specialist checking jigs are essential. If a body is left misaligned, it is first of all dangerous, as the car will not handle properly, and secondly, uneven stresses will be imposed on the steering, engine and transmission, causing abnormal wear or complete failure. Tyre wear may also be excessive.

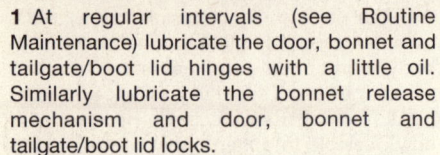

6 Maintenance - hinges and locks

1 At regular intervals (see Routine Maintenance) lubricate the door, bonnet and tailgate/boot lid hinges with a little oil. Similarly lubricate the bonnet release mechanism and door, bonnet and tailgate/boot lid locks.
2 At the same time lubricate the door check straps with a little multi-purpose grease.
3 Do not attempt to lubricate the steering lock.

7 Door rattles - tracing and rectification

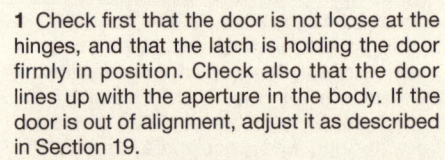

1 Check first that the door is not loose at the hinges, and that the latch is holding the door firmly in position. Check also that the door lines up with the aperture in the body. If the door is out of alignment, adjust it as described in Section 19.
2 If the latch is holding the door in the correct position, but the latch still rattles, the lock mechanism is worn and should be renewed.
3 Other rattles from the door could be caused by wear in the window operating mechanism, interior lock mechanism, or loose glass channels.

8 Bonnet - removal, refitting and adjustment

1 Support the bonnet in its open position, and place some cardboard or rags beneath the corners by the hinges.
2 Mark the location of the hinges with a pencil then loosen the four retaining bolts (photo).
3 Where applicable, disconnect the windscreen washer tubes from the jets on the bonnet (photo).
4 With the help of an assistant, release the stay, remove the bolts, and withdraw the bonnet from the car.

5 Refitting is a reversal of removal, but adjust the hinges to their original positions and check that the bonnet is level with the surrounding bodywork. If necessary adjust the height of the bonnet front edge by screwing the rubber buffers in or out (photo).
6 Check that the bonnet lock operates in a satisfactory manner.

9 Bonnet lock and release cable - removal and refitting

1 The bonnet lock is not adjustable for position and is secured to the front cross panel by four pop-rivets (photo). To remove the lock, disconnect the lock release cable, as described below, then carefully drill down through the rivets and withdraw the lock.
2 Refit the lock reversing the removal procedure. Ensure that the new pop-rivets secure the lock firmly.
3 To remove the bonnet lock release cable, raise and support the bonnet. See paragraph 8 if the cable has broken. Remove the radiator grille (Section 10).
4 Reaching through the aperture in the front, press the release to one side and disconnect the cable from it (photo). Release the cable from the retaining clip on the underside of the front panel.
5 Unclip the cable from the retainers in the engine compartment.
6 Detach the cable from the release handle

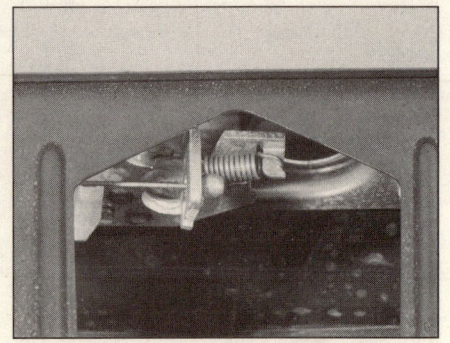

9.1 Bonnet lock and securing rivets

9.4 Bonnet release cable-to-lock attachment

Bodywork and fittings 11•5

10.2 Undoing the front grille retaining screws

10.3 Front grille securing clips

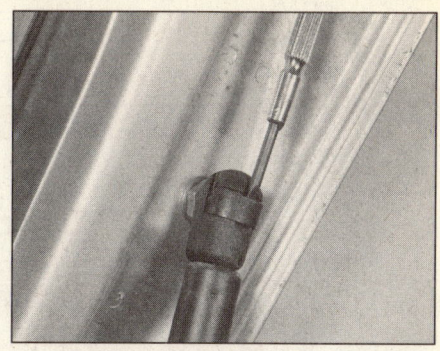

11.2 Releasing the tailgate strut balljoint clip

inside the vehicle and pull the cable through the bulkhead grommet and remove it.
7 Refit in the reverse order to removal. Pull the release lever to operate and check the satisfactory operation of the catch before closing the bonnet.
8 If the cable should break with the bonnet shut it is possible to release the catch by hand. A largish screwdriver will just reach the lock release when inserted through the grille centre badge, and by pushing the screwdriver, or carefully using the badge as a pivot, the bonnet can be unlocked.

10 Radiator grille - removal and refitting

1 Raise and support the bonnet.
2 Undo and remove the two grille retaining screws on the top front edge (photo).
3 Release the clips from the top of the grille (photo). Withdraw the grille lifting it upwards from the front valance.
4 Refit in the reverse order of removal.

11 Tailgate support strut - removal and refitting

1 Open and support the tailgate.
2 Unhook the spring clip from the end of the strut attached to the body, pull up the ball-head and disconnect the strut from the ball-pin (photo).
3 Lever the spring clip from the other end of the strut, remove the washer, and withdraw the strut from the pivot pin.
4 Refit in the reverse order of removal.

12 Tailgate - removal and refitting

1 Open and support the tailgate. Disconnect the straps supporting the rear shelf.
2 Remove the trim panel using a wide-bladed screwdriver, and disconnect the wiring from the heated rear window and wiper motor. Disconnect the washer tube and pull the wiring and tube from the tailgate.
3 Pull the weatherseal from the body aperture by the hinge positions.
4 Carefully pull the headlining down to reveal the hinge bolts.
5 Lever the spring clips from the struts, remove the washers, and disconnect the struts from the tailgate.
6 Unscrew the hinge bolts and withdraw the tailgate from the car.
7 Refitting is a reversal of removal, but before tightening the hinge bolts make sure that the tailgate closes centrally within the body aperture. If necessary adjust the lock as described in Section 13.

13 Tailgate lock, grip and lock cylinder - removal, refitting and adjustment

1 Open the tailgate and, using an Allen key, unscrew the two lock retaining screws. Withdraw the lock (photo).

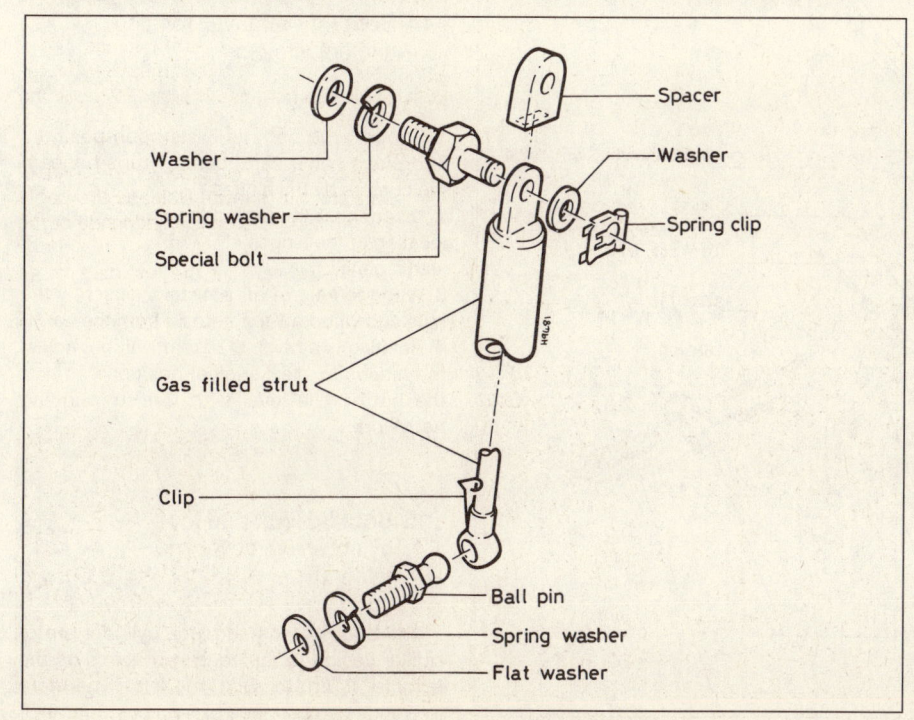

Fig. 11.1 Tailgate support strut end fittings (Sec 11)

13.1 Tailgate lock

11•6 Bodywork and fittings

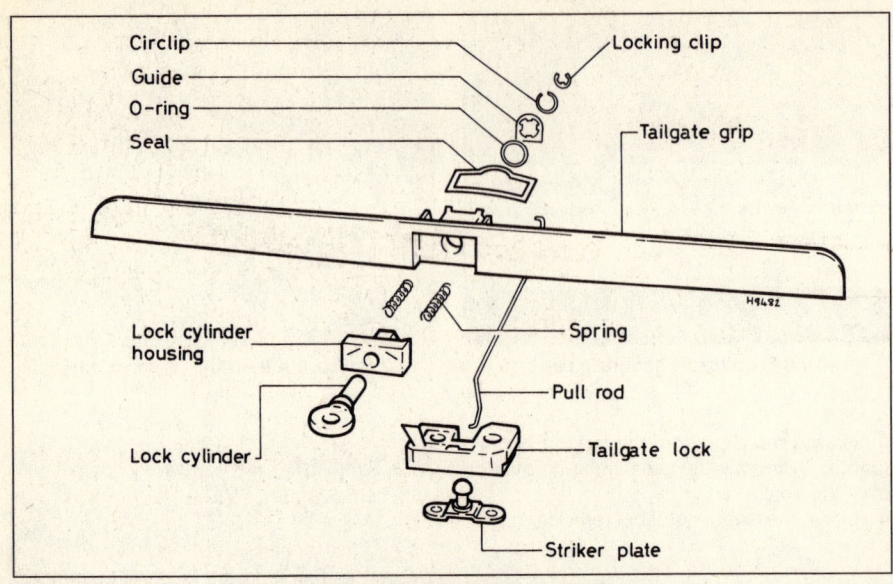

Fig. 11.2 Tailgate lock components (Sec 13)

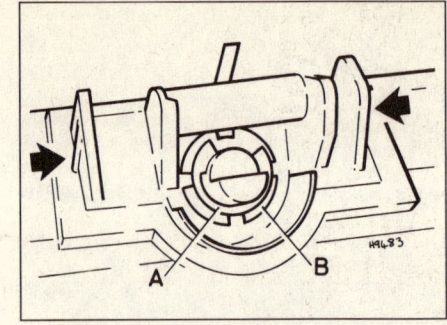

Fig. 11.3 Tailgate grip/lock cylinder retaining clip (A) and securing ring (B). Compress lugs (arrowed) in direction indicated (Sec 13)

2 The striker plate can be removed by undoing the two retaining screws.
3 To remove the tailgate grip and lock cylinder, undo the cross-head screws on the outside, then compress the retaining lug each side of the
lock cylinder together (on the inside) and pull free the grip.
4 Fit the key to the lock cylinder, prise free the retaining clip and withdraw the lock cylinder by pulling on the key.
5 To remove the cylinder housing, prise free the retaining ring and withdraw the housing from the grip.
6 Refitting is a reversal of removal, but before fully tightening the striker, close and open the tailgate two or three times to centralise it.

14 Boot lid - removal, refitting and adjustment

1 Support the boot lid in its open position, and place some cardboard or rags beneath the corners by the hinges.
2 Disconnect the wiring loom and mark the location of the hinges
with a pencil.
3 With the help of an assistant, unscrew the nuts and withdraw the boot lid from the car.
4 Refitting is a reversal of removal, but adjust the hinges to their original positions so that the boot lid is level with the surrounding bodywork

15 Boot lid lock and lock cylinder - removal and refitting

The boot lid lock and lock cylinder are of similar design to the equivalent items on the tailgate fitted to Golf models. Therefore reference can be made to Section 13 for their removal and refitting details.

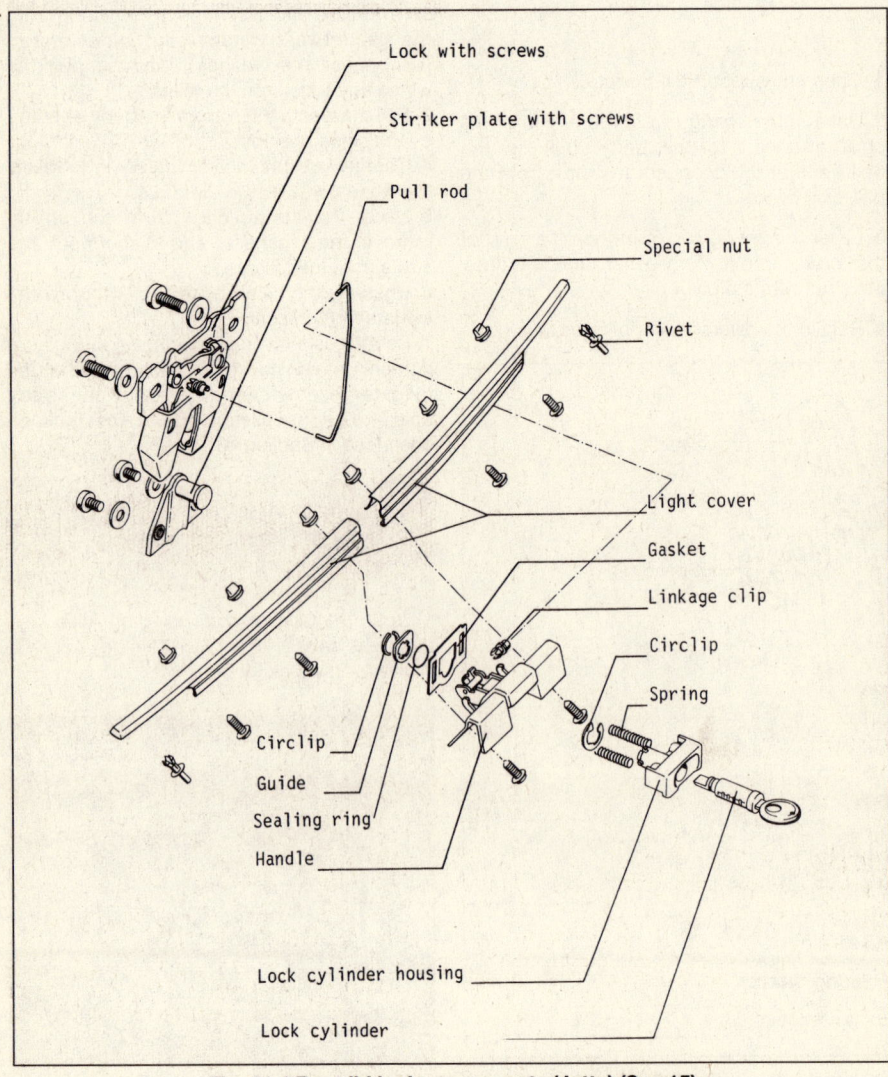

Fig. 11.4 Boot lid lock components (Jetta) (Sec 15)

Bodywork and fittings 11•7

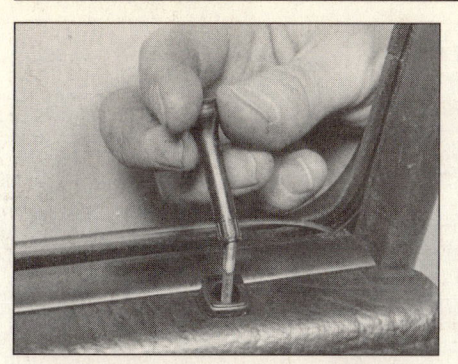

16.1 Unscrew the door locking knob

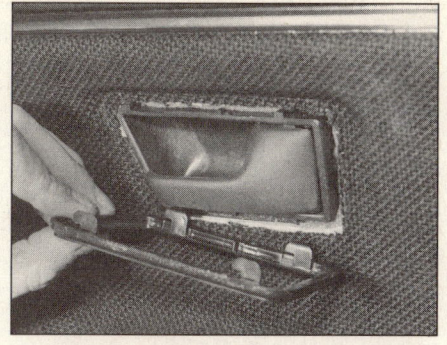

16.2 Removing the door inner handle surround

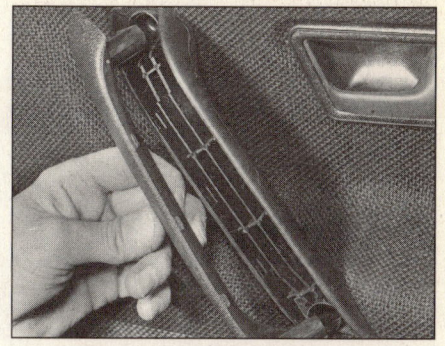

16.3A Remove the door pull cover

16 Door trim panel - removal and refitting

1 Unscrew and remove the locking knob (photo).
2 Remove the inner handle surround by sliding it to the rear (photo).
3 Prise the cover from the door pull with a small screwdriver, remove the cross-head screws, and withdraw the door pull (photos).
4 Note the position of the window regulator handle with the window shut then prise off the cover, remove the cross-head screw and withdraw the handle and washer (photos).
5 Where applicable, prise free the door mirror adjuster knob and remove the gaiter (photo).
6 Remove the self-tapping screws and withdraw the storage compartment panel (where applicable).
7 Prise out the stoppers and remove the cross-head screws from the trim panel (photos).
8 Using a wide-bladed screwdriver, prise the trim panel clips from the door, taking care not to damage the panel. Remove the panel.
9 Remove the window regulator handle packing (where applicable).
10 Carefully prise free the plastic cover for access to the inner door components (photo).
11 Refitting is a reversal of removal. However, it is recommended that the window regulator handle retaining screw is locked by coating its threads with a liquid locking agent.

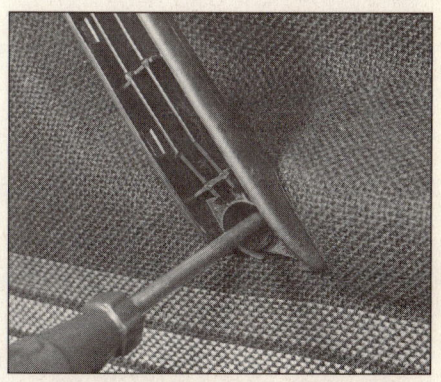

16.3B Remove the door pull retaining screws

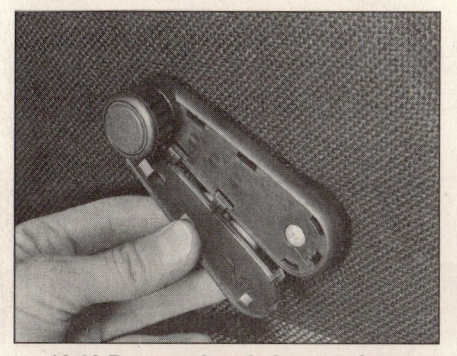

16.4A Remove the window regulator handle cover . . .

16.4B . . . and remove the handle retaining screw

16.5 Removing the door mirror adjuster knob

16.7A Remove stoppers (where necessary) for access to trim panel screws

16.7B Trim panel retaining screw removal (rear edge)

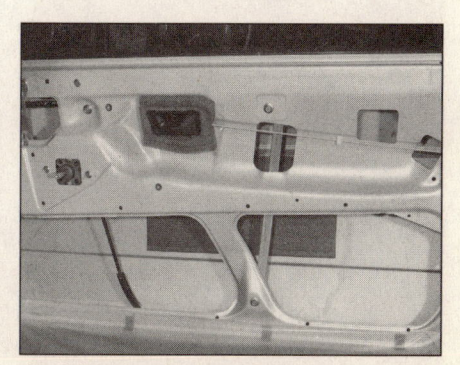

16.10 Plastic cover peeled back for access to door components

11•8 Bodywork and fittings

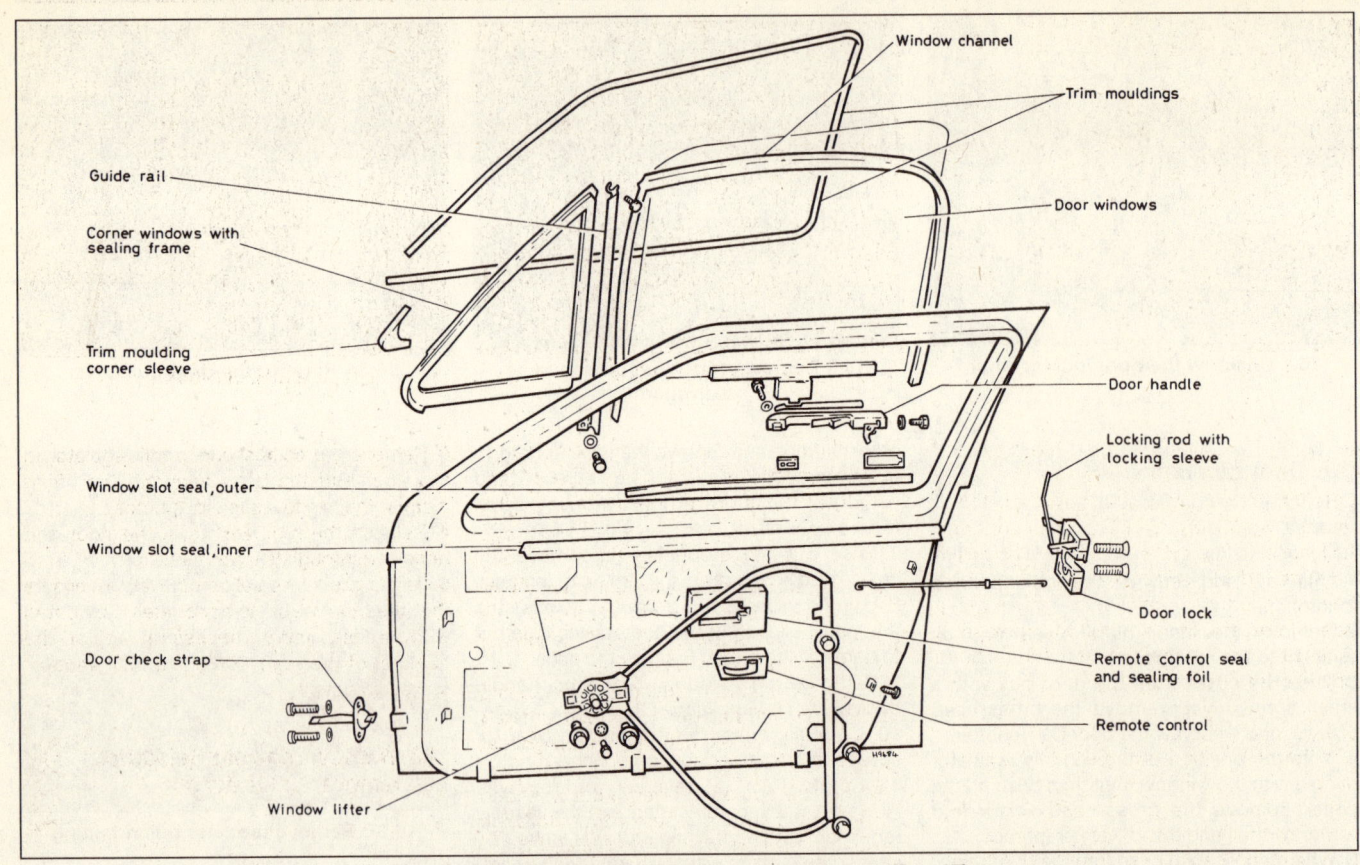

Fig. 11.5 Exploded view of the door components (Sec 17)

17 Door handle (interior) - removal and refitting

1 Remove the trim panel, as described in Section 16.
2 Pull the foam seal away then prise the retainer from the bottom of the handle.
3 Press the fingerplate forwards out of the door and unhook it from the rod (photo).
4 Refitting is a reversal of removal.

18 Door handle (exterior) - removal and refitting

1 Remove the trim panel as described in Section 16.
2 Using a small screwdriver, lever the plastic strip from the exterior door handle.
3 Remove the cross-head screws from the handle grip and the end of the door.
4 Withdraw the handle and release it from the lock (photo). Remove the gaskets.
5 Refitting is a reversal of removal, but fit new gaskets if necessary.

19 Door - removal and refitting

1 Open the door and use a punch to drive the pivot pin up from the check strap (photo).
2 Mark the position of the door on the hinges.
3 Support the door then unscrew and remove the lower hinge bolt followed by the upper

17.3 Removing the interior door handle and finger plate

18.4 View of exterior door handle from inside the door

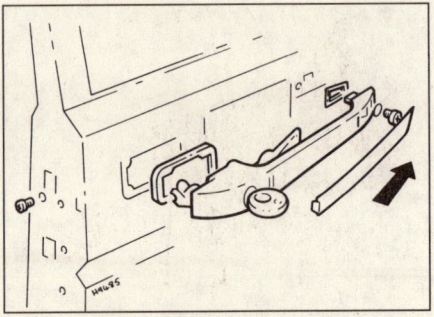

Fig. 11.6 Exterior door handle components. Remove handle in direction of arrow (Sec 18)

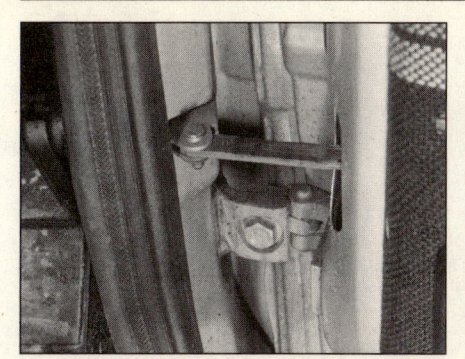

Bodywork and fittings 11•9

19.1 Door check strap and hinge

19.4 Door striker

21.2 Door lock

hinge bolt, and withdraw the door from the car.
4 Refitting is a reversal of removal, but if necessary adjust the position of the door on the hinges so that, when closed, it is level with the surrounding bodywork and central within the body aperture. Lubricate the hinges with a little oil and the check strap with grease. If necessary adjust the door striker position (photo) - see Section 20.

20 Door striker - adjustment

1 Mark round the door striker with a pencil, or a fine ballpoint pen.
2 Fit a spanner to the hexagon on the striker and unscrew the striker about one turn so that the striker moves when tapped with a soft-headed hammer.
3 Tap the striker towards the inside of the car if the door rattles, or towards the outside of the car if the door fits too tightly, but be careful to keep the striker in the same horizontal line, unless it also requires vertical adjustment. Only move the striker a small amount at a time; the actual amount moved can be checked by reference to the pencil marks made before the striker was loosened.
4 When a position has been found in which the door closes firmly, but without difficulty, tighten the striker.

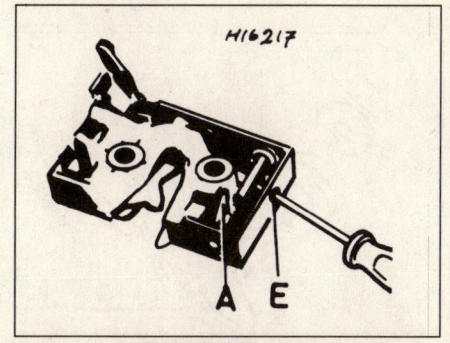

21 Door lock - removal and refitting

1 It is not necessary to remove the trim panel. First open the door and set the lock in the locked position either by moving the interior knob or by turning the exterior key.
2 Using an Allen key, unscrew the retaining screws and withdraw the lock approximately 12 mm (0.5 in) to expose the operating lever (photo).
3 Retain the operating lever in the extended position by inserting a screwdriver through the hole in the bottom of the lock (Fig. 11.7).
4 Unhook the remote control rod from the operating lever and pull the upper lever from the sleeve. Withdraw the lock from the door.
5 Refitting is a reversal of removal, but remember to set the lock in the locked position first, and make sure that the lugs on the plastic sleeve are correctly seated.

22 Window regulator (manual) - removal and refitting

1 Remove the trim panel, as described in Section 16.
2 Temporarily refit the window regulator handle and lower the window until the lifting plate is visible.
3 Remove the bolts securing the regulator to the door and the bolts securing the lifting plate to the window channel (photos).
4 Release the regulator from the door and remove it through the aperture.
5 Refitting is a reversal of removal, but ensure that the inner cable is adequately lubricated with grease and if necessary adjust the position of the regulator so that the window moves smoothly.

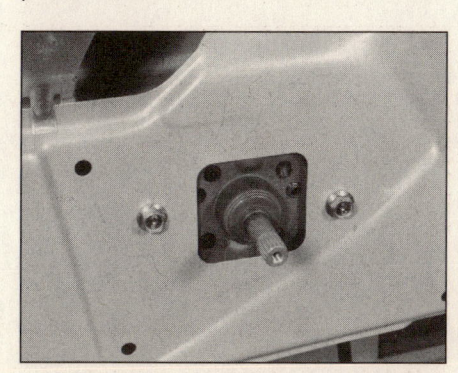

23 Window regulator (electric) - removal and refitting

1 Disconnect the battery earth lead.
2 Remove the door trim panel, as described in Section 16.
3 Lower the window to enable the bolts securing the lifting plate to the window channel to be unscrewed.
4 Disconnect the wiring connector.
5 Unscrew and remove the window regulator motor securing bolts and the three bolts securing the guide rail (Fig. 11.8).
6 Withdraw the window regulator assembly, ie the motor, cables and guide rails, from the aperture at the bottom end of the door.
7 Refit in the reverse order of removal. Ensure that the upper cable is located underneath the guide rail securing bracket and, when refitting the door trim panel, the plastic cover is crease free.

Fig. 11.7 Using a screwdriver through the door lock hole (E) to retain the operating lever (A) in the extended position (Sec 21)

22.3A Window regulator securing bolts

22.3B Lifting plate-to-window channel bolts

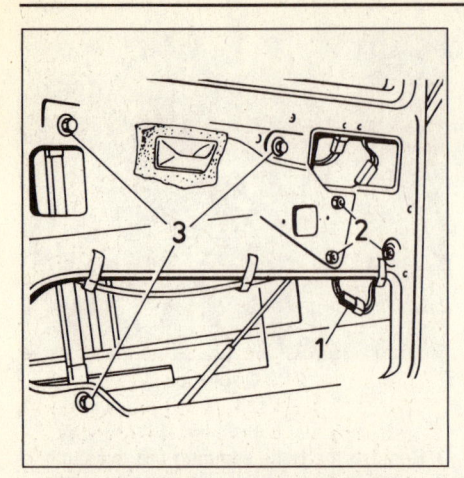

11•10 Bodywork and fittings

Fig. 11.8 Window regulator (electric) (Sec 23)

1 Wiring connector
2 Motor securing bolts
3 Guide rail bolts

24 Windows - removal and refitting

Door windows

1 Remove the window regulator, as described in Section 22 or 23.
2 With the window fully lowered, unclip the inner and outer mouldings from the window aperture.
3 Remove the bolt and screw and pull out the front window channel abutting the corner window.
4 Withdraw the corner window and seal.
5 Lift the glass from the door.
6 Refitting is a reversal of removal. If the glass is being renewed, make sure that the lift channel is located in the same position as in the old glass.

Windscreen and fixed glass

7 Removal and refitting of the windscreen and fixed glass windows is best left to a VW garage or windscreen specialist who will have the necessary equipment and expertise to complete the work properly.

25 Bumpers - removal and refitting

Front bumper

Warning: Under no circumstances should the vehicle be driven with the front bumper and bumper brackets not securely fitted, as in this condition the front crossmember which supports the engine is no longer properly secured.

1 Working inside the engine compartment, first disconnect the battery negative lead, then disconnect the wiring to the direction indicator lights.
2 Raise the front of the car, and support securely on axle stands. Place a jack (with interposed block of wood) under the engine front mounting, and raise the jack head until it is just taking the weight of the engine.
3 Working underneath the front end of the car, undo and remove the bumper brackets from the longitudinal member on each side then withdraw the bumper (photo).
4 Refitting is a reversal of removal Check that the indicators operate in a satisfactory manner on completion.

Rear bumper

5 Raise and support the car securely at the rear.
6 Working underneath the rear end of the car undo and remove the two bumper support bracket retaining bolts on each side (photo).
7 Withdraw the bumper by pulling it rearwards and disengaging it from the guide on each side quarter panel (Fig. 11.9).
8 Refitting is a reversal of removal.

26 Bumper trim covering - removal and renewal

1 Remove the bumper concerned, as described in the previous Section.
2 Use a suitable lever to carefully prise free the old covering from the bumper.
3 To fit the new covering, locate the covering on the bumper then support the covering and bumper with the covering underneath (bumper inverted). Use a firmly padded support if possible to protect the new covering.
4 Press or tap the bumper down onto the covering so that the securing clips engage in the bumper. Start from the centre and work progressively outwards, alternating from side to side.
5 Refit the bumper on completion.

27 Exterior mirrors - removal and refitting

Non remote control type

1 Prise the plastic cover from inside the door.
2 Unscrew the cross-head screws and remove the clips.
3 Withdraw the outer cover and mirror.
4 Refitting is a reversal of removal.

Remote control type

5 Pull off the adjusting knob and bellows from the inside of the door.
6 Remove the door trim panel, as described in Section 16.
7 Unscrew the locknut and remove the adjusting knob from the bracket.
8 Prise off the plastic cover then unscrew the cross-head screws and remove the clips.
9 Withdraw the mirror, together with the adjusting knob and gasket.
10 Refitting is a reversal of removal, but fit a new gasket if necessary.

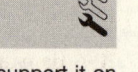

28 Front wheel housing liner - removal and refitting

1 Raise the front of the car and support it on axle stands.
2 Remove the roadwheel from the side concerned.
3 Remove the two cross-head screws from the positions indicated in Fig. 11.11.

25.3 Front bumper bracket securing points to longitudinal member (arrowed)

25.6 Rear bumper bracket bolts (arrowed)

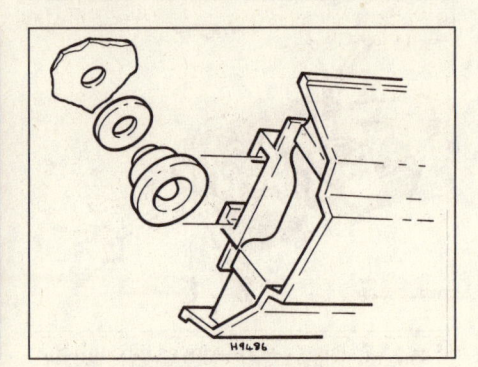

Fig. 11.9 Bumper side quarter panel location guide (Sec 25)

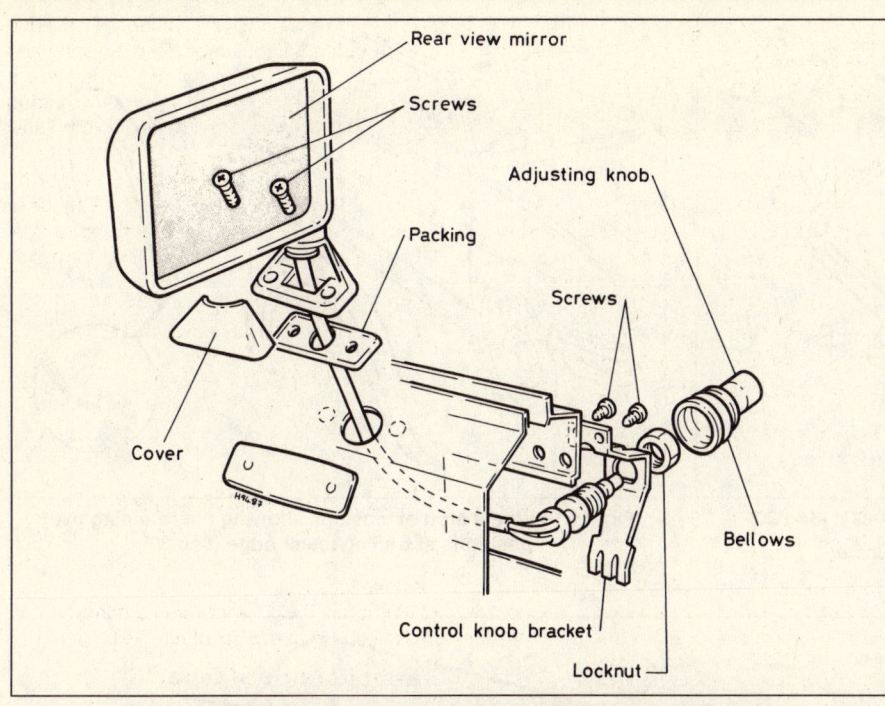

Bodywork and fittings 11•11

Fig. 11.10 Exploded view of remote control exterior mirror (Sec 27)

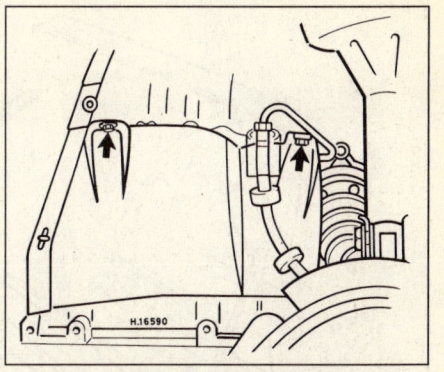

Fig. 11.11 Remove wheel housing liner retaining screws (arrowed) (Sec 28)

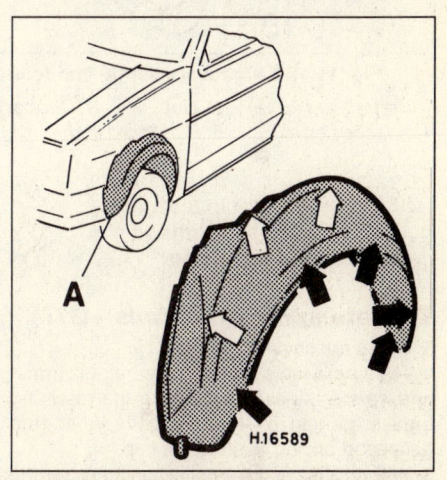

Fig. 11.12 Wheel housing liner securing screw locations – arrowed (Sec 28)

4 Swivel the liner 90° downwards and pull it free from the elongated hole.
5 Undo and remove the cross-head screws (with washers) from the points indicated in Fig. 11.12 then withdraw the liner after disengaging its location peg A from the leading lower edge.
6 Renew any retaining screw location rivets which are damaged.
7 Refit in the reverse order of removal.

necessary warm the sealing joints with a blowlamp to melt the adhesive underseal, *but be sure to take the necessary fire precautions.*
5 Clean the mating faces and treat with rust inhibitor if necessary.
6 Apply sealant along the line of the screws before fitting the wing. Once in place, apply underseal as necessary. Paint the wing then fit the liner and front bumper.

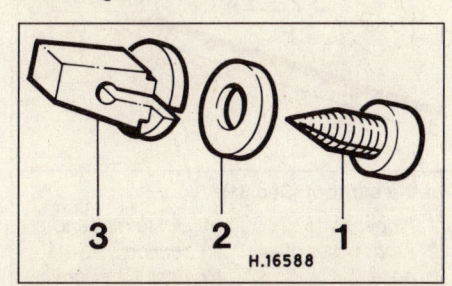

29 Front wing - removal and refitting

1 A damaged front wing may be renewed complete. First remove the front bumper, as described in Section 25.
2 Remove the screws and withdraw the liner from inside the wing (see previous Section).
3 Where applicable disconnect/remove the wing-mounted radio aerial.
4 Remove all the screws and lever the wing from the guides. If

Fig. 11.13 Wheel housing liner securing screw (1), washer (2) and special rivet (3) (Sec 28)

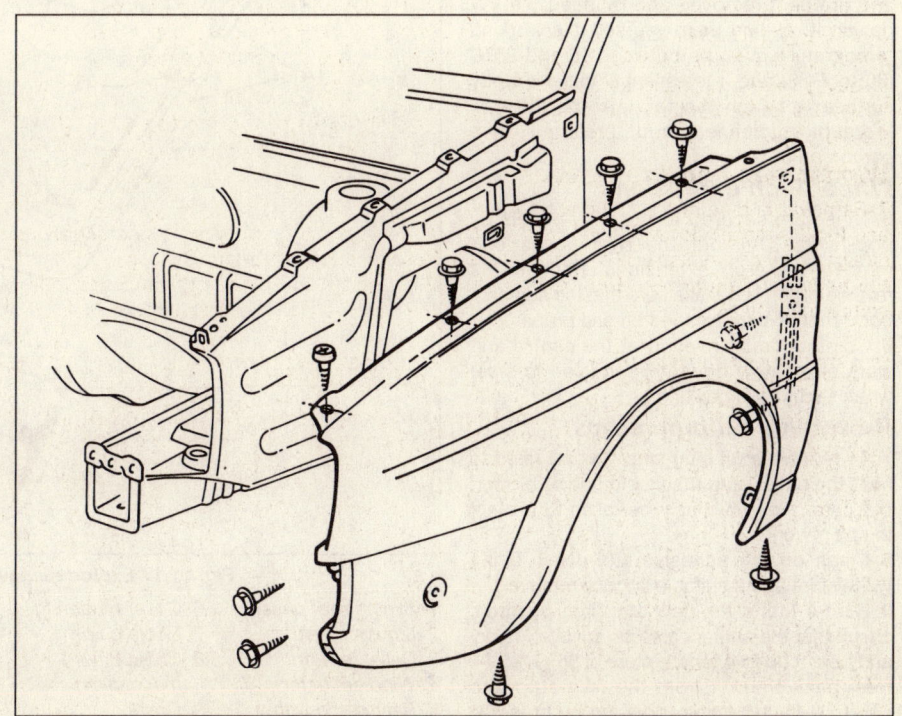

Fig. 11.14 Front wing retaining screw positions – Jetta (Sec 29)

11•12 Bodywork and fittings

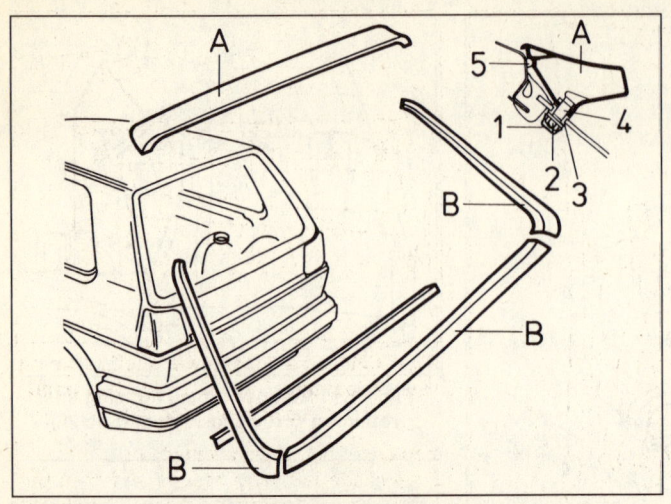

Fig. 11.15 Tailgate spoiler (A) and foils (B) – GTI (Sec 30)

1 Protective cap
2 Nut
3 Rubber grommet
4 Spacer sleeve
5 Butyl cord (5 mm dia.)

Fig. 11.16 Wheel arch extensions showing the retaining rivet positions at trailing lower edge (Sec 30)

30 Body protective and decorative trim fittings - removal and refitting

Tailgate spoiler and foils - GTI

1 These are shown in Fig. 11.15.
2 The spoiler is secured by a nut, grommet and spacer sleeve. Access to the retaining nuts is gained by removing the inner trim panel and prising free the nut cap.
3 When refitting the spoiler, ensure that the body surface is clean.
4 The foils are stuck in position with adhesive and are best removed and refitted by a VW dealer. If refitting them yourself, the working temperature must be between 15 and 25°C (60 to 77°F) and it is essential that the body surface to which the foil is to be fitted is thoroughly cleaned and prepared (see paragraph 8).

Wheel arch extensions

5 These are secured to the wing panels by pop-rivets. Drill out the rivet heads and remove the arch extensions. Refit in the reverse order, but make sure that the adjacent body sections are cleaned off and prepared.
6 Commence by riveting at the centre and work alternately down from it (side to side) when securing in position.

Protective rubbing strips

7 To remove a rubbing strip you will need to heat the strip using a suitable hot air blower, but care must obviously be taken to protect the paintwork.
8 Clean off the adhesive and polish using white spirit and a suitable silicone remover.
9 Before fitting the new strip into position, check that the contact area on the body is dry and heat it up to a temperature of 35°C (95°F). Peel back the foil from the new strip and carefully locate it into position by pressing firmly home, particularly at each end.

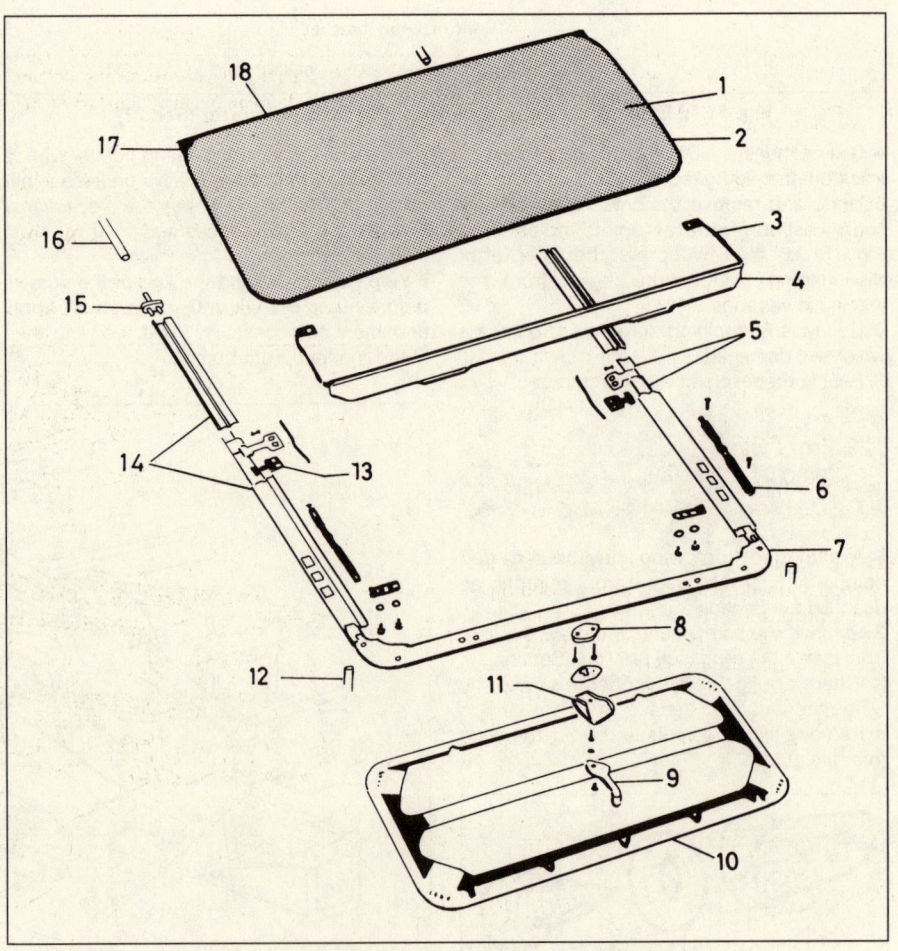

Fig. 11.17 Exploded view of the sunroof (Sec 31)

1 Sliding roof panel
2 Moulded seal
3 Deflector arm
4 Wind deflector
5 Rear guide with cable (one part)
6 Cover moulding
7 Cable guide
8 Cable drive mechanism
9 Crank
10 Panel headlining
11 Finger plate
12 Front water drain hose
13 Support plate
14 Guide rail
15 Guide rails end section
16 Rear water drain hose
17 Water trap plate
18 Panel seat

Bodywork and fittings 11•13

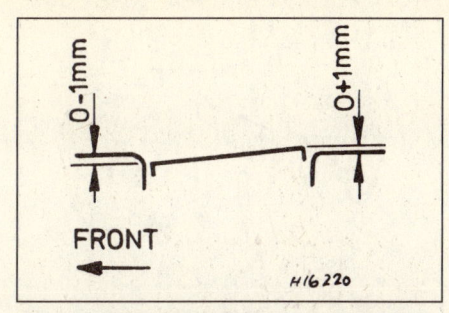

Fig. 11.18 Sunroof adjustment dimensions (Sec 31)

31 Sunroof - removal, refitting and adjustment

1 Half open the sunroof then prise off the five steel trim clips.
2 Close the sunroof and push the trim to the rear.
3 Unscrew the guide screws from the front of the sunroof and remove the guides.
4 Disengage the leaf springs from the rear guides by pulling them inwards.
5 Remove the screws and withdraw the rear support plates.
6 Lift the sunroof from the car.
7 To refit the sunroof, locate it in the aperture and fit the front guides.
8 With the sunroof closed and correctly aligned, fit the rear guides and leaf springs.
9 The correct adjustment of the sunroof is shown in Fig. 11.18 - the front edge must be level with or a maximum of 1.0 mm (0.040 in) below the roof panel, and the rear edge must be level with or a maximum of 1.0 mm (0.040 in) above the roof panel.
10 To adjust the front edge of the sunroof, loosen the front guide screws and turn the adjustment screws as necessary, then tighten the guide screws.
11 To adjust the rear edge, detach the leaf springs, loosen the slotted screws and move the sunroof as necessary in the serrations. Tighten the screws and refit the leaf springs after making the adjustment.
12 Refit the trim with the clips.

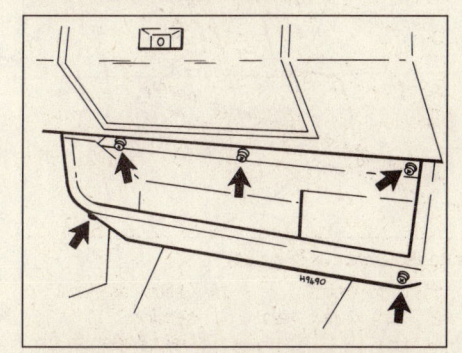

Fig. 11.21 Facia panel lower shelf retaining screw locations – passenger side (left-hand drive shown) (Sec 33)

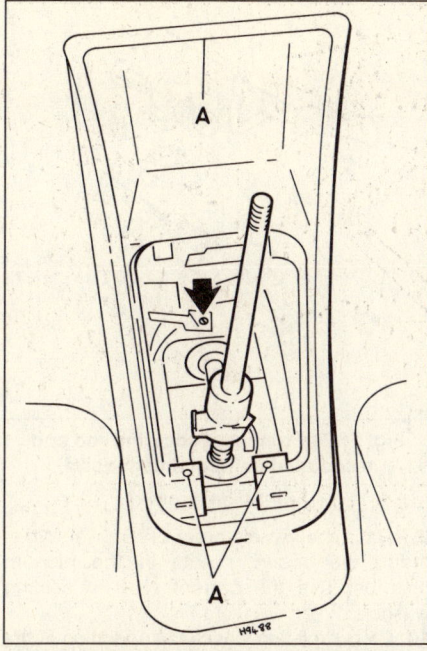

Fig. 11.19 Centre console retaining screw (arrowed) and guide locations (A) (Sec 32)

32 Centre console - removal and refitting

1 Disconnect the battery earth lead.
2 Unscrew and remove the gear lever knob then unclip and withdraw the boot.
3 Undo the retaining screws and then pull free the console from its guides at the rear. Disconnect any console switch lead connectors (Fig. 11.19).
4 Refit in the reverse order of removal. Check operation of the console switches (where fitted) on completion.

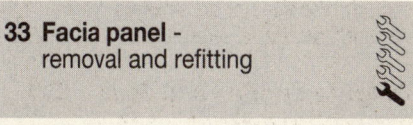

33 Facia panel - removal and refitting

1 Remove the steering wheel, as described in Chapter 10.
2 Undo the retaining screws and withdraw the undertray on the driver and passenger sides (see Figs. 11.20 and 11.21).

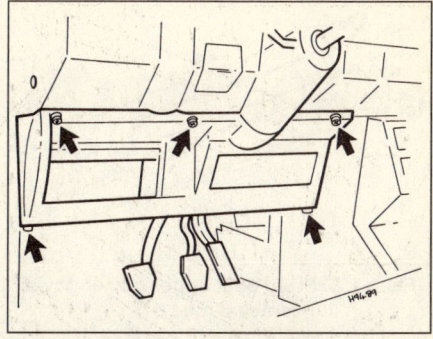

Fig. 11.20 Facia panel lower shelf retaining screw locations – driver's side (left-hand drive shown) (Sec 33)

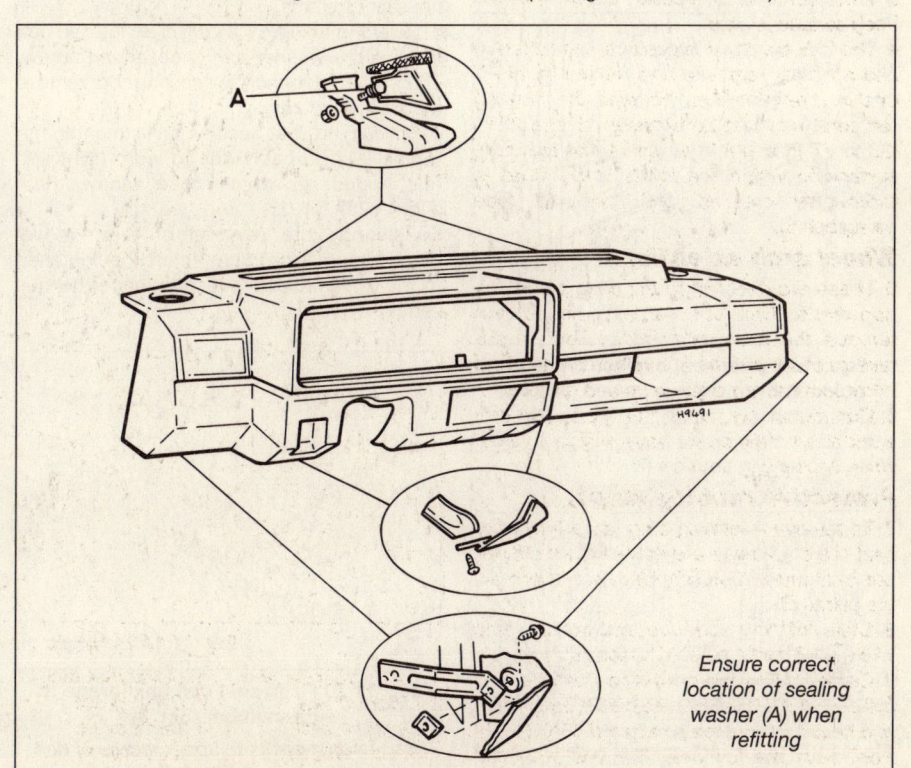

Ensure correct location of sealing washer (A) when refitting

Fig. 11.22 Facia panel securing points (left-hand drive shown) (Sec 33)

11•14 Bodywork and fittings

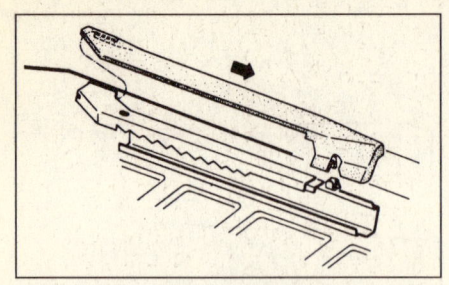

Fig. 11.23 Front seat upper runner cover removal (Sec 34)

Unclip cover and remove in direction arrowed

3 Remove the centre console, as described in the previous Section.
4 Pull free the heater/fresh air control knobs then carefully unclip the control panel trim and detach the electrical connectors.
5 Referring to Chapter 9, remove the radio/cassette unit or cubby hole, the instrument panel cluster, and the loudspeaker and grille.
6 Remove the air vent pivot grilles by carefully levering them free, then undo the screws securing the air vent housing and lever out the housing.
7 Referring to Fig. 11.22, undo and remove the facia panel retaining screws from the points indicated. To remove the nuts/bolts at the front, access is from the plenum chamber in the engine compartment.
8 Check that the facia panel is fully disconnected then carefully withdraw it from the car.

Fig. 11.26 Rear seat cushion pressure points for removal – arrowed (Sec 35)

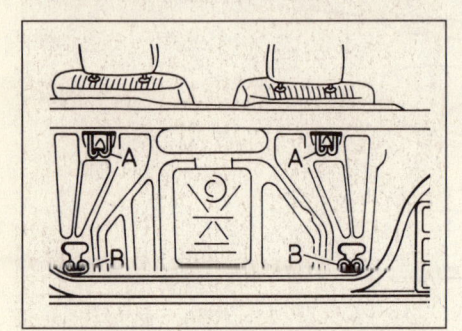

Fig. 11.27 Rear seat backrest retaining hook locations in luggage compartment – A and B (Jetta and Golf convertible) (Sec 35)

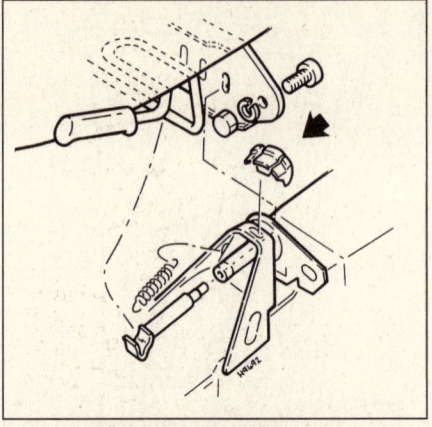

Fig. 11.24 Front seat securing rod and associated components (Sec 34)

Front slide arrowed

9 Refit in the reverse order of removal. When fitting the securing nuts in the plenum chamber use the correct type of sealing washers.
10 On completion, check the operation of the various instruments, switches and controls.

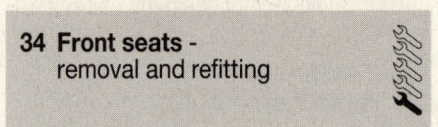

34 Front seats - removal and refitting

1 Prise free the lower runner cover and clip towards the rear of the seat.
2 Pull the cover from the runner and then pull the seat forwards.
3 Referring to Fig. 11.24 unscrew the cap nut, remove the washer and cheesehead screw. Then, after releasing the securing rod, remove the seat rearwards.
4 Difficulty in seat position adjustment longitudinally is probably due to worn front and rear slides, in which case renew them (Fig. 11.25).
5 Refitting is a reversal of the removal procedure, but the cap nut must be tightened to the manufacturer's recommended torque setting.

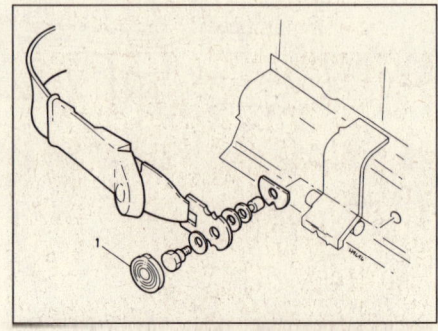

Fig. 11.28 Front seat belt anchorage to side-member (Sec 36)

Spring end (1) points to upper recess of belt link and is then tensioned 270° and hooked onto link pin

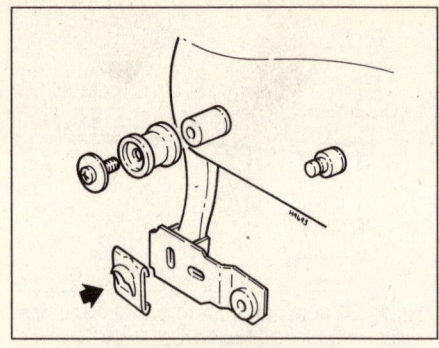

Fig. 11.25 Front seat rear slide (arrowed) – renew if worn (Sec 34)

35 Rear seat - removal and refitting

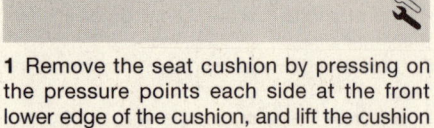

1 Remove the seat cushion by pressing on the pressure points each side at the front lower edge of the cushion, and lift the cushion out (Fig. 11.26).
2 On the luggage compartment side, release the backrest retaining hooks whilst an assistant pushes the backrest downwards (Fig. 11.27).
3 Refitting is a reversal of the removal procedure, but ensure that the backrest retaining hooks fully engage.

36 Seat belts - maintenance

1 Periodically check the belts for fraying or other damage. If evident, renew the belt.
2 If the belts become dirty, wipe them with a damp cloth using a little liquid detergent only.
3 Check the tightness of the anchor bolts and if they are ever disconnected, make quite sure that the original sequence of fitting of washers, bushes, and anchor plate is retained - See Figs. 11.28 to 11.33 inclusive.
4 Never modify the belt or alter its attachment point to the body.

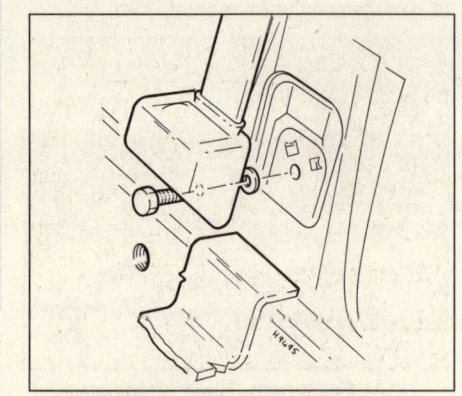

Fig. 11.29 Front seat belt anchorage to B pillar – lower (Sec 36)

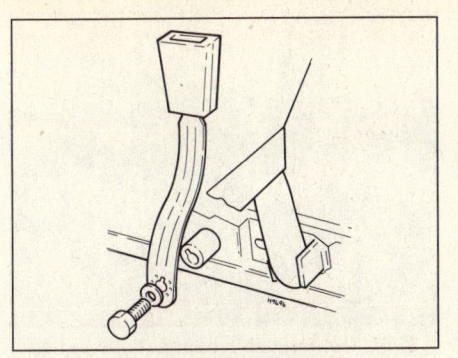

Fig. 11.30 Front seat frame anchorage (Sec 36)

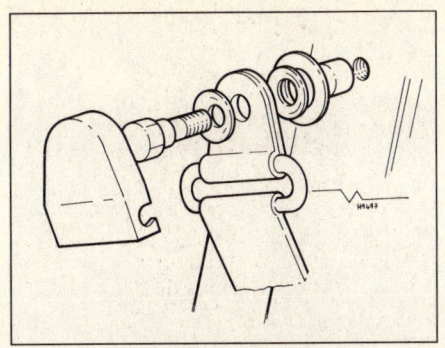

Fig. 11.31 Front seat belt anchorage to B pillar – upper (Sec 36)

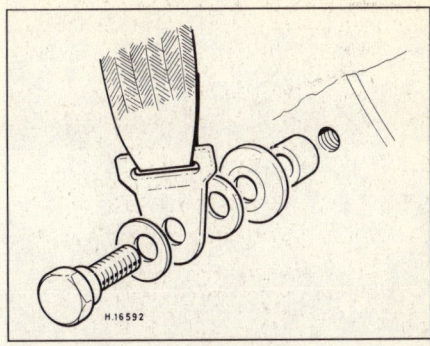

Fig. 11.32 Rear seat belt anchorage to floor (Sec 36)

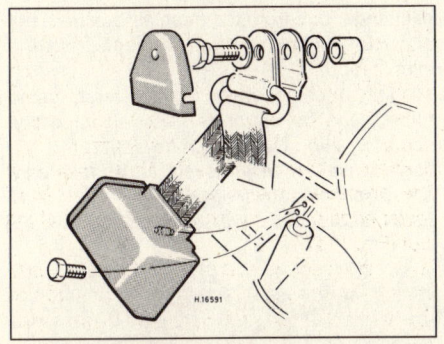

Fig. 11.33 Rear seat belt anchorage to C pillar (Sec 36)

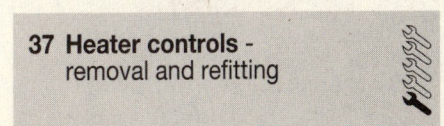

37 Heater controls - removal and refitting

1 The control unit is located in the centre of the dashboard. It is accessible after the radio has been removed or, on cars without a radio, the cubby hole. Once the radio is extracted the control unit may be seen. Disconnect the battery earth lead.
2 Pull off the control knobs and unclip the trim panel (photos).
3 Remove the three cross-head screws holding the control unit and it may be eased forward (photo).
4 The cables can now be unhooked from the control unit levers and their outer body unclipped from the control unit body.

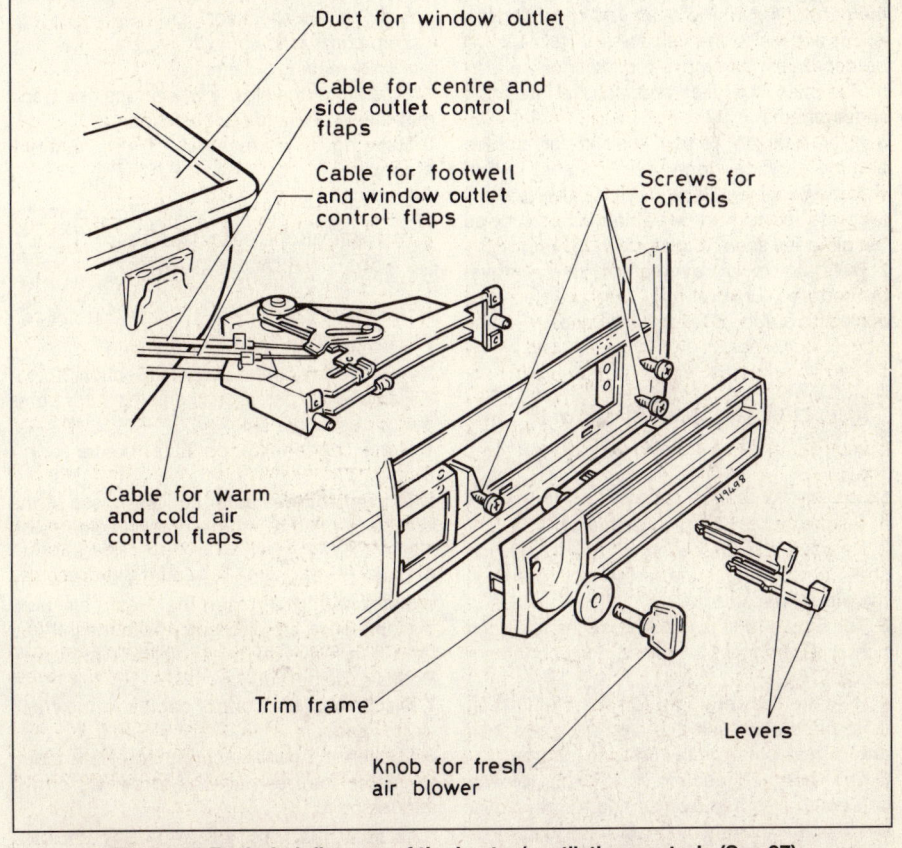

Fig. 11.34 Exploded diagram of the heater/ventilation controls (Sec 37)

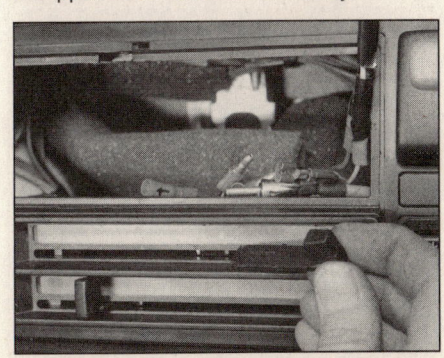

Duct for window outlet
Cable for centre and side outlet control flaps
Cable for footwell and window outlet control flaps
Screws for controls
Cable for warm and cold air control flaps
Trim frame
Knob for fresh air blower
Levers

37.2A Pull free the heater/ventilation control knobs

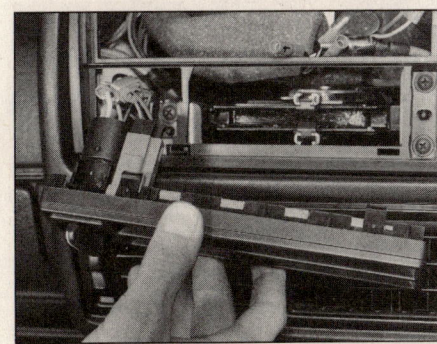

37.2B Unclip and withdraw the trim panel

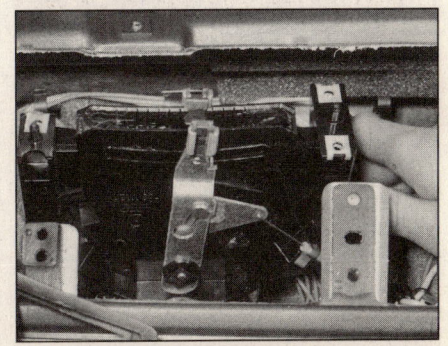

37.3 Detaching the control unit

11•16 Bodywork and fittings

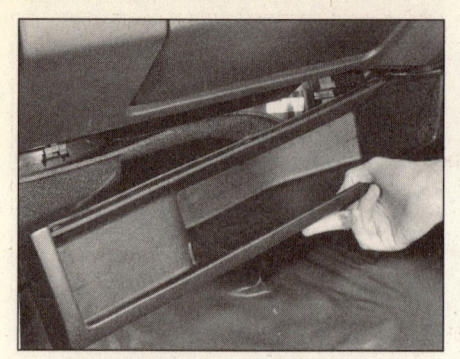

37.5A Remove the parcel shelf...

37.5B ... and insulation sheet

37.5C Control cable connections to flap valves at heater distribution box unit (arrowed)

5 If a cable is to be renewed, unhook it from the control flap at the other end and withdraw it. For access to the flap control valves it will be necessary to remove the lower parcel tray on the passenger side and also the insulation sheet (photos).
6 It is best to renew the heater cables completely if the inner cable snaps. In this way the exact length required is obtained. It is a good idea to fit new cable clamps too, as the old ones seem to distort when removed.
7 Refitting is a reversal of the removal procedure. Ensure that the cables are correctly routed with no sharp bends.

38 Heater and fresh air blower unit - removal and refitting

1 Disconnect the battery earth lead.
2 Remove the parcel shelf and insulation sheet on the underside of the facia panel on the passenger side.
3 The blower unit is mounted in the left-hand corner. Disconnect the wiring multi-connector (photo).
4 Release the retaining tab (carefully) then twist the blower unit in a clockwise direction and withdraw it from the housing (photo).
5 The wiring connection plate on the blower can be levered free by inserting a screwdriver blade under the retaining tab at the top.

6 If an ohmmeter is available the thermo cut-out can be checked:
   Zero ohms reading = OK
   Infinity reading = Defective
7 Check that the blower wheel runs freely and that the air ducts are not blocked up.
8 Refitting is a reversal of the removal procedure.

39 Heat exchanger/fresh air box - removal and refitting

1 Disconnect the battery earth lead.
2 Remove the centre console (Section 32).
3 Remove the parcel shelf and insulator panel on the passenger side.
4 Drain the engine coolant (heater on) - Chapter 2.
5 Disconnect the heater coolant hoses at the bulkhead on the engine compartment side (Fig. 11.35).
6 Undo the retaining nuts and withdraw the outlet distributor from the fresh air box, disconnecting the distributor from the left and right-hand air ducts as it is withdrawn. Remove the gasket.
7 Disconnect the control cables at the fresh air box end.
8 Loosen the dash securing screws enough to enable the fresh air box to be withdrawn and removed.
9 Release the clips and withdraw the heat exchanger unit from the fresh air box unit, but allow for further coolant drainage from the inlet and outlet pipes.
10 The housing upper and lower housing halves can be separated by releasing the securing clips (photo). Once separated the flap valves can be removed. **Note:** *take care not to split or crack the housings.*

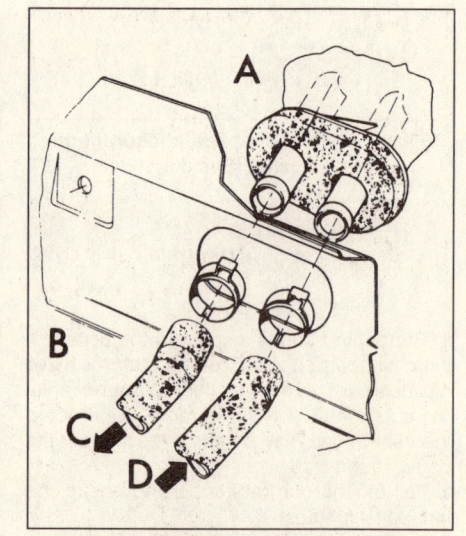

Fig. 11.35 Bulkhead coolant hose connections (Sec 39)

A Passenger compartment   C Return hose
B Engine compartment   C Supply hose

38.3 Blower unit and wiring connection

38.4 Blower unit withdrawal from housing

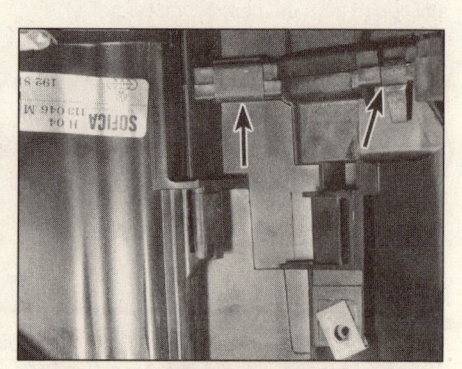

39.10 Upper-to-lower housing retaining clips (arrowed)

Bodywork and fittings 11•17

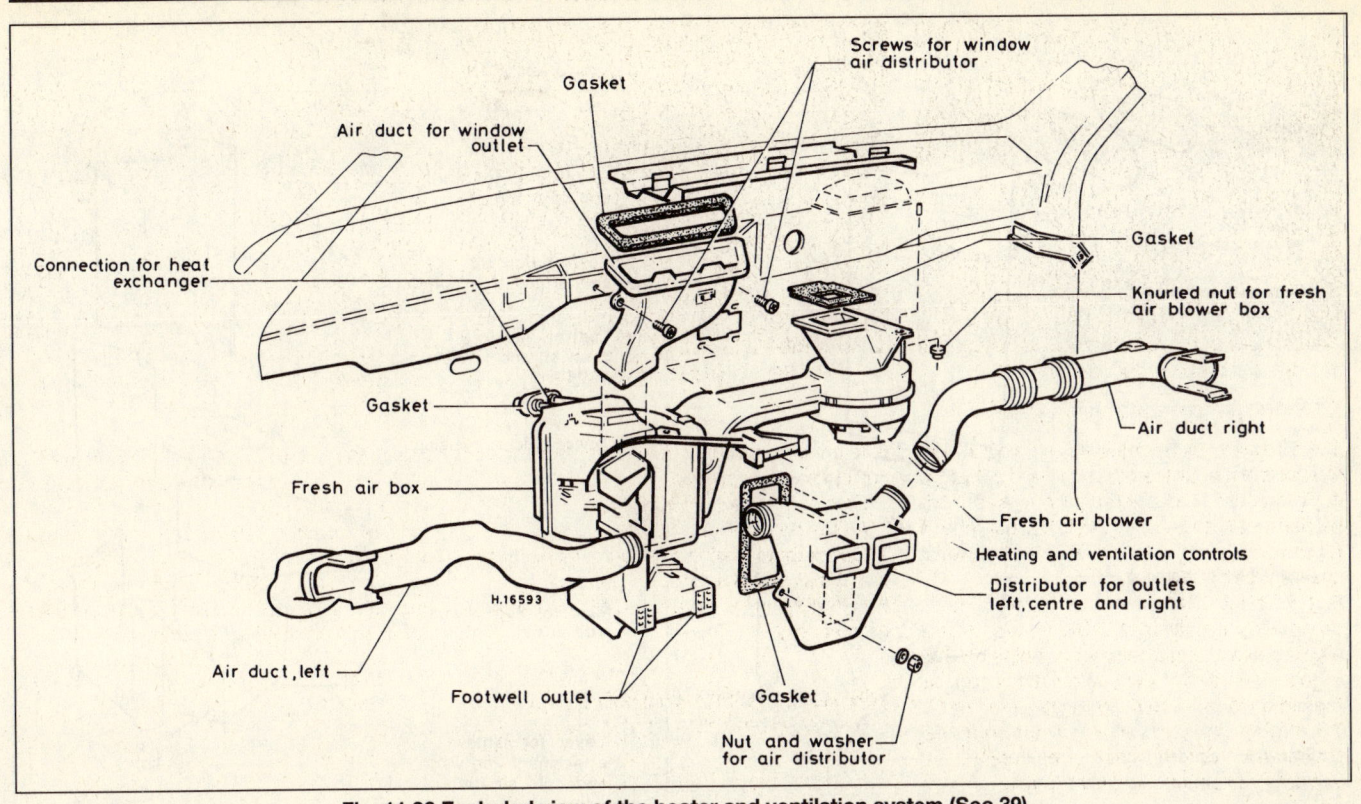

Fig. 11.36 Exploded view of the heater and ventilation system (Sec 39)

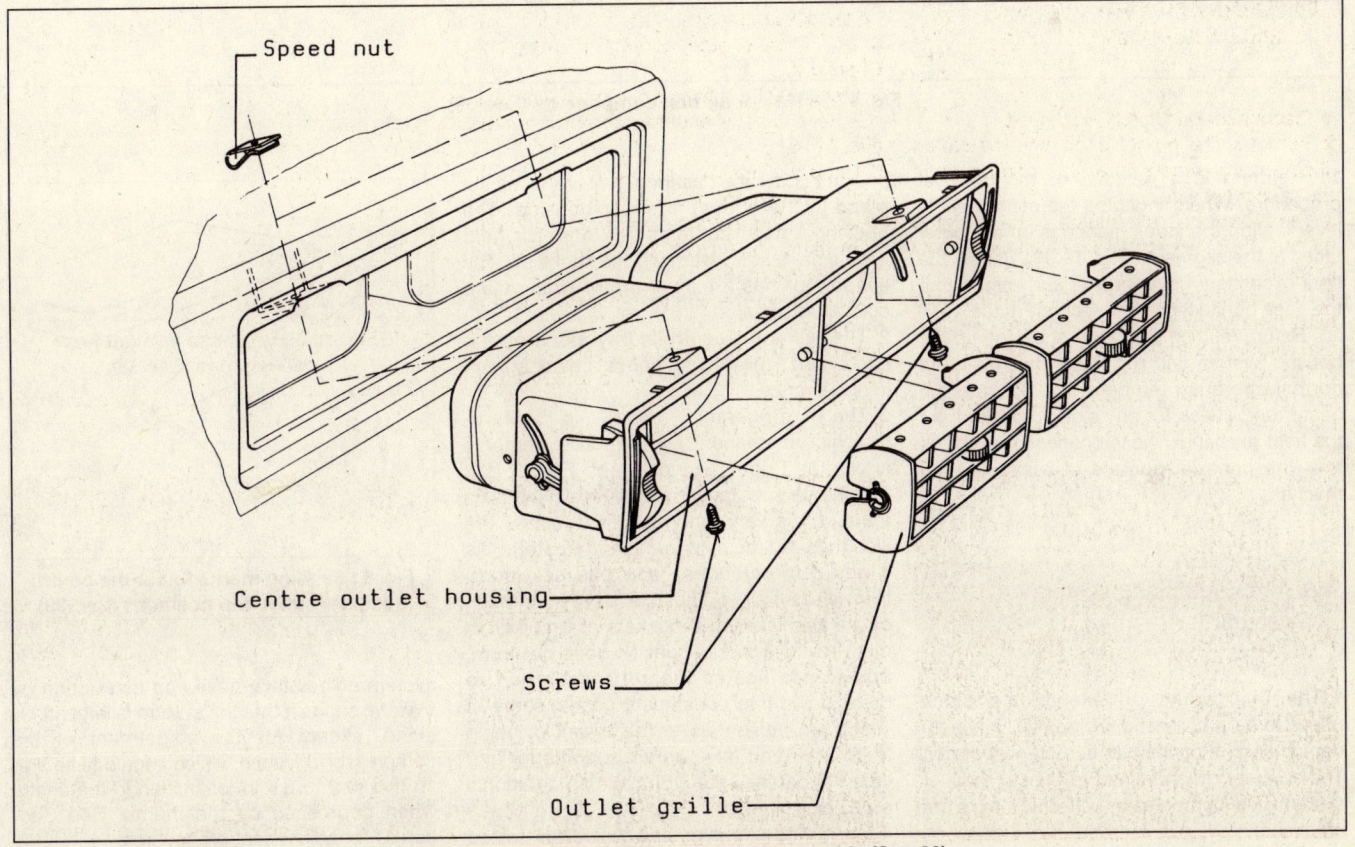

Fig. 11.37 Central air outlet housing assembly (Sec 39)

11•18 Bodywork and fittings

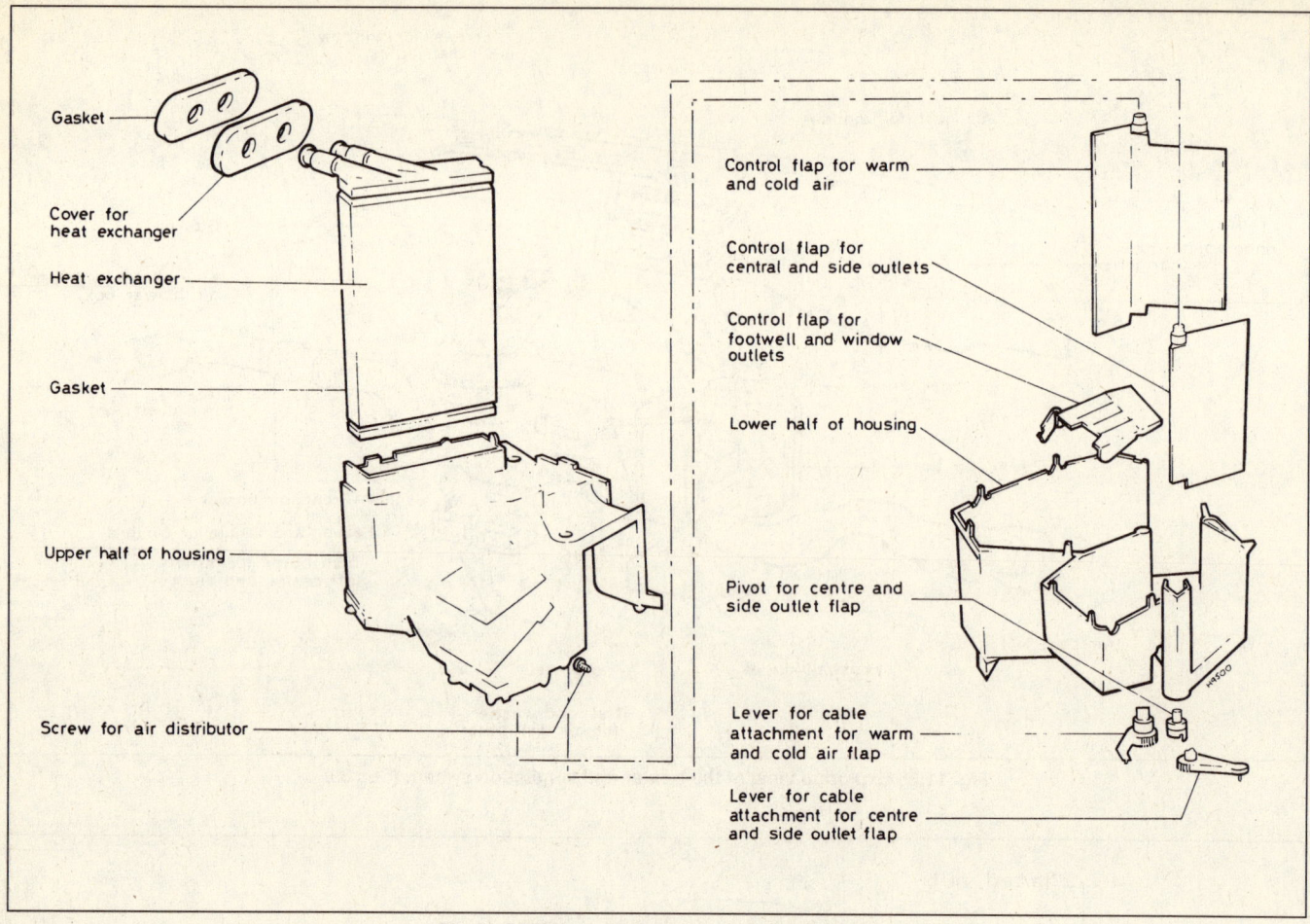

Fig. 11.38 Heater air box components (Sec 39)

11 Refitting is a reversal of the removal procedure. When engaging the control cable levers, align the index markings on the outer faces of the segments (Fig. 11.39). Renew the heat exchanger cover gasket and ensure that the hose connections are securely made.

12 Before refitting the parcel shelf, top up the cooling system and run the engine up to its normal operating temperature. Operate the heater and check for any signs of leaks from the heat exchanger hose connections. Check that the controls operate in a satisfactory manner.

40 Air conditioning system - general

1 The unit works on exactly the same principle as a domestic refrigerator, having a compressor, a condenser and an evaporator. The condenser is attached to the car radiator system. The compressor, belt-driven from the crankshaft pulley, is installed on a bracket on the engine. The evaporator is installed in a housing under the dashboard which takes the place of the normal fresh air housing. The housing also contains a normal heat exchanger unit for warming the intake air. The evaporator has a blower motor to circulate cold air as required.

2 The system is controlled by a unit on the dashboard similar to the normal heater control in appearance.

3 The refrigerant used is difluorodichloromethane (CF_2Cl_2) more commonly known as Frigen F12 or Freon F12. It is a dangerous substance in unskilled hands. As a liquid it is very cold and if it touches the skin there will be cold burns and frostbite. As a gas it is colourless and has no odour. Heavier than air, it displaces oxygen and can cause asphyxiation if pockets of it collect in pits or similar workplaces. It does not burn, but even a lighted cigarette causes it to break down into constituent gases, some of which are poisonous to the extent of being fatal. So if you have an air-conditioner and your car catches fire, you have an additional problem.

4 We strongly recommend that even trained refrigeration mechanics do not adjust the system unless they have had instruction by VW. We suggest that the system is left entirely alone, except for the adjustment of the compressor/drivebelt, which should have 5 to 10 mm (0.2 to 0.4 in) deflection in the centre when depressed by the thumb. See Section 41 for adjustment procedures.

5 Removal and refitting of the air conditioner

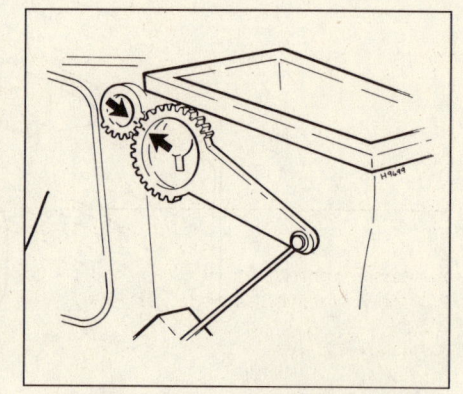

Fig. 11.39 Align marks to set the centre and side outlet flap positions (Sec 39)

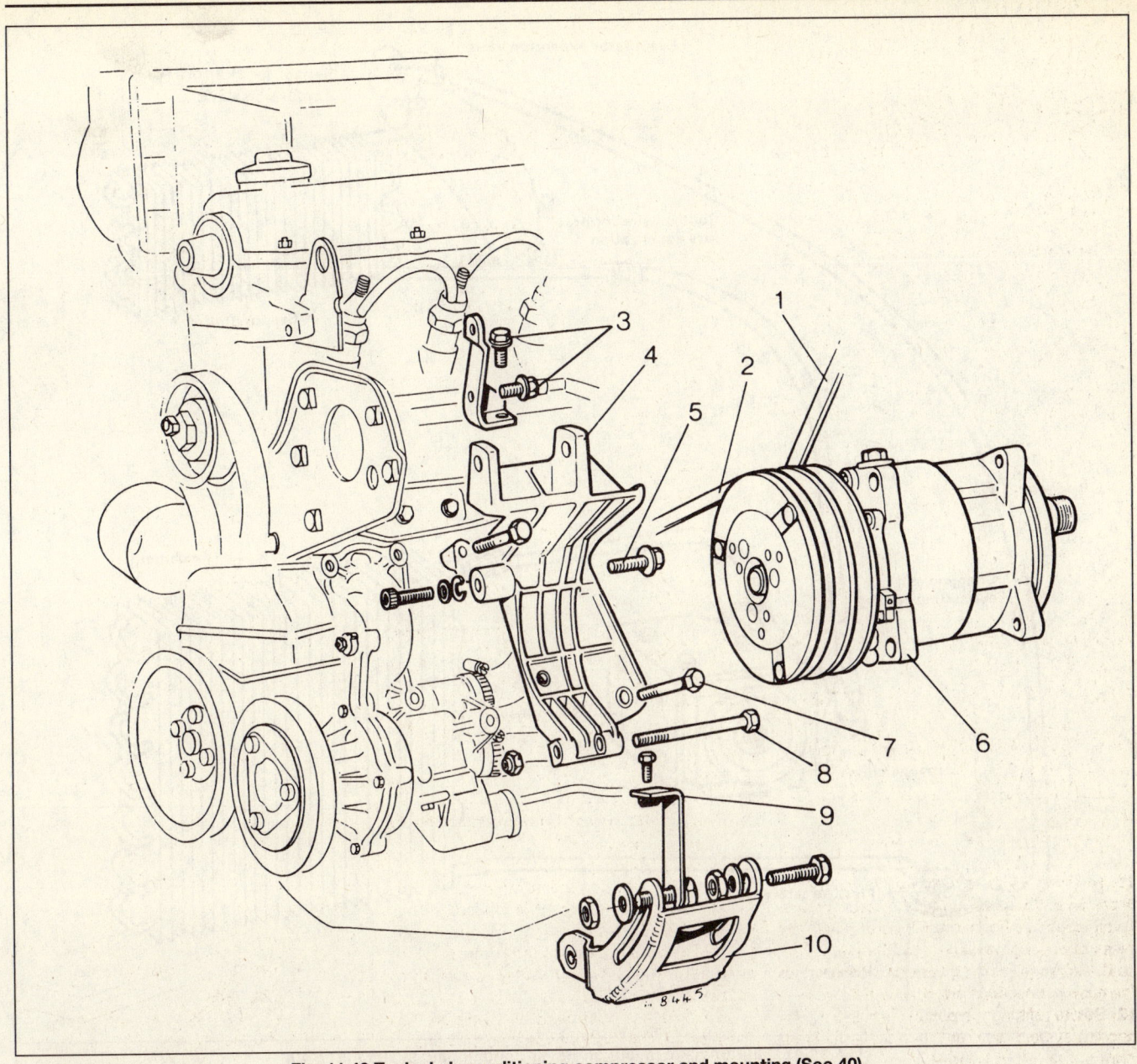

Bodywork and fittings 11•19

Fig. 11.40 Typical air conditioning compressor and mounting (Sec 40)

1 Alternator drivebelt
2 Water pump and compressor drivebelt
3 Bolts
4 Bracket
5 Bolt
6 Compressor – bolt must be at top
7 Bolt
8 Bolt
9 Hose bracket
10 Tensioner

compressor is straight-forward, as can be seen from Fig. 11.40 but the refrigerant circuit must not be opened. The compressor must be placed on the side of the engine compartment when removing the engine, but only move it to the point where the flexible refrigerant hoses are in no danger of being stretched.
6 When a situation arises which calls for the removal of one of the air conditioning system components, have the system discharged by your VW agent or a qualified refrigeration engineer. Similarly have the system recharged by him on completion.
7 During the winter period operate the air conditioner for a few minutes each week to keep the system in good order.
8 Periodically, clean the condenser of dirt and insects, either by
washing with a cold water hose or by air pressure. Use a soft bristle brush to assist removal of dirt jammed in the condenser fins.

41 Drivebelt - air conditioning system

1 Drivebelt tension is adjusted by adding or subtracting shims from between the halves of the compressor pulley.
2 When correctly adjusted the belt should give a deflection of 5 to 10 mm (0.2 to 0.4 in) on its longest run.

11•20 Bodywork and fittings

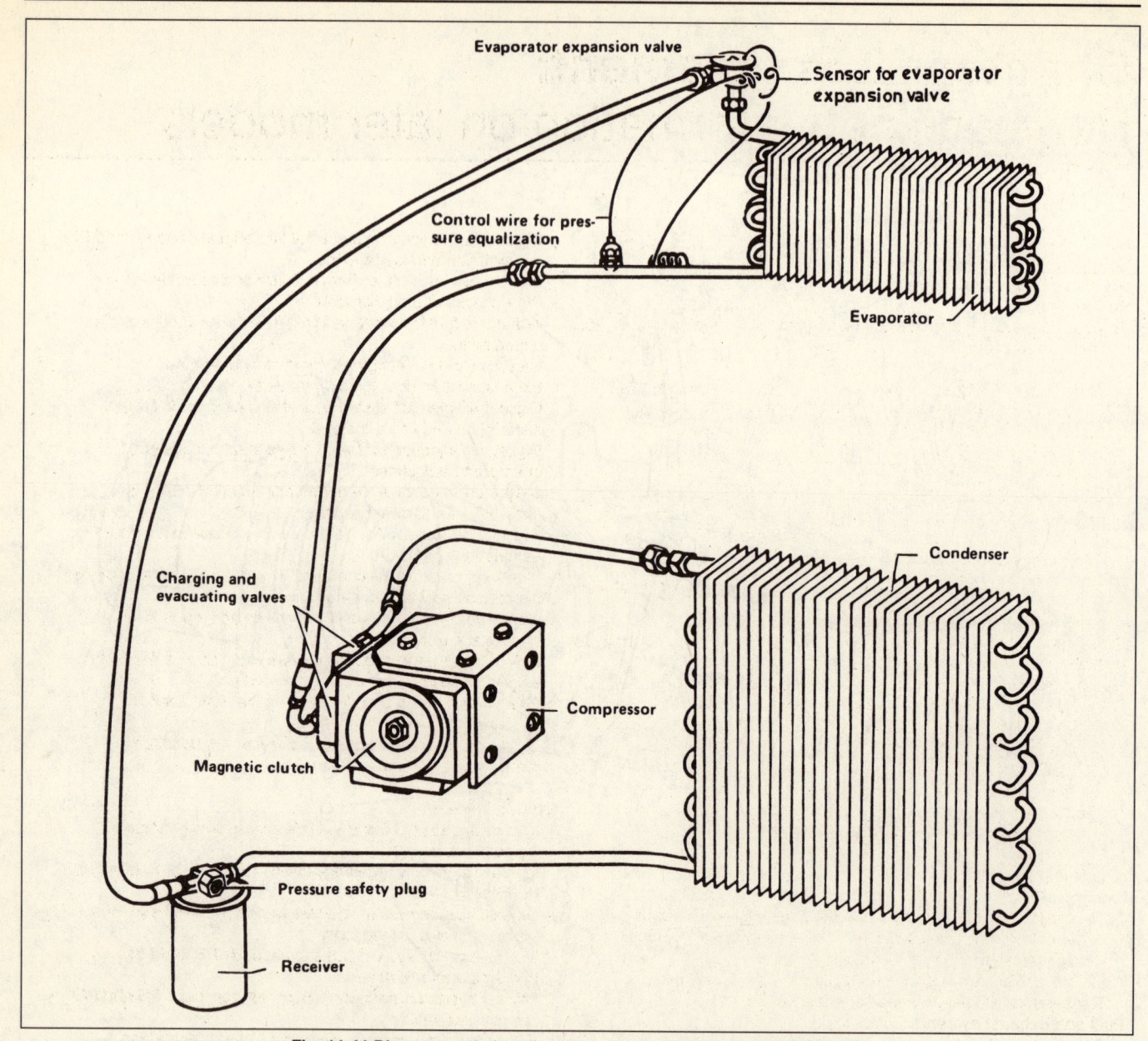

Fig. 11.41 Diagrammatic layout of the air conditioning system (Sec 40)

Chapter 12 Supplement:
Revisions and information on later models

Contents

Introduction 1
Vehicle kerb weights - general 2
Specifications 3
Routine maintenance 4
Engine (1.05 and 1.3 litre with hydraulic tappets) 5
   General description
   Cylinder head - removal
   Camshaft - removal and inspection
   Camshaft oil seal - renewal
   Camshaft endfloat
   Camshaft - refitting
   Cylinder head - inspection
   Hydraulic bucket tappets - removal, inspection and refitting
   Hydraulic bucket tappets - checking free travel
   Inlet and exhaust valves - removal, inspection and refitting
   Valve stem oil seals - renewal
   Cylinder head - refitting
   Oil pump
   Crankshaft sprocket - modification
Engine (1.6 and 1.8 litre) 6
   Engine front mounting - modification
   Camshaft and cylinder head - examination and renovation
   Hydraulic bucket tappets - description
   Sump - modification
   Oil cooler - renewal
   16-valve (16V) engine - general description
   Timing belt (16V engine) - removal and refitting
   Camshafts (16V engine) - removal and refitting
   Exhaust valves (16V engine) - description
   Big-end caps (16V engine) - description
   Engine (1986-on) - removal
Cooling system 7
   Thermostat housing (1.05 and 1.3 litre engines) - modification
   Water pump (1.05 and 1.3 litre engines) - removal and refitting
   Cooling fan and motor - removal and refitting
   Electric cooling fan (fuel injection engines) - modifications
   Temperature sender (16V engine) - description
Fuel and exhaust systems 8
   Carburettor (32 TLA and 1B3) - description
   Carburettor (32 TLA and 1B3) cleaning - general
   Pierburg 1B3 carburettor - servicing and adjustment
   Weber 32 TLA carburettor - servicing and adjustment
   Solex/Pierburg 2E2 carburettor - choke valve gap (wide open kick) adjustment
   Solex/Pierburg 2E2 carburettor - choke pull-down unit - modification
   Solex/Pierburg 2E2 carburettor - three/four point unit - checking
   K-Jetronic fuel injection system (except PB, PF and 16V engines) - modifications

Digifant fuel injection system (1.8 litre engine code PB and PF) - description and precautions
Digifant fuel injection system (1.8 litre engine, code PB and PF) - checks and adjustments
K-Jetronic fuel injection system (16V engine) checks and adjustments
Inlet manifold (16V engine) - removal and refitting
Exhaust system (fuel injection models) - description
Digijet fuel injection system (1.3 litre engine, code NZ) - description and precautions
Digijet fuel injection system (1.3 litre engine, code NZ) - checks and adjustment
Digijet fuel injection system components (1.3 litre engine, code NZ) - removal and refitting
Evaporative fuel control (1.3 litre engine, code NZ) - description
Mono-Jetronic fuel injection system (1.8 litre engine, code RP) - description and precautions
Mono-fuel injection system (1.8 litre engine, code RP) - checks and adjustments
Mono-Jetronic fuel injection system components (1.8 litre engine, code RP) - removal and refitting
Fuel pump - Mono-Jetronic and Digifant fuel injection systems
Exhaust system with catalytic converter - description, removal and refitting
Ignition system 9
   Ignition system (1.05 and 1.3 litre engine with hydraulic tappets) - description
   Ignition system (1.6 litre engine with automatic transmission) - description
   Digifant ignition system (1.8 litre engine code PB and PF) - description and precautions
   Digifant ignition system (1.8 engine, code PB and PF) - checking and adjustment
   Digifant system distributor (1.8 engine code PB and PF) - removal and refitting
   FEI system (16V engine) - description and precautions
   FEI system distributor (16V engine) - removal and refitting
   FEI system distributor (16V engine) - overhaul
   FEI system switch unit (16V engine) - testing
   FEI control unit (16V engine) - testing
   FEI system Hall sender unit (16V engine) - testing
   FEI system ignition timing (16V engine) - checking and adjustment
   Spark plugs - removal and refitting
   Spark plugs and coil - general
   Ignition system (1.3 litre engine, code NZ and 1.8 litre engine, code RP) - general

Degrees of difficulty

Easy, suitable for novice with little experience	Fairly easy, suitable for beginner with some experience	Fairly difficult, suitable for competent DIY mechanic	Difficult, suitable for experienced DIY mechanic	Very difficult, suitable for expert DIY or professional

12•2 Supplement: Revisions and information on later models

Clutch 10
   Clutch cable (self-adjusting type with 085 and 020 gearbox) -
   removal and refitting
   Clutch (085 gearbox) - description
   Flywheel bolts (085 gearbox) - tightening
   Clutch release mechanism (085 gearbox) - removal and refitting
   Clutch disc and pressure plate - anti-corrosion protection
Manual gearbox and automatic transmission 11
   Gearbox oil level (084) - checking
   Manual gearbox (085) - general description
   Manual gearbox (085) - removal and refitting
   Gearshift mechanism (085) - removal, refitting and adjustment
   Gearbox oil level (020 5-speed) - checking
   Gearshift modification (later 4 and 5-speed manual gearboxes)
   Gear lever boot (manual gearboxes) - refitting procedure
   Automatic transmissions
Electrical system 12
   Battery
   Alternator drivebelt - adjustment
   Oil pressure warning system - description
   Multi-function indicator - description
   Windscreen and rear window washer system - modifications
   Headlamps (twin) - alignment
Suspension and steering 13
   Front suspension camber adjustment - general
   Rear suspension mounting bracket - modification
   Power steering gear pinion - modification
   Wheels and tyres - care and maintenance
Bodywork and fittings 14
   Seat belts with height adjustment - description
   Central locking system - description
   Central locking system components - removal and refitting
   Front door (1988-on) - dismantling and reassembly
   Exterior mirror and glass (1988-on) - removal and refitting
   Front seat (1986-on) - removal and refitting
   Side rubbing strip - removal and refitting
   Knee-bar - removal and refitting
   Rear spoiler (Jetta GT) - removal and refitting
   Dust and pollen filter

1 Introduction

This Supplement contains information which has become available since the manual was first written. This includes the introduction of hydraulic bucket tappets, the Digifant, Digijet and Mono-Jetronic fuel injection systems, the 16-valve engine fitted to the GTI, additional carburettors, the fully electronic ignition system (FEI), the 085 five-speed gearbox, and several other minor modifications and revisions.

In order to use the Supplement to the best advantage it is suggested that it is referred to before the main Chapters of the manual. This will ensure than any relevant information can be noted and incorporated within the procedures given in Chapters 1 to 11. Time and cost will therefore be saved and the particular job will be completely corrected.

2 Vehicle kerb weights - general

Space limitations have prevented the incorporation of vehicle kerb weights for later models. These have increased marginally over those given in the manual's preliminary pages but, if more accurate information is required, a VW dealer should be contacted.

The Specifications below are revisions of, or

3 Specifications

supplementary to, those at the beginning of the preceding Chapters

Engine (1.05 and 1.3 litre) - 1986-on

General
Code letters:
  1.05 litre .... HZ
  1.3 litre .... MH
  1.3 litre .... NZ
  1.3 litre 2G
Bore:
  1.05 litre .... 75 mm (2.95 in)
  1.3 litre..... .... 75 mm (2.95 in)
Stroke:
  1.05 litre .... 59 mm (2.33 in)
  1.3 litre... .... 72 mm (2.84 in)
Compression ratio:
  1.05 litre.. .... 9.5:1
  1.3 litre... .... 9.5:1
Output:
  1.05 litre.. .... 37 kW (50 bhp) at 5900 rpm
  1.3 litre......... .... 40 kW (54 bhp) at 5200 rpm
Torque (max):
  1.05 litre...... .... 74 Nm at 3600 rpm
  1.3 litre .... 96 Nm at 3400 rpm

Cylinder head
Minimum dimension after machining (skimming) .. .. 135.6 mm (5.34 in)

Camshaft
Run-out (max) .... 0.01 mm (0.0004 in)
Radial Play (max) .. .. 0.1 mm (0.004 in)

Valves

Head diameter:
- Inlet .... 36 mm (1.42 in)
- Exhaust .... 29 mm (1.14 in)

Valve length:
- Inlet .... 98.9 mm (3.897 in)
- Exhaust .... 99.1 mm (3.905 in)

Seat width (max) .... 2.2 mm (0.087 in)

Hydraulic bucket tappets

Free travel (max) .... 0.1 mm (0.004 in)

Valve timing

(at 1.0 mm/0.04 in valve lift, zero valve clearance)

	HZ	MH/NZ/2G
Inlet opens	12°ATDC	5°ATDC
Inlet closes	28°ABDC	29°ABDC
Exhaust opens	25°BBDC	33°BBDC
Exhaust closes	9°BTDC	9°BTDC

Lubrication system

Capacity:
- Without filter change .... 3.0 litres (5.3 pints)
- With filter change .... 3.5 litres (6.2 pints)

Dipstick MIN to MAX .... 1 litre (1.8 pints)

Oil pump:
- Gear teeth backlash:
  - New .... 0.05 mm (0.002 in)
  - Wear limit .... 0.20 (0.008 in)
- Gear teeth axial play (wear limit) .... 0.15 mm (0.006 in)
- Chain drive deflection .... 1.5 to 2.5 mm (0.059 to 0.10 in)

Torque wrench settings

	Nm	lbf ft
Camshaft sprocket bolt	80	59.0
Timing belt cover:		
Upper bolt	10	7.3
Lower bolt	20	14.7
Camshaft bearing cap nuts:		
Stage 1	6	4.4
Stage 2	Tighten by further 90°	Tighten by further 90°
Number 5 cap screws	10	7.3
Cylinder head bolts:		
Stage 1	40	29.5
Stage 2	60	44.3
Stage 3	Tighten by further 180° (or 2 turns of 90°)	
Oil pump bolts	20	14.7
Stay bracket bolts	10	7.3
Strainer assembly to pump body	10	7.3
Socket-headed screws in sump (new)	8	5.9
Crankshaft sprocket bolt (oiled) - 1986-on:		
Stage 1	90	66
Stage 2	Tighten by a further 180°	Tighten by a further 180°
Flywheel bolt (with shoulder)	100	74

Engine (1.6 and 1.8 litre)

General

Code letters:
- 1.6 litre .... RF with catalytic converter
- 1.8 litre, GTI 16V .... KR with catalytic converter
- 1.8 litre, GTI 8V (January 1987 on) .... PB, GU (RH, RP, PF with catalytic converter)

Compression ratio:
- Engine codes KR, PB, GU, RH and PF 10.0:1
- Engine codes RF and RP 9.0:1

Piston rings

End gap (new) - except 16V:
- Oil scraper ring (2 part) .... 0.25 to 0.45 mm (0.010 to 0.018 in)
- Oil scraper ring (3 part) .... 0.25 to 0.50 mm (0.010 to 0.020 in)

End gap (max) - all engines .... 1.0 mm (0.040 in)

Cylinder head

Minimum height:
- Except 16V .... 132.6 mm (5.221 in)
- 16V .... 118.1 mm (4.650 in) measured through cylinder head bolt hole

Valves (except 16V)

Head diameter:
- Inlet (model codes PB and PF) .... 40.0 mm (1.57 in)
- Inlet (all other model codes) .... 38.0 mm (1.50 in)
- Exhaust .... 33.0 mm (1.30 in)

Stem diameter:
- Inlet .... 7.97 mm (0.314 in)
- Exhaust .... 7.95 mm (0.313 in)

Overall length:
- Inlet .... 91.0 mm (3.59 in)
- Exhaust (model codes PB, PF and RP) .... 90.95 mm (3.58 in)
- Exhaust .... 90.8 mm (3.57 in)

Seat angle .... 45°

Valves (16V)

Head diameter:
- Inlet .... 32.0 mm (1.260 in)
- Exhaust .... 28.0 mm (1.102 in)

Stem diameter:
- Inlet .... 6.97 mm (0.274 in)
- Exhaust .... 6.94 mm (0.273 in)

Overall length:
- Inlet .... 95.5 mm (3.760 in)
- Exhaust .... 98.2 (3.866 in)

Valve timing

(at 1.0 mm (0.04 in) valve lift)

1.8 litre KR, PB and PF engines:

	KR engine	**PB and PF engines**
Inlet opens	3° ATDC	3° ATDC
Inlet closes	35° ABDC	43° ABDC
Exhaust opens	43° BBDC	37° BBDC
Exhaust closes	3° BTDC	3° ATDC

1.6 litre EZ and 1.8 litre GU engines with hydraulic tappets - from August 1985 to March 1986:

	EZ engine	**GU engine**
Inlet opens	3° BTDC	3° BTDC
Inlet closes	19° ABDC	33° ABDC
Exhaust opens	27° BBDC	41° BBDC
Exhaust closes	5° BTDC	5° BTDC

1.6 litre EZ and 1.8 litre GU engines with hydraulic tappets - from March 1986:

	EZ engine	**GU engine**
Inlet opens	TDC	2° BTDC
Inlet closes	22° ABDC	34° ABDC
Exhaust opens	28° BBDC	44° BBDC
Exhaust closes	6° BTDC	8° BTDC

1.6 litre RF and 1.8 litre RH engines:

	RF engine	**RH engine**
Inlet opens	TDC	2° BTDC
Inlet closes	22° ABDC	34° ABDC
Exhaust opens	28° BBDC	44° BBDC
Exhaust closes	6° BTDC	8° BTDC

1.8 litre RP engine:

	Up to July 1988	**From August 1988**
Inlet opens	2° ATDC	5° BTDC
Inlet closes	38° ABDC	41° ABDC
Exhaust opens	40° BBDC	37° BBDC
Exhaust closes	4° BTDC	1° BTDC

Lubrication

Oil capacity (all engines from August 1985):
- With filter change .... 4.0 litres (7.0 Imp pints)
- Without filter change .... 3.5 litres (6.2 Imp pints)

Torque wrench settings (16V)

	Nm	lbf ft
Vibration damper	20	15
Intermediate shaft sprocket bolt	65	48
Valve cover	10	7
Oil cooler	25	19
Camshaft sprocket bolt	65	48
Camshaft bearing caps	15	11
Oil temperature sender	10	7
Oil pump cover	10	7
Oil pump mounting bolts	20	15
Oil jet	10	7
Crankshaft sprocket bolt (oiled)	180	133

Cooling system

Thermostat
1.05 and 1.3 litre hydraulic tappet engines:
- Opening temperature .... 87°C (189°F)
- Fully open temperature .... 102°C (216°F)
- Minimum stroke .... 7.0 mm (0.276 in)

Cooling fan thermo-switch (in radiator)
Fuel injection engines (except 16V):
- Switch-on temperature (single speed and 1st stage of twin speed) .... 92° to 97°C (198° to 207°F)
- Switch-off temperature (single speed and 1st stage of twin speed) .... 84° to 91°C (183° to 196°F)
- Switch-on temperature (2nd stage of twin speed) .... 99° to 105°C (210° to 221°F)
- Switch-off temperature (2nd stage of twin speed) .... 91° to 98°C (196° to 208°F)

Cooling fan thermo-switch (for injector cooling)
- Switch-on temperature .... 110°C (230°F)
- Switch-off temperature .... 103°C (217°F)

Torque wrench settings

	Nm	lbf ft
Radiator	10	7
Thermo-switch (radiator)	25	19

Fuel and exhaust systems

Air cleaner element
Application:
- 1781 cc 16V engine .... Champion U502
- 1781 cc 8V engine (code RP) .... Champion U572

Fuel filter
Application:
- 1781 cc 16V engine (Golf) .... Champion L203
- 1781 cc 16V engine (Jetta) .... Champion L206
- 1781 cc 8V engine (code RP) .... Champion L206

Carburettor (1.05 litre engine) - Pierburg 1B3
- Venturi .... 23 mm
- Main jet 105
- Air correction jet 57.5
- Idling fuel/air jet 50/130
- Pump injection tube 32.5/150
- Needle valve 1.5
- Accelerator pump capacity (cc/stroke) ... 1.0 ± 0.15
- Choke valve gap .... 1.8 ± 0.2 mm
- Fast idle speed .... 2000 ± 100 rpm
- Idle speed .... 800 ± 50 rpm
- CO content .... 2.0 ± 0.5%

Carburettor (1.05 litre engine) - Weber 32 TLA

Venturi	22 mm
Main jet:	
Code 030 129 016	105
Code 030 129 016 D	102
Air correction jet:	
Code 030 129 016	80
Code 030 129 016 D	100
Emulsion tube	F96
Idling fuel jet	47
Idling air jet:	
Code 030 129 016	110
Code 030 129 016D	145
Auxiliary fuel jet (code 030 129 016D)	30
Auxiliary air jet (code 030 129 016D)	170
Pump injection tube	0.35/0.35
Needle valve	1.75
Needle valve washer thickness	0.75 mm
Accelerator pump capacity (cc/stroke)	1.05 ± 0.15
Choke valve gap (pull-down):	
Without vacuum	2.5 ± 0.2 mm
With 300 mbar vacuum	2.0 ± 0.2 mm
Choke valve gap (wide open kick):	
Code 030 129 016	2.0 ± 0.5 mm
Code 030 129 01 6D	2.5 ± 0.5 mm
Float level	28.0 ± 1.0 mm
Fast idle speed	2000 ± 100 rpm
Idle speed	800 ± 50 rpm
CO content	2.0 ± 0.5%

Carburettor (1.6 litre engine, code RF) - Solex/Pierburg 2E2

	Stage 1	Stage 2
Venturi	22 mm	26mm
Main jet	102.5	127.5
Air correction jet with emulsion tube	80	105
Idle fuel/air jet	42.5	-
Fuel throttle enrichment	-	0.7
Accelerator pump injection tube	0.5	-
Choke valve gap (± 0.15 mm):		
Manual gearbox	2.5 mm	5.0 mm
Automatic transmission	1.9 mm	5.3 mm
Accelerator pump capacity (cc/stroke)	0.85 to 1.15	
Fast idle speed	2800 to 3200 rpm	
Idle speed	700 to 800 rpm	
CO content	1.0 to 1.5%	

K-Jetronic fuel injection (1.8 litre engine, code KR (16V) and EV)

System pressure - from March 1986	5.2 to 5.9 bars (75 to 86 lbf/in²)
Idle speed - from September 1984 (except 16V)	900 ± 100 rpm
Idle speed (16V)	950 + 50 rpm

Torque wrench settings (K-Jetronic fuel injection)

	Nm	lbf ft
Injector insert	20	15
Thermo-time switch	30	22
Inlet manifold nuts/bolts	20	15

Digifant II fuel injection (1.8 litre engine, codes PB and PF)

Idle speed	800 ± 50 rpm
CO content	1.0 ± 0.5%
System pressure - at idling speed:	
On	Approximately 2.5 bars
Off	Approximately 3.0 bars
Holding (10 minutes after switching off ignition)	2.0 bars minimum

Torque wrench settings (Digifant II fuel injection)

	Nm	lbf ft
Throttle valve housing	20	15
Inlet manifold	25	19
Fuel pressure regulator	15	11
Injector insert	20	15

Digijet fuel injection (1.3 litre engine, code NZ)
Speed limiter .... 6400 to 6500 rpm
Control unit code colour:
  Up to July 1989 .... Copper-brown sticker
  From July 1989 .... Blue sticker
Idle speed:
  Up to July 1989 .... 750 to 850 rpm
  July 1989 .... 880 to 980 rpm
CO content:
  Up to July 1989 .... 0.3 to 0.11%
  July 1989 .... 0.3 to 1.5%
Injectors:
  Resistance .... 15 to 20 ohms
  Spray pattern .... Conical
Fuel pressure (approx):
  Vacuum hose connected .... 2.5 bars
  Vacuum hose disconnected .... 3.0 bars
Fuel octane rating .... 91 RON (unleaded only)

Mono-Jetronic fuel injection (1.8 litre engine, code RP)
Fuel octane rating .... 91 RON (unleaded only)
Idle speed .... 750 to 950 (not adjustable)
Co content .... 0.2 to 1.2%
Fuel system pressure .... 0.8 to 1.2 bars
Holding pressure (after being switched off for 5 minutes) .... 0.5 bar
Injector resistance .... 1.2 to 1.6 ohm

Torque wrench settings (Mono-Jetronic fuel injection)

	Nm	lbf ft
Air intake manifold	10	7
Injector holder	5	3.7
Throttle valve positioner	6	4.4
Inlet manifold-to-injector unit flange	13	9
Inlet manifold	25	18
Inlet manifold pre-heater	10	7

Ignition system

Ignition coil from August 1987
Primary winding resistance .... 0.6 to 0.8 ohm
Secondary winding resistance .... 6900 to 8500 ohm

Distributor
Rotor cut-out speed:
  1.05 and 1.3 litre (transistorized)* .... 6600 to 7000 rpm
  1.6 and 1.8 litre (transistorized)** .... 6150 to 6460 rpm
Discontinued from 1986 models
**Only on engine without hydraulic tappets*

Ignition timing
1.3 litre engine (code NZ) - TCI-H .... 4 to 6° BTDC at 750 to 850 rpm, with vacuum hose disconnected
1.6 litre engine (code RF) - TCI-H .... 17 to 19° BTDC at 700 to 800 rpm, with vacuum hose disconnected
1.8 litre engine (code PB and PF) - Digifant .... 5 to 7° BTDC at 2000 to 2500 rpm, with temperature sender disconnected
1.8 litre engine (code GU and RH) - TCI-H .... 17 to 19° BTDC at 675 to 825 rpm, with vacuum hose connected
1.8 litre engine (code RP) - TCI-H .... 5 to 7° BTDC at 950 rpm, with vacuum hose disconnected
1.8 litre engine (16V) - FEI .... 5 to 7° BTDC at 950 to 1050 rpm, with vacuum hose connected

Spark plugs
Type - from September 1985:
  1.3 litre engine .... Champion N7BYC or N7YCC
  1.6 litre engine:
    Coil with green sticker .... Champion N9BYC4 or N9YCC
    Coil with grey sticker .... Champion N9YCC
  1.8 litre engine (except 16V) .... Champion N7BYC or N7YCC
  1.8 litre engine (16V) .... Champion C6BYC or C6YCC
Electrode gap:
  1.3 litre engine .... 0.8 mm (0.031 in)
  1.6 litre engine:
    Coil with green sticker .... 1.0 mm (0.039 in)
    Coil with grey sticker .... 0.8 mm (0.031 in)
  1.8 litre engines .... 0.8 mm (0.031 in)

12•8 Supplement: Revisions and information on later models

Torque wrench settings	Nm	lbf ft
Spark plugs:		
1.05 and 1.3 litre engines	25	18
1.06 and 1.8 litre engines	20	15
Knock sensor (1.8 litre engine)	20	15

Clutch - models with 085 gearbox

General

Clutch friction disc diameter	190 mm (7.48 in)
Pressure plate maximum inward taper	0.3 mm (0.012 in)
Friction disc maximum run-out - measured 2.5 mm (0.099 in) from outer edge	0.4 mm (0.016 in)

Torque wrench settings

	Nm	lbf ft
Flywheel:		
Bolt with collar	100	74
Bolt without collar	75	55
Guide sleeve	18	13
Pressure plate	25	18

Manual gearbox

Identification codes

1.3 litre engine (five-speed)	085 (8N)
1.6 litre engine	085 (AEN)
1.8 litre engine	085 (ACD, AEN, 2Y, AUG, ATH or AVZ)

Ratios (1.3 litre engine)

1st	3.455:1
2nd	1.958:1
3rd	1.250:1
4th	0.891:1
5th	0.740:1
Reverse	3.384:1
Final drive	4.267:1

Ratios (1.6 and 1.8 litre engines)

	ACD, AEN	2Y	AUG	ATH	AVZ
1st	3.45:1	3.45:1	3.45:1	3.45:1	3.45:1
2nd	2.11:1	2.11:1	1.94:1	1.94:1	1.94:1
3rd	1.44:1	1.44:1	1.44:1	1.28:1	1.28:1
4th	1.12:1	1.12:1	1.12:1	0.90:1	0.90:1
5th	0.89:1	0.91:1	0.89:1	0.74:1	0.74:1
Reverse	3.16:1	3.16:1	3.16:1	3.16:1	3.16:1
Final drive	3.66:1	3.66:1	3.66:1	3.66:1	3.94:1

Lubrication

Capacity:	
1.3 litre engine (5-speed)	3.1 litres (5.5 Imp pints)
1.6 and 1.8 litre engines	2.0 litres (3.5 Imp pints)
Lubricant type	Gear oil, viscosity SAE 80

Torque wrench settings

	Nm	lbf ft
End cover bolt - 085 gearbox	8	6
Gear lever bracket (inside gearbox) - 085 gearbox	16	12
Selector arm pinch-bolt - 085 gearbox	25	19
Selector shaft location screw* - 020 gearbox from 1989	20	15

*Smear threads with sealant prior to fitting screw

Automatic transmission

Torque wrench settings

	Nm	lbf ft
Driveplate-to-crankshaft bolts:		
Stage 1	30	22
Stage 2	Further tighten 90°	Further tighten 90°

Supplement: Revisions and information on later models

Electrical system
Fuses (August 1989-on)

Fuse	Component	Rating (amps)
1	Low beam, left	10
2	Low beam, right	10
3	Instrument and number plate lights	10
4	Glovebox light	15
5	Windscreen wash/wipe system	15
6	Fresh air blower	20
7	Side/tail lights, right	10
8	Side/tail lights, left	10
9	Heated rear window	20
10	Foglights	10
11	High beam, left	10
12	High beam, right	10
13	Horn	10
14	Reversing lights, heated washer jets	10
15	Electromagnetic cut-off, fuel pump run-on	10
16	Dash panel insert	15
17	Emergency light system	10
18	Fuel pump Lambda probe heating	20
19	Radiator fan, A/C relay	30
20	Brake stoplights	30
21	Interior light, digital clock	15
22	Radio system/cigarette lighter	10

Suspension and steering
Power-assisted steering fluid type (April 1989-on) ... VW Oil G 002000

Torque wrench setting — Nm / lbf ft
Rear suspension mounting bracket (1988-on) ... 70 / 52

4 Routine maintenance

The routine maintenance intervals for models manufactured from August 1985 (ie 1986 models) are as follows.

Every 250 miles (400 km) or weekly - whichever comes first
- [ ] Refer to this section of Routine maintenance at the beginning of the Manual.

Every 12 months
- [ ] Change engine oil and filter (Chapter 1)
- [ ] Check engine for oil, fuel and coolant leaks (Chapters 1, 2 and 3)
- [ ] Check antifreeze strength and adjust if necessary (Chapter 2)
- [ ] Check exhaust system for leaks and damage (Chapter 3)
- [ ] Check and adjust idling speed and mixture (Chapter 3)
- [ ] Check clutch pedal play and adjust where applicable (Chapter 5)
- [ ] Check gearbox/transmission for oil leaks and damage (Chapter 6)
- [ ] Check automatic transmission fluid level and top up if necessary (Chapter 6)
- [ ] Check driveshaft boots for leaks and damage (Chapter 7)
- [ ] Check front and rear brake linings for wear (Chapter 8)
- [ ] Check brake hydraulic lines for leaks and damage (Chapter 8)
- [ ] Check brake fluid level and top up if necessary (Chapter 8)
- [ ] Check battery electrolyte level and top up with distilled water if necessary (Chapter 9)
- [ ] Check operation of all lights, direction indicators and horns (Chapter 9)
- [ ] Check operation of washer system and top up levels if necessary (Chapter 9)
- [ ] Check headlight beam alignment and adjust if necessary (Chapter 9)
- [ ] Check steering tie-rod balljoints for wear and damage (Chapter 10)
- [ ] Check front suspension lower balljoints for wear and damage (Chapter 10)
- [ ] Check all tyres for wear and damage (Chapter 10)
- [ ] Check power steering fluid level and top up if necessary (Chapter 10)
- [ ] Grease door check straps (Chapter 11)
- [ ] Check underbody sealant and re-seal where necessary (Chapter 11)

Every 10 000 miles (15 000 km) if completing more than 10 000 miles (15 000 km) per annum
- [ ] Change engine oil and filter (Chapter 1)
- [ ] Check disc pad linings for wear (Chapter 8)

Every 20 000 miles (30 000 km)
- [ ] Renew air cleaner element and clean housing (Chapter 3)
- [ ] Renew fuel filter, where applicable (Chapter 3)
- [ ] Renew the spark plugs (Chapter 4)
- [ ] Renew automatic transmission fluid, clean sump and filter screen (Chapter 6)
- [ ] Check drivebelt(s) for wear and damage and adjust tension if necessary (Chapter 9)
- [ ] Clean sunroof guide rails (where applicable) and lubricate with silicone spray

Every 2 years
- [ ] Renew the brake fluid

Every 40 000 miles (160 000 km)
- [ ] Renew the timing belt (Chapter 1)

12•10 Supplement: Revisions and information on later models

5.4 New type valve cover

5.5 Plastic oil shield

5 Engine (1.05 and 1.3 litre with hydraulic tappets)

General description

1 The 1.05 litre and 1.3 litre engines (code letters HZ, MH, NZ and 2G), produced since August 1985 have a redesigned cylinder head, incorporating hydraulic 'bucket' type tappets in place of the previous rocker finger tappets, and a redesigned engine oil pump, driven by chain from the crankshaft.
2 Additionally, different ancillary components are fitted such as the carburettor and distributor.

Cylinder head - removal

3 The procedure for removing the cylinder head on engines with hydraulic tappets is basically the same as described in Chapter 1, but the following points should be borne in mind.
4 The valve cover is different, being held in place by three bolts (photo).
5 There is a plastic oil shield located at the distributor end of the engine (photo).
6 The fuel and coolant pipes differ, depending on model.
7 Spring type re-usable hose clips may be fitted. These are removed by pinching the ends together to expand the clip and then sliding it down the hose.
8 The clips on the fuel hoses are designed to be used only once, so obtain new ones or replace them with screw type clips.

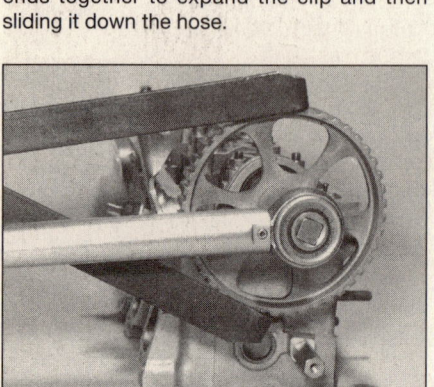

Camshaft - removal and inspection

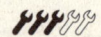

Removal

9 Refer to Chapter 1, Section 11, paragraphs 1 to 4 (inclusive).
10 Devise a method to prevent the camshaft turning, and remove the sprocket bolt (photo). Remove the camshaft sprocket and where applicable, the Woodruff key.
11 The camshaft bearing caps must be refitted in their original locations, and the same way round. They are usually numbered, but centre-punch marks on them, if necessary, to ensure correct refitting.
12 Remove bearing caps 5, 1 and 3 in that order. Now undo the nuts holding 2 and 4 in a diagonal pattern and the camshaft will lift them up as the pressure of the valve springs is exerted. When they are free, lift the caps off.
13 If the caps are stuck, give them a sharp tap with a soft-faced mallet to loosen them. Do not try to lever them off with a screwdriver.
14 Lift out the camshaft complete with the oil seal.

Inspection

15 Clean the camshaft in solvent, then inspect its journals and cam peaks for pitting, scoring, cracking and wear.

16 The camshaft bearings are machined directly into the cylinder head and the bearing caps.
17 Radial play in the bearings can be measured using the Plastigage method. Compare the results with the dimension in the Specifications.
18 If wear is evident, consult your VW dealer.

Camshaft oil seal - renewal

19 This is a straightforward task if the camshaft is removed, but it is possible to renew the oil seal without removing the camshaft.
20 A VW special tool exists for this job, but if it is not available the old seal will have to be removed by securing self-tapping screws into it and pulling it out with pliers. Note which way round it is fitted.
21 Whichever method is used, the timing cover and camshaft sprocket will have to be removed. Slacken the water pump bolts to release the tension in the timing belt.
22 Lightly oil the new seal and slide in onto the camshaft - the same way round as the one which was removed. Use a suitable socket and a bolt in the end of the shaft to press the new seal home. Push it in as far as it will go.

Camshaft endfloat

23 To check the camshaft endfloat, remove the camshaft and all the tappets.
24 Refit the camshaft using only number 3 bearing cap.
25 Set up a dial test indicator or use feeler gauges to measure the endfloat (photo). If the endfloat is greater than specified (see Chapter 1 Specifications), consult your VW dealer.

Camshaft - refitting

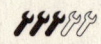

26 Oil the bucket tappets, the camshaft journals and the camshaft liberally with clean engine oil.

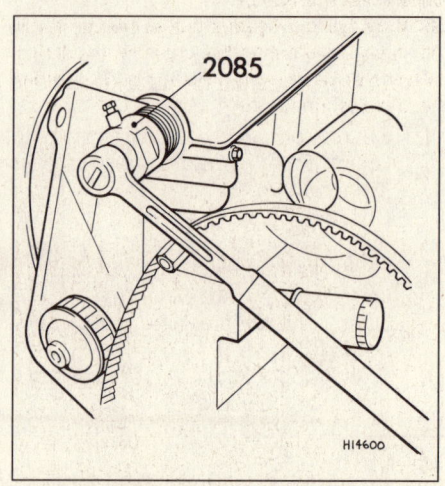

5.10 Two lengths of metal used to lock camshaft sprocket

5.25 Measuring camshaft endfloat

Fig. 12.1 Renewing the camshaft oil seal using VW special tool 2085 (Sec 5)

Supplement: Revisions and information on later models 12•11

5.27 Refitting the camshaft

5.28 Camshaft oil seal

5.30 Tightening a camshaft bearing cap nut

27 Place the camshaft in position on the cylinder head (photo).
28 Fit a new camshaft oil seal (photo).
29 Refit the bearing caps, ensuring they are the right way and in their correct position (they should be numbered 1 to 5, readable from the exhaust manifold side of the head).
30 Thread on the cap retaining nuts loosely, then tighten the nuts on number 2 and 4 caps in a diagonal sequence to the Stage 1 torque figure given in the Specifications (photo).
31 Tighten the nuts on caps 1, 3 and 5 to the Stage 1 torque.
32 Once all nuts have been tightened to the Stage 1 torque, tighten all nuts a further 90° (Stage 2). Fit and tighten No. 5 cap screws to the correct torque.
33 Refit the Woodruff key into its slot in the camshaft, where applicable. Fit the camshaft sprocket and tighten the bolt to the specified torque (photo).
34 If the work is being carried out in the engine compartment, follow the procedure given in Chapter 1, Section 37, paragraphs 9 to 18.
35 Ignore any reference to the oil spray tube, and be sure to refit the oil shield at the distributor end of the camshaft before the valve cover is refitted.
36 If the cylinder head is out of the car it will obviously have to be refitted before the timing belt can be reconnected. Refitting the cylinder head is described later in this Section.

Cylinder head - inspection

37 If, on examination, the valve seats are badly pitted or eroded they can be reworked, but this is a specialist job best left to a VW dealer or an engine overhaul specialist.
38 Similarly, the cylinder head surfaces can be skimmed, again by specialist engineers, if the head is warped.
39 On inspection, if it is found that there are cracks from the valve seats or valve seat inserts to the spark plug threads, the cylinder head may still be serviceable. Consult your VW dealer for advice.

Hydraulic bucket tappets - removal inspection and refitting

40 Remove the camshaft, as previously described.
41 Lift out the tappets one by one, ensuring they are kept in their correct order and can be returned to their original bores (photo).
42 Place them, face down (cam contact surface), on a clean sheet of paper as they are removed.
43 Inspect the tappets for wear, indicated by ridging on the clean surface, pitting and cracks.
44 Tappets cannot be repaired, and if worn must be renewed.
45 Before fitting the tappets, oil all parts liberally and slip each tappet back into its original bore.

⚠ **Caution: If new tappets are fitted, the engine must not be started after fitting for approximately 30 minutes, or the valves will strike the pistons.**

Hydraulic bucket tappets - checking free travel

46 Start the engine and run it until the radiator cooling fan has switched on once.
47 Increase engine speed to about 2500 rpm for about two minutes.
48 Irregular noises are normal when starting, but should become quiet after a few minutes running.
49 If the valves are still noisy carry out the following check to identify worn tappets.
50 Stop the engine and remove the valve cover from the cylinder head.
51 Turn the crankshaft clockwise, using a wrench on the crankshaft pulley securing bolt, until the cam of the tappet to be checked is facing upward, and is not exerting any pressure on the tappet.
52 Press the tappet down using a wooden or plastic wedge.
53 If free travel of the tappet exceeds that given in the Specifications, the tappet must be renewed.

Inlet and exhaust valves - removal inspection and refitting

54 Remove the cylinder head, camshaft and tappets, as described previously.

5.33 Fitting the camshaft sprocket bolt

5.41 Removing an hydraulic bucket tappet

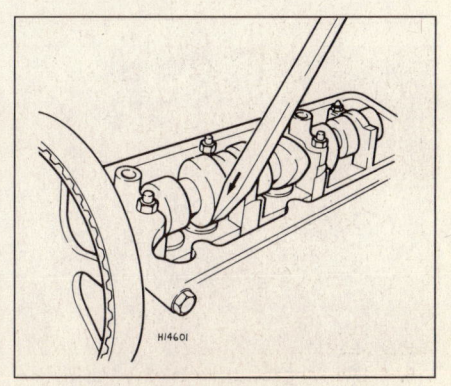

Fig. 12.2 Checking hydraulic tappet free travel (Sec 5)

12•12 Supplement: Revisions and information on later models

5.56 Removing the valve spring upper seat

5.57A Removing an outer valve spring

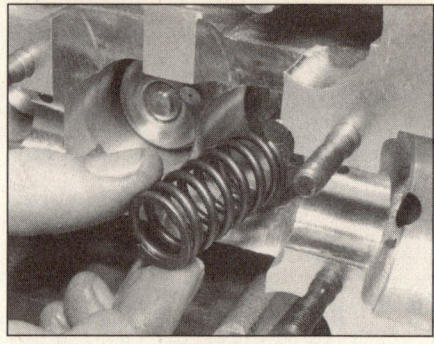

5.57B Removing an inner valve spring

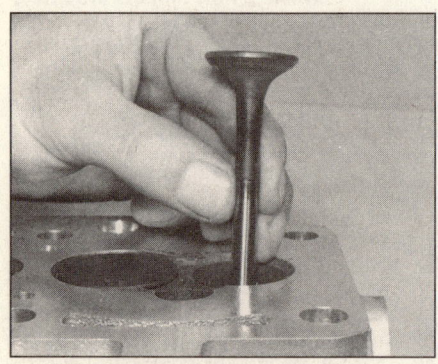

5.58 Removing a valve

55 Using a valve spring compressor with a deep reach, compress the valve springs, remove the two cotters and release the compressor and springs.
56 Lift out the upper spring seat (photo).
57 Remove the outer and inner valve springs (photos).
58 Lift out the valve (photo).
59 The valves should be inspected as described in Chapter 1, Section 12.
60 Valves cannot be reworked, but must be renewed if they are worn. They should be ground in the normal manner.
61 If possible, check the valve spring lengths against new ones. Renew the whole set if any are too short.
62 Refitting is a reversal of removal.

Valve stem oil seals - renewal

63 The valve stem oil seals should be renewed whenever the valves are removed, by prising them from the ends of the valve guides (photo). With the oil seals removed the lower spring seats can also be lifted out for cleaning. Press the new oil seals onto the ends of the valve guides.

Cylinder head - refitting

64 Clean all traces of old gasket from the cylinder block and cylinder head faces,

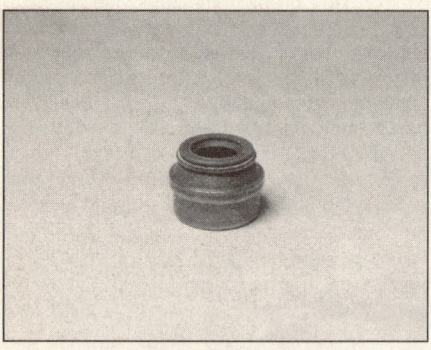

5.63 A valve stem oil seal

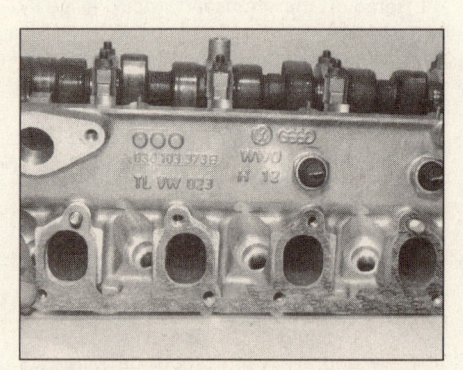

5.65A Fitting a new inlet manifold gasket

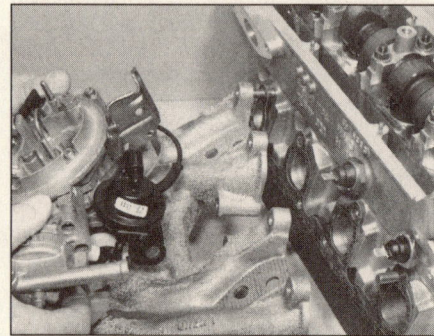

5.65B Fitting the inlet manifold complete with carburettor

5.66 Refitting the oil pressure switch

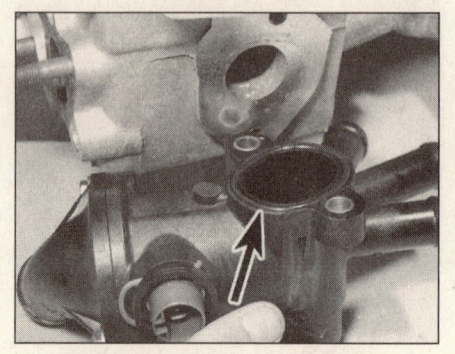

5.67 O-ring seal (arrowed) in the thermostat housing

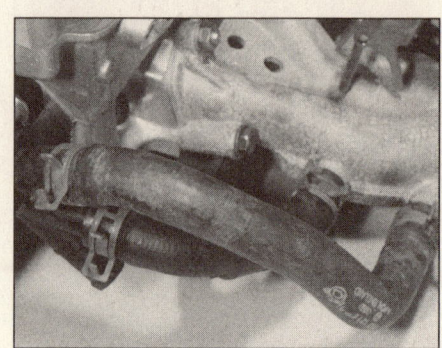

5.68 Coolant hoses in position

Supplement: Revisions and information on later models 12•13

5.69 Fitting the fuel pump plunger (arrowed)

5.70A Fitting the fuel pump

5.70B Location of engine lifting eye

taking great care not to mark the gasket surfaces.
65 Using a new gasket, fit the inlet manifold (photos).
66 If they have been removed, refit the oil pressure switches, using new copper sealing washers (photo).
67 Refit the thermostat housing, using a new O-ring seal (photo).
68 Refit the coolant hoses, ensuring they are connected up in the correct position (photo).
69 Lubricate the fuel pump plunger with clean engine oil and slip it into its housing in the cylinder head (photo).
70 Refit the fuel pump and tighten the bolts, not forgetting the engine lifting eye (photos).

71 Slide the distributor into position, and ensure that it goes fully home (photo). Hand-tighten the retaining bolts.
72 Fit the distributor rotor arm (photo).
73 Fit the distributor cap and connect up the earth lead (photo).
74 Check the timing marks on the cylinder head and camshaft sprocket are lined up.
75 Note that none of the pistons **must** be at TDC when refitting the cylinder head.
76 Position a new cylinder head gasket on the cylinder block (photo).
77 Lower the cylinder head gently into position. Special guides are used by the manufacturer both to line up the gasket and

guide the cylinder head into position, but this can be done using suitable sized rods inserted in two cylinder head bolt holes.
78 Install the cylinder head bolts. Refer to Fig. 1.11 of Chapter 1 for the tightening sequence, but use the torque figures and stages given in the Specifications section of this Chapter.
79 It is not necessary to retighten the bolts after a period of service, as is normally the case.
80 Refit the plastic oil shield (photo).
81 Using a new rubber sealing gasket, properly located over the dowels, refit the valve cover (photo).

5.71 Refitting the ignition distributor

5.72 Fitting the rotor arm

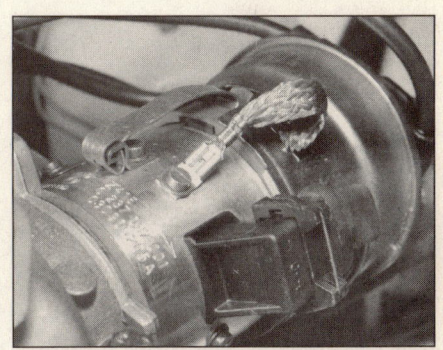

5.73 Fitting the distributor cap and earth lead

5.76 Cylinder head gasket in position

5.80 Plastic oil shield correctly located

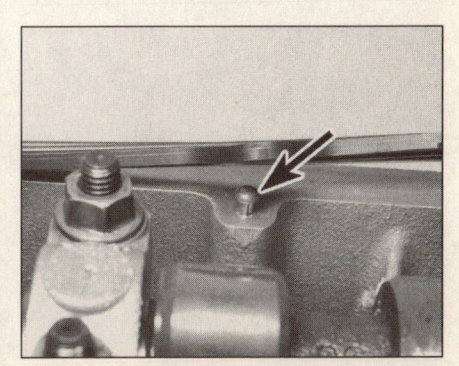

5.81 Locating dowel for valve cover gasket (arrowed)

12•14 Supplement: Revisions and information on later models

5.82 Fitting a new exhaust manifold gasket

5.83A Exhaust manifold bolted in position

5.83B Fitting the hot air shroud

82 Fit a new gasket to the exhaust manifold (photo).
83 Fit the exhaust manifold, tightening its nuts securely, then fit the hot air shroud (photos).
84 Connect up the exhaust downpipe and any other exhaust brackets loosened during removal.
85 Refit all remaining hoses of the cooling system and fuel system, referring to the relevant Chapter where necessary.
86 Refit all electrical connections disturbed during dismantling (distributor, carburettor, oil pressure and coolant temperature switches, inlet manifold preheater, etc.) (photos). Do not forget the earth lead under the inlet manifold nut.

87 Refit the distributor vacuum hose.
88 With reference to Chapter 1, Section 39, refit the timing belt and covers.
89 Refer to Chapter 3 and refit the throttle cable.
90 Refit the spark plugs, air cleaner and associated pipework and electrical leads.
91 Check oil and coolant levels, refilling as necessary, then adjust the ignition timing with reference to Chapter 4.

Oil pump
General description
92 The oil pump fitted to engines produced since August 1985 has been changed from the crescent type to a gear type pump, driven by chain from the engine crankshaft.
93 Only the oil pump has been changed, the rest of the lubrication system remains as before.

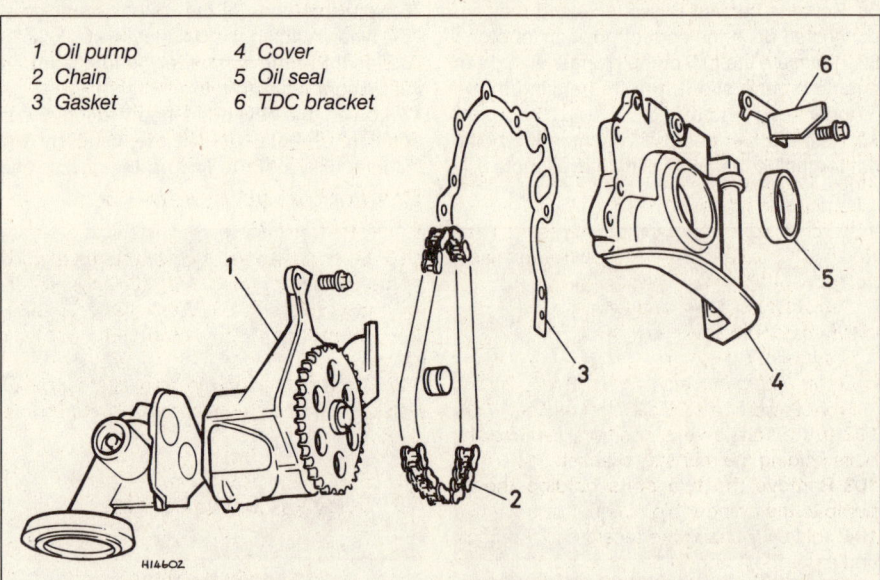

1 Oil pump
2 Chain
3 Gasket
4 Cover
5 Oil seal
6 TDC bracket

Fig. 12.3 Components of the gear type oil pump (Sec 5)

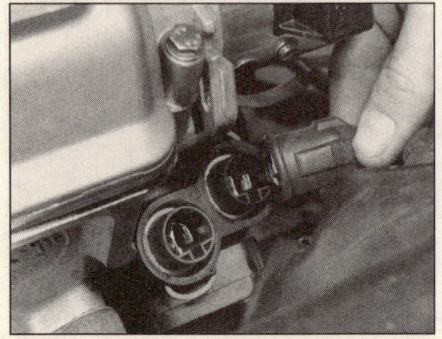

5.86A Ignition distributor electrical connection

5.86B Coolant temperature switch/sender electrical connection

5.86C Oil pressure switch electrical connection

5.86D The earth lead under the inlet manifold bolt head

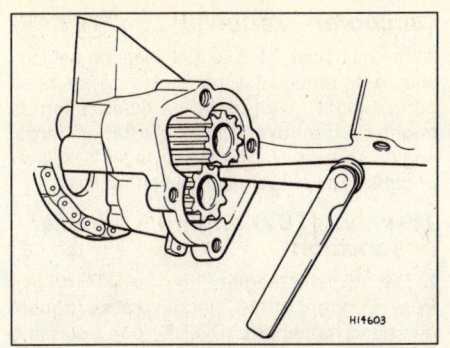

Supplement: Revisions and information on later models 12•15

Fig. 12.4 Checking the oil pump backlash (Sec 5)

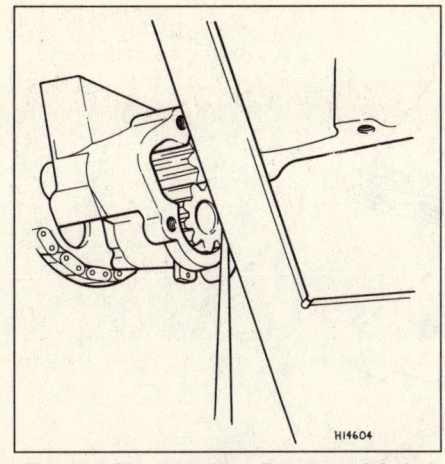

Fig. 12.5 Checking the oil pump axial play (Sec 5)

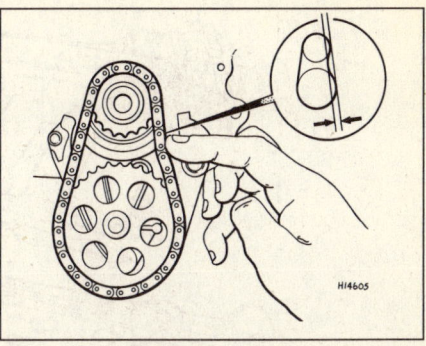

Fig. 12.6 Checking the oil pump drive chain tension (Sec 5)

Removal and inspection

94 The oil pump can be removed with the engine still in the vehicle.
95 Drain the oil from the sump.
96 Referring to the relevant Chapters, disconnect the exhaust downpipe and the inboard end of the right-hand driveshaft to permit sump removal.
97 Remove the sump.
98 If it is only desired to check backlash in the gears, this can be done by removing the oil pump cover and strainer assembly from the back of the pump.
99 Refer to Figs. 12.4 and 12.5 and check backlash and axial play against the tolerances in the Specifications.
100 If the tolerances are exceeded then the oil pump should be renewed.
101 To remove the oil pump, refer to the relevant Chapters and remove the following components
  Camshaft drivebelt (timing belt)
  Alternator drivebelt
  Crankshaft pulley
  Lower timing belt cover
  Front cover and TDC setting bracket
102 If they are still in position, remove the bolts holding the rear stay bracket.
103 Remove the two bolts holding the oil pump to the cylinder block.
104 This will release the tension on the chain and allow the pump to be removed.
105 If sufficient slack in the chain cannot be achieved by this method, then slide the pump, chain and crankshaft drive sprocket forward together.
106 Check the chain and teeth of the drive sprockets and renew any parts which are worn.
107 If a new pump is being fitted, it would be as well to renew all associated parts at the same time.

Refitting

108 Refitting is a reversal of removal, but bear in mind the following points.
109 Use new gaskets on all components.
110 Oil all new parts liberally.
111 If the small plug in the front cover is at all damaged, renew it.
112 Similarly, fit a new crankshaft oil seal to the cover. The oil seal can be prised out and a new one pressed fully home.
113 The chain is tensioned by moving the pump housing against its mounting bolts.
114 With light finger pressure exerted on the chain, deflection should be as given in the Specifications.
115 Whenever the sump is removed with the engine *in situ*, the two hexagon screws in the sealing flange at the flywheel end should be replaced by socket-headed screws and spring washers, and tightened to the figure given in the Specifications.

Crankshaft sprocket - modification

116 As from August 1986 the crankshaft sprocket incorporates a lug for engagement with the groove in the crankshaft, replacing the Woodruff key arrangement used previously.
117 When tightening the crankshaft sprocket bolt observe the stages given in the Specifications.

6 Engine (1.6 and 1.8 litre)

Engine front mounting - modification

1 As from December 1984 the engine front mounting is changed from the bonded rubber type to a 'hydro' type with damping action. Refer to Fig. 12.7 - the tightening torques of the nuts and bolts with letters are given in the Specifications section of Chapter 1.

Camshaft and cylinder head - examination and renovation

2 On exchange engines or cylinder heads, the camshaft is supplied with bearing shells instead of running directly in the head and bearing caps. Exchange units supplied by VW may have an undersized camshaft with corresponding bearing shells, and where this is the case the camshaft will have a yellow paint spot on it and the journal diameter will be 25.75 mm (1.014 in) An unmarked camshaft supplied with bearing shells will be of standard size with a journal diameter of 26.00 mm (1.024 in).

Hydraulic bucket tappets - description

3 All 1986-on engines are fitted with a redesigned cylinder head incorporating hydraulic bucket tappets in place of the previous shim bucket tappets. Camshaft bearing number 4 is deleted on all single camshaft engines, and in order to identify the type of tappets fitted a sticker is normally affixed to the valve cover, indicating that valve clearance adjustment is neither necessary nor possible.
4 All the relevant procedures given in Section 5, concerning the hydraulic bucket tappets, apply also to 1.6 and 1.8 litre engines. In particular note that the valves should not be re-cut as this will adversely affect the operation of the hydraulic tappets. Regrinding is permissible but if the valves are deeply pitted they should be renewed.

Sump - modification

5 As from August 1985 a larger sump is fitted and the oil capacity is increased as given in the Specifications.

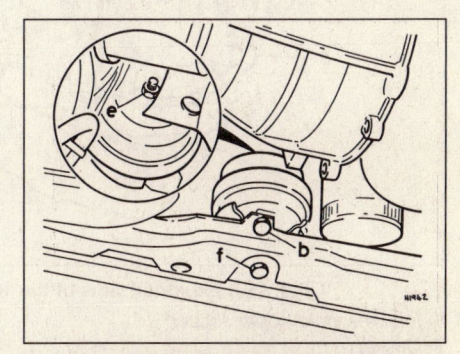

Fig. 12.7 'Hydro' type front engine mounting (Sec 6)

Refer to Chapter 1 for torque wrench settings for nuts and bolts b, e and f

12•16 Supplement: Revisions and information on later models

Oil cooler - renewal

6 The oil cooler fitted to fuel injection engines should be renewed if the engine oil has been contaminated with metal particles, such as might be the case following total or partial engine seizure. Renew it anyway if it is likely to contain any other harmful contaminant.

16-valve (16V) engine - general description

7 The 16-valve engine fitted to GTI models from October 1986, incorporates double overhead camshafts (DOHC), one operating the exhaust valves and the other the inlet valves, with four valves per cylinder. The valves operate in pairs simultaneously and provide the engine with a much improved breathing capability, resulting in greater power output. A single camshaft sprocket is attached to the exhaust camshaft, and a chain and sprocket at the opposite end of the cylinder head is used to drive the inlet camshaft.

8 Apart from the obvious differences mentioned in paragraph 7, most overhaul procedures for the 16-valve engine are basically the same as those for the 8-valve engine; the following paragraphs describe procedures which differ.

Timing belt (16V engine) - removal and refitting

9 Besides the timing mark on the camshaft sprocket shown in Chapter 1, Fig. 1.15, an additional timing mark is provided on the

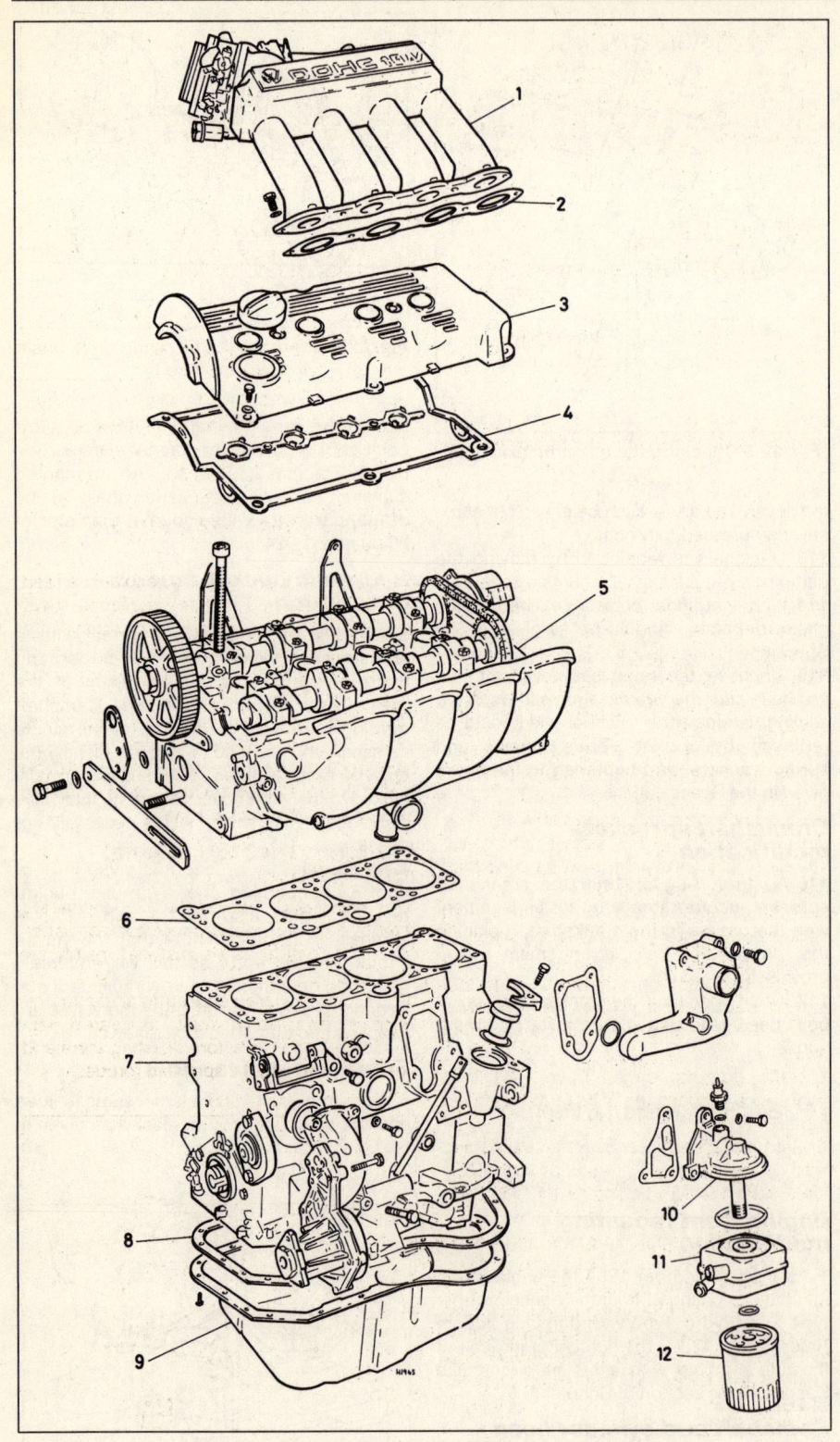

Fig. 12.8 Exploded view of the 16V fuel injection engine (Sec 6)

1 Inlet manifold upper section
2 Gasket
3 Valve cover
4 Gasket
5 Cylinder head assembly with camshafts
6 Cylinder head gasket
7 Cylinder block assembly
8 Gasket
9 Sump
10 Oil filter head
11 Oil cooler
12 Oil filter

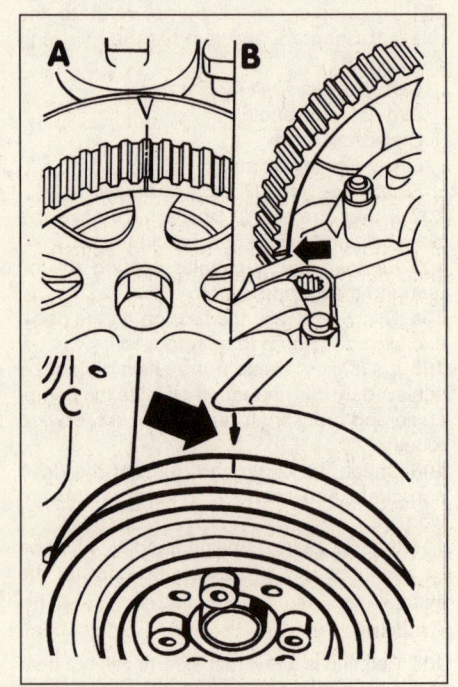

Fig. 12.9 Valve timing marks on the 16V engine (Sec 6)

A Camshaft sprocket outer marks
B Camshaft sprocket inner marks
C Crankshaft vibration damper marks

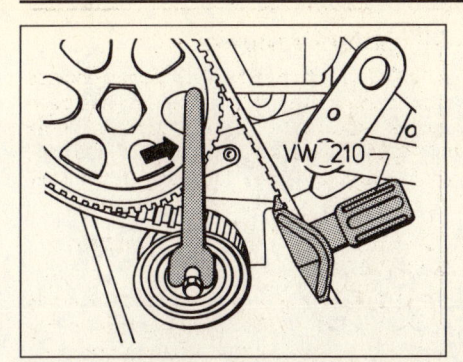

Supplement: Revisions and information on later models 12•17

Fig. 12.10 Adjusting the timing belt tension using VW special tool 210 (Sec 6)

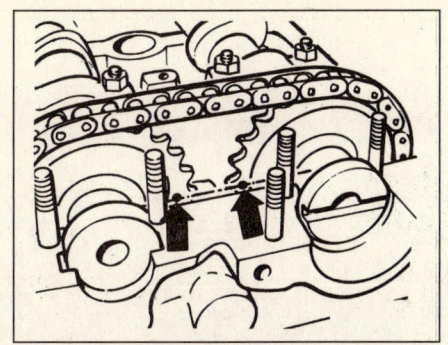

Fig. 12.11 TDC timing marks in alignment on the camshaft drive chain sprockets (Sec 6)

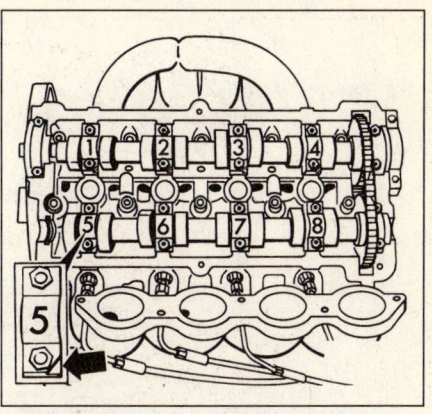

Fig. 12.12 Camshaft bearing cap identification on the 16V engine (Sec 6)

Inset shows recessed corner position (arrowed)

outside of the camshaft sprocket (Fig. 12.9) which aligns with a mark on the valve cover. This means that if the timing belt alone is being renewed it is not necessary to remove the valve cover in order to check the alignment marks.

10 When fitting the timing belt it is recommended that VW tool 210 is used to set the tension accurately as this is more critical with the dohc arrangement. Using this tool the tension should be set to record a reading of between 13 and 14 on the scale. The tool can be obtained from a VW dealer.

Camshafts (16V engine) - removal and refitting

11 Remove the cover from the camshaft sprocket.
12 Unbolt and remove the upper section of the inlet manifold.
13 Unbolt and remove the valve cover after disconnecting the HT leads from the spark plugs. Remove the main gasket and the central gasket from around the spark plug locations.
14 Align the timing marks with reference to Chapter 1, then check also that the marks on the chain sprockets are aligned (Fig. 12.11).
15 Remove the timing belt and camshaft sprocket with reference to Chapter 1.
16 Note the fitted positions of the camshaft bearing caps, if necessary marking them to ensure correct refitment. Refer to Fig. 12.12 for details.
17 Progressively unscrew the nuts and bolts from the end caps and bearing caps 1 and 3 on the exhaust camshaft.
18 Progressively unscrew the bolts from the bearing caps 2 and 4; the exhaust valve springs will force the exhaust camshaft up as the bolts are loosened. Remove the bearing caps keeping them identified for position.
19 Working on the inlet camshaft, progressively unscrew the nuts and bolts from the end cap and bearing caps 5 and 7.
20 Progressively unscrew the bolts from bearing caps 6 and 8, then remove all the caps keeping them identified for position.
21 Lift both camshafts from the cylinder head, then release them from the drive chain.
22 If necessary, remove the hydraulic bucket

tappets with reference to paragraph 3 of this Section and the relevant paragraphs in Section 5. Check the camshafts and drive chain for wear, referring also to Section 5.
23 Oil all the bucket tappets and the camshaft journals, then insert the tappets in their original bores.
24 Locate the drive chain on the camshaft sprockets so that the timing marks are aligned as shown in Fig. 12.11, then lower the camshafts into position on the cylinder head. Recheck the timing mark alignment.
25 Fit a new oil seal to the front end of the exhaust camshaft.
26 When refitting the bearing caps make sure that they are located the correct way round. They are numbered as shown in Fig. 12.12 and the numbers must be readable from the inlet manifold side of the head. The recessed corners of the caps must also face the inlet manifold side of the head.
27 Refit bearing caps 6 and 8, then progressively tighten the bolts to the specified torque.
28 Refit the inlet camshaft end cap and bearing caps 5 and 7, then progressively tighten the nuts and bolts to the specified torque.
29 Refit bearing caps 2 and 4, then progressively tighten the bolts to the specified torque.
30 Refit the exhaust camshaft end caps and bearing caps 1 and 3, then progressively tighten the nuts and bolts to the specified torque.
31 Refit the camshaft sprocket and timing belt with reference to Chapter 1, and paragraphs 9 and 10 of this Section.
32 Check that all the timing marks including the drive chain sprocket marks are aligned.
33 Refit the valve cover together with new gaskets and reconnect the spark plug HT leads.
34 Refit the inlet manifold upper section and the camshaft sprocket cover.

Caution: *If new hydraulic tappets have been fitted, do not start the engine before 30 minutes have elapsed otherwise the valves may strike the pistons.*

Exhaust valves (16V engine) - description

35 Exhaust valves on the 16V engine are filled with sodium to provide improved heat dissipation, and special precautions are necessary when disposing of this type of valve, particularly where recycling of scrap metal is concerned.
36 To render the valve safe it should be wiped dry, then cut through the stem with a hacksaw. Throw the valve into a bucket of water, keeping well away from it until the chemical reaction has subsided.

Big-end caps (16V engine) - description

37 The big-end caps on the 16V engine are fitted with oil jets which direct a stream of oil to the underside of the pistons, mainly for cooling purposes.
38 The oil jets are secured to the caps by small screws which must be coated with thread-locking fluid before inserting them and tightening them to the specified torque.

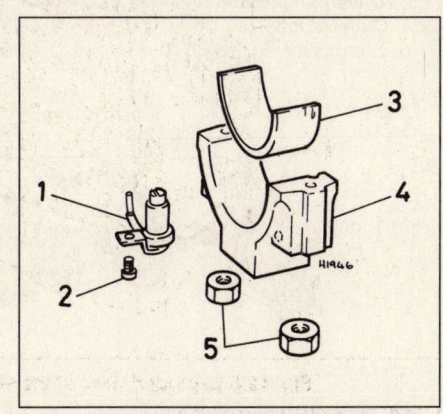

Fig. 12.13 Big-end cap components on the 16V engine (Sec 6)

1 Oil jet
2 Screw
3 Bearing shell
4 Cap
5 Nuts

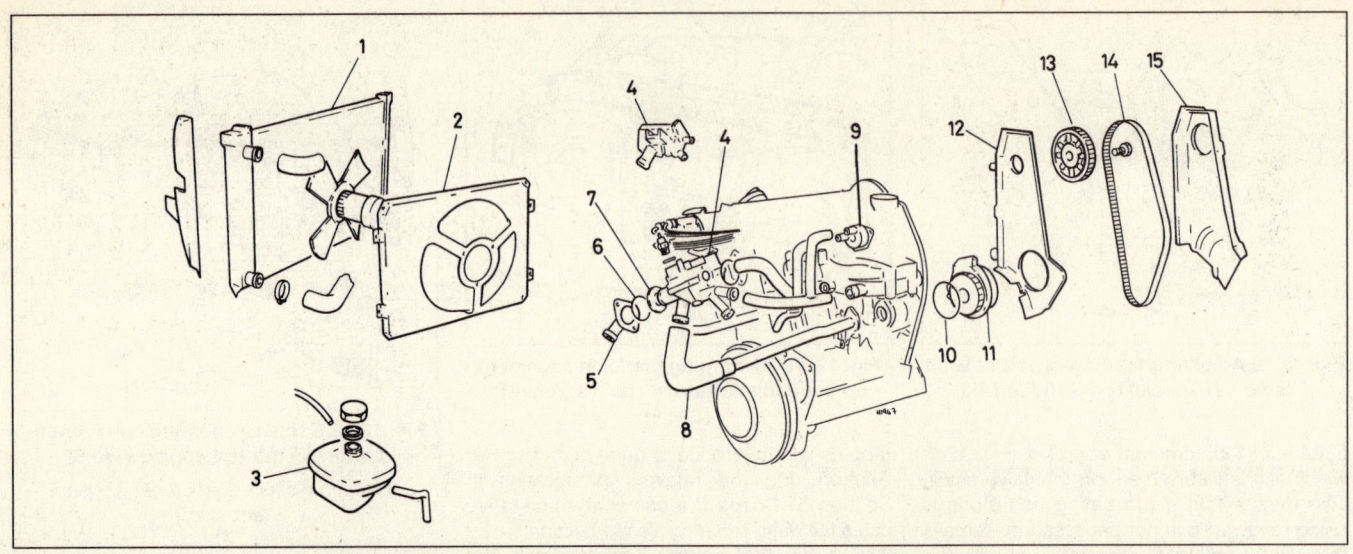

12•18 Supplement: Revisions and information on later models

Fig. 12.14 Cooling system components for the 1.05 and 1.3 litre engines with hydraulic 'bucket' tappets (Sec 7)

1 Radiator
2 Fan ring
3 Expansion tank
4 Thermostat housing
5 Cover
6 O-ring
7 Thermostat
8 Hose
9 Automatic choke
10 O-ring
11 Water pump
12 Inner timing cover
13 Camshaft sprocket
14 Timing belt
15 Outer timing cover

Engine (1986-on) - removal

39 When removing 1.6 and 1.8 litre engines from later models, the operations described in Chapter 1 generally apply, but note the following points.
40 Remove the front panel before removing the radiator.
41 If power-assisted steering is fitted, remove the hydraulic pump drivebelt, and unbolt the pump, belt tensioner and fluid reservoir. Tie them to one side of the engine compartment.

7 Cooling system

Thermostat housing (1.05 and 1.3 litre engines) - modification

1 The carburettor on 1.05 and 1.3 litre hydraulic 'bucket' tappet engines incorporates a coolant-operated automatic choke, and the coolant supply and return hoses are routed from the thermostat housing. The modified components are shown in Fig. 12.14; however, the removal and refitting procedures remain basically as given in Chapter 2.

Water pump (1.05 and 1.3 litre engines) - removal and refitting

2 When fitting a water pump which has been reconditioned by VW, a check should be made to see if the sealing ring groove has been reworked. If it has, the 'Y' will be stamped on the pump mounting flange

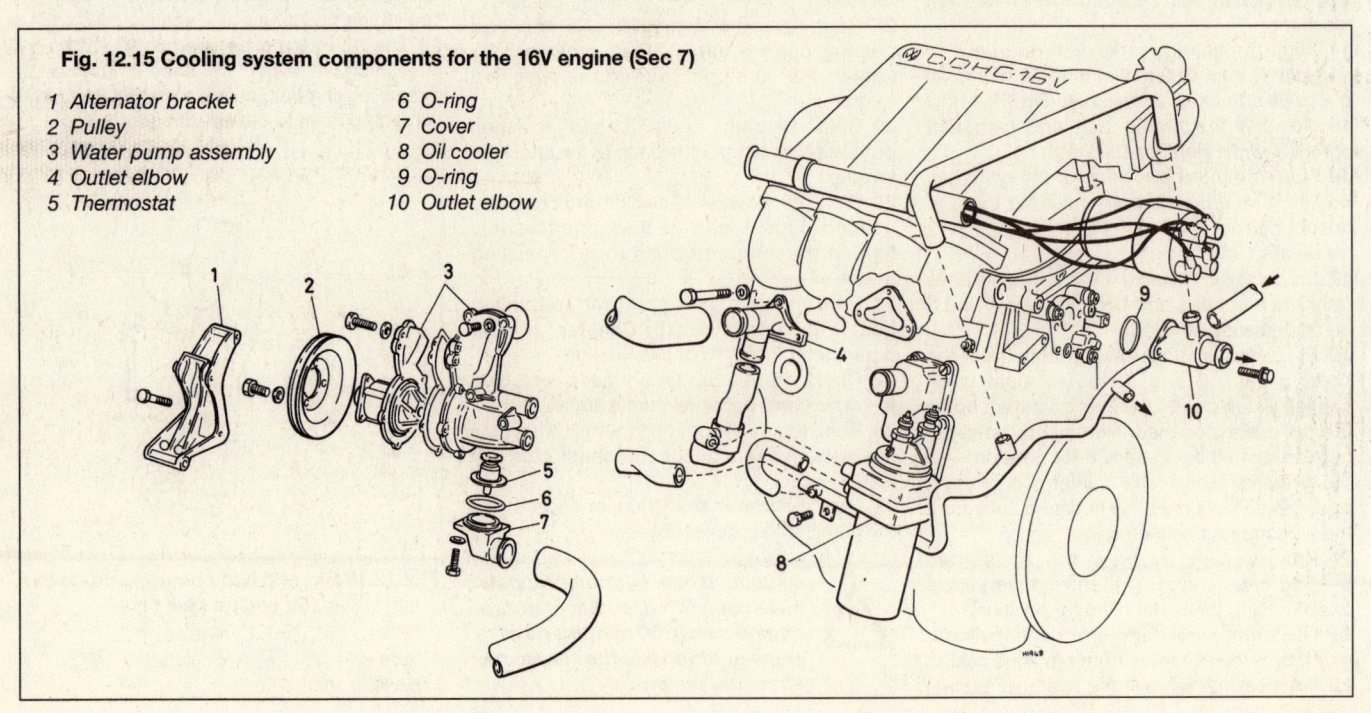

Fig. 12.15 Cooling system components for the 16V engine (Sec 7)

1 Alternator bracket
2 Pulley
3 Water pump assembly
4 Outlet elbow
5 Thermostat
6 O-ring
7 Cover
8 Oil cooler
9 O-ring
10 Outlet elbow

Supplement: Revisions and information on later models 12•19

indicating that a 5 mm diameter sealing ring should be fitted instead of the normal 4 mm diameter ring.

Cooling fan and motor - removal and refitting

3 As from January 1986, the wiring on all new cooling fan motors obtained from VW incorporates a standardised connector. Where necessary, the old connector must be cut from the main harness and the standardised part fitted instead. The relevant parts are obtainable from a VW dealer.

Electric cooling fan (fuel injection engines) - modifications

4 From September 1985, on fuel injection engines (except 16V) the cooling fan motor thermo-switch in the bottom of the radiator is of three-pin type, replacing the previous two-pin type. The new switch has two operation temperature ranges (see Specifications) the first range operates the coolant fan at normal speed and the second range operates the fan at boost speed.

5 The cooling fan fitted to 16V engines is of six-blade type; however, on other engines it may be of four or six-blade type.

6 From March 1986 the electric cooling fan is also controlled by a temperature sensor located between injectors 1 and 2. A time relay is also incorporated in the wiring circuit to keep the system functional for ten to twelve minutes after switching off the ignition.

7 To prevent personal injury do not work near the cooling fan blades on a warm engine within the time relay operating period in paragraph 6. As a precaution, disconnect the battery negative lead when working in this area of the engine.

Temperature sender (16V engine) - description

8 On the 16V engine the temperature sender is located on the flywheel end of the cylinder block below the outlet elbow. It controls the temperature gauge.

8 Fuel and exhaust systems

Carburettor (32 TLA and 1B3) - description

1 From March 1985, 1.05 litre engines are fitted with a Weber 32 TLA carburettor, although from July 1985 they may also be fitted with a Pierburg 1B3 carburettor.

Carburettor (32 TLA and 1B3) cleaning - general

2 Wash the exterior of the carburettor with a suitable solvent and allow to dry.

3 Dismantle the carburettor with reference to the relevant illustrations. Before dismantling, obtain a set of gaskets. Be sure to mark the relationship of the automatic choke to the carburettor body before separating them.

4 Clean the internal components with a suitable solvent. Do not probe any jets or orifices with wire or similar to remove dirt, blow them through with an air line.

5 Do not alter or remove the full throttle stop, or adjust the Stage II throttle valve screw settings (if applicable).

6 Reassembly is a reversal of dismantling, but renew all gaskets and sealing rings. Refer to the following sub-Sections for checks and adjustments.

Pierburg 1B3 carburettor - servicing and adjustment

7 Before undertaking any carburettor adjustments, be sure all jets, etc., are clean.

8 When inserting the accelerator pump piston seal, press it towards the opposite side of the vent drilling. The piston retaining ring must be pressed flush into the carburettor body.

General

9 All checks and adjustments are as described for the Pierburg 2E3 carburettor in Chapter 3, with the following additions.

Enrichment tube

10 With the choke valve closed, the bottom of the enrichment tube should be 1.0 mm (0.039 in) from the valve (see Fig. 12.18).

Idle speed and mixture

11 Before making any adjustment, make sure that the automatic choke is fully open, otherwise the throttle valve linkage may still be on the fast idle cam.

Idle speed boost valve

12 The idle speed adjustment screw incorporates a vacuum-operated valve which opens if the idle speed drops below 700 rpm and causes an increase in the idle speed. The

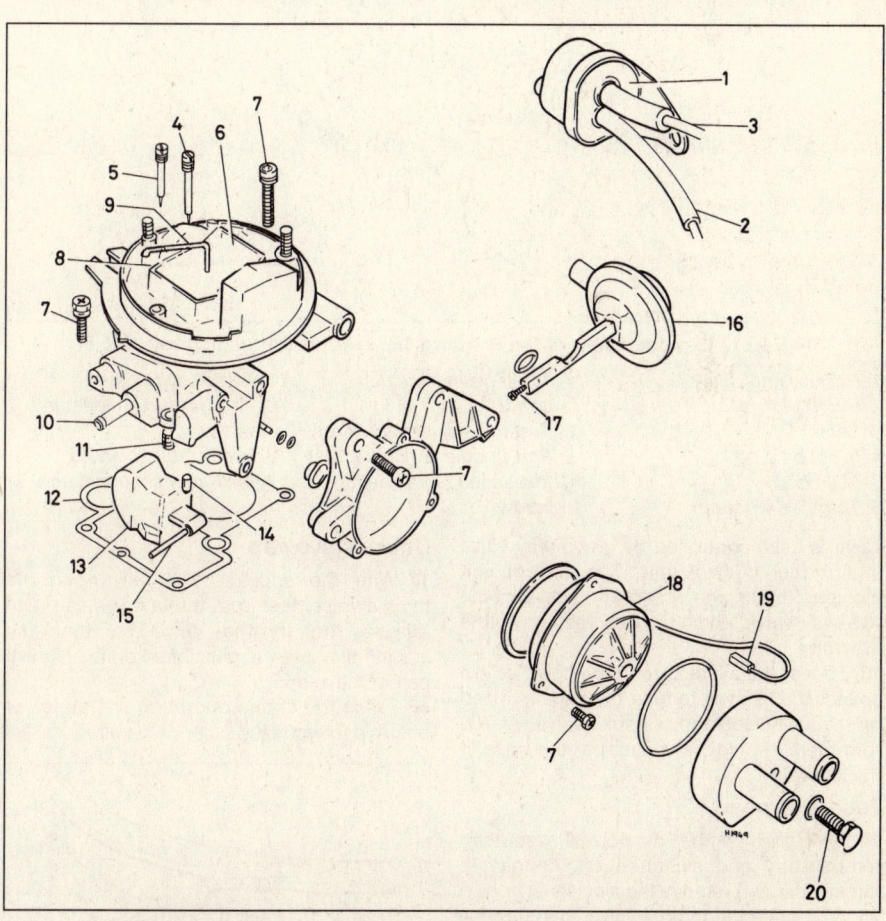

Fig. 12.16 Exploded view of the Pierburg 1B3 carburettor top cover (Sec 8)

1 Idle speed boost two-way valve
2 To idle adjustment screws
3 To vacuum line and brake servo
4 Idling fuel/air jet
5 Auxiliary fuel/air jet
6 Choke valve
7 Screw
8 Cover
9 Enrichment tube
10 Fuel supply
11 Main jet
12 Gasket
13 Float
14 Needle valve
15 Pivot pin
16 Pull-down unit
17 Adjustment screw
18 Automatic choke
19 Wiring connector
20 Screw

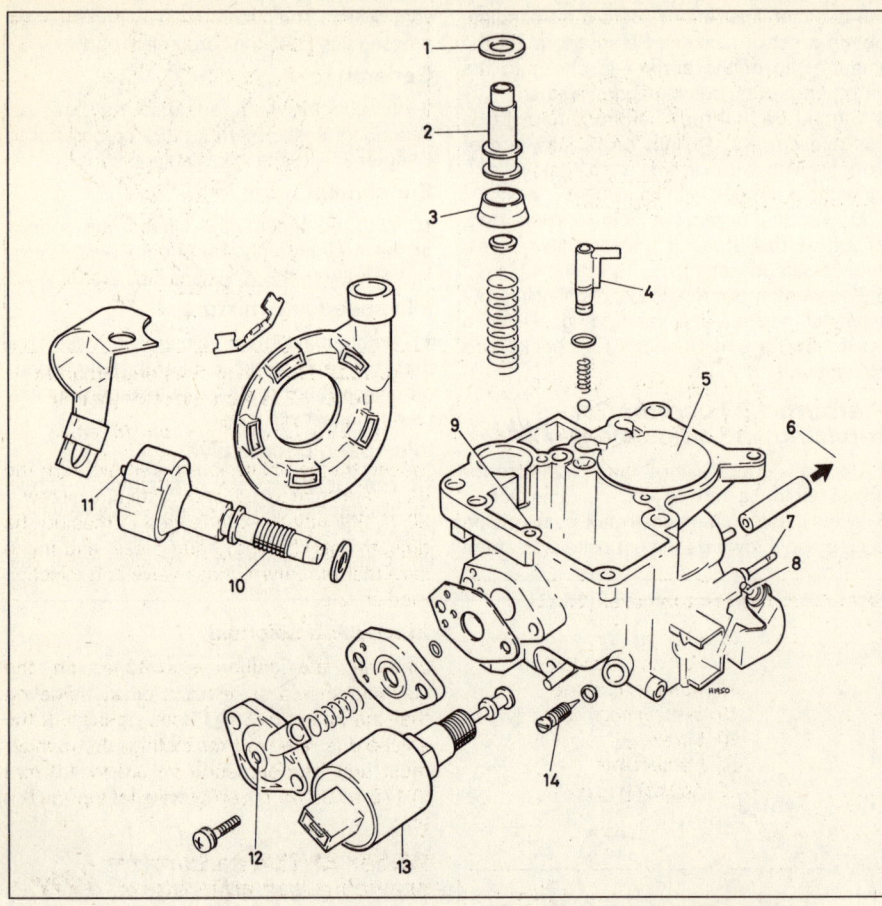

12•20 Supplement: Revisions and information on later models

Fig. 12.17 Exploded view of the Pierburg 1B3 carburettor main body (Sec 8)

1 Bearing ring
2 Pump plunger
3 Seal
4 Injection tube
5 Main body
6 To pull-down unit
7 To air cleaner vacuum control
8 Fast idle adjustment screw
9 Part throttle enrichment jet
10 Idle speed adjustment screw
11 To two-way valve
12 Part throttle enrichment valve
13 Idle cut-off solenoid
14 Mixture adjustment screw

valve is itself controlled by a two-way valve and further control unit. The control unit monitors the engine speed and activates the two-way valve which applies vacuum to the idle valve.

13 To test the system, run the engine at idle speed, then slowly reduce the engine speed by manually closing the choke valve. At 700 rpm there should be vacuum at the hose in the idle valve.

Fast idle speed

14 With the engine at normal operating temperature and switched off, connect a tachometer and remove the air cleaner.

15 Fully open the throttle valve, then turn the fast idle cam and release the throttle valve so that the adjustment screw is positioned on the second highest part of the cam.

16 Without touching the accelerator pedal, start the engine and check that the fast idle speed is as given in the Specifications. If not, turn the adjustment screw on the linkage as necessary. If a tamperproof cap is fitted, renew it after making the adjustment.

Choke valve gap

17 With the engine cold, fully open the throttle valve, then turn the fast idle cam and release the throttle valve so that the adjustment screw is positioned on the highest part of the cam.

18 Press the choke operating rod as far as possible towards the pull-down unit.

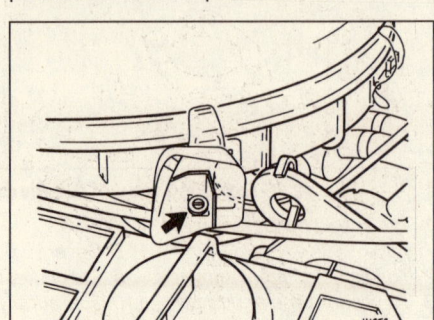

Fig 12.20 Mixture (CO content) adjustment screw location – Pierburg 1B3 carburettor (Sec 8)

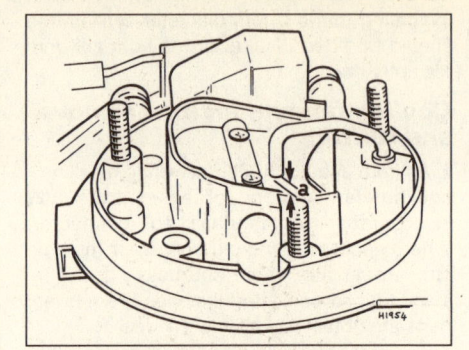

Fig. 12.18 Enrichment tube adjustment – Pierburg 1B3 carburettor (Sec 8)

$a = 1.0 \pm 0.3$ mm (0.039 ± 0.012 in)

Fig. 12.19 Idle speed adjustment screw location – Pierburg 1B3 carburettor (Sec 8)

19 Using the shank of a twist drill, check that the distance from the choke valve to the carburettor wall is as given in the Specifications. If not, adjust the screw behind the automatic choke.

Accelerator pump capacity

20 Hold the carburettor over a funnel and measuring glass.

21 Turn the fast idle cam so that the adjusting screw is off the cam.

Hold the cam in this position during the following procedure.

22 Fully open the throttle ten times, allowing at least three seconds per stroke. Divide the total quantity by ten and check that the resultant injection capacity is as given in Specifications. If not, refer to Fig. 12.21 and

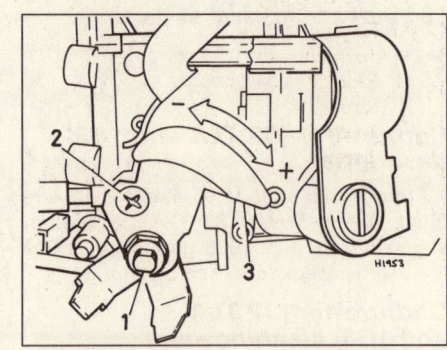

Fig. 12.21 Accelerator pump adjustment – Pierburg 1B3 carburettor (Sec 8)

1 Nut
2 Camplate locking screw
3 Camplate

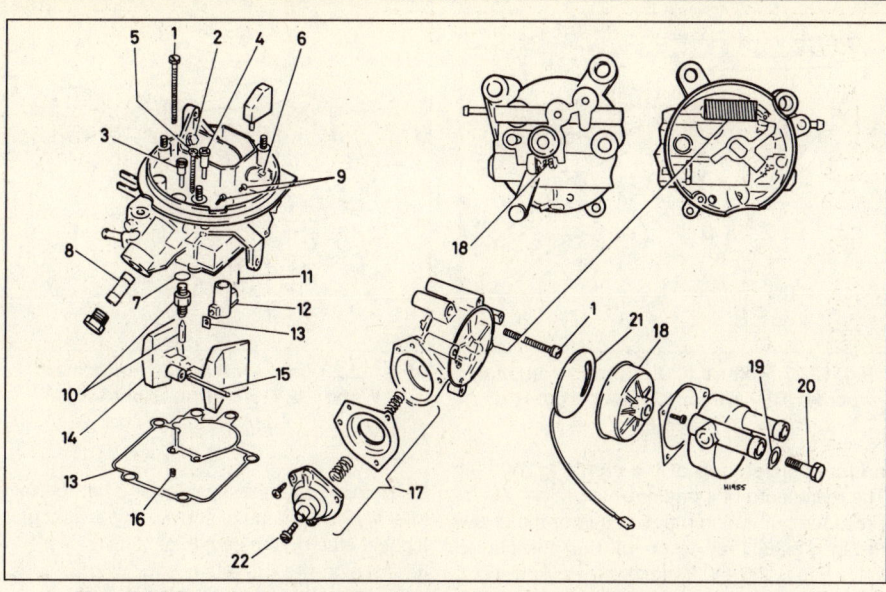

Supplement: Revisions and information on later models 12•21

Fig. 12.22 Exploded view of the Weber 32 TLA carburettor top cover (Sec 8)

1 Screw
2 Air correction jet
3 Auxiliary fuel jet (if applicable)
4 Idling fuel jet
5 Emulsion tube
6 Choke valve and lever
7 Washer
8 Gauze filter
9 Plugs
10 Needle valve
11 Pin
12 Atomizer
13 Gasket
14 Float
15 Pin
16 Main jet
17 Pull-down unit
18 Automatic choke
19 Sealing ring
20 Screw
21 Heater plate
22 Adjusting screw

1 Accelerator pump
2 Injection pipe
3 Part throttle enrichment valve
4 Idle speed boost two-way valve
5 To idle adjusting screw
6 To vacuum line and brake servo
7 Gasket
8 Clip
9 Idle speed adjustment screw
10 Throttle housing
11 Sealing ring
12 Idle cut-off solenoid
13 To air cleaner
14 To distributor
15 Fast idle adjustment screw
16 Mixture adjustment screw

Fig. 12.23 Exploded view of the Weber 32 TLA carburettor main body (Sec 8)

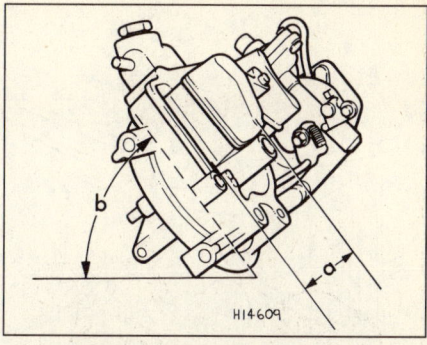

Fig. 12.24 Float level checking diagram – Weber 32 TLA carburettor (Sec 8)

a = 28 ± 1.0 mm   b = 45° angle

loosen the camplate locking screw, turn the camplate as required, and tighten the screw.

23 If difficulty is experienced in making the adjustment, check the pump seal and make sure that the return check valve and injection tube are clear.

Idle cut-off solenoid

24 When the ignition is switched on, the solenoid should be heard to click, indicating that the idle circuit has been opened. If the solenoid is removed for testing, the plunger must first be depressed by 3.0 to 4.0 mm (0.118 to 0.158 in) before switching on the unit.

Weber 32 TLA carburettor – servicing and adjustment

25 Before undertaking any carburettor adjustments, be sure all jets, etc., are clean.

Float level

26 With the upper part of the carburettor inverted and held at an angle of approximately 45°, the measurement 'a' in Fig. 12.24 should be as shown. The ball of the float needle should not be pressed in against the spring when making the measurement.

Idle speed and mixture

27 The procedure for checking and adjusting the idle speed and CO content are basically the same as given in Chapter 3, Section 17. However, refer to Figs. 12.25, 12.26 and 12.27

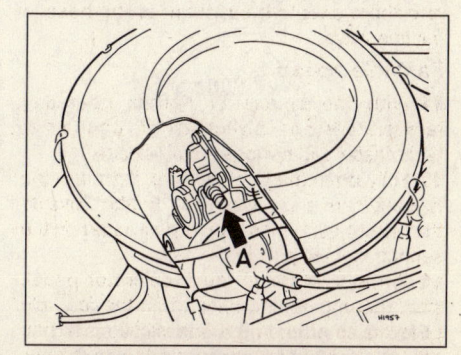

Fig. 12.25 Idle speed adjusting screw (A) for models up to June 1985 – Weber 32 TLA carburettor (Sec 8)

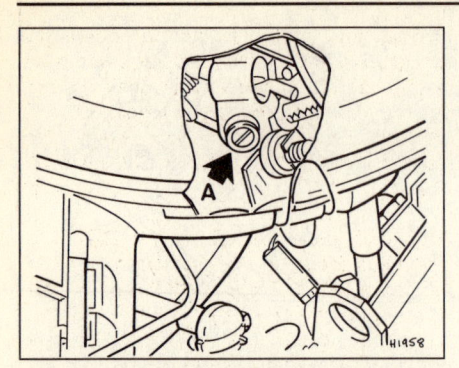

12•22 Supplement: Revisions and information on later models

Fig. 12.26 Idle speed adjusting screw (A) for models from July 1985-on – Weber 32 TLA carburettor (Sec 8)

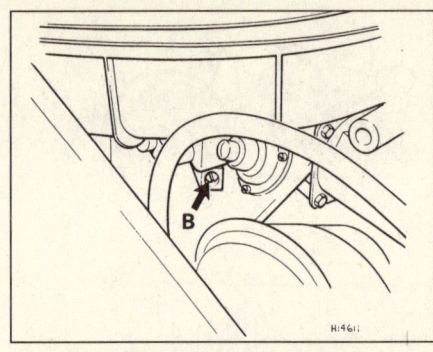

Fig. 12.27 Mixture (CO content) adjusting screw (B) – Weber 32 TLA carburettor (Sec 8)

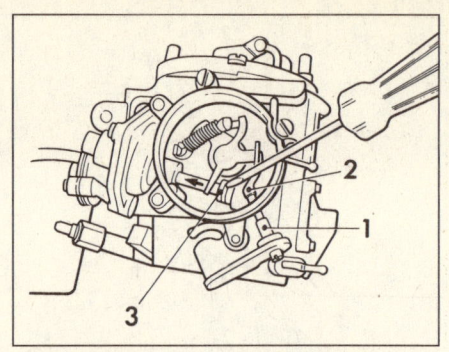

Fig. 12.28 Choke valve gap adjustment – Weber 32 TLA carburettor (Sec 8)

1 Fast idle adjustment screw
2 Cam   3 Pull rod

for the location of adjustment screws and to the Specifications in this Supplement for settings.

Idle speed boost valve

28 The idle speed boost valve is identical to the unit on the Pierburg 1B3 carburettor described in paragraphs 12 and 13.

Choke valve gap (pull-down)

29 Remove the choke cover.
30 Place the fast idle speed adjusting screw on the highest step of the cam (Fig. 12.28). The manufacturer's original instruction was to press the pull rod in the direction of the arrow in Fig. 12.28, then to check that the choke valve gap is 2.5 ± 0.2 mm. As from April 1987 however, this instruction is revised, and it is now necessary to use a vacuum pump to apply 300 mbar vacuum on the pull-down unit. The choke valve gap in this case must be 2.0 ± 0.2 mm.
31 Adjustment is made on the screw at the end of the pull-down device. Ensure that the spring (2 in Fig. 12.29) is not compressed when making the check.

Idle cut-off valve

32 To check the cut-off valve, apply battery voltage. The valve must be heard to click when voltage is applied.

Fast idle speed

33 Before carrying out this check, ensure that the ignition timing and manual idling adjustments are correct. The engine should be at normal operating temperature.
34 Remove the air cleaner.
35 Plug the temperature regulator connection.
36 Connect the tachometer.
37 Remove the choke cover and set the fast idle speed adjusting screw on the second highest step on the cam (Fig. 12.30).
38 Tension the operating lever with a rubber band so that the choke valve is fully open.
39 Without touching the accelerator pedal, start the engine, which should run at the fast idle speed given in the Specifications.
40 Adjust the screw as necessary.

Choke valve gap (wide open kick)

41 Remove the air cleaner.
42 Fully open the throttle and hold it in this position.
43 Refer to Fig. 12.31 and press the lever (1) upwards.
44 Check the gap with a twist drill which should be as given in the Specifications. Adjust by bending the lever (Fig. 12.32).

Accelerator pump capacity

45 This can be checked by following the procedure in Chapter 3, Section 16 with the following differences.
46 Open the throttle valve quickly when operating the pump (ie one second per stroke, with pauses of three seconds between strokes).

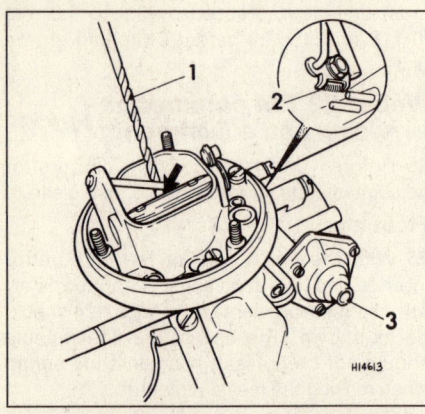

Fig. 12.29 Checking the choke valve gap (pull-down) Weber 32 TLA carburettor (Sec 8)

1 Twist drill   2 Spring   3 Adjusting screw

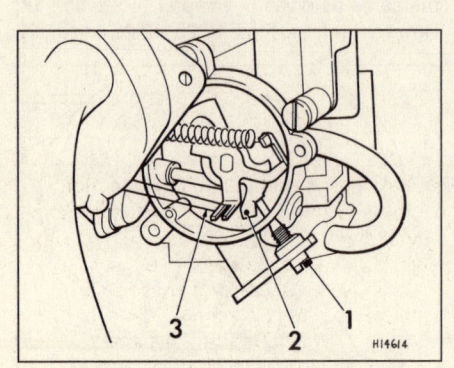

Fig. 12.30 Adjusting the fast idle speed – Weber 32 TLA carburettor (Sec 8)

1 Fast idle adjusting screw
2 Cam   3 Rubber band

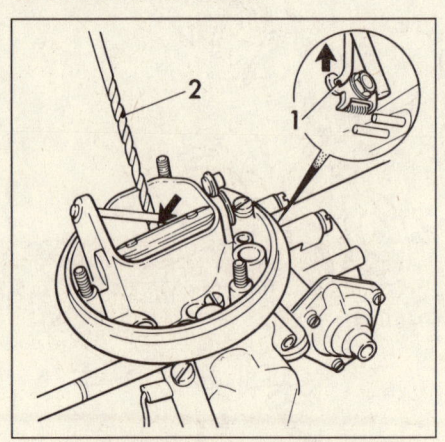

Fig. 12.31 Checking the choke valve gap (wide open kick) – Weber 32 TLA carburettor (Sec 8)

1 Pressure applied upwards   2 Twist drill

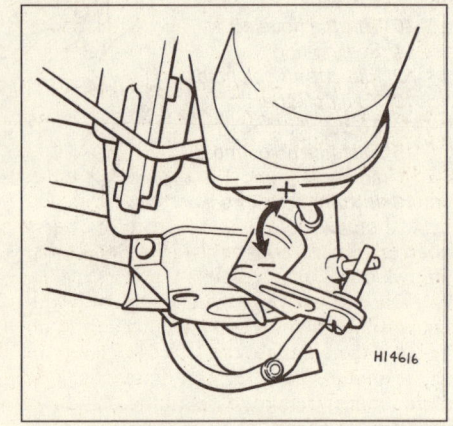

Fig. 12.32 Adjusting the choke valve gap (wide open kick) – Weber 32 TLA carburettor (Sec 8)

Bend the lever as required

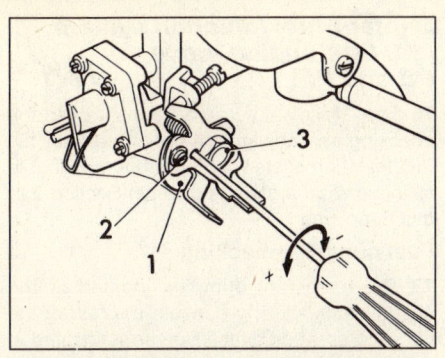

Supplement: Revisions and information on later models 12•23

Fig. 12.33 Accelerator pump adjustment – Weber 32 TLA carburettor (Sec 8)

1 Cam 2 Camplate
3 Camplate locking nut

47 The amount of fuel injected can be altered, but only very slightly, as follows.
48 Take the accelerator cable cam off the throttle valve lever.
49 Secure the accelerator pump cam with an M4 screw (Fig. 12.33).
50 Loosen the locknut on the camplate securing screw. Loosen the screw and turn the camplate with a screwdriver clockwise to decrease injected fuel and anti-clockwise to increase injected fuel. Tighten the screw and locknut and recheck the injection capacity.

Solex/Pierburg 2E2 carburettor - choke valve gap (wide open kick) adjustment

51 Remove the automatic choke cover and fit a rubber band to the operating pin, so that the choke valve is held in the closed position.
52 Hold the primary throttle valve open 45°. To do this, temporarily insert a 10 mm nut between the fast idling adjustment screw and the vacuum unit plunger.
53 Using a twist drill, check that the gap between the choke valve and carburettor wall is 6.3 + 0.3 mm (0.248 + 0.012 in). If not, bend the choke operating lever as required.
54 After making an adjustment, check and adjust the choke pull-down unit as described in Chapter 3.

Solex/Pierburg 2E2 carburettor choke pull-down unit - modification

55 As of February 1987, the choke pull-down unit is both temperature and time-controlled by a thermotime valve. When the valve is open (starting a cold engine) the vacuum to the pull-down unit is reduced, and the choke valve will open by a small amount. After between one and six seconds (depending on ambient temperature), the valve heats up (to approximately 20 to 30°C) and closes. This allows more vacuum to reach the pull-down unit, and the choke valve will open by a larger amount. The choke is of course fully released by the heat of the engine coolant and the electric heater acting on the automatic choke bi-metallic spring.

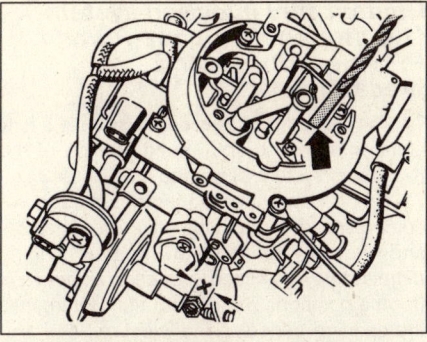

Fig. 12.34 Checking the choke valve gap on the Solex/Pierburg 2E2 (Sec 8)

Using a drill of correct diameter as a gauge (arrowed)
Note dimension x (10 mm)

Solex/Pierburg 2E2 carburettor - three/four point unit checking

56 The method described in Chapter 3, Section 20 requires the use of a vacuum pump, whereas the following method uses engine vacuum.
57 Run the engine to normal operating temperature then switch it off, remove the air cleaner, and close the vacuum line from the carburettor to the temperature regulator.
58 With the engine stopped, check the diaphragm pushrod (A in Fig. 3.27) is fully extended to approximately 14.5 mm (0.571 in).
59 Start the engine and let it idle. The diaphragm pushrod must now be extended approximately 8.5 mm (0.335 in) for the three-point unit, or 9.5 mm (0.374 in) for the four-point unit, and must just contact the fast idle adjustment screw.
60 On models with air conditioning, switch on the air conditioner with the blower on maximum speed. The diaphragm pushrod dimension should be approximately 12.0 mm (0.472 in).
61 To check the overrun cut-off point, run the engine at idle speed.
62 On the four-point unit, disconnect and plug the pink-coloured hose at the control valve.
63 Using a screwdriver, hold the primary throttle valve fully closed to prevent it moving to the overrun cut-off point.

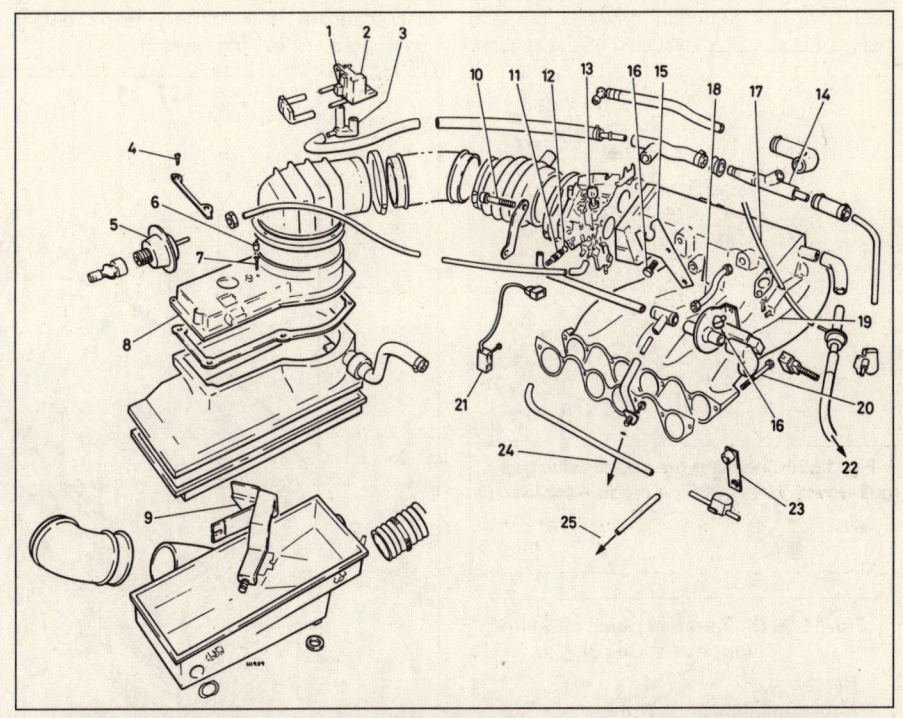

Fig. 12.35 Exploded view of the K-Jetronic system inlet manifold and fuel injection components (except code PB, PF and 16V engines) – from September 1984 (Sec 8)

1 Two-way valve (II)	9 Temperature control flap (where applicable)	17 To multi-function indicator
2 Two-way valve (I)	10 Screw	18 To valve cover
3 T-piece	11 Idle speed adjustment screw	19 Auxiliary air valve
4 Screw	12 O-ring	20 Screw
5 Diaphragm pressure valve	13 Throttle housing	21 Throttle valve switch
6 Plug	14 Vacuum booster	22 To brake servo unit
7 Mixture (CO) adjustment screw	15 Bracket	23 Bracket
8 Airflow meter	16 Screw	24 To cylinder head
		25 To distributor

12•24 Supplement: Revisions and information on later models

64 Disconnect the plug from the idling/overrun control valve, then check that the diaphragm pushrod dimension is approximately 1.5 mm (0.059 in).
65 To check the unit for leaks, first, on the three-point unit only, pinch the hose between the unit and Y-piece.
66 Stop the engine by disconnecting the coil terminal 15, and check that the diaphragm rod remains in the overrun/cut-off position for a minimum of five seconds.
67 Reconnect the coil wiring, control valve plug and hose where applicable, and refit the air cleaner.

K-Jetronic fuel injection system (except PB, PF and 16V engines) - modifications

68 As from September 1984, the components associated with the inlet manifold were modified as shown in Fig. 12.35. All work procedures remain as described in Chapter 3, Part B
69 As from March 1986, a temperature sensor is located between injectors 1 and 2. This switches on the electric cooling fan when the temperature of the cylinder head exceeds 110°C (230°F) after switching off the ignition. A time relay is incorporated in the circuit, to switch off the function between ten and twelve minutes after switching off the ignition

Digifant fuel injection system (1.8 litre engine, code PB and PF) - description and precautions

70 The Digifant fuel injection system is a fully electronic and computerised version of the K-Jetronic system described in Chapter 3.
71 The main components include a computerised control unit, electronic injectors and various sensors to monitor engine temperature and speed, induction air flow and throttle position. The control unit determines the opening period of the injectors, and also continuously adjusts the ignition timing according to engine speed, load and temperature.
72 When working on the system, take extra care to prevent dust and dirt entering the various components. It is recommended not to use compressed air or fluffy cloths for cleaning purposes.
73 Switch off the ignition before disconnecting any relevant wiring or when washing the engine.
74 Boost-charging the battery is only permissible for one minute at 16.5 volts maximum.
75 Disconnect both battery leads before carrying out any electric welding.

Digifant fuel injection system (1.8 litre engine, code PB and PF)

76 The following paragraphs describe checking and adjustment procedures for the fuel injection system. Information applicable to the ignition system is given in Section 9 of this Supplement.

Fuel pumps - checking

77 The main fuel pump is located in the accumulator housing beneath the rear of the car, and an additional lift pump is located in the fuel tank, together with the fuel gauge sender.
78 With the engine stopped, have an assistant switch on the ignition. It should be possible to hear both pumps running for a short period. If not, check fuse 5 for continuity, and also check all wiring connections.
79 With the ignition on, disconnect each wire connector from the pumps and check that there is a 12 volt supply using a voltmeter.
80 Should there be no voltage at the pumps with the ignition switched on, the fuel pump relay (No 2 on fusebox) may be faulty. This is best checked by substituting a new relay.

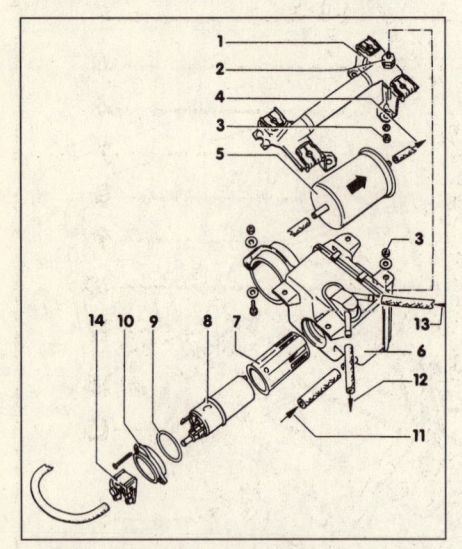

Fig. 12.36 Digifant fuel pump and filter components (Sec 8)

1 Bracket
2 Rubber mounting
3 Nut
4 Fuel supply to fuel distributor
5 Fuel filter
6 Pump accumulator
7 Strainer
8 Fuel pump
9 O-ring
10 Retainer
11 From fuel lift pump in fuel tank
12 Return to fuel tank
13 Return from pressure regulator
14 Adapter

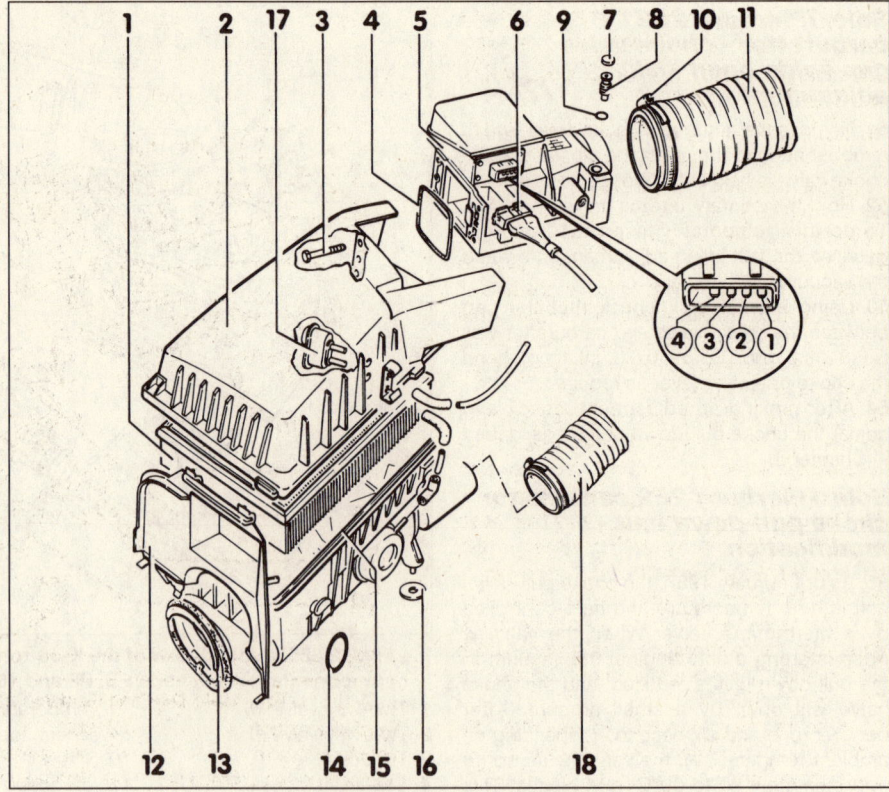

Fig. 12.37 Digifant airflow meter components (Sec 8)

1 Air cleaner element
2 Cover
3 Bolt
4 Seal
5 Airflow meter
6 Connector
7 Tamperproof plug
8 Mixture (CO content) adjustment screw
9 O-ring
10 Clip
11 Air inlet hose
12 Plate
13 Seal
14 Retaining ring
15 Air cleaner body
16 Rubber washer
17 Temperature regulator
18 Warm air hose

Supplement: Revisions and information on later models 12•25

Fig. 12.38 Intake air temperature sender resistance graph – Digifant and Digijet systems (Sec 8)

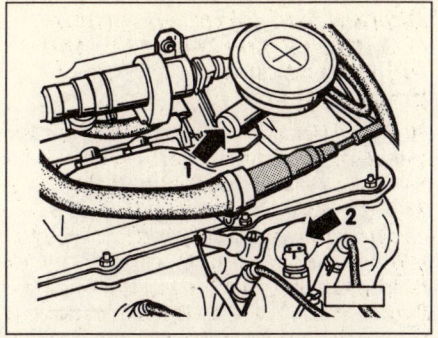

Fig. 12.39 Digifant crankcase ventilation pressure regulating valve (1) and temperature sender (2) (Sec B)

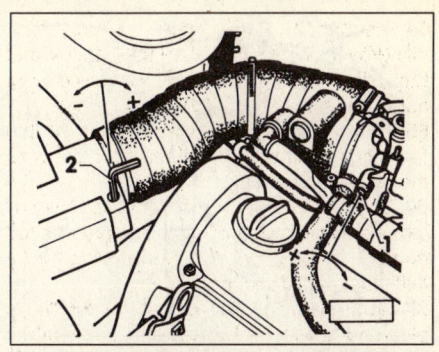

Fig. 12.40 Digifant idle speed adjusting screw (1) and mixture (CO content) adjusting screw (2) (Sec 8)

Airflow meter - checking

81 Refer to Fig. 12.37 and disconnect the wiring plug from the airflow meter.
82 Connect an ohmmeter between terminals 1 and 4 and check that the resistance of the intake air temperature sender is as shown in Fig. 12.38, according to the ambient air temperature.
83 Connect the ohmmeter between terminals 3 and 4 and check that the resistance of the potentiometer is between 0.5 and 1.0 k ohms.
84 Connect the ohmmeter between terminals 2 and 3, and check that the resistance fluctuates as the airflow meter plate is moved.

Idle speed and mixture (CO content) adjustment

85 Run the engine until the oil temperature is at least 80°C (176°F) - this should correspond to normal operating temperature.
86 Switch off all electrical components, including the air conditioning, where fitted. Note that the radiator fan must also be stationary during the adjustment procedure.
87 For accurate adjustment, the throttle valve switch and idling stabilisation control valve must be functioning correctly, and the ignition timing must be correct.
88 With the engine stopped, connect a tachometer to the engine. Plug one of the exhaust tailpipes, and position the probe of an exhaust gas analyser in the remaining tailpipe.
89 Disconnect the crankcase ventilation hose from the pressure regulating valve on the valve cover, and plug the hose.
90 Run the engine at idle speed, then, after approximately one minute, disconnect the wire from the temperature sender (Fig. 12.39) and quickly increase the engine speed to 3000 rpm three times.
91 With the engine idling, check the idle speed and CO content. If necessary, adjust the screws shown in Fig. 12.40. The CO adjustment screw is fitted with a tamperproof plug at the factory, and should be prised out before making an adjustment.
92 Reconnect the temperature sender wire, and again quickly increase the engine speed to 3000 rpm three times. With the engine idling, the idle speed and CO content should be as specified, but if necessary make any small corrections required.
93 Fit a new tamperproof plug.
94 Reconnect the crankcase ventilation hose. Note that if this increases the CO content, do not alter the adjustment. The cause is fuel dilution of the engine oil due to frequent stop/start use, and a long fast drive should reduce the CO content to the correct level again. Alternatively, an oil change will achieve the same objective.

Automatic air cleaner temperature control - checking

95 Disconnect the hose from the vacuum unit, then remove the air cleaner cover and element.
96 Check that the flap in the lower body is closing the warm air inlet.

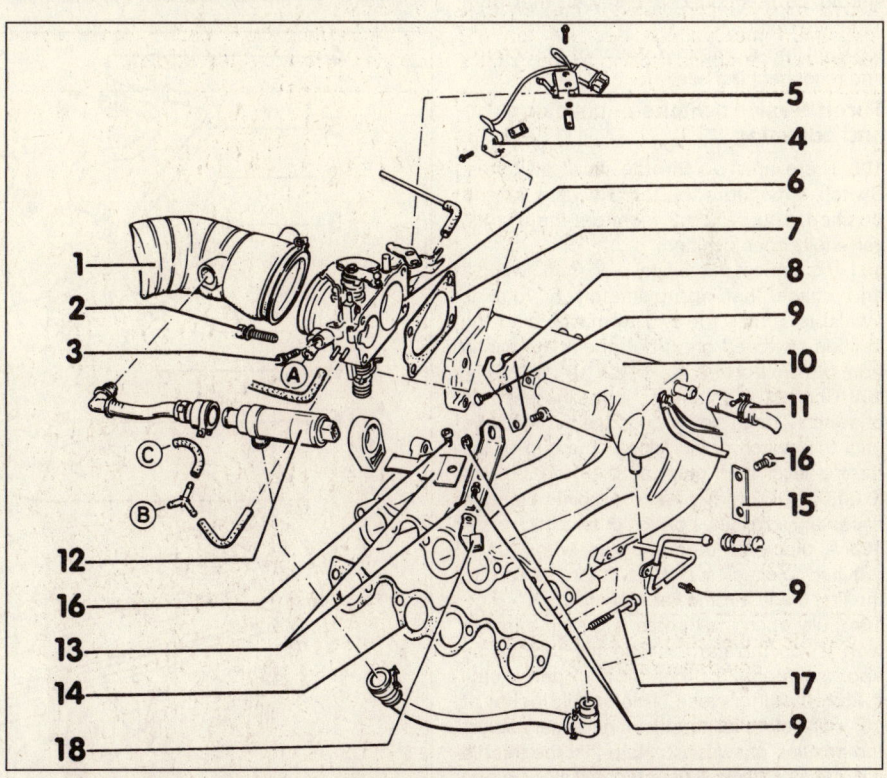

Fig. 12.41 Digifant throttle valve housing components (Sec 8)

A Front crankcase ventilation valve
B Vacuum hose connection from fuel pressure regulator
C Vacuum hose from air cleaner temperature regulator

1 Air inlet hose
2 Bolt
3 Idle speed adjustment
4 Throttle valve switch 1
5 Throttle valve switch 2
6 Throttle valve housing
7 Gasket
8 Bracket
9 Bolt
10 Inlet manifold
11 Vacuum hose to brake servo unit
12 Idle speed stabilization control valve
13 Support
14 Gasket
15 Support
16 & 17 Bolt
18 Bracket

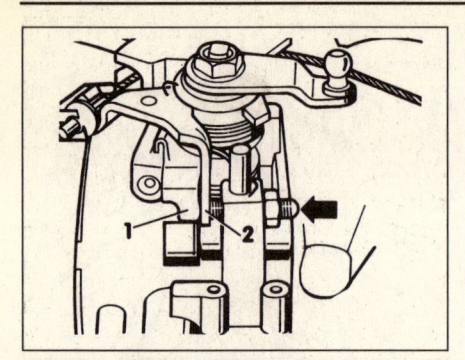

12•26 Supplement: Revisions and information on later models

Fig. 12.42 Digifant throttle stop adjustment (Sec 8)

1 Carrier lever   2 Stop lever
Arrow indicates adjustment screw

97 Suck on the vacuum hose, and check that the flap moves freely to close the cold air inlet.
98 The flap operation may be checked with the engine idling by extending the vacuum hose and positioning a thermometer by the temperature regulator. Below 20°C (68°F) the cold air inlet must be closed, above 30°C (86°F) the warm air inlet must be closed, and between 20 and 30°C (68 and 86°F), the flap should be positioned midway so that both inlets are open.
99 Refit the air cleaner element and cover, and reconnect the hose.

Throttle valve switches - checking and adjusting

100 There are two throttle valve switches. Switch 1 monitors the throttle valve closed position, and switch 2 monitors the throttle valve fully open position.
101 Disconnect the supply plug from switch 2 and check that approximately 5 volts is available across the two terminals with the ignition switched on. If not check the wiring from the control unit.
102 Connect an ohmmeter across the terminals of switch 2, then slowly open the throttle valve until the switch points close. The gap at the throttle lever stop must be 0.20 to 0.60 mm (0.008 to 0.024 in) when the points close. If necessary adjust the position of switch 1.
103 A piece of card marked with 10° is required to check switch 2. Attach the card to the first stage throttle valve shaft.
104 Fully open the throttle and align a datum with 0° on the card. Close the throttle by approximately 20°, then slowly open it until switch 2 points close. This should occur at 10° ± 2° before full throttle. If necessary adjust the position of switch 2. Note that the throttle valve lever roller must contact the sloping part of switch 2.

Throttle stop - adjustment

105 The throttle stop adjustment is initially set at the factory, and should not be tampered with. However, if it is accidentally loosened, proceed as follows.
106 Back off the adjustment screw until a gap exists between the carrier lever and stop lever (Fig. 12.42).

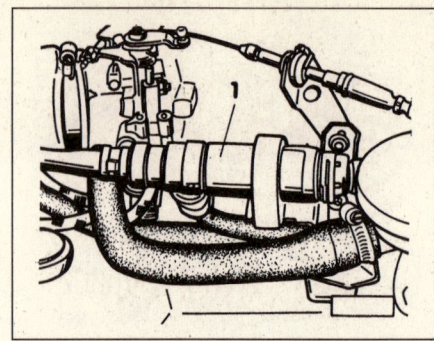

Fig. 12.43 Digifant idle speed stabilization control valve (1) (Sec 8)

107 Turn the adjustment screw until the two levers just make contact, then continue to turn it a further half-turn. Tighten the lockout.
108 After making an adjustment, readjust the throttle valve switches, and the idle speed and mixture.

Idle speed stabilization system - checking

109 Check that the stabilization control valve buzzes when the ignition is switched on. If not, use an ohmmeter to check the continuity valve after pulling off the connector (Fig.12.43).
110 Run the engine until the oil temperature is at least 80°C (176°F) - this should correspond to normal operating temperature.
111 Connect a multi-meter to the stabilization control valve in series with the existing wiring.
112 Run the engine at idle speed, then, after approximately one minute, quickly increase the engine speed to 3000 rpm three times. At idling speed, the control current should be approximately 420 ± 30 mA and *fluctuating*. With the temperature sender plug disconnected, the current should be approximately 420 ± 30 mA but *constant*. All electrical components must be switched off during the check, and power steering (where fitted) centralised.

Fuel pressure regulator - checking

113 An accurate pressure gauge and adapter is required for the work, and as these will not normally be available to the home mechanic, it is recommended that a VW dealer carry out the check.

Fuel injectors - checking

114 Refer to Chapter 3, Section 37, paragraphs 1 to 3, but in addition, carry out the following electrical tests.

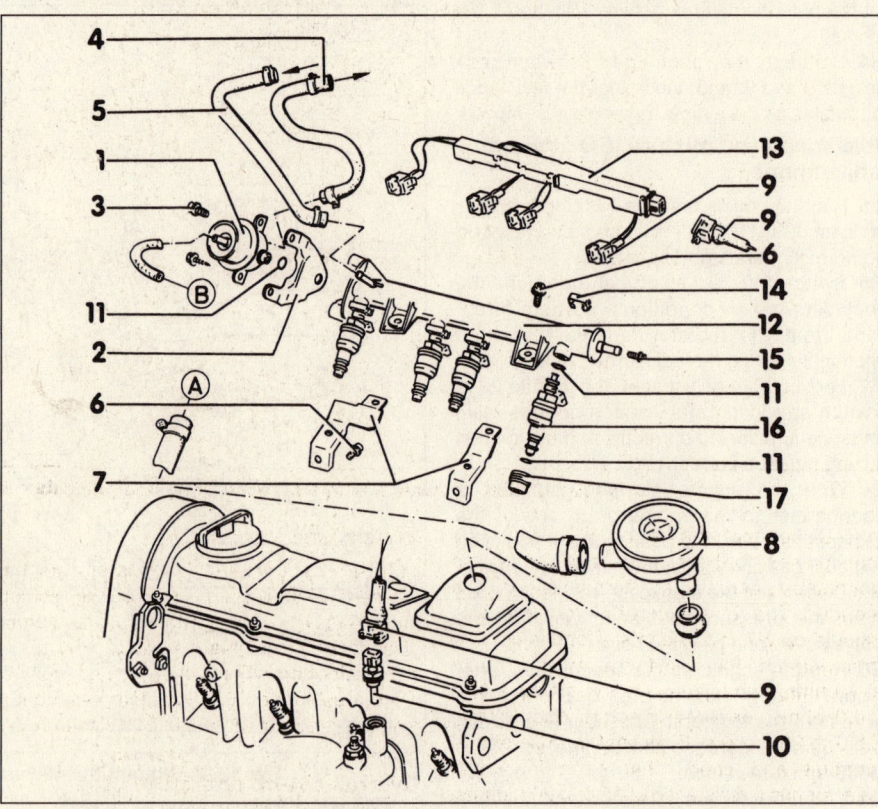

Fig. 12.44 Digifant fuel injectors and pressure regulator components (Sec 8)

A Crankcase, ventilation hose	6 Bolt	12 Fuel distributor
B Vacuum hose	7 Bracket	13 Wiring conduit
1 Fuel pressure regulator	8 Crankcase ventilation pressure regulator valve	14 Clip
2 Bracket		15 Plug
3 Bolt	9 Connector	16 Injector
4 Fuel return hose (blue)	10 Temperature sender	17 Insert
5 Fuel supply hose (black)	11 O-ring	

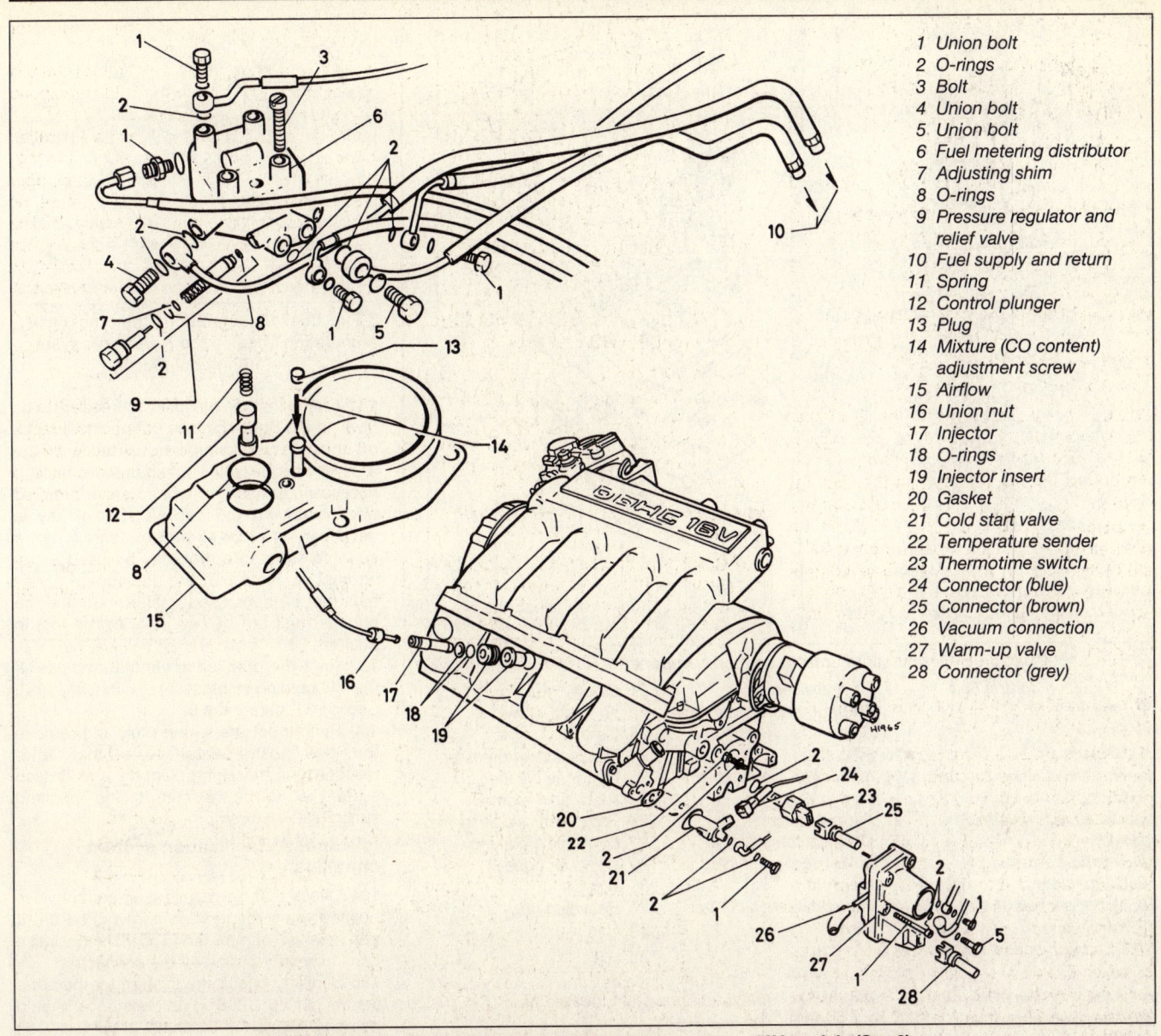

Supplement: Revisions and information on later models 12•27

1 Union bolt
2 O-rings
3 Bolt
4 Union bolt
5 Union bolt
6 Fuel metering distributor
7 Adjusting shim
8 O-rings
9 Pressure regulator and relief valve
10 Fuel supply and return
11 Spring
12 Control plunger
13 Plug
14 Mixture (CO content) adjustment screw
15 Airflow
16 Union nut
17 Injector
18 O-rings
19 Injector insert
20 Gasket
21 Cold start valve
22 Temperature sender
23 Thermotime switch
24 Connector (blue)
25 Connector (brown)
26 Vacuum connection
27 Warm-up valve
28 Connector (grey)

Fig.12.45 K-Jetronic fuel injection metering components – 16V models (Sec 8)

115 Disconnect the wiring plug from the conduit next to the injectors, and connect an ohmmeter across the terminals on the conduit. The resistance of all four injectors should be 3.7 to 5.0 ohms. If one injector is open-circuit, the resistance will be 5.0 to 6.7 ohms, two injectors open-circuit 7.5 to 10.0 ohms, or three injectors open-circuit 15.0 to 20.0 ohms. If necessary, prise off the conduit and check that each individual injector has a resistance of 15.0 to 20.0 ohms.
116 Checking the injector spray patterns cannot be performed as described in Chapter 3, due to the position of the fuel distributor. However, the injectors may be removed together with the fuel distributor and wiring conduit, and the engine turned on the starter for a few seconds. Use a suitable container to catch the fuel.

Control unit - general
117 The control unit is located on the left-hand side of the bulkhead. The ignition must always be switched off before disconnecting the plug.
118 It is not possible to check the control unit without using the VW test appliances, so if a fault is suspected, it should be taken to a VW dealer.

Overrun cut-off and full throttle enrichment - checking
119 Run the engine until the oil temperature is at least 80°C (176°F) normal operating temperature then let the engine idle.
120 Manually close the full throttle valve switch 2 and hold it closed. Open the throttle until the engine speed is approximately 2000 rpm, and check that the engine speed surges,

indicating that the overrun cut-off is functioning.
121 If the engine does not surge, disconnect the wiring from the temperature sender and connect a bridging wire between the two contacts on the plug.
122 Repeat the procedure in paragraph 120. If the engine now surges, the temperature sender is proved faulty. However, if it still refuses to surge, check the associated wiring and throttle valve switch 2. If no fault is found, renew the control unit.

K-Jetronic fuel injection system (16V engine) - checks and adjustments

123 The fuel injection components for the 16V engine are shown in Figs.12.45 and 12.46. Procedures are the same as described

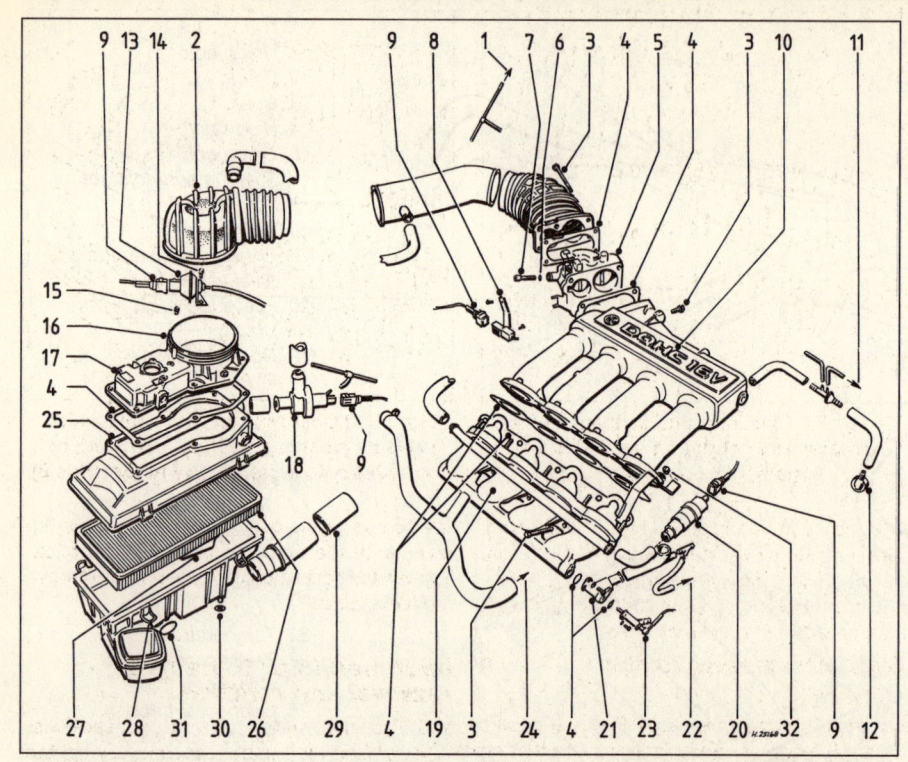

12•28 Supplement: Revisions and information on later models

Fig. 12.46 K-Jetronic inlet manifold and associated components – 16V models (Sec 8)

1 To ignition control unit
2 Intake elbow
3 Screw
4 Gaskets
5 Throttle valve housing
6 O-ring
7 Idle speed adjustment screw
8 Throttle valve switch
9 Connector
10 Upper section of inlet manifold
11 To multi-function indicator
12 To brake servo unit
13 Diaphragm pressure valve
14 Screw
15 Plug
16 Mixture (CO) adjustment screw
17 Airflow meter
18 Overrun cut-off valve
19 Lower section of inlet manifold
20 Idle stabilization control valve
21 Elbow
22 To warm-up valve
23 Cold start valve
24 To crankcase breather
25 Upper air cleaner
26 Air cleaner element
27 Temperature control flap
28 Lower air cleaner
29 Warm air hose
30 Washer
31 Retaining ring
32 Nut

in Chapter 3, Part B except as given in the following paragraphs.

Idle speed - adjustment

124 Run the engine to normal operating temperature, then check that all electrical components are switched off. Note that the electric cooling fan must not be running during the adjustment procedure.
125 Disconnect the crankcase ventilation hose, referring to Fig.12.47.
126 Connect a tachometer and an exhaust gas analyser to the engine.
127 If the injector pipes have been removed and refitted just prior to making the adjustment, run the engine to 3000 rpm several times, then allow it to idle for at least two minutes.
128 Check that when the ignition is switched on the idling stabilization control valve is heard to buzz. If not, check the system with reference to paragraph 134 to 137.
129 Disconnect the wiring plug for the idle stabilization system located near the ignition coil (see Fig.12.48).
130 Allow the engine to idle, then check that the idle speed is 1000 ± 50 rpm. If necessary remove the cap and turn the idle speed adjustment screw as required.

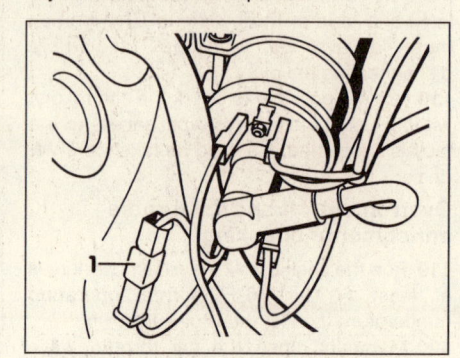

Fig. 12.48 K-Jetronic idle stabilization wiring plug (1) – 16V model (Sec 8)

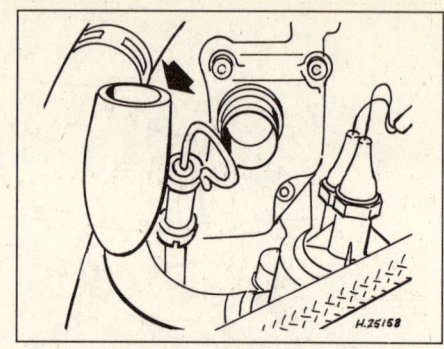

Fig. 12.47 Disconnecting the crankcase ventilation hose on the K-Jetronic system – 16V model (Sec 8)

131 Check that the mixture (CO reading) is as given in the Specifications - temporarily block off the exhaust tailpipe not fitted with the analyser probe while making the check. If necessary, turn the mixture screw as required after removing the cap. A special key is necessary in order to turn the screw, but a suitable substitute tool may be used as an alternative. Note that the adjustment screw must not be depressed or lifted and that the engine must not be revved with the tool in position.
132 Refit the crankcase ventilation hose. If the CO reading increases, refer to Chapter 3, Section 31, paragraph 9.
133 Reconnect the wiring plug and remove the test instruments. Note that after reconnecting the wiring plug, the stabilization system will return the idling to the specified speed (950 + 50 rpm).

Idle speed stabilization system - checking

134 Check that the stabilization control valve buzzes when the ignition is switched on. If not, use an ohmmeter to check the valve continuity after pulling off the connector.
135 Similarly check the system temperature sender. At 20°C (68°F) its resistance should be approximately 1000 ohms, at 60°C (140°F) the resistance should be approximately 250 ohms, and at 100°C (212°F) it should be approximately 75 ohms.
136 If the system fault cannot be traced using

Fig. 12.49 K-Jetronic idle speed screw (A) and mixture (CO content) screw (B) 16V model (Sec 8)

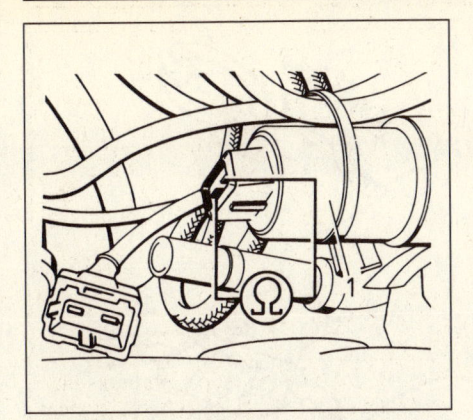

Supplement: Revisions and information on later models 12•29

Fig. 12.50 Checking the continuity of wiring for the idling stabilization control valve on the K-Jetronic system 16V model (Sec 8)

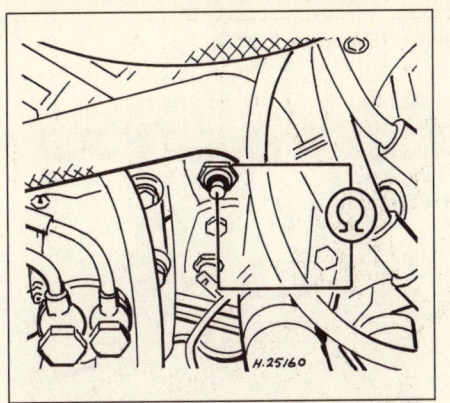

Fig. 12.51 Checking the resistance of the temperature sender on the K-Jetronic system – 16V model (Sec 8)

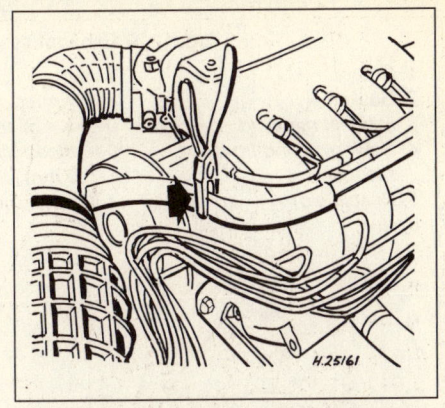

Fig. 12.52 Checking the idle stabilization valve by pinching the hose (arrowed) on the K-Jetronic system – 16V model (Sec 8)

the previous test, check all the associated wiring and finally, if necessary, renew the control unit located behind the centre console.

137 The operations of the control valve may be checked by connecting a multi-meter to it. With a tachometer connected, run the engine (hot) at idle speed and note the control current. Now pinch the hose shown in Fig.12.52 and check that the current rises. Release the hose, increase the engine speed to 1300 rpm, and actuate the throttle valve switch. The control current should drop below 430 mA. With the wiring disconnected as described in paragraph 129, the control current should be constant between 415 and 445 mA.

Overrun cut-off valve - checking

138 With a tachometer connected, run the engine (hot) at 2500 rpm, then operate the throttle valve switch and check that the engine hunts (ie speed fluctuates). If not, let the engine idle, disconnect the valve wiring and connect a voltmeter to the terminals as shown if Fig.12.53. Zero volts should be registered.

139 Increase the engine speed to 4000 rpm, then quickly close the throttle. At 1400 rpm battery voltage should be indicated.

140 If necessary renew the control unit located behind the centre console.

Diaphragm pressure switch - checking

141 Pull the wiring connector from the switch, then connect an ohmmeter to the switch terminals. With the engine idling, the reading should be infinity. Quickly open and close the throttle and check that the resistance drops briefly then rises to infinity.

Throttle valve switch - checking

142 Pull the wiring connector from the throttle valve switch.

143 Refer to Fig. 12.55 then using an ohmmeter check that with the throttle closed there is zero resistance between terminals 1 and 2, but a reading of infinity between terminals 2 and 3. With the throttle open the readings should be reversed.

144 To adjust the switch, insert a 0.10 mm (0.004 in) feeler blade between the throttle lever and stop (see Fig. 12.56), then loosen the screws and move the switch towards the lever until the contacts are heard to click. Tighten the screws on completion and remove the feeler blade.

Inlet manifold (16V engine) - removal and refitting

145 The inlet manifold is in two sections. When refitting the upper section, fully tighten the nuts securing it to the lower section first before attaching it to the rear support bracket.

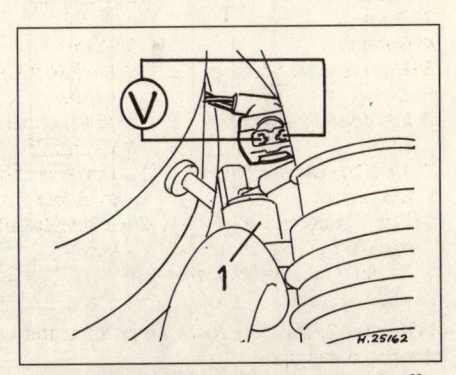

Fig. 12.53 Checking the overrun cut-off valve (1) on the K-Jetronic system – 16V system model (Sec 8)

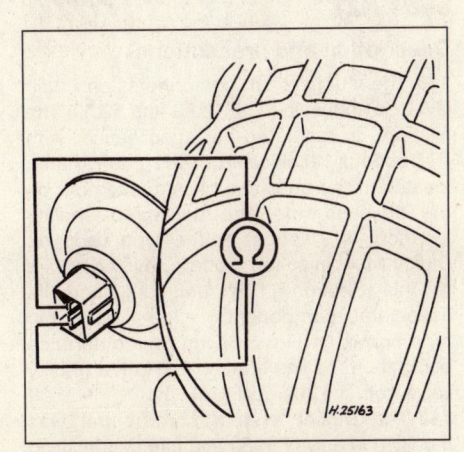

Fig. 12.54 Checking the diaphragm pressure switch on the K-Jetronic system – 16V model (Sec 8)

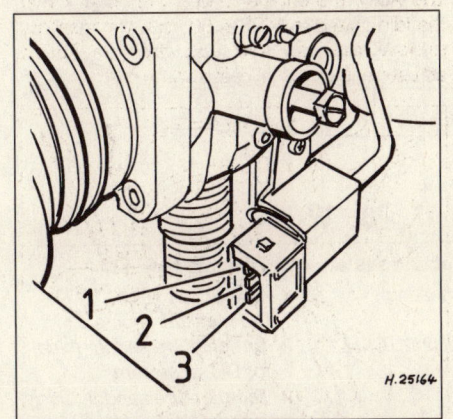

Fig. 12.55 K-Jetronic throttle valve switch connector terminals – 16V model (Sec 8)

See text for terminal identification

Fig. 12.56 Throttle valve switch adjustment on the K-Jetronic system – 16V model (Sec 8)

12•30 Supplement: Revisions and information on later models

Fig. 12.57 Exhaust system – 16V model (Sec 8)

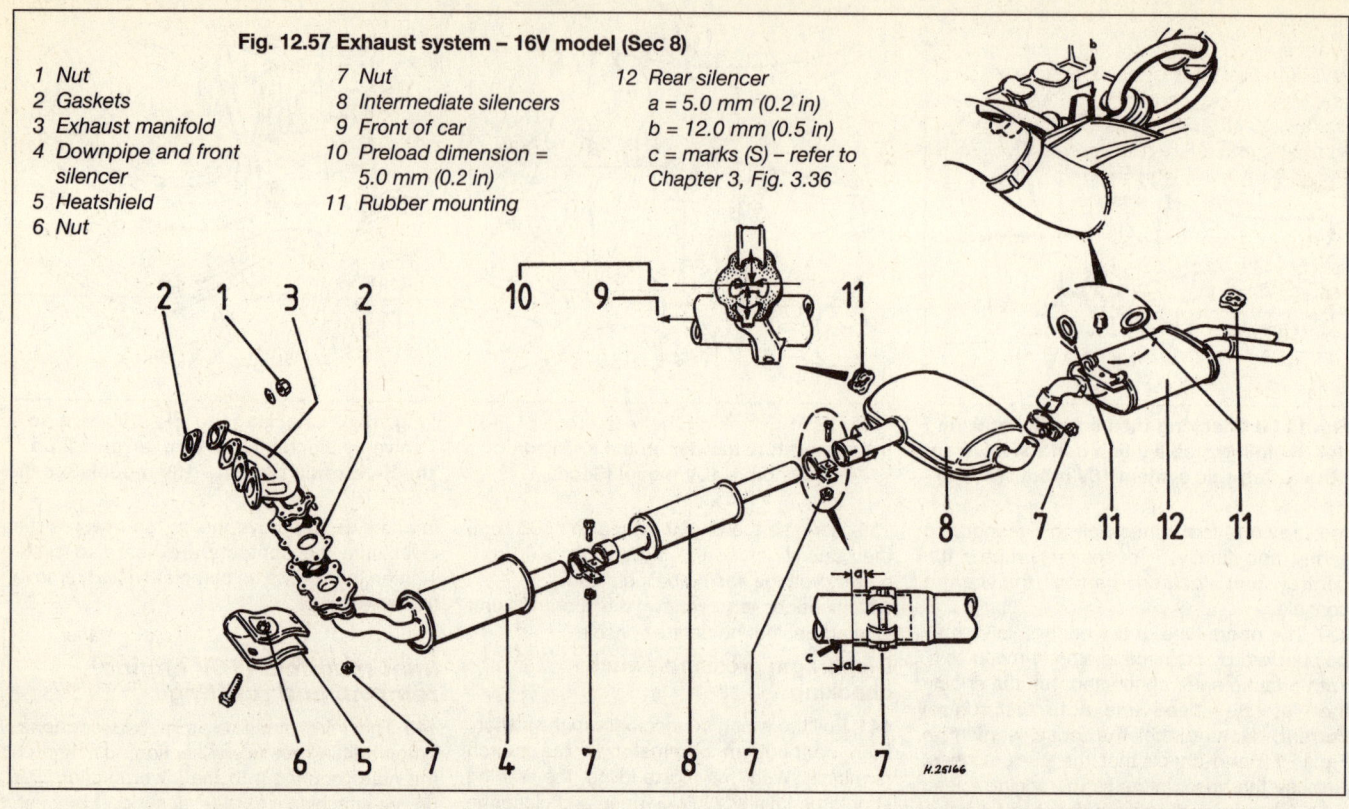

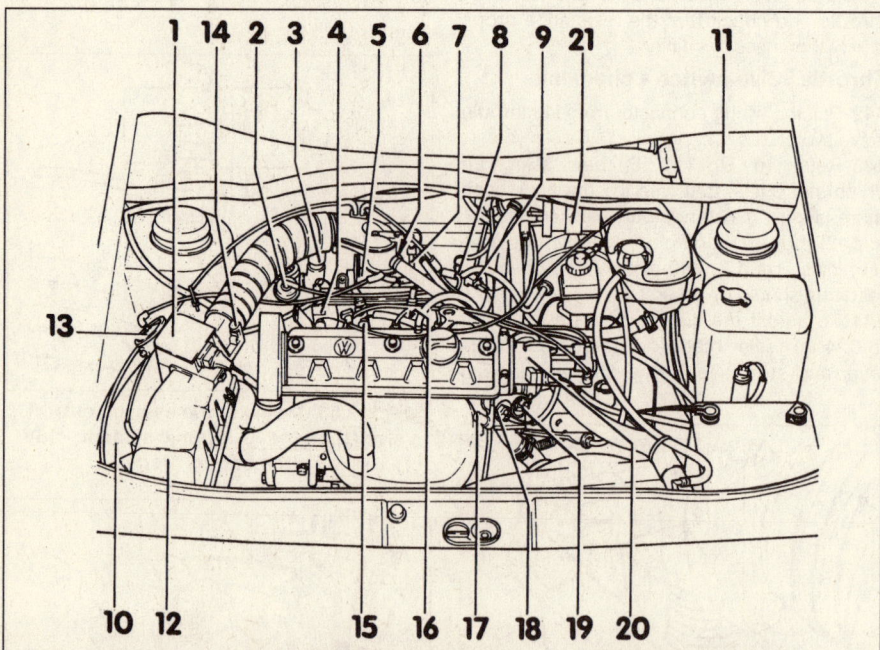

1 Nut
2 Gaskets
3 Exhaust manifold
4 Downpipe and front silencer
5 Heatshield
6 Nut
7 Nut
8 Intermediate silencers
9 Front of car
10 Preload dimension = 5.0 mm (0.2 in)
11 Rubber mounting
12 Rear silencer
   a = 5.0 mm (0.2 in)
   b = 12.0 mm (0.5 in)
   c = marks (S) – refer to Chapter 3, Fig. 3.36

Fig. 12.58 Location of Digijet fuel injection system components (Sec 8)

1 Airflow meter
2 Fuel pressure regulator
3 Heater element
4 Injector
5 Throttle valve housing
6 Idle speed adjustment screw
7 Throttle valve switch
8 Auxiliary air valve connector
9 Lambda probe connector
10 Intake air preheating vacuum unit
11 Digijet control unit/TCI-H switch unit
12 Air cleaner
13 Cut-off valve
14 Mixture (CO) adjustment screw
15 Spark plug
16 Auxiliary air valve
17 CO measuring pipe
18 Temperature sender (blue) for Digijet system
19 Temperature sender (black) for coolant gauge
20 Distributor (with Hall sender)
21 Ignition coil

Exhaust system (fuel injection models) - description

146 The exhaust system for the 16V engine is shown in Fig. 12.57. It incorporates four silencers together with twin downpipes and tailpipes. The manifold/downpipe flange is of standard type with a gasket. Refer to Chapter 3, Section 24 for the relevant procedures.
147 Non-16V models manufactured from August 1985 are also fitted with a manifold/downpipe flange incorporating a gasket instead of spring clips.

Digijet fuel injection system (1.3 litre engine, code NZ)

Description and precautions

148 The main system components and their layout is shown in Figs. 12.58 and 12.59. The system is regulated in accordance with instructions received from the control unit, located in the bulkhead plenum chamber on the left-hand side. The fuel pump (and its location) is identical to the type used on Digifant fuel injection models covered earlier in this Section. The fuel tank and its associated components is identical to the type shown in Fig. 3.5, the only difference being the feed line attachment to the gravity valve from the charcoal filter.
149 The Digijet system control unit was modified in July of 1989 and can be identified by a blue sticker on the unit (earlier models had a copper-brown sticker).
150 The precautions and general

Supplement: Revisions and information on later models 12•31

maintenance notes in Section 26 of Chapter 3 concerning the K-Jetronic fuel injection system are also applicable to the Digijet system. Having observed these notes, the following checks and adjustments can be made to the system if the appropriate test equipment is available.

Digijet fuel injection system (1.3 litre engine, code NZ) - checks and adjustments

Air cleaner element - removal, cleaning/renewal and refitting

151 Refer to Chapter 3, Section 27.

Idle speed and mixture - check and adjustment

152 The idle speed can only be accurately checked using a suitable tachometer and an exhaust CO analyser. VW recommend that the intake air temperature sender in the airflow meter must ideally be set to 1.8 K ohms to provide a neutral air intake temperature, but as this requires the use of specialised VW equipment to achieve, an approximate check/setting will therefore have to suffice.

153 When checking or making any adjustments to the idle speed, it is important that the following are adhered to.
(a) The engine must be at its normal operating temperature.
(b) All electrical components must be switched off (including the cooling fan).
(c) The ignition timing adjustment must be correct.

154 Pull free the crankcase ventilation hose from the pressure regulating valve and plug it.

155 With the ignition switched off, connect up a tachometer in accordance with the manufacturer's instructions, then connect up the CO analyser to the measuring pipe (Fig. 12.62). An adaptor will probably be needed to ensure a good seal between the analyser hose and the measuring pipe. Disconnect the Lambda probe wiring plug from its in-line connector.

156 Start the engine and check that the idle speed and the CO content are as specified. If the idle speed is too high, check that the throttle valve is fully closing before making any adjustments to the idle speed.

157 If adjustment to the idle speed and/or the mixture (CO content) are required, turn the appropriate adjuster screw as necessary (see Fig. 12.63). If the CO content is to be adjusted, the mixture screw's tamperproof cap will have to be carefully prised free and a suitable Allen key used to make the adjustment. On models produced from July 1989 on, the idle speed should initially be between 900 to 1000 rpm and the CO content between 1.0 and 1.4%; when the Lambda probe is reconnected the idle speed and the CO content should settle down to the specified setting. Fit a new tamperproof cap over the mixture screw on completion.

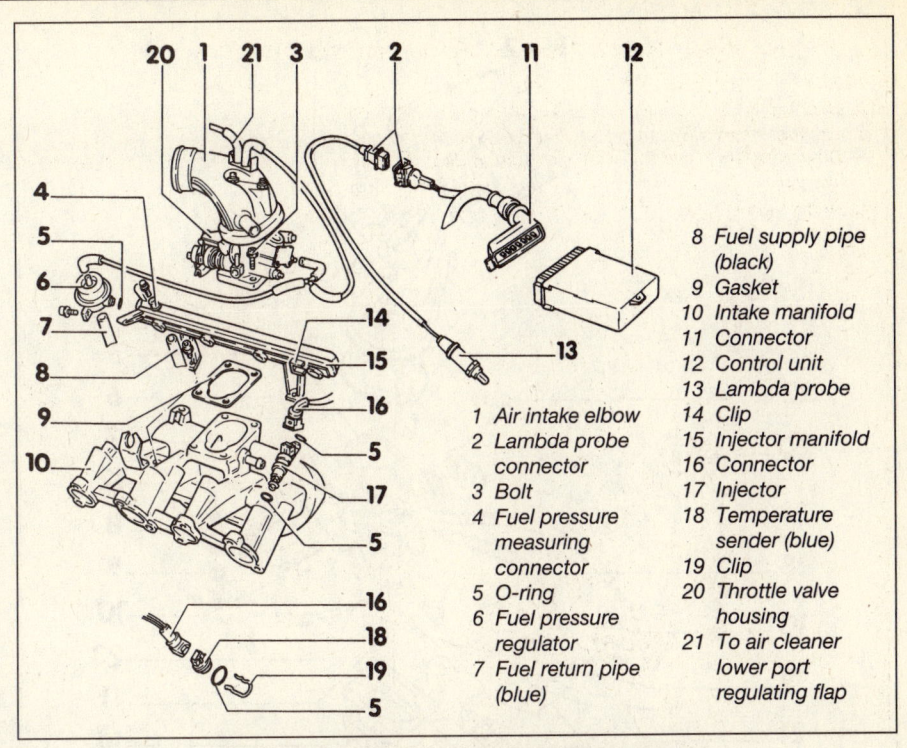

Fig. 12.59 Digijet fuel system components (Sec 8)

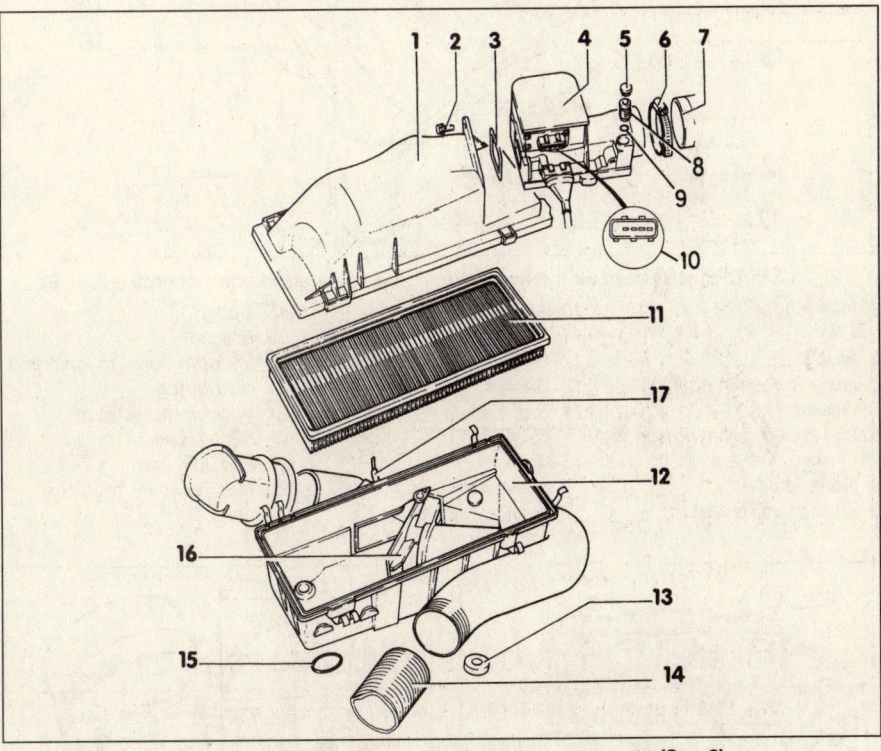

1 Air intake elbow
2 Lambda probe connector
3 Bolt
4 Fuel pressure measuring connector
5 O-ring
6 Fuel pressure regulator
7 Fuel return pipe (blue)
8 Fuel supply pipe (black)
9 Gasket
10 Intake manifold
11 Connector
12 Control unit
13 Lambda probe
14 Clip
15 Injector manifold
16 Connector
17 Injector
18 Temperature sender (blue)
19 Clip
20 Throttle valve housing
21 To air cleaner lower port regulating flap

Fig. 12.60 Digijet system – air cleaner components (Sec 8)

1 Upper cover
2 Screws
3 O-ring
4 Airflow meter
5 Tamperproof plug
6 Hose clip
7 Intake hose
8 Mixture (CO content) adjusting screw
9 O-ring
10 Connector
11 Air cleaner element
12 Lower body
13 Rubber washer
14 Pre-heater hose
15 Retaining ring
16 Air intake pre-heater regulator flap
17 To inlet elbow

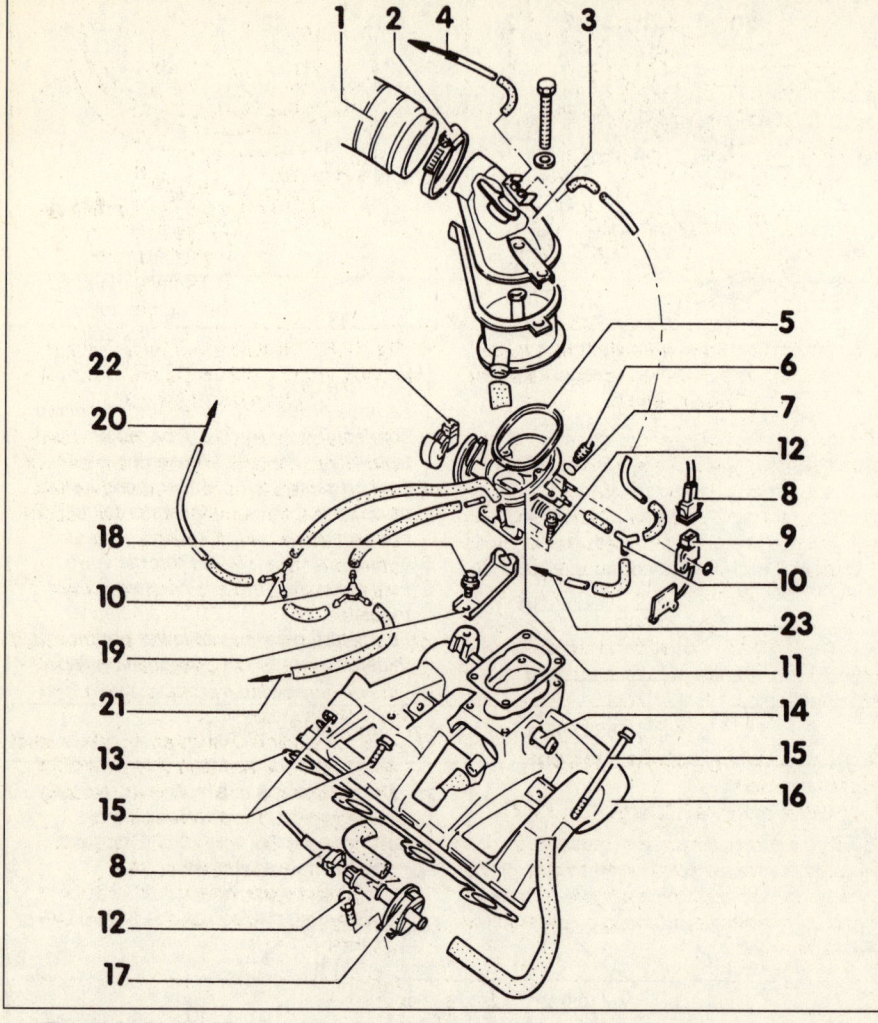

12•32 Supplement: Revisions and information on later models

Fig. 12.61 Digijet system air intake manifold and associated components – (Sec 8)

1 Intake hose
2 Clip
3 Elbow
4 Hose to regulating flap
5 Gasket
6 Idle speed adjusting screw
7 O-ring
8 Connector
9 Throttle valve switch
10 Angled connector
11 Throttle valve housing
12 Screw
13 Gasket
14 Brake servo vacuum connection
15 Bolt
16 Intake manifold
17 Auxiliary air valve
18 Bolt
19 Bracket
20 Vacuum hose (to ignition distributor)
21 Vacuum hose (to non-return valve)
22 Fast idle cam
23 Fuel pressure regulator hose

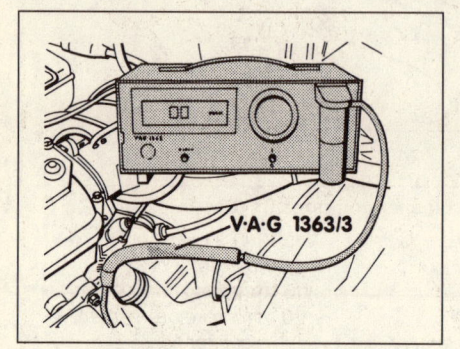

Fig. 12.62 CO analyser and connecting pipe fitted to the Digijet (Sec 8)

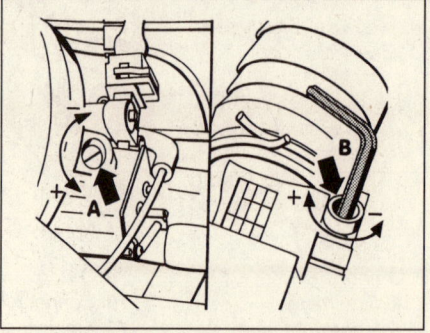

Fig. 12.63 Idle speed (A) and mixture adjustment screw (B) – Digijet system (Sec 8)

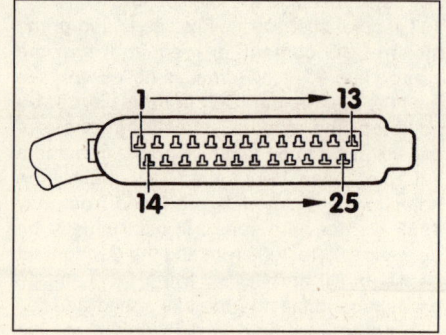

Fig. 12.64 Digijet control unit plug showing terminal connectors (Sec 8)

158 Disconnect the analyser when the idle speed/CO content is correct. Reconnect the Lambda probe wiring plug.

Airflow meter - checking

159 The efficiency of the airflow meter in the intake manifold is checked by measuring the resistance value between contacts 1 and 4 of the control unit plug (Figs. 12.64 and 12.38). The potentiometer is measured in the same manner by connecting the probes to terminals 2 and 3 and simultaneously operating the airflow sensor plate. The resistance reading must be seen to fluctuate.

Intake air pre-heater (from September 1989) - checking

160 A hot air blower such as a hair dryer can be used to make this check. First release the retaining clips, lift the lid from the air cleaner unit and remove the element.

161 With the engine cold, and with the air temperature around the pre-heater between 5 to 15° C (41 to 59°F), the warm air flap valve must be seen to be open. On heating up the air temperature in the area of the air intake valve to over 20°C (68°F), the valve should be seen to close.

Fuel injectors - checking

162 Refer to Section 37 in Chapter 3 and proceed as described but note the dribble test in paragraph 5 differs from that specified. Switch on the ignition for a period of 5 seconds, and check that no more than 2 drips per minute leak from any of the injectors.

Throttle valve switch - checking

163 A multi-meter (set to the resistance scale) will be required to make this check. Pull free the wiring connector from the throttle valve switch, connect up the meter probes between the switch contacts and check that the reading is zero ohms. Operate the throttle to fully open it (a high 'infinite' resistance reading will be shown on the meter), then slowly close the throttle to the point where 0.3 mm (0.0118 in) clearance exists between the throttle lever and the stop screw and check that zero ohms is shown on the meter. Insert a feeler gauge of this thickness between the lever and the stop screw to ensure the correct

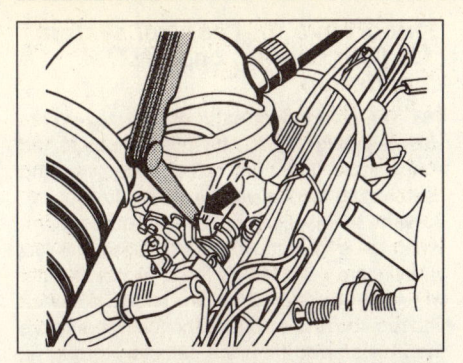

Supplement: Revisions and information on later models 12•33

Fig. 12.65 Feeler gauge location for throttle valve switch check on Digijet system (Sec 8)

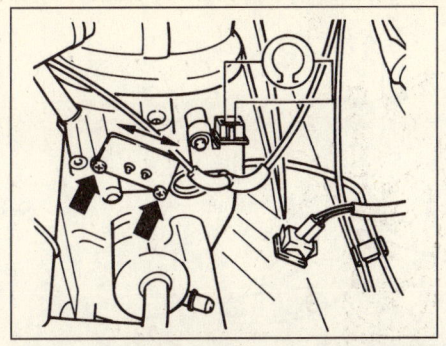

Fig. 12.66 Throttle valve switch test meter connections and securing screws – Digijet system (Sec 8)

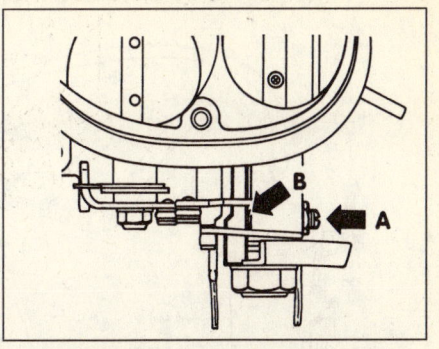

Fig. 12.67 Throttle valve basic setting showing limiting screw (A) and stop (B) – Digijet system (Sec 8)

clearance (see Fig. 12.65). If adjustment is required, loosen off the throttle valve switch screws, then move the switch in the required direction to the point where the zero ohms reading is shown, then retighten the screws. Fully open the throttle valve and check that it is switched 'on' as described above. Reconnect the wiring connector to the switch on completion of the check.

164 It should be noted that the throttle valve basic setting is made during production and in normal circumstances, it should not require any further adjustment. If minor adjustment to the valve setting is necessary, it can be made by loosening off the limiting screw to provide a minimal clearance between the screw and the stop, then tightening the screw until it just comes into contact with the stop (see Fig. 12.67). This setting is critical and to judge when the contact point is made, a piece of thin paper should be positioned between the lever and stop screw, then move the paper and simultaneously tighten the screw to the point where the paper is just clamped by the screw. From this point, tighten the screw a further half turn.

165 If adjustment has been made, the idle speed and mixture should be checked, as should the throttle valve switch; these are described earlier in this Section.

Pre-throttle valve clearance check

166 The pre-throttle valve clearance is set during production and under normal circumstances should not require checking and adjustment. If the clearance is to be checked, first remove the air cleaner unit, then using a suitable 0.5 mm diameter feeler blade or twist drill at the point shown in Fig. 12.68, check that the clearance at the point is indicated. If adjustment is required, loosen off the locknut and turn the adjuster screw in the required direction to set the clearance at 0.5 mm, then retighten the locknut.

Digijet fuel injection system components - removal and refitting

167 By reference to the accompanying illustrations, the removal and refitting of the various components of the system are self explanatory, but the following special points should be noted.

(a) Observe the precautions described in Section 26 of Chapter 3 whenever any parts of the system are to be removed and refitted.
(b) Ensure that the routings and connections of the system wiring, fuel and vacuum components are noted prior to disconnecting them (to ensure correct reassembly).
(c) If the injector manifold is to be removed, it is first necessary to detach and remove the air intake elbow complete with the throttle valve housing.
(d) Any component O-rings and gaskets must always be renewed during reassembly.
(e) The accelerator cable removal, refitting and adjustment procedures are as described in Section 11 of Chapter 3.
(f) The fuel tank and its associated components are removed in a similar manner to that described in Section 46 of Chapter 3.

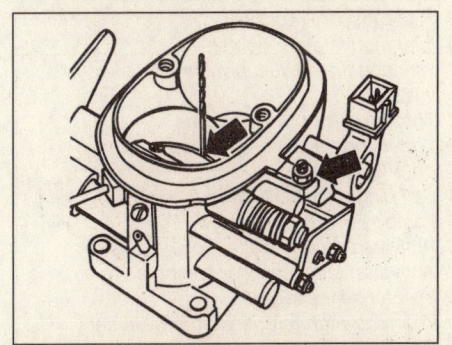

Fig. 12.68 Measuring the pre-throttle valve clearance using a 0.5 mm feeler blade or twist drill. Adjustment screw and locknut are also indicated – Digijet system (Sec 8)

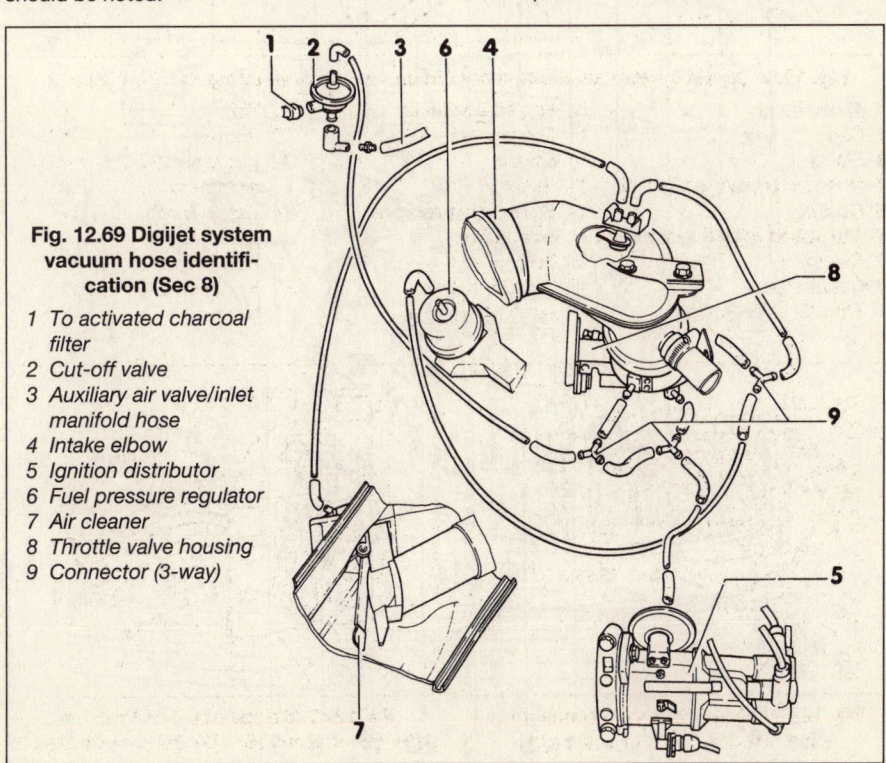

Fig. 12.69 Digijet system vacuum hose identification (Sec 8)

1 To activated charcoal filter
2 Cut-off valve
3 Auxiliary air valve/inlet manifold hose
4 Intake elbow
5 Ignition distributor
6 Fuel pressure regulator
7 Air cleaner
8 Throttle valve housing
9 Connector (3-way)

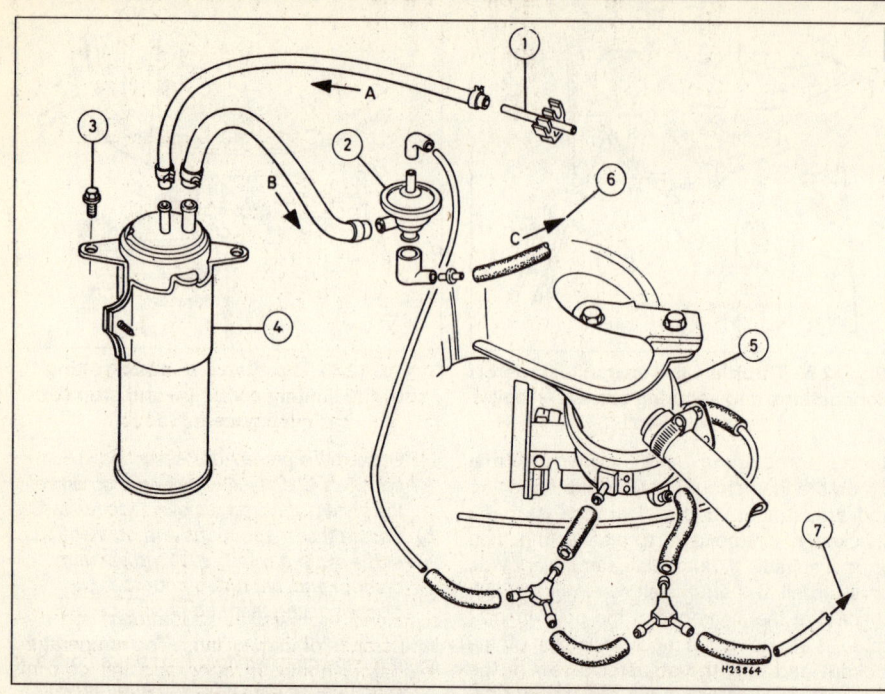

12•34 Supplement: Revisions and information on later models

Fig. 12.70 Activated charcoal filter system components (Sec 8)

A   Fuel tank vapour route when engine is idling or stopped
B/C Fuel tank vapour route when engine is run above idle speed
1   Pipe (to fuel tank gravity valve in filler line)
2   Cut-off valve
3   Fixing screw
4   Activated charcoal canister
5   Throttle valve housing
6   Hose (auxiliary air valve/inlet manifold)
7   Hose (to ignition distributor)

Evaporative fuel control system (1.3 litre engine, code NZ) - description

168 The component parts of this system are shown in Fig. 12.70. Its function is to aid evaporative fuel control by collecting and recirculating the fuel vapours in the fuel tank to prevent them escaping to the atmosphere. When the engine is stopped or idling, the fuel vapours are collected by the charcoal canister where they are stored until the engine is started and run above idle speed. The fuel vapours are then transferred from the canister, through a cut-off valve, then into the air filter and inlet manifold to be burnt off during the normal combustion process. The charcoal canister is secured to the base of the air cleaner unit and access to it for inspection of renewal is made after first removing the air cleaner.

Mono-Jetronic fuel injection system (1.8 litre engine, code RP) - description and precautions

169 The Mono-Jetronic central fuel injection system fitted to the 1.8 litre RP engine model is a simplified method of fuel injection. The system layout and component location is shown in Fig. 12.71.

170 Fuel is injected into the inlet manifold by a single solenoid valve (fuel injector) mounted centrally in the top of the injector unit housing. The length of time for which the injector

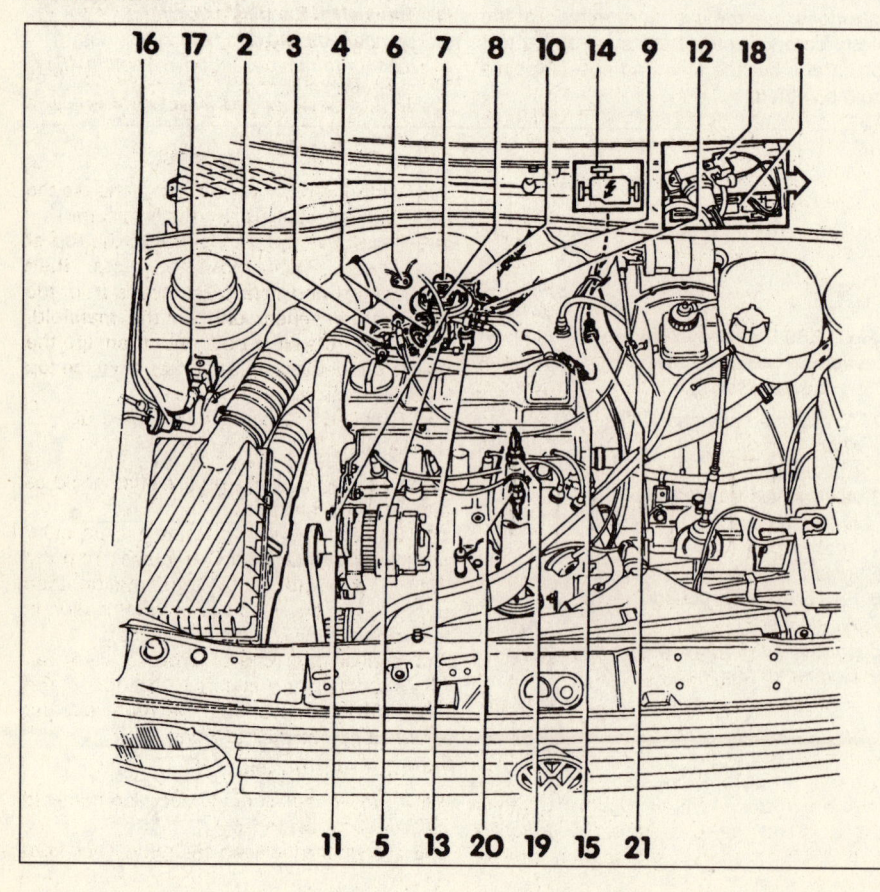

Fig. 12.71 Location of Mono-Jetronic system components (Sec 8)

1 Electronic Control unit (ECU)
2 Connector (throttle valve positioner and idle switch)
3 Throttle damper
4 Connector (injector and air intake temperature sender)
5 Throttle valve positioner and idle switch
6 Intake air pre-heater temperature regulator
7 Injector and air temperature sender
8 Fuel pressure regulator
9 Inlet manifold pre-heater
10 Injection timing vacuum control valve
11 Injector
12 Throttle valve potentiometer
13 Water separator (throttle valve potentiometer)
14 Self diagnosis fault warning lamp
15 Lambda probe connector
16 Activated charcoal filter solenoid valve
17 Activated charcoal filter solenoid valve
18 Injector series resistor
19 Thermoswitch for manifold pre-heater
20 Coolant temperature sender
21 Self diagnosis plug

Supplement: Revisions and information on later models 12•35

remains open determines the quantity of fuel reaching the cylinders for combustion. The electrical signals which determine the fuel injector opening duration are calculated by the Electronic Control Unit (ECU) from information supplied by its network of sensors. Fuel pressure is regulated mechanically.

171 The signals fed to the ECU include engine speed and crankshaft position from the distributor; the position of the throttle valve plate from the throttle position sensor; the engine coolant temperature; and the oxygen content in the exhaust gases via a sensor in the exhaust manifold (Lambda probe).

172 Using the information gathered from the various sensors, the ECU sends out signals to control the system actuators as required.

173 The ECU also has a diagnostic function which can be used in conjunction with special VW test equipment for fault diagnosis. With the exception of basic checks to ensure that all relevant wiring and hoses are in good condition and securely connected, fault diagnosis should be entrusted to a VW dealer.

Mono-Jetronic fuel injection system (1.8 litre engine, code RP) - checks and adjustments

174 The following basic checks can be made on the system components. More detailed checks can be made using specialised equipment, but this must be entrusted to a VW dealer.

Idle speed and mixture (CO content) checks

175 The prerequisites for this check are that the ignition timing must be correct and the engine must be at its normal operating temperature. During the checks, all electrical circuits including the engine cooling fan and, where applicable, the air conditioning, must be switched off.

176 The ignition must be switched off before the test meter is attached to check the engine speed. An exhaust gas analyzer must be used to check the CO content from the exhaust.

177 The idle speed and mixture are not adjustable on this system and if they are not as specified, all that can be done is to inspect the various fuel system and associated vacuum electrical connections to ensure that they are in good condition and securely connected. If found to be in good condition, it will be necessary to have the system checked out by a VW dealer using specialised testing equipment to identify and rectify the fault.

Idle switch control valve

178 This device is attached to the throttle position sensor and its function is to control the ignition timing vacuum advance. If defective, it can cause problems with the idle speed and/or the overrun cut-off. A simple check can be made by switching on the ignition, then opening and closing throttle valve. Listen to hear if the control valve clicks twice. If this is proved to be in order, start the engine, allow it to idle and then momentarily

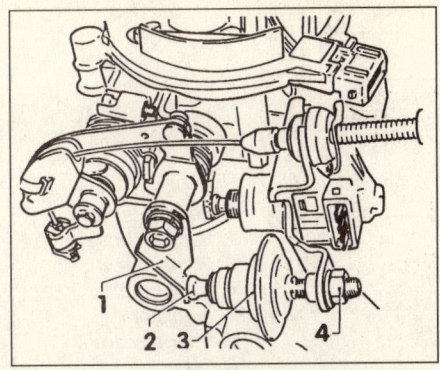

Fig. 12.72 Throttle damper assembly on the Mono-Injection system (Sec 8)

1 Throttle lever 3 Damper
2 Plunger 4 Locknut

detach the wiring connector from the control valve and reconnect it. The idle speed should momentarily increase and then drop back to normal; if not, the control valve is faulty and should be renewed.

Injector

179 Run the engine up to its normal operating temperature, then detach and remove the air intake duct from the top of the injector unit.

180 With the engine running at idle speed, look into the top of the injector unit and check the fuel spray pattern which should be visible on the throttle valve.

181 Increase the engine speed to 3000 rpm then snap shut the throttle and check that the fuel spray from the injector is momentarily interrupted. Turn the ignition off and then check that no more than two drops of fuel per minute leak from the injector. This indicates that the overrun cut-off is functioning in a satisfactory manner.

Throttle damper

182 When the throttle valve is in the closed position, the throttle damper plunger should be pressed into the damper a minimum distance of 4 mm by the operating lever (Fig. 12.72). If adjustment is required, loosen off the adjuster locknut, then rotate the damper screw to the point where the lever is just in contact with the plunger. Now turn the damper four and a half turns towards the lever, then retighten the locknut.

Air intake pre-heater

183 With the engine cold, detach and remove the upper section of the air cleaner and the filter element. Check the air flap valve in the base of the lower section of the air cleaner for freedom of movement. Ensure that when closed, it shuts off the warm air passage.

184 Start the engine and whilst running it at idle speed, check that the flap closes off the cold air passage.

185 To check that the temperature regulator is operating correctly, disconnect the two hoses from it, connect them together and then note if the warm air passage remains closed off. If this is the case, the vacuum unit is

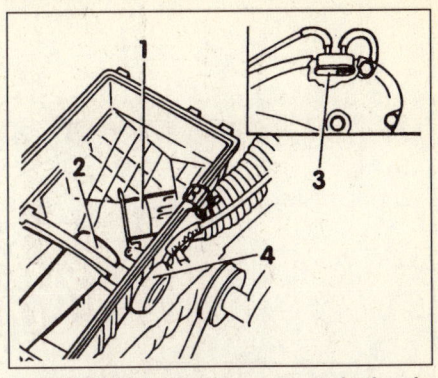

Fig. 12.73 Air intake components in the air cleaning housing (Sec 8)

1 Warm air nozzle 3 Temperature regulator
2 Cold air nozzle 4 Vacuum unit

defective. Where the flap valve closes off the cold air passage, the temperature regulator is at fault and in need of replacement.

186 The position of the flap valve when the engine is running is dependent on the temperature of the regulator. The temperature regulator should be open and the cold air passage closed off, when the temperature is below 35°C (95°F). At temperatures above 45°C (113°F), the regulator should be closed and the warm air passage sealed off.

Mono-Jetronic fuel injection system components (1.8 litre engine, code RP) - removal and refitting

Air cleaner element

187 The procedure is the same as that described for other fuel injection models in Section 27 of Chapter 3.

Air intake duct and manifold

188 Undo the retaining clips and release the duct from the manifold and the air cleaner.

189 To remove the manifold from the top of the injector unit housing, note their connections and detach the hoses from the temperature sensor unit on the manifold. Undo the retaining bolt and then lift the manifold together with its gasket, from the top face of the injector unit.

190 Refit in the reverse order of removal.

Injector

191 Remove the intake duct and manifold as previously described.

192 Undo the retaining screw and lift clear the injector holder and O-ring seal from the top of the injector. Note its orientation, then grip and pull the injector from its location in the housing. Remove the O-ring seals.

193 Refit in the reverse order of removal. When refitting the injector, the upper and lower O-ring seals must be renewed and lightly lubricated prior to fitting.

Injector unit housing

194 Remove the air intake duct and manifold as previously described.

195 Detach the fuel feed and return lines from

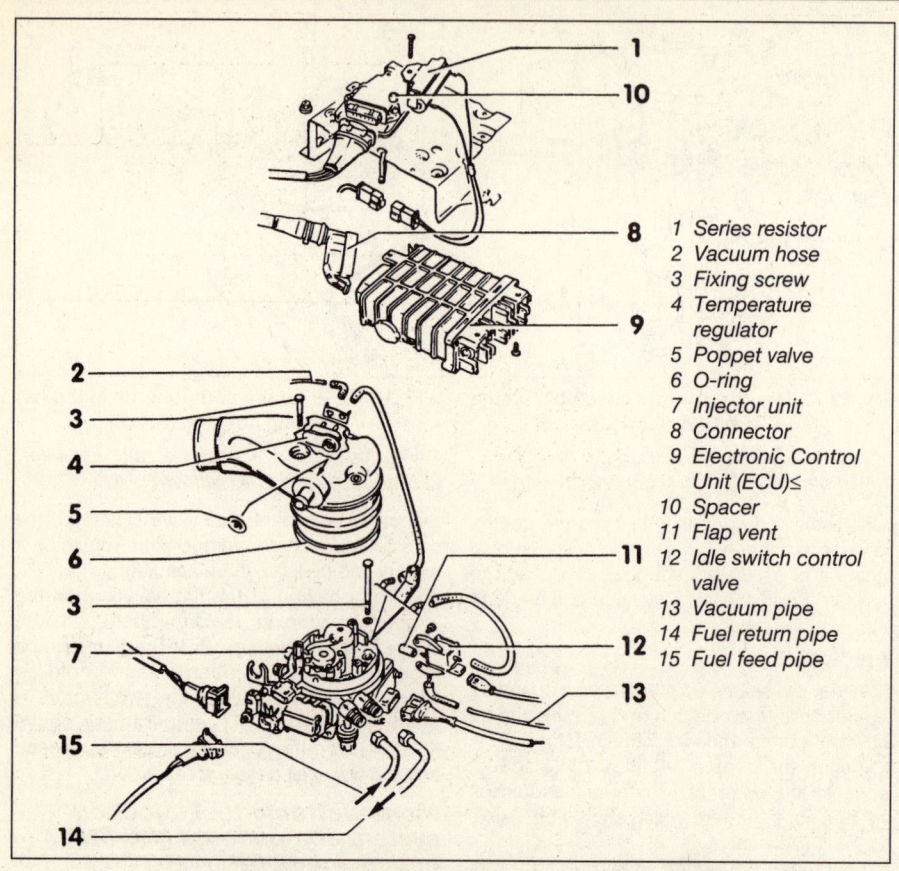

12•36 Supplement: Revisions and information on later models

Fig. 12.74 Injector, ECU and associated components (Sec 8)

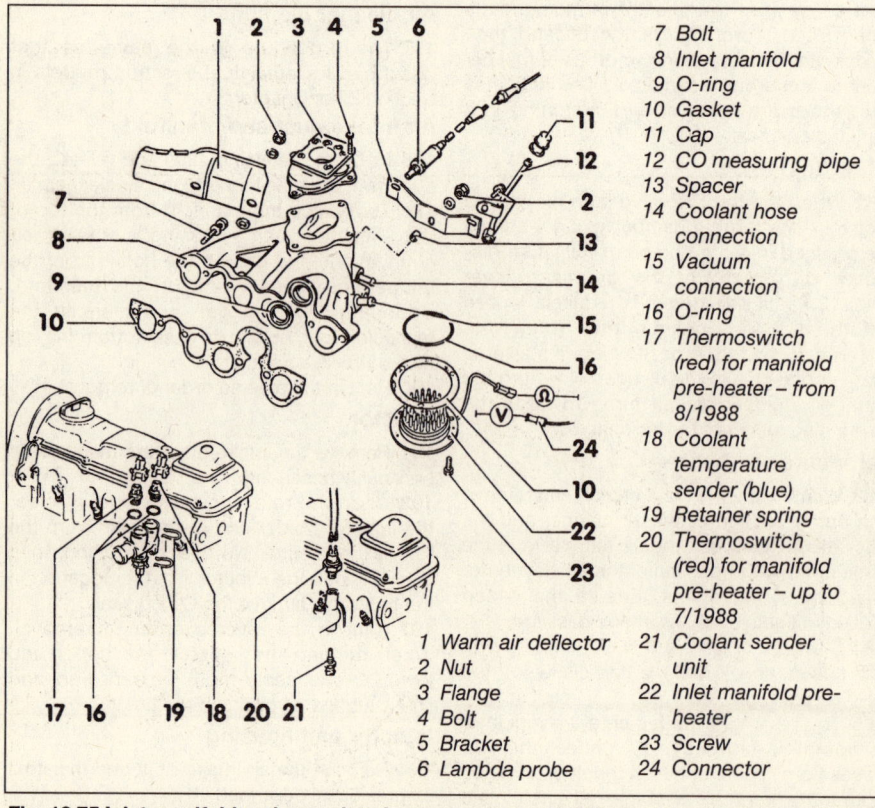

1 Series resistor
2 Vacuum hose
3 Fixing screw
4 Temperature regulator
5 Poppet valve
6 O-ring
7 Injector unit
8 Connector
9 Electronic Control Unit (ECU)≤
10 Spacer
11 Flap vent
12 Idle switch control valve
13 Vacuum pipe
14 Fuel return pipe
15 Fuel feed pipe

Fig. 12.75 Inlet manifold and associated components on the Mono-Jetronic system (Sec 8)

1 Warm air deflector
2 Nut
3 Flange
4 Bolt
5 Bracket
6 Lambda probe
7 Bolt
8 Inlet manifold
9 O-ring
10 Gasket
11 Cap
12 CO measuring pipe
13 Spacer
14 Coolant hose connection
15 Vacuum connection
16 O-ring
17 Thermoswitch (red) for manifold pre-heater – from 8/1988
18 Coolant temperature sender (blue)
19 Retainer spring
20 Thermoswitch (red) for manifold pre-heater – up to 7/1988
21 Coolant sender unit
22 Inlet manifold pre-heater
23 Screw
24 Connector

their connections on the side of the injector unit. Allow for fuel spillage as they are detached and plug the hoses to prevent further leakage and the ingress of dirt.

196 Disconnect the wiring plugs from their connections on the injector unit.

197 Disconnect the accelerator cable from the throttle lever at the injector unit.

198 Undo the retaining screws and withdraw the injector unit housing from the inlet manifold. Remove the gasket and if damaged or in doubtful condition, renew it when refitting the injector unit.

199 Refit in the reverse order of removal. Ensure that the mating faces of the housing and fuel lines are clean as they are reconnected.

Fuelpump - Mono-Jetronic and Digifant fuel injection systems

200 From mid 1989, certain models fitted with Mono-Jetronic or Digifant systems were fitted with a single fuel pump (in the fuel tank) rather than the previous arrangement of one in the tank and a secondary pump outside the tank. The pump can be checked in the same manner as that for the 'in-tank' dual pump type (refer to paragraphs 77 to 80 in this Section).

201 The fuel pump can be removed in a similar manner to that described for the fuel gauge sender unit in Section 9 of Chapter 3.

Exhaust system with catalytic converter - description, removal and refitting

202 A catalytic converter is fitted as standard on certain models.

203 The device is fitted into the forward end of the exhaust system, and consists of a steel casing over a ceramic body. It incorporates a longitudinal multi-passage honeycomb unit, which is coated with a layer of platinum or rhodium.

204 As the exhaust gases pass through the converter, the harmful constituents are converted into water, nitrogen and carbon dioxide.

205 For the correct operation of the catalytic converter, it is essential that **only unleaded** fuel is used, and that the fuel system is correctly adjusted and tuned.

206 The catalytic converter reaches very high temperatures, and consequently, the vehicle should not be parked directly over any inflammable material, especially long dry grass, as it may catch fire. Also, take care that the converter is not subject to impact when traversing uneven ground.

207 A typical exhaust system is shown in Fig. 12.78. Removal is simply a matter of releasing the flange or socket type couplings and separating the components. When working on the exhaust system note that the catalytic converter is fragile - do not strike it with tools and take care not to allow it to contact jacks or lifting gear.

208 When reassembling and refitting, use new coupling seals and gaskets.

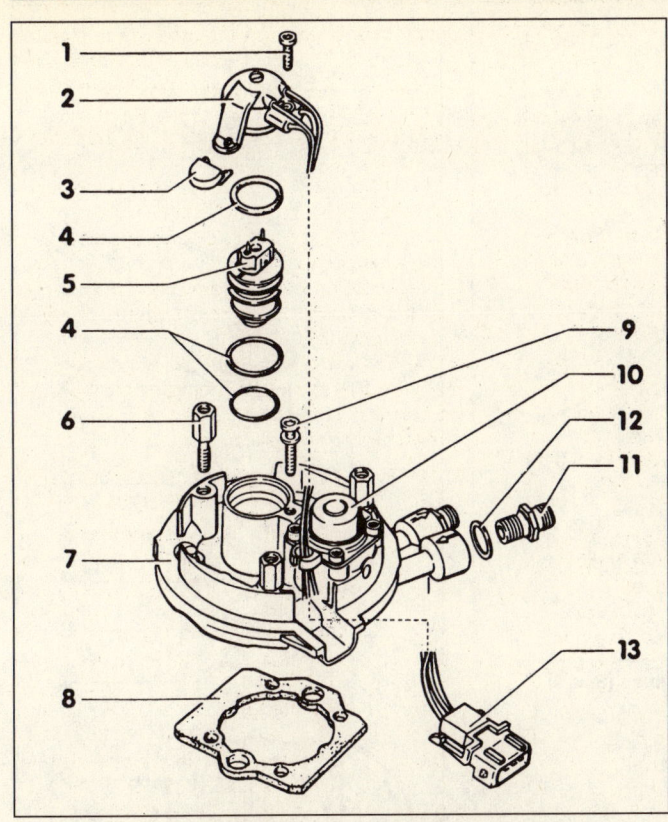

Supplement: Revisions and information on later models 12•37

Fig. 12.76 Injector unit and upper body components – Mono-Jetronic system (Sec 8)

1 Screw
2 Injector holder
3 Protector cap
4 O-ring
5 Injector
6 Stud
7 Injector upper body
8 Gasket
9 Screw
10 Pressure regulator
11 Fuel pipe adaptor
12 Seal ring
13 Connector

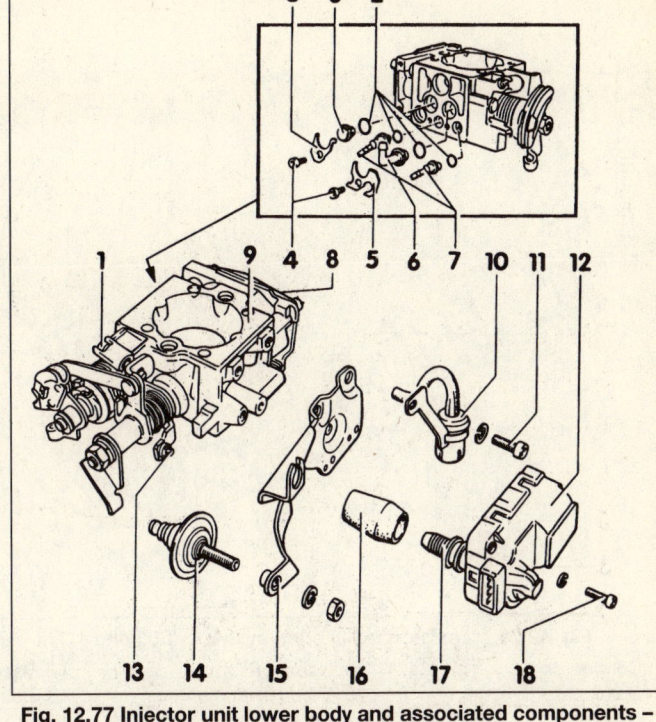

Fig. 12.77 Injector unit lower body and associated components – Mono-Jetronic system (Sec 8)

1 Throttle valve stop screw
2 O-ring
3 Plug
4 Screw
5 Retainer
6 Connector
7 Connector
8 Throttle valve potentiometer
9 Injector lower body
10 Water separator
11 Screw
12 Throttle valve positioner
13 Throttle damper adjuster screw
14 Throttle damper
15 Bracket
16 Protector grommet (for idle switch)
17 Idle switch
18 Screw

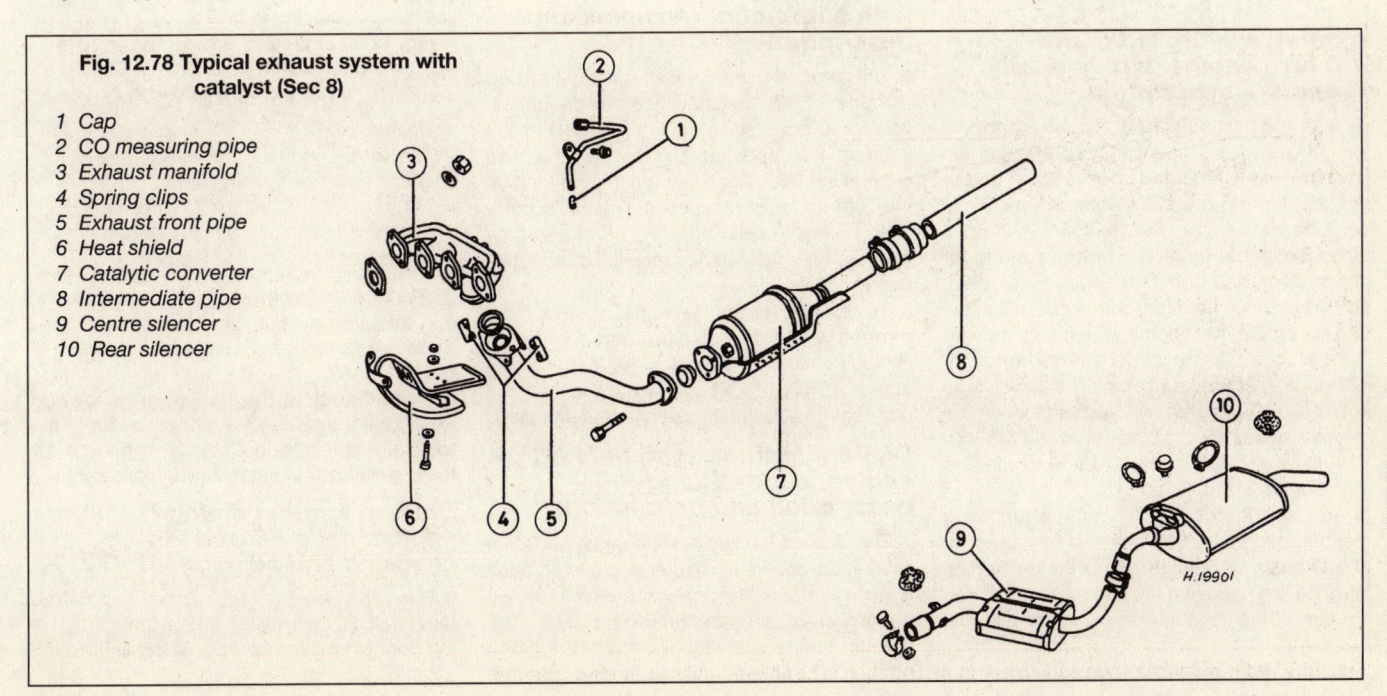

Fig. 12.78 Typical exhaust system with catalyst (Sec 8)

1 Cap
2 CO measuring pipe
3 Exhaust manifold
4 Spring clips
5 Exhaust front pipe
6 Heat shield
7 Catalytic converter
8 Intermediate pipe
9 Centre silencer
10 Rear silencer

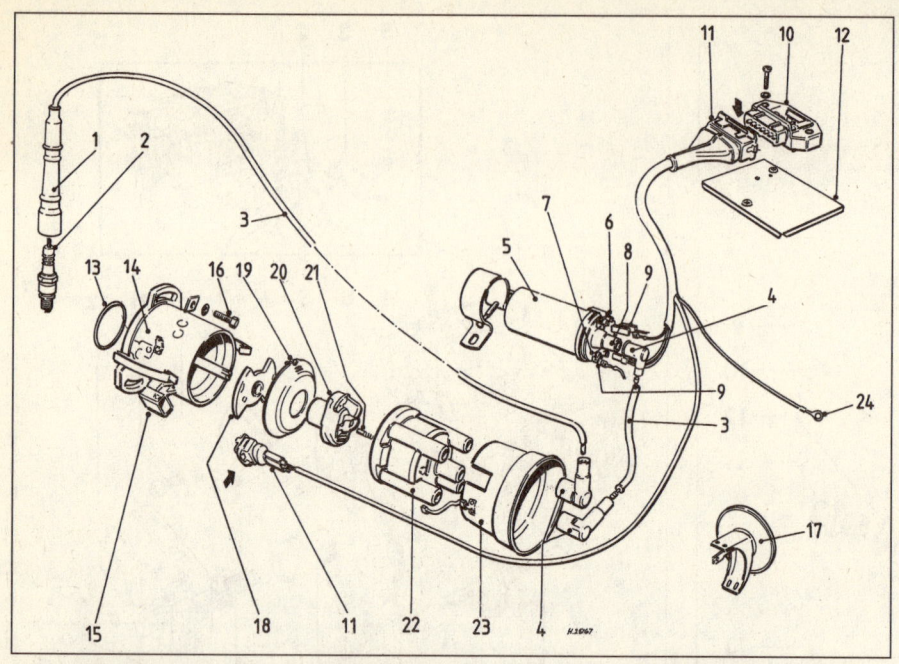

12•38 Supplement: Revisions and information on later models

Fig. 12.79 Transistorized ignition system – 1.05 and 1.3 litre engines (Sec 9)

1 Connector
2 Spark plug
3 HT lead
4 Suppression connector
5 Ignition coil
6 Terminal (–)
7 Terminal 15 (+)
8 Terminal 4
9 Connectors
10 TCI-H switch unit
11 Connector
12 Heat sink
13 O-ring
14 Distributor
15 Hall sender
16 Screw
17 Vacuum unit
18 Bearing plate
19 Dust cover
20 Rotor arm
21 Carbon brush with spring
22 Distributor cap
23 Screening ring
24 Earth lead

9 Ignition system

Ignition system (1.05 and 1.3 litre engine with hydraulic tappets) - description

1 With the introduction of hydraulic tappets on 1.05 and 1.3 litre engines the ignition system was changed from the contact breaker type to the transistorized type. Refer to Chapter 4 for the relevant Sections describing the function and precautions for the system, and note that as from late 1986, the rotor arm is not fitted with a speed limiter.
2 Test procedures for the switch unit and Hall sender are as described in Chapter 4. Distributor removal and refitting is basically as for the contact breaker type, and overhaul procedures as for the transistorized type with reference also to Fig. 12.79 and the following paragraphs 3 and 4.
3 The distributor shaft is supported by a bearing plate which is removed by loosening the two screws securing it to the tensioning ring. Before removing the ring make a mark on the rim of the distributor body in line with the guide lug.
4 Shims are provided above and below the Hall sender and these should be selected to eliminate axial clearance and to provide for movement by the vacuum unit.

Ignition system (1.6 litre engine with automatic transmission) - description

5 On automatic transmission models fitted with the 1.6 litre engine a thermo-pneumatic valve and non-return valve are fitted in the vacuum line between the carburettor and distributor. This effectively retains the ignition vacuum advance when the engine is cold, even during acceleration. At normal engine temperature, vacuum advance is not effective during acceleration.
6 To test the thermo-pneumatic valve blow through it with the unit in heated water. It should be closed under 30°C (86°F) and open above 46°C (115°F). Check also that the non-return valve is only open in one direction.

Digifant ignition system (1.8 litre engine, code PB and PF) - description and precautions

7 The Digifant ignition system uses the TCI-H ignition described in Chapter 4, but in addition it incorporates a knock sensor, which senses the onset of pre-ignition and retards the ignition timing accordingly. Normal ignition timing is automatically adjusted by the Digifant control unit, which also controls the fuel injection system, and because of this, there are no centrifugal advance weights in the distributor.
8 Components of the system are shown in Figs. 12.81 and 12.82. Work procedures are basically as given in Chapter 4, except for those described in the following paragraphs.

Digifant ignition timing (1.8 litre engine, code PB and PF) - checking and adjustment

9 Run the engine to normal operating temperature, then switch off the ignition.
10 Connect a stroboscopic timing light to the engine.

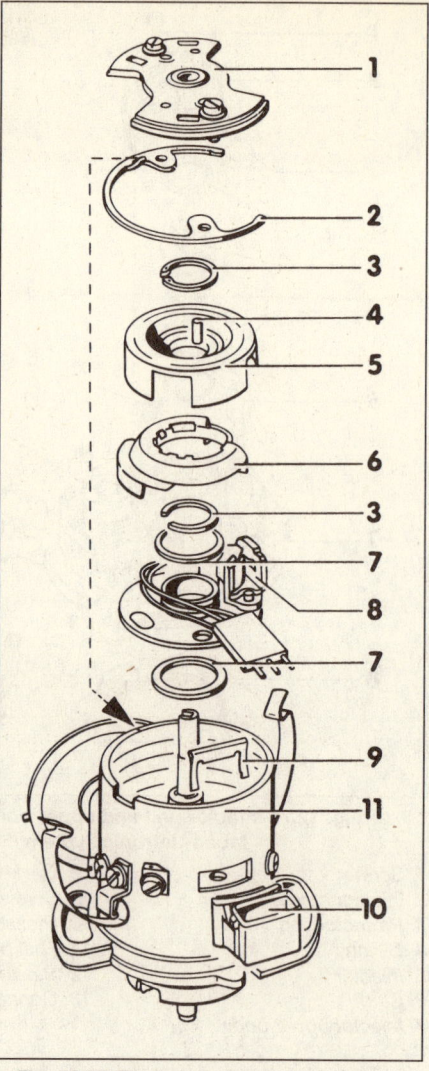

Fig. 12.80 Exploded view of the transistorized ignition distributor – 1.05 and 1.3 litre engines (Sec 9)

1 Bearing plate
2 Tensioning ring
3 Circlip
4 Pin
5 Rotor
6 Cover
7 Shims
8 Hall sender
9 Clip
10 Connector
11 Main body

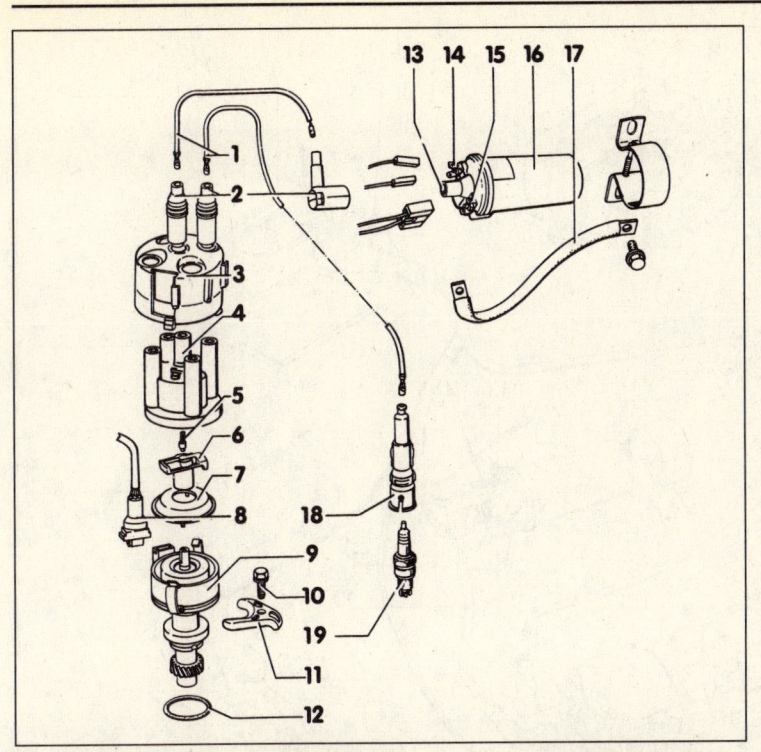

Supplement: Revisions and information on later models 12•39

Fig. 12.81 Digifant ignition distributor and coil components (Sec 9)

1 HT leads
2 Suppression connectors
3 Screen
4 Distributor cap
5 Carbon brush and spring
6 Rotor arm
7 Dust cover
8 Connector
9 Distributor
10 Bolt
11 Clamp
12 O-ring
13 Coil terminal 4
14 Coil terminal 15 (+)
15 Coil terminal 1 (–)
16 Coil
17 Earth strap
18 Spark plug connector
19 Spark plug

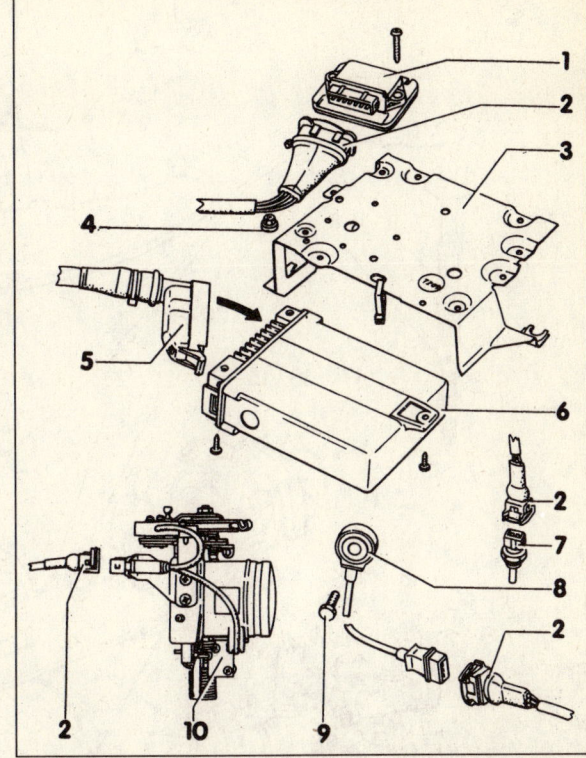

Fig. 12.82 Digifant ignition system control components (Sec 9)

1 TCI-H switch unit
2 Connector
3 Plate
4 Nut
5 Connector
6 Digifant control unit
7 Temperature sender
8 Knock sensor
9 Bolt
10 Throttle valve switch 1

11 Run the engine at idle speed.
12 Disconnect the wiring from the temperature sender (Fig.12.83).
13 Increase the engine speed to between 2000 and 2500 rpm, then point the timing light at the aperture over the flywheel. The timing marks should be aligned (Chapter 4, Fig. 4.12), but if not, loosen the clamp bolt, turn the distributor as required, and retighten the bolt.
14 While checking the ignition timing, the opportunity should be taken to check the temperature and knock sensor controls.
15 With the temperature sender wiring disconnected, increase the engine speed to 2300 rpm and note the exact ignition timing. Hold the engine speed at 2300 rpm, then reconnect the wiring and check that the ignition timing advances by 30° ± 3° from the previously noted value.
16 If the ignition timing only advances about 20°, slacken the knock sensor securing bolt, retighten to 20 Nm (15 lbf ft) and repeat the test. If there is no difference, check the associated wiring for an open-circuit, or as a last resort, renew the knock sensor.
17 If there is no advance in ignition timing, check the temperature sender wiring for an open-circuit. A fault is indicated in the Digifant control unit if there is no open-circuit.

Digifant system distributor (1.8 litre engine, code PB and PF) - removal and refitting

18 Release the distributor cap and place it to one side complete with HT leads.
19 Disconnect the wiring harness plug from the side of the distributor body.
20 Unscrew the clamp plate screw, remove the clamp plate and withdraw the distributor.

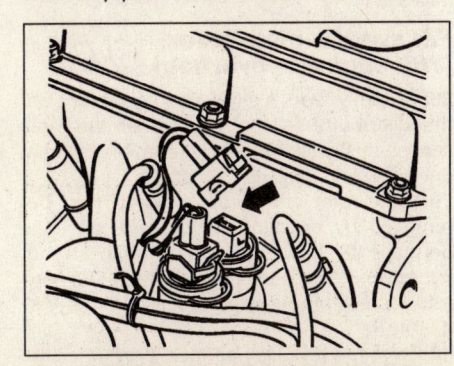

Fig. 12.83 Disconnecting the temperature sender wire – Digifant system (Sec 9)

21 Before fitting the distributor, set No 1 piston to TDC. When correctly set, the flywheel mark or the crankshaft pulley vibration damper mark should be aligned with the matching mark on the casing or belt cover. The mark on the camshaft sprocket must be aligned with the joint of the camshaft cover.
22 Using a screwdriver, turn the slot in the end of the oil pump driveshaft so that it is parallel with the crankshaft centre-line.
23 Set the rotor arm so that it points to the mark (No 1) on the distributor body rim.
24 Install the distributor so that the wiring harness LT plug socket is in the position shown in Fig. 12.84. Check and if necessary adjust the ignition timing.

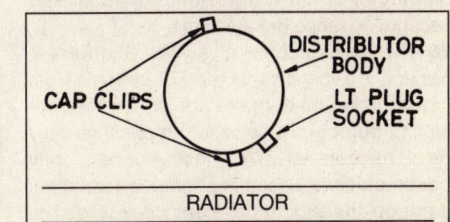

Fig. 12.84 Distributor installation position – Digifant system (Sec 9)

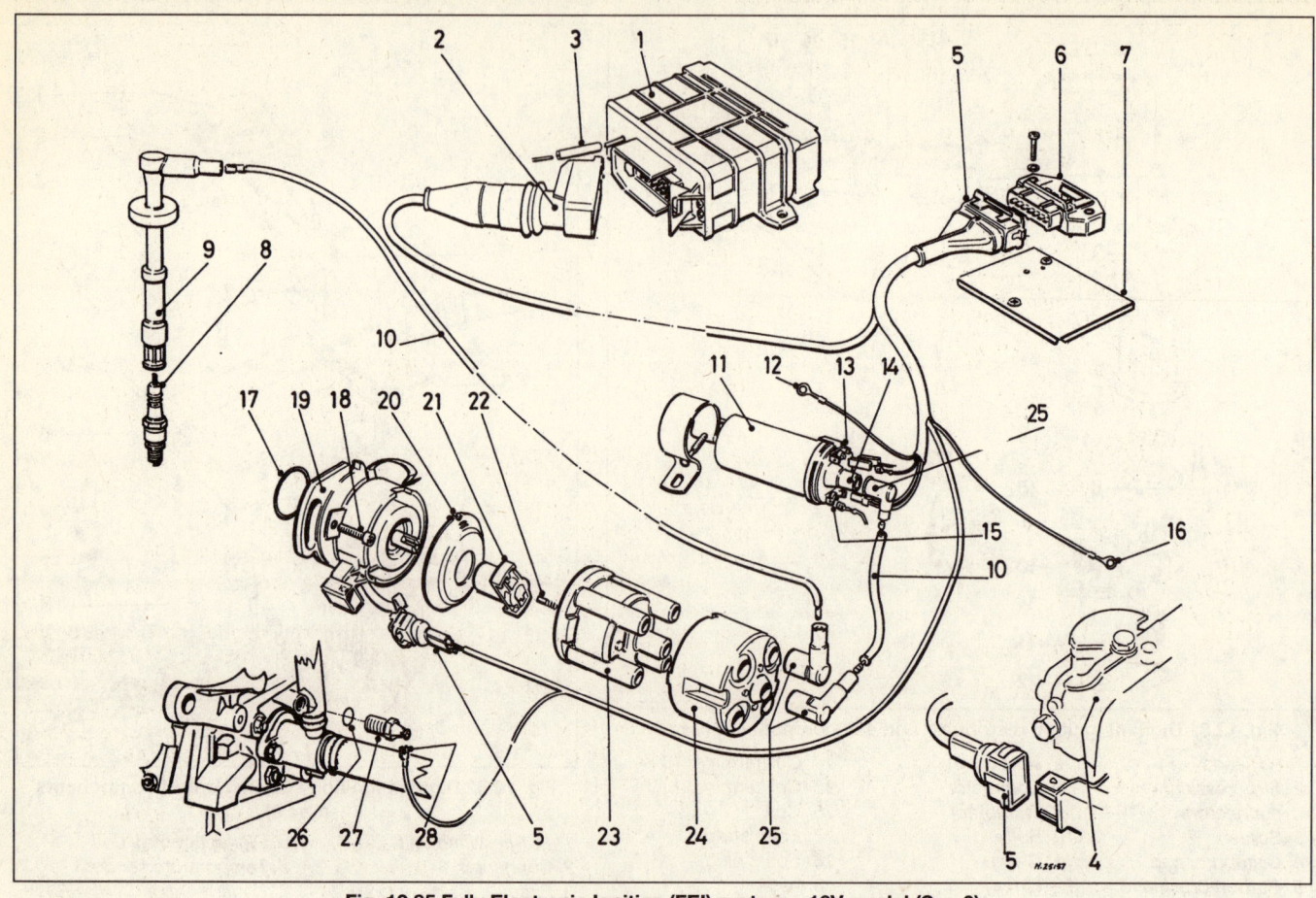

12•40 Supplement: Revisions and information on later models

Fig. 12.85 Fully Electronic Ignition (FEI) system – 16V model (Sec 9)

1 FEI control unit
2 Connector
3 Vacuum line
4 Throttle valve switch
5 Connector
6 TCI-H switch unit
7 Heat sink
8 Spark plug
9 Connector
10 HT lead
11 Ignition coil
12 Earth lead
13 Terminal 1 (–)
14 Terminal 4
15 Terminal 15 (+)
16 Earth lead
17 O-ring
18 Screw
19 Distributor
20 Dust cover
21 Rotor arm
22 Carbon brush and spring
23 Distributor cap
24 Suppression cap
25 Suppression connectors
26 Washer
27 Temperature sender
28 Connector

FEI system (16V engine) - description and precautions

25 The 16V engine is fitted with a Fully Electronic Ignition (FEI) system as shown in Fig. 12.85. It functions in a similar manner to the transistorized system described in Chapter 4, but in addition it incorporates an electronic control unit which adjusts the ignition timing electronically according to engine speed, load, and temperature. The distributor is not fitted with centrifugal and vacuum advance mechanisms.

26 The precautions given in Chapter 4, Section 7 apply also to the FEI system. Note that a digital multi-meter should be used for testing purposes otherwise the readings may be inaccurate. **Do not** under any circumstances use a testlamp, as this will damage the electronic components of the system. When using the multi-meter **do not** switch between ranges during the test as this also may damage the components.

FEI system distributor (16V engine) - removal and refitting

27 This is basically as described in Chapter 4, Section 10, but ignore the reference to the vacuum pipe and renew the O-ring if necessary.

FEI system distributor (16V engine) - overhaul

28 The only work likely to be necessary on the distributor is the renewal of the Hall sender; this is available in kit form including a drive coupling, pin and circlip.

29 If the rotor arm is defective it must be removed by crushing with pliers, as it is permanently fixed to the shaft with strong adhesive. Clean the shaft and secure the new rotor arm with adhesive obtained from a VW dealer.

30 To renew the Hall sender, first note the position of the drive coupling offset in relation to the rotor arm.

31 Support the drive coupling in a vice, then drive out the roll pin after removing the circlip.

32 Remove the coupling followed by the shims and plastic washer.

33 Remove the shaft complete with rotor arm, followed by the plastic dust cover, shim and plastic washer.

34 Remove the screws and lift the Hall sender from inside the distributor body.

35 Clean all the components, then fit the new Hall sender using a reversal of the removal procedure, but lubricate the shaft with a little grease.

FEI system switch unit (16V engine) - testing

36 The switch unit is located in the left-hand side of the plenum chamber beneath a plastic cover. The ignition coil should be in good condition before making this test.

37 Depress the wire clip and pull the connector from the switch unit.

38 Connect a voltmeter between terminals 4

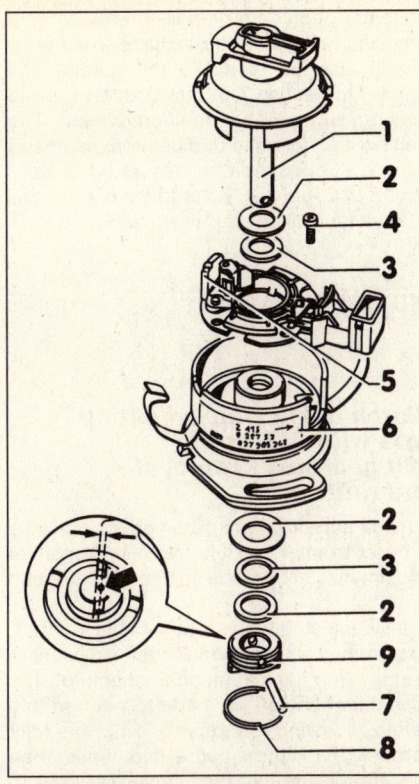

Supplement: Revisions and information on later models

Fig. 12.86 Exploded view of the FEI distributor – 16V model (Sec 9)

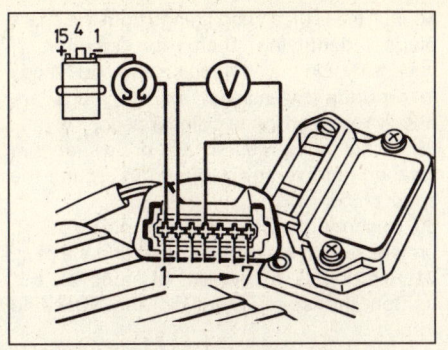

1 Shaft
2 Shims
3 Plastic washers
4 Screw
5 Hall sender
6 Main body
7 Roll pin
8 Circlip
9 Drive coupling

Fig. 12.87 Testing the FEI switch unit – 16V model (Sec 9)

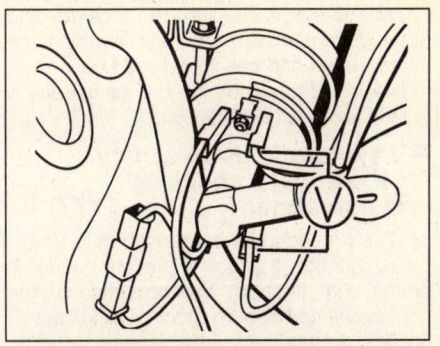

Fig. 12.88 Voltmeter connection across ignition coil's LT terminals when testing the FEI switch unit – 16V model (Sec 9)

and 2 on the connector, then switch on the ignition and check that battery voltage is available. Switch off the ignition.

39 Using an ohmmeter, check that there is continuity between terminal 1 on the connector and terminal 1 on the coil.

40 Refit the connector to the switch unit, then connect a voltmeter across the low tension terminals on the coil as shown in Fig. 12.88.

41 Release the spring and pull the connector from the control unit, then switch on the ignition. Check that initially a reading of 2 volts is registered on the voltmeter, dropping to zero after one to two seconds. If this is not the case, renew the switch unit, and also if necessary the ignition coil.

42 Using a temporary length of wire, briefly earth terminal 12 on the connector. The voltage should rise to at least 2 volts. If this is not the case, renew the switch unit.

FEI control unit (16V engine) - testing

43 Check the switch unit as previously described before checking the control unit.

44 Release the spring and pull the connector from the control unit located in the right-hand side of the plenum chamber.

45 Switch on the ignition, then use a voltmeter to check that battery voltage is available between terminals 3 and 5 on the connector.

46 Check also that battery voltage is available between terminals 6 and 3, then operate the throttle valve switch and check that the voltage drops to zero. Switch off the ignition.

47 Using an ohmmeter, measure the resistance between the connector terminals 1 to 3. These are the temperature sender terminals and the resistance varies according to the coolant temperature, as described in Section 8, paragraph 69.

48 Press the clip and pull the connector from the side of the distributor. Connect the voltmeter to the two outer terminals of the connector, then switch on the ignition. A reading of 5 volts should be registered. Switch off the ignition.

49 Connect a voltmeter across the low tension terminals of the ignition coil. Switch on the ignition.

50 Using a temporary length of wire, briefly earth the centre terminal of the distributor connector. The voltage should rise to at least 2 volts and the fuel pump should be heard to operate. If this is not the case, renew the control unit and if necessary check the fuel pump relay.

FEI system Hall sender unit (16V engine) - testing

51 Refer to paragraph 26 in this Section for notes concerning the applicable test equipment and precautions necessary before proceeding with the following checks.

52 Release the lead connector from the Hall sender unit. Check the voltage supply to the Hall sender unit by connecting the tester between the outer contacts of the plug, then switch on the ignition. A minimum reading of 5 volts should be indicated, if not check the FEI control unit and wiring.

53 To check the signal from the Hall sender unit, slide the rubber grommet away from the Hall sender plug and with the plug connected,

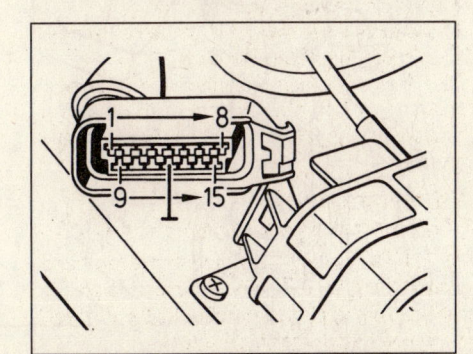

Fig. 12.89 FEI control unit connector terminals – 16V model (Sec 9)

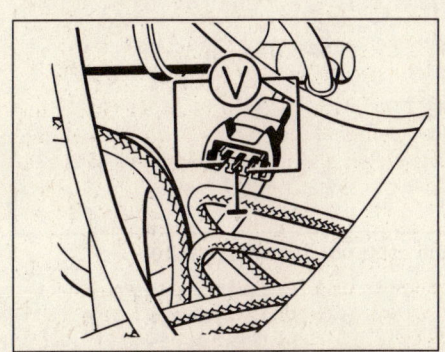

Fig. 12.90 Testing Hall sender connector on the side of the distributor – 16V model (Sec 9)

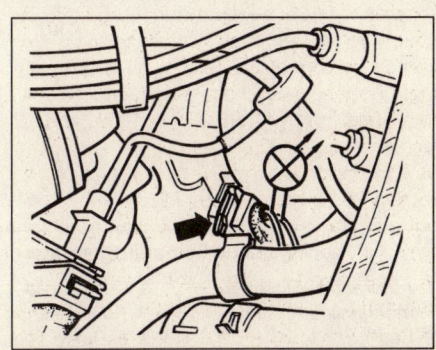

Fig. 12.91 Signal check method from the Hall sender unit – 16V model (Sec 9)

12•42 Supplement: Revisions and information on later models

attach the diode test light to its centre and outer (brown/white) terminals. Operate the starter motor and check that the LED is seen to flicker. If it does not, the Hall sender unit is at fault and must be renewed.

FEI system ignition timing (16V engine) - checking and adjustment

54 The procedure is as described in Chapter 4, Section 12, using the stroboscopic timing light method. The operation of the control unit can also be checked as follows.
55 Run the engine at idling speed and note the basic ignition timing. Pull the vacuum hose from the control unit, then increase the engine speed to 4600 rpm and read off the ignition advance. Deduct the basic advance and the resultant value should be 18°, this being the advance attributable to engine speed.
56 Reconnect the vacuum hose, then run the engine to 4600 rpm. Note the ignition timing. Pull off the vacuum hose and again increase the engine speed to 4600 rpm. The ignition timing should be approximately 20° retarded from the previously-noted figure. This amount indicates the advance attributable to engine vacuum.

Spark plugs - removal and refitting

57 Where applicable remove the air cleaner.
58 Pull the HT lead and fittings from the spark plugs, identifying them for location if necessary. On the 16V engine, the end fittings incorporate extensions, as the plugs are deeply recessed in the cylinder head.
59 Using compressed air or a vacuum cleaner, remove any debris from around the spark plugs.
60 Unscrew the plugs using a plug socket, preferable with a rubber insert to grip the plug.
61 Refitting is a reversal of removal, but tighten the spark plugs to the specified torque.

Spark plugs and coil - general

62 From August 1987 on, some models are fitted with a modified ignition coil and single earth electrode spark plugs. The modified ignition coil is identified by a grey- rather than green-coloured sticker (as used on some other models). Refer to the Specifications at the start of this Chapter for the recommended plug types.
63 Note that it is not permissible to use new plugs with an old coil, or vice versa.

Ignition system (1.3 litre engine, code NZ and 1.8 litre engine, code RP) - general

64 The TCI-H transistorised ignition system fitted to both of these engine types is similar to that used on other models in the range and dealt with in Chapter 4. Reference should be made to Chapter 4 for details on testing, and removal and refitting procedures. Reference should also be made to the precautions outlined in Section 7 of that Chapter prior to working on the TCI-H ignition system. The ignition timing check/adjustment is made using a stroboscope as described in Section 12 of Chapter 4. Refer to the start of this Chapter for ignition specifications.

10 Clutch

Clutch cable (self-adjusting type with 085 and 020 gearbox) - removal and refitting

1 A self-adjusting type clutch operating cable is fitted to later models. Note that manual adjustment can be made so that the cable can be
initially adjusted when a new cable is fitted. Also, in the event of the full cable adjustment being taken up, a manual check of the adjustment should be made to confirm this before renewing the cable. To do this fully depress the clutch pedal five times then check to ensure that the clutch release lever cannot be pressed downwards, in which case the cable is in need of renewal.
2 To remove the cable, first disconnect the battery negative lead.
3 Depress the clutch pedal several times, then compress the adjusting mechanism within the dust excluding boot, and retain it in this state. A special tool is shown in Fig. 12.93, but wire or a ratchet-type cable strap can be used as an alternative device.

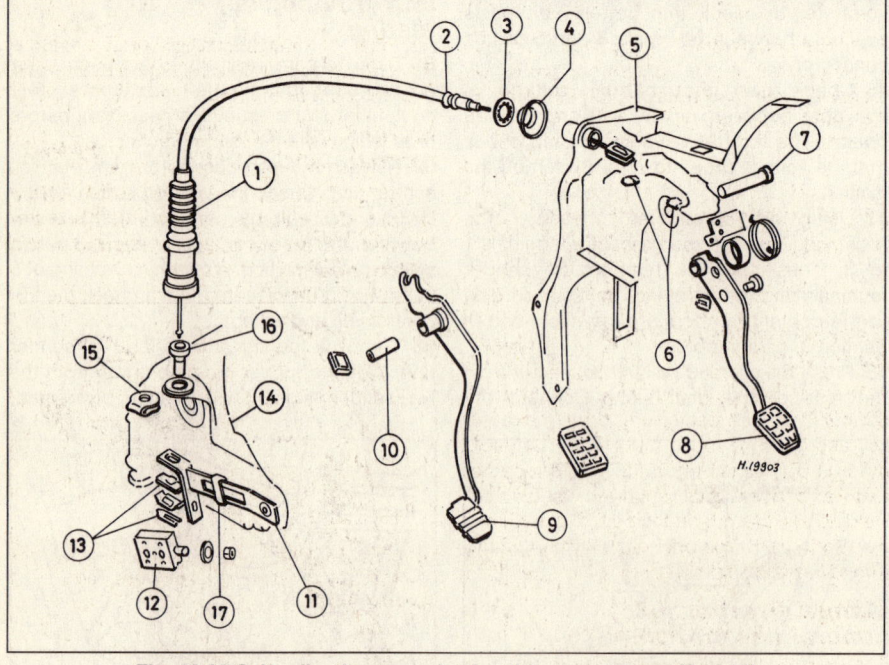

Fig. 12.92 Self-adjusting type clutch cable components (Sec 10)

1 Automatic adjustment mechanism	6 Stop clip	12 Balance weight
2 Seal	7 Pedal shaft	13 Cable fixings
3 Clamping washer	8 Brake pedal	14 Gearbox casing
4 Sleeve	9 Clutch pedal	15 Rubber washer
5 Mounting bracket	10 Bush	16 Rubber guide
	11 Release lever	17 Buffer

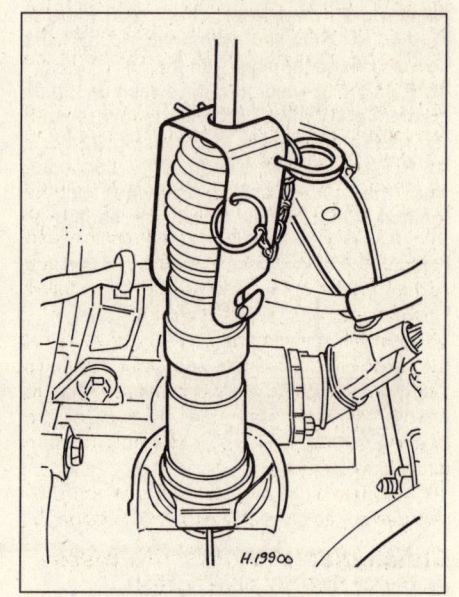

Fig. 12.93 Self-adjusting clutch cable mechanism compressed using special tool 3151 (Sec 10)

Supplement: Revisions and information on later models 12•43

4 Release the cable from the release lever, and unhook the cable eye from the clutch pedal. Withdraw the cable through the bulkhead grommet.
5 Fit a new cable, and connect it to the clutch pedal only.
6 Depress the clutch pedal by hand while an assistant pulls the release lever end of the cable. Compress the adjusting mechanism within the dust excluding boot, and retain it as previously described.
7 Connect the cable to the release lever.
8 Depress the clutch pedal a minimum of five times. Grip the release lever and push it in the opposite direction to its normal direction of travel to a distance of about 10.0 mm (0.4 in). Check that the release lever moves freely.
9 On no account attempt to dismantle the automatic adjustment mechanism.

Clutch (085 gearbox) - description

10 The clutch fitted with the 085 gearbox is similar to the 084 gearbox version described in Chapter 5. Most of the work procedures are as given in Chapter 5, but refer also to the information given in the following paragraphs.

Flywheel bolts (085 gearbox) - tightening

11 The threads of the flywheel bolts should be coated with locking fluid before inserting and tightening them. Bolts with a collar have a different tightening torque to those without (see Specifications).

Clutch release mechanism (085 gearbox) - removal and refitting

12 The clutch release mechanism on the 085 gearbox is shown in Fig. 12.94. It differs from the 084 version by having a release lever splined to the release shaft. This enables the shaft to be removed without first removing the guide sleeve.
13 To remove the release shaft, prise out the two locking clips, then slide out the shaft and withdraw the release lever.
14 The bushes may be driven from the clutch housing with a suitable drift, although special VW tools may be required for the removal and fitting of the inner bush (consult a VW dealer if in doubt). The outer bush should be installed to allow flush fitting of the seal.
15 Refit the release shaft using a reversal of the removal procedure. A master spline is incorporated on the shaft and release lever to ensure correct assembly. Lubricate the bearing surfaces with a molybdenum disulphide grease.
16 All other clutch release mechanism procedures are as given in Chapter 5, Section 7.

Clutch disc and pressure plate - anti-corrosion protection

17 Both the friction disc and pressure plate are treated with anticorrosion grease during manufacture in order to prolong the service life of the components. The grease must only be removed from the contact surface of the pressure plate, and **must** be left intact on all the remaining areas.

11 Manual gearbox and automatic transmission

Gearbox oil level (084) - checking

1 The oil filler plug on the 084 gearbox is difficult to reach using the normal hexagon key and it will be found much easier to use a nut and bolt as shown in Fig. 12.95 together with a conventional spanner. Instead of welding a single nut on the bolt, two nuts may be tightened against each other using thread-locking fluid.

Manual gearbox (085) - general description

2 Certain models may be fitted with the 085 manual gearbox which is a five-speed version of the 084 gearbox. Although the construction of the 085 gearbox appears similar to the 084, there are major differences which make most procedures different. Where necessary however reference is made to Chapter 6 in the following paragraphs. Note that special tools are required for certain procedures, therefore the complete sub-Section should be read prior to commencing work.

Manual gearbox (085) - removal and refitting

3 Refer to Chapter 6, Section 4. Before refitting the gearbox make sure that the location dowels are correctly inserted in the cylinder block.

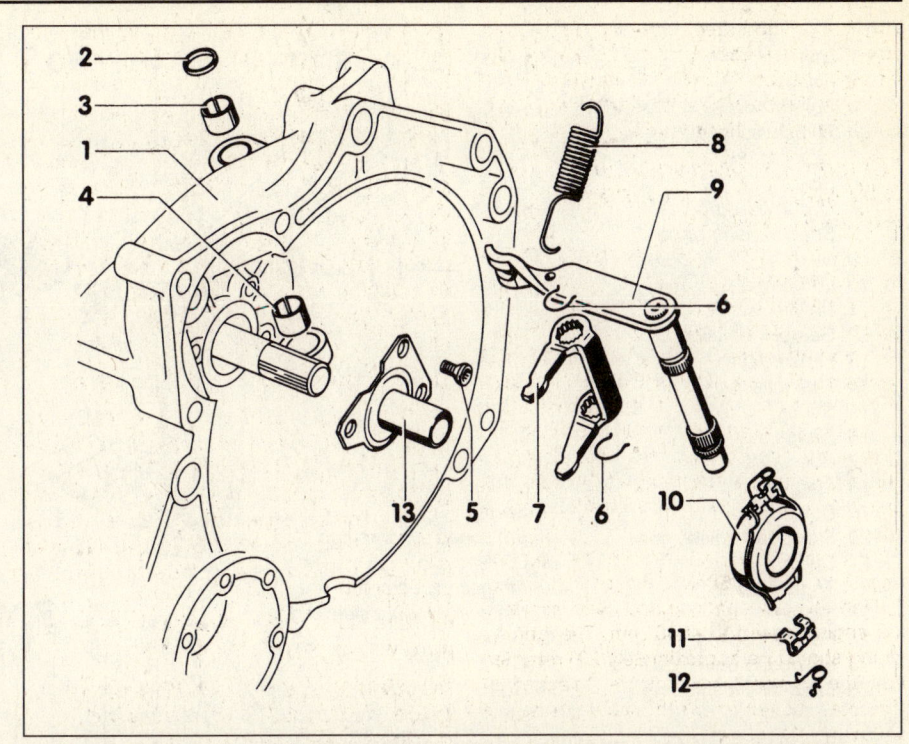

Fig. 12.94 Exploded view of the clutch release mechanism on the 085 gearbox (Sec 10)

1 Clutch housing	5 Screw	8 Return spring	11 Retaining clip
2 Seal	6 Locking clips	9 Release shaft	12 Retaining spring
3 Outer bush	7 Release lever	10 Release bearing	13 Guide sleeve
4 Inner bush			

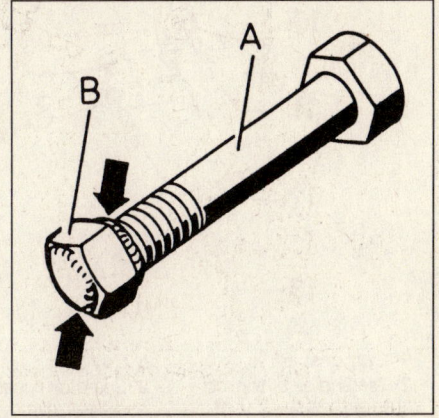

Fig. 12.95 Nut and bolt welded together to make oil level plug removal tool on the 084 gearbox (Sec 11)

A Bolt M10 x 100 mm   B Welded nut
Arrows show area of weld

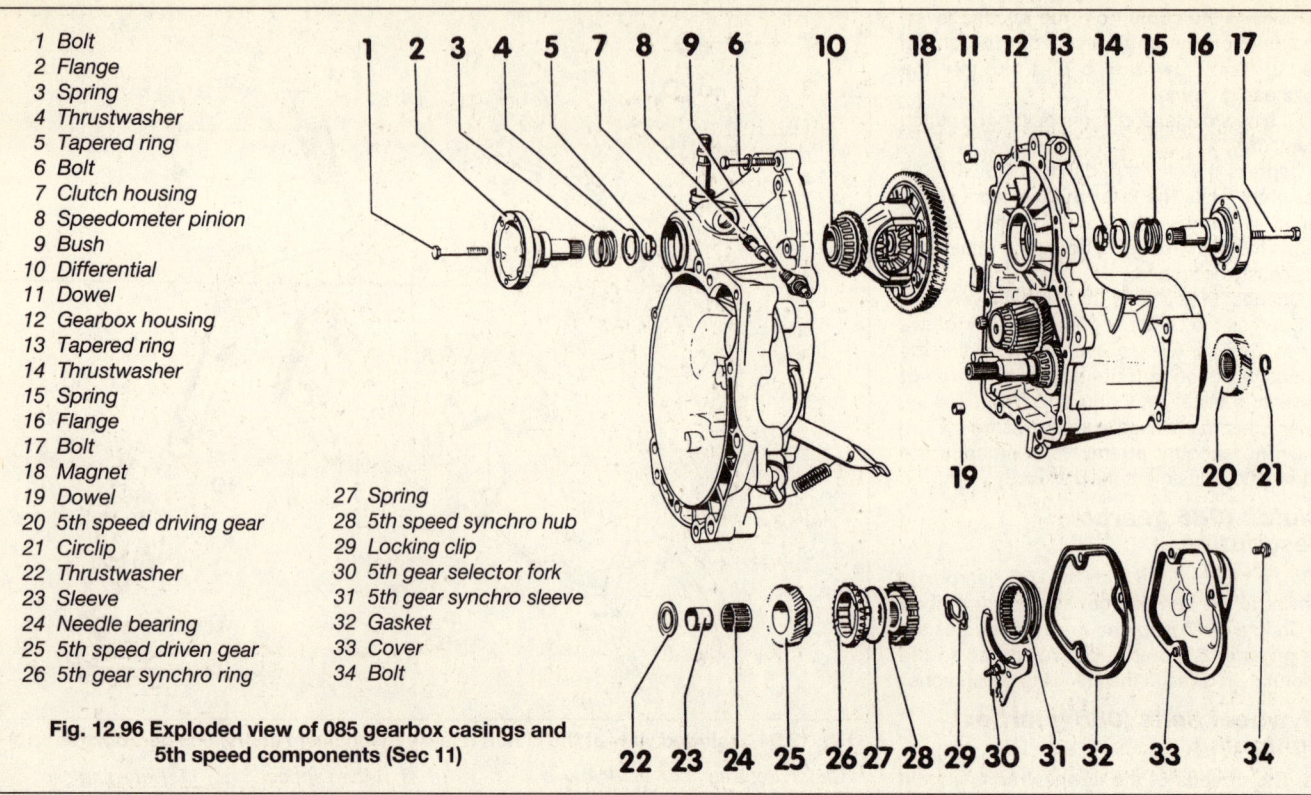

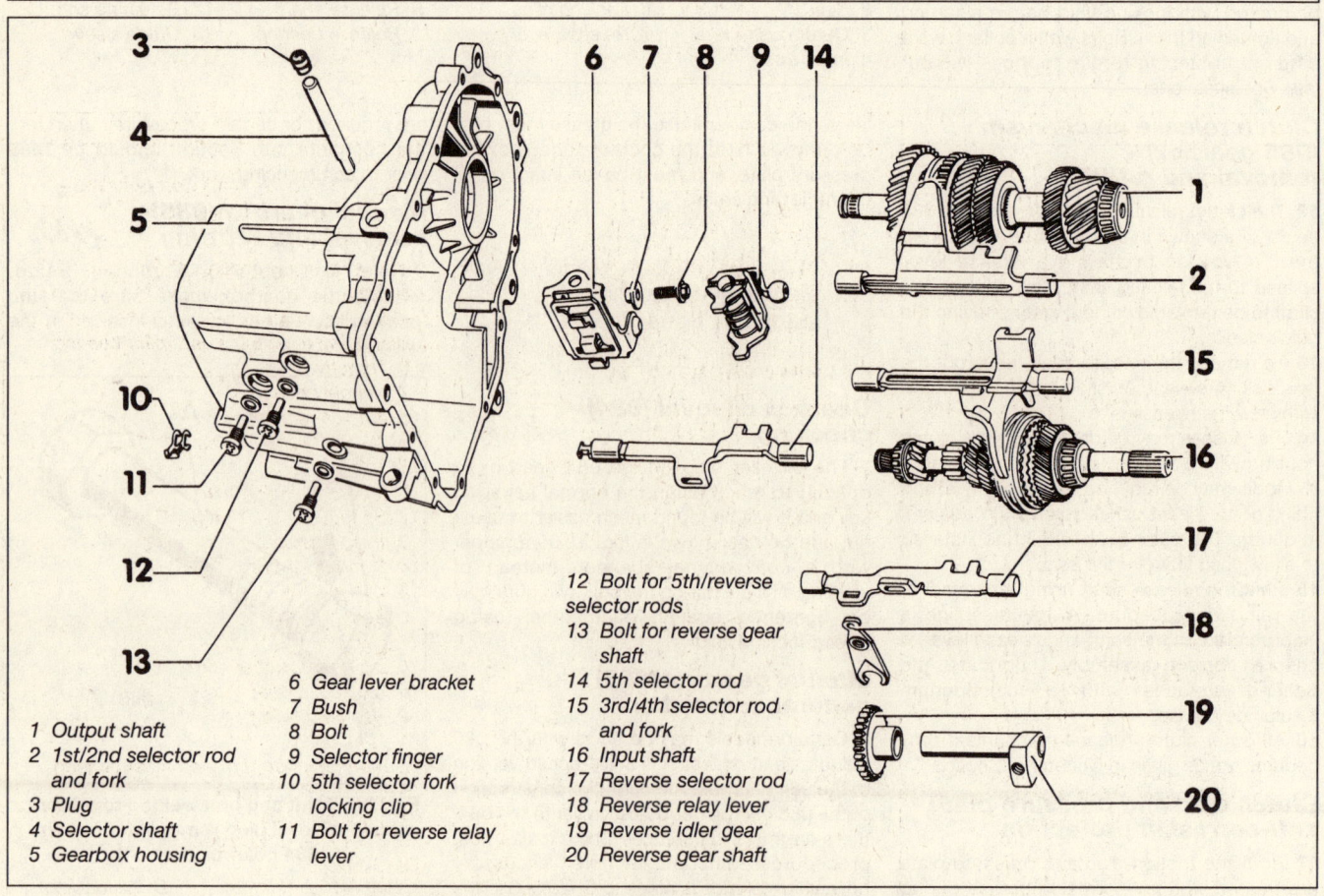

12•44 Supplement: Revisions and information on later models

1 Bolt
2 Flange
3 Spring
4 Thrustwasher
5 Tapered ring
6 Bolt
7 Clutch housing
8 Speedometer pinion
9 Bush
10 Differential
11 Dowel
12 Gearbox housing
13 Tapered ring
14 Thrustwasher
15 Spring
16 Flange
17 Bolt
18 Magnet
19 Dowel
20 5th speed driving gear
21 Circlip
22 Thrustwasher
23 Sleeve
24 Needle bearing
25 5th speed driven gear
26 5th gear synchro ring
27 Spring
28 5th speed synchro hub
29 Locking clip
30 5th gear selector fork
31 5th gear synchro sleeve
32 Gasket
33 Cover
34 Bolt

Fig. 12.96 Exploded view of 085 gearbox casings and 5th speed components (Sec 11)

1 Output shaft
2 1st/2nd selector rod and fork
3 Plug
4 Selector shaft
5 Gearbox housing
6 Gear lever bracket
7 Bush
8 Bolt
9 Selector finger
10 5th selector fork locking clip
11 Bolt for reverse relay lever
12 Bolt for 5th/reverse selector rods
13 Bolt for reverse gear shaft
14 5th selector rod
15 3rd/4th selector rod and fork
16 Input shaft
17 Reverse selector rod
18 Reverse relay lever
19 Reverse idler gear
20 Reverse gear shaft

Fig. 12.97 Gearbox casing components – 085 gearbox (Sec 11)

Supplement: Revisions and information on later models 12•45

Fig. 12.98 Clutch housing components – 085 gearbox (Sec 1)

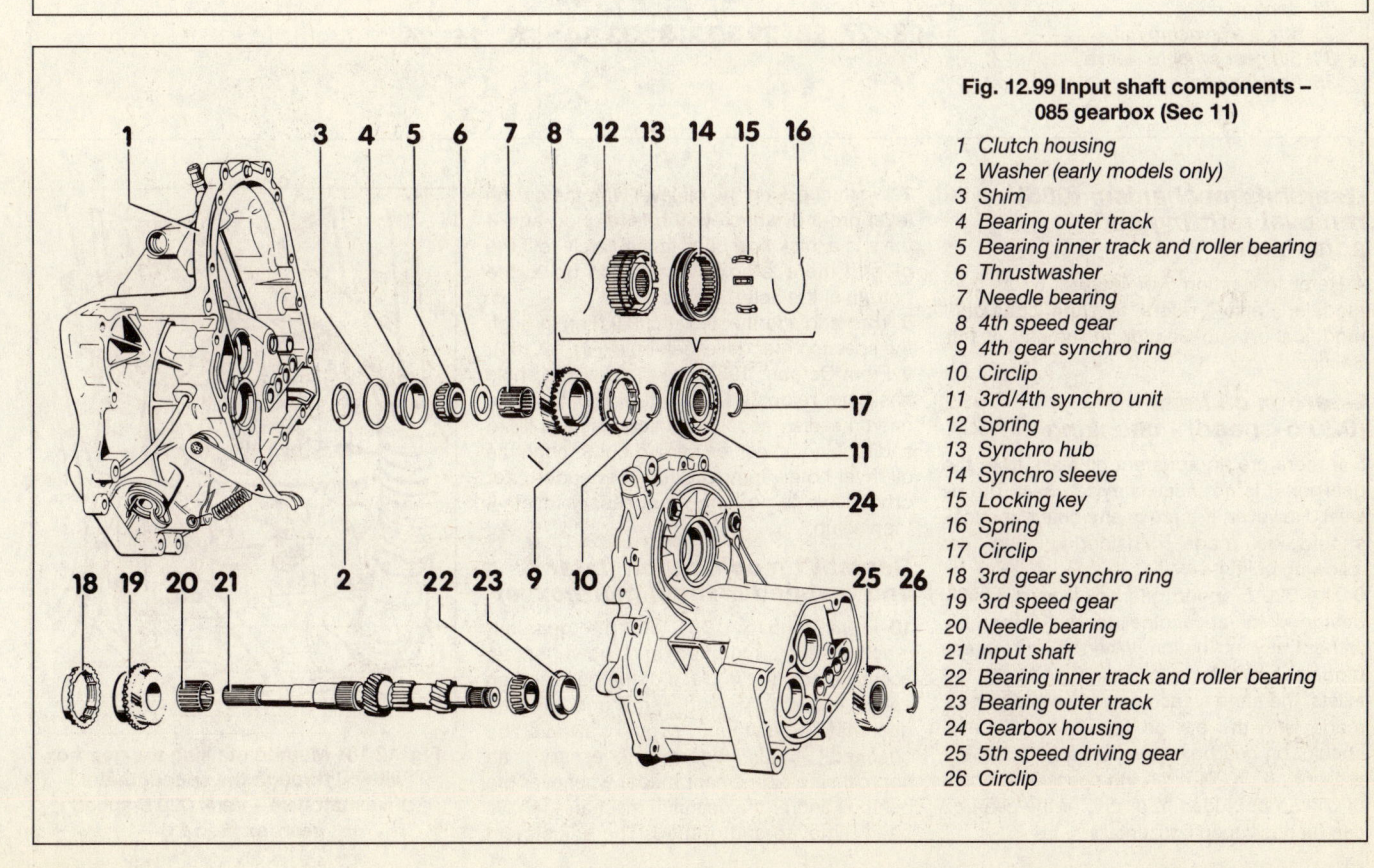

1 Inner shift lever detent
2 Clutch housing
3 Input shaft bearing outer track
4 Shim
5 Washer (early models only)
6 Output shaft bearing outer track
7 Shim
8 Selector arm
9 Pinch-bolt
10 Inner shift lever
11 Bush
12 Seal
13 Differential bearing outer track
14 Shim
15 Sleeve
16 Seal
17 Speedometer pinion
18 Bush
19 Seal
20 Guide sleeve
21 Bolt
22 Release bearing
23 Starter bush
24 Breather pipe
25 Plug

Fig. 12.99 Input shaft components – 085 gearbox (Sec 11)

1 Clutch housing
2 Washer (early models only)
3 Shim
4 Bearing outer track
5 Bearing inner track and roller bearing
6 Thrustwasher
7 Needle bearing
8 4th speed gear
9 4th gear synchro ring
10 Circlip
11 3rd/4th synchro unit
12 Spring
13 Synchro hub
14 Synchro sleeve
15 Locking key
16 Spring
17 Circlip
18 3rd gear synchro ring
19 3rd speed gear
20 Needle bearing
21 Input shaft
22 Bearing inner track and roller bearing
23 Bearing outer track
24 Gearbox housing
25 5th speed driving gear
26 Circlip

12•46 Supplement: Revisions and information on later models

Fig. 12.100 Output shaft components – 085 gearbox (Sec 11)

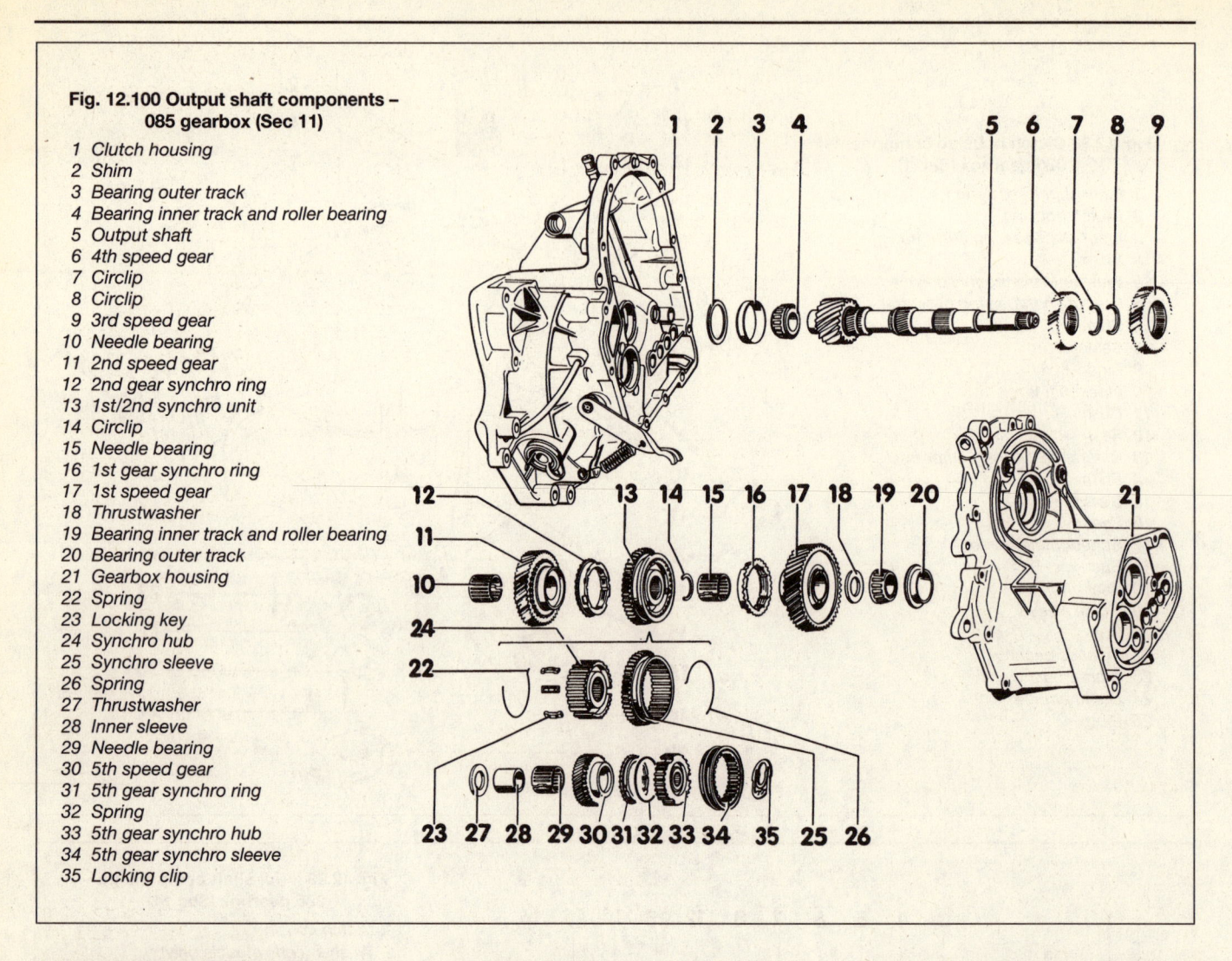

1 Clutch housing
2 Shim
3 Bearing outer track
4 Bearing inner track and roller bearing
5 Output shaft
6 4th speed gear
7 Circlip
8 Circlip
9 3rd speed gear
10 Needle bearing
11 2nd speed gear
12 2nd gear synchro ring
13 1st/2nd synchro unit
14 Circlip
15 Needle bearing
16 1st gear synchro ring
17 1st speed gear
18 Thrustwasher
19 Bearing inner track and roller bearing
20 Bearing outer track
21 Gearbox housing
22 Spring
23 Locking key
24 Synchro hub
25 Synchro sleeve
26 Spring
27 Thrustwasher
28 Inner sleeve
29 Needle bearing
30 5th speed gear
31 5th gear synchro ring
32 Spring
33 5th gear synchro hub
34 5th gear synchro sleeve
35 Locking clip

Gearshift mechanism (085) - removal refitting and adjustment

4 Refer to Section 5 of Chapter 6. On later models, also refer to the gearshift modification sub-Section at the end of this Section.

Gearbox oil level (020 5-speed) - checking

5 If there are no apparent oil leaks from the gearbox it is not necessary to check the oil level. However, if there is any doubt, a check should be made considering also the following points.

6 The 020 5-speed gearbox was originally designed for an engine gearbox/assembly without any inclination. When fitted to these models, however, a 2° inclination to the left exists, therefore an accurate check cannot be made with the car on ground level. Level checks on gearboxes removed from the car present no problem, as the specified amount of oil can be added from dry, or the gearbox can be positioned horizontally.

7 When checking the oil level with the car on level ground, unscrew the level plug and if there is a thick flow of oil immediately refit the plug. If there is no flow, first top up to the bottom of the hole, refit the plug.

8 Then add a further 0.5 litre (0.9 pint) through the speedometer driveshaft hole (Fig. 12.101).

9 From October 1987, the oil level plug hole has been relocated 7.0 mm higher than the one on earlier models. Consequently all filling and topping up can be carried out through the oil level hole. Removal of the speedometer drive cable is no longer necessary for final topping up.

Gearshift modification (later 4 and 5-speed manual gearboxes)

10 From January 1991 on, the gearshift mechanism is modified and now has an eccentric adjuster in place of the ball used on earlier models. As with earlier models, the gearshift adjustment should always be checked (and where necessary an approximate adjustment made) whenever the gearbox and/or the gearshift mechanism have been removed and refitted. The adjustment

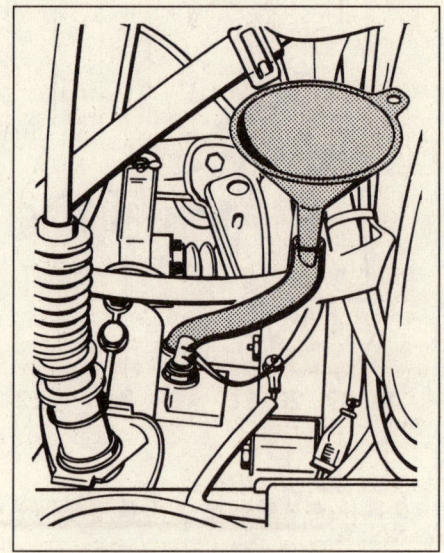

Fig. 12.101 Method of filling the gearbox with oil through the speedometer driveshaft hole – early 020 5-speed gearbox (Sec 11)

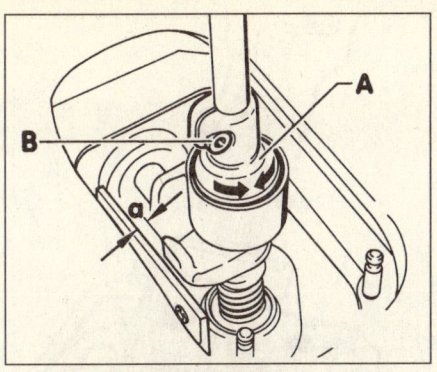

Supplement: Revisions and information on later models 12•47

Fig. 12.102 Manual gearshift showing eccentric adjuster (A) and securing screw (B) – later models (Sec 11)

Clearance 'a' must be set at 1.0 to 1.5 mm (0.04 to 0.06 in)

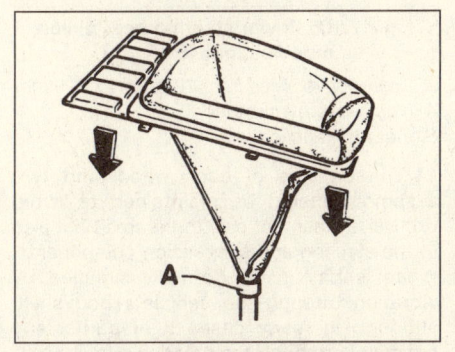

Fig. 12.103 Gear lever boot fitting method showing collar 'A' (Sec 11)

procedure for the eccentric type is as described in Section 19 of Chapter 6, but the following additional check should also be made.

11 Referring to Fig. 12.102, check that with 1st gear engaged, dimension 'a' is as specified. If required, fine adjustment can be made by pressing the lever knob down and to the left to take up any minor play in the shift mechanism, then loosen off the eccentric securing screw and turn the eccentric as required to provide the specified clearance. Retighten the screw to set the fine adjustment. Ensure that the lever remains in the 1st gear selected position as the adjustment is made.

12 Unlike the gear lever balljoint on earlier models, the eccentric can if required, be removed and renewed by simply loosening off the retaining screw and levering the eccentric up from the lever. Refit in the reverse order of removal and adjust the position of the eccentric as described in the previous paragraph.

Gear lever boot (manual gearboxes) - refitting procedure

13 When the gear lever boot is being refitted to the lever, it is essential to fit it in the correct manner to avoid possible damage. Manipulate the boot so that it is inside-out then slide it down the lever so that it is located against the collar flange (55 mm down the shaft). Now pull the frame down so that it turns the boot back the correct way and engage its locating lugs with the central console. Ensure that the boot is not twisted.

Automatic transmission

14 New driveplate-to-crankshaft retaining bolts with their threads coated in a black locking agent are fitted to later models. These bolts must be tightened to the stages given in the Specifications at the start of this Chapter.

12 Electrical system

Battery

1 Where battery renewal is required, it should be noted that a centralised ventilation type battery is recommended rather than one with ventilation plugs. If a battery with ventilated plugs is fitted, it will be necessary to fit a protective cover over the battery to prevent water spray entering and causing it to be over-filled. This would cause the acid level within the battery to overflow and damage the surrounding components.

Alternator drivebelt - adjustment

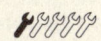

2 From early 1985, some models are fitted with a rack type alternator adjustment link. To adjust the drivebelt tension, first fully loosen the adjustment locknut and bolt, the link pivot bolt and the alternator pivot bolt, so that the alternator falls to one side under its own weight.

3 Using a socket and torque wrench on the adjustment bolt, apply a torque of 8 to 10 Nm (6 to 7 lbf ft). Secure the adjustment bolt in the set position by tightening its locknut to 35 Nm (26 lbf ft).

4 If the special VW tool is being used the adjustment bolt can now be tightened, but if not, tighten the pivot bolt then remove the socket and immediately tighten the adjustment bolt, making sure that the alternator does not move.

5 Tighten the link pivot bolt and alternator pivot bolt.

Oil pressure warning system - description

6 Some models are equipped with an optical and acoustic oil pressure warning system. The system incorporates two oil pressure switches, a 0.3 bar switch with brown insulation on the cylinder head and a 1.8 bar switch with white insulation on the oil filter head.

7 On starting the engine, as soon as the oil pressure rises above 0.3 bar, the oil pressure warning light will go out. At engine speeds above 2000 rpm the high pressure switch comes into operation, and should the oil

Fig. 12.104 Rack type alternator drivebelt tensioner link (A), locknut (B) and adjustment bolt (C) (Sec 12)

pressure drop below 1.8 bar, the oil warning light will come on and the buzzer will sound.

8 Apart from changing the oil pressure switches, little can be done by way of maintenance, and your VW dealer should be consulted if the system malfunctions.

Multi-function indicator - description

9 Some models are equipped with a multi-function indicator consisting of an electronic processor and a digital display unit. With the ignition switched on the following information can be accessed by repeatedly pressing the MFA recall button on the end of the windscreen wiper control stalk.
  Current time
  Driving time
  Distance driven
  Average speed
  Average fuel consumption
  Engine oil temperature
  Ambient temperature

10 Should a fault occur in the system the associated wiring should be checked for security and damage, particularly where it connects to the various sensors. Further checks should be made by a VW dealer using the special test instruments necessary.

Windscreen and rear window washer system - modifications

11 As from early 1986, the washer system described in Chapter 9, Section 41 is modified. The new system has a single reservoir and pump located in the engine compartment, with a plastic tube to the rear window incorporated in the rear wiring loom.

12 The wiper motor switch incorporates two sets of contacts which energise the pump with opposite polarities, causing rotation of the pump vane in two alternative directions. Using in-line non-return valves, the water is directed either to the windscreen or rear window according to which direction the pump is rotating.

Headlamps (twin) - alignment

13 On models with twin headlamps, the inner lamps are adjusted laterally with the *lower* adjustment screw, and vertically with the *upper* screw.

13 Suspension and steering

Front suspension camber adjustment - general

1 On early models, front suspension camber adjustment was possible by loosening the two bolts securing the strut to the wheel bearing housing, then turning the eccentric top bolt as required. Where this arrangement is fitted, the position of the eccentric bolt must be accurately marked before removing it, otherwise the camber adjustment will have to be reset.
2 On later models no adjustment was possible as the assembly tolerances were reduced sufficiently to make any adjustment unnecessary. However, in isolated instances it may be found that even on later models slight correction of the camber angle within 1° or 2° is required. In this case a special bolt, part number N 903-334-01 can be obtained from a VW dealer. The bolt shank is of 11 mm diameter instead of the standard 12 mm diameter and allows a small amount of adjustment to be made.
3 The special bolt should first be fitted in the top bolt position, but if this does not provide sufficient adjustment, the lower bolt should also be changed for the special type. No attempt should be made to reduce the diameter of the original bolts.

Rear suspension mounting bracket - modification

4 On 1988 models, the rear suspension mounting bracket bolts incorporate a modified shoulder, and the tightening torque is reduced to that given in the Specifications.

Power steering gear pinion - modification

5 As from May 1985 the pinch-bolt clamping the intermediate shaft to the steering gear pinion is located approximately 1.0 mm (0.040 in) nearer the centre line of the pinion. To identify the modified pinion a flat is cut opposite the pinch-bolt location.
6 When renewing either of the components separately it may be necessary to increase the depth of the pinch-bolt recess in the pinion by 1.0 mm (0.040 in) so that the two components match. Do not alter the hole in the intermediate shaft.
7 As from April 1989, VW hydraulic oil (part number G 002 000) is used in the power-assisted steering system. This oil will mix safely with the ATF type fluid used previously.

Wheels and tyres - care and maintenance

8 Wheels and tyres should give no real problems in use provided that a close eye is kept on them with regard to excessive wear or damage. To this end, the following points should be noted.
9 Ensure that tyre pressures are checked regularly and maintained correctly. Checking should be carried out with the tread cold and not immediately after the vehicle has been in use. If the pressures are checked with the tyres hot, an apparently high reading will be obtained owing to heat expansion. Under no circumstances should an attempt be made to reduce the pressures to the quoted cold reading in this instance, or effective underinflation will result.
10 Underinflation will cause overheating of the tyre owing to excessive flexing of the casing, and the tread will not sit correctly on the road surface. This will cause a consequent loss of adhesion and excessive wear, not to mention the danger of sudden tyre failure due to heat build-up.
11 Overinflation will cause rapid wear of the centre part of the tyre tread coupled with reduced adhesion, harsher ride, and the danger of shock damage occurring in the tyre casing.
12 Regularly check the tyres for damage in the form of cuts or bulges, especially in the sidewalls. Remove any nails or stones embedded in the tread before they penetrate the tyre to cause deflation. If removal of a nail *does* reveal that the tyre has been punctured, refit the nail so that its point of penetration is marked. Then immediately change the wheel and have the tyre repaired by a tyre dealer. Do *not* drive on a tyre in such a condition. In many cases a puncture can be simply repaired by the use of an inner tube of the correct size and type. If in any doubt as to the possible consequences of any damage found, consult your local tyre dealer for advice.
13 Periodically remove the wheels and clean any dirt or mud from the inside and outside surfaces. Examine the wheel rims for signs of rusting, corrosion or other damage. Light alloy wheels are easily damaged by 'kerbing' whilst parking, and similarly steel wheels may become dented or buckled. Renewal of the wheel is very often the only course of remedial action possible.

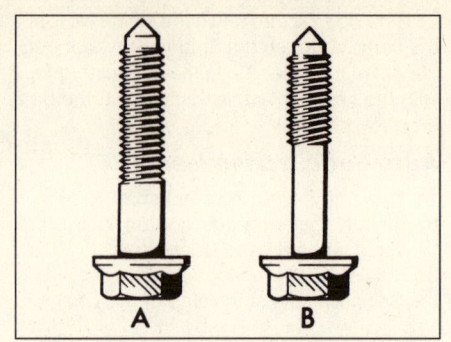

Fig. 12.105 Front suspension camber adjustment bolts – later models (Sec 13)

A Standard 12.0 mm diameter bolt
B Special 11.0 mm diameter bolt

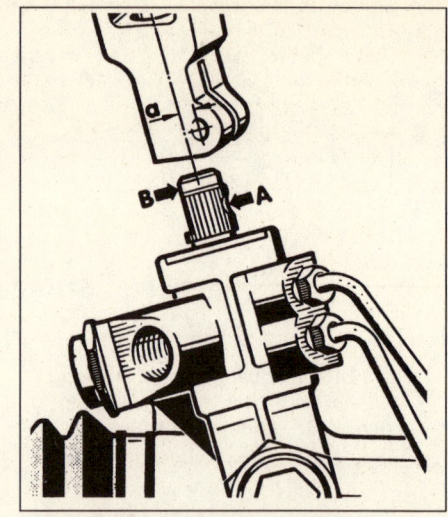

Fig. 12.106 Power steering gear pinion modifications (Sec 13)

a Dimension reduced from 12.1 mm to 11.0 mm
A Notch depth increased
B Flat for identification

14 The balance of each wheel and tyre assembly should be maintained to avoid excessive wear, not only to the tread but also to the steering and suspension components. Wheel imbalance is normally signified by vibration through the vehicle's bodyshell, although in many cases it is particularly noticeable through the steering wheel. Conversely, it should be noted that wear or damage in suspension or steering components may cause excessive tyre wear. Out-of-round or out-of-true tyres, damaged wheels and wheel bearing wear/maladjustment also fall into this category. Balancing will not usually cure vibration caused by such wear.
15 Wheel balancing may be carried out with the wheel either on or off the vehicle. If balanced on the vehicle, ensure that the wheel-to-hub relationship is marked in some way prior to subsequent wheel removal so that it may be refitted in its original position.
16 General tyre wear is influenced to a large degree by driving style - harsh braking and acceleration or fast cornering will all produce more rapid tyre wear. Interchanging of tyres may result in more even wear, but this should only be carried out where there is no mix of tyre types on the vehicle. However, it is worth bearing in mind that if this is completely effective, the added expense of replacing a complete set of tyres simultaneously is incurred, which may prove financially restrictive for many owners.
17 Front tyres may wear unevenly as a result of wheel misalignment. The front wheels should always be correctly aligned according to the settings specified by the vehicle manufacturer.
18 Legal restrictions apply to the mixing of tyre types on a vehicle. Basically this means that a vehicle must not have tyres of differing

Supplement: Revisions and information on later models 12•49

construction on the same axle. Although it is not recommended to mix tyre types between front axle and rear axle, the only legally permissible combination is crossply at the front and radial at the rear. When mixing radial ply tyres, textile braced radials must always go on the front axle, with steel braced radials at the rear. An obvious disadvantage of such mixing is the necessity to carry two spare tyres to avoid contravening the law in the event of a puncture.

19 In the UK, the Motor Vehicles Construction and Use Regulations apply to many aspects of tyre fitting and usage. It is suggested that a copy of these regulations is obtained from your local police if in doubt as to the current legal requirements with regard to tyre condition, minimum tread depth, etc.

14 Bodywork and fittings

Seat belts with height adjustment - description

1 As from early 1986 some models are fitted with front seat belts incorporating height adjustment of the 'B' pillar attachment point. The components involved are shown in Fig. 12.107.
2 The adjustable seat belts can be fitted to any model having a chassis number later than 16/19 G 054 900, but a new 'B' pillar trim must also be fitted.

Central locking system - description

3 The central locking system fitted to some models comprises a pressure/vacuum pump, control element (on the driver's door), shift elements (on the remaining doors and fuel tank flap), and interconnecting tubing.

Central locking system components - removal and refitting

4 To remove the pressure/vacuum pump, release the rubber strap in the luggage compartment, remove the cover, then withdraw the pump and disconnect the wiring and tube.
5 To remove a control or shift element, first remove the door, tailgate, or luggage compartment trim panel (as appropriate) On door elements carefully peel back the protective foil. Remove the element mounting screws and disconnect the tubing. On the driver's door only, disconnect the wiring. Disconnect the operating rod (except on the fuel tank flap) and withdraw the element.
6 Refitting is a reversal of removal, but make sure that the door protective foil is firmly stuck to prevent water penetration. Use double-sided tape to secure it if necessary.

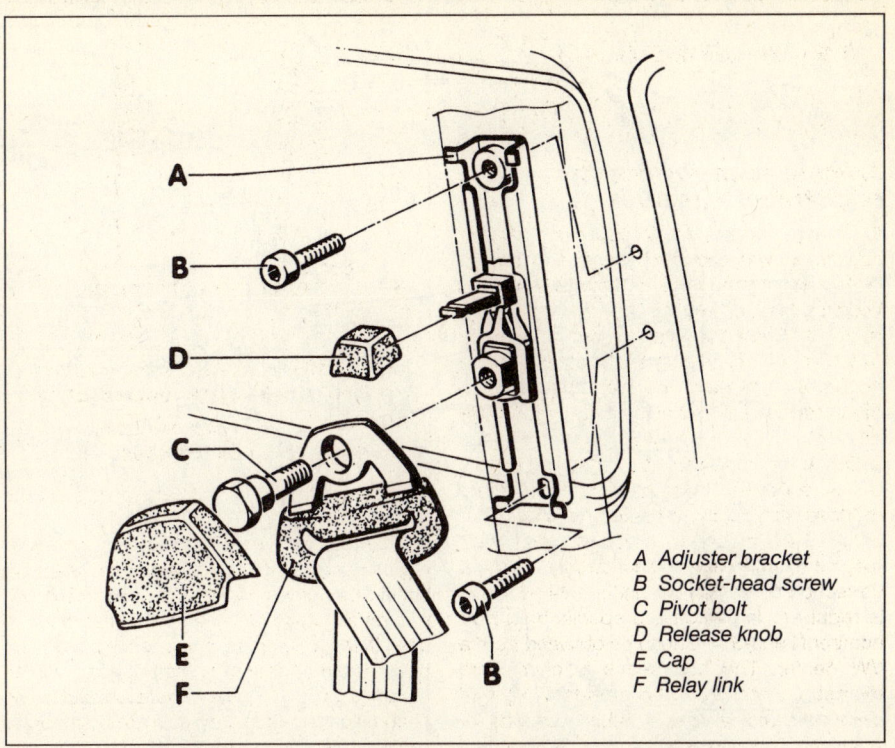

A Adjuster bracket
B Socket-head screw
C Pivot bolt
D Release knob
E Cap
F Relay link

Fig. 12.107 Height-adjustable seat belt components (Sec 14)

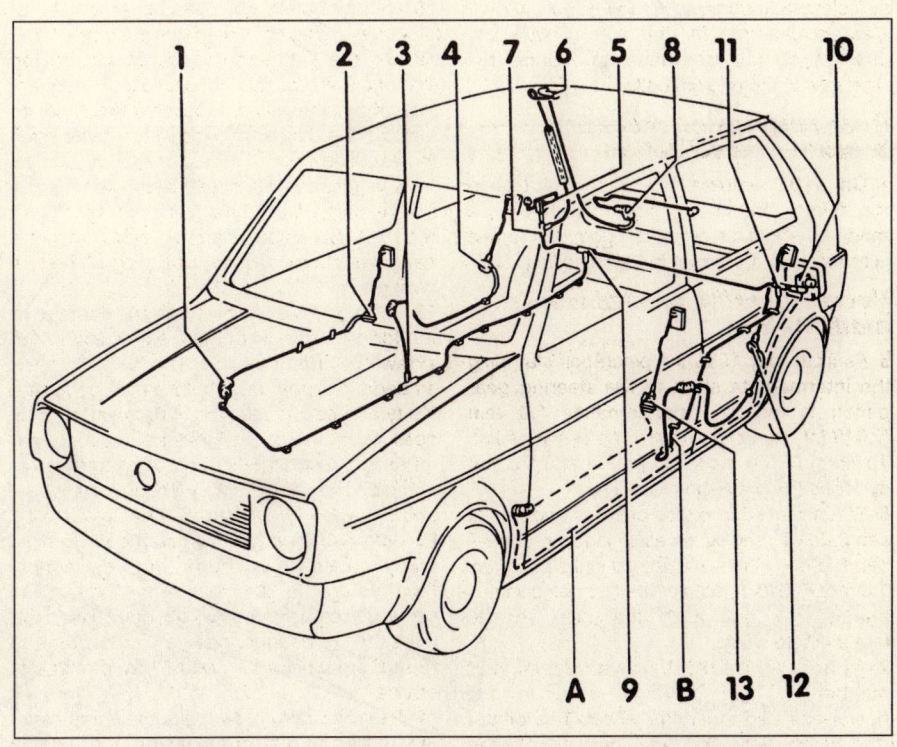

Fig. 12.108 Central locking system – left-hand drive shown (Sec 14)

A Wiring
B Tubing
1 Bellows
2 Front door shift element (or control element on RHD)
3 Connector
4 Rear door shift element
5 Fuel tank flap shift element
6 Grommet
7 Connector
8 Tailgate shift element
9 Connector
10 Pressure/vacuum pump
11 Connector
12 Rear door shift element
13 Front door control element (or shift element on RHD)

12•50 Supplement: Revisions and information on later models

Fig. 12.109 Front door components – 1988-on models (Sec 14)

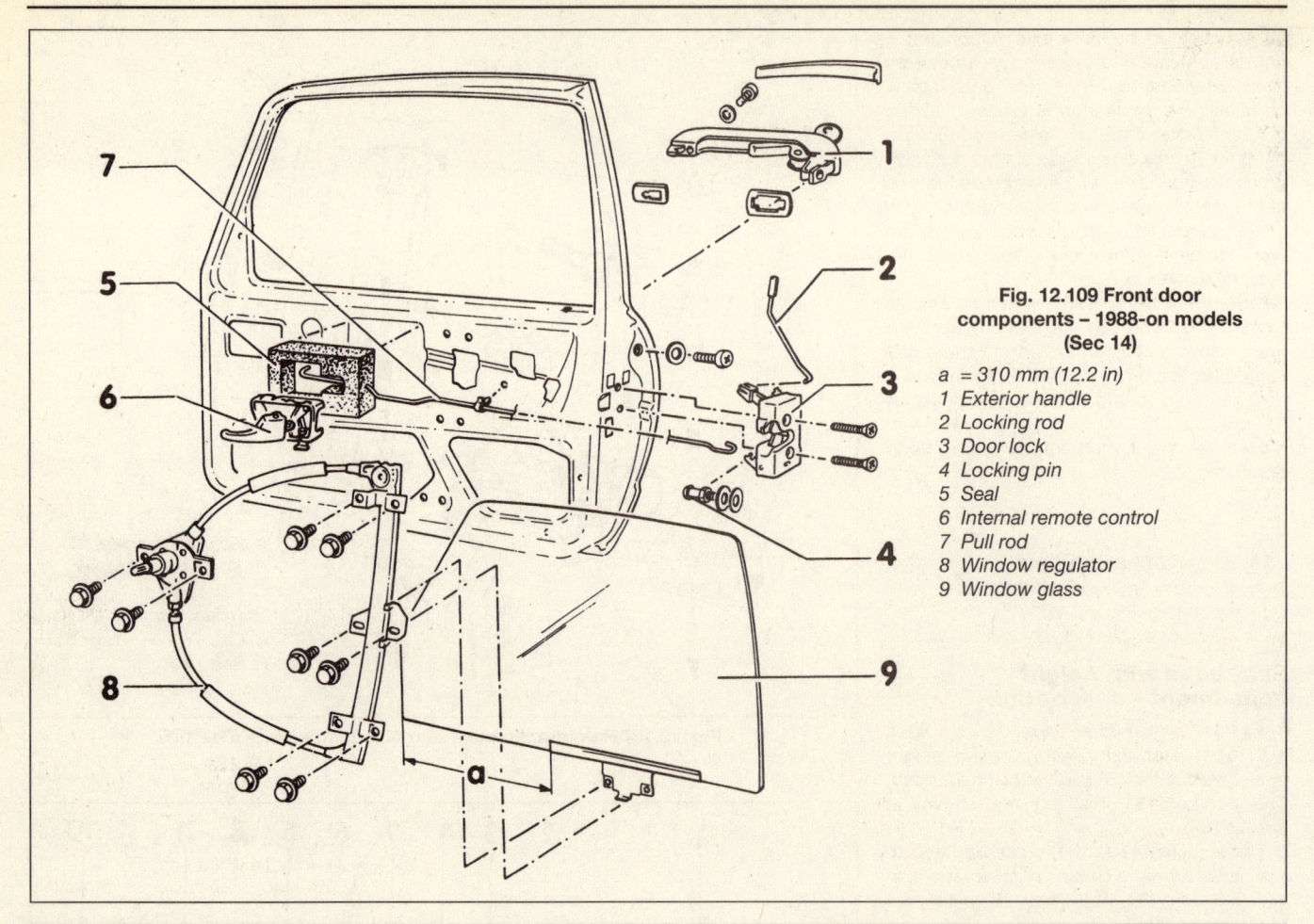

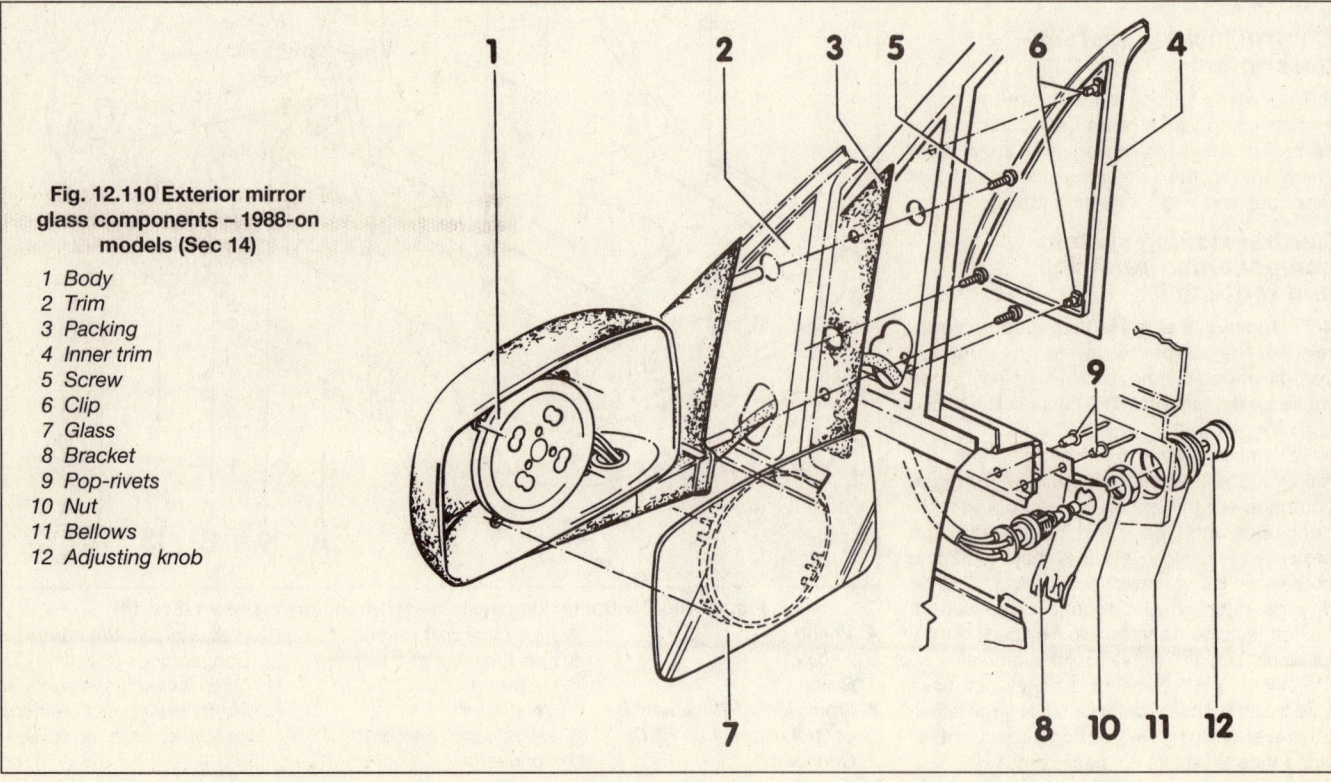

a = 310 mm (12.2 in)
1 Exterior handle
2 Locking rod
3 Door lock
4 Locking pin
5 Seal
6 Internal remote control
7 Pull rod
8 Window regulator
9 Window glass

Fig. 12.110 Exterior mirror glass components – 1988-on models (Sec 14)

1 Body
2 Trim
3 Packing
4 Inner trim
5 Screw
6 Clip
7 Glass
8 Bracket
9 Pop-rivets
10 Nut
11 Bellows
12 Adjusting knob

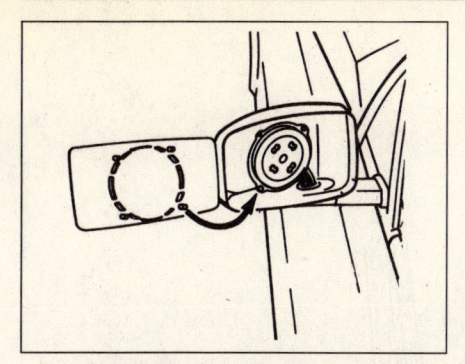

Supplement: Revisions and information on later models

Fig. 12.111 Exterior mirror glass fixing – 1988-on models (Sec 14)

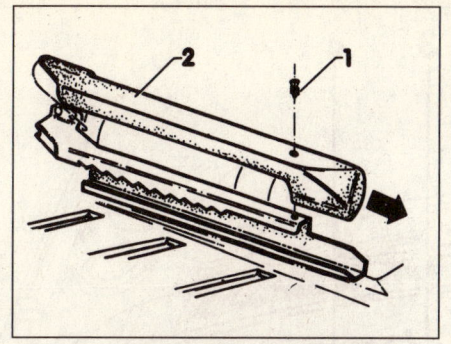

Fig. 12.112 Front seat runner and cover – 1986-on models (Sec 14)
1 Screw   2 Cover

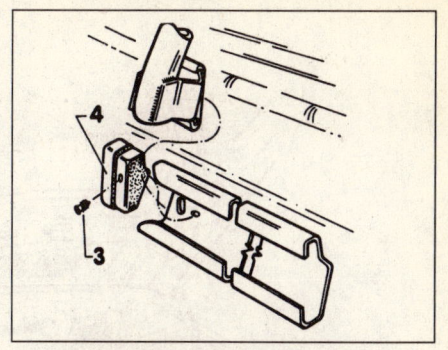

Fig. 12.113 Front seat guide fixing – 1986-on models (Sec 14)
3 Screw   4 Cap

Front door (1988-on) - dismantling and reassembly

7 The front door components for 1988-on models are shown in Fig. 12.109. Dismantling and reassembly procedures are basically the same as for earlier models.

Exterior mirror and glass (1988-on) - removal and refitting

8 On 1988-on models, the exterior mirrors are mounted in the triangular area in front of the window glass.

9 The removal and refitting procedures are basically the same as for earlier models. Note that the mirror glass is clipped in position and may be removed by carefully levering out the bottom edge, then the top edge, using a plastic or wooden tool. When refitting the glass, align the guide pins and use a wad of cloth, pressing only on the middle of the glass.

Front seat (1986-on) - removal and refitting

10 Referring to Fig. 12.112, remove screw (1) and slide off the cover (2) from the runner.
11 Referring to Fig. 12.113, remove the cross-head screw (3) and pull the cap (4) from the seat guide.
12 Slide the seat fully forward and then unscrew the cap nut, extract the circlip and fillister head screw see Fig. 11.24 (Chapter 11).
13 Release the locking bar and slide the seat rearwards out of the guide rails.
14 Refitting is a reversal of removal.

Side rubbing strip - removal and refitting

15 The side rubbing strips may be removed using a lever to prise them from their fixing clips. Protect the paintwork by taping the end of the lever.
16 When fitting a strip, engage the lower edge under the clip and give a sharp blow with the hand to force the upper edge into engagement.

Knee-bar - removal and refitting

17 On certain models, a protective knee-bar is fitted across the lower edge of the facia panel.
18 To remove the bar, first peel back the weatherstrip from the edge of the door aperture and the trim in the vicinity of the knee-bar end brackets.
19 Extract the bracket fixing screws and withdraw the bar.
20 Refitting is a reversal of removal.

Rear spoiler (Jetta GT) - removal and refitting

21 Open the boot lid and unscrew the nuts which secure the spoiler retaining clips.
22 Lift the spoiler from the boot lid.

Dust and pollen filter

23 This filter is fitted (or can be fitted) to all models covered by this manual. The filter is located in the air intake within the plenum chamber at the right-hand side of the underbonnet area. Access to the filter is gained after removing the anti-leaf mesh and the water deflector.

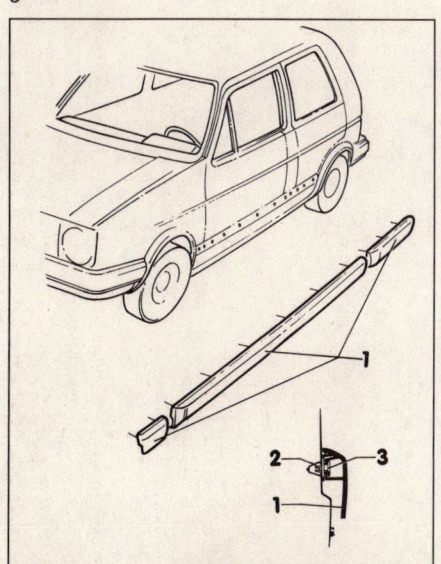

Fig. 12.114 Side rubbing strip components (Sec 14)
1 Rubbing strip   2 Retainer   3 Clip

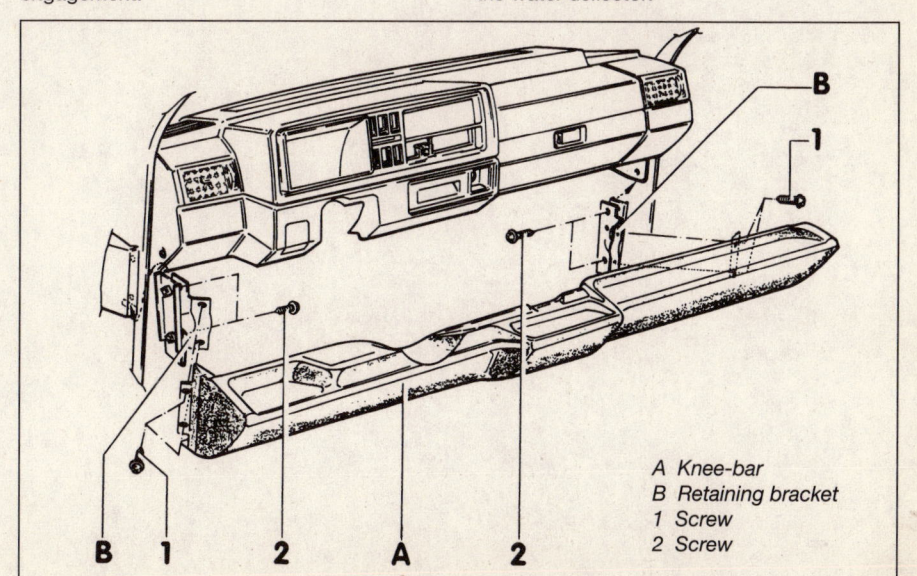

Fig. 12.115 Knee-bar fixing (Sec 14)
A Knee-bar
B Retaining bracket
1 Screw
2 Screw

Fig. 12.116 Dust/pollen filter location (Sec 14)

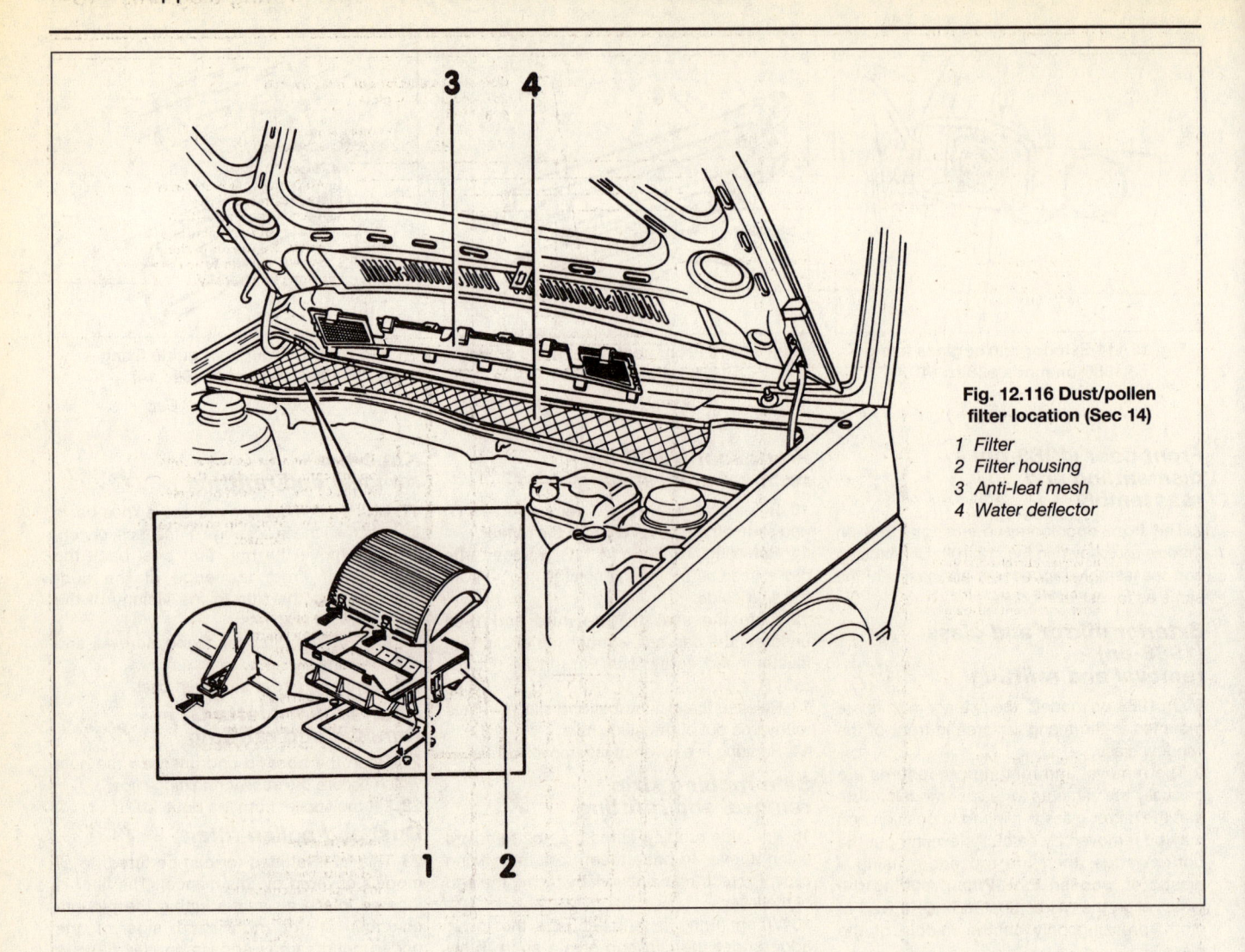

1 Filter
2 Filter housing
3 Anti-leaf mesh
4 Water deflector

Wiring diagrams 13•1

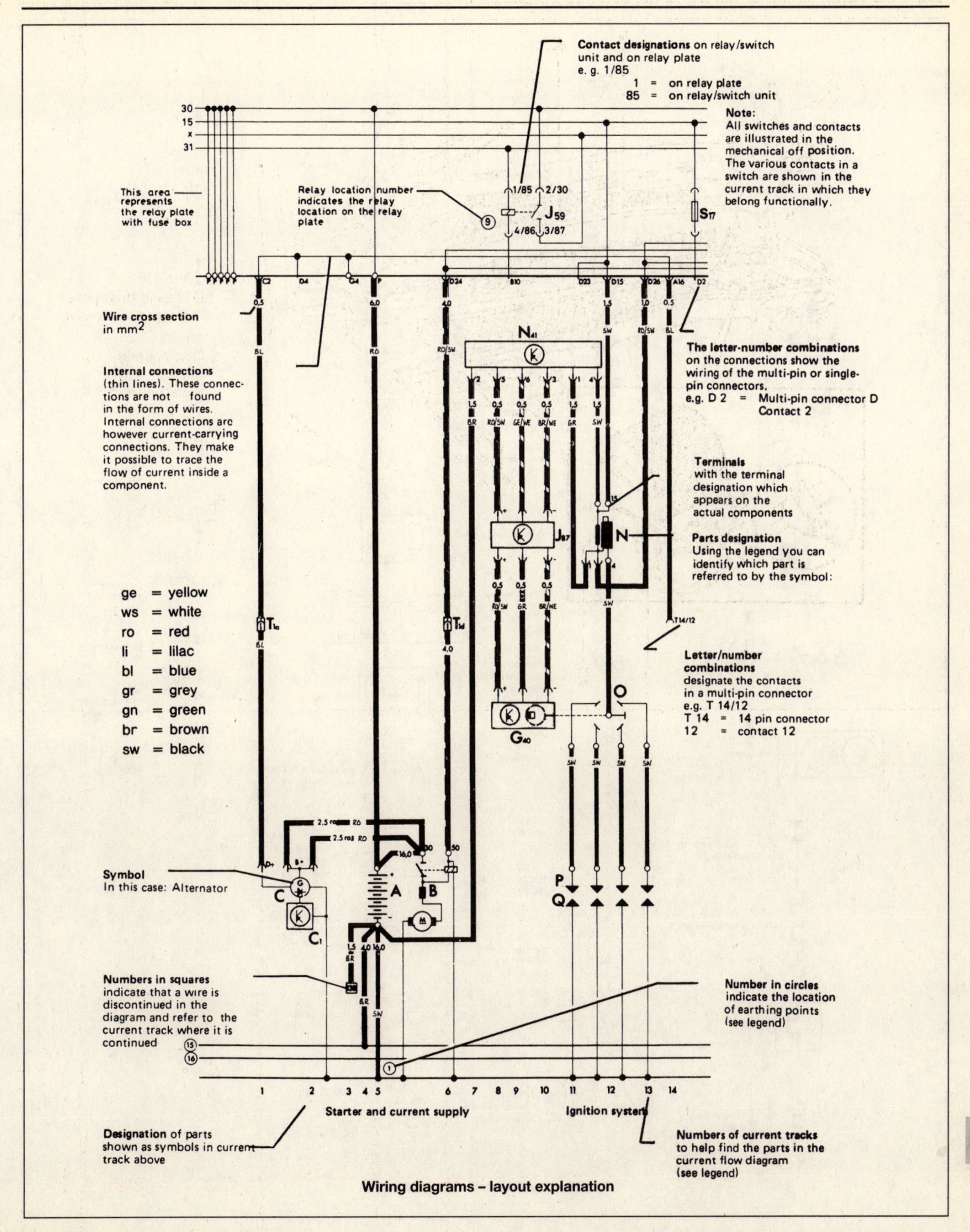

Wiring diagrams – layout explanation

13•2 Wiring diagrams

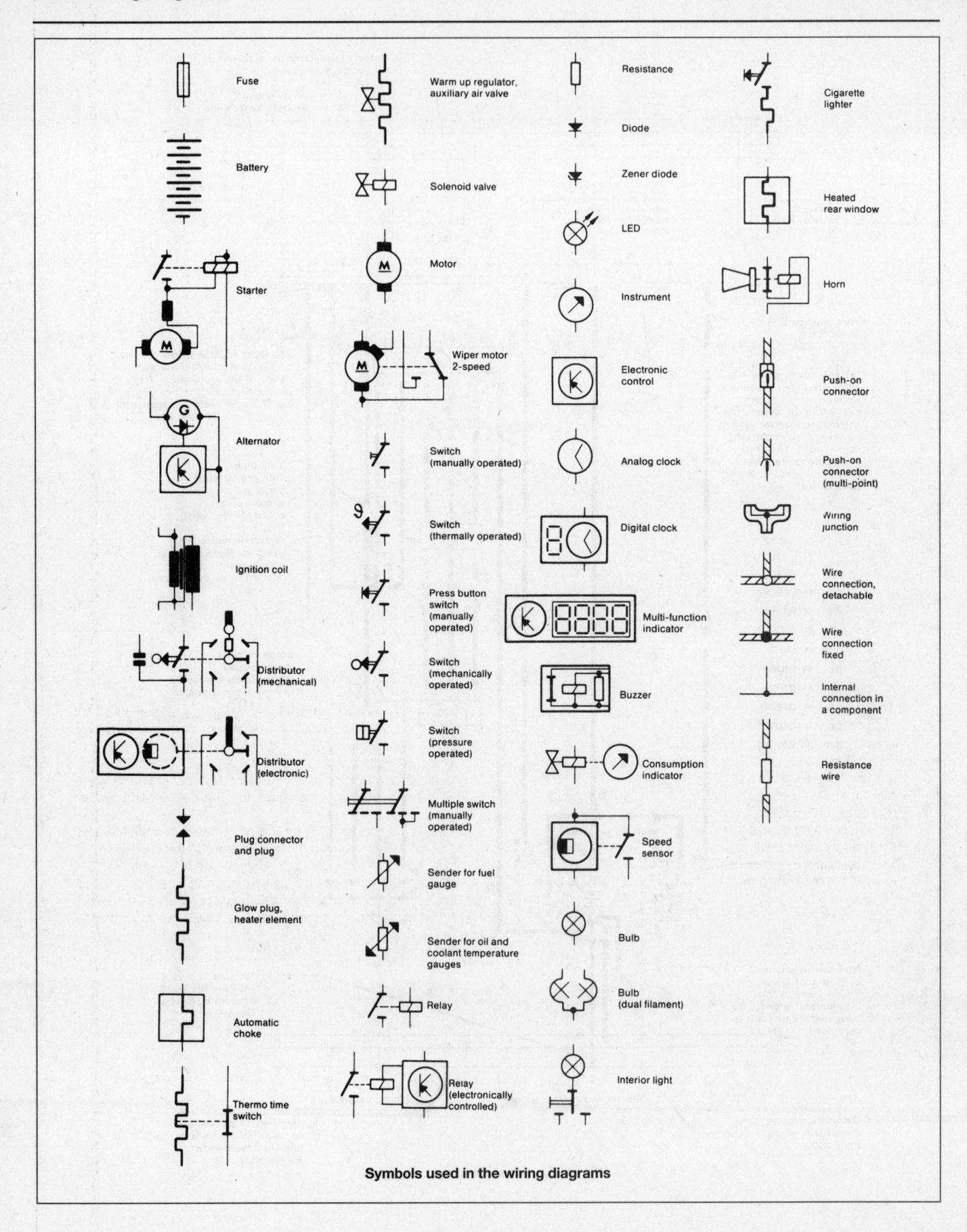

Symbol	Description
	Fuse
	Battery
	Starter
	Alternator
	Ignition coil
	Distributor (mechanical)
	Distributor (electronic)
	Plug connector and plug
	Glow plug, heater element
	Automatic choke
	Thermo time switch
	Warm up regulator, auxiliary air valve
	Solenoid valve
	Motor
	Wiper motor 2-speed
	Switch (manually operated)
	Switch (thermally operated)
	Press button switch (manually operated)
	Switch (mechanically operated)
	Switch (pressure operated)
	Multiple switch (manually operated)
	Sender for fuel gauge
	Sender for oil and coolant temperature gauges
	Relay
	Relay (electronically controlled)
	Resistance
	Diode
	Zener diode
	LED
	Instrument
	Electronic control
	Analog clock
	Digital clock
	Multi-function indicator
	Buzzer
	Consumption indicator
	Speed sensor
	Bulb
	Bulb (dual filament)
	Interior light
	Cigarette lighter
	Heated rear window
	Horn
	Push-on connector
	Push-on connector (multi-point)
	Wiring junction
	Wire connection, detachable
	Wire connection fixed
	Internal connection in a component
	Resistance wire

Symbols used in the wiring diagrams

Wiring diagrams 13•3

Relay locations

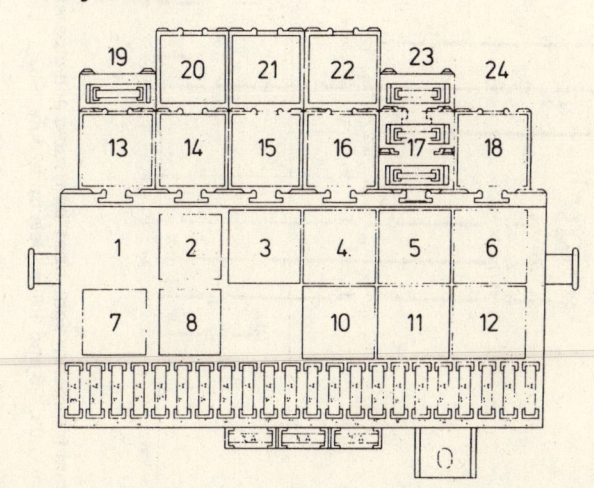

Connections

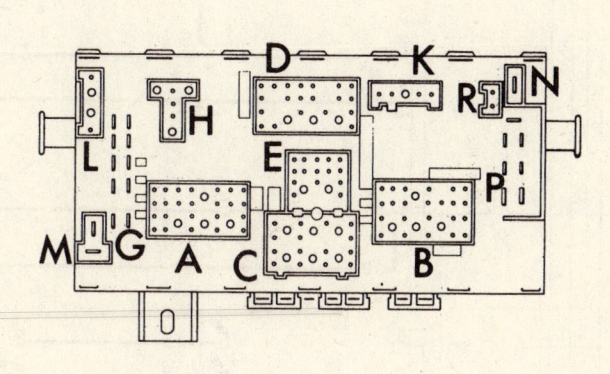

Relays and connections – all models

Relays (typical)
1. Vacant
2. Intake manifold preheating relay (carburettor models) or fuel pump relay (injection models)
3. Seat belt warning system relay
4. Gearshift indicator control unit
5. Air conditioner relay
6. Dual tone horn relay
7. Relay for foglights and rear foglight
8. Relief relay for X contact
10. Intermittent wash/wipe relay
11. Rear window wiper relay
12. Turn signal flasher or trailer towing warning relay
13. Seat belt warning system (interlock) or rear window, driving lights and oil pressure warning relay
14. Window lift or seat belt warning system relay
15. Headlight washer relay
16. Control unit for idling speed increase
17. Fuse for rear foglight
18. Control unit for coolant shortage indicator
19. Thermo fuse for window lifters
20. Switch unit for heated driver's seat
21. Switch unit for heated passenger's seat
22. Switch unit for overrun cut-off
23. Vacant
24. Vacant

Relays are symbolised as a number in a black box

Not all relays are fitted to all models

Connections
A Multi-pin connector (blue) for dash panel loom
B Multi-pin connector (red) for dash panel loom
C Multi-pin connector (yellow) for engine compartment loom left
D Multi-pin connector (white) for engine compartment loom right
E Multi-pin connector (black) for rear wiring loom
G Single connector
H Multi-pin connector (brown) for air conditioner or wiring loom
K Multi-pin connector (transparent) for seat belt warning system loom
L Multi-pin connector (black) for lighting switch terminal 56 and dip and flasher switch terminal 56b (carburettor models) or multi-pin connector (grey) for dual tone horn (injection models)
M Multi-pin connector (black) for lighting switch terminal 56 and dip and flasher switch terminal 56b (injection models)
N Single connector for separate fuse (manifold heater element)
P Single connector (terminal 30)
R Not in use

Fuse colours
Blue	5A
Green	30A
Red	10A
Yellow	20A

13•4 Wiring diagrams

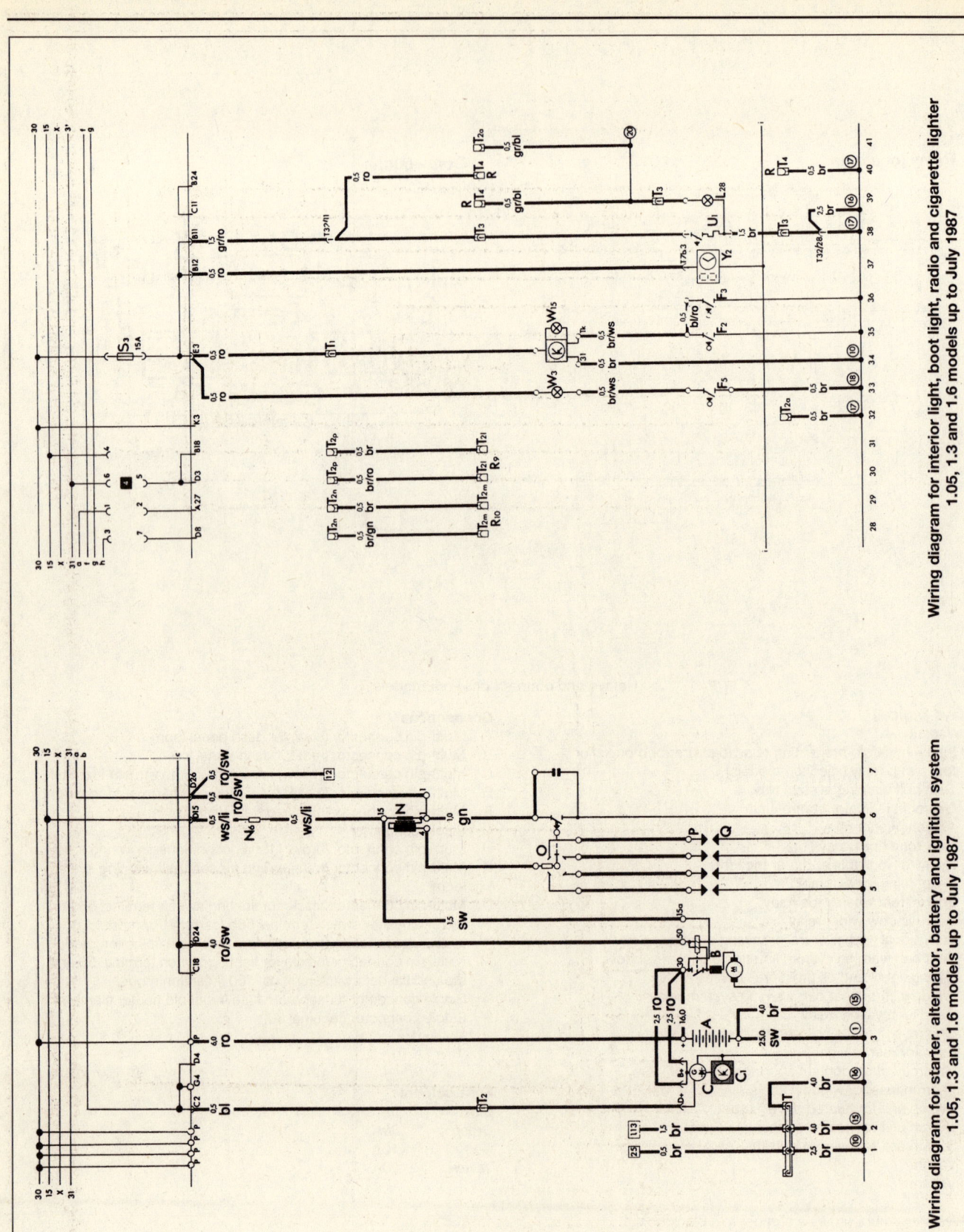

Wiring diagram for interior light, boot light, radio and cigarette lighter
1.05, 1.3 and 1.6 models up to July 1987

Wiring diagram for starter, alternator, battery and ignition system
1.05, 1.3 and 1.6 models up to July 1987

Wiring diagrams 13•5

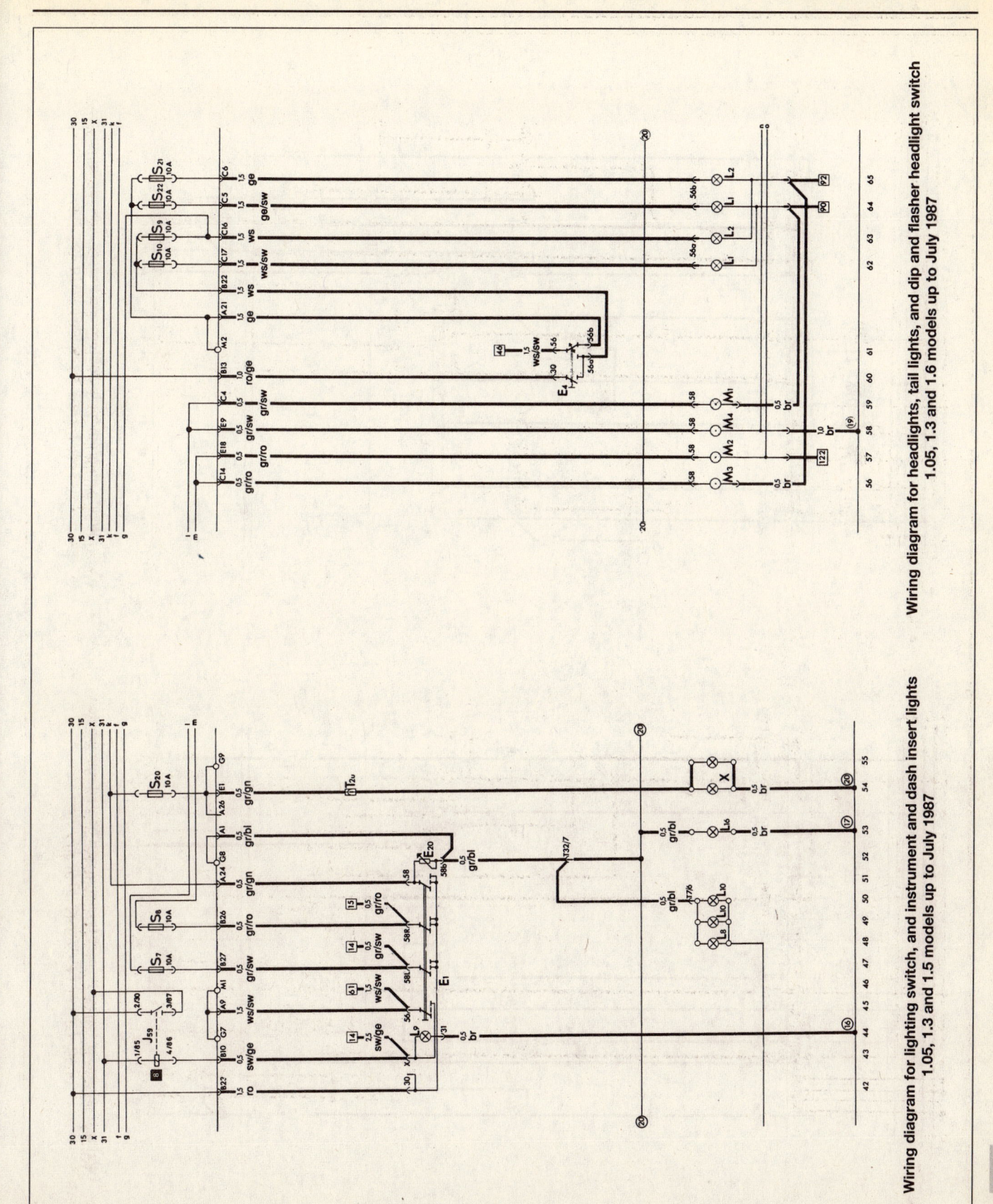

Wiring diagram for headlights, tail lights, and dip and flasher headlight switch 1.05, 1.3 and 1.6 models up to July 1987

Wiring diagram for lighting switch, and instrument and dash insert lights 1.05, 1.3 and 1.5 models up to July 1987

13•6 Wiring diagrams

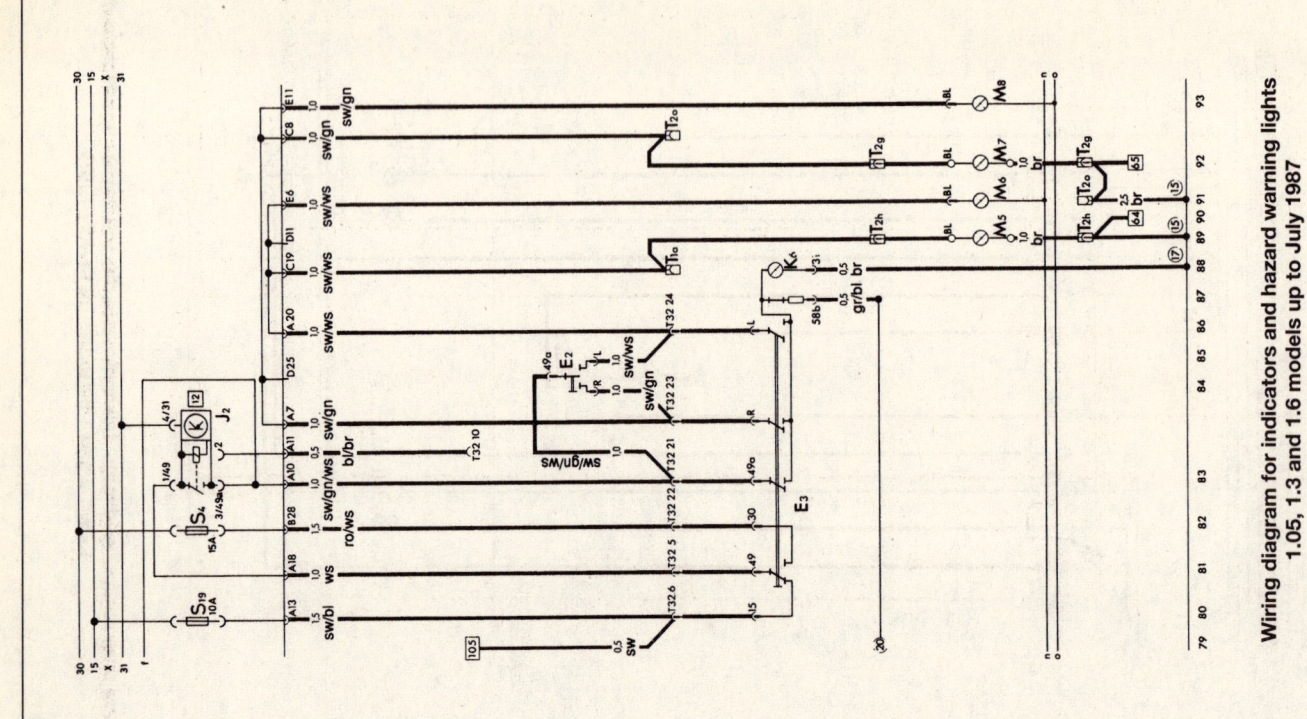

Wiring diagram for indicators and hazard warning lights 1.05, 1.3 and 1.6 models up to July 1987

Wiring diagram for foglights, rear foglights and heated rear window 1.05, 1.3 and 1.6 models up to July 1987

Wiring diagrams

Wiring diagram for dual tone horn, and handbrake and brake fluid level warning 1.05, 1.3 and 1.6 models up to July 1987

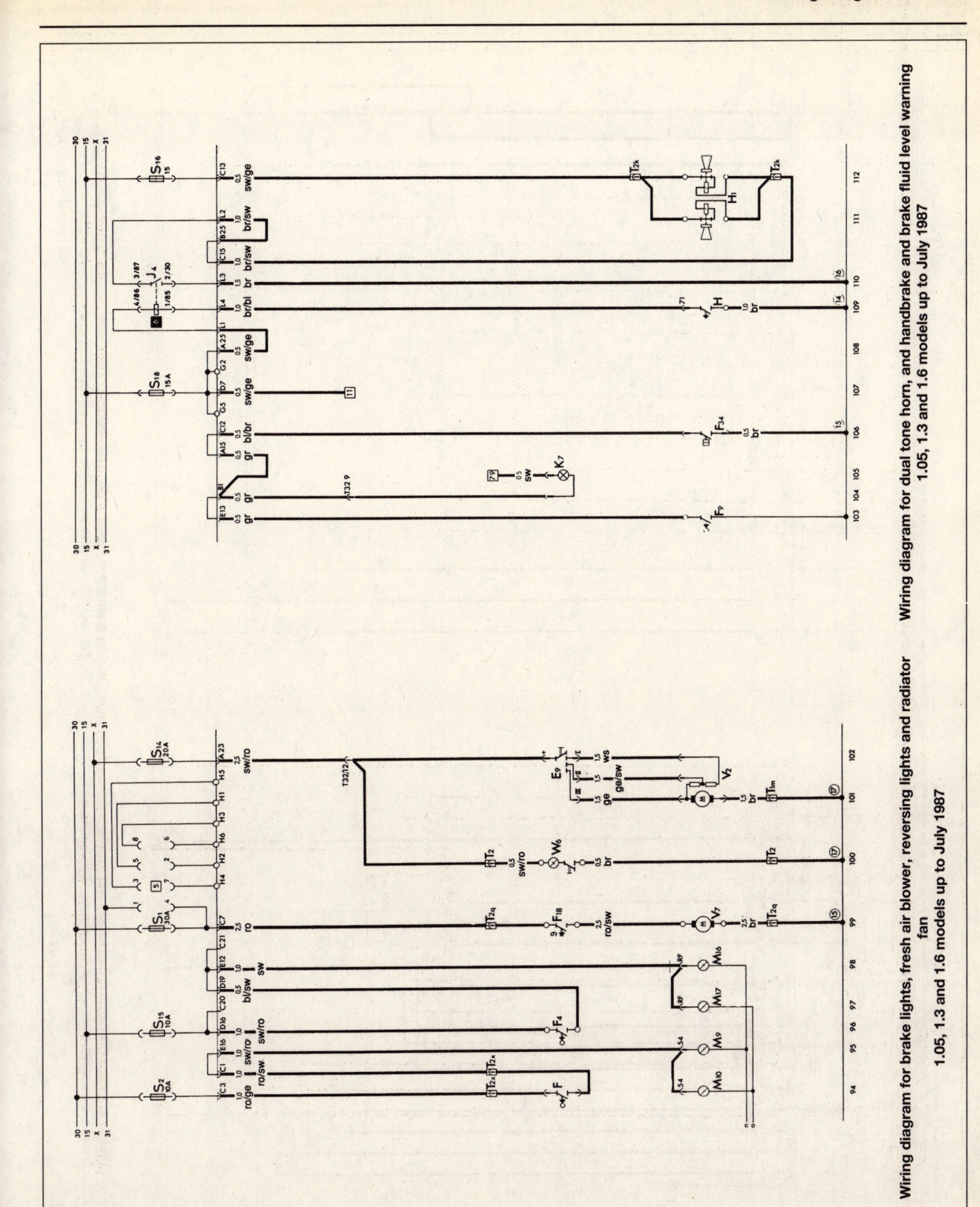

Wiring diagram for brake lights, fresh air blower, reversing lights and radiator fan 1.05, 1.3 and 1.6 models up to July 1987

13•8 Wiring diagrams

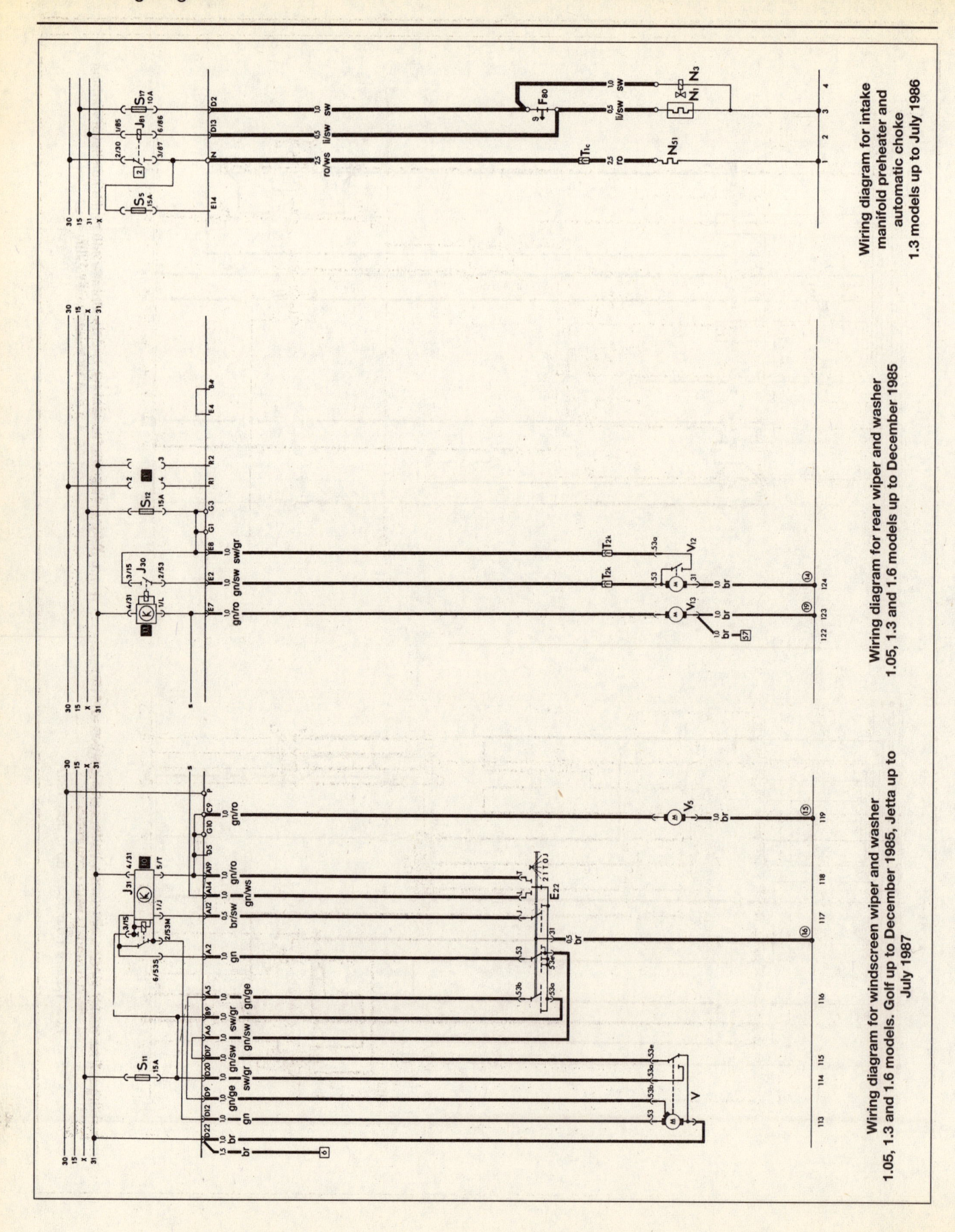

Wiring diagram for intake manifold preheater and automatic choke 1.3 models up to July 1986

Wiring diagram for rear wiper and washer 1.05, 1.3 and 1.6 models up to December 1985

Wiring diagram for windscreen wiper and washer 1.05, 1.3 and 1.6 models. Golf up to December 1985, Jetta up to July 1987

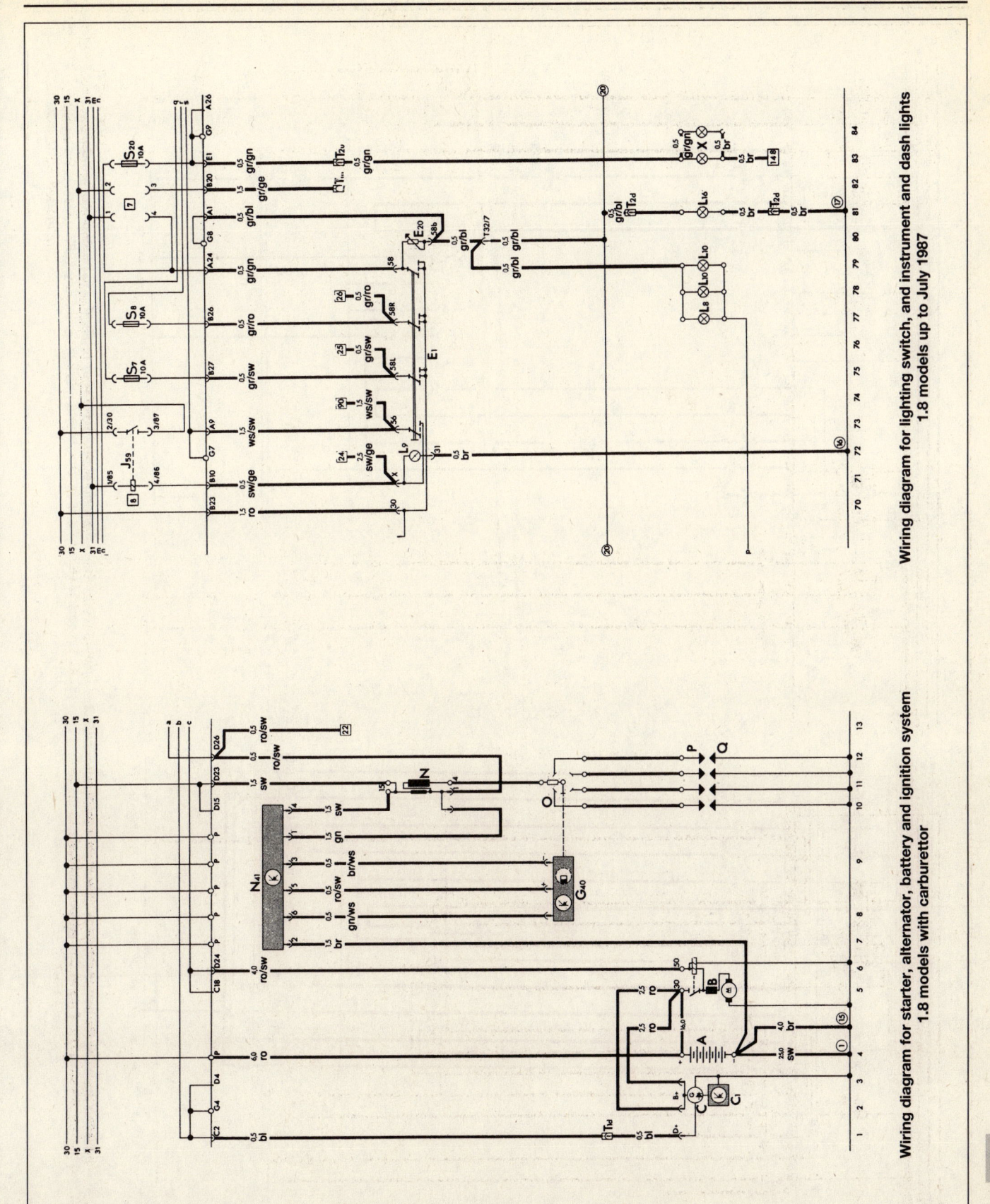

Wiring diagrams

**Wiring diagram for lighting switch, and instrument and dash lights
1.8 models up to July 1987**

**Wiring diagram for starter, alternator, battery and ignition system
1.8 models with carburettor**

13•10 Wiring diagrams

Wiring diagram for rear foglight and heated rear window
1.8 models up to July 1987

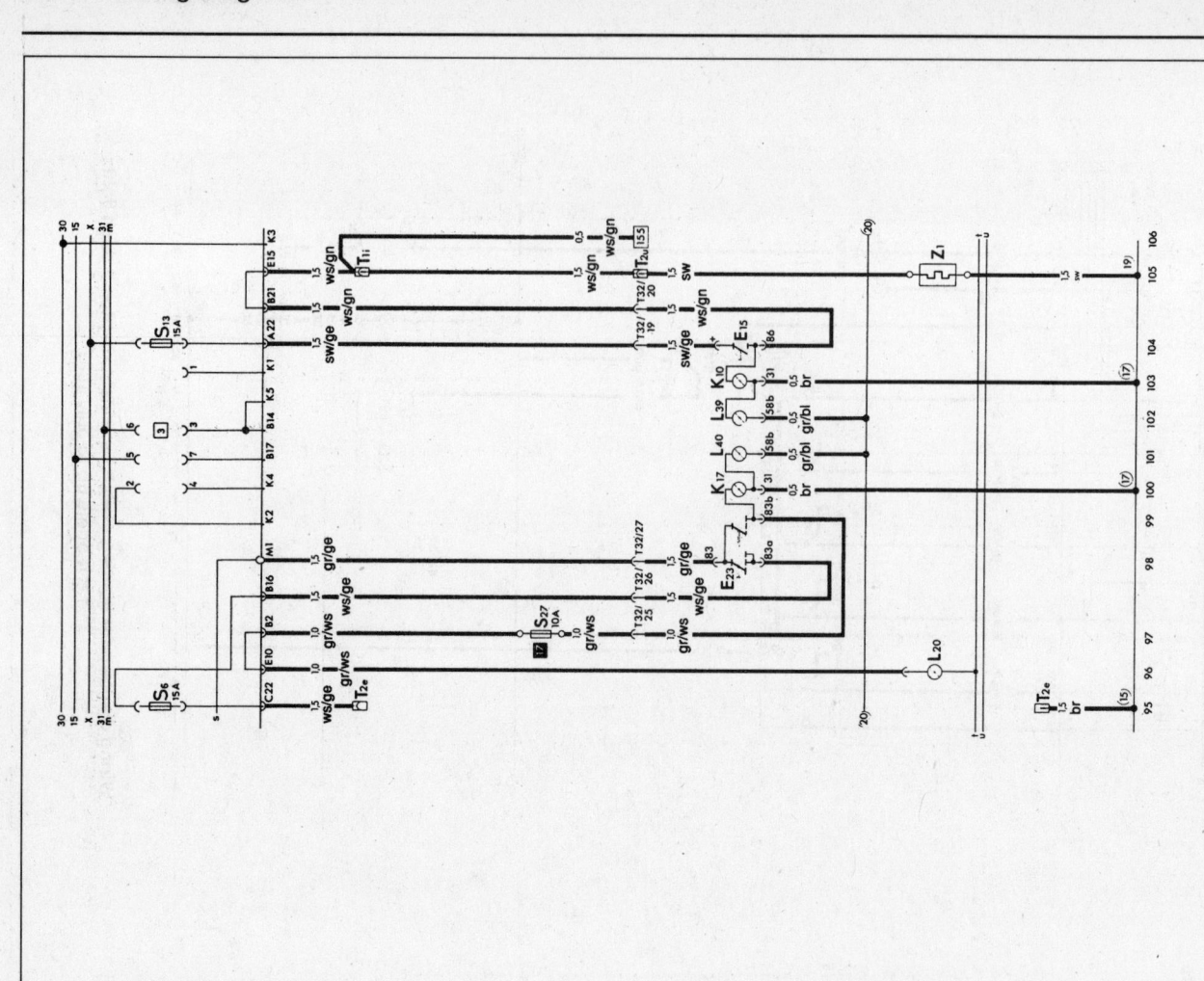

Wiring diagram for headlights, tail lights, and dip flasher switch
1.8 models up to July 1987

Wiring diagrams

Wiring diagram for brake lights, fresh air blower, reversing lights and radiator fan – 1.8 models up to July 1987

Wiring diagram for indicators and hazard warning lights – 1.8 models up to July 1987

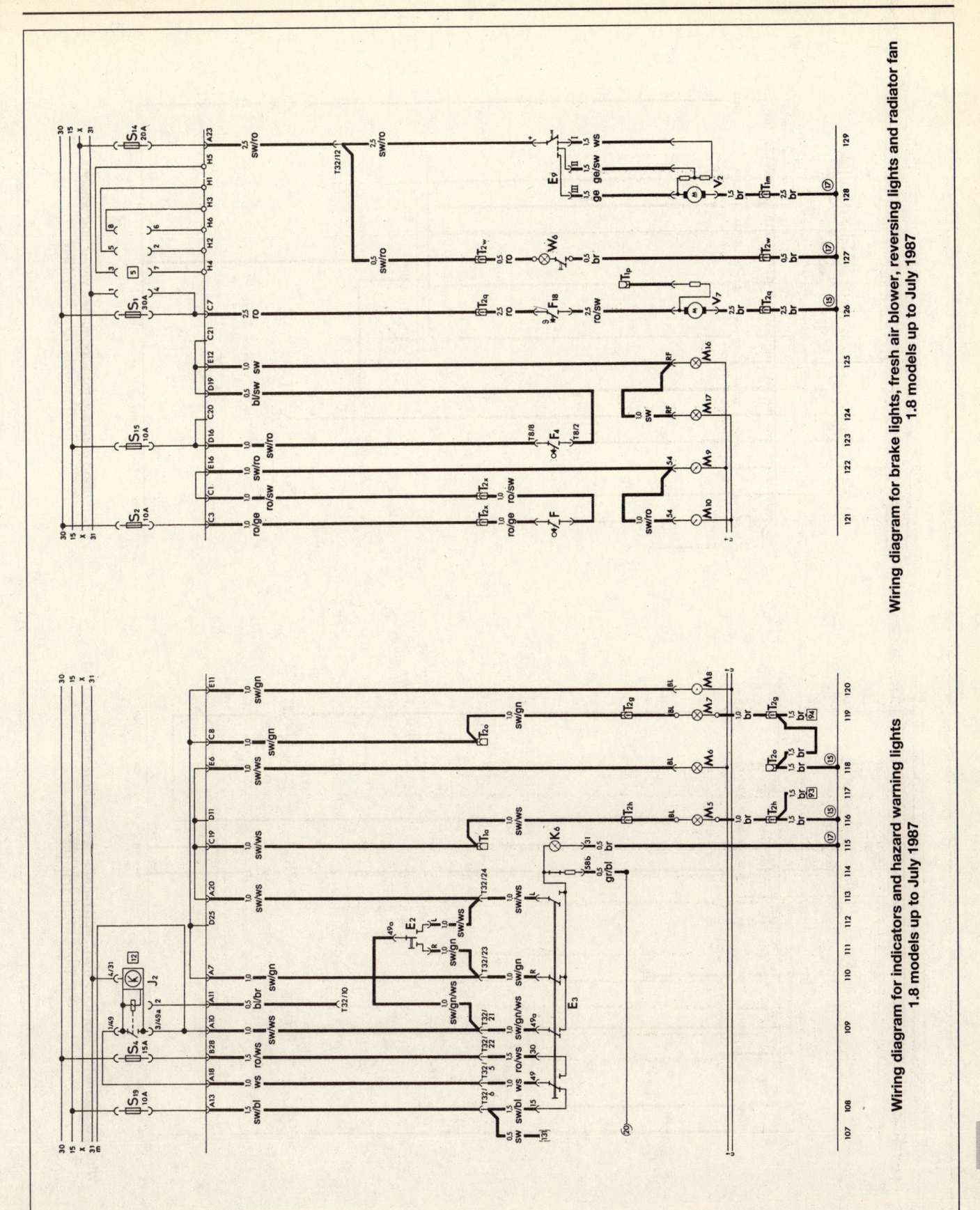

13•12 Wiring diagrams

Wiring diagram for windscreen wiper and washer 1.8 models up to July 1987

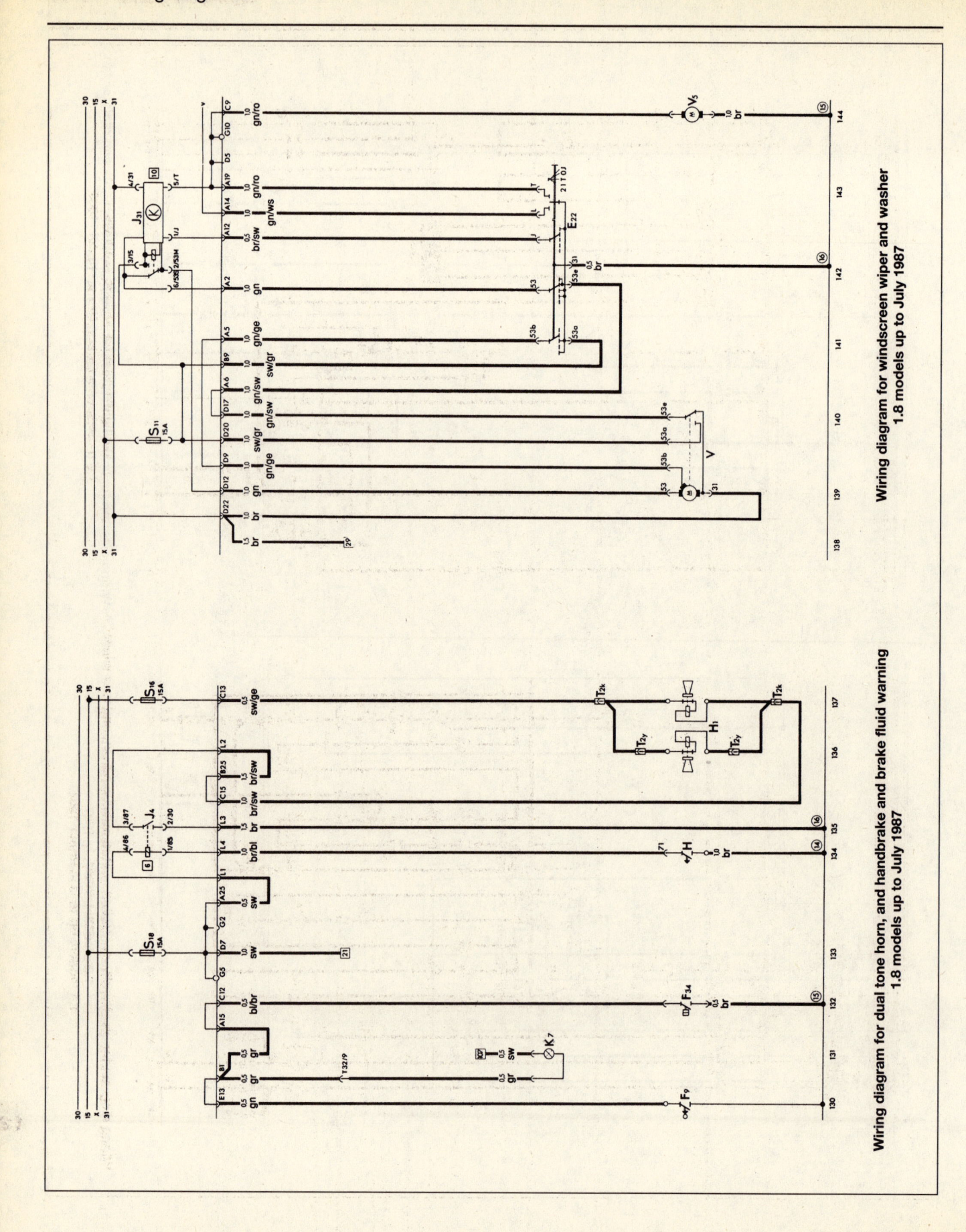

Wiring diagram for dual tone horn, and handbrake and brake fluid warning 1.8 models up to July 1987

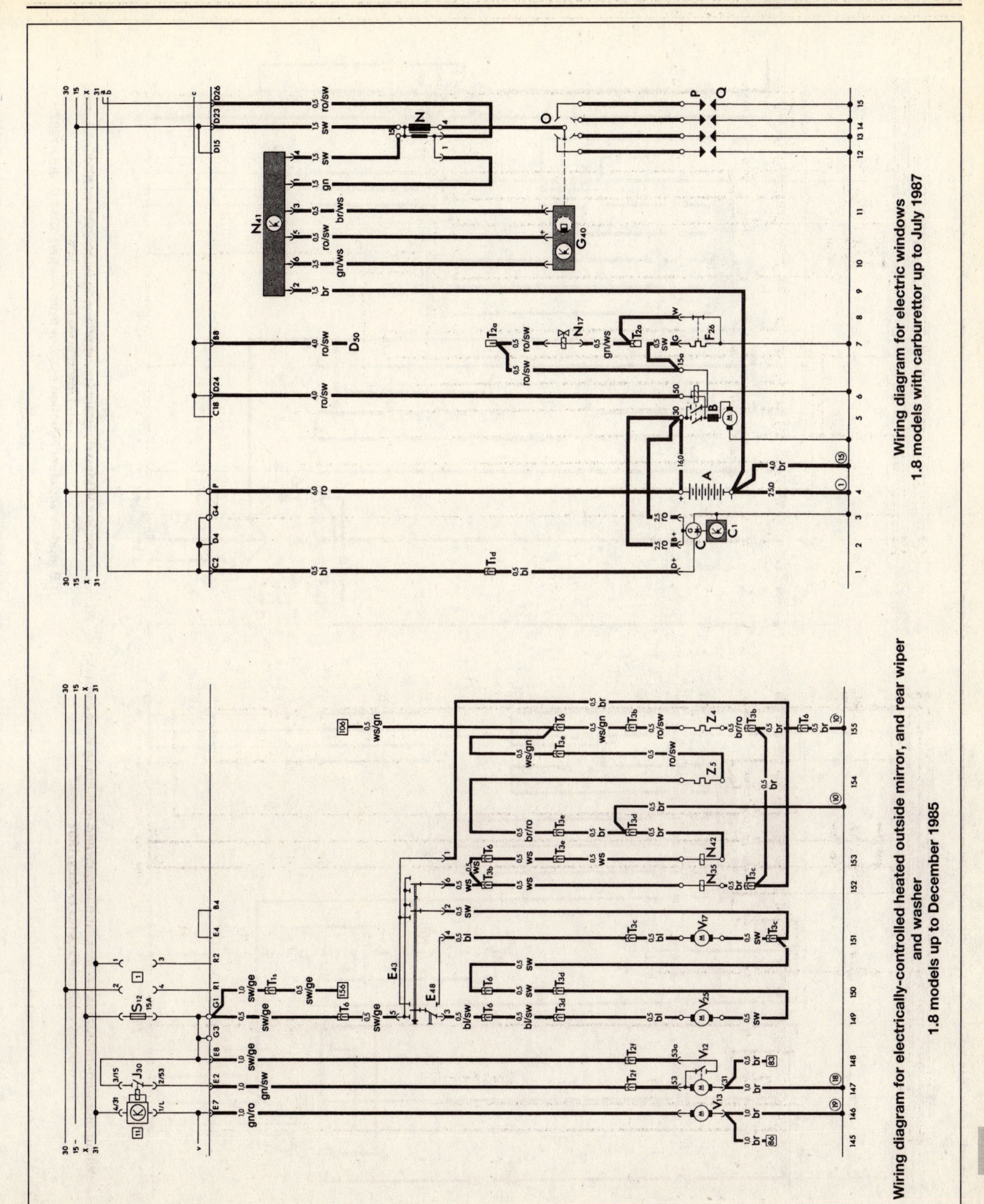

Wiring diagrams 13•13

Wiring diagram for electric windows 1.8 models with carburettor up to July 1987

Wiring diagram for electrically-controlled heated outside mirror, and rear wiper and washer 1.8 models up to December 1985

13•14 Wiring diagrams

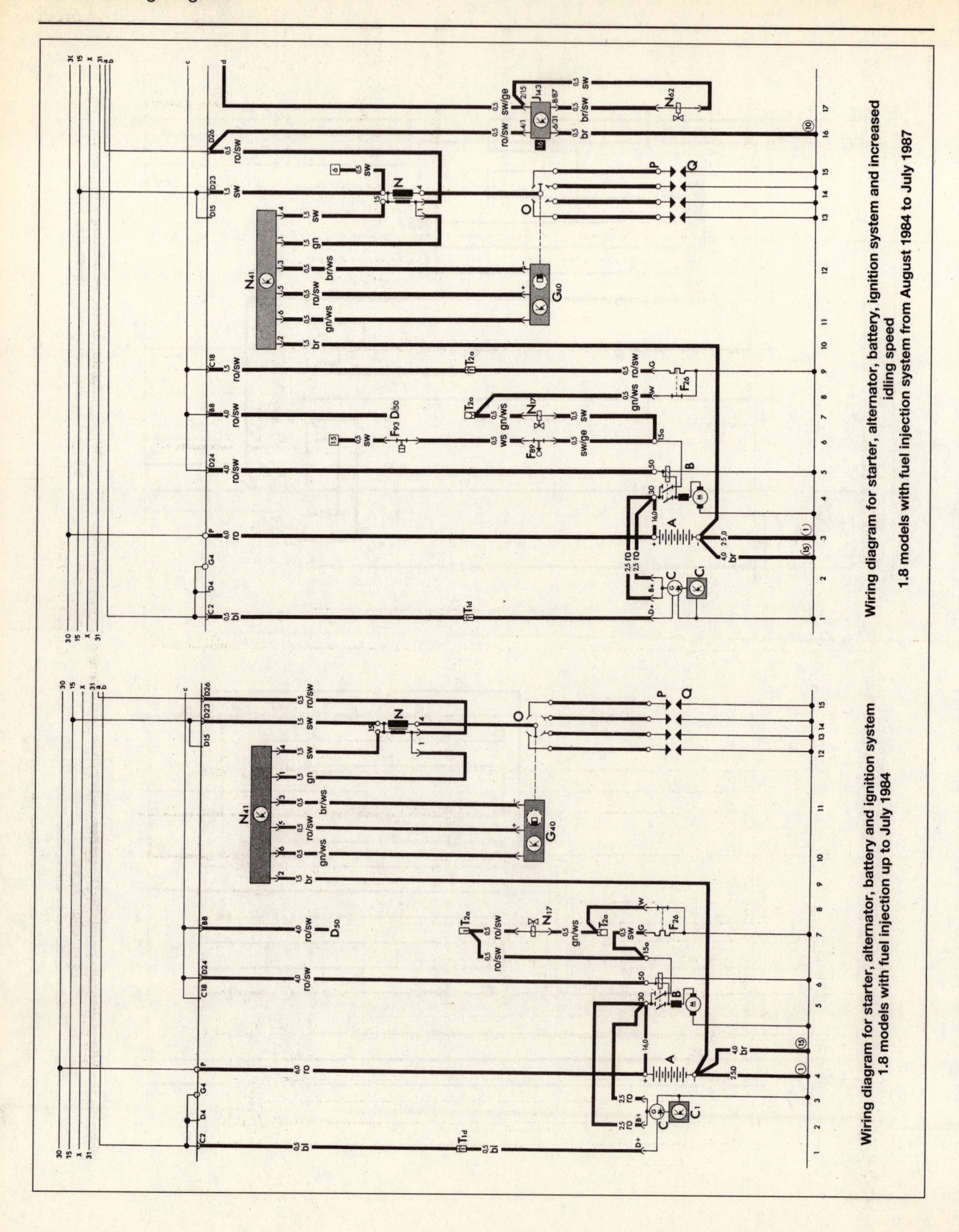

Wiring diagram for starter, alternator, battery, ignition system and increased idling speed
1.8 models with fuel injection system from August 1984 to July 1987

Wiring diagram for starter, alternator, battery and ignition system
1.8 models with fuel injection up to July 1984

Wiring diagrams 13•15

Wiring diagram for automatic gearbox 1.6 models

Wiring diagram for 250W radiator fan 1.6 and 1.8 models

Wiring diagram for headlight washer All models

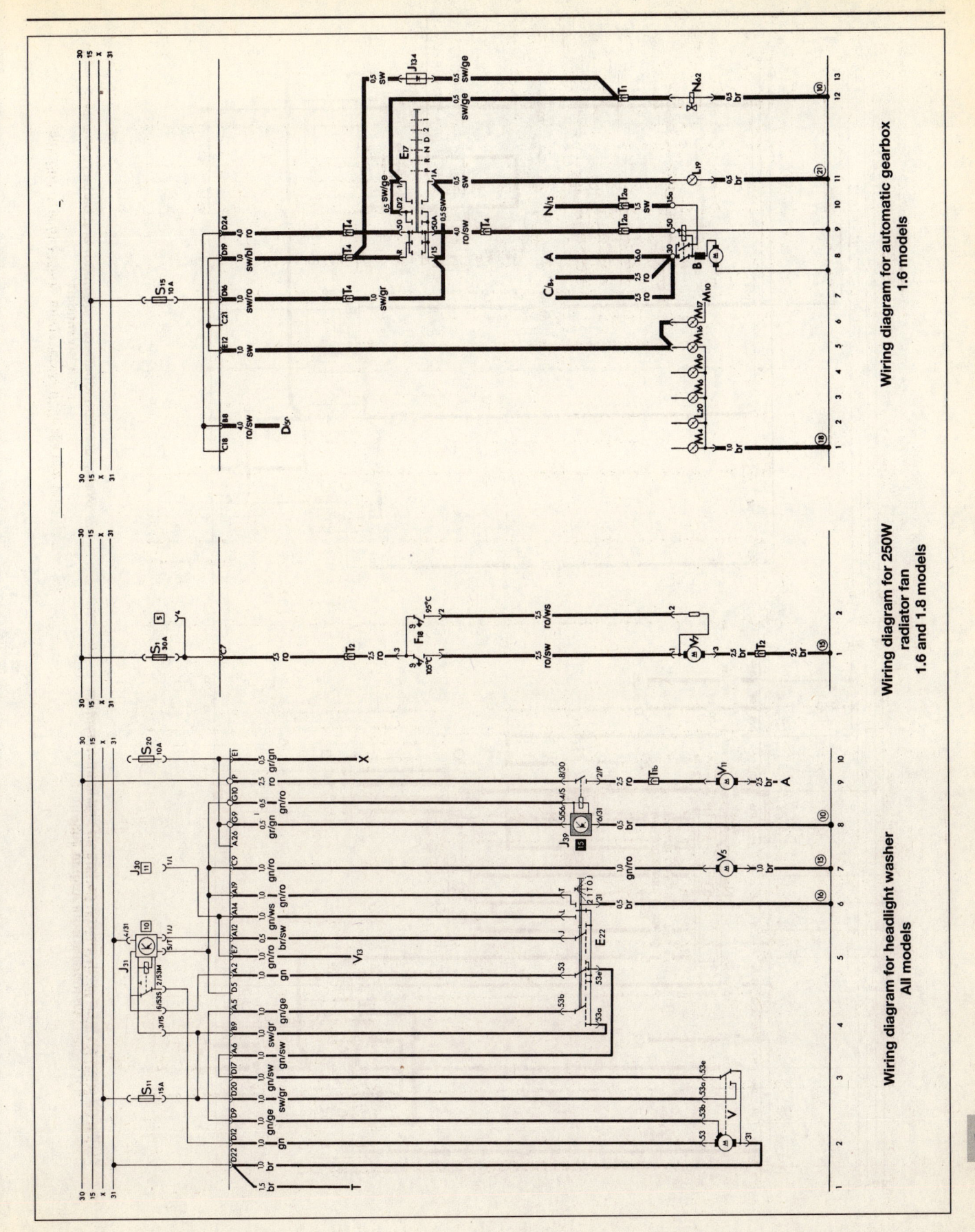

13•16 Wiring diagrams

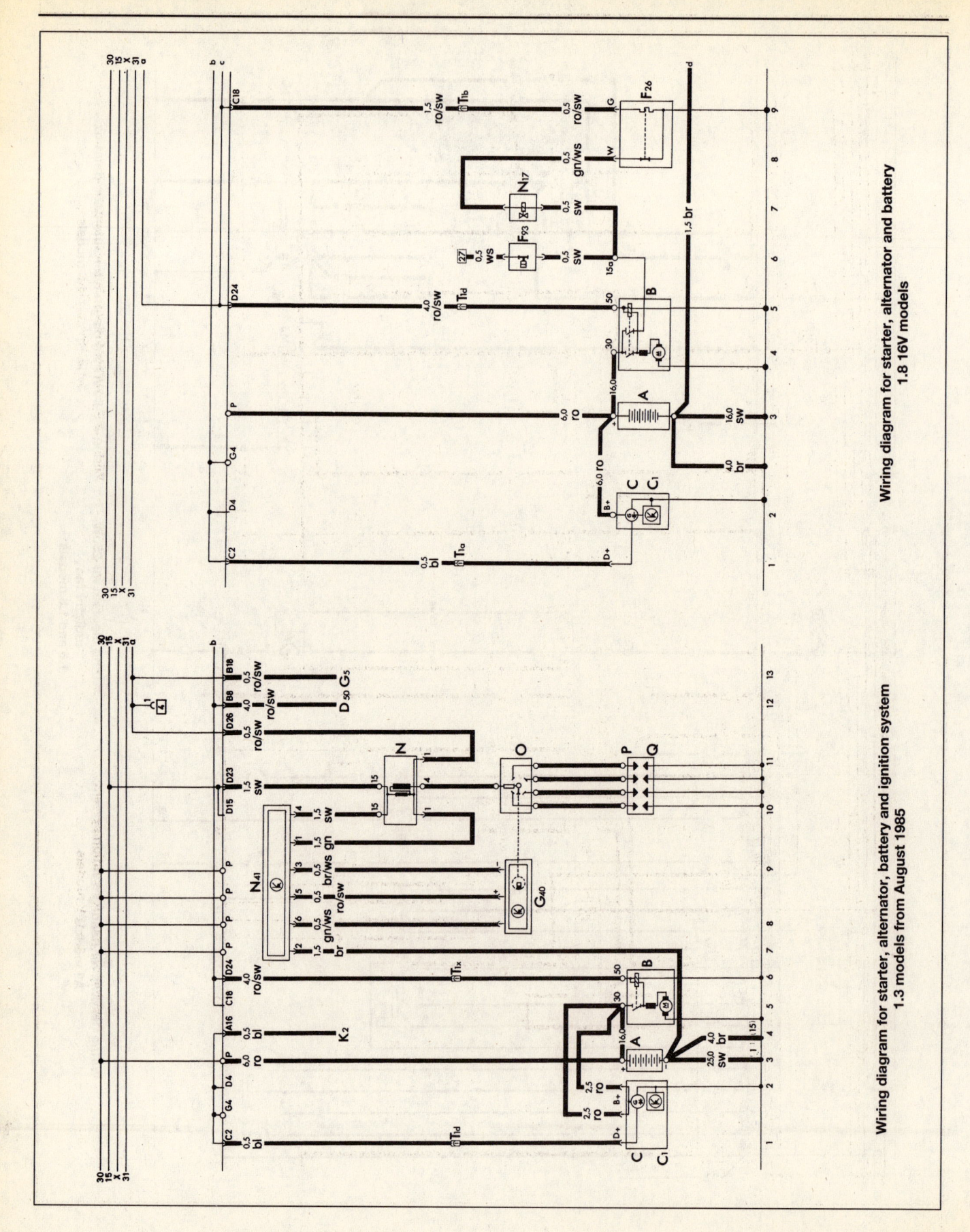

Wiring diagram for starter, alternator and battery
1.8 16V models

Wiring diagram for starter, alternator, battery and ignition system
1.3 models from August 1985

Wiring diagrams

Wiring diagram for low coolant level warning 1.8 16V models

Wiring diagram for ignition system 1.8 16V models

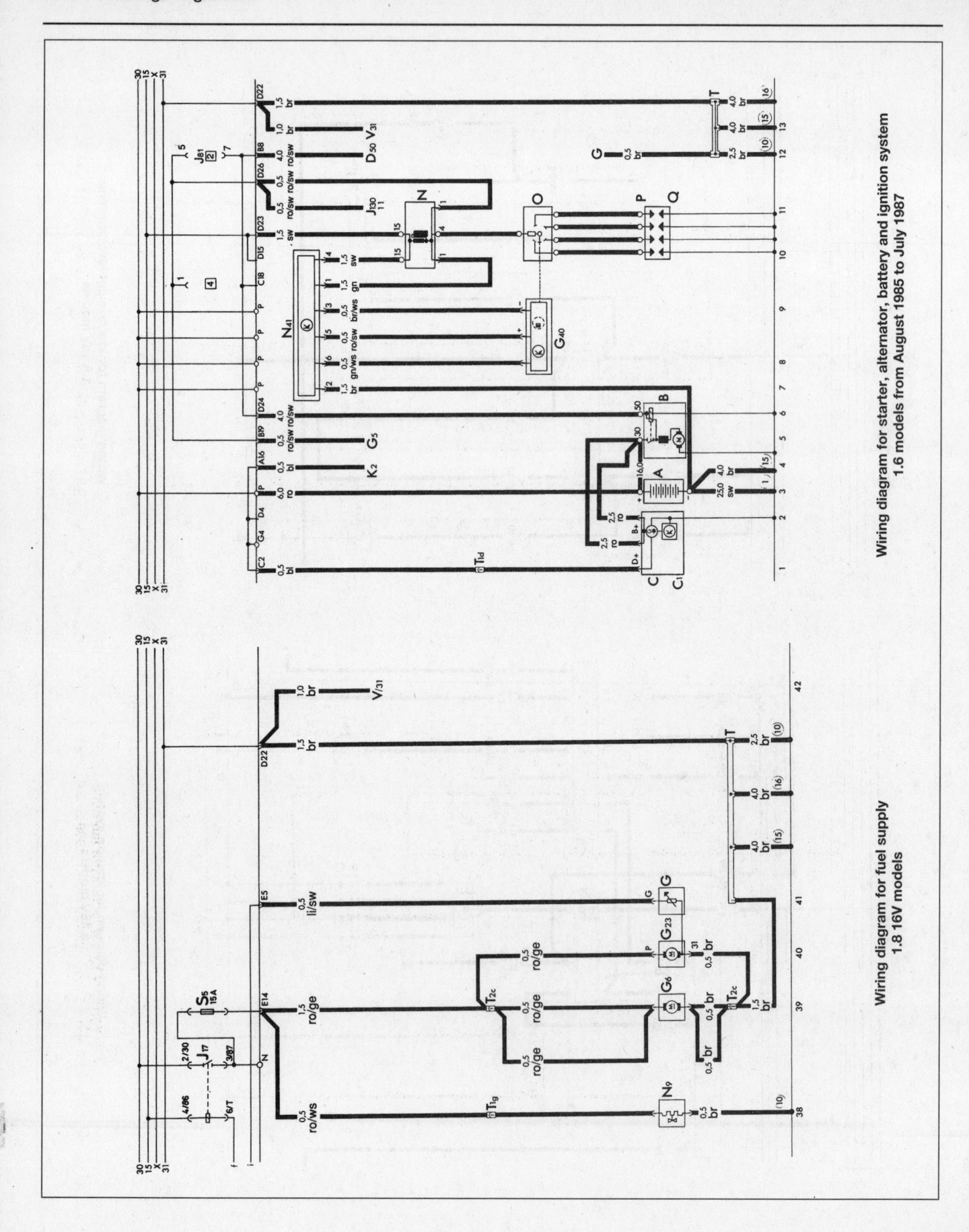

Wiring diagram for starter, alternator, battery and ignition system 1.6 models from August 1985 to July 1987

Wiring diagram for fuel supply 1.8 16V models

Wiring diagrams 13•19

Wiring diagram for windscreen wiper
All Golf models from January 1986 to July 1987

Wiring diagram for radiator fan run-on
1.6 and 1.8 models from March 1986 to July 1987

13•20 Wiring diagrams

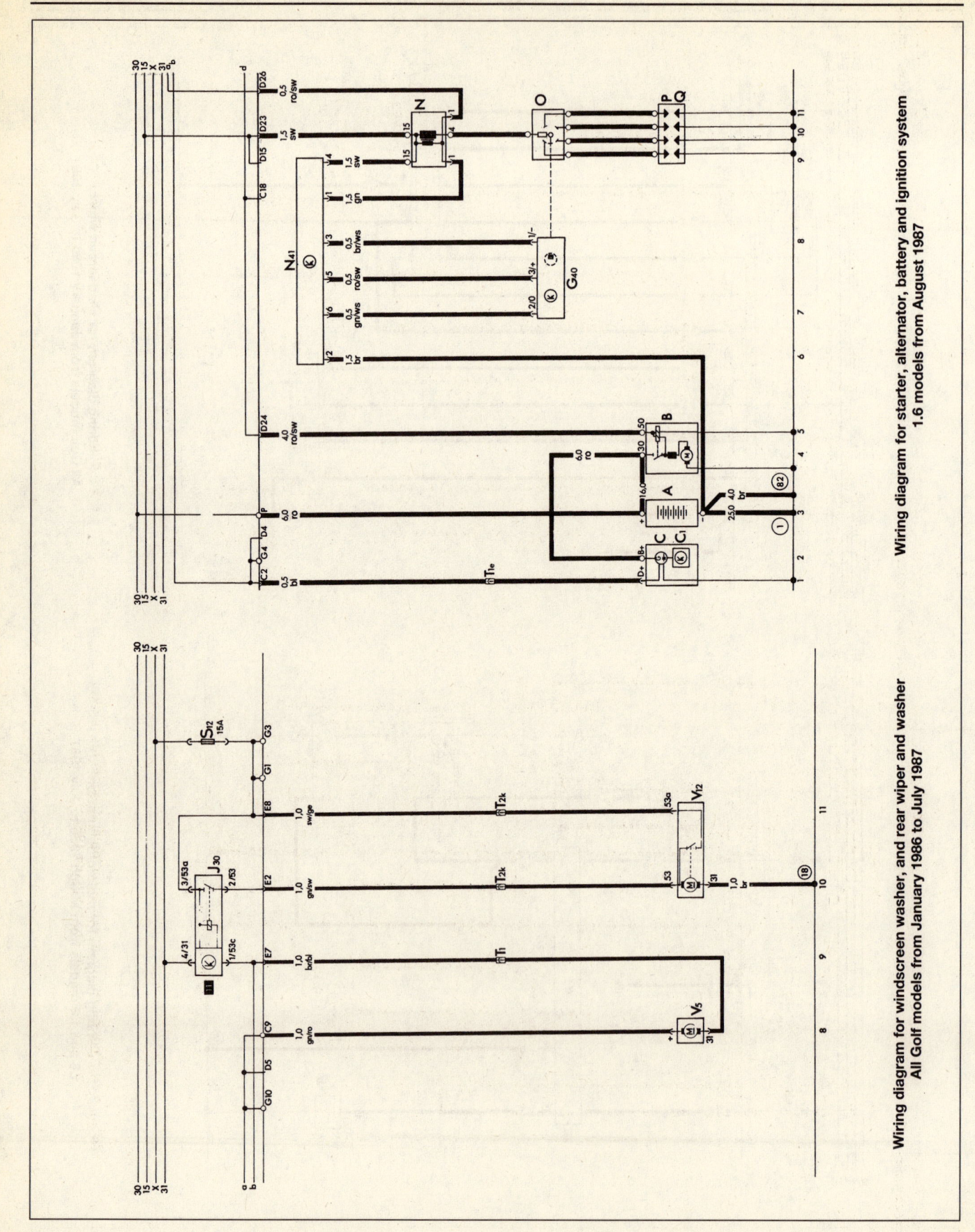

**Wiring diagram for starter, alternator, battery and ignition system
1.6 models from August 1987**

**Wiring diagram for windscreen washer, and rear wiper and washer
All Golf models from January 1986 to July 1987**

Wiring diagrams 13•21

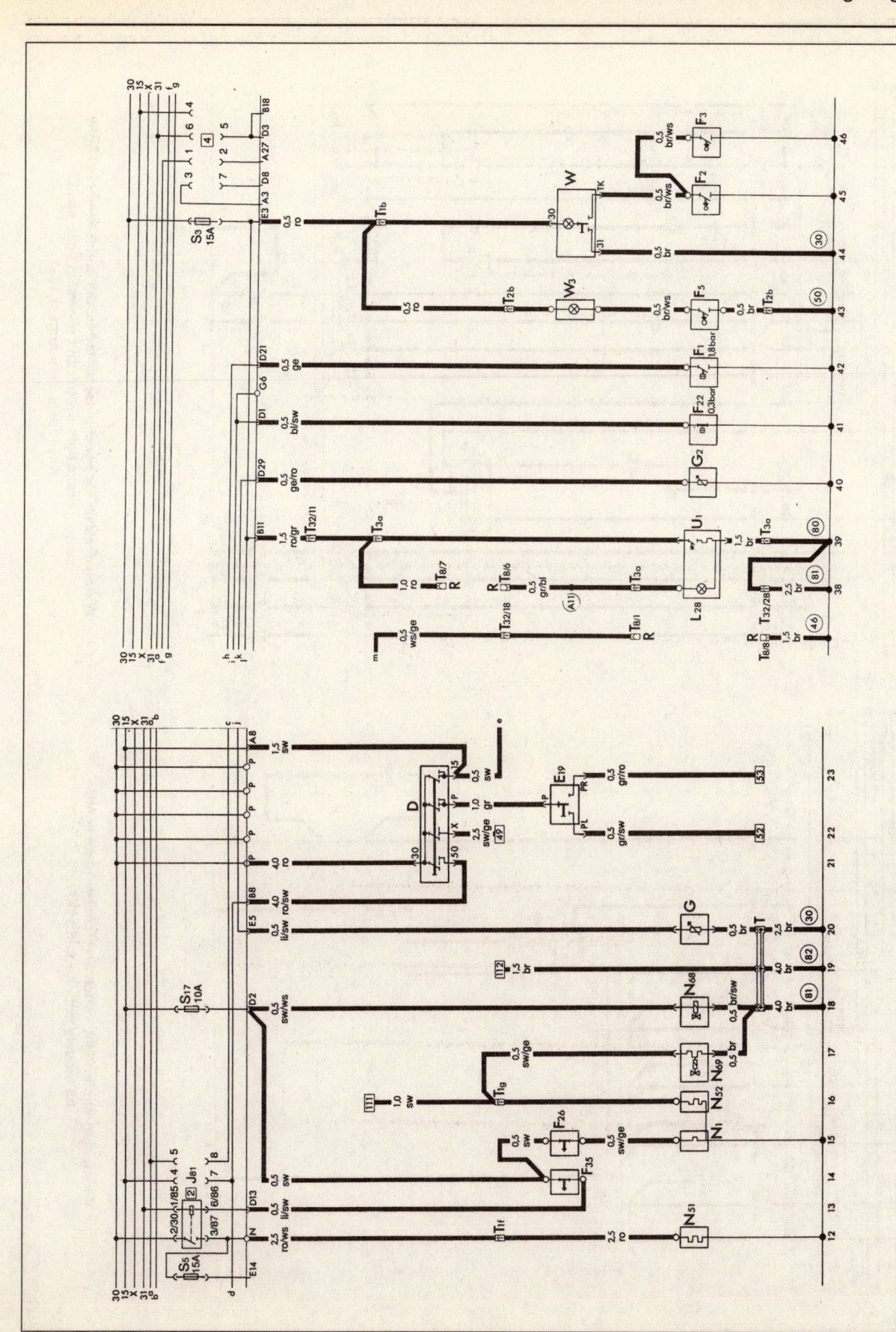

Wiring diagram for interior lights, boot light and radio
All models from August 1987

Wiring diagram for inlet manifold preheating and automatic choke
1.6 models from August 1987

13•22 Wiring diagrams

Wiring diagram for headlights, tail lights, dip and flasher headlight switch, brake light switch and reversing light switch — All models from August 1987

Wiring diagram for light switch and number plate lights — All models from August 1987

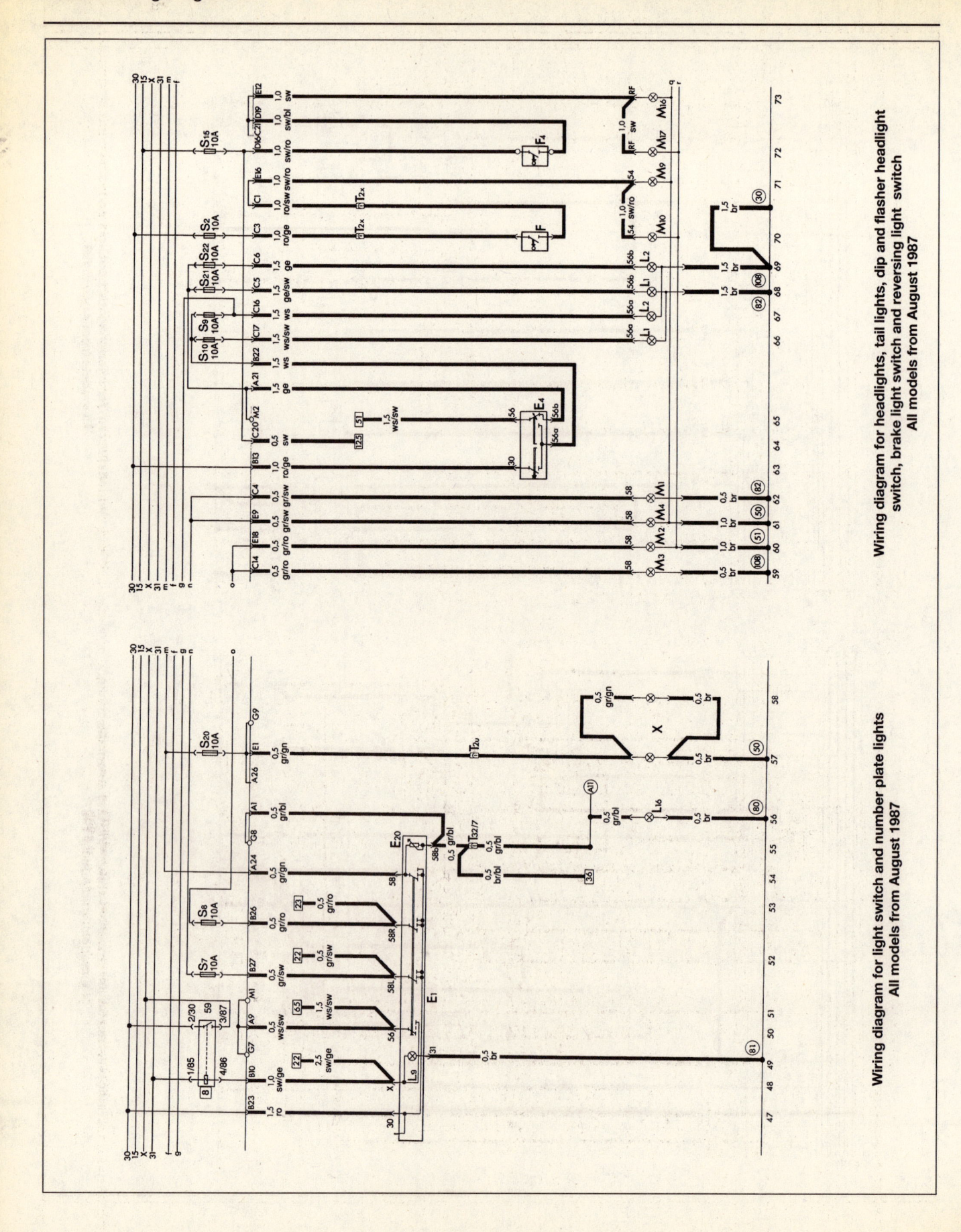

Wiring diagrams 13•23

Wiring diagram for foglights, rear foglights and heated rear window
All models from August 1987

Wiring diagram for indicators and hazard warning lights
All models from August 1987

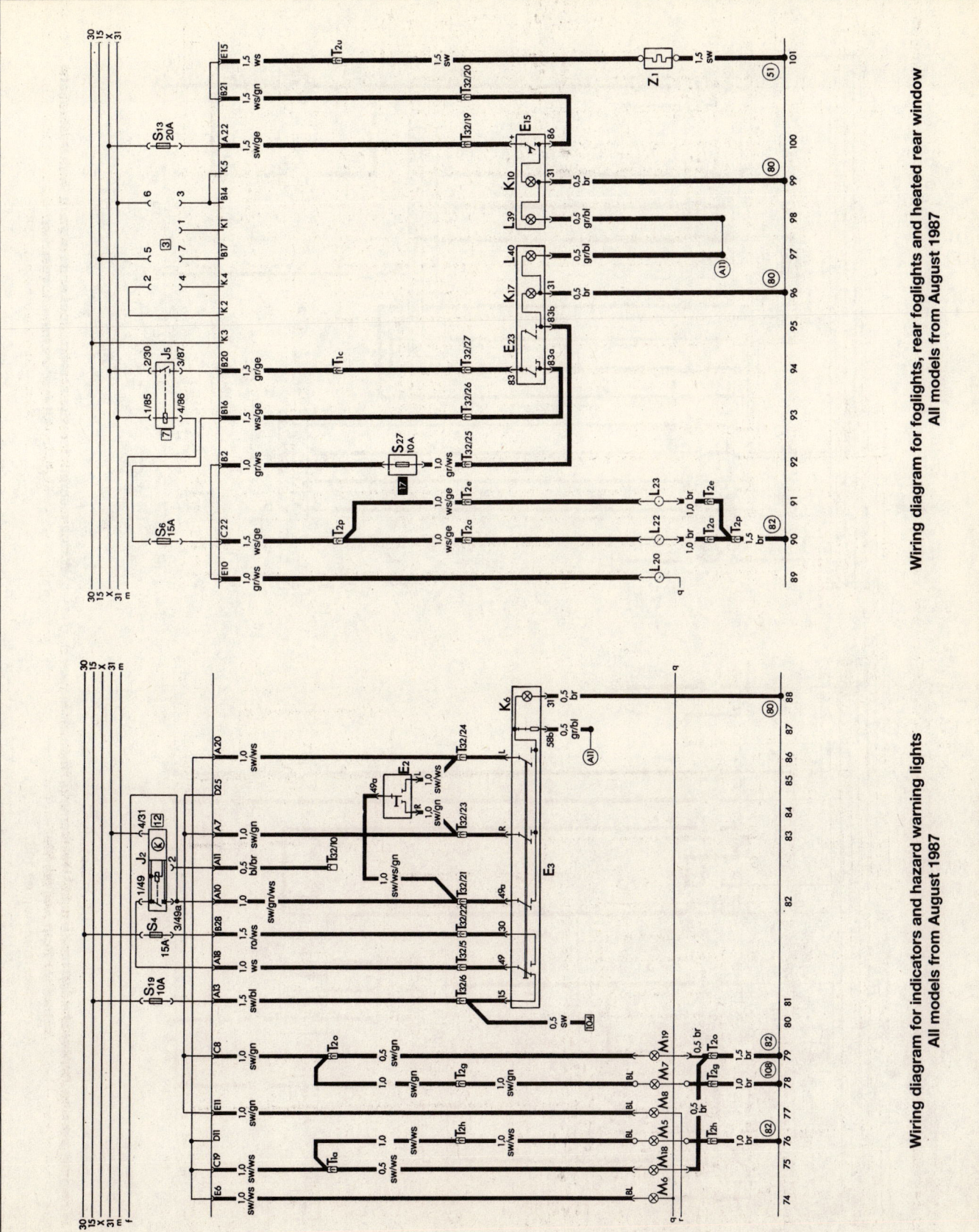

13•24 Wiring diagrams

Wiring diagram for windscreen wiper and washers (with heated jets)
All models from August 1987

Wiring diagram for handbrake and brake fluid level warning, fresh air blower, glovebox light and horn
All models from August 1987

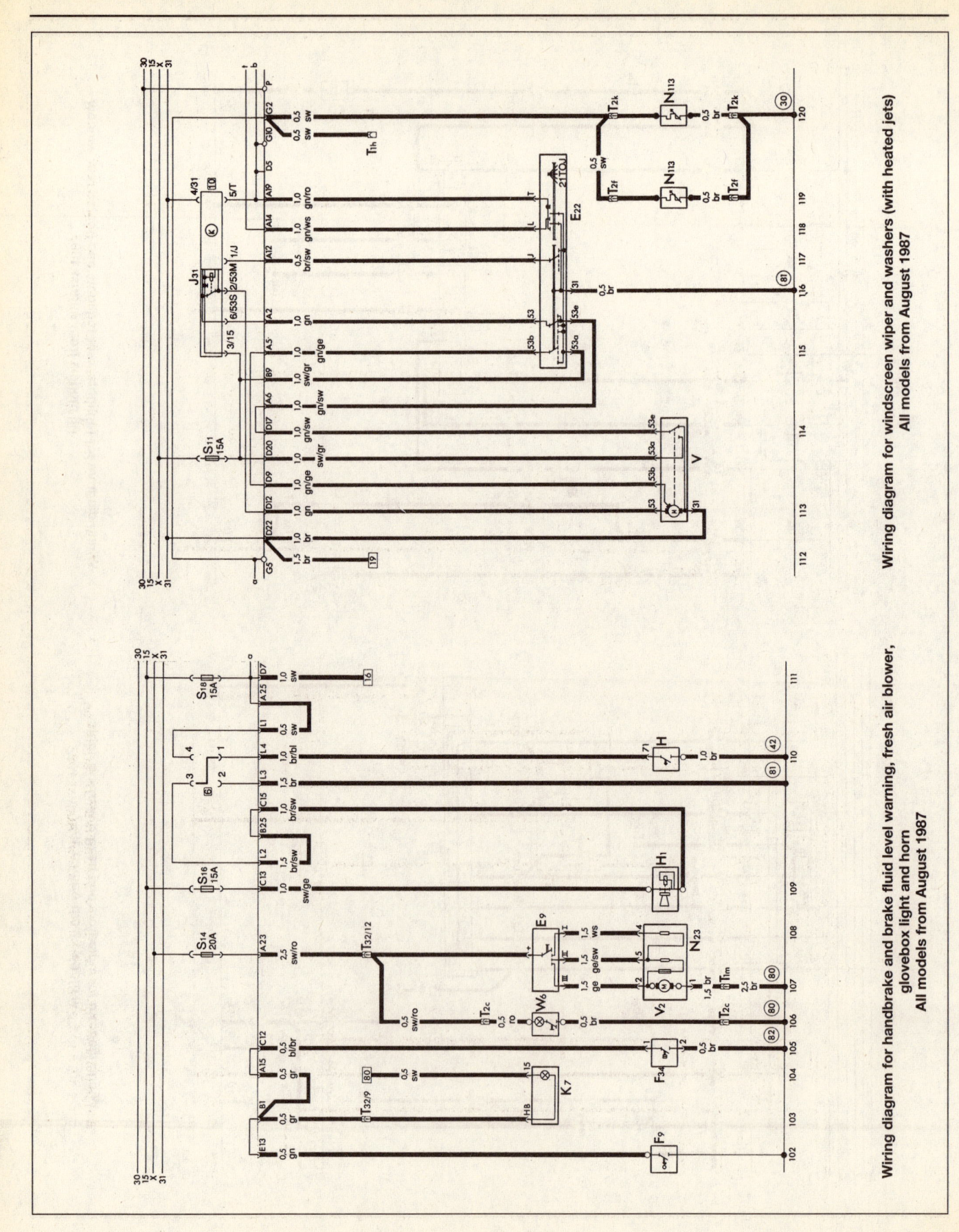

Wiring diagrams

Wiring diagram for electric windows
1.6 models from August 1987

Wiring diagram for rear window wiper and radiator fan run-on
1.6 and 1.8 carburettor models from August 1987

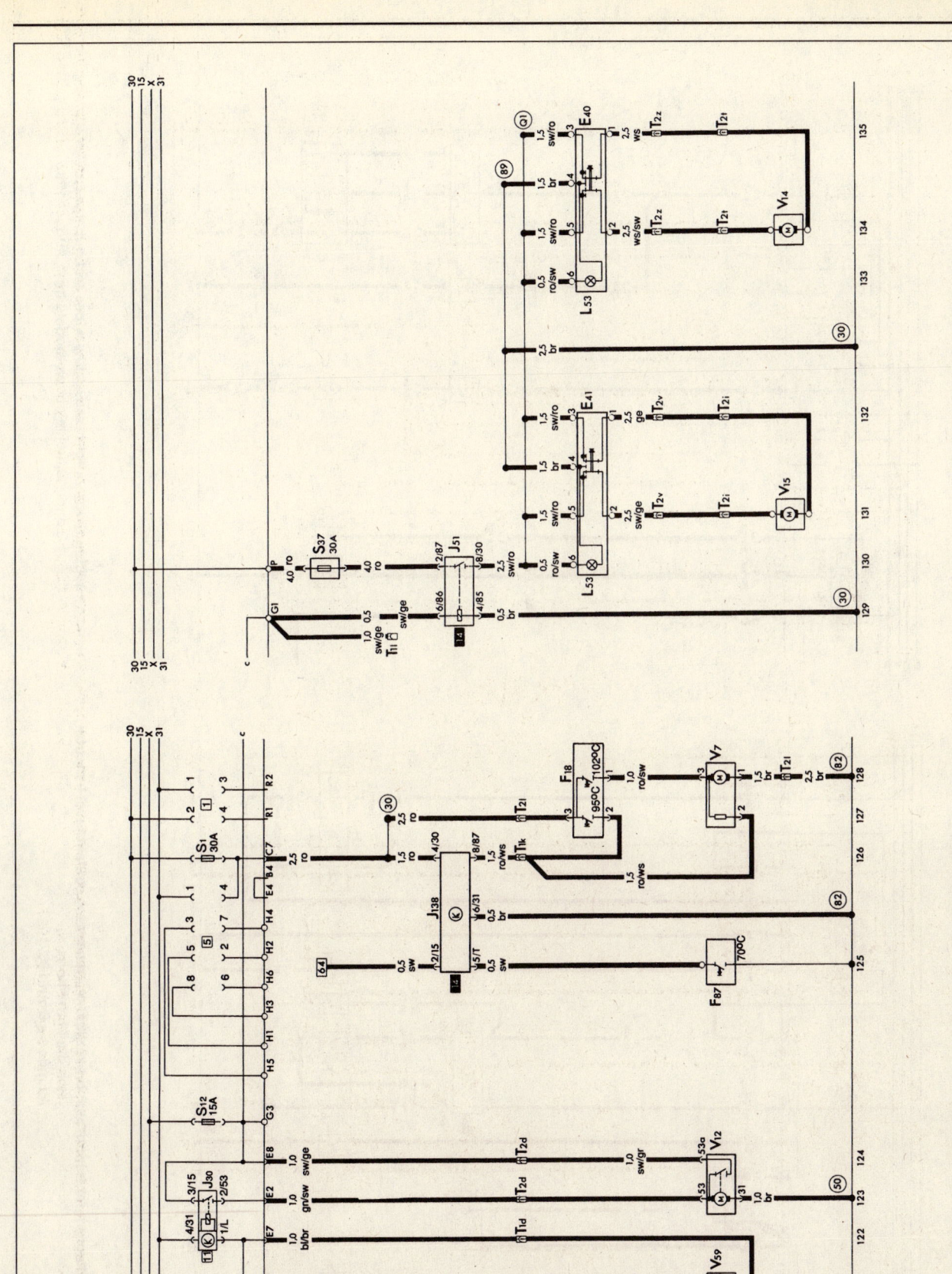

13•26 Wiring diagrams

Wiring diagram for rear window wiper and radiator fan 1.05, 1.3 and 1.8 fuel injection models from August 1987

Wiring diagram for handbrake, brake fluid warning, low coolant level indicator, and dual tone horn All models from 1987

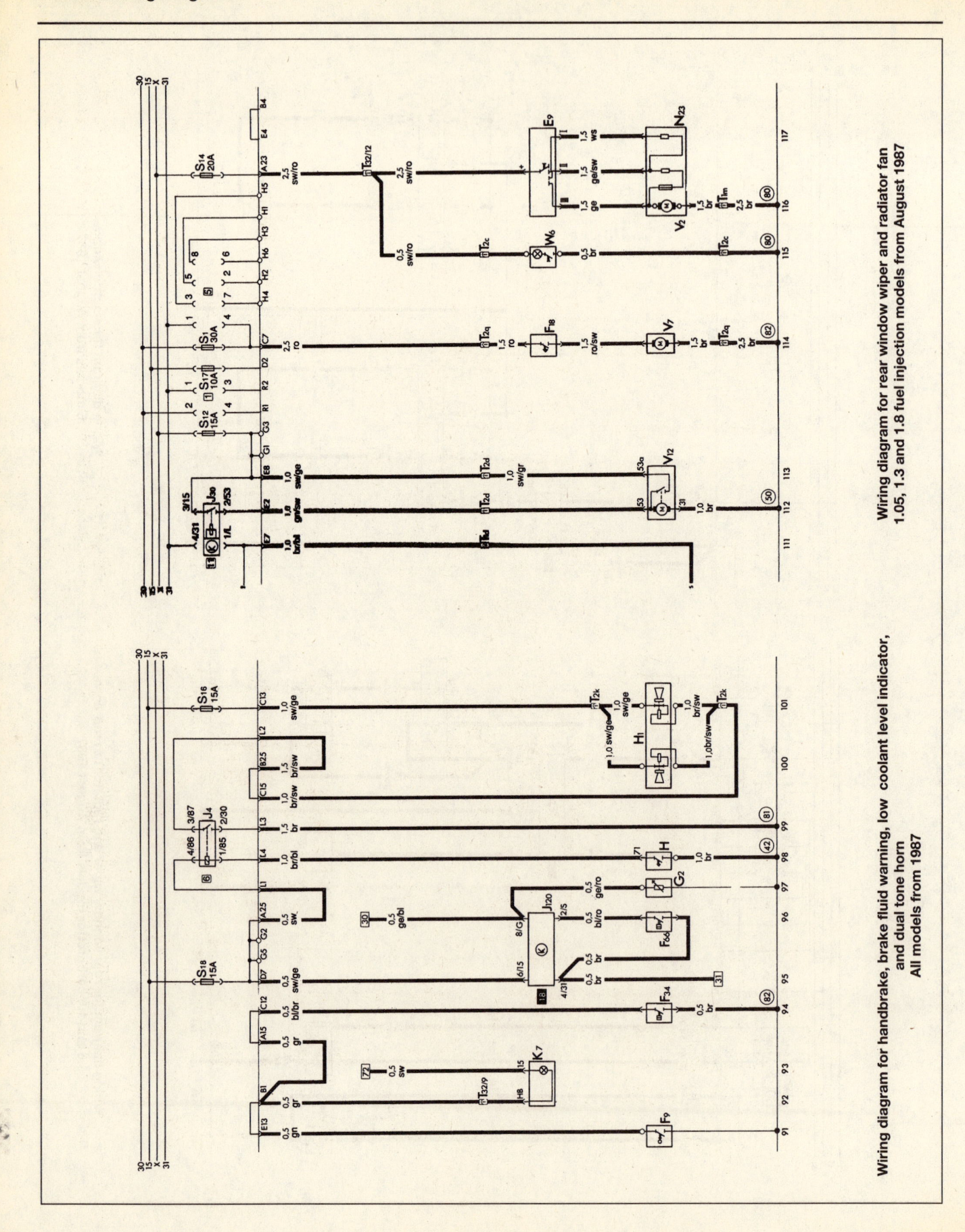

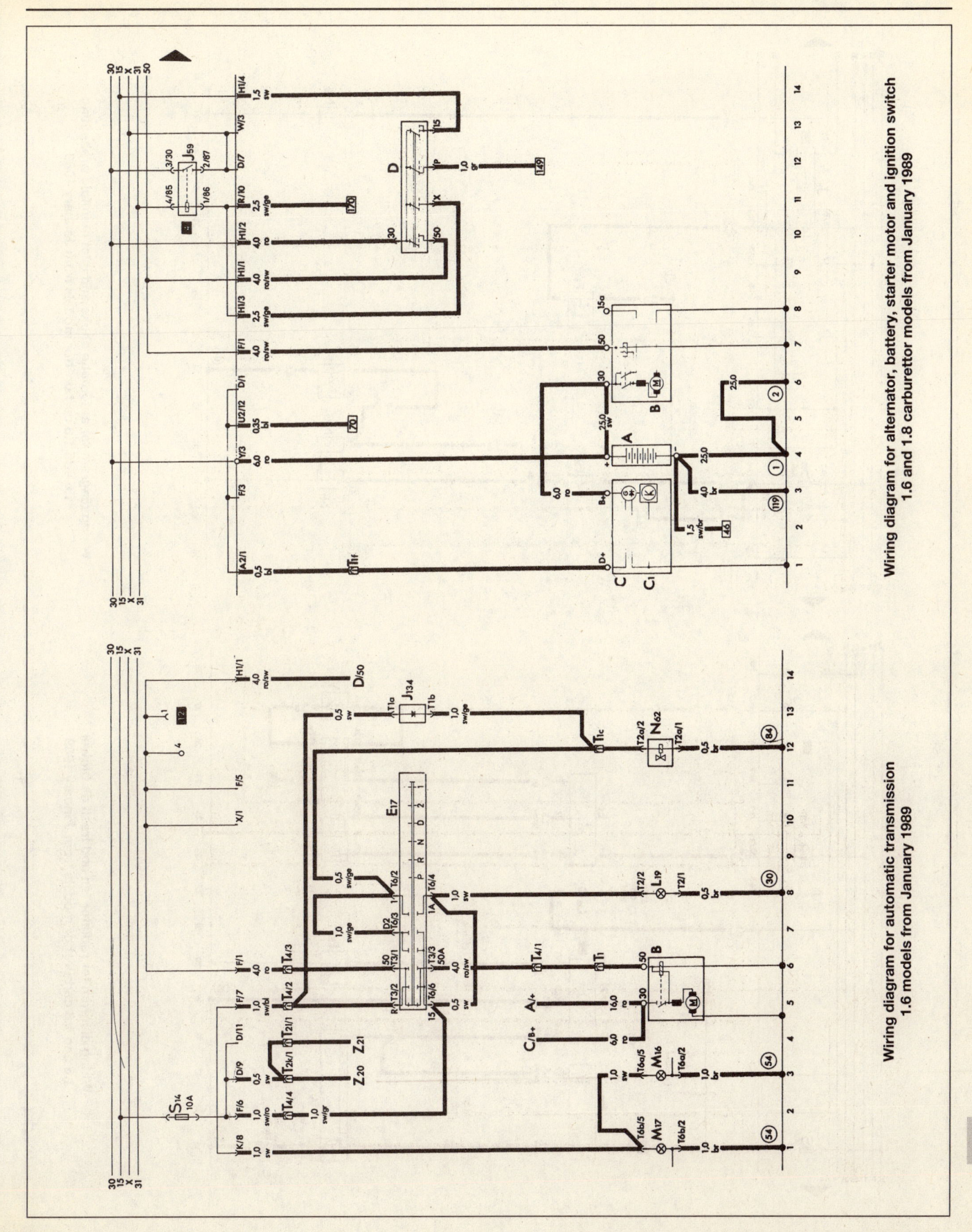

Wiring diagrams 13•27

Wiring diagram for alternator, battery, starter motor and ignition switch 1.6 and 1.8 carburettor models from January 1989

Wiring diagram for automatic transmission 1.6 models from January 1989

13•28 Wiring diagrams

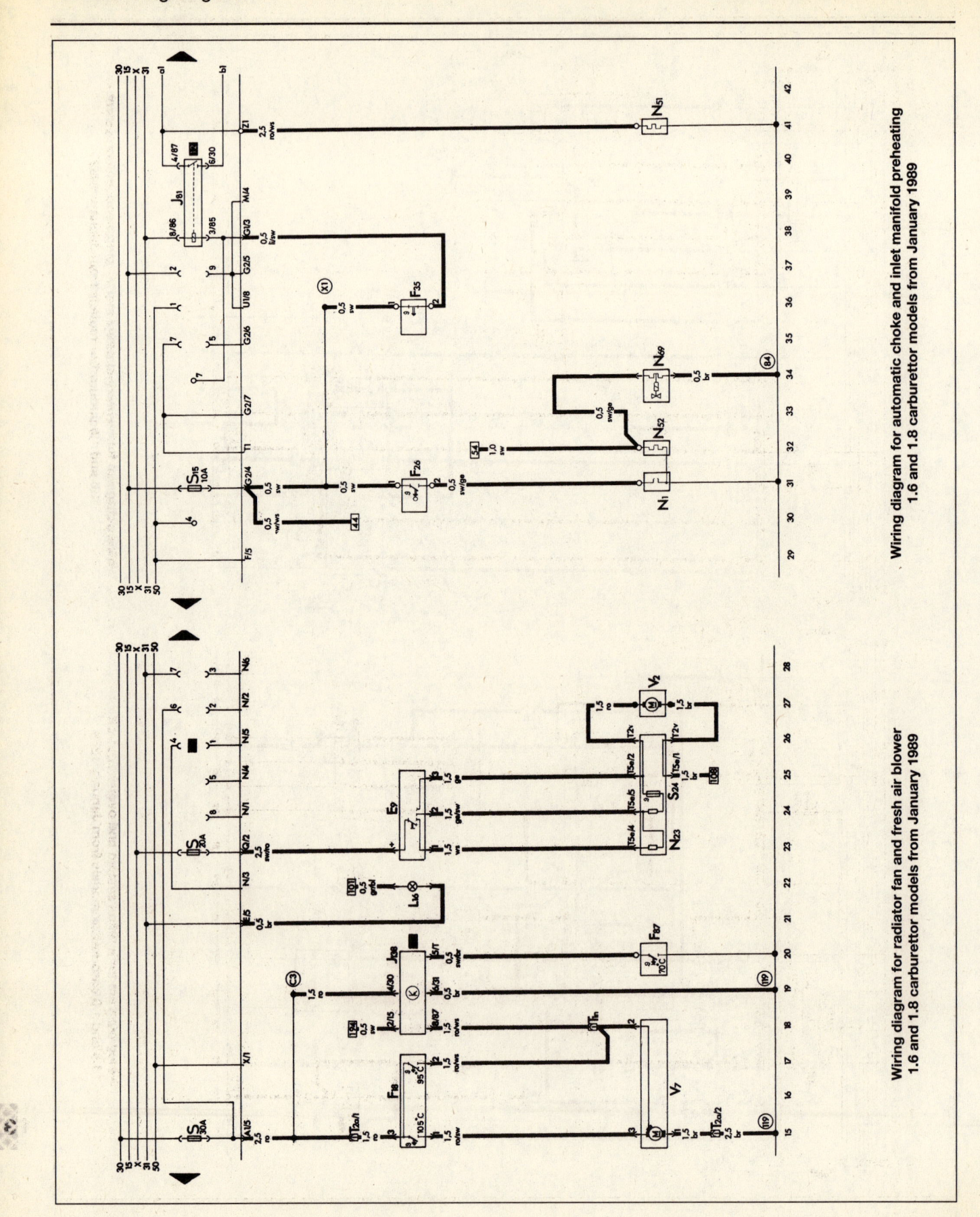

Wiring diagram for automatic choke and inlet manifold preheating 1.6 and 1.8 carburettor models from January 1989

Wiring diagram for radiator fan and fresh air blower 1.6 and 1.8 carburettor models from January 1989

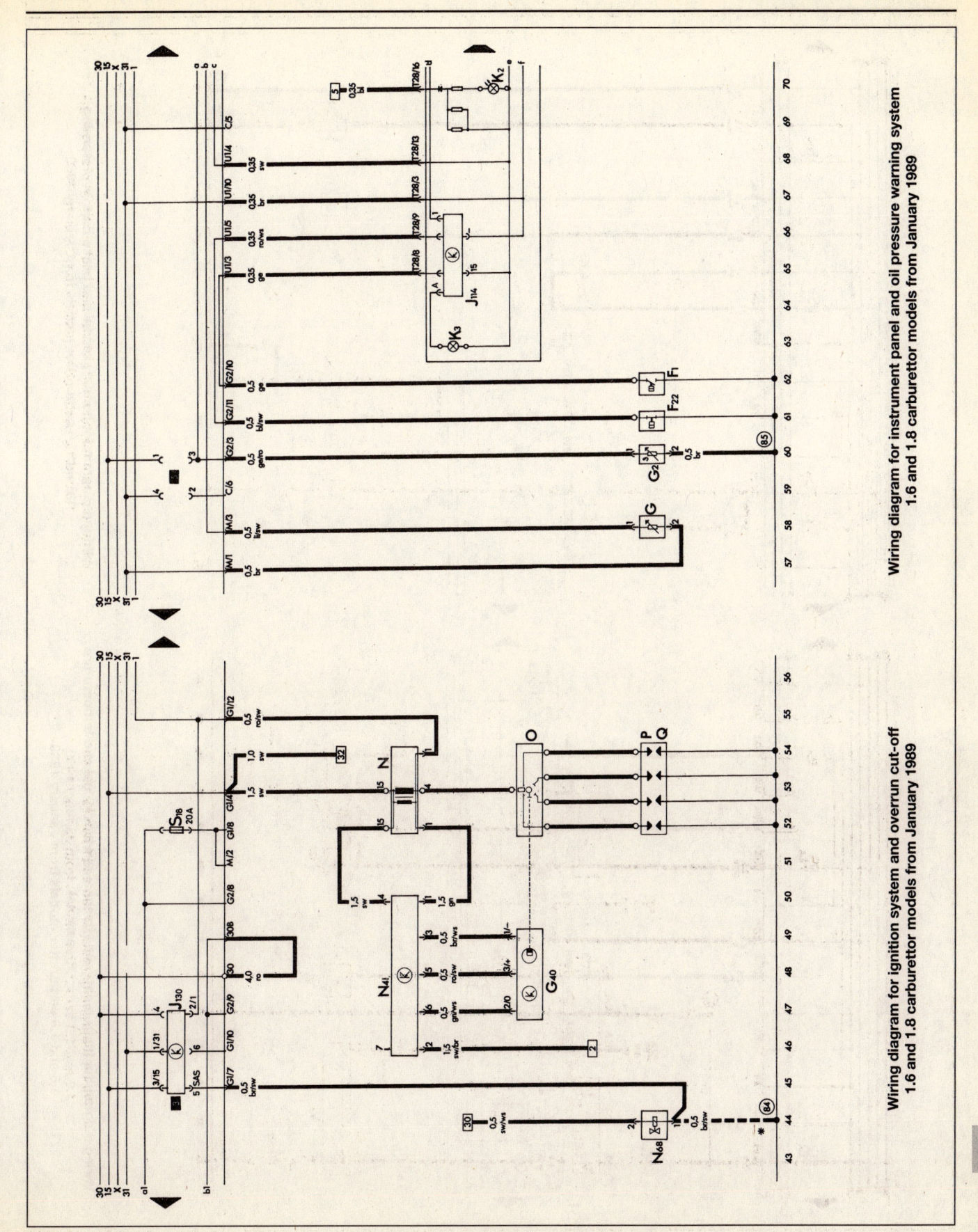

Wiring diagrams 13•29

Wiring diagram for instrument panel and oil pressure warning system 1.6 and 1.8 carburettor models from January 1989

Wiring diagram for ignition system and overrun cut-off 1.6 and 1.8 carburettor models from January 1989

13•30 Wiring diagrams

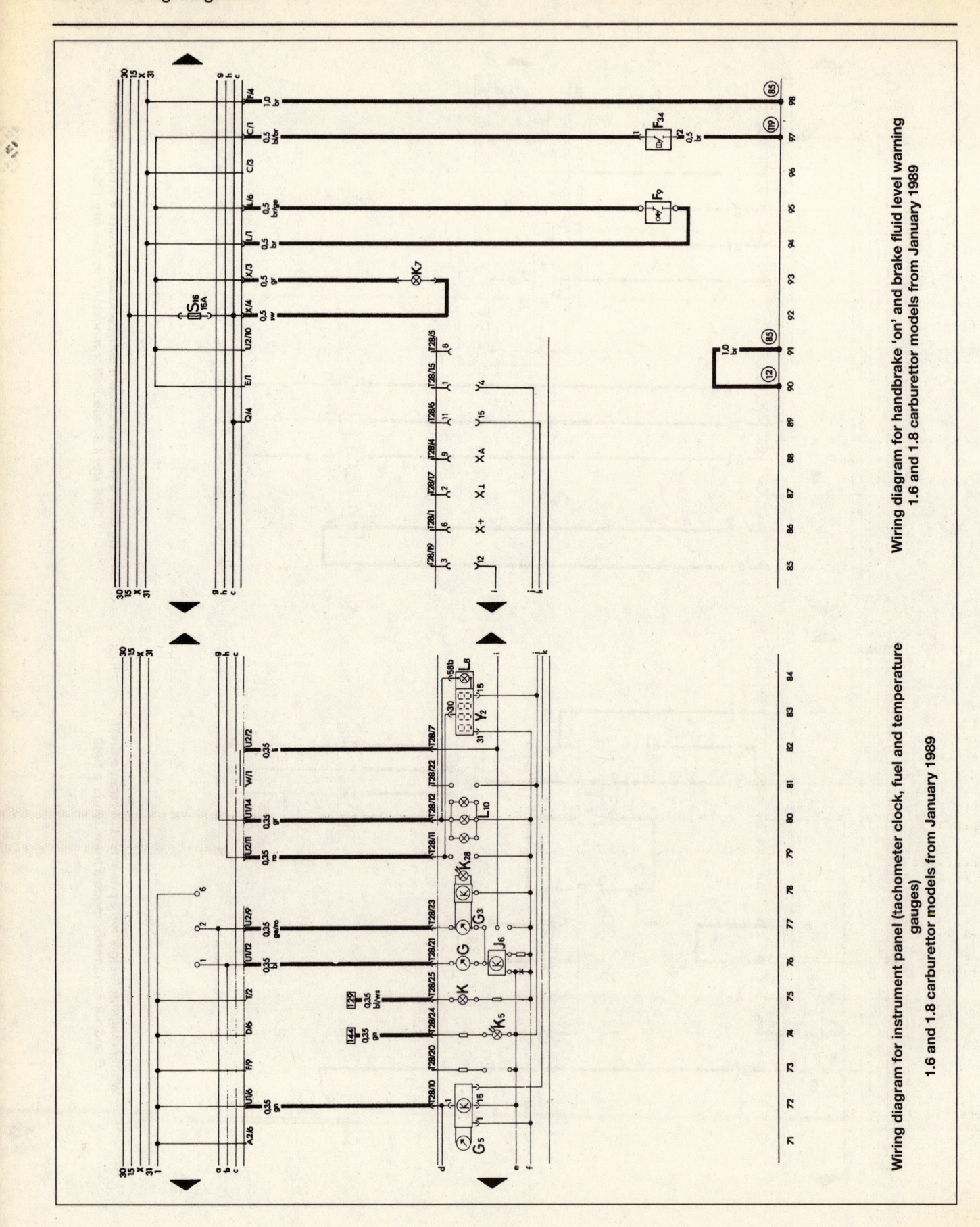

Wiring diagram for instrument panel (tachometer clock, fuel and temperature gauges) 1.6 and 1.8 carburettor models from January 1989

Wiring diagram for handbrake 'on' and brake fluid level warning 1.6 and 1.8 carburettor models from January 1989

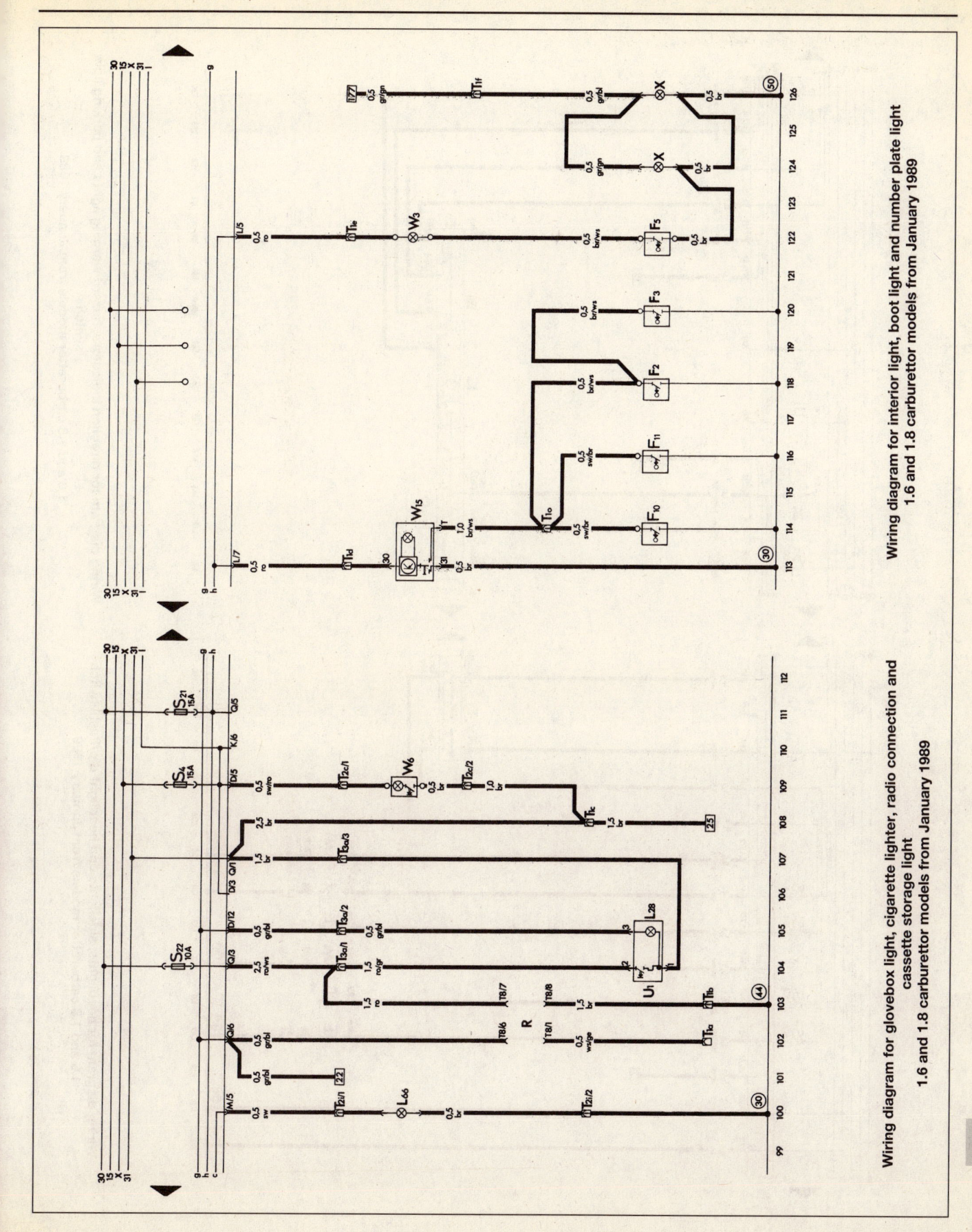

Wiring diagrams 13•31

Wiring diagram for interior light, boot light and number plate light 1.6 and 1.8 carburettor models from January 1989

Wiring diagram for glovebox light, cigarette lighter, radio connection and cassette storage light 1.6 and 1.8 carburettor models from January 1989

13•32 Wiring diagrams

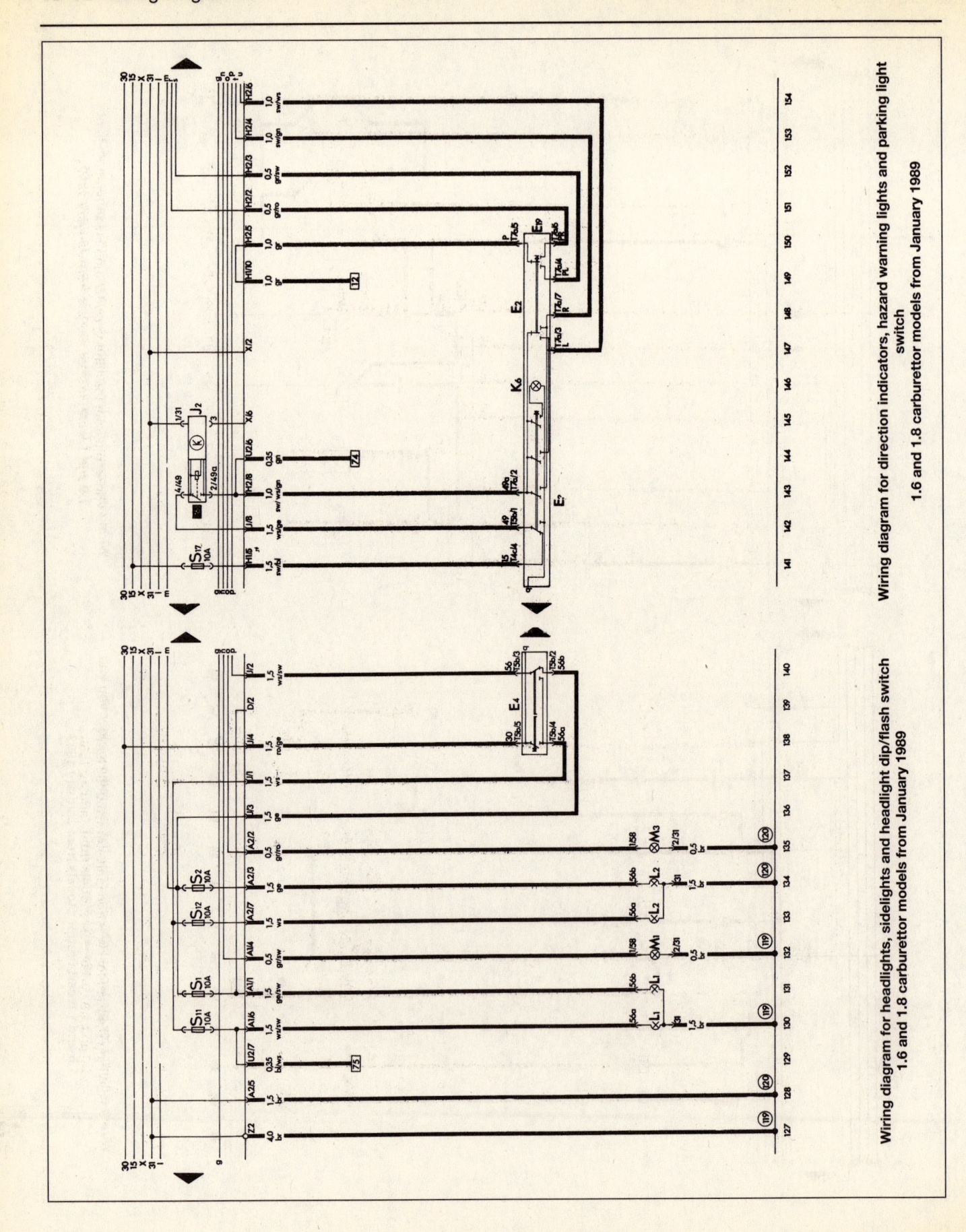

Wiring diagram for direction indicators, hazard warning lights and parking light switch
1.6 and 1.8 carburettor models from January 1989

Wiring diagram for headlights, sidelights and headlight dip/flash switch
1.6 and 1.8 carburettor models from January 1989

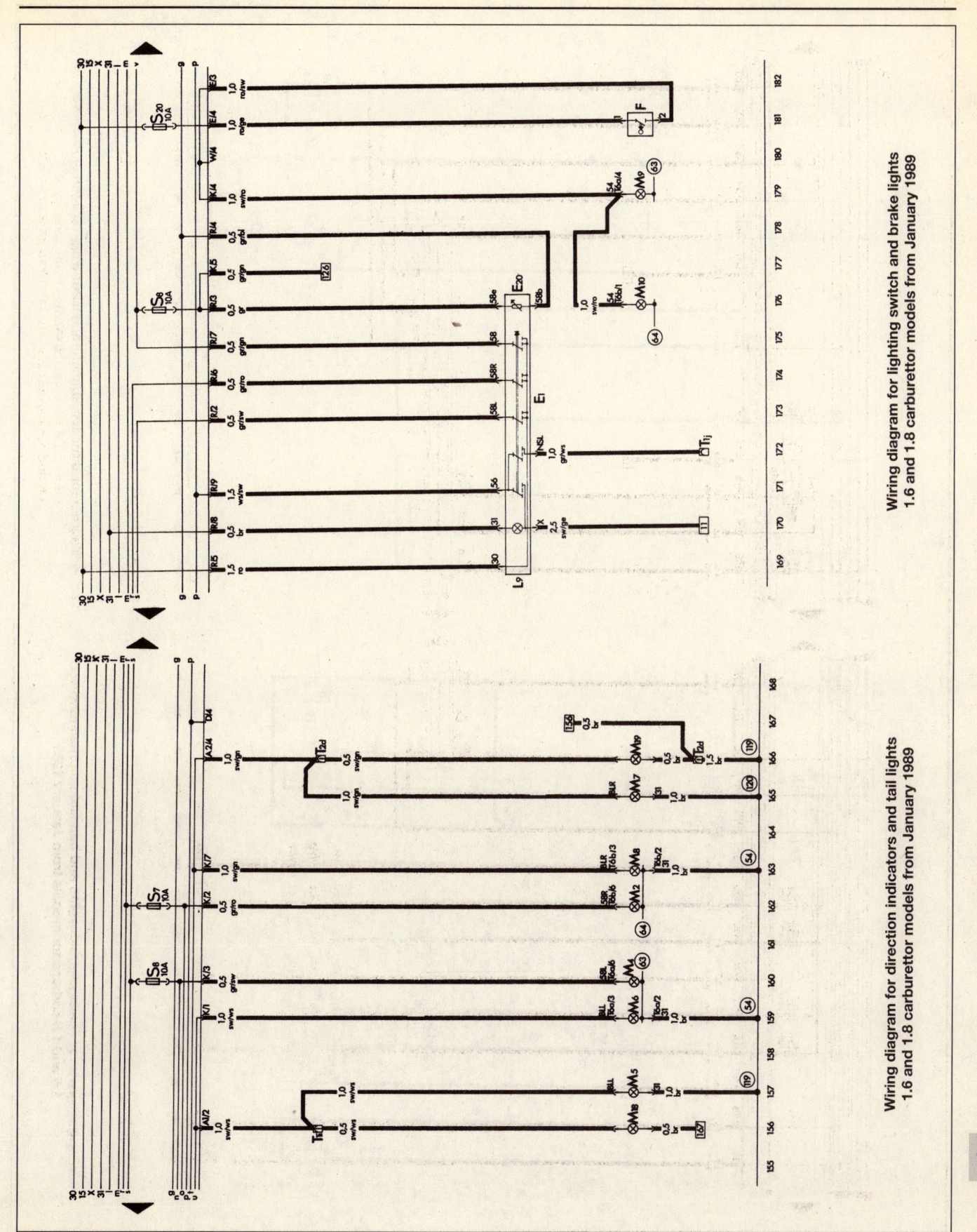

Wiring diagram for lighting switch and brake lights 1.6 and 1.8 carburettor models from January 1989

Wiring diagram for direction indicators and tail lights 1.6 and 1.8 carburettor models from January 1989

13•34 Wiring diagrams

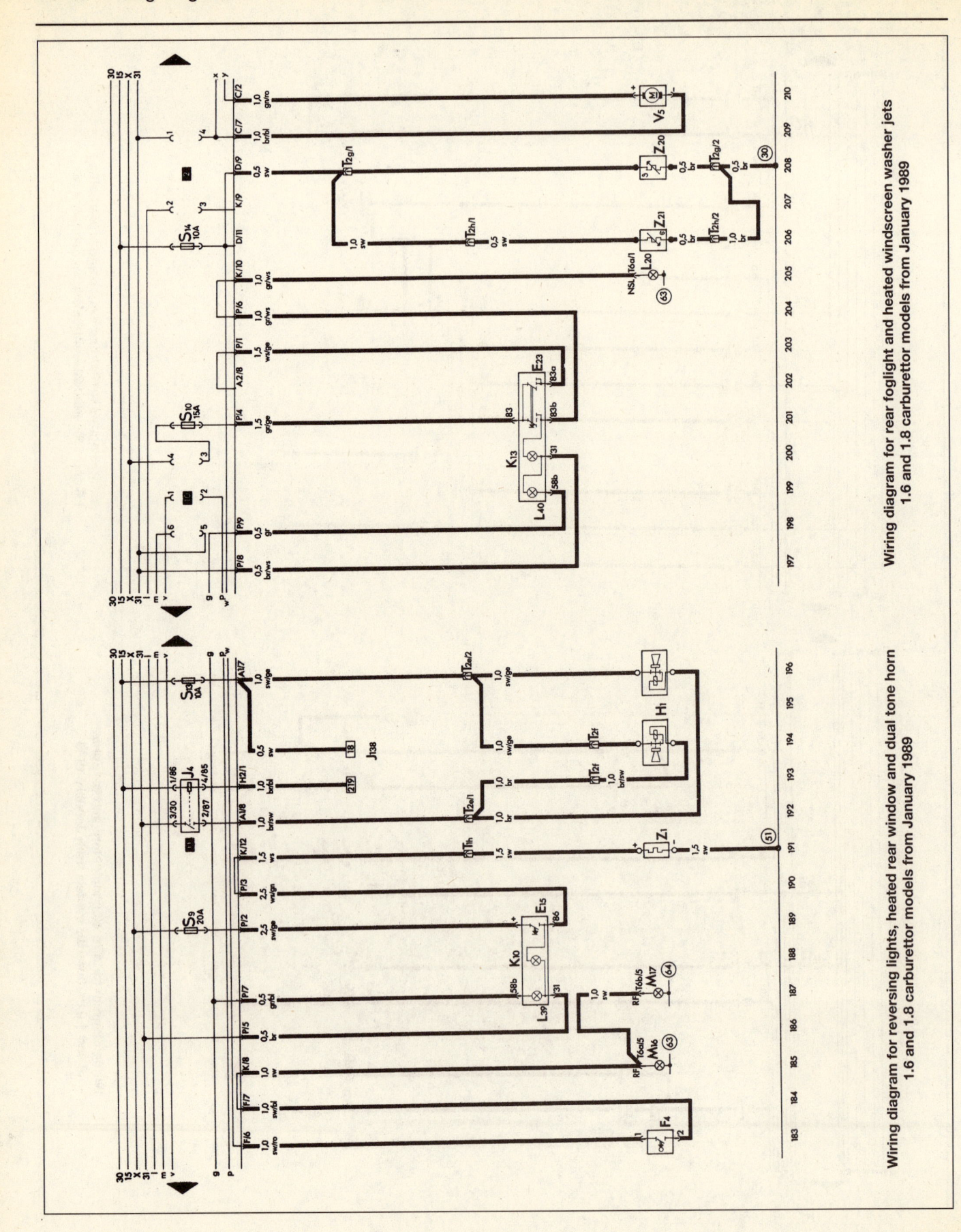

Wiring diagram for rear foglight and heated windscreen washer jets 1.6 and 1.8 carburettor models from January 1989

Wiring diagram for reversing lights, heated rear window and dual tone horn 1.6 and 1.8 carburettor models from January 1989

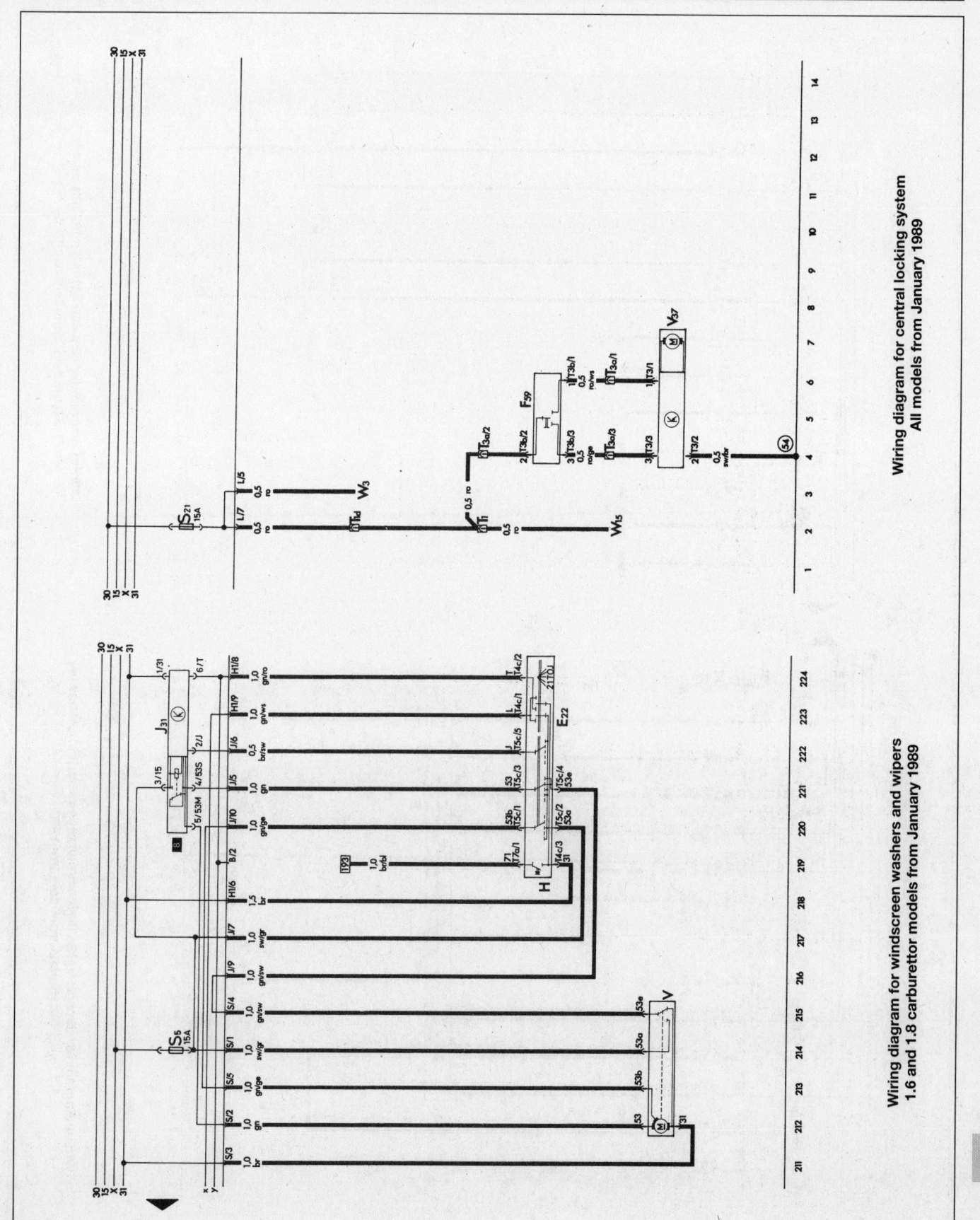

Wiring diagrams 13•35

Wiring diagram for central locking system
All models from January 1989

Wiring diagram for windscreen washers and wipers
1.6 and 1.8 carburettor models from January 1989

13•36 Wiring diagrams

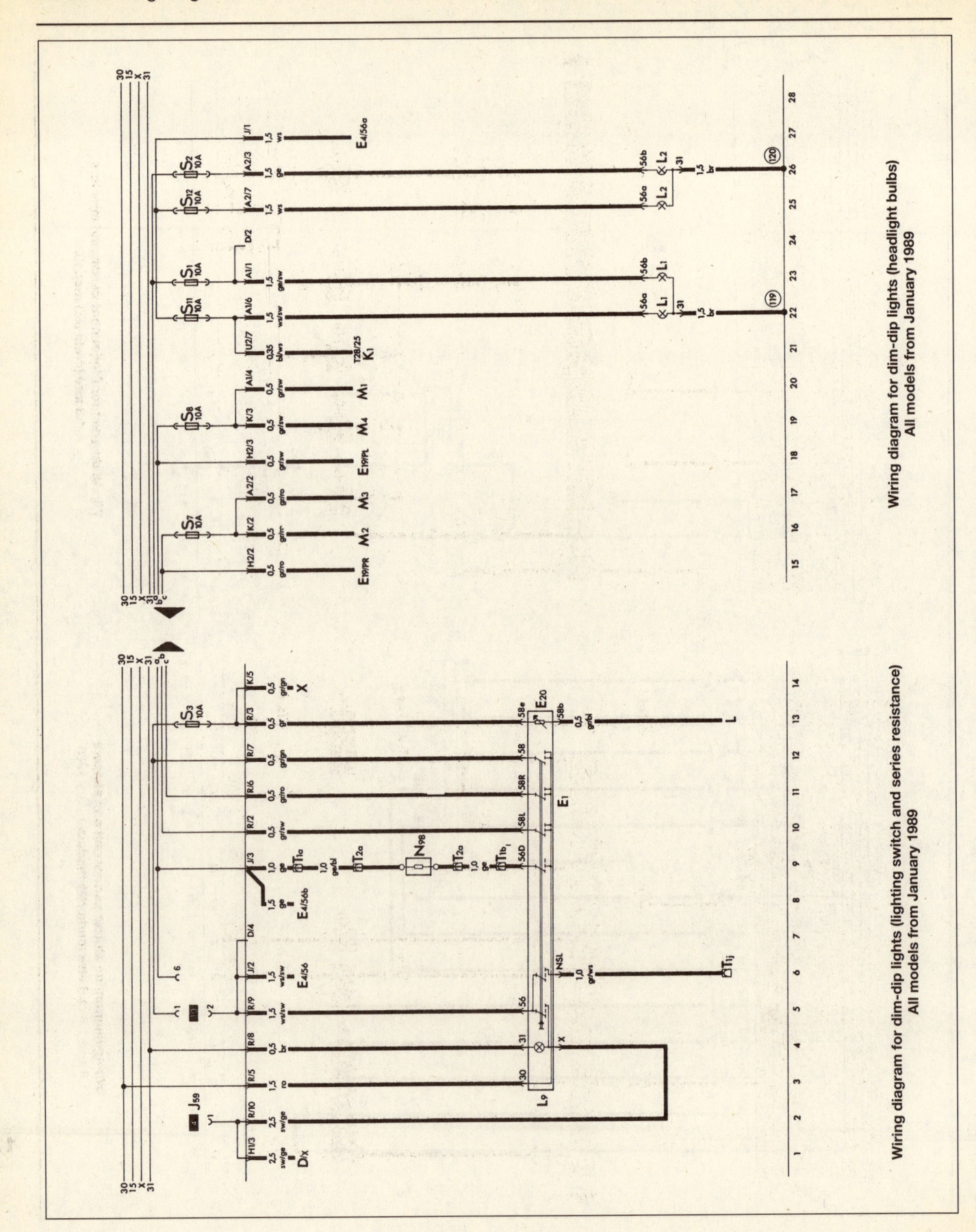

Wiring diagram for dim-dip lights (headlight bulbs)
All models from January 1989

Wiring diagram for dim-dip lights (lighting switch and series resistance)
All models from January 1989

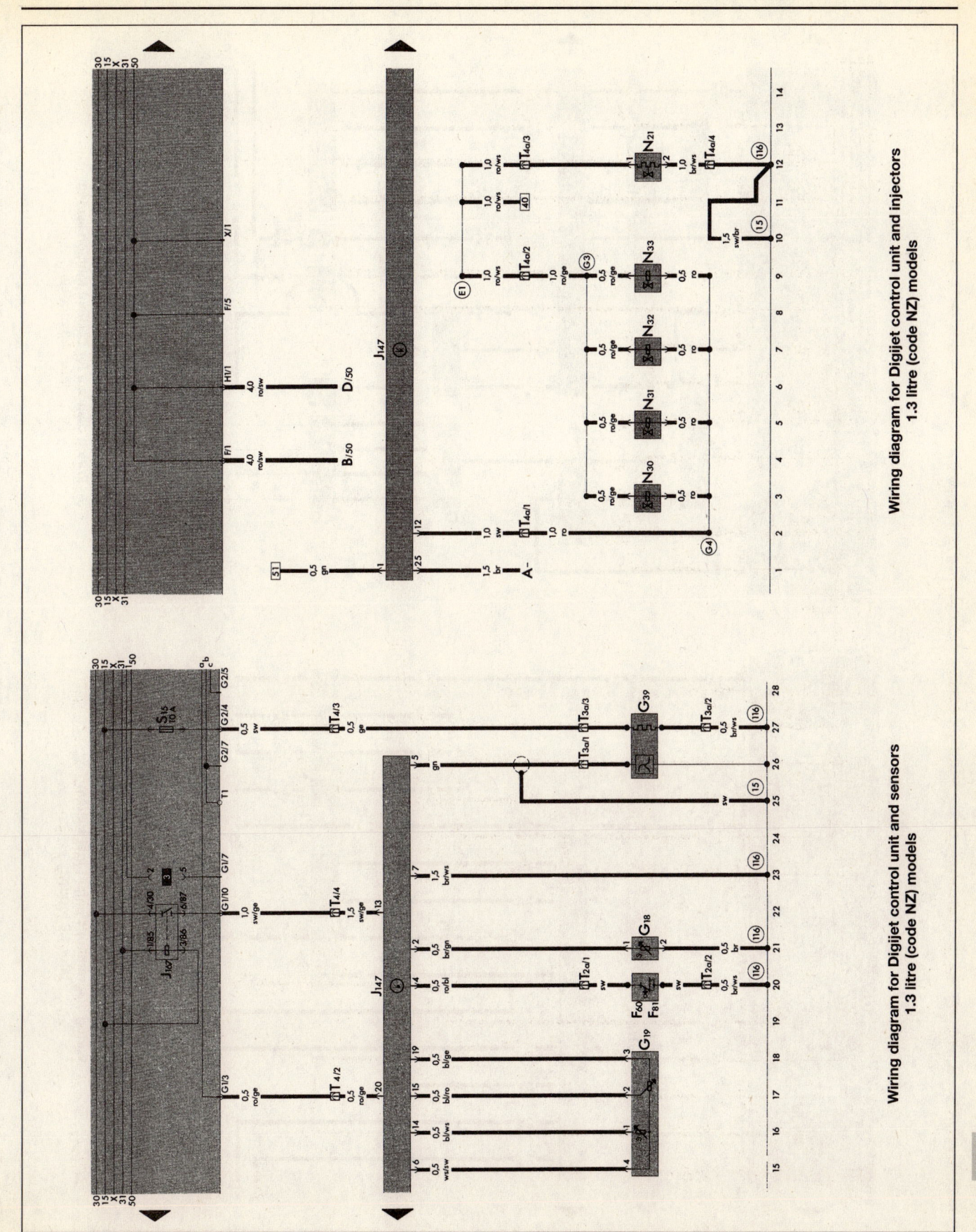

Wiring diagrams 13•37

Wiring diagram for Digijet control unit and injectors
1.3 litre (code NZ) models

Wiring diagram for Digijet control unit and sensors
1.3 litre (code NZ) models

13•38 Wiring diagrams

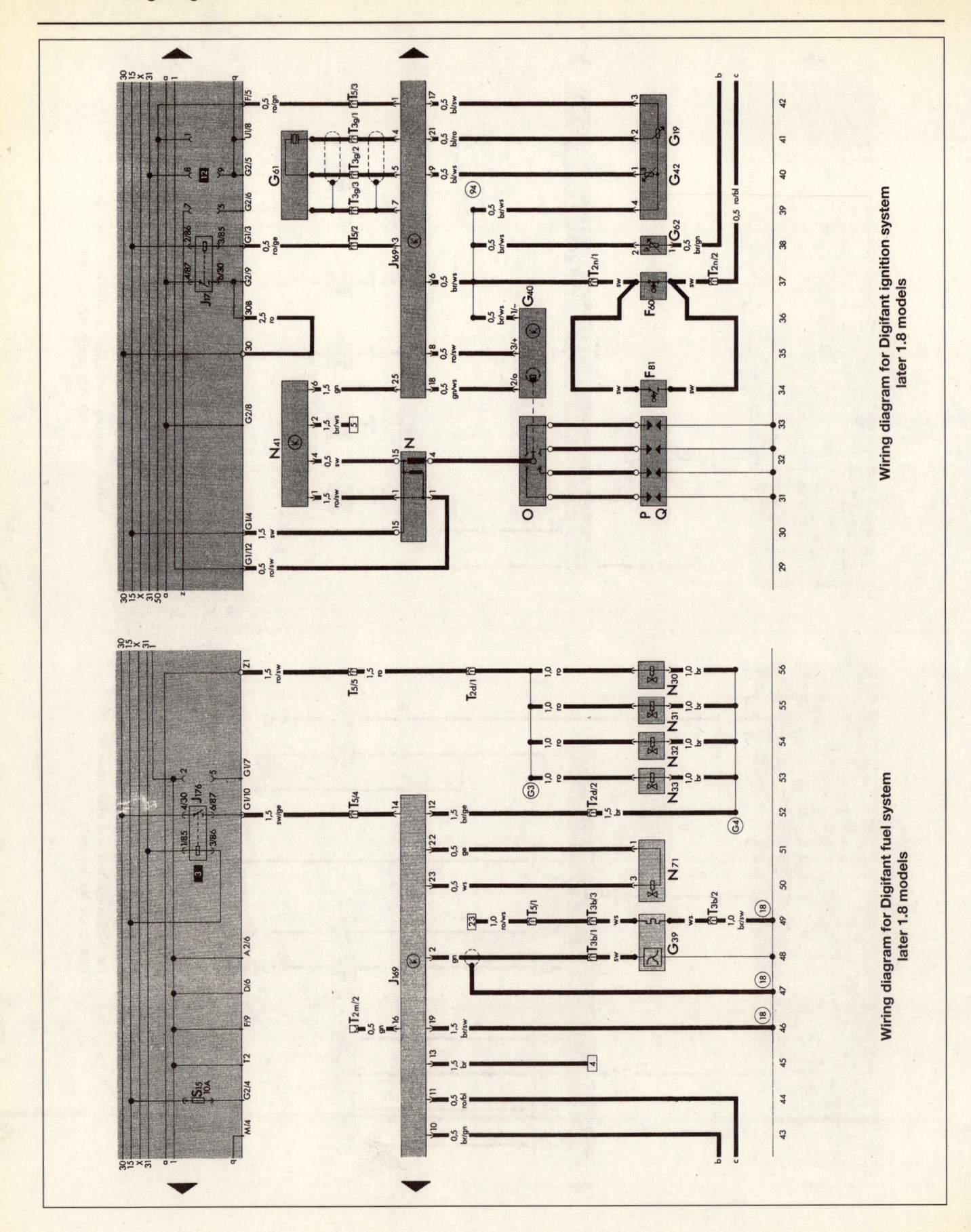

Wiring diagram for Digifant ignition system later 1.8 models

Wiring diagram for Digifant fuel system later 1.8 models

Wiring diagrams 13•39

Key for all wiring diagrams

No	Description
A	Battery
B	Starter
C	Alternator
C1	Voltage regulator
D	Ignition switch
E1	Lighting switch
E2	Indicator switch
E3	Hazard warning light switch
E4	Headlight dip and flasher switch
E9	Fresh air blower switch
E15	Heated rear window switch
E17	Starter/inhibitor and reversing light switch
E19	Parking light switch
E20	Instrument/dash insert lighting control
E22	Intermittent wiper switch
E23	Foglight and rear foglight switch
E39	Electric window switch
E40	Electric window switch, left
E41	Electric window switch, right
E43	Mirror adjustment switch
E48	Mirror adjustment changeover switch
E52	Electric window switch, rear left, in door
E53	Electric window switch, rear left, in console
E54	Electric window switch, rear right, in door
E55	Electric window switch, rear right, in console
E86	Call-up button for multi-function indicator
E102	Headlight beam adjuster
E109	Memory switch for multi-function indicator
F	Brake light switch
F1	Oil pressure switch (1.8 bar)
F2	Door contact switch, front left
F3	Door contact switch, front right
F4	Reversing light switch
F5	Boot light
F9	Handbrake warning switch
F10	Thermo-switch for radiator fan
F18	Radiator fan thermal switch
F22	Oil pressure switch (0.3 bar)
F25	Throttle valve switch
F26	Thermo-switch for choke
F34	Brake fluid level warning contact
F35	Thermo-switch for intake preheating
F59	Central locking system switch
F60	Idle switch
F62	Gearchange indicator vacuum switch
F66	Low level coolant switch
F68	Switch for gearchange and consumption indicator
F69	Central locking switch (driver's door)
F80	Thermo-switch for N52
F81	Full-throttle switch
F87	Thermo-switch for radiator from run-on
F89	Switch for accelerator enrichment
F93	Vacuum timeswitch
G	Fuel gauge sender
G1	Fuel gauge
G2	Coolant temperature sender
G3	Coolant temperature gauge
G5	Rev counter
G6	Fuel pump
G8	Oil temperature sender

No	Description
G17	Feeler for outside temperature
G18	Temperature sensor
G19	Potentiometer for airflow meter
G23	Electric fuel pump II
G32	Low coolant level indicator sender unit
G39	Lambda probe with heater
G40	Hall sender
G42	Intake air temperature sender
G51	Consumption indicator
G54	Speed sensor for multi-function indicator
G55	Vacuum sensor for multi-function indicator
G61	Knock sensor
G62	Coolant temperature sender unit
G114	Switch unit for oil pressure warning
H	Horn control
H1	Dual tone horn
J2	Indicators flasher relay
J4	Dual tone horn relay
J5	Foglight relay
J6	Voltage stabiliser
J17	Fuel pump relay
J20	Emergency lamp – trailer towing
J26	Radiator fan relay
J30	Rear wash/wipe relay
J31	Intermittent wash/wipe relay
J39	Headlamp wash system relay
J51	Electric window relay
J59	Relief valve (for X contact)
J81	Intake preheating relay
J86	Electronic ignition control unit
J88	Electronic ignition control unit (in plenum chamber, LH side)
J98	Gearchange indicator switch unit
J114	Oil pressure monitor switch unit
J119	Multi-function indicator
J120	Switch unit for low coolant indicator
J130	Switch unit for overrun cut-off valve
J134	Diode
J138	Control unit for radiator fan run-on
J143	Switch unit for speed increase
J147	Digijet control unit
J159	Control unit for idle speed stabiliser and overrun cut-off
J167	Digijet relay and idle speed stabilization unit
J169	Control unit for Digifant
J176	Digifant current supply and idle speed stabilization
K	Dash insert
K1	High beam warning lamp
K2	Alternator warning lamp
K3	Oil pressure warning lamp
K5	Indicators warning lamp
K6	Warning lamp for hazard lights
K7	Dual circuit and handbrake warning lamp
K10	Heated rear window warning lamp
K13	Rear foglight warning lamp
K17	Foglight warning lamp
K18	Trailer operation warning lamp
K28	Coolant temperature warning lamp (too hot, red)
K48	Gearchange indicator warning lamp
L1	Twin filament headlight bulb, left
L2	Twin filament headlight bulb, right

No	Description
L8	Clock light bulb
L9	Lighting switch bulb
L10	Dash insert bulb
L16	Fresh air control bulb
L19	Gear selector bulb
L20	Rear foglight bulb
L22	Foglight bulb
L23	Foglight bulb, right
L28	Cigarette lighter bulb
L39	Heated rear window switch bulb
L40	Foglight switch bulb
L52	Connection for fader control unit
L53	Electric window switch light
L54	Headlight beam adjuster bulb
L66	Cassette storage illumination
M1	Parking light bulb, left
M2	Tail light bulb, right
M3	Parking light bulb, right
M4	Tail light bulb, left
M5	Indicator bulb, front left
M6	Indicator bulb, rear left
M7	Indicator bulb, front right
M8	Indicator bulb, rear right
M9	Brake light bulb, left
M10	Brake light bulb, right
M16	Reversing light bulb, left
M17	Reversing light bulb, right
M18	Side indicator bulb, left
M19	Side indicator bulb, right
N	Ignition coil
N1	Automatic choke
N3	Bypass cut-off valve
N6	Resistance wire
N9	Warm-up valve
N10	Temperature sensor (NTC resistance)
N17	Cold start valve
N21	Auxiliary air valve
N23	Series resistance for fresh air blower
N30	Fuel injector, cylinder No 1
N31	Fuel injector, cylinder No 2
N32	Fuel injector, cylinder No 3
N33	Fuel injector, cylinder No 4
N35	Mirror adjustment solenoid (driver's side)
N39	Radiator fan series resistance
N41	TCI control unit
N42	Mirror adjustment solenoid, passenger's
N51	Heater element for manifold preheating
N52	Heater element for carburettor throttle passage
N60	Solenoid valve for consumption indicator
N62	Idling speed – acceleration valve
N65	Overrun cut-off valve
N68	Idling – overrun cut-off valve
N69	Thermotime valve for overrun cut-off
N71	Control valve for idling stabilisation
N98	Series resistance, headlamp dim-dip system (front right of engine compartment)
N113	Heater resistance for washer jets
O	Distributor
P	Spark plug connector
Q	Spark plug
R	Connection for radio
R9	Loudspeaker, front left
R10	Loudspeaker, front right

Key for all wiring diagrams (continued)

No	Description
S24	Overheating fuse
S27	Separate fuse for rear foglight
S37	Fuse for electric windows
T	Connector, behind relay plate
T1	Single connector, various locations
T1a	Single connector, various locations
T1b	Single connector, left of engine compartment or behind relay plate
T1c	Single connector, various locations
T1d	Single connector, various locations
T1e	Single connector, right of engine compartment or behind relay plate
T1f	Single connector, near carburettor or coil
T1g	Single connector, various locations
T1h	Single connector, behind relay plate
T1i	Single connector, behind relay plate
T1k	Single connector, behind relay plate or on radiator cowl
T11	Single connector, behind relay plate
T1m	Single connector, behind dash
T1n	Single connector, behind relay plate or near carburettor
T1p	Single connector, on radiator cowl
T1q	Single connector behind relay plate
Tr	Single connector – luggage boot
T1s	Single connector behind relay plate
T1v	Single connector behind steering wheel switch trim
T1x	Single connector, near coil
T1y	Single connector, near carburettor or behind relay
T2	2-pin connector, various locations
T2a	2-pin connector, various locations
T2b	2-pin connector, various locations
T2c	2-pin connector, left of boot or behind dash
T2d	2-pin connector, left of boot or behind dash (near inlet manifold on Digifant system)
T2e	2-pin connector, left of engine compartment
T2f	2-pin connector. various locations
T2g	2-pin connector, right of engine compartment
T2h	2-pin connector, left of engine compartment
T2i	2-pin connector, behind door trim
T2k	2-pin connector, various locations
T21	2-pin connector, behind dash or front of engine compartment
T2m	2-pin connector, behind dash
T2n	2-pin connector, behind dash
T20	2-pin connector, right of engine compartment
T2p	2-pin connector, various locations
T2q	2-pin connector, right of engine compartment
T2r	2-pin connector, behind door trim
T2s	2-pin connector, behind door trim
T2t	2-pin connector, behind door trim
T2u	2-pin connector, left of boot
T2v	2-pin connector, behind right A-pillar trim or in engine compartment
T2w	2-pin connector, behind dash
T2x	2-pin connector, front of engine compartment or behind dash

No	Description
T2y	2-pin connector, front of engine compartment
T2z	2-pin connector, behind left A-pillar trim
T3	3-pin connector, on throttle valve housing or behind relay plate
T3a	3-pin connector, behind relay plate (in plenum chamber on Digijet system)
T3b	3-pin connector, behind door trim (in rear of engine compartment on Digifant system)
T3c	3-pin connector, behind door trim
T3d	3-pin connector, behind door trim
T3e	3-pin connector, behind door trim
T3f	3-pin connector, behind right B-pillar trim
T3g	3-pin connector, behind left B-pillar trim (near starter on Digifant system)
T3h	3-pin connector, behind relay plate
T4	4-pin connector, behind dash (in plenum chamber on Digijet system)
T4a	4-pin connector, behind steering column trim (near inlet manifold on Digijet system)
T4c	4-pin connector, behind steering column trim
T5	5-pin connector on left of bulkhead
T5b	5-pin connector, behind steering column switch trim
T5c	5-pin connector, behind steering column switch trim
T5e	5-pin connector, on series resistance N23
T6	6-pin connector, behind relay plate
T6a	6-pin connector, rear left-hand tail lamp
T6b	6-pin connector, rear right-hand tail lamp
T7	7-pin connector, on dash insert or behind steering column trim
T7a	7-pin connector, on dash insert
T7b	7-pin connector, on dash insert
T7c	7-pin connector, on dash insert
T8	8-pin connector, on gearbox or behind dash
T16	16-pin connector, on multi-function indicator
T28	28-pin connector, on instrument panel
T32	32-pin connector, behind facia panel
U	Socket
U1	Cigarette lighter
V	Windscreen wiper motor
V2	Fresh air blower
V5	Windscreen washer pump
V7	Radiator fan
V11	Headlight washer pump
V12	Wiper motor
V13	Washer pump motor
V14	Window motor, left
V15	Window motor, right
V17	Mirror adjustment motor, driver's
V25	Mirror adjustment motor, passenger's
V26	Window motor, rear left
V27	Window motor, rear right
V37	Central locking motor
V48	Headlight motor, left
V49	Headlight motor, right
V59	Washer pump
W	Interior light, front

No	Description
W3	Boot light
W6	Glovebox light
W15	Delayed interior light
X	Number plate light
Y2	Digital clock
Z1	Heated rear window
Z4	Heated mirror, driver's
Z5	Heated mirror, passenger's
Z20	Heater resistance, LH washer jet
Z21	Heater resistance, RH washer jet

Earth connections

No	Description
1	Battery earth strap
10	Near relay plate
12	On cylinder head cover or distributor
14	Near steering column or in tailgate
15	In front loom or on cylinder head
16	In instrument loom
17	In instrument loom
17	On intake manifold (1989 on)
18	On cylinder block
19	In boot on right
20	On front seat crossmember, in tailgate or in instrument loom
21	In electric window loom
22	In electric window loom
23	In electric window loom
30	In front loom or next to relay plate
42	Next to steering column
44	Base of LH A-pillar
46	Next to relay plate
50	In boot on left
51	In boot on right
54	On rear cross panel
63	Bulbholder, left-hand tail lamp
64	Bulbholder, right-hand tail lamp
80	In instrument loom
81	In instrument loom
82	In front loom
84	Engine block wiring loom
85	In engine compartment wiring loom
89	In electric window loom
94	In Digifant wiring loom
107	In exterior mirror wiring loom
108	In front loom
116	In Digijet wiring loom
119	In headlamp wiring loom
120	In headlamp wiring loom
A11	In instrument loom
C3	Positive (+) connector (30) in headlamp wiring loom
C10	Positive connector (30) in headlamp wiring loom
E1	Positive (+) connector in Digijet wiring loom
G3	Positive (+) connector in cable sleeve – injector
G4	Connector in cable sleeve – injector
Q1	In electric window loom
Q9	In window lift wiring loom
X1	Positive connector (15) in carburettor wiring loom

MOT Test Checks   REF•1

This is a guide to getting your vehicle through the MOT test. Obviously it will not be possible to examine the vehicle to the same standard as the professional MOT tester. However, working through the following checks will enable you to identify any problem areas before submitting the vehicle for the test.

Where a testable component is in borderline condition, the tester has discretion in deciding whether to pass or fail it. The basis of such discretion is whether the tester would be happy for a close relative or friend to use the vehicle with the component in that condition. If the vehicle presented is clean and evidently well cared for, the tester may be more inclined to pass a borderline component than if the vehicle is scruffy and apparently neglected.

It has only been possible to summarise the test requirements here, based on the regulations in force at the time of printing. Test standards are becoming increasingly stringent, although there are some exemptions for older vehicles. For full details obtain a copy of the Haynes publication Pass the MOT! (available from stockists of Haynes manuals).

An assistant will be needed to help carry out some of these checks.

The checks have been sub-divided into four categories, as follows:

1 Checks carried out **FROM THE DRIVER'S SEAT**

2 Checks carried out **WITH THE VEHICLE ON THE GROUND**

3 Checks carried out **WITH THE VEHICLE RAISED AND THE WHEELS FREE TO TURN**

4 Checks carried out on **YOUR VEHICLE'S EXHAUST EMISSION SYSTEM**

---

1 Checks carried out **FROM THE DRIVER'S SEAT**

Handbrake

☐ Test the operation of the handbrake. Excessive travel (too many clicks) indicates incorrect brake or cable adjustment.

☐ Check that the handbrake cannot be released by tapping the lever sideways. Check the security of the lever mountings.

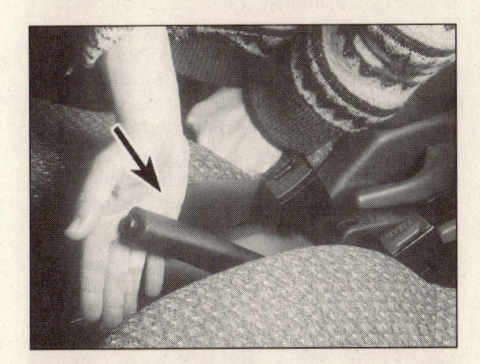

Footbrake

☐ Depress the brake pedal and check that it does not creep down to the floor, indicating a master cylinder fault. Release the pedal, wait a few seconds, then depress it again. If the pedal travels nearly to the floor before firm resistance is felt, brake adjustment or repair is necessary. If the pedal feels spongy, there is air in the hydraulic system which must be removed by bleeding.

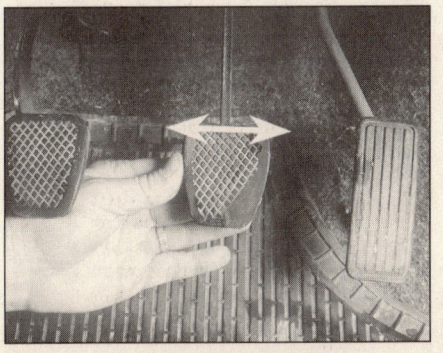

☐ Check that the brake pedal is secure and in good condition. Check also for signs of fluid leaks on the pedal, floor or carpets, which would indicate failed seals in the brake master cylinder.

☐ Check the servo unit (when applicable) by operating the brake pedal several times, then keeping the pedal depressed and starting the engine. As the engine starts, the pedal will move down slightly. If not, the vacuum hose or the servo itself may be faulty.

Steering wheel and column

☐ Examine the steering wheel for fractures or looseness of the hub, spokes or rim.

☐ Move the steering wheel from side to side and then up and down. Check that the steering wheel is not loose on the column, indicating wear or a loose retaining nut. Continue moving the steering wheel as before, but also turn it slightly from left to right.

☐ Check that the steering wheel is not loose on the column, and that there is no abnormal movement of the steering wheel, indicating wear in the column support bearings or couplings.

Windscreen and mirrors

☐ The windscreen must be free of cracks or other significant damage within the driver's field of view. (Small stone chips are acceptable.) Rear view mirrors must be secure, intact, and capable of being adjusted.

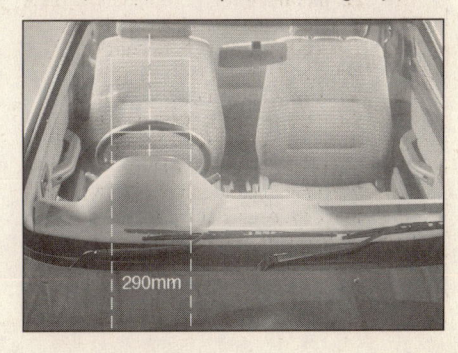

REF•2 MOT Test Checks

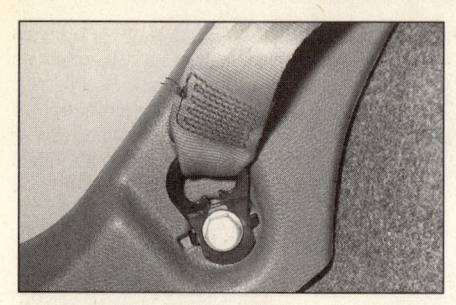

Seat belts and seats

Note: *The following checks are applicable to all seat belts, front and rear.*

☐ Examine the webbing of all the belts (including rear belts if fitted) for cuts, serious fraying or deterioration. Fasten and unfasten each belt to check the buckles. If applicable, check the retracting mechanism. Check the security of all seat belt mountings accessible from inside the vehicle.

☐ The front seats themselves must be securely attached and the backrests must lock in the upright position.

Doors

☐ Both front doors must be able to be opened and closed from outside and inside, and must latch securely when closed.

2 Checks carried out WITH THE VEHICLE ON THE GROUND

Vehicle identification

☐ Number plates must be in good condition, secure and legible, with letters and numbers correctly spaced – spacing at (A) should be twice that at (B).

☐ The VIN plate and/or homologation plate must be legible.

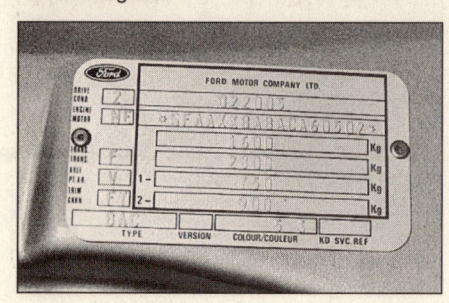

Electrical equipment

☐ Switch on the ignition and check the operation of the horn.

☐ Check the windscreen washers and wipers, examining the wiper blades; renew damaged or perished blades. Also check the operation of the stop-lights.

☐ Check the operation of the sidelights and number plate lights. The lenses and reflectors must be secure, clean and undamaged.

☐ Check the operation and alignment of the headlights. The headlight reflectors must not be tarnished and the lenses must be undamaged.

☐ Switch on the ignition and check the operation of the direction indicators (including the instrument panel tell-tale) and the hazard warning lights. Operation of the sidelights and stop-lights must not affect the indicators - if it does, the cause is usually a bad earth at the rear light cluster.

☐ Check the operation of the rear foglight(s), including the warning light on the instrument panel or in the switch.

Footbrake

☐ Examine the master cylinder, brake pipes and servo unit for leaks, loose mountings, corrosion or other damage.

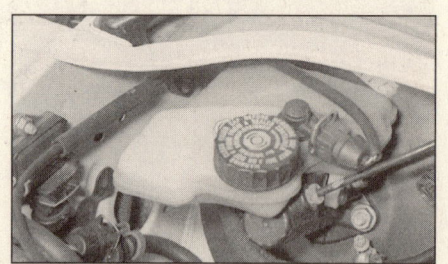

☐ The fluid reservoir must be secure and the fluid level must be between the upper (A) and lower (B) markings.

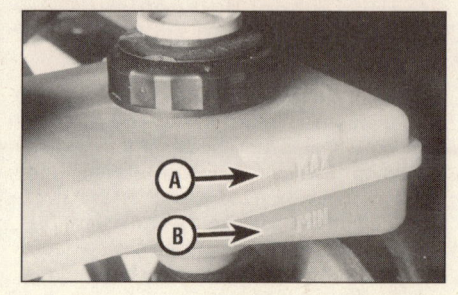

☐ Inspect both front brake flexible hoses for cracks or deterioration of the rubber. Turn the steering from lock to lock, and ensure that the hoses do not contact the wheel, tyre, or any part of the steering or suspension mechanism. With the brake pedal firmly depressed, check the hoses for bulges or leaks under pressure.

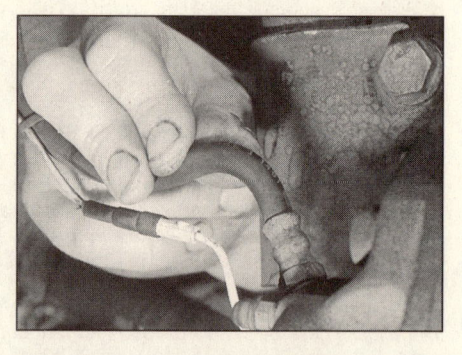

Steering and suspension

☐ Have your assistant turn the steering wheel from side to side slightly, up to the point where the steering gear just begins to transmit this movement to the roadwheels. Check for excessive free play between the steering wheel and the steering gear, indicating wear or insecurity of the steering column joints, the column-to-steering gear coupling, or the steering gear itself.

☐ Have your assistant turn the steering wheel more vigorously in each direction, so that the roadwheels just begin to turn. As this is done, examine all the steering joints, linkages, fittings and attachments. Renew any component that shows signs of wear or damage. On vehicles with power steering, check the security and condition of the steering pump, drivebelt and hoses.

☐ Check that the vehicle is standing level, and at approximately the correct ride height.

Shock absorbers

☐ Depress each corner of the vehicle in turn, then release it. The vehicle should rise and then settle in its normal position. If the vehicle continues to rise and fall, the shock absorber is defective. A shock absorber which has seized will also cause the vehicle to fail.

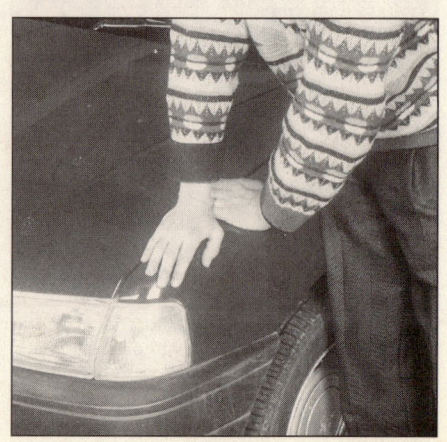

MOT Test Checks REF•3

Exhaust system

☐ Start the engine. With your assistant holding a rag over the tailpipe, check the entire system for leaks. Repair or renew leaking sections.

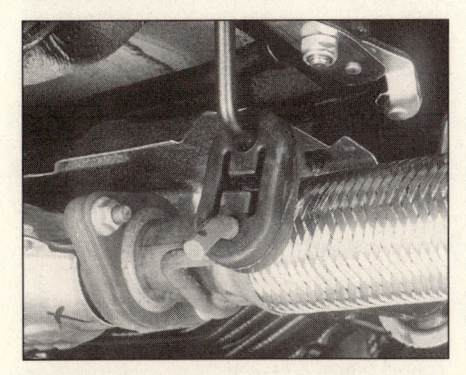

3 Checks carried out WITH THE VEHICLE RAISED AND THE WHEELS FREE TO TURN

Jack up the front and rear of the vehicle, and securely support it on axle stands. Position the stands clear of the suspension assemblies. Ensure that the wheels are clear of the ground and that the steering can be turned from lock to lock.

Steering mechanism

☐ Have your assistant turn the steering from lock to lock. Check that the steering turns smoothly, and that no part of the steering mechanism, including a wheel or tyre, fouls any brake hose or pipe or any part of the body structure.

☐ Examine the steering rack rubber gaiters for damage or insecurity of the retaining clips. If power steering is fitted, check for signs of damage or leakage of the fluid hoses, pipes or connections. Also check for excessive stiffness or binding of the steering, a missing split pin or locking device, or severe corrosion of the body structure within 30 cm of any steering component attachment point.

Front and rear suspension and wheel bearings

☐ Starting at the front right-hand side, grasp the roadwheel at the 3 o'clock and 9 o'clock positions and shake it vigorously. Check for free play or insecurity at the wheel bearings, suspension balljoints, or suspension mountings, pivots and attachments.

☐ Now grasp the wheel at the 12 o'clock and 6 o'clock positions and repeat the previous inspection. Spin the wheel, and check for roughness or tightness of the front wheel bearing.

☐ If excess free play is suspected at a component pivot point, this can be confirmed by using a large screwdriver or similar tool and levering between the mounting and the component attachment. This will confirm whether the wear is in the pivot bush, its retaining bolt, or in the mounting itself (the bolt holes can often become elongated).

☐ Carry out all the above checks at the other front wheel, and then at both rear wheels.

Springs and shock absorbers

☐ Examine the suspension struts (when applicable) for serious fluid leakage, corrosion, or damage to the casing. Also check the security of the mounting points.

☐ If coil springs are fitted, check that the spring ends locate in their seats, and that the spring is not corroded, cracked or broken.

☐ If leaf springs are fitted, check that all leaves are intact, that the axle is securely attached to each spring, and that there is no deterioration of the spring eye mountings, bushes, and shackles.

☐ The same general checks apply to vehicles fitted with other suspension types, such as torsion bars, hydraulic displacer units, etc. Ensure that all mountings and attachments are secure, that there are no signs of excessive wear, corrosion or damage, and (on hydraulic types) that there are no fluid leaks or damaged pipes.

☐ Inspect the shock absorbers for signs of serious fluid leakage. Check for wear of the mounting bushes or attachments, or damage to the body of the unit.

Driveshafts (fwd vehicles only)

☐ Rotate each front wheel in turn and inspect the constant velocity joint gaiters for splits or damage. Also check that each driveshaft is straight and undamaged.

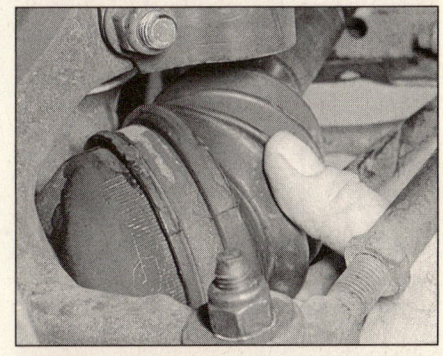

Braking system

☐ If possible without dismantling, check brake pad wear and disc condition. Ensure that the friction lining material has not worn excessively, (A) and that the discs are not fractured, pitted, scored or badly worn (B).

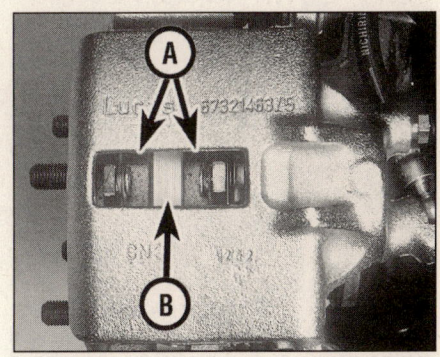

☐ Examine all the rigid brake pipes underneath the vehicle, and the flexible hose(s) at the rear. Look for corrosion, chafing or insecurity of the pipes, and for signs of bulging under pressure, chafing, splits or deterioration of the flexible hoses.

☐ Look for signs of fluid leaks at the brake calipers or on the brake backplates. Repair or renew leaking components.

☐ Slowly spin each wheel, while your assistant depresses and releases the footbrake. Ensure that each brake is operating and does not bind when the pedal is released.

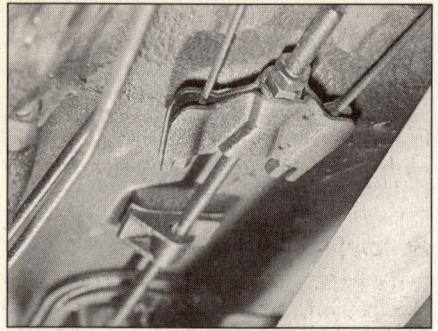

MOT Test Checks

☐ Examine the handbrake mechanism, checking for frayed or broken cables, excessive corrosion, or wear or insecurity of the linkage. Check that the mechanism works on each relevant wheel, and releases fully, without binding.

☐ It is not possible to test brake efficiency without special equipment, but a road test can be carried out later to check that the vehicle pulls up in a straight line.

Fuel and exhaust systems

☐ Inspect the fuel tank (including the filler cap), fuel pipes, hoses and unions. All components must be secure and free from leaks.

☐ Examine the exhaust system over its entire length, checking for any damaged, broken or missing mountings, security of the retaining clamps and rust or corrosion.

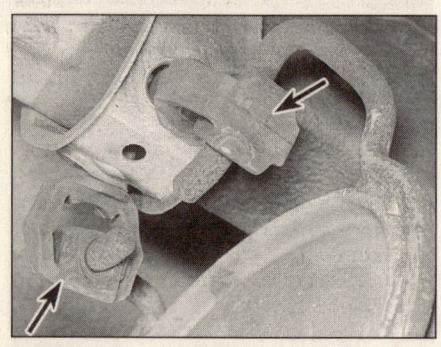

Wheels and tyres

☐ Examine the sidewalls and tread area of each tyre in turn. Check for cuts, tears, lumps, bulges, separation of the tread, and exposure of the ply or cord due to wear or damage. Check that the tyre bead is correctly seated on the wheel rim, that the valve is sound and properly seated, and that the wheel is not distorted or damaged.

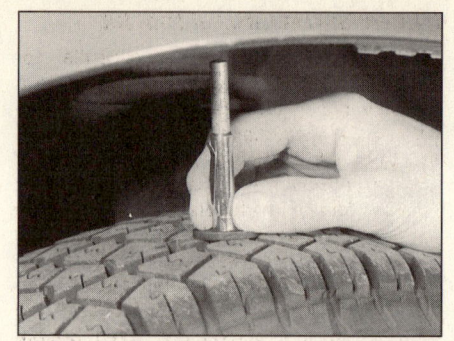

☐ Check that the tyres are of the correct size for the vehicle, that they are of the same size and type on each axle, and that the pressures are correct.

☐ Check the tyre tread depth. The legal minimum at the time of writing is 1.6 mm over at least three-quarters of the tread width. Abnormal tread wear may indicate incorrect front wheel alignment.

Body corrosion

☐ Check the condition of the entire vehicle structure for signs of corrosion in load-bearing areas. (These include chassis box sections, side sills, cross-members, pillars, and all suspension, steering, braking system and seat belt mountings and anchorages.) Any corrosion which has seriously reduced the thickness of a load-bearing area is likely to cause the vehicle to fail. In this case professional repairs are likely to be needed.

☐ Damage or corrosion which causes sharp or otherwise dangerous edges to be exposed will also cause the vehicle to fail.

4 Checks carried out on YOUR VEHICLE'S EXHAUST EMISSION SYSTEM

Petrol models

☐ Have the engine at normal operating temperature, and make sure that it is in good tune (ignition system in good order, air filter element clean, etc).

☐ Before any measurements are carried out, raise the engine speed to around 2500 rpm, and hold it at this speed for 20 seconds. Allow the engine speed to return to idle, and watch for smoke emissions from the exhaust tailpipe. If the idle speed is obviously much too high, or if dense blue or clearly-visible black smoke comes from the tailpipe for more than 5 seconds, the vehicle will fail. As a rule of thumb, blue smoke signifies oil being burnt (engine wear) while black smoke signifies unburnt fuel (dirty air cleaner element, or other carburettor or fuel system fault).

☐ An exhaust gas analyser capable of measuring carbon monoxide (CO) and hydrocarbons (HC) is now needed. If such an instrument cannot be hired or borrowed, a local garage may agree to perform the check for a small fee.

CO emissions (mixture)

☐ At the time of writing, the maximum CO level at idle is 3.5% for vehicles first used after August 1986 and 4.5% for older vehicles. From January 1996 a much tighter limit (around 0.5%) applies to catalyst-equipped vehicles first used from August 1992. If the CO level cannot be reduced far enough to pass the test (and the fuel and ignition systems are otherwise in good condition) then the carburettor is badly worn, or there is some problem in the fuel injection system or catalytic converter (as applicable).

HC emissions

☐ With the CO emissions within limits, HC emissions must be no more than 1200 ppm (parts per million). If the vehicle fails this test at idle, it can be re-tested at around 2000 rpm; if the HC level is then 1200 ppm or less, this counts as a pass.

☐ Excessive HC emissions can be caused by oil being burnt, but they are more likely to be due to unburnt fuel.

Diesel models

☐ The only emission test applicable to Diesel engines is the measuring of exhaust smoke density. The test involves accelerating the engine several times to its maximum unloaded speed.

Note: *It is of the utmost importance that the engine timing belt is in good condition before the test is carried out.*

☐ Excessive smoke can be caused by a dirty air cleaner element. Otherwise, professional advice may be needed to find the cause.

Tools and Working Facilities

Introduction

A selection of good tools is a fundamental requirement for anyone contemplating the maintenance and repair of a motor vehicle. For the owner who does not possess any, their purchase will prove a considerable expense, offsetting some of the savings made by doing-it-yourself. However, provided that the tools purchased meet the relevant national safety standards and are of good quality, they will last for many years and prove an extremely worthwhile investment.

To help the average owner to decide which tools are needed to carry out the various tasks detailed in this manual, we have compiled three lists of tools under the following headings: *Maintenance and minor repair*, *Repair and overhaul*, and *Special*. Newcomers to practical mechanics should start off with the *Maintenance and minor repair* tool kit, and confine themselves to the simpler jobs around the vehicle. Then, as confidence and experience grow, more difficult tasks can be undertaken, with extra tools being purchased as, and when, they are needed. In this way, a *Maintenance and minor repair* tool kit can be built up into a *Repair and overhaul* tool kit over a considerable period of time, without any major cash outlays. The experienced do-it-yourselfer will have a tool kit good enough for most repair and overhaul procedures, and will add tools from the *Special* category when it is felt that the expense is justified by the amount of use to which these tools will be put.

Maintenance and minor repair tool kit

The tools given in this list should be considered as a minimum requirement if routine maintenance, servicing and minor repair operations are to be undertaken. We recommend the purchase of combination spanners (ring one end, open-ended the other); although more expensive than open-ended ones, they do give the advantages of both types of spanner.

- [ ] *Combination spanners: 8, 9, 10, 11, 12, 13, 14, 15, 16, 17, 19, 21, 22, 24 & 26 mm*
- [ ] *Adjustable spanner - 35 mm jaw (approx)*
- [ ] *Gearbox drain plug key*
- [ ] *Set of feeler gauges*
- [ ] *Spark plug spanner (with rubber insert)*
- [ ] *Spark plug gap adjustment tool*
- [ ] *Brake bleed nipple spanner*
- [ ] *Brake adjuster spanner*
- [ ] *Screwdrivers: Flat blade and cross blade – approx 100 mm long x 6 mm dia*
- [ ] *Combination pliers*
- [ ] *Hacksaw (junior)*
- [ ] *Tyre pump*
- [ ] *Tyre pressure gauge*
- [ ] *Grease gun*
- [ ] *Oil can*
- [ ] *Oil filter removal tool*
- [ ] *Fine emery cloth*
- [ ] *Wire brush (small)*
- [ ] *Funnel (medium size)*

Repair and overhaul tool kit

These tools are virtually essential for anyone undertaking any major repairs to a motor vehicle, and are additional to those given in the *Maintenance and minor repair* list. Included in this list is a comprehensive set of sockets. Although these are expensive, they will be found invaluable as they are so versatile - particularly if various drives are included in the set. We recommend the half-inch square-drive type, as this can be used with most proprietary torque wrenches. If you cannot afford a socket set, even bought piecemeal, then inexpensive tubular box spanners are a useful alternative.

The tools in this list will occasionally need to be supplemented by tools from the *Special* list:

- [ ] *Sockets (or box spanners) to cover range in previous list*
- [ ] *Reversible ratchet drive (for use with sockets) (see illustration)*
- [ ] *Extension piece, 250 mm (for use with sockets)*
- [ ] *Universal joint (for use with sockets)*
- [ ] *Torque wrench (for use with sockets)*
- [ ] *Self-locking grips*
- [ ] *Ball pein hammer*
- [ ] *Soft-faced mallet (plastic/aluminium or rubber)*
- [ ] *Screwdrivers:*
  Flat blade - long & sturdy, short (chubby), and narrow (electrician's) types
  Cross blade - Long & sturdy, and short (chubby) types
- [ ] *Pliers:*
  Long-nosed
  Side cutters (electrician's)
  Circlip (internal and external)
- [ ] *Cold chisel - 25 mm*
- [ ] *Scriber*
- [ ] *Scraper*
- [ ] *Centre-punch*
- [ ] *Pin punch*
- [ ] *Hacksaw*
- [ ] *Brake hose clamp*
- [ ] *Brake bleeding kit*
- [ ] *Selection of twist drills*
- [ ] *Steel rule/straight-edge*
- [ ] *Allen keys (inc. splined/Torx type) (see illustrations)*
- [ ] *Selection of files*
- [ ] *Wire brush*
- [ ] *Axle stands*
- [ ] *Jack (strong trolley or hydraulic type)*
- [ ] *Light with extension lead*

Special tools

The tools in this list are those which are not used regularly, are expensive to buy, or which need to be used in accordance with their manufacturers' instructions. Unless relatively difficult mechanical jobs are undertaken frequently, it will not be economic to buy many of these tools. Where this is the case, you could consider clubbing together with friends (or joining a motorists' club) to make a joint purchase, or borrowing the tools against a deposit from a local garage or tool hire specialist. It is worth noting that many of the larger DIY superstores now carry a large range of special tools for hire at modest rates.

The following list contains only those tools and instruments freely available to the public, and not those special tools produced by the vehicle manufacturer specifically for its dealer network. You will find occasional references to these manufacturers' special tools in the text of this manual. Generally, an alternative method of doing the job without the vehicle manufacturers' special tool is given. However, sometimes there is no alternative to using them. Where this is the case and the relevant tool cannot be bought or borrowed, you will have to entrust the work to a franchised garage.

- [ ] *Valve spring compressor (see illustration)*
- [ ] *Valve grinding tool*
- [ ] *Piston ring compressor (see illustration)*
- [ ] *Piston ring removal/installation tool (see illustration)*
- [ ] *Cylinder bore hone (see illustration)*
- [ ] *Balljoint separator*
- [ ] *Coil spring compressors (where applicable)*
- [ ] *Two/three-legged hub and bearing puller (see illustration)*

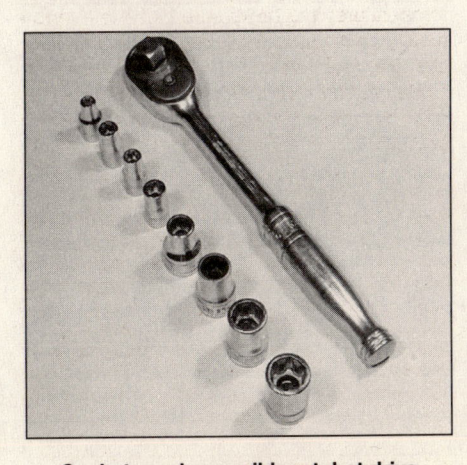

Sockets and reversible ratchet drive

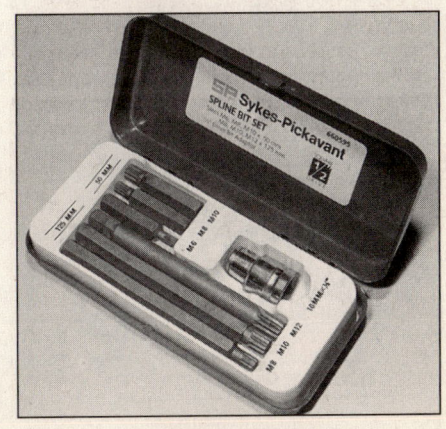

Spline bit set

REF•6 Tools and Working Facilities

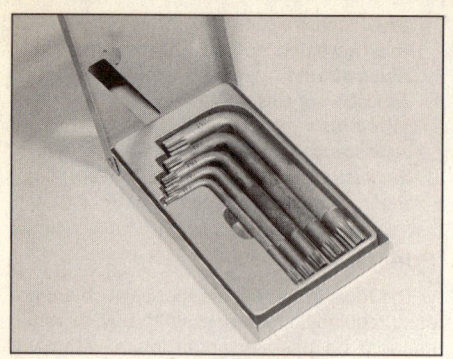

Spline key set

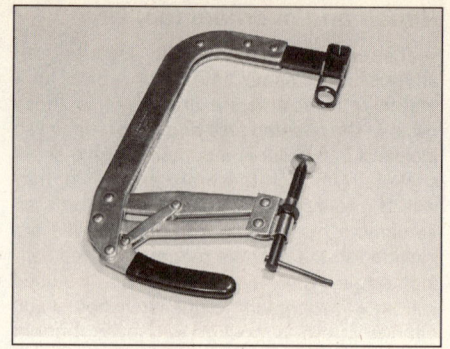

Valve spring compressor

Piston ring compressor

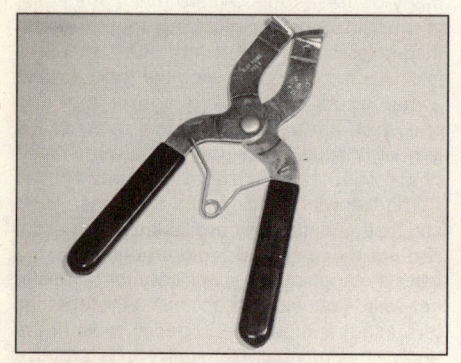

Piston ring removal/installation tool

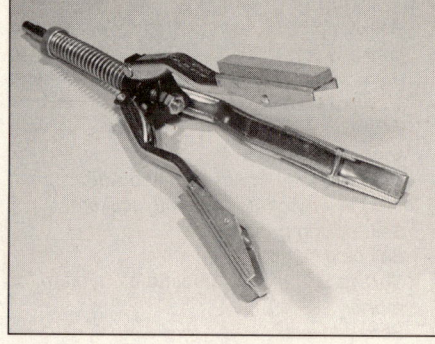

Cylinder bore hone

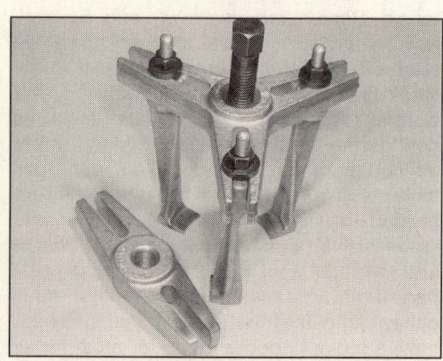

Three-legged hub and bearing puller

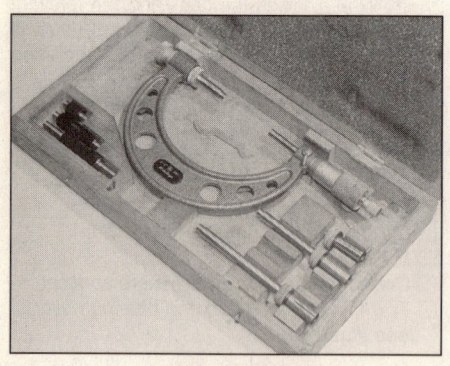

Micrometer set

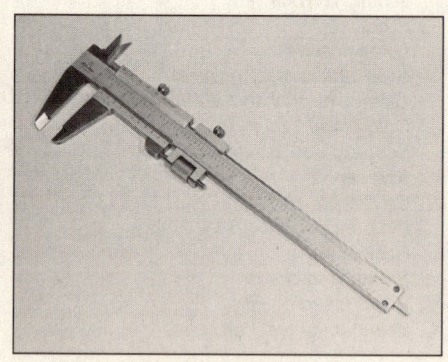

Vernier calipers

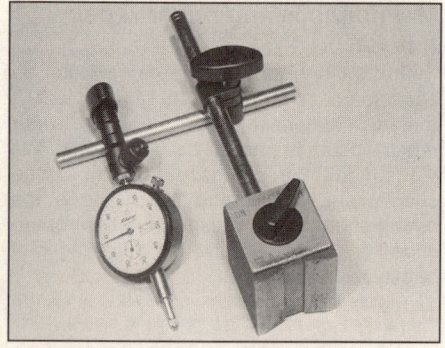

Dial test indicator and magnetic stand

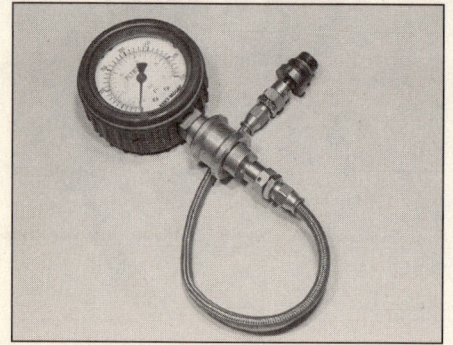

Compression testing gauge

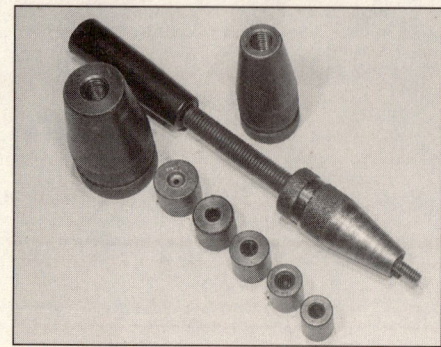

Clutch plate alignment set

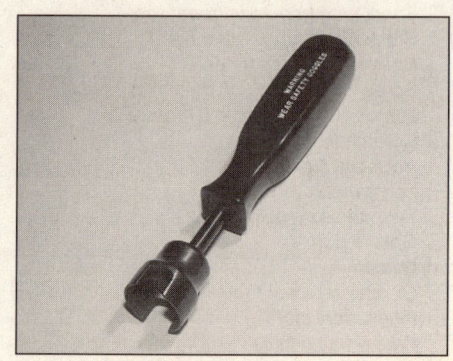

Brake shoe steady spring cup removal tool

Tools and Working Facilities   REF•7

- ☐ Impact screwdriver
- ☐ Micrometer and/or vernier calipers *(see illustrations)*
- ☐ Dial gauge *(see illustration)*
- ☐ Universal electrical multi-meter
- ☐ Cylinder compression gauge *(see illustration)*
- ☐ Clutch plate alignment set *(see illustration)*
- ☐ Brake shoe steady spring cup removal tool *(see illustration)*
- ☐ Bush and bearing removal/installation set *(see illustration)*
- ☐ Stud extractors *(see illustration)*
- ☐ Tap and die set *(see illustration)*
- ☐ Lifting tackle
- ☐ Trolley jack

Buying tools

For practically all tools, a tool factor is the best source, since he will have a very comprehensive range compared with the average garage or accessory shop. Having said that, accessory shops often offer excellent quality tools at discount prices, so it pays to shop around.

Remember, you don't have to buy the most expensive items on the shelf, but it is always advisable to steer clear of the very cheap tools. There are plenty of good tools around at reasonable prices, but always aim to purchase items which meet the relevant national safety standards. If in doubt, ask the proprietor or manager of the shop for advice before making a purchase.

Care and maintenance of tools

Having purchased a reasonable tool kit, it is necessary to keep the tools in a clean and serviceable condition. After use, always wipe off any dirt, grease and metal particles using a clean, dry cloth, before putting the tools away. Never leave them lying around after they have been used. A simple tool rack on the garage or workshop wall for items such as screwdrivers and pliers is a good idea. Store all normal spanners and sockets in a metal box. Any measuring instruments, gauges, meters, etc, must be carefully stored where they cannot be damaged or become rusty.

Take a little care when tools are used. Hammer heads inevitably become marked, and screwdrivers lose the keen edge on their blades from time to time. A little timely attention with emery cloth or a file will soon restore items like this to a good serviceable finish.

Working facilities

Not to be forgotten when discussing tools is the workshop itself. If anything more than routine maintenance is to be carried out, some form of suitable working area becomes essential.

It is appreciated that many an owner-mechanic is forced by circumstances to remove an engine or similar item without the benefit of a garage or workshop. Having done this, any repairs should always be done under the cover of a roof.

Wherever possible, any dismantling should be done on a clean, flat workbench or table at a suitable working height.

Any workbench needs a vice; one with a jaw opening of 100 mm is suitable for most jobs. As mentioned previously, some clean dry storage space is also required for tools, as well as for any lubricants, cleaning fluids, touch-up paints and so on, which become necessary.

Another item which may be required, and which has a much more general usage, is an electric drill with a chuck capacity of at least 8 mm. This, together with a good range of twist drills, is virtually essential for fitting accessories.

Last, but not least, always keep a supply of old newspapers and clean, lint-free rags available, and try to keep any working area as clean as possible.

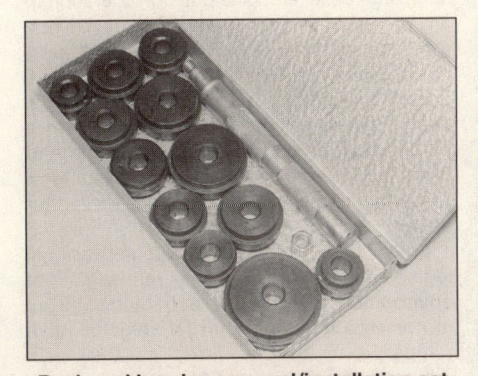

Bush and bearing removal/installation set

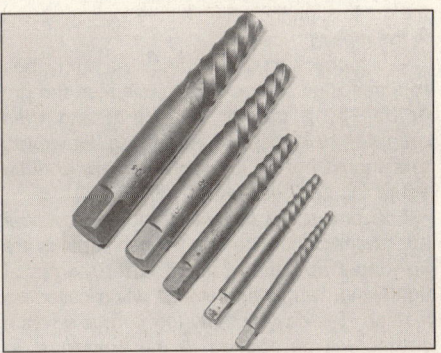

Stud extractor set

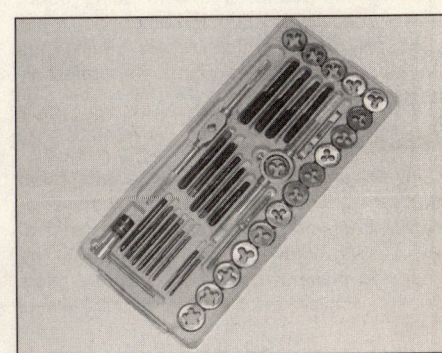

Tap and die set

General Repair Procedures

Whenever servicing, repair or overhaul work is carried out on the car or its components, it is necessary to observe the following procedures and instructions. This will assist in carrying out the operation efficiently and to a professional standard of workmanship.

Joint mating faces and gaskets

When separating components at their mating faces, never insert screwdrivers or similar implements into the joint between the faces in order to prise them apart. This can cause severe damage which results in oil leaks, coolant leaks, etc upon reassembly. Separation is usually achieved by tapping along the joint with a soft-faced hammer in order to break the seal. However, note that this method may not be suitable where dowels are used for component location.

Where a gasket is used between the mating faces of two components, ensure that it is renewed on reassembly, and fit it dry unless otherwise stated in the repair procedure. Make sure that the mating faces are clean and dry, with all traces of old gasket removed. When cleaning a joint face, use a tool which is not likely to score or damage the face, and remove any burrs or nicks with an oilstone or fine file.

Make sure that tapped holes are cleaned with a pipe cleaner, and keep them free of jointing compound, if this is being used, unless specifically instructed otherwise.

Ensure that all orifices, channels or pipes are clear, and blow through them, preferably using compressed air.

Oil seals

Oil seals can be removed by levering them out with a wide flat-bladed screwdriver or similar implement. Alternatively, a number of self-tapping screws may be screwed into the seal, and these used as a purchase for pliers or some similar device in order to pull the seal free.

Whenever an oil seal is removed from its working location, either individually or as part of an assembly, it should be renewed.

The very fine sealing lip of the seal is easily damaged, and will not seal if the surface it contacts is not completely clean and free from scratches, nicks or grooves.

Protect the lips of the seal from any surface which may damage them in the course of fitting. Use tape or a conical sleeve where possible. Lubricate the seal lips with oil before fitting and, on dual-lipped seals, fill the space between the lips with grease.

Unless otherwise stated, oil seals must be fitted with their sealing lips toward the lubricant to be sealed.

Use a tubular drift or block of wood of the appropriate size to install the seal and, if the seal housing is shouldered, drive the seal down to the shoulder. If the seal housing is unshouldered, the seal should be fitted with its face flush with the housing top face (unless otherwise instructed).

Screw threads and fastenings

Seized nuts, bolts and screws are quite a common occurrence where corrosion has set in, and the use of penetrating oil or releasing fluid will often overcome this problem if the offending item is soaked for a while before attempting to release it. The use of an impact driver may also provide a means of releasing such stubborn fastening devices, when used in conjunction with the appropriate screwdriver bit or socket. If none of these methods works, it may be necessary to resort to the careful application of heat, or the use of a hacksaw or nut splitter device.

Studs are usually removed by locking two nuts together on the threaded part, and then using a spanner on the lower nut to unscrew the stud. Studs or bolts which have broken off below the surface of the component in which they are mounted can sometimes be removed using a proprietary stud extractor. Always ensure that a blind tapped hole is completely free from oil, grease, water or other fluid before installing the bolt or stud. Failure to do this could cause the housing to crack due to the hydraulic action of the bolt or stud as it is screwed in.

When tightening a castellated nut to accept a split pin, tighten the nut to the specified torque, where applicable, and then tighten further to the next split pin hole. Never slacken the nut to align the split pin hole, unless stated in the repair procedure.

When checking or retightening a nut or bolt to a specified torque setting, slacken the nut or bolt by a quarter of a turn, and then retighten to the specified setting. However, this should not be attempted where angular tightening has been used.

For some screw fastenings, notably cylinder head bolts or nuts, torque wrench settings are no longer specified for the latter stages of tightening, "angle-tightening" being called up instead. Typically, a fairly low torque wrench setting will be applied to the bolts/nuts in the correct sequence, followed by one or more stages of tightening through specified angles.

Locknuts, locktabs and washers

Any fastening which will rotate against a component or housing in the course of tightening should always have a washer between it and the relevant component or housing.

Spring or split washers should always be renewed when they are used to lock a critical component such as a big-end bearing retaining bolt or nut. Locktabs which are folded over to retain a nut or bolt should always be renewed.

Self-locking nuts can be re-used in non-critical areas, providing resistance can be felt when the locking portion passes over the bolt or stud thread. However, it should be noted that self-locking stiffnuts tend to lose their effectiveness after long periods of use, and in such cases should be renewed as a matter of course.

Split pins must always be replaced with new ones of the correct size for the hole.

When thread-locking compound is found on the threads of a fastener which is to be re-used, it should be cleaned off with a wire brush and solvent, and fresh compound applied on reassembly.

Special tools

Some repair procedures in this manual entail the use of special tools such as a press, two or three-legged pullers, spring compressors, etc. Wherever possible, suitable readily-available alternatives to the manufacturer's special tools are described, and are shown in use. Unless you are highly-skilled and have a thorough understanding of the procedures described, never attempt to bypass the use of any special tool when the procedure described specifies its use. Not only is there a very great risk of personal injury, but expensive damage could be caused to the components involved.

Environmental considerations

When disposing of used engine oil, brake fluid, antifreeze, etc, give due consideration to any detrimental environmental effects. Do not, for instance, pour any of the above liquids down drains into the general sewage system, or onto the ground to soak away. Many local council refuse tips provide a facility for waste oil disposal, as do some garages. If none of these facilities are available, consult your local Environmental Health Department for further advice.

With the universal tightening-up of legislation regarding the emission of environmentally-harmful substances from motor vehicles, most current vehicles have tamperproof devices fitted to the main adjustment points of the fuel system. These devices are primarily designed to prevent unqualified persons from adjusting the fuel/air mixture, with the chance of a consequent increase in toxic emissions. If such devices are encountered during servicing or overhaul, they should, wherever possible, be renewed or refitted in accordance with the vehicle manufacturer's requirements or current legislation.

OIL CARE — FOLLOW THE CODE

OIL BANK LINE
0800 66 33 66

Note: It is antisocial and illegal to dump oil down the drain. To find the location of your local oil recycling bank, call this number free.

Fault Finding   REF•9

Introduction

The vehicle owner who does his or her own maintenance according to the recommended schedules should not have to use this section of the manual very often. Modern component reliability is such that, provided those items subject to wear or deterioration are inspected or renewed at the specified intervals, sudden failure is comparatively rare. Faults do not usually just happen as a result of sudden failure, but develop over a period of time. Major mechanical failures in particular are usually preceded by characteristic symptoms over hundreds or even thousands of miles. Those components which do occasionally fail without warning are often small and easily carried in the vehicle.

With any fault finding, the first step is to decide where to begin investigations. Sometimes this is obvious, but on other occasions a little detective work will be necessary. The owner who makes half a dozen haphazard adjustments or replacements may be successful in curing a fault (or its symptoms), but he will be none the wiser if the fault recurs and he may well have spent more time and money than was necessary. A calm and logical approach will be found to be more satisfactory in the long run. Always take into account any warning signs or abnormalities that may have been noticed in the period preceding the fault – power loss, high or low gauge readings, unusual noises or smells, etc – and remember that failure of components such as fuses or spark plugs may only be pointers to some underlying fault.

The pages which follow here are intended to help in cases of failure to start or breakdown on the road. There is also a Fault Diagnosis Section at the end of each Chapter which should be consulted if the preliminary checks prove unfruitful. Whatever the fault, certain basic principles apply. These are as follows:

Verify the fault. This is simply a matter of being sure that you know what the symptoms are before starting work. This is particularly important if you are investigating a fault for someone else who may not have described it very accurately.

Don't overlook the obvious. For example, if the vehicle won't start, is there petrol in the tank? (Don't take anyone else's word on this particular point, and don't trust the fuel gauge either!) If an electrical fault is indicated, look for loose or broken wires before digging out the test gear.

Cure the disease, not the symptom. Substituting a flat battery with a fully charged one will get you off the hard shoulder, but if the underlying cause is not attended to, the new battery will go the same way. Similarly, changing oil-fouled spark plugs for a new set will get you moving again, but remember that the reason for the fouling (if it wasn't simply an incorrect grade of plug) will have to be established and corrected.

Don't take anything for granted. Particularly, don't forget that a 'new' component may itself be defective (especially if it's been rattling round in the boot for months), and don't leave components out of a fault diagnosis sequence just because they are new or recently fitted. When you do finally diagnose a difficult fault, you'll probably realise that all the evidence was there from the start.

Electrical faults

Electrical faults can be more puzzling than straightforward mechanical failures, but they are no less susceptible to logical analysis if the basic principles of operation are understood. Vehicle electrical wiring exists in extremely unfavourable conditions – heat, vibration and chemical attack and the first things to look for are loose or corroded connections and broken or chafed wires, especially where the wires pass through holes in the bodywork or are subject to vibration.

All metal-bodied vehicles in current production have one pole of the battery 'earthed', ie connected to the vehicle bodywork, and in nearly all modern vehicles it is the negative (–) terminal. The various electrical components – motors, bulb holders, etc – are also connected to earth, either by means of a lead or directly by their mountings. Electric current flows through the component and then back to the battery via the bodywork. If the component mounting is loose or corroded, or if a good path back to the battery is not available, the circuit will be incomplete and malfunction will result. The engine and/or gearbox are also earthed by means of flexible metal straps to the body or subframe; if these straps are loose or missing, starter motor, generator and ignition trouble may result.

Assuming the earth return to be satisfactory, electrical faults will be due either to component malfunction or to defects in the current supply. Individual components are dealt with in Chapter 9. If supply wires are broken or cracked internally this results in an open-circuit, and the easiest way to check for this is to bypass the suspect wire temporarily with a length of wire having a crocodile clip or suitable connector at each end. Alternatively, a 12V test lamp can be used to verify the presence of supply voltage at various points along the wire and the break can be thus isolated.

If a bare portion of a live wire touches the bodywork or other earthed metal part, the electricity will take the low-resistance path thus formed back to the battery: this is known as a short-circuit. Hopefully a short-circuit will blow a fuse, but otherwise it may cause burning of the insulation (and possibly further short-circuits) or even a fire. This is why it is inadvisable to bypass persistently blowing fuses with silver foil or wire.

REF•10 Fault Finding

Spares and tool kit

Most vehicles are supplied only with sufficient tools for wheel changing; the *Maintenance and minor repair* tool kit detailed in *Tools and working facilities*, with the addition of a hammer, is probably sufficient for those repairs that most motorists would consider attempting at the roadside. In addition a few items which can be fitted without too much trouble in the event of a breakdown should be carried. Experience and available space will modify the list below, but the following may save having to call on professional assistance:

- [ ] Spark plugs, clean and correctly gapped
- [ ] HT lead and plug cap – long enough to reach the plug furthest from the distributor
- [ ] Distributor rotor, condenser and contact breaker points (where applicable)
- [ ] Drivebelt(s) — emergency type may suffice
- [ ] Spare fuses
- [ ] Set of principal light bulbs
- [ ] Tin of radiator sealer and hose bandage
- [ ] Exhaust bandage
- [ ] Roll of insulating tape
- [ ] Length of soft iron wire
- [ ] Length of electrical flex
- [ ] Torch or inspection lamp (can double as test lamp)
- [ ] Battery jump leads
- [ ] Tow-rope
- [ ] Ignition waterproofing aerosol
- [ ] Litre of engine oil
- [ ] Sealed can of hydraulic fluid
- [ ] Emergency windscreen
- [ ] Wormdrive clips
- [ ] Tube of filler paste

If spare fuel is carried, a can designed for the purpose should be used to minimise risks of leakage and collision damage. A first aid kit and a warning triangle, whilst not at present compulsory in the UK, are obviously sensible items to carry in addition to the above. When touring abroad it may be advisable to carry additional spares which, even if you cannot fit them yourself, could save having to wait while parts are obtained. The items below may be worth considering:

- [ ] Clutch and throttle cables
- [ ] Cylinder head gasket
- [ ] Alternator brushes
- [ ] Tyre valve core

One of the motoring organisations will be able to advise on availability of fuel, etc, in foreign countries.

Engine will not start

Engine fails to turn when starter operated

- [ ] Flat battery (recharge use jump leads or push start)
- [ ] Battery terminals loose or corroded
- [ ] Battery earth to body defective
- [ ] Engine earth strap loose or broken
- [ ] Starter motor (or solenoid) wiring loose or broken
- [ ] Automatic transmission selector in wrong position, or inhibitor switch faulty
- [ ] Ignition/starter switch faulty
- [ ] Major mechanical failure (seizure)
- [ ] Starter or solenoid internal fault (see Chapter 12)
- [ ] Faulty stop-start system (where fitted)

Starter motor turns engine slowly

- [ ] Partially discharged battery (recharge, use jump leads, or push start)
- [ ] Battery terminals loose or corroded
- [ ] Battery earth to body defective
- [ ] Engine earth strap loose
- [ ] Starter motor (or solenoid) wiring loose
- [ ] Starter motor internal fault (see Chapter 9)

Starter motor spins without turning engine

- [ ] Flywheel gear teeth damaged or worn
- [ ] Starter motor mounting bolts loose

Engine turns normally but fails to start

- [ ] Damp or dirty HT leads and distributor cap (crank engine and check for spark)
- [ ] No fuel in tank (check for delivery at carburettor)
- [ ] Excessive choke (hot engine) or insufficient choke (cold engine)
- [ ] Fouled or incorrectly gapped spark plugs (remove, clean and regap)
- [ ] Other ignition system fault (see Chapter 4)
- [ ] Other fuel system fault (see Chapter 3)
- [ ] Poor compression (see Chapter 1)
- [ ] Major mechanical failure (eg camshaft drive)

Engine fires but will not run

- [ ] Insufficient choke (cold engine)
- [ ] Air leaks at carburettor or inlet manifold
- [ ] Fuel starvation (see Chapter 3)
- [ ] Ballast resistor defective, or other ignition fault (see Chapter 4)

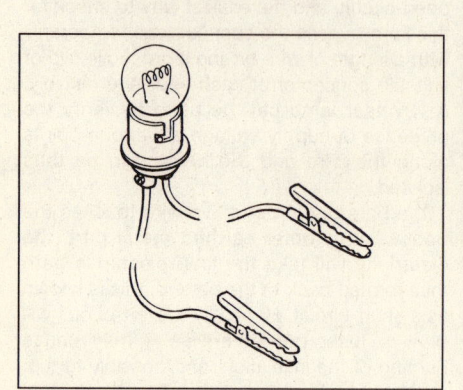

A simple test lamp is useful for checking electrical faults

Carrying a few spares may save you a long walk!

Fault Finding REF•11

Engine cuts out and will not restart

Engine cuts out suddenly – ignition fault
- ☐ Loose or disconnected LT wires
- ☐ Wet HT leads or distributor cap (after traversing water splash)
- ☐ Coil failure (check for spark)
- ☐ Other ignition fault (see Chapter 4)

Engine misfires before cutting out – fuel fault
- ☐ Fuel tank empty
- ☐ Fuel pump defective or filter blocked (check for delivery)
- ☐ Fuel tank filler vent blocked (suction will be evident on releasing cap)
- ☐ Carburettor needle valve sticking
- ☐ Carburettor jets blocked (fuel contaminated)
- ☐ Other fuel system fault (see Chapter 3)

Engine cuts out – other causes
- ☐ Serious overheating
- ☐ Major mechanical failure (eg camshaft drive)

Crank engine and check for a spark. Note use of insulated tool

Engine overheats

Ignition (no-charge) warning light illuminated
- ☐ Slack or broken drivebelt — retension or renew (Chapter 9)

Ignition warning light not illuminated
- ☐ Coolant loss due to internal or external leakage (see Chapter 2)
- ☐ Thermostat defective
- ☐ Low oil level
- ☐ Brakes binding
- ☐ Radiator clogged externally or internally
- ☐ Electric cooling fan not operating correctly
- ☐ Engine waterways clogged
- ☐ Ignition timing incorrect or automatic advance malfunctioning
- ☐ Mixture too weak

Note: *Do not add cold water to an overheated engine or damage may result*

Low engine oil pressure

Note: *Low oil pressure in a high-mileage engine at tickover is not necessarily a cause for concern. Sudden pressure loss at speed is far more significant. In any event check the gauge or warning light sender before condemning the engine.*

Gauge reads low or warning light illuminated with engine running
- ☐ Oil level low or incorrect grade
- ☐ Defective gauge or sender unit
- ☐ Wire to sender unit earthed
- ☐ Engine overheating
- ☐ Oil filter clogged or bypass valve defective
- ☐ Oil pressure relief valve defective
- ☐ Oil pick-up strainer clogged
- ☐ Oil pump worn or mountings loose
- ☐ Worn main or big-end bearings

Engine noises

Pre-ignition (pinking) on acceleration
- ☐ Incorrect grade of fuel
- ☐ Ignition timing incorrect
- ☐ Distributor faulty or worn
- ☐ Worn or maladjusted carburettor
- ☐ Excessive carbon build-up in engine

Whistling or wheezing noises
- ☐ Leaking vacuum hose
- ☐ Leaking carburettor or manifold gasket
- ☐ Blowing head gasket

Tapping or rattling
- ☐ Incorrect valve clearances (where applicable)
- ☐ Worn valve gear
- ☐ Worn timing chain or belt
- ☐ Broken piston ring (ticking noise)

Knocking or thumping
- ☐ Unintentional mechanical contact (eg fan blades)
- ☐ Worn drivebelt
- ☐ Peripheral component fault (generator, water pump, etc)
- ☐ Worn big-end bearings (regular heavy knocking, perhaps less under load)
- ☐ Worn main bearings (rumbling and knocking, perhaps worsening under load)
- ☐ Piston slap (most noticeable when cold)

Conversion Factors

Length (distance)
Inches (in)	25.4	= Millimetres (mm)	x 0.0394	=	Inches (in)
Feet (ft)	0.305	= Metres (m)	x 3.281	=	Feet (ft)
Miles	1.609	= Kilometres (km)	x 0.621	=	Miles

Volume (capacity)
Cubic inches (cu in; in^3)	x 16.387	= Cubic centimetres (cc; cm^3)	x 0.061	=	Cubic inches (cu in; in^3)
Imperial pints (Imp pt)	x 0.568	= Litres (l)	x 1.76	=	Imperial pints (Imp pt)
Imperial quarts (Imp qt)	x 1.137	= Litres (l)	x 0.88	=	Imperial quarts (Imp qt)
Imperial quarts (Imp qt)	x 1.201	= US quarts (US qt)	x 0.833	=	Imperial quarts (Imp qt)
US quarts (US qt)	x 0.946	= Litres (l)	x 1.057	=	US quarts (US qt)
Imperial gallons (Imp gal)	x 4.546	= Litres (l)	x 0.22	=	Imperial gallons (Imp gal)
Imperial gallons (Imp gal)	x 1.201	= US gallons (US gal)	x 0.833	=	Imperial gallons (Imp gal)
US gallons (US gal)	x 3.785	= Litres (l)	x 0.264	=	US gallons (US gal)

Mass (weight)
Ounces (oz)	x 28.35	= Grams (g)	x 0.035	=	Ounces (oz)
Pounds (lb)	x 0.454	= Kilograms (kg)	x 2.205	=	Pounds (lb)

Force
Ounces-force (ozf; oz)	x 0.278	= Newtons (N)	x 3.6	=	Ounces-force (ozf; oz)
Pounds-force (lbf; lb)	x 4.448	= Newtons (N)	x 0.225	=	Pounds-force (lbf; lb)
Newtons (N)	x 0.1	= Kilograms-force (kgf; kg)	x 9.81	=	Newtons (N)

Pressure
Pounds-force per square inch (psi; lbf/in^2; lb/in^2)	x 0.070	= Kilograms-force per square centimetre (kgf/cm^2; kg/cm^2)	x 14.223	=	Pounds-force per square inch (psi; lbf/in^2; lb/in^2)
Pounds-force per square inch (psi; lbf/in^2; lb/in^2)	x 0.068	= Atmospheres (atm)	x 14.696	=	Pounds-force per square inch (psi; lbf/in^2; lb/in^2)
Pounds-force per square inch (psi; lbf/in^2; lb/in^2)	x 0.069	= Bars	x 14.5	=	Pounds-force per square inch (psi; lbf/in^2; lb/in^2)
Pounds-force per square inch (psi; lbf/in^2; lb/in^2)	x 6.895	= Kilopascals (kPa)	x 0.145	=	Pounds-force per square inch (psi; lbf/in^2; lb/in^2)
Kilopascals (kPa)	x 0.01	= Kilograms-force per square centimetre (kgf/cm^2; kg/cm^2)	x 98.1	=	Kilopascals (kPa)
Millibar (mbar)	x 100	= Pascals (Pa)	x 0.01	=	Millibar (mbar)
Millibar (mbar)	x 0.0145	= Pounds-force per square inch (psi; lbf/in^2; lb/in^2)	x 68.947	=	Millibar (mbar)
Millibar (mbar)	x 0.75	= Millimetres of mercury (mmHg)	x 1.333	=	Millibar (mbar)
Millibar (mbar)	x 0.401	= Inches of water (inH$_2$O)	x 2.491	=	Millibar (mbar)
Millimetres of mercury (mmHg)	x 0.535	= Inches of water (inH$_2$O)	x 1.868	=	Millimetres of mercury (mmHg)
Inches of water (inH$_2$O)	x 0.036	= Pounds-force per square inch (psi; lbf/in^2; lb/in^2)	x 27.68	=	Inches of water (inH$_2$O)

Torque (moment of force)
Pounds-force inches (lbf in; lb in)	x 1.152	= Kilograms-force centimetre (kgf cm; kg cm)	x 0.868	=	Pounds-force inches (lbf in; lb in)
Pounds-force inches (lbf in; lb in)	x 0.113	= Newton metres (Nm)	x 8.85	=	Pounds-force inches (lbf in; lb in)
Pounds-force inches (lbf in; lb in)	x 0.083	= Pounds-force feet (lbf ft; lb ft)	x 12	=	Pounds-force inches (lbf in; lb in)
Pounds-force feet (lbf ft; lb ft)	x 0.138	= Kilograms-force metres (kgf m; kg m)	x 7.233	=	Pounds-force feet (lbf ft; lb ft)
Pounds-force feet (lbf ft; lb ft)	x 1.356	= Newton metres (Nm)	x 0.738	=	Pounds-force feet (lbf ft; lb ft)
Newton metres (Nm)	x 0.102	= Kilograms-force metres (kgf m; kg m)	x 9.804	=	Newton metres (Nm)

Power
Horsepower (hp)	x 745.7	= Watts (W)	x 0.0013	=	Horsepower (hp)

Velocity (speed)
Miles per hour (miles/hr; mph)	x 1.609	= Kilometres per hour (km/hr; kph)	x 0.621	=	Miles per hour (miles/hr; mph)

Fuel consumption*
Miles per gallon (mpg)	x 0.354	= Kilometres per litre (km/l)	x 2.825	=	Miles per gallon (mpg)

* It is common practice to convert from miles per gallon (mpg) to litres/100 kilometres (l/100km), where mpg x l/100 km = 282

Temperature
Degrees Fahrenheit = (°C x 1.8) + 32   Degrees Celsius (Degrees Centigrade; °C) = (°F - 32) x 0.56

Buying spare parts & Vehicle identification numbers REF•13

Buying spare parts

Spare parts are available from many sources, for example: VW garages, other garages and accessory shops, and motor factors. Our advice regarding spare parts is as follows:

Officially appointed VW garages – This is the best source of parts which are peculiar to your car and otherwise not generally available (eg complete cylinder heads, internal gearbox components, badges, interior trim, etc). It is also the only place at which you should buy parts if your vehicle is still under warranty – non-VW components may invalidate the warranty. To be sure of obtaining the correct parts it will always be necessary to give the storeman your car's engine and chassis number, and if possible, to take the 'old' part along for positive identification. Remember that many parts are available on a factory exchange scheme – any parts returned should always be clean! It obviously makes good sense to go straight to the specialists on your car for this type of part for they are best equipped to supply you.

Other garages and accessory shops – These are often very good places to buy material and components needed for the maintenance of your car (eg oil filters, spark plugs, bulbs, drivebelts, oils and grease, touch-up paint, filler paste, etc). They also sell general accessories, usually have convenient opening hours, charge lower prices and can often be found not far from home.

Motor factors – Good factors stock all of the more important components which wear out relatively quickly (eg clutch components, pistons, valves, exhaust systems, brake cylinders/pipes/hoses/ seals/shoes and pads, etc). Motor factors will often provide new or reconditioned components on a part exchange basis – this can save a considerable amount of money.

Vehicle identification numbers

It is most important to identify the vehicle accurately when ordering spare parts or asking for information. There have been many modifications to this range already.

The vehicle identification plate is located within the engine compartment on the right-hand side panel.

The chassis number is in the engine compartment on the bulkhead.

The engine number on 1.05 and 1.3 litre models is located on the cylinder block next to the alternator bracket.

The engine number on 1.6 and 1.8 litre models is located on the left-hand side of the cylinder block.

These numbers should be identified and recorded by the owner; they are required when ordering spares, going through the customs, and by the police if the vehicle is stolen.

When ordering spares remember that VW output is such that inevitably spares vary, are duplicated. and are held on a usage basis. If the storeman does not have the correct identification, he cannot produce the correct item. It is a good idea to take the old part if possible to compare it with a new one.

When fitting accessories it is best to fit VW recommended ones. They are designed specifically for the vehicle.

Identification number locations in the engine compartment
1 Vehicle identification plate
2 Engine number
3 Chassis number

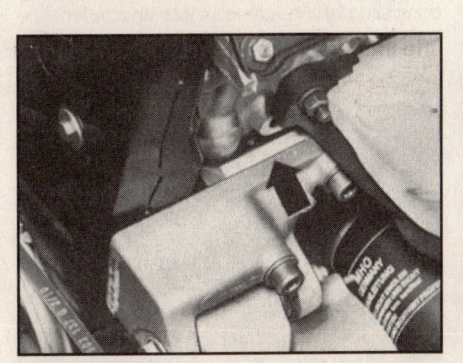

Engine number location – 1.05 and 1.3 litre

Engine number location – 1.6 and 1.8 litre

Glossary of Technical Terms

A

ABS (Anti-lock brake system) A system, usually electronically controlled, that senses incipient wheel lockup during braking and relieves hydraulic pressure at wheels that are about to skid.

Air bag An inflatable bag hidden in the steering wheel (driver's side) or the dash or glovebox (passenger side). In a head-on collision, the bags inflate, preventing the driver and front passenger from being thrown forward into the steering wheel or windscreen.

Air cleaner A metal or plastic housing, containing a filter element, which removes dust and dirt from the air being drawn into the engine.

Air filter element The actual filter in an air cleaner system, usually manufactured from pleated paper and requiring renewal at regular intervals.

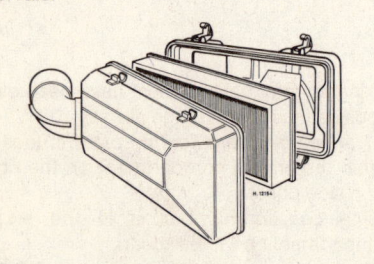

Air filter

Allen key A hexagonal wrench which fits into a recessed hexagonal hole.

Alligator clip A long-nosed spring-loaded metal clip with meshing teeth. Used to make temporary electrical connections.

Alternator A component in the electrical system which converts mechanical energy from a drivebelt into electrical energy to charge the battery and to operate the starting system, ignition system and electrical accessories.

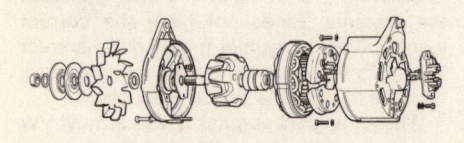

Alternator (exploded view)

Ampere (amp) A unit of measurement for the flow of electric current. One amp is the amount of current produced by one volt acting through a resistance of one ohm.

Anaerobic sealer A substance used to prevent bolts and screws from loosening. Anaerobic means that it does not require oxygen for activation. The Loctite brand is widely used.

Antifreeze A substance (usually ethylene glycol) mixed with water, and added to a vehicle's cooling system, to prevent freezing of the coolant in winter. Antifreeze also contains chemicals to inhibit corrosion and the formation of rust and other deposits that would tend to clog the radiator and coolant passages and reduce cooling efficiency.

Anti-seize compound A coating that reduces the risk of seizing on fasteners that are subjected to high temperatures, such as exhaust manifold bolts and nuts.

Anti-seize compound

Asbestos A natural fibrous mineral with great heat resistance, commonly used in the composition of brake friction materials. Asbestos is a health hazard and the dust created by brake systems should never be inhaled or ingested.

Axle A shaft on which a wheel revolves, or which revolves with a wheel. Also, a solid beam that connects the two wheels at one end of the vehicle. An axle which also transmits power to the wheels is known as a live axle.

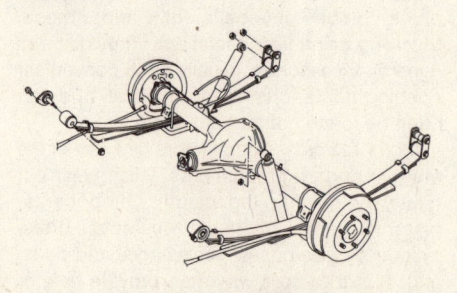

Axle assembly

Axleshaft A single rotating shaft, on either side of the differential, which delivers power from the final drive assembly to the drive wheels. Also called a driveshaft or a halfshaft.

B

Ball bearing An anti-friction bearing consisting of a hardened inner and outer race with hardened steel balls between two races.

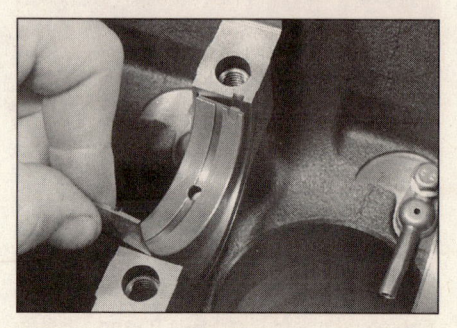

Bearing

Bearing The curved surface on a shaft or in a bore, or the part assembled into either, that permits relative motion between them with minimum wear and friction.

Big-end bearing The bearing in the end of the connecting rod that's attached to the crankshaft.

Bleed nipple A valve on a brake wheel cylinder, caliper or other hydraulic component that is opened to purge the hydraulic system of air. Also called a bleed screw.

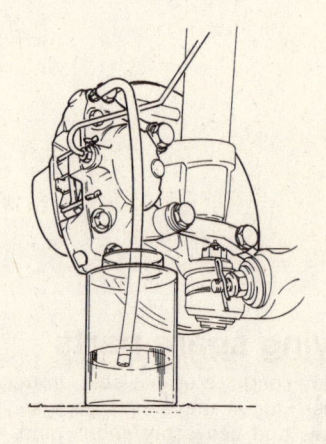

Brake bleeding

Brake bleeding Procedure for removing air from lines of a hydraulic brake system.

Brake disc The component of a disc brake that rotates with the wheels.

Brake drum The component of a drum brake that rotates with the wheels.

Brake linings The friction material which contacts the brake disc or drum to retard the vehicle's speed. The linings are bonded or riveted to the brake pads or shoes.

Brake pads The replaceable friction pads that pinch the brake disc when the brakes are applied. Brake pads consist of a friction material bonded or riveted to a rigid backing plate.

Brake shoe The crescent-shaped carrier to which the brake linings are mounted and which forces the lining against the rotating drum during braking.

Braking systems For more information on braking systems, consult the *Haynes Automotive Brake Manual*.

Breaker bar A long socket wrench handle providing greater leverage.

Bulkhead The insulated partition between the engine and the passenger compartment.

C

Caliper The non-rotating part of a disc-brake assembly that straddles the disc and carries the brake pads. The caliper also contains the hydraulic components that cause the pads to pinch the disc when the brakes are applied. A caliper is also a measuring tool that can be set to measure inside or outside dimensions of an object.

Glossary of Technical Terms REF•15

Camshaft A rotating shaft on which a series of cam lobes operate the valve mechanisms. The camshaft may be driven by gears, by sprockets and chain or by sprockets and a belt.

Canister A container in an evaporative emission control system; contains activated charcoal granules to trap vapours from the fuel system.

Canister

Carburettor A device which mixes fuel with air in the proper proportions to provide a desired power output from a spark ignition internal combustion engine.

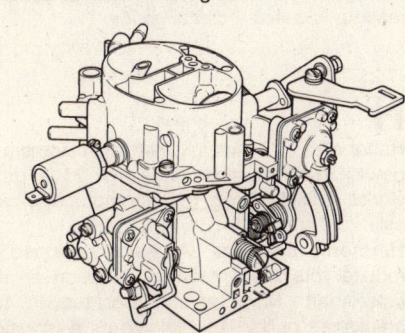

Carburettor

Castellated Resembling the parapets along the top of a castle wall. For example, a castellated balljoint stud nut.

Castellated nut

Castor In wheel alignment, the backward or forward tilt of the steering axis. Castor is positive when the steering axis is inclined rearward at the top.

Catalytic converter A silencer-like device in the exhaust system which converts certain pollutants in the exhaust gases into less harmful substances.

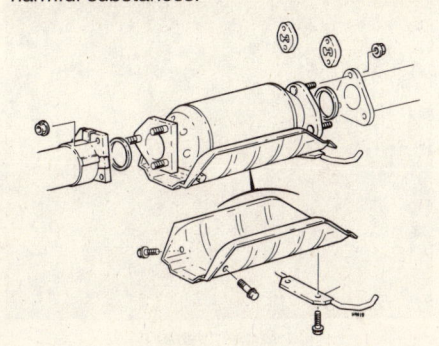

Catalytic converter

Circlip A ring-shaped clip used to prevent endwise movement of cylindrical parts and shafts. An internal circlip is installed in a groove in a housing; an external circlip fits into a groove on the outside of a cylindrical piece such as a shaft.

Clearance The amount of space between two parts. For example, between a piston and a cylinder, between a bearing and a journal, etc.

Coil spring A spiral of elastic steel found in various sizes throughout a vehicle, for example as a springing medium in the suspension and in the valve train.

Compression Reduction in volume, and increase in pressure and temperature, of a gas, caused by squeezing it into a smaller space.

Compression ratio The relationship between cylinder volume when the piston is at top dead centre and cylinder volume when the piston is at bottom dead centre.

Constant velocity (CV) joint A type of universal joint that cancels out vibrations caused by driving power being transmitted through an angle.

Core plug A disc or cup-shaped metal device inserted in a hole in a casting through which core was removed when the casting was formed. Also known as a freeze plug or expansion plug.

Crankcase The lower part of the engine block in which the crankshaft rotates.

Crankshaft The main rotating member, or shaft, running the length of the crankcase, with offset "throws" to which the connecting rods are attached.

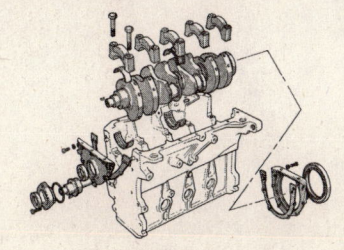

Crankshaft assembly

Crocodile clip See Alligator clip

D

Diagnostic code Code numbers obtained by accessing the diagnostic mode of an engine management computer. This code can be used to determine the area in the system where a malfunction may be located.

Disc brake A brake design incorporating a rotating disc onto which brake pads are squeezed. The resulting friction converts the energy of a moving vehicle into heat.

Double-overhead cam (DOHC) An engine that uses two overhead camshafts, usually one for the intake valves and one for the exhaust valves.

Drivebelt(s) The belt(s) used to drive accessories such as the alternator, water pump, power steering pump, air conditioning compressor, etc. off the crankshaft pulley.

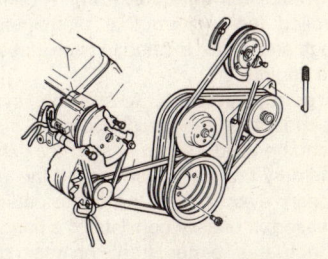

Accessory drivebelts

Driveshaft Any shaft used to transmit motion. Commonly used when referring to the axleshafts on a front wheel drive vehicle.

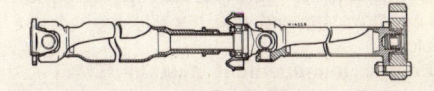

Driveshaft

Drum brake A type of brake using a drum-shaped metal cylinder attached to the inner surface of the wheel. When the brake pedal is pressed, curved brake shoes with friction linings press against the inside of the drum to slow or stop the vehicle.

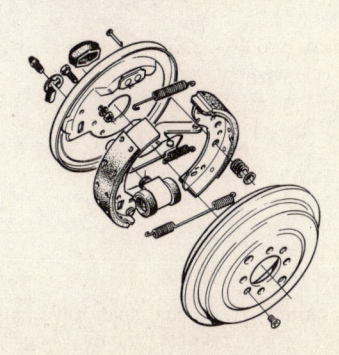

Drum brake assembly

Glossary of Technical Terms

E

EGR valve A valve used to introduce exhaust gases into the intake air stream.

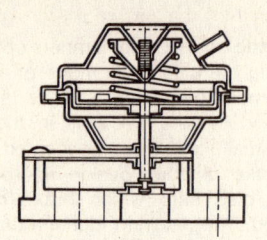

EGR valve

Electronic control unit (ECU) A computer which controls (for instance) ignition and fuel injection systems, or an anti-lock braking system. For more information refer to the *Haynes Automotive Electrical and Electronic Systems Manual*.

Electronic Fuel Injection (EFI) A computer controlled fuel system that distributes fuel through an injector located in each intake port of the engine.

Emergency brake A braking system, independent of the main hydraulic system, that can be used to slow or stop the vehicle if the primary brakes fail, or to hold the vehicle stationary even though the brake pedal isn't depressed. It usually consists of a hand lever that actuates either front or rear brakes mechanically through a series of cables and linkages. Also known as a handbrake or parking brake.

Endfloat The amount of lengthwise movement between two parts. As applied to a crankshaft, the distance that the crankshaft can move forward and back in the cylinder block.

Engine management system (EMS) A computer controlled system which manages the fuel injection and the ignition systems in an integrated fashion.

Exhaust manifold A part with several passages through which exhaust gases leave the engine combustion chambers and enter the exhaust pipe.

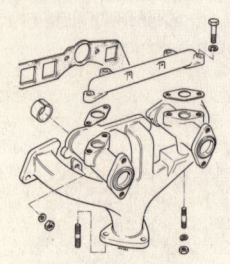

Exhaust manifold

F

Fan clutch A viscous (fluid) drive coupling device which permits variable engine fan speeds in relation to engine speeds.

Feeler blade A thin strip or blade of hardened steel, ground to an exact thickness, used to check or measure clearances between parts.

Feeler blade

Firing order The order in which the engine cylinders fire, or deliver their power strokes, beginning with the number one cylinder.

Flywheel A heavy spinning wheel in which energy is absorbed and stored by means of momentum. On cars, the flywheel is attached to the crankshaft to smooth out firing impulses.

Free play The amount of travel before any action takes place. The "looseness" in a linkage, or an assembly of parts, between the initial application of force and actual movement. For example, the distance the brake pedal moves before the pistons in the master cylinder are actuated.

Fuse An electrical device which protects a circuit against accidental overload. The typical fuse contains a soft piece of metal which is calibrated to melt at a predetermined current flow (expressed as amps) and break the circuit.

Fusible link A circuit protection device consisting of a conductor surrounded by heat-resistant insulation. The conductor is smaller than the wire it protects, so it acts as the weakest link in the circuit. Unlike a blown fuse, a failed fusible link must frequently be cut from the wire for replacement.

G

Gap The distance the spark must travel in jumping from the centre electrode to the side electrode in a spark plug. Also refers to the spacing between the points in a contact breaker assembly in a conventional points-type ignition, or to the distance between the reluctor or rotor and the pickup coil in an electronic ignition.

Gasket Any thin, soft material - usually cork, cardboard, asbestos or soft metal - installed between two metal surfaces to ensure a good seal. For instance, the cylinder head gasket seals the joint between the block and the cylinder head.

Gasket

Gauge An instrument panel display used to monitor engine conditions. A gauge with a movable pointer on a dial or a fixed scale is an analogue gauge. A gauge with a numerical readout is called a digital gauge.

H

Halfshaft A rotating shaft that transmits power from the final drive unit to a drive wheel, usually when referring to a live rear axle.

Harmonic balancer A device designed to reduce torsion or twisting vibration in the crankshaft. May be incorporated in the crankshaft pulley. Also known as a vibration damper.

Hone An abrasive tool for correcting small irregularities or differences in diameter in an engine cylinder, brake cylinder, etc.

Hydraulic tappet A tappet that utilises hydraulic pressure from the engine's lubrication system to maintain zero clearance (constant contact with both camshaft and valve stem). Automatically adjusts to variation in valve stem length. Hydraulic tappets also reduce valve noise.

I

Ignition timing The moment at which the spark plug fires, usually expressed in the number of crankshaft degrees before the piston reaches the top of its stroke.

Inlet manifold A tube or housing with passages through which flows the air-fuel mixture (carburettor vehicles and vehicles with throttle body injection) or air only (port fuel-injected vehicles) to the port openings in the cylinder head.

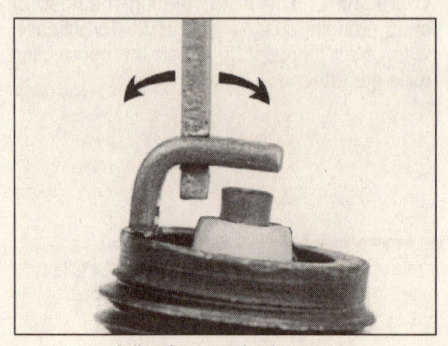

Adjusting spark plug gap

Glossary of Technical Terms REF•17

J
Jump start Starting the engine of a vehicle with a discharged or weak battery by attaching jump leads from the weak battery to a charged or helper battery.

L
Load Sensing Proportioning Valve (LSPV) A brake hydraulic system control valve that works like a proportioning valve, but also takes into consideration the amount of weight carried by the rear axle.
Locknut A nut used to lock an adjustment nut, or other threaded component, in place. For example, a locknut is employed to keep the adjusting nut on the rocker arm in position.
Lockwasher A form of washer designed to prevent an attaching nut from working loose.

M
MacPherson strut A type of front suspension system devised by Earle MacPherson at Ford of England. In its original form, a simple lateral link with the anti-roll bar creates the lower control arm. A long strut - an integral coil spring and shock absorber - is mounted between the body and the steering knuckle. Many modern so-called MacPherson strut systems use a conventional lower A-arm and don't rely on the anti-roll bar for location.
Multimeter An electrical test instrument with the capability to measure voltage, current and resistance.

N
NOx Oxides of Nitrogen. A common toxic pollutant emitted by petrol and diesel engines at higher temperatures.

O
Ohm The unit of electrical resistance. One volt applied to a resistance of one ohm will produce a current of one amp.
Ohmmeter An instrument for measuring electrical resistance.
O-ring A type of sealing ring made of a special rubber-like material; in use, the O-ring is compressed into a groove to provide the sealing action.

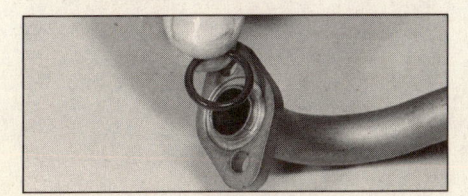

O-ring

Overhead cam (ohc) engine An engine with the camshaft(s) located on top of the cylinder head(s).
Overhead valve (ohv) engine An engine with the valves located in the cylinder head, but with the camshaft located in the engine block.
Oxygen sensor A device installed in the engine exhaust manifold, which senses the oxygen content in the exhaust and converts this information into an electric current. Also called a Lambda sensor.

P
Phillips screw A type of screw head having a cross instead of a slot for a corresponding type of screwdriver.
Plastigage A thin strip of plastic thread, available in different sizes, used for measuring clearances. For example, a strip of Plastigage is laid across a bearing journal. The parts are assembled and dismantled; the width of the crushed strip indicates the clearance between journal and bearing.

Plastigage

Propeller shaft The long hollow tube with universal joints at both ends that carries power from the transmission to the differential on front-engined rear wheel drive vehicles.
Proportioning valve A hydraulic control valve which limits the amount of pressure to the rear brakes during panic stops to prevent wheel lock-up.

R
Rack-and-pinion steering A steering system with a pinion gear on the end of the steering shaft that mates with a rack (think of a geared wheel opened up and laid flat). When the steering wheel is turned, the pinion turns, moving the rack to the left or right. This movement is transmitted through the track rods to the steering arms at the wheels.
Radiator A liquid-to-air heat transfer device designed to reduce the temperature of the coolant in an internal combustion engine cooling system.
Refrigerant Any substance used as a heat transfer agent in an air-conditioning system. R-12 has been the principle refrigerant for many years; recently, however, manufacturers have begun using R-134a, a non-CFC substance that is considered less harmful to the ozone in the upper atmosphere.
Rocker arm A lever arm that rocks on a shaft or pivots on a stud. In an overhead valve engine, the rocker arm converts the upward movement of the pushrod into a downward movement to open a valve.
Rotor In a distributor, the rotating device inside the cap that connects the centre electrode and the outer terminals as it turns, distributing the high voltage from the coil secondary winding to the proper spark plug. Also, that part of an alternator which rotates inside the stator. Also, the rotating assembly of a turbocharger, including the compressor wheel, shaft and turbine wheel.
Runout The amount of wobble (in-and-out movement) of a gear or wheel as it's rotated. The amount a shaft rotates "out-of-true." The out-of-round condition of a rotating part.

S
Sealant A liquid or paste used to prevent leakage at a joint. Sometimes used in conjunction with a gasket.
Sealed beam lamp An older headlight design which integrates the reflector, lens and filaments into a hermetically-sealed one-piece unit. When a filament burns out or the lens cracks, the entire unit is simply replaced.
Serpentine drivebelt A single, long, wide accessory drivebelt that's used on some newer vehicles to drive all the accessories, instead of a series of smaller, shorter belts. Serpentine drivebelts are usually tensioned by an automatic tensioner.

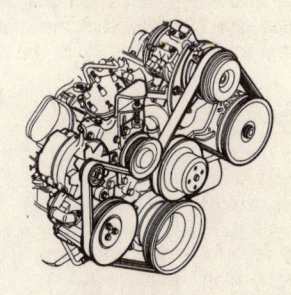

Serpentine drivebelt

Shim Thin spacer, commonly used to adjust the clearance or relative positions between two parts. For example, shims inserted into or under bucket tappets control valve clearances. Clearance is adjusted by changing the thickness of the shim.
Slide hammer A special puller that screws into or hooks onto a component such as a shaft or bearing; a heavy sliding handle on the shaft bottoms against the end of the shaft to knock the component free.
Sprocket A tooth or projection on the periphery of a wheel, shaped to engage with a chain or drivebelt. Commonly used to refer to the sprocket wheel itself.
Starter inhibitor switch On vehicles with an

Glossary of Technical Terms

automatic transmission, a switch that prevents starting if the vehicle is not in Neutral or Park.

Strut See MacPherson strut.

T

Tappet A cylindrical component which transmits motion from the cam to the valve stem, either directly or via a pushrod and rocker arm. Also called a cam follower.

Thermostat A heat-controlled valve that regulates the flow of coolant between the cylinder block and the radiator, so maintaining optimum engine operating temperature. A thermostat is also used in some air cleaners in which the temperature is regulated.

Thrust bearing The bearing in the clutch assembly that is moved in to the release levers by clutch pedal action to disengage the clutch. Also referred to as a release bearing.

Timing belt A toothed belt which drives the camshaft. Serious engine damage may result if it breaks in service.

Timing chain A chain which drives the camshaft.

Toe-in The amount the front wheels are closer together at the front than at the rear. On rear wheel drive vehicles, a slight amount of toe-in is usually specified to keep the front wheels running parallel on the road by offsetting other forces that tend to spread the wheels apart.

Toe-out The amount the front wheels are closer together at the rear than at the front. On front wheel drive vehicles, a slight amount of toe-out is usually specified.

Tools For full information on choosing and using tools, refer to the *Haynes Automotive Tools Manual*.

Tracer A stripe of a second colour applied to a wire insulator to distinguish that wire from another one with the same colour insulator.

Tune-up A process of accurate and careful adjustments and parts replacement to obtain the best possible engine performance.

Turbocharger A centrifugal device, driven by exhaust gases, that pressurises the intake air. Normally used to increase the power output from a given engine displacement, but can also be used primarily to reduce exhaust emissions (as on VW's "Umwelt" Diesel engine).

U

Universal joint or U-joint A double-pivoted connection for transmitting power from a driving to a driven shaft through an angle. A U-joint consists of two Y-shaped yokes and a cross-shaped member called the spider.

V

Valve A device through which the flow of liquid, gas, vacuum, or loose material in bulk may be started, stopped, or regulated by a movable part that opens, shuts, or partially obstructs one or more ports or passageways. A valve is also the movable part of such a device.

Valve clearance The clearance between the valve tip (the end of the valve stem) and the rocker arm or tappet. The valve clearance is measured when the valve is closed.

Vernier caliper A precision measuring instrument that measures inside and outside dimensions. Not quite as accurate as a micrometer, but more convenient.

Viscosity The thickness of a liquid or its resistance to flow.

Volt A unit for expressing electrical "pressure" in a circuit. One volt that will produce a current of one ampere through a resistance of one ohm.

W

Welding Various processes used to join metal items by heating the areas to be joined to a molten state and fusing them together. For more information refer to the *Haynes Automotive Welding Manual*.

Wiring diagram A drawing portraying the components and wires in a vehicle's electrical system, using standardised symbols. For more information refer to the *Haynes Automotive Electrical and Electronic Systems Manual*.

Index

Note: *References throughout this index relate to Chapter•page number*

A

Accelerator cable - 3•8, 3•9, 3•24, 6•18
Accelerator pedal - 3•9
Accelerator pump - 12•20, 12•22
Acknowledgements - 0•4
Air bags - 0•5
Air cleaner - 3•4, 3•5, 3•6, 3•23, 12•25, 12•31, 12•35
Air conditioning system - 11•18
Air intake duct - 12•35
Airflow meter - 3•21, 3•27, 12•25, 12•32
Airflow sensor plate - 3•26
Alternator - 9•4, 9•5, 9•7, 12•47
Anti-corrosion protection - 12•43
Anti-roll bar - 10•5
Antifreeze - 0•6, 2•1, 2•4
Asbestos - 0•5
ATF - 0•6, 0•16, 6•2
Automatic transmission - See *Manual gearbox and automatic transmission*
Automatic transmission fault finding - 6•19
Automatic transmission fluid - 0•6, 0•16, 6•2
Auxiliary air device - 3•21, 3•25
Axle - 10•7

B

Backfire - 1•37, 3•30
Battery - 0•5, 9•3, 9•4, 12•47
Battery fault - 9•22
Bellows - 10•10
Big-end caps - 12•17
Bleeding brakes - 8•11
Blower unit - 11•16
Bodywork and fittings - 11•1 et seq, 12•49 et seq, REF•4
Bonnet - 11•4, 11•6
Brake fluid - 0•16, 8•1
Braking system - 8•1 et seq, REF•1, REF•2, REF•3
Braking system fault finding - 8•14

Bulbs - 9•17
Bumpers - 11•10
Burning - 0•5

C

Cables - 3•8, 3•9, 3•24, 5•2, 6•18, 8•13, 9•11, 11•4, 12•42
Calipers - 8•3, 8•6
Camber - 12•48
Camshafts - 1•10, 1•18, 1•21, 1•27, 1•32, 12•10, 12•15, 12•17
Capacities - 0•6
Carburettor - 3•10, 3•12, 3•15, 3•16, 6•18, 12•19, 12•21, 12•23
Carpets - 11•2
Cassette player - 9•21
Catalytic converter - 12•36
Central locking system - 12•49
Centre console - 11•13
Choke cable - 3•9
Choke valve gap - 12•20, 12•22
Cigarette lighter - 9•11
Clutch - 5•1 et seq, 12•42 et seq
Clutch fault finding - 5•8
CO emissions (mixture) - REF•4
Coil - 4•10, 12•42
Coil springs - 10•4, 10•7
Cold acceleration enrichment system - 3•25
Cold start valve - 3•21, 3•25
Condenser - 4•4
Connecting rods - 1•15, 1•17, 1•19, 1•33, 1•35
Console - 11•13
Consumption gauge - 9•8
Contact breaker points - 4•3, 4•4
Contents - 0•2
Conversion factors - REF•12
Coolant pump - 2•6, 12•18
Cooling fan - 2•4, 2•5, 12•19
Cooling system - 2•1 et seq, 12•18 et seq
Cooling system fault finding - 2•7
Corrosion inhibitor - 2•4
Courtesy light - 9•10, 9•17

Crankcase - 1•16, 1•33
Crankcase ventilation system - 1•16, 1•32
Crankshaft - 1•13, 1•15, 1•16, 1•18, 1•31, 1•32, 1•33, 1•34, 12•15
Crushing - 0•5
Cylinder block - 1•16, 1•33
Cylinder head - 1•9, 1•12, 1•20, 1•21, 1•28, 1•36, 12•10, 12•11, 12•12, 12•15

D

Dents in bodywork - 11•2
Diaphragm pressure switch - 12•29
Dimensions - 0•6
Direction indicators - 9•9, 9•17
Discs - 8•4, 8•7
Distributor - 4•5, 4•7, 4•8, 12•39, 12•40
Doors - 11•4, 11•7, 11•8, 11•9, 12•51, REF•2
Drivebelts - 9•4, 10•14, 11•19, 12•47
Driveplate - 1•33
Driveshafts - 7•1 et seq, REF•3
Driveshafts fault finding - 7•4
Drums - 8•10
Dust filter - 12•51

E

Electric shock - 0•5
Electrical system - 9•1 et seq, 12•47 et seq, REF•2
Electrical system fault finding - 9•22, REF•9
Electrolyte - 9•4
Engine - 1•1 et seq, 12•10 et seq, 12•15 et seq
Engine fault finding - 1•37, 3•30, REF•10, REF•11
Engine oil - 0•6, 0•16, 1•4, 1•5, 12•3, 12•4
Environmental considerations - REF•8
Evaporative fuel control system - 12•34
Exhaust emission checks - REF•4
Exhaust manifold - 3•19, 3•29
Exhaust system - 3•19, 3•29, 12•30, 12•36, REF•3

Index

F

Facia - 9•10, 9•14, 9•18, 9•22, 11•13
Fan - 2•4, 2•5, 12•19
Fast idle speed adjustment - 3•12, 3•15, 3•16, 12•20, 12•22
Fault finding - REF•9 *et seq*
Fault finding - automatic transmission - 6•19
Fault finding - braking system - 8•14
Fault finding - clutch - 5•8
Fault finding - cooling system - 2•7
Fault finding - driveshafts - 7•4
Fault finding - electrical system - 9•22
Fault finding - engine - 1•37
Fault finding - fuel system - 3•30
Fault finding - ignition system - 4•10
Fault finding - manual gearbox - 6•19
Fault finding - suspension and steering - 10•14
Final drive oil - 0•6, 0•16, 6•2
Fire - 0•5
Fixed glass - 11•10
Float level - 12•21
Flywheel - 1•13, 1•18, 1•20, 1•33, 12•43
Foglights - 9•16
Fuel accumulator - 3•29
Fuel and exhaust systems - 3•1 *et seq*, 12•19 *et seq*, REF•4
Fuel and exhaust systems fault finding - 3•30, REF•10
Fuel distributor - 3•21
Fuel filler gravity valve - 3•8
Fuel filter - 3•29
Fuel gauge - 3•8
Fuel gauge fault - 9•22
Fuel injectors - 3•26, 12•26, 12•32
Fuel meter distributor - 3•27
Fuel pressure regulator - 12•26
Fuel pump - 3•6, 3•27, 3•28, 12•24, 12•36
Fuel reservoir - 3•7
Fuel tank - 3•7, 3•29
Full throttle enrichment - 12•27
Fume or gas intoxication - 0•5
Fuses - 9•8

G

Gaiters - 10•10
Gashes in bodywork - 11•2
Gear lever - 6•14, 12•47
Gearbox - See *Manual gearbox*
Gearchange gauge - 9•8
Gearshift mechanism - 6•7, 6•14, 12•46
Glossary of technical terms - REF•14 *et seq*
Glovebox light - 9•18
Grille - 11•5

H

Hall sender - 4•7, 12•41
Handbrake - 8•13, REF•1
Handle - 11•8
Hazard flasher system - 9•9
HC emissions - REF•4
Headlamps - 9•14, 9•15, 9•16, 9•21, 12•47
Heater - 11•15, 11•16

Hinges - 11•4
Horn - 9•21
HT leads - 4•10
Hub bearings - 8•7, 10•8
Hydraulic bucket tappets - 12•11, 12•15
Hydraulic pipes and hoses - 8•11
Hydraulic system - bleeding - 8•11
Hydrofluoric acid - 0•5

I

Idle cut-off - 12•21, 12•22
Idle speed adjustment - 3•23, 3•24, 12•19, 12•21, 12•25, 12•28, 12•31, 12•35
Idle speed adjustment fault - 3•30
Idle speed boost - 3•23, 12•19, 12•22
Idle speed stabilization system - 12•26, 12•28
Idle switch control valve - 12•35
Ignition light fault - 9•22, REF•11
Ignition switch - 4•7, 9•9
Ignition system - 4•1 *et seq*, 12•38 *et seq*
Ignition system fault finding - 4•10, REF•11
Ignition timing - 4•9, 12•38, 12•42
Indicators - 9•9, 9•17
Injectors - 3•26, 12•26, 12•32, 12•35
Inlet manifold - 3•17, 3•18, 3•29, 12•29
Instrument panel - 9•11, 9•18
Intake air pre-heater - 12•32
Interior light - 9•10, 9•17
Intermediate shaft - 1•31, 1•32, 1•33, 1•35
Introduction to the Volkswagen Golf and Jetta - 0•4

J

Jacking - 0•8
Joint mating faces and gaskets - REF•8

K

Knee-bar - 12•51

L

Leaks - 0•7
Lights inoperative - 9•22
Locknuts, locktabs and washers - REF•8
Locks - 9•9, 10•10, 11•4, 11•5, 11•6, 11•9, 12•49
Loudspeakers - 9•22
Lubricants and fluids - 0•16
Luggage compartment light - 9•10, 9•18

M

Main bearings - 1•15, 1•18, 1•31, 1•33, 1•34
Manifolds - 3•17, 3•18, 3•19, 3•29, 12•29, 12•35
Manual gearbox and automatic transmission - 1•8, 1•23, 1•25, 6•1 *et seq*, 12•43 *et seq*
Manual gearbox fault finding - 6•19
Manual gearbox oil - 0•6, 0•16, 6•1, 12•8, 12•43, 12•46

Master cylinder - 8•10
Mirrors - 9•18, 11•10, 12•51, REF•1
Misfire - 1•37, 3•30, 4•11, REF•11
Mixture adjustment - 3•24, 12•19, 12•21, 12•25, 12•31, 12•35
MOT test checks - REF•1 *et seq*
Mountings - 12•15
Multi-function indicator - 12•47

N

Number plate light - 9•17

O

Oil - engine - 0•6, 0•16, 1•4, 1•5, 12•3, 12•4
Oil - final drive - 0•6, 0•16, 6•2
Oil - manual gearbox - 0•6, 0•16, 6•1, 12•8, 12•43, 12•46
Oil consumption high - 1•37
Oil cooler - 12•16
Oil filter - 1•6, 1•16, 1•31
Oil pressure fault - REF•11
Oil pressure warning system - 12•47
Oil pump - 1•14, 1•17, 1•20, 1•30, 1•33, 12•14
Oil seals - 1•13, 1•32, 7•4, 12•10, 12•12, REF•8
Overheating - 2•7
Overrun cut-off - 12•27, 12•29

P

Pads - 8•2, 8•4
Parking lights - 9•17
Pedals - 3•9, 5•3, 8•13
Pinking - REF•11
Pistons - 1•15, 1•17, 1•19, 1•30, 1•33, 1•35
Plastic components - 11•3
Points - 4•3, 4•4
Poisonous or irritant substances - 0•5
Pollen filter - 12•51
Power-assisted steering - 10•4, 10•14, 12•48
Power steering fluid - 0•16, 10•1, 10•13, 12•9
Pre-throttle valve - 12•33
Pre-ignition - REF•11
Pressure regulator - 8•11
Pressure relief valve - 3•27

R

Radiator - 2•4, 11•5
Radio - 9•21
Rear axle - 10•7
Rear lights - 9•17
Rear window washer - 9•21, 12•47
Regulator (window) - 11•9
Relays - 9•8
Repair procedures - REF•8
Roadwheels - 10•14
Routine maintenance - 0•10 *et seq*, 12•9
Routine maintenance - automatic transmission - 6•16
Routine maintenance - bodywork and underframe - 11•1

Index

Routine maintenance - braking system - 8•2
Routine maintenance - cooling system - 2•2
Routine maintenance - electrical system - 9•3
Routine maintenance - engine - 1•5, 1•23
Routine maintenance - fuel and exhaust system - 3•4, 3•21
Routine maintenance - hinges and locks - 11•4
Routine maintenance - ignition system - 4•3
Routine maintenance - manual gearbox - 6•3
Routine maintenance - seat belts - 11•14
Routine maintenance - suspension and steering - 10•4
Routine maintenance - upholstery and carpets - 11•2
Rubbing strips - 11•12, 12•51
Rust holes in bodywork - 11•2

S

Safety first! - 0•5
Scalding - 0•5
Scratches in bodywork - 11•2
Screw threads and fastenings - REF•8
Seat belts - 11•14, 12•49, REF•2
Seats - 11•14, 12•51, REF•2
Selector cable - 6•18
Servo unit - 8•13, 8•14
Shock absorbers - REF•2, REF•3
Shoes - 8•8
Sidelights - 9•17
Slow running adjustment - 3•12, 3•15, 3•16
Spares - REF•13
Spark plugs - 4•10, 12•42
Speedometer cable - 9•11
Spoiler - 11•12, 12•51
Springs - 10•4, 10•7, REF•3
Starter motor - 9•7
Starter motor fault finding - 9•22, REF•10
Steering column - 9•9, 10•9, REF•1
Steering fault - 10•14
Steering gear - 10•10, 10•11, 10•12, REF•3
Steering lock - 10•10
Steering wheel - 10•8, REF•1
Stop-start system - 9•8
Struts - 10•4, 10•7
Sump - 1•14, 1•20, 1•30, 12•15
Sunroof - 11•13
Supplement: Revisions and information on later models - 12•1 *et seq*
Suspension and steering - 10•1 *et seq*, 12•48 *et seq*, REF•2, REF•3
Suspension and steering fault finding - 10•14
Switches - 2•5, 2•6, 3•25, 4•7, 9•9, 9•10

T

Tailgate - 11•5, 11•12
Tappets - 12•11, 12•15
Temperature gauge fault - 9•22
Temperature sender - 2•6, 12•19
Thermostat - 2•5, 12•18
Throttle cable - 3•8, 3•9, 3•24, 6•18
Throttle damper - 12•35
Throttle valve switch - 12•32, 12•26
Tie-rods - 10•10, 10•11
Timing - 4•9, 12•38, 12•42
Timing belt - 1•12, 1•18, 1•22, 1•26, 1•34, 1•36, 12•16
Tools - REF•5, REF•7, REF•8, REF•10
Towing - 0•8
Track control arm - 10•6
Trim fittings - 11•10, 11•12
Trim panels - 9•14, 11•7
Tyres - 0•15, 10•4, 10•14, 12•48, REF•4
Tyre fault - 10•14

U

Underframe - 11•1
Upholstery - 11•2

V

Vacuum servo unit - 8•13, 8•14
Valve clearances - 1•6, 1•22, 1•35
Valves - 12•11, 12•12, 12•17
Vehicle identification - REF•2, REF•13

W

Warm-up regulator (valve) - 3•21, 3•25
Warning lamp cluster - 9•10
Water pump - 2•6, 12•18
Weights - 0•6, 12•2
Wheel alignment - 10•14
Wheel arch extensions - 11•12
Wheel bearings - 10•5, 10•6, 10•8, REF•3
Wheel cylinder - 8•9
Wheel housing liner - 11•10
Wheels - 12•48, REF•4
Window regulator - 11•9
Windows - 11•10
Windscreen - 11•10, REF•1
Windscreen washer - 9•21, 12•47
Wing - 11•10, 11•11, 11•12
Wipers - 9•19, 9•20
Wiring diagrams - 13•1 *et seq*
Wishbone - 10•6
Working facilities - REF•7

Preserving Our Motoring Heritage

The Model J Duesenberg Derham Tourster. Only eight of these magnificent cars were ever built – this is the only example to be found outside the United States of America

Almost every car you've ever loved, loathed or desired is gathered under one roof at the Haynes Motor Museum. Over 300 immaculately presented cars and motorbikes represent every aspect of our motoring heritage, from elegant reminders of bygone days, such as the superb Model J Duesenberg to curiosities like the bug-eyed BMW Isetta. There are also many old friends and flames. Perhaps you remember the 1959 Ford Popular that you did your courting in? The magnificent 'Red Collection' is a spectacle of classic sports cars including AC, Alfa Romeo, Austin Healey, Ferrari, Lamborghini, Maserati, MG, Riley, Porsche and Triumph.

A Perfect Day Out

Each and every vehicle at the Haynes Motor Museum has played its part in the history and culture of Motoring. Today, they make a wonderful spectacle and a great day out for all the family. Bring the kids, bring Mum and Dad, but above all bring your camera to capture those golden memories for ever. You will also find an impressive array of motoring memorabilia, a comfortable 70 seat video cinema and one of the most extensive transport book shops in Britain. The Pit Stop Cafe serves everything from a cup of tea to wholesome, home-made meals or, if you prefer, you can enjoy the large picnic area nestled in the beautiful rural surroundings of Somerset.

John Haynes O.B.E., Founder and Chairman of the museum at the wheel of a Haynes Light 12.

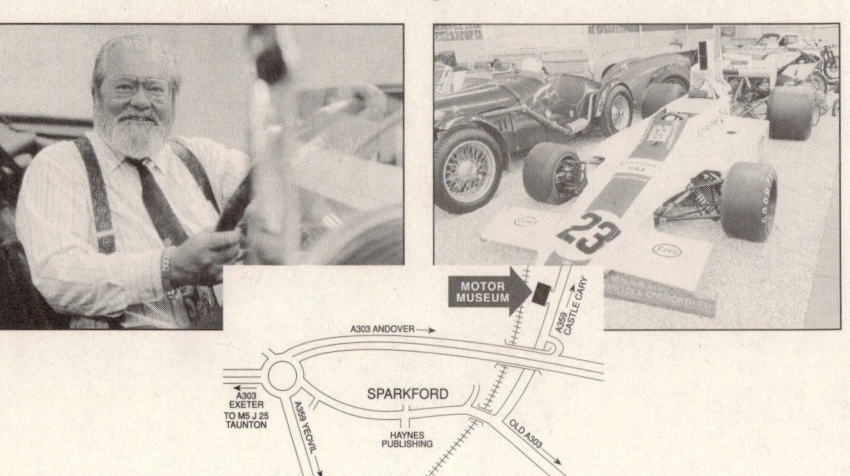

Graham Hill's Lola Cosworth Formula 1 car next to a 1934 Riley Sports.

The Museum is situated on the A359 Yeovil to Frome road at Sparkford, just off the A303 in Somerset. It is about 40 miles south of Bristol, and 25 minutes drive from the M5 intersection at Taunton.
Open 9.30am - 5.30pm (10.00am - 4.00pm Winter) 7 days a week, *except Christmas Day, Boxing Day and New Years Day*
Special rates available for schools, coach parties and outings Charitable Trust No. 292048